The Downfall of GOD

The Downfall of GOD

A History of Atheism in the West

Volume 1: From Prehistory to 1600

S. T. Joshi

Pitchstone Publishing
Durham, North Carolina

Pitchstone Publishing
Durham, North Carolina
www.pitchstonebooks.com

Printed in the United States of America

Library of Congress Cataloging-in-Publication Data

Names: Joshi, S. T., 1958- author.
Title: The downfall of God : a history of atheism in the West / S.T. Joshi.

Description: Durham, North Carolina : Pitchstone Publishing, [2024]- | Includes bibliographical references and index. | Contents: v. 1 From prehistory to 1600 — | Summary: "Atheism has been on the rise in the West for several decades, but its roots, including those belonging to secularism, agnosticism, and freethought, run deep in Western history, philosophy, and thought. Drawing on a multitude of sources from a number of disciplines, S. T. Joshi outlines the natural origins of religious belief in primitive times and charts the slow development of secular accounts of natural phenomena in the Greco-Roman world. Adopting the " Christ myth" theory, he surveys the emergence of a new faith- Christianity- that grew out of Judaism and explores its evolution through the medieval period. He then examines the increasing schisms within the church and conflicts between religious and political entities that caused a fracturing of the monolith of Christianity and the birth of the Renaissance, which not only brought to light the literary glories of the Greco-Roman world but also led to a scientific resurgence and the development of a secular view of the cosmos. By the end of the sixteenth century, as he concludes, the stage was set for the emergence of a worldview free of religion"— Provided by publisher.
Identifiers: LCCN 2024031248 (print) | LCCN 2024031249 (ebook) | ISBN 9781634312585 (paperback) | ISBN 9781634312592 (ebook)
Subjects: LCSH: Atheism—History. | Secularism—History. | Free thought—History. | BISAC: RELIGION / Atheism | PHILOSOPHY / Religious
Classification: LCC BL2747.3 .J66 2024 (print) | LCC BL2747.3 (ebook) | DDC 211/.8—dc23/eng/20240725
LC record available at https://lccn.loc.gov/2024031248
LC ebook record available at https://lccn.loc.gov/2024031249

Contents

Preface ix

I. The Origin and Development of Religion 3

A. Religion in the Palaeolithic Age 3
B. Religion in the Neolithic and Bronze Ages 8
C. Egyptian Religion 14
D. Religion in the Near East 18
E. Israelite Religion 24
F. Early Religion in North America 32

II. The Greeks 37

A. The Development of Greek Religion 37
B. The Beginnings of Greek Philosophy 48
C. The Ionian Tradition 51
D. The Challenge of Parmenides 61
E. The Sophists 74
F. Socrates and Plato 81
G. Atheism and Religion in Greek Literature 90
H. Aristotle and His Legacy 99
I. Hellenistic Thought 107
J. Hellenistic Literature and Culture 124

III. The Romans 134

A. The Romans and the Etruscans 134
B. Roman Politics and Religion to the End of the Republic 141
C. Religion in Early Roman Literature 149
D. Philosophy in Early Rome 158

E. Lucretius: The Exponent of Epicureanism 162
F. Cicero: Sceptical Critic of Epicureans and Stoics 170
G. The Augustan Age 178
H. Rome, Britain, and the Jews 201
I. Seneca: Eclectic Stoic 206
J. Literature During the First and Second Centuries C.E. 212
K. Greek and Latin Literature and Philosophy in the Later Empire 228
L. Greek and Roman Science 245

IV. The Triumph of Christianity 252

A. Was There a Jesus? 253
B. The Spread of Christianity 270
C. The Evolution of Christian Doctrine 278
D. Heaven, Hell, and the Devil 292
E. The Pagan Response 304
F. The Consolidation of Christian Rule 314

V. The Mediaeval Era 325

A. The Emergence and Spread of Islam 326
B. The Basic Doctrines of Islam 330
C. Politics, Society, and the Church in Mediaeval Europe 332
D. Intraction of Christians and Muslims 335
E. Muslim and Christian Science and Philosophy 341
F. The Rise of Scholasticism 347
G. Christian Heresy and Its Consequences 354
H. Troubles in Church and State 359
I. Mediaeval Literature 362
J. Mediaeval Art and Music 374
K. Norse Mythology 378
L. Religion, Society, and Literature in Great Britain 381

VI. The Renaissance 391

A. The Emergence of Humanism 393
B. Erasmus, Luther, and the Reformation 401
C. The Spread of Reformation Theology 407

D. England's Break with the Papacy 410
E. Toleration and Inquisition 418
F. Secularism in Continental European Literature 425
G. Secularism in English Literature 438
H. Renaissance Art and Music 456
I. Europe's Encounters with New World Cultures 465
J. Renaissance Science and Its Ramifications 472

Epilogue 479
Bibliography 484
Index 493
About the Author

Preface

I had initially conceived this work as a *world* history of atheism, but I gradually became aware that the relative paucity of academic work on the subject beyond the West—or, more plausibly, the deficiencies of my own scholarly faculties—made such a broad compass impossible, to say nothing of expanding this work even beyond its current length. And so I focused on the development of atheism in Western civilisation.

It soon became evident to me that a history of atheism—and, more generally, secularism, or the evolution of a worldview in which religion plays little or no part—is inseparable from the history of religion itself. Accordingly, I have felt the need to provide at least a broad overview of the major religions that have dominated Western culture: Judaism, Christianity, Islam, as well as Norse mythology, Native American religion, and others. I was obliged to omit discussion of Hinduism, Buddhism, and other Asian religions, for all that they have had some bearing on Western thought and society. My portrayal of religion is perforce restricted to a focus on certain key principles that are specifically related to atheism: the existence and nature of god(s), the existence and nature of something called the soul, the existence and nature of the afterlife, and the ramifiations of religious (or atheistic) belief upon intellectual, social, political, and cultural history. This is a large enough canvass without the attempt to write (*per impossibile*) a full-scale history of world religions.

It is probably best to state at the outset that I am myself a supporter and advocate of atheism, as even a casual examination of my publishing history will attest. I am not shy in stating that I regard nearly all aspects of religious belief, ancient and modern, to be arrant nonsense and, taken as a whole, harmful to human thought, society, and culture. I would not have undertaken a work of this magnitude if I did not have such a belief, and the expectation that anyone writing a treatise of this kind should be neutral or objective is not credible. The best one can hope is that the writer will expound the views of all thinkers and intellectual movements fairly, and I like to think I have done that.

A greater danger, as I see it, is one that is endemic to any work of this sort—a work that focuses on a single strain of thought, when in most cases that strain is intimately tied to a wide array of other elements in a given thinker or movement. The result is frequently an inadvertently teleological approach that, in this instance, sees atheism as inevitably emerging triumphant as religious belief subsides or is overthrown in a given culture. But given that religion today, even if weakened in many societies (especially in the West), still commands widespread adherence, it can hardly be said that atheism has attained a definitive victory. We are all too aware that the ebb and flow of cultures make very few "triumphs" permanent.

I have made efforts to examine the central issue of atheism not only by examination of philosophers but also of literature and the other arts, the role of religion and atheism in political and social history, and (where possible) an assessment of the development of religious belief among a given society's people as a whole; for it is they, and not the intellectual class, who have frequently made the expression of atheism possible.

I did not wish to burden this book down with an excess of academic jargon or paraphernalia, but I have included internal page citations to scholarly and other works, as included in my bibliography. For the chapters on Greek and Roman thought, I have not cited in the bibliography the translations I quote in the text, merely listing the translator in a footnote. I do, however, provide full bibliographic information on primary works in subsequent chapters. In most instances, I have checked (and, in a few cases, modified) the translations by comparison with the original texts in those languages with which I am familiar.

I trust I shall be excused for not citing religious titles (Saint, Reverend, Father, and so on) when referring to certain figures, since I would regard it as hypocritical for me to do so. I do not intend any disrespect in this matter. I generally capitalise "God" when referring to the Christian god.

I did most of my research on this book at the various libraries of the University of Washington; but I have been preparing for this book, wittingly or not, for several decades. My studies of classical philosophy at Brown (under the instruction of Michael C. J. Putnam, Kurt A. Raaflaub, Charles Fornara, and others) and Princeton (where I worked with David Furley, Michael Frede, Froma Zeitlin, and others), and my wide-ranging discussions of this general subject with such colleagues as Robert M. Price, Steven J. Mariconda, Donald R. Burleson, Tom Flynn, and many others have been of inestimable value to me. It is needless to say that I bear sole responsibility for any errors or misinterpretations found in this work.

S. T. Joshi
Seattle, Washington
September 2022

The Downfall of GOD

I. The Origin and Development of Religion

> If we think that this search for God is a vain search, and that there is no reality to be discovered, . . . then the history of religion becomes a study of the aberrations of the human mind.
>
> —Cyril Bailey

A. Religion in the Palaeolithic Age

More than a century and a half ago, the pioneering anthropologist Edward Burnett Tylor wrote in *Primitive Culture* (1871), "Are there, or have there been, tribes of men so low in culture as to have no religious conceptions whatever?"[1] For all the mountains of research done on this question, Tylor's rhetorical question remains fundamentally sound (with the exclusion of his apparent prejudice toward "low" cultures). And even though much of the scholarship of Tylor and other nineteenth- and early twentieth-century anthropologists has been superseded by later, more precise work or discarded altogether as being based on flawed premises, the notion that there is such a thing as a "natural history of religion" (a methodology by which the origin and development of religion from "primitive"[2] times to the present day), and that it can account far more plausibly and accurately for the prevalence of religion in our time, are central hermeneutical tools in presenting a compelling case for the

1. Tylor, *Primitive Culture* 2.2.
2. I do not intend any pejorative connotation in the use of this word; I employ it merely to avoid tedious circumlocution, and intend by it a level of society chronologically prior to the establishment of what can (also with a neutral signification) be termed "civilisation."

validity of a secularist outlook on human life, culture, and society.[3]

Although it was David Hume who first published a full-fledged treatise on this subject, precisely titled *The Natural History of Religion* (1757), speculation on the subject can be traced to Greco-Roman antiquity at the very latest. Such speculations—including Hume's—were largely founded on philosophical presuppositions and were, therefore, almost wholly cognitive in their approach. In some popular accounts, such as John Fiske's *Myths and Myth-Makers* (1872), the thrust appeared to be that primitive people were simply bad philosophers who misconstrued natural phenomena—ranging from the growth of trees to the course of the sun over the sky to the flow of rivers downstream—as the product of human-like forces (although infinitely more powerful than themselves), leading to the development of the concept of deity. And the facile theory that Sir James George Frazer (*The Golden Bough,* 1890–1915) and others put forth—that early animism (the personification or deification of natural forces) and the practice of magic led first to polytheism, then to monotheism, and at last to the proper understanding of Nature through science—has been shown to be crude and erroneous, even if some of these scholars gathered together valuable information on the issues in question.

Many of these scholars overused the principle of analogy; that is, they attempted to extrapolate the contours of primitive religion by a study of the primitive peoples in their own midst; but the utility of this approach is now under strong question, chiefly because it is impossible to determine to what extent such present-day peoples have been affected by the civilised people they may have come into contact with. Today, the natural history of religion is overwhelmingly based on such disciples as evolutionary neuroscience, archaeology, sociology, psychology, and of course anthropology; and there is a significant emphasis on the *social* context of religious belief.

---

3. I am not qualified to assess the soundness of the notion—propounded in some treatises early in this century (see, e.g., Hamer and Wade)—that our brains are "hardwired" toward belief in God, or more generally toward some kind of "faith." It appears that this view has now been widely rejected (see, e.g., Wightman, *Origins of Religion* 8). The notion strikes me as highly speculative and also incapable of accounting plausibly for the growing secularism of world society over the past several centuries, even if—as W. E. H. Lecky hypothesised more than a century and a half ago—"faith" has for many been transferred from the realm of religion to that of politics.

What these disciplines tell us is that, although the precise origin of religion—even, or indeed especially, in its earliest stages, when it may have been manifested as magic, ritual, shamanism, animism, and totemism—is lost in the mists of time, we can make compelling conjectures on how it developed over millions of years, stretching back to the earliest species of hominin[4] life. Numerous strands of primitive thought, belief, and action—especially those that contributed to the protection and expansion of the group, therefore rendering them evolutionally beneficial—all fused into what can only be regarded as an inescapable tendency toward belief in gods, a soul, and an afterlife.

It has been observed that, in human groups at all levels of development, empathy is in fact favourable to the preservation of the group. Those who can show empathy—often through the triggering of the so-called "mirror" neurons[5]—can modify their own behaviour for the benefit of the group. This allows the group to be more than the sum of its parts, even though the resulting "ingrouping" can also have deleterious effects—for example, it can lead to xenophobia and tribalism. When a group engages in synchronic action, such as ritual dancing, a state of ecstasy can occur from the intensifying rhythmic and repetitive action that results. But, for purposes of self-preservation, the group is compelled to find ways to control this ecstasy, especially during key rites of passage—birth, sexual maturation, marriage, and so on. In this way, collective or corporate ritual develops. As one scholar has put it, "Corporate ritual is about enacting shared ideas and values."[6] Ritual, by allowing individuals to place themselves within the group structure, allows the individual's brain to accept information sanctioned by the group.

Anthropomorphism is, from the evolutionary standpoint, a vital and even necessary component of human survival, stemming from the human need to guard against threats in the natural world and the tendency to recognise (or imagine) patterns that might be human faces. In primitive societies there is less likelihood of a clear distinction between the human and the non-human, leading to a kind of identification with the animals

4. The term hominin is now applied to all human species, extinct and modern. Hominid refers to modern humans and the extinct Great Apes.

5. These are neurons in the premotor cortex that are triggered when an individual watches a given action being performed by another and then copies it.

6. Wightman, *Origins of Religion* 34.

that are needed to maintain the group. As the killing of animals for food increases, the need arises for rituals to atone for the act. The celebrated cave paintings found in the south of France and elsewhere, probably dating to the Upper Palaeolithic (50,000 to 10,000 years ago), are a vivid testament to this. Some paintings point to a magical belief that depicting the killing or injuring of the animals will result in the death of the animals in real life; other paintings suggest rituals—sometimes involving a shaman or sorcerer, sometimes a group of dancing women—that are enacted to ensure the animals' fertility so that they can continue to provide sustenance to the group.

Just as individuals are inclined to perceive that they are part of something greater (i.e., the social group), the group itself comes to feel the need to see itself as part of something greater. As the social group becomes larger, the need for hierarchies arises, with select individuals attaining supremacy for the sake of the efficient performance of social needs. The whole society then looks to a non-human external leader who becomes a kind of parent of the group. Rules come into being for the preservation of the group; eventually these rules become concretised as a coherent and recognisable morality. Ritual and punishment play significant roles in the development of morality, as do anthropomorphised non-human agents.

It is now conjectured that belief in spirits, ghosts, and other such phenomena was a result of the brain's need to "keep alive" individuals of significant value to the individual. Death is, in a sense, the most significant "rite of passage" in human existence, and it is no surprise that it has long been regarded with fear and awe, with efforts made to deny or circumvent it reaching back to the remotest antiquity. Indeed, earlier generations of scholars believed that the phenomenon of death was either the chief or even the only factor that led to the birth of religion, but it is evident that many other factors come into play. In any case, the primitive need to take account of death led to the concept of the ghost or phantom of the dead, who then came to be regarded as part of the natural order. But this can only happen on a social level when communication systems have developed to such a degree that sharing of such experiences can occur. The existence of material objects associated with the dead also play a role. Grief over the death of a loved one, and a desire (wish-fulfilment) that the dead still be present, contribute to the idea of life after death.

The social group as a whole adopts this belief, resulting in the practice of ancestor-worship. Animals and natural phenomena are endowed with agency and thus with spirit. Then all such manifestations are attributed to a single agent—in other words, a supreme deity.

The role of dreams is also critical. Probably all hominins dreamed, but the ability to remember and communicate dreams only occurred once certain parts of the brain—specifically, the hippocampus—developed; this probably occurred over a long period in the Lower Palaeolithic period, from about 800,000 to 200,000 years ago. Individuals' dreams then became co-opted by the group, although this process probably did not begin until about 50,000 years ago. Daydreams, hallucinations, and other altered states of consciousness may have been particularly prevalent among certain primitive peoples, especially those who lived or spent a significant amount of time in caves or in featureless landscapes such as the African savannah or the sub-arctic regions of northern Europe. Such terrains are conductive to altered states of consciousness.

Language obviously plays an immense role in both the development of the human race (especially in regard to its mental functions) and the growth of religion. But ritual developed on a separate track from language and probably preceded it, since many if not most rituals are inherently non-verbal. Such non-linguistic phenomena as music, gesture, and the like also come into play here. But when did language emerge? Some scholars place it as early as one million years ago, but this view has not gone unchallenged. Probably language developed very slowly over a long period; it may possibly—although not certainly—have done so in conjunction with tool-making.

The dating of all the phenomena just described is necessarily a matter of conjecture. Evidence of primitive peoples fashioning or collecting anthromorphic or zoomorphic objects can be traced to as far back as the period from 500,000 to 200,000 years ago—in other words, from the Lower to Middle Palaeolithic. The use of red ochre as a pigment—traditionally thought to symbolise blood—probably dates to about 400,000 years ago and suggests that the ritualisation of death was beginning to occur. The burial of the dead by *Homo sapiens* probably began around 120,000 to 80,000 years ago; and the fact that grave goods—objects ranging from food to clothing to items of many other sorts—have been found clearly suggests belief in an afterlife when the dead could make use of these objects.

Groups of *Homo sapiens* are believed to have emerged in Africa as far back as 300,000 years ago. The period from 150,000 to 50,000 years ago saw the evolution of *Homo sapiens* as culturally and cognitively distinct from *Homo neanderthalensis.* In the period from 80,000 to 45,000 years ago there began an extensive migration of peoples from East Africa to southwest Asia, the Near East, the Caucasus, and Europe. We find death rituals, objects signifying the development of a mother-goddess concept, and other elements of proto-religious belief by around 30,000 years ago. By the Neolithic period (12,000 to as late as 4000 years ago or even later in some regions of the world), all the elements were in place for a full flowering of religion throughout the world.

B. Religion in the Neolithic and Bronze Ages

The chief distinguishing characteristic of the Neolithic period is the establishment of settled life through the introduction of agriculture and the domestication of animals and livestock, notably dogs, cattle, sheep, and pigs. Earlier scholars believed this period to be still "primitive" in many senses, but more recent research establishes that Neolithic peoples in Europe and elsewhere no longer lived in caves but constructed houses of stone, wood, and sod, sometimes quite large and elaborate. Circular ditches around settlements, beginning around 3600 B.C.E., may have served some kind of ritual purpose in addition to defining the borders of a community. There were even some signs of class stratification in Neolithic society, although nothing approaching an aristocratic elite as found in the succeeding Bronze Age. There also appear to be some early signs of specialisation in the performance of tasks—such as the making of flint axes or in trade between communities. No tombs for kings have been found, although there may well have been a leader or chieftain of a given group. These groups were apparently largely self-governing and relatively small in numbers. Shamans and priests probably existed, but only as part-time occupations.

The repetitive acts of planting crops in spring and harvesting in autumn, and the careful attention that Neolithic societies were thereby compelled to pay to the succession of the seasons, appears to have led to a perception of cyclical growth, death, and rebirth—and this conception was then applied to human life, augmenting the belief in life after death brought on by other factors. There was, accordingly, a close connexion between death cults and fertility cults, as well as the evolution of profound symbolism surrounding the spring and autumn equinoxes and the summer and winter solstices. All this led to the concept of the Earth Mother, statuettes of whom (generally depicted as heavy-set if not actually pregnant, with exaggerated breasts and other distinctively feminine features) have been found in Neolithic remains. Multiple cycles of myth developed whereby the Earth Mother mates with the sun- or sky-god (invariably male) to generate crops and also to foster human growth; in winter she retreats underground, and the sky-god also suffers an actual or symbolic death, only to be revived in spring. The death and resurrection of Jesus Christ falls into this schema.

The sun, as the source of life, was freighted with symbolism. Earth circles (a feature unique to England) symbolised the sun; and it is in this context that we must understand the more than 700 groups of standing stones constructed throughout Great Britain—again, almost exclusively there, although a few such monuments exist elsewhere in Europe. Construction of Stonehenge, for example, began around 3000 B.C.E., although at this juncture it appears to have consisted only of a circular bank or berm and an external ditch. A circle of small sarsen stones was set up around 2800; much later, around 2250, larger stones were brought to the site, from as far away as Wales (probably by boat). These are the so-called bluestones; but they were then abandoned and large sarsen stones were brought from the nearby site of Overton Down. This site also served as the source of the sarsen stones at the much larger site of Avebury, which was built around 2600–2500.

While these henges could serve both secular and sacred purposes (although the Neolithic peoples probably did not acknowledge such a distinction), they were clearly utulised for the sake of ritual. Numerous fanciful theories have been made as to the exact purpose of Stonehenge and analogous sites, many of them now rejected; for example, the notion that it was some sort of astronomical observatory where eclipses were predicted has now been discredited. In all probability, Stonehenge was constructed to establish a connexion between the earth, the sun, and the moon; there are also indirect indications of a relation to the summer solstice. In effect, Stonehenge is a sun temple, and rituals whereby the power of the sun and moon were harnessed were probably performed, possibly to foster the growth of crops.

Other circles may have served as funerary sites. We find, indeed, two different types of death customs practised by the Neolithic peoples of England. The first is the use of the long barrow, generally in the east of England, which date to as early as 4255 B.C.E. These barrows, or mounds, could be as long as 550 metres, and they were encased by vertical timbers. In a sense, they replicated the houses of the living, clearly suggesting a belief in life after death. This practice died out around 2500. The second is the megalithic chambered tomb, chiefly in the west of England, the earliest of which dates to around 4300 B.C.E. These are found in a wide variety of styles and forms. Sometimes the two traditions were fused to produce hybrid forms. There is evidence that the tombs were carefully maintained for many centuries. These tombs were communal, not individual. The barrows probably contained only a fraction of the dead of a given community; as such, they were not cemeteries but rather were thought of as "magic gateways through which life could be started anew and where the living and the dead could meet."[7] Birds or animals were sacrificed in front of the tombs, suggesting a totem function. Actual totem poles are known to have existed at many of the barrow sites. Totemism implies belief in the transmigration of souls—from animals to human beings and back again.

The transition from the Stone Age to the Bronze Age probably led to (or was brought about by) an increase in population, which resulted in the emergence of kings and an aristocratic warrior class to lead a more complex society that may have had conflicts with neighbouring communities. It is not necessary to assume invasions from outside to account for this social transition.

It may be helpful to study the religious beliefs of the Celts, as they were a group that dominated western and central Europe (including England and Ireland) from the late Neolithic and into the Bronze Ages before at last succumbing to the Romans in the early centuries of the Common Era. Because the Celts did not produce a written literature until very late in their history, we are largely reliant on archaeology, as well as the testimony of other groups, for information about their rituals

7. Castleden, *The Stonehenge People* 185.

and practices. These groups, chiefly the Greeks and the Romans from as early as 500 B.C.E. to the fourth century C.E., often spoke about the Celts from a hostile perspective, since the Celts made incursions into territory they controlled from the third century B.C.E. onward; moreover, the Romans in particular were inclined to identify the gods of the Celts with members of their own pantheon, even though these identifications were frequently inexact given that the Celtic gods do not appear to have had the fairly precise functions and attributes of the Greco-Roman pantheon.

What we can learn about the Celtic religion in general is the manner in which religious belief made a transition from the Neolithic to the Bronze Age—a transition that is highlighted by the progression from an approximately animistic set of beliefs to the conception of gods who gradually took on specific traits and were imagined to be increasingly anthropomorphic. While it is not possible, given the state of the evidence, to establish a chronological development along these lines, we can see that the Celts did evolve their religion in accordance with the evolution of their own society (or societies, since Celtic groups did not develop in any uniform or systematic way over the broad areas they controlled).

The Celts emerged among Neolithic farmers in the fifth or fourth millennium B.C.E. The so-called Urnfield people (c. 1300 B.C.E.), who practised cremation burial, are now regarded as proto-Celtic. Around 700 we see extensive use of metalworking as well as the use of the horse as the Celts developed a warrior culture. The La Tène culture (c. 500 B.C.E.) is the first true Celtic culture, typified by fortified towns across Europe and a society based on kingship and a martial aristocracy.

A prominent facet of early Celtic religious belief is reverence for natural features such as rivers, lakes, trees, and the like. Indeed, although the Celts appear to have had temples made of wood, they also used open-air venues for rituals, notably sacred groves. Water was held in especially high regard: it not only had curative powers (as in hot springs), but there was a need to propitiate it to ward off its potentially destructive effects. The reverence for water is indicated by numerous deposits of undamaged weapons and other metalwork in rivers, lakes, or bogs; the names of actual river gods and goddesses are also known. Bogs in particular were regarded with dread because the danger they presented made them seem alive. Human sacrifices were offered to them or to the underworld deity thought to live in them. Temples sprang up around springs, especially those containing mineralised water, which was found to be beneficial to treat human ailments. One of the most celebrated of the water goddesses was Sulis, a Celtic goddess of the spring who gave her name to the Roman colony in Bath, England (Aquae Sulis). In England, the healing god Nodens was equated with Mars and at times with the sea god Neptune, again suggesting the healing powers of water.

The Celts had a priesthood, and paraphernalia worn by them (masks, staffs, and the like) has been found. The Druids were the chief Celtic priests, prevalent in Gaul and Britain as prophets and soothsayers. Roman authors state that they were in charge of all religious ceremonies, and go on to claim that human sacrifices (mostly of criminals or prisoners of war) were carried out by the Druids for purposes of divination. Archaeology appears to confirm the practice. The Celts developed a reverence for the human head, as representative of the body as a whole; heads of defeated enemies were placed on poles or in niches in the walls of shrines, apparently as ritual offerings.

Pure animism—or, more precisely, animatism—is indicated by the extent to which the Celts venerated a wide array of animals. Animals were depicted as accompanying Celtic gods but were also visualised independently in cave paintings, figurines, and other artifacts. The chief Celtic god, Cernunnos ("the horned one"), was often depicted as a horned man, accompanied by ram-headed snakes. He was essentially a god of nature, crops, and prosperity. Some gods were seen as shapeshifters, metamorphosing from animal to human and back again. Horses, dogs, and bulls were all depicted as cult animals. Epona was a horse-goddess widely portrayed in Gaul (France); she also functioned as a fertility goddess and earth mother. Dogs, bulls, boars, and stags were associated with healing or fertility, or were all endowed with supernatural properties, as were aquatic birds (especially swans), geese (associated with war-gods), and ravens (associated with the underworld because of their carrion-eating).

The need to foster the growth of crops and livestock engendered the worship of the sun. Extensive survivals of spoked wheels and other imagery on jewellery suggest the prevalence of a sun- or sky-god; initially he appears not to have been anthropomorphised, but later (perhaps through Roman influence) the sun-god was depicted as quasi-human.

Oftentimes the sky-god is shown riding a horse; this cannot be a Roman feature but must be Celtic.

Fertility goddesses were common. The so-called Celtic Mother was associated with both procreation and death. The prevalence of such goddesses may signal the prominence that women had in Celtic society; the Romans discovered that some of their most valiant opponents were Boudicca and other warrior queens. Often the Celtic Mothers were depicted in groups of three, since three was a sacred or magic number for the Celts. Fertility goddesses had a wide array of functions or aspects ranging from war, good luck, commercial prosperity, and protection of the domestic hearth.

Given that a warrior elite existed in Celtic society from at least the early first millennium B.C.E., it is understandable that gods or goddesses of war would be worshipped. One of them, Andraste of the Iceni (a tribe in Britain), is definitely known. The Celts readily adapted the Roman war-god Mars to their own purposes—or it is possible that the Romans applied the name Mars to a number of different Celtic war-gods.

Extensive evidence points to the Celts' belief in an active afterlife. Grave goods for fallen warriors feature weapons of all sorts. A shift occurring in the Bronze Age from cremation to inhumation signalled that "the otherworld was clearly one where earthly status was recognised and prolonged to eternity."[8] Warriors were often buried with chariots and even horses in chambered tombs, along with food, weapons, clothing, and other items. Even a few women were so buried. The existence of pits that serve no utilitarian purpose, and that contain traces of what may be human or animal sacrifices, suggests attempts to placate the gods of the underworld. Irish vernacular sources name Donn as a god of the dead, from whom human beings were thought to be descended.[9] Aside from this detail, however, there is little evidence that the Celts devised any sort of "creation story" to account for the existence of the universe and of the humans and animals within it.

8. Green, *The Gods of the Celts* 123.

9. Cf. Caesar, *Bellum Gallicum* 6.18: "All the Gauls assert that they are descended from the god Dis, and say that this tradition has been handed down by the Druids" (tr. W. A. McDevitte). Dis was the Roman god of the underworld.

C. Egyptian Religion

The earliest organised religious system on earth appears to be the Egyptian religion. The settlement of the region—probably by migrants from Africa and western Asia—can be traced to the Neolithic period (about 5000 B.C.E.). In the so-called Protodynastic period (3200–3100),[10] the hieroglyphic script was created; Upper Egypt (in the south, and featuring a more African populace) and Lower Egypt (in the north, more significantly influenced by Asia and Lybia) were united, traditionally under the kingship of Mena (Menes in Greek), who established the capital at Memphis, near the Nile delta. It is evident that at least some aspects of Egyptian religion—especially the cult of the dead—were already established at this time.

Two of the central facts of Egyptian religion are its intimate connexion with kingship and its relations with the unusual climate of the terrain, especially the dominance of the Nile (which in ancient Egyptian didn't even have a name; the name Nile [Neilos] was coined by the Greeks). It is, for example, unsurprising that the Egyptians regarded the sun-god Ra as the creator of the universe, under his aspect as Atum ("the All"); significantly, Atum is depicted as a king of Egypt. The god Horus (the Greek name for Heru) is also an aspect of Ra and symbolises the sky. The two gods' power over the earth is embodied in the worship of Ra-Horakhty ("Ra/Horus of the horizon").

The basic creation story in Egyptian religion—the coming to be of Ra out of an infinite expanse of dark waters called Nun, and his subsequent creation of the rest of the universe—was in all likelihood inspired by the yearly inundation of the Nile valley in summer by the river and the subsequent retreat of the waters in autumn. Human beings were engendered out of the "eye" of Ra. Upon his return to the sky, he appointed a human king to be his successor; this king is himself a god. The birth of a (male) child to the king and queen was regarded as a divine event. (All this created a problem for the queen Hapshepsut [r. 1479–58], who had some difficulty establishing her right to rule after the death of her father, Thutmose II.)

The Egyptians envisioned a multitude of gods with varying and at

10. All dates for Egyptian history until about the 7th century B.C.E. should be considered approximate.

times overlapping powers. Nut (a female goddess of the sky) and Geb (a male god of dry land), by their union, begat four offspring: Seth (god of disorder), Osiris (god of order), Nephthys, and Isis. We also have Bastet (a fertility goddess), Thoth (god of wisdom, language, and writing), and numerous others. Many of these were depicted as animals or as fusions of the animal and the human. These depictions were widely misunderstood by other cultures (including our own) as signifying Egyptian worship of animals; in fact, it appears that these animals merely symbolised the multifarious powers of the god in question (Horus, as symbolising the sky, is often portrayed as a falcon). It is also erroneous to believe that the Egyptians engaged in the crude animism of deifying trees, mountains, and other natural objects; even the Nile was not deified, although the flood that it periodically engendered was depicted as the god Hapy.

Osiris, whose name appears in funerary texts as early as around 2400 B.C.E., became a dominant figure thereafter. This was during the Old Kingdom (Dynasties 1–3, 2686–2181). Osiris came to be regarded as the god of those who had led a good life and had had a good burial (an expensive process not available to the poor). This explicit connexion of religion and morality is of interest. It was at this time that the process of mummification began, and it is no surprise that Osiris was the god of dead kings. But, startlingly, Osiris was murdered by his immoral counterpart, Seth. This seeming triumph of disorder over order was, of course, short-lived: even though a tomb of Osiris was constructed at Abydos (Upper Egypt), he was brought back to life by his sister (and, later, wife) Isis. It is likely that this myth was fostered by the revival of the earth and its fertility by the yearly inundation caused by the Nile. In any event, Osiris became the ruler of the underworld. Horus and Seth subsequently engaged in a battle over Egypt; Horus ultimately prevailed, but Seth remained as a lurking menace.

Isis herself became a force of healing, specifically in the cure of bites from poisonous animals—a stark necessity in a land populated by snakes, scorpions, and other dangerous creatures. It was, however, only at a very late stage of Egyptian history (the fourth century B.C.E.) that temples to Isis were constructed. These continued to be in use all the way up to the time when the Byzantine emperor Justinian closed them in the sixth century C.E.

The Egyptians evolved an elaborate conception of the nature of the human body. In essence, they imagined not a single "soul" occupying the body but two distinct if related elements: the *ba* (that which endows the body with motion) and the *ka* (that which nurtures or sustains the body). It was only to be expected that the phenomenon of childbirth was surrounded by all manner of divine forces; and so, of course, was the phenomenon of death. The degree to which the Egyptians had some kind of awe of or fascination with death has been much exaggerated;[11] but they clearly exhibited a fascination with the afterlife. Grave goods have been found in Egyptian graves from as early a period as 4000 B.C.E., far antedating the Dynastic period. The climate may well have enhanced the Egyptians' belief in a material afterlife where (some) dead people could make use of food, clothing, and other objects they enjoyed in life. The dry climate causes bodily decomposition to be much delayed, and the Egyptians' use of dry natron for treating the dead resulted in the disinfection and desiccation of corpses, who were then mummified (once their internal organs were removed) after treatment with other substances. It is, however, not entirely clear how the dead were supposed to function without their internal organs.

A kind of class system emerged in the treatment of the dead—or, rather, in the manner in which the dead could act in the afterlife. The overwhelming emphasis on the intimate relations between the gods and earthly kings resulted in the construction of the pyramids, the most impressive visible symbol of the Egyptians' focus on life after death. This work began with the building of the Step Pyramid (c. 2600) for Djoser (r. 2670–50); it is plain that the pyramid form symbolises the ascent of the king to heaven. Later pyramids were constructed with smooth, sloping sides, and the great pyramids at Giza (Lower Egypt), as well as the Sphinx, date to the 26th century B.C.E. While it is not entirely true that the pyramids were solely built for kings (a few were built for courtiers), it is certainly not the case that average citizens could expect

11. Perhaps the most amusing example of this is Théophile Gautier's lurid tale of Egyptian horror, "One of Cleopatra's Nights" (1838), where Cleopatra laments: "'Menacing and funereal symbols alone meet the eye . . . the Unknown, death, nothingness. In the place of any vegetation only *stelae* limned with weird characters; instead of avenues of trees, avenues of granite obelisks; in lieu of soil, vast pavements of granite for which whole mountains could each furnish but one slab; in place of a sky, ceilings of granite—eternity made palpable, a bitter and everlasting sarcasm upon the frailty and brevity of life . . ." *The Mummy's Foot* 70 (the translation is by Lafcadio Hearn [1882]).

such august memorials to their life, and gateways to the afterlife, to be built for them.

Moreover, the moral element we have seen in some aspects of Osiris' rulership of the underworld enhanced the clear distinction between royalty and everyone else. The *Book of the Dead* (whose earliest texts date to around 1600 B.C.E.) identify two types of people: the *akh* (transfigured spirits who have quasi-divine powers) and the *mut* (the ordinary dead, who remain dead and do not attain a good afterlife). In later stages of Egyptian history, it was believed that a tribunal of the gods sat in judgment on the dead; only those who had led a good life (however that may have been defined) would be allowed to enter the underworld and join Osiris.

A curious attempt at a wholesale revision of Egyptian religion occurred under the reign of Amenhotep IV (r. 1353–36). His name reflects the prominence given to the god Amun, a "hidden" god who, under the aspect of Amun-Ra, became the chief god of the New Kingdom (1550–1069). At this time Egypt had emerged from a century of foreign invasion to reunify itself and expand its own territorial reach. Amenhotep attempted to obliterate the worship of Amun-Ra, maintaining that the sun-god was merely the disk of the sun. He substituted the worship of the solar creator god Aten; he himself changed his named to Akhenaten. This apparent enforcement of monotheism (albeit accompanied by a demythologising of the sun) was in fact a self-aggrandising move, since he also decreed that the people were to worship the god only through the king, not directly. But Akhenaten's successor, Tutankhamun, restored the old religion.

Egyptian science down to the time of the nation's conquest by Alexander (332 B.C.E.) is of some interest, only because much of it seems subservient to religion rather than staking out positions independent of theology. Egyptian medicine is a case in point. While various medical texts did present diagnoses and treatments based on experience and observation, they were almost uniformly melded with incantations and other elements of magic. Clearly the Egyptians did not conceive of a distinction between these phenomena. Upon the birth of a child, an oracle was summoned to issue a decree providing protection of the child through life. The so-called Harris Magical Papyrus is a series of incantations to ward off disasters on the Nile. Egyptian astronomy, although making a number of landmark discoveries, was purely utilitarian in purpose; the Egyptians appeared to take no particular interest in the nature or constitution of the stars. As arranged in constellations, these stars were associated with the various gods of their pantheon. The Egyptians did evolve the twenty-four-hour day, but their mathematics was also used mostly for practical ends. It hardly needs to be said that the existence of the pyramids point to the fact that their knowledge of geometry was formidable.

The literature of the pharaonic period does consist of some secular texts, both in prose and verse, and we do have some prose romances involving supernatural creatures apparently unrelated to their theology. But most of the literature that has survived is plainly religious in origin and purpose. There does not appear to have been anything that could be termed philosophical speculation during this entire period.

D. Religion in the Near East

In examining the highly complex development of civilisation (and, hence, religion) in the Near East from the third to the first millennium B.C.E., we must focus on the region known as Mesopotamia. Far from being any sociopolitical or ethnic terrain, this region is simply a geographical designation: "between the rivers," i.e., the area (extending from eastern Turkey to the Persian Gulf) between the Tigris and Euphrates rivers. During the period in question, portions of this area were successively ruled by the Sumerians, Babylonians, Assyrians, and Persians; in addition, other groups (distinguished by language or ethnicity) such as the Hittites, the Chaldeans, and the Medes figured at various times.

If we focus on the city of Babylon (now in Iraq) and its immediate environs, we can trace human settlement from at least 5000 B.C.E. Two millennia later we see the establishment of large cities, extensive work in stone and metal, and the invention of writing: Sumerian (which does not belong to any recognised linguistic group) and Akkadian (a Semitic language). The latter progressed from pictographs to the familiar cuneiform script found in an enormous array of documents on clay tablets, making it evident that the language evolved chiefly for the keeping of accounts in regard to the increasing domestic and international trade that was then developing.

It was during the so-called Early Dynastic period (2900–2350) that the region came together as a single administrative entity, called the Akkadian Empire. The central figure in this movement of consolidation was Sargon (r. 2371–16). Late in the third millennium, the Sumerian city of Ur gained prominence. Ur was sacked by the Elamites (residents of the city of Elam and environs) around 1940, leading to the emergence of Babylon (Bab-ili, "Gateway of the Gods") to geopolitical significance. During the First Babylonian Empire (1894–1595), Hammurabi (1792–50) became celebrated as establishing one of the most detailed law codes in the ancient world. He also conquered neighbouring Assyria and other regions, but under his successors some of this territory was lost.

In 1595 the Hittites, an Indo-European-speaking tribe from modern-day Turkey, plundered Babylon but did not remain. The city was taken over by a shadowy group called the Kassites, who ruled until 1155. Assyria, which had been gaining economic and political power since the third millennium, especially in such of its cities as Ashur (the capital) and Nineveh, sacked Babylon around 1225, whereupon the Kassite kings became vassals of Assyria. From 1200 to 1000 there was considerable instability in the region from attacks by Hittites, Aramaeans (a Semitic-speaking people from the land of Aram, in modern-day Syria), and other groups. Assyria managed to reassert itself and form the Neo-Assyrian Empire (911–609), chiefly under kings Tiglath-pileser III (r. 745–27), Sargon II (r. 721–05), and Sennacherib (r. 705–681), during which time the empire extended as far as the borders of Egypt (including Palestine) and Nineveh became the capital. Under Ashurbanipal (r. 668–31), the region was increasingly under attack from Cimmerians and Scythians from the northwest and Medes from the east.

The Assyrians were definitively defeated by a Babylonian ruler, Nabopolassar, who sacked Nineveh in 612, ushering in the Neo-Babylonian Empire. It was this empire, under Nebuchadnezzar (r. 605–562), who destroyed Jerusalem in 586 after capturing it in 597. But the empire gave way to Cyrus, king of the Medes and Persians, who sacked Babylon in 539, ending Babylonia's (and Assyria's) independent existence. The region remained under Persian rule until 331, when Alexander the Great swept in and conquered it.

During this long period, religion developed in a multitude of ways. Insofar as the earliest traces of religious belief can be identified, we can state that the distinction between what we would call magic and what could be termed a formal religion (as constituting a coherent theology specifying the functions of personal gods) did not exist. Magical thinking is evident in the widespread belief in demons capable of directly harming human beings in a wide variety of ways; protection against them could be had by the use of amulets containing incantations against the demon. Demonic possession, especially as a cause of disease, was widely credited, leading to the emergence of exorcists and witch-doctors as distinct occupations in Sumerian and Assyrian culture. One of these demons, as we shall have reason to discuss later, was Lilitu, who in the Israelite religion became known as Lilith. She was thought to be a succubus who tempted men into unwanted sexual activity in their sleep.

Ghosts of the dead—especially those who died by violence—were thought to stalk the land, and all manner of rituals were developed to lay them. Witchcraft was so commonly accepted that the Code of Hammurabi decrees the death penalty for practitioners (as does the Hebrew Bible). Omens and divination were extensively used, the latter mostly taking the form of examining livers, the interpretation of dreams and peculiar events, and astrology.

As early as the early third millennium B.C.E., we find evidence of religious practices in Erech (the first major city in Mesopotamia) revolving around the fertility goddess Inanna (the "Lady of Heaven"), to whom animal and plant offerings were made. Eventually a formal pantheon and theology developed in the region, as the gods associated with individual cities were consolidated, although irregularities remained. Anu was thought to be the father of the gods. Accompanying him was Enlil, who became the national god of Sumer. He was king of the earth; later he was believed to be Anu's son. He created the objects of the world and granted divine status to Sumerian rulers. Enki was lord of the underworld, and Ea was god of the water. These three gods were themselves created out of the offspring of Apsu (the Deep) and Tiamat (Ocean). Inanna-Ishtar was the most powerful female deity, as the goddess of war, love, and sex. Ereshkigal was the sister of Ishtar and had been the original goddess of the underworld, but she eventually gave way to Enki.

In the early to mid-second millennium B.C.E., a new god, Marduk, gained supremacy in the pantheon, taking over many functions from Enlil. In the *Enuma Elish,* the Babylonian account of creation, Marduk becomes the son of Ea who defeats Tiamat and becomes chief among the gods. It was the gods in general, and Marduk in particular, who were explicitly stated as commissioning Hammurabi to fashion his law code.[12] Marduk was in the most visible possible manner adopted by the Assyrians during their ascendancy over the region, when the Assyrian king Tukulti-ninurta I (r. 1244–08) removed the massive statue of Marduk from Babylon and brought it to the Assyrian capital, Ashur.

From an early period, priests gained enormous economic power by establishing temple estates that had vast groups of workers to till the land and do other work; as one scholar notes, the priests essentially became "powerful and rich corporations, with huge estates and thousands of personnel."[13] The king, who was also a priest, would enact the Sacred Marriage with the goddess of the city; in the case of male gods, royal females would enact the ceremony. Sumerian and Akkadian myths speak of gods who themselves had to toil before the creation of human beings; this was, indeed, why humans were created in the first place, at the behest of Enlil.

There is considerable evidence of the widespread use of temple prostitutes and concubines (usually slaves) connected with the goddess Inanna-Ishtar, who was explicitly declared to be a harlot (presumably not in a pejorative sense). The high-priestess (*Entu*) of the temple was chaste, but that was because she functioned as the "wife of the god" in Sacred Marriage ceremonies (even if these were sometimes carried out by human males serving as the god in a symbolic sense). The gods were "fed" all manner of foodstuffs from animals to milk, dates, figs, and other products. Even architecture contributed to the religious ambiance: the distinctive Babylonian feature of the ziggurat almost always existed as part of a temple compound and was believed to be the residence of the god. Mentions of the Tower of Babel and Jacob's ladder in the Hebrew Bible are clear allusions to the ziggurat.

The *Epic of Gilgamesh* contains vital features of early Sumerian religion. It is now believed that Gilgamesh was an actual ruler during the Early Dynastic Period, and the epic was probably fashioned in oral form from as early as 2100 B.C.E.; the text as we have it was set down in Akkadian, perhaps as early as 1600 B.C.E. The myth reveals the utter

12. See Saggs, *The Greatness That Was Babylon* 74–75.

13. Saggs 144.

saturation of the culture by religious concepts. Gilgamesh himself is said to be two-thirds divine (as the son of the goddess Ninsun and a human father), and we find other elements such as the idea of Gilgamesh as a priest-king, temple prostitutes, prophetic dreams and omens, Gilgamesh's rejection of sacred marriage with Ishtar, constant intervention of gods in human affairs, and, most relevant to our purposes, his trip to the realm of the dead, where he learns of the deluge that overwhelmed the city of Shuruppak, after which the god Ea instructs Utnapishtim to build a ship filled with his family and also livestock and wild animals.

This account is now believed to have been inserted into the *Epic of Gilgamesh* from another epic, the *Atrahasis* (c. 1650), which tells the creation story of the three main gods of the Sumerians, Anu, Enlil, and Enki. It need hardly be noted that this account later found its way into the Hebrew Bible in the form of Noah's ark. Other myth-cycles speak extensively of the underworld, and there is some evidence that the Babylonians gave some thought to the age-old problem of evil—how a god can allow bad things to happen to innocent people. But it cannot be said that the discussion of this issue was notably searching or profound.

The Persians who conquered the region in the sixth century B.C.E. of course had their own religious traditions. Settlements in the area (now Iran) can be traced back to about 7000 B.C.E., but the Medes (who spoke their own language, Median, and who occupied what is now western and northern Iran) became a force to be reckoned with under the reign of king Phraortes, who subjugated the Persians around 640. But a century later, the Persian king Cyrus II (r. 560?–530) conquered the Medes (c. 550), the Lydians at the western end of Turkey (c. 546), and Babylon (539). His successor, Cambyses (r. 530–22), conquered Egypt in 525, thereby granting Persia an enormous terrain stretching from the Mediterranean to the boundary with India.

It was around 650 B.C.E. that the dominant Persian religion, Zoroastrianism, emerged. Zarathustra (rendered in Greek as Zoroastres and thence into English as Zoroaster) is a highly obscure figure whose *floruit* has been dated as early as the second millennium B.C.E. and as late as the sixth century B.C.E. (his canonical dates in some documents are given as 628–551). Whatever the case, his chief theological virtue (if it is that) is to envision a god that is pure good, Ahura Mazda, the creator of earth, sky, and human beings; he is also the embodiment of justice. But this god was evidently created in conjunction with a cosmic force of evil, falsehood, and disorder (*druj*), who was eventually given the name Ahriman. It is evidently our choice whether to follow the one entity or the other. At death, the good go to heaven and the bad to hell; but the latter will not remain there for eternity. Zoroaster envisioned a four-stage cycle of cosmic history, each extending to 3000 years, in the final cycle of which Ahura Mazda will conquer Ahriman, at which time the distinction between heaven and earth will be destroyed and everyone will live in the presence of Ahura Mazda.

Persian rulers regarded themselves as the regents of Ahura Mazda; and—although they were absolute monarchs who had the power of life and death over their citizens—in their culture they themselves were not regarded as divine and were not deified after death. The Persians also regarded fire as a divine substance, and Anahita became the goddess of fire. The Persians also appear to have worshipped natural forces (the sun, the moon, the earth, wind, etc.). Their priests, known as Magi, had purely ceremonial functions and did not engage in theological debate. Nor did the Persians practise religious exclusivity: when conquering other nations, they rarely interfered in native religious beliefs and engaged (as did the Greeks and other cultures) in elaborate attempts to synthesise their own deities with those of the local populations they governed.

In the eastern Mediterranean, the Phoenicians are worth noting. They had settled the area now designated by Syria, Lebanon, and Israel no later than 2000 B.C.E., establishing the city of Byblos. They arrived in the region before the Israelites, who called them the Canaanites. Beginning around 1580, Egypt conquered the Levant, but the Phoenicians were also threatened by the Hittites and Amorites from the north. By 1200, Egypt was in decline, the Hittites destroyed, and the Mycenaeans of early Greece (who had given the Phoenicians the name by which we now know them) were under attack. It was at this time (c. 1200–600) that the Phoenicians became a dominant force, especially at sea. With such major cities as Tyre and Sidon, they controlled the eastern end of the Mediterranean and expanded their reach along North Africa as well.

But the Israelites defeated the Phoenicians in the eleventh and tenth centuries, and the Assyrians were a menace in the ninth. Intermarriage between the Phoenicians and the Israelites led to such figures as Jezebel and Athaliah, who occupy prominent roles in the Hebrew Bible.

Nebuchadnezzar destroyed Tyre in 574, and the Persians took over the region in 539. They ruled until Alexander's conquest in 332. But, so early as the thirteenth century, the Phoenicians established trading posts and colonies from one end of the Mediterranean to the other, including Carthage, traditionally founded around 814—a date that seems approximately correct.

Traces of the Phoenician religion can be found as early as the fourteenth century B.C.E., in the form of clay tablets depicting fertility cults and a cult of the dead. A distinct pantheon began to emerge, with El as the supreme god and king, portrayed variously as a bull or as a sun-god. His wife, Asherat-by-the-sea, was a mother goddess, and they gave birth to Baal, a god of the mountains, storms, and rain. Dagon was a god of grain. From an early period, Phoenician religion was influenced by its counterparts in Egypt and Mesopotamia, as can be seen in the fertility goddess Astarte, equivalent to the Babylonian Ishtar and the Egyptian Isis. As in Mesopotamia and elsewhere, local gods were worshipped in individual cities—Melqart in Tyre and Eshmun in Sidon, for example.

Priests and priestesses operated the numerous temples and sanctuaries throughout the areas controlled by the Phoenicians; the position was often handed down from generation to generation in the same family. Priests were sometimes married to priestesses. But kings, queens, and generals could also preside over religious rituals. There were also religious prostitutes, both male and female. Sacrifices included both animals and humans, including infants. The Phoenicians practised both cremation and inhumation. Grave goods in tombs and cremation urns (food, clothing, etc.) clearly suggest a belief in life after death.

E. Israelite Religion

We now come to one of the most difficult issues in the early history of religion. It is not simply that both the history and the religion of the inhabitants of what came to be called Israel, Palestine, and Canaan have, for obvious reasons, been studied with incredible minuteness for well over two millennia, but that nearly every aspect of these subjects is engulfed by controversy, disputes, and contradictory opinions. These disputes extend even to the smallest matters of terminology and nomenclature.[14] And because Judaism is a living religion as the religions of ancient Egypt, Assyria, and many other cultures (as well as those of the Greeks and Romans, to be studied in the next chapter) are not, some of its defenders have a vested interest in maintaining the veracity of the traditional accounts (specifically in the HB), not excluding the supernatural episodes featured in them. Given this situation, I will preface my own discussion by declaring that I have at least some superficial awareness of the differing opinions on the subjects in question and that my purpose is to portray the development of Israelite religion over the millennium that extended from approximately 1200 to 160 B.C.E. Indeed, it becomes apparent that this development proceeded in an unusually close manner with the course of the political, military, and social history of the Israelite people.

The word "Israel" first appears in an Egyptian stela dating to the late 13th century B.C.E. How much earlier a people whom we can recognise as Israelites lived in the area is unclear. The Canaanites (Phoenicians) occupied the area from at least the Middle Bronze Age (c. 2000–1550 B.C.E.), establishing a series of what appear to be independent city-states. Egypt controlled the region toward the end of this period, but a West Semitic people called the Hyksos took over Egypt around 1650. They were expelled from Egypt about a century later, and Egypt resumed rule over Canaan; but it withdrew from the region around 1200.

It appears that during this period a tribe whom some scholars call the Proto-Israelites established hundreds of settlements in the highlands of Canaan. It is now thought unlikely that there was any "conquest" of Canaan, as recounted in the book of Joshua; the highlands were sparsely populated, in contrast to the Egyptian-Canaanite cities in the lowlands. The Proto-Israelites may have come from various locales and settled the region over a long period, mingling with the Canaanite population.

After the Egyptian withdrawal, the Philistines (a seafaring people that may have come from Crete or other islands in the eastern Mediterranean) took over the coast, establishing the city of Ashkelon and others. To some degree they encroached upon the Israelites, who appear to have banded together and established customs (including

14. For the purposes of this discussion, I shall refer to the ancient inhabitants of Israel as Israelites and their scripture as the Hebrew Bible (abbreviated as HB).

circumcision and a ban on the eating of pork) as a means of distinguishing themselves from the Philistines.

This is the historical background from which we should now study the story of the Exodus from Egypt. There is no credible archaeological support for any such event; if it is not simply a recollection of the expulsion of the Hyksos from Egypt, the story may have been based on memories of a small number of Israelites who emigrated from Egypt to Canaan. The very existence of a figure named Moses is in grave doubt, and I trust we can dispense with the supernatural episodes leading up to the Exodus. Much the same can be said of certain figures of a purpotedly later date, such as Samson, whose battles with the Philistines have all the earmarks of a folktale handed down orally over the generations. It was at this time that, for a variety of factors, the region was split into two parts, Judah on the south and Israel on the north.

There is even some doubt as to the historicity of Saul, whom the HB declares to be the first king of Israel. His successor, David, is probably the first authentically historical king of Israel, his reign traditionally dating to c. 1000 to c. 960. It was he who united Israel and Judah. Current scholarship believes that David did not conquer the Philistines, as stated in the HB; rather, he probably made a truce with them, although he apparently expanded his territory in other directions, including areas east of the Jordan River. David probably did take over Jerusalem (located in the northern part of Judah), although it seems to have been a relatively small community at this time.

David was followed by his son Solomon (r. 960–30), although it is highly likely that the territory he (and David) controlled was considerably smaller than is indicated in the HB. Indeed, given that there is no evidence in the HB itself that Solomon fought any major battles, it becomes difficult to believe how he could control a vast area that purportedly extended from Egypt to Asia Minor (Turkey). In effect, it is now believed that the story of Solomon in the HB "is essentially a folktale about an Oriental potentate—it is a royal legend."[15] But Solomon's signal religious achievement—the building of a temple to Yahweh, called the First Temple—is likely to be historical.

After the death of Solomon, battles between Israel and Judah over the

15. Lester L. Grabbe, "Iron Age: Tribes to Monarchy," in Hoyland and Williamson, *The Oxford Illustrated History of the Holy Land* 56.

next fifty years resulted in the separation of the two regions into distinct monarchies. Both Israel and Judah became vassals to the Aramaeans (whose capital was Damascus) around 800. Meanwhile, the Assyrians had begun encroaching upon the region; for a time Israel was freed from Aramaean control and underwent a brief period of prosperity, where trade with the Phoenicians and other peoples expanded. But internal political turbulence and the increasing menace of the Assyrian Empire, beginning around 750, led to the fall of Israel in 722. As many as 27,000 Israelites were deported to Assyria. The kingdom of Judah retained independence but was obliged to pay tribute to Assyria. Later, in 701, Sennacherib suppressed a revolt from Judah and other regions; portions of Judah were given to the Philistines, who were vassals of Assyria.

The waning of Assyrian power allowed Josiah, king of Judah (r. 640–609), to expand his territory to the coast of the Mediterranean and also to the east; he also established the celebration of Passover, an indication that the Exodus story had now become firmly lodged as a central element in Israelite history. But now the Israelites had to face the resurgent Babylonians. Nebuchadnezzar overran the entire area, including Judah, beginning in 604; he undertook a siege of Jerusalem, and it fell in 597, ending the monarchy and beginning the period of the Babylonian Exile. A revolt in Judah (in conjunction with Egypt, which had also succumbed to Babylon) in 587 was suppressed by Nebuchadnezzar the next year. Jerusalem was looted and burned to the ground, its inhabitants deported to Babylon, and the Temple of Solomon was demolished.

Ironically, these events, catastrophic as they were, had the result of preserving the ethnic integrity of the Israelites. Some Jews (as we can now call them) fled to Egypt. Babylon itself fell to the emerging Persians, as Cyrus I overthrew the city in 539. In regard to Israel and Judah (now referred to as Judea), he allowed the people to run their own affairs and to preserve their traditional forms of worship; some exiles returned to the region at this time. The Temple was rebuilt during the reign of Darius I; it was completed in 515. Otherwise, not much is known of Israel and Judea during Persian rule. There is evidence that Ezra, a priest who may have been some sort of official in the Persian government, began enforcing many aspects of Mosaic law as recorded in the Pentateuch (the first five books of the HB; also called the Torah[16]), especially relating to marriage with "foreigners." Clearly, a need for social cohesion was felt. In a sense, Judaism as a religion that fused sacred doctrine with ethnic identity began with Ezra.

The Persian Empire fell to the Greeks in the course of the fifth and fourth centuries, as shall be related in greater detail in the next chapter. Following the death of Alexander the Great in 323, one of his successors, Ptolemy I of Egypt, captured Jerusalem in 312. During the following century many Greek-speaking cities were established in the region. Jerusalem was conquered by Antiochus III, a monarch of the Seleucid Empire that controlled enormous stretches of the Near East at this juncture; but he allowed the residents of the city to retain their ancestral laws.

One of the books of the Apocrypha, 1 Maccabees, tells the story of Antiochus IV Epiphanes preventing Jews from practising their religion, leading to a revolt by Judas Maccabaeus (Judah of the Maccabees); but this account is now thought to be a reversal of the historical event, since it is unlikely that Antiochus would have troubled to undertake a suppression of this sort. It is now believed that the suppression was punishment for a previous revolt by the Maccabees. In any event, Judas did lead a new revolt (167–60), resulting in the recapture of Jerusalem in 164. Israel did not regain full control of its territory until the reign of John Hyrcanus (r. 134–04), of the Hasmonean dynasty.

It will become apparent that the overall contours of the Israelite religion, as well as many of its particulars, are intimately related to the fluctuating fortunes of the Israelites over the millennium during which they emerged as a distinct people. Recent scholarship not only has made it likely that the HB was set down somewhat later than previously believed (mostly from the seventh to the fifth century B.C.E., with some texts dating as late as the mid-second century B.C.E.), but has traced possible influences on the figures and narratives in the text from neighbouring regions, ranging from Mesopotamia to Greece. Writing in Israel only emerged around 1000 B.C.E., and very few texts are available for this early period. Writing became more widespead around the seventh century,

16. The term Torah, however, can have a wider meaning. During the mediaeval period (and perhaps earlier), it could refer to the entire HB or even include the so-called Oral Torah, the totality of Jewish teaching and practice.

and so it is likely—given the complexity and sophistication of many of the books of the HB—that they were set down at an even later date, for all that some features of the texts are likely to reflect oral traditions dating back centuries earlier.

The earliest extant manuscripts of any portions of the HB are among the documents found in the Dead Sea Scrolls, dating to around the third century B.C.E. It is difficult to know when the HB as we know it achieved canonisation; this may have occurred as late as the third or fourth century C.E., and the current text of the HB includes books that are now classified as deuterocanonical or apocryphal.

The Pentateuch was probably codified during the Babylonian Exile. Its authorship by Moses was assumed from an early period—certainly no later than the Hellenistic Jews of the third century B.C.E. onward—in spite of the fact that Deuteronomy 29–34 presents an elaborate account of Moses' death. Some scholars believe that Genesis 1–11, which is largely separate from the rest of the Bible and records some of the most celebrated (and most incredible) narratives—the creation of the universe, Adam and Eve, the flood and Noah's ark, the Tower of Babel—may be of even more recent date. The creation story is in fact two narratives not very well fused together, since in one account (Gen. 1:20–26) animals were created before human beings, and in the other (Gen. 2:15–20) humans were created before animals. The overall thrust of the story is, as we have seen, common to many cultures, in regard to such elements as the separation of sky and earth, the creation of animal life, and so on. The name Adam (*'ādām*) simply means "man"; it is not used as a proper name for the first man until Gen. 4:25. Some scholars believe that the name is derived from Admu, the "god of the fathers" as cited in texts from the West Semitic city of Ebla (now in Syria), or the earth mother Adamma.[17] His consort, Eve, is in fact Hawwah in the HB, approximately meaning "source of life."[18] We have already seen that the story of the flood and Noah's ark is very likely derived from Assyrian sources. The Tower of Babel may have been based on a Sumerian myth.

In regard to the rest of the Pentateuch, it becomes apparent that the elaborate genealogies—extending from Adam onward and recounting

17. See Hess, *Israelite Religions* 82.

18. The odd belief that Lilith—a kind of demon figure cited only once in the HB (Isaiah 34:14)—was Adam's first wife is a legend that originated in the later rabbinic tradition.

how some of the patriarchs lived ludicrously long lives (Methuselah is credited with being 969 years old)—are a reflection of some kind of ancestor worship, whereby the Israelites of the post-exilic period wished to establish a direct lineage between themselves and the chief figures of their myths of origins. One scholar, Jean Louis Ska, has recently put forth the provocative thesis that the elaborate stipulations—legal, social, religious, and so on—found in Exodus, Leviticus, and Deuteronomy were a result of Persian influence: it was, so the theory goes, a condition of Persia granting the Israelites legal and social autonomy that they fashion their own law code.

One critical issue facing us is the origin of the monotheism that is one of the most prominent features of the HB, as enunciated most emphatically in one of the two versions of the Decalogue: "You must have no other god besides me" (Exod. 20:3).[19] There is considerable archaeological and textual evidence that the early Israelites worshipped (or at least knew of) the Canaanite gods El and Baal; indeed, the very name Isra*el* suggests as much. It is well known that the god mentioned in the first sentence of the Bible is *Elohim,* the plural of *El* (although it is probably being used in a singular sense). In Genesis 12–50, there is little evidence that Yahweh is hostile to other gods, and Abraham and his family are seen to live at peace with the Canaanites and other tribes.

Monotheism is, as we have seen, a relative rarity among ancient peoples, and the question remains why or from what source (if any) the Israelites came to adopt it. Some scholars have proposed a dualism among the early Israelites, whereby the official religion was monotheistic (based on Yahweh, whose worship may have originated in Sinai) and a popular religion inclined toward polytheism. But this is not posited as a straightforward dichotomy. In any event, the former triumphed not through any kind of oppression of "the people" by religious elites, but probably because it was genuinely supported by the majority of Israelites. The notion that monotheism was adopted from a recollection of the attempt by the Egyptian pharaoh Akhenaten to enforce such a principle does not seem plausible; it is more likely that the Israelites came to monotheism as a means of preserving both their religious and their socio-ethnic integrity amidst the numerous peoples and nations

19. I use the text of the *Revised English Bible* (Oxford/Cambridge, 1989).

in which they found themselves, including long periods of vassalage or actual subjugation.

Other elements of the Israelite religion call for attention. To what extent did they believe in a life after death? In the HB, Sheol is put forth as a realm of the dead. Some texts begin tentatively to assert a moral distinction between the righteous (who may be rescued from Sheol) and the wicked (who will remain there). Such appears to be the import of Ps. 16:10 ("for you will not abandon me to Sheol or suffer your faithful servant to see the pit") and Ps. 49:15 ("But God will ransom my life and take me from the power of Sheol"). There are almost no references in the HB to the physical resurrection of the dead; the closest we get is Isa. 26:19: "But your dead will live, their bodies will rise again. Those who sleep in the earth will awake and shout for joy." Daniel 12:2 is of similar import, but this is a very late text, written around the time of the revolt of the Maccabees in the mid-second century C.E.

The figure of Satan is also of some interest. The word *sātān* appears sporadically in the HB as a generic term for an adversary, both human and supernatural. But on some occasions it is also used as a proper noun, notably in the early chapters of Job ("The day came when the members of the court of heaven took their places in the presence of the Lord, and the Adversary, Satan, was there among them" [1:6]).[20] But there is no suggestion in the HB that Satan was in or was the ruler of Sheol. Some scholars believe the HB was influenced by the dualism of Zoroastrianism, but others doubt this as a source.

It is striking that there is virtually no evidence of non-religious writing among the Israelites during this entire period; in particular, no extant texts treat Israelite history as other than an aspect or result of their god's intervention in their affairs or the affairs of their neighbours. As one scholar has declared, "Israel did not make a fundamental distinction between historical and mythological time."[21] Overall, the HB itself is a concatenation of a wide array of material—from the creation story to legal and religious strictures to elaborate genealogies to wisdom literature to prophetic literature to apocalyptic texts to the exquisite poetry of the

20. The talking serpent who tempts Eve in Gen. 3:1–7 was only identified with Satan in the late *Wisdom of Solomon* (mid-first century B.C.E.).

21. Marc Zvi Brettler, "The Hebrew Bible and History," in Chapman and Sweeney, *The Cambridge Companion to the Hebrew Bible/Old Testament* 111.

Song of Solomon and the Psalms. And the widely differing tone of the work—the naïveté of the creation story, the bitter denunciation of God found in Job (which addresses, but fails to resolve, the perennial issue of the "problem of evil"), the triumphalism of Joshua, the world-weariness of Ecclesiastes—bespeaks not only a multiplicity of authors over a long period but a radical variance in temperament as the authors faced the fluctuating fortunes of their people. Whether a unitary vision of God and his role in human life and society emerges from the text is strongly to be doubted.

F. Early Religion in North America

The difficulties in ascertaining the origin and development of religion in the Indigenous tribes and cultures of North and South America are formidable. Given the general absence of written records and the fact that accounts of their religion largely derive from Europeans who came into contact with them no earlier than the later fifteenth century C.E. (and in some cases did not record their religious beliefs until a much later date), the question will inevitably arise as to whether we can pinpoint with any precision when the central religious conceptions of these cultures emerged.[22]

Archaeology allows us to trace the migration of these cultures across the Bering Strait (which at the time may have been a solid land mass, now called Beringia) as far back as 16,500 years ago. Evidence of hunting tribes in the southwestern United States can be found as early as 9000 years ago, while human settlement as far south as Tierra del Fuego can be dated to at least 8000 years ago. By no later than 2000 B.C.E. numerous tribes had settled into an agrarian way of life on both continents. In my judgment, the religious beliefs that we know from later reports bear a striking similarity to those evolved during the Neolithic period, so that even if they cannot be definitively dated to that period, it is worth treating them here. It is of course impossible to discuss every tribe's views separately; and while some there is some danger of

22. There is greater evidence for the religious views of the three main cultures of Mesoamerica—the Aztecs, the Mayans, and the Incas—but as their *floruit* generally occurred in the mid- to late first millennium C.E. and later, I will postpone discussion of them until chapter III.

suggesting a uniformity of belief among the tribes, certain broad patterns and tendencies can be distinguished.

There is no question that nearly all Indigenous tribes have a profound, complex, and multifaceted conception of the supernatural, and most envision a Supreme Being.[23] In some instances this Supreme Being is a creator god; in other instances he is not. (He is universally regarded as male.) In many cultures (such as the Lenape in the northeastern United States) the Supreme Being is worshipped by means of a central pole; this is regarded as a cosmic pillar that upholds the sky, and is analogous to the world tree of other religions (such as the Norse). The Supreme Being is usually thought of as a somewhat remote deity, although not indifferent to human life. But he frequently entrusts other gods to act more directly with human beings.

Many tribes focus less on the Supreme Being and more on a culture hero who has endowed humans with their "material and spiritual heritage."[24] In many cultures he is a capricious trickster figure: this may be a means of accounting for the dangers in the natural world, and in human society, that result in death or injury. The culture hero is rarely worshipped, but he is the focus of many myths. Among the Navajo, the Coyote is such a figure; the Raven is such among the tribes of the Pacific Northwest.

The deities actually worshipped by tribes are by and large nature spirits. The sun, the moon, thunder, and lightning are the forces most commonly deified; in some instances these are associated with the Supreme Being (the Natchez, Sioux, Crow, and other tribes connect the Supreme Being with the sun). Stars are also related to gods or are thought of as gods themsevles. Many North American tribes associate thunder and lightning with an eagle-like bird called the thunderbird. A variety of spirits are thought to control rain.

Many agrarian tribes worship an earth goddess as a virtually all-powerful deity, a sort of Earth Mother capable of begetting all life on her own, without any role by the (male) sky god. In some cultures (such as the Pueblo and others in North and Central America) there is a separate corn goddess or corn mother. Tree and bush spirits are common. Mountains

23. Darwin made the error of believing that the Tierra del Fuegans did not have such a conception.

24. Hultkrantz, *The Religions of the American Indians* 33.

(especially volcanic ones) are thought to be the home of spirits that must be placated through dance or other rituals. Even stones and boulders are revered, leading to the creation of statuettes or fetishes out of stone. Water is regarded as the source of life and perhaps as a means for the rejuvenation of life. Ponce de León in 1513 sought the Fountain of Youth in Florida as a result of stories he had heard from Mexican tribes. The Mississippi River is the "father of waters." Oftentimes, however, sea deities take the form of monsters of various sorts (notably a giant snake or serpent), perhaps as an indication of the dangers the sea can pose to human welfare.

Animals of all sorts are revered, and some cultures envision a "master of animals" as a protector of animal life. This conception, understandably, prevails among hunting tribes. As a result, due care and oftentimes a precise ritual must be practised in the killing of animals. The importance of animals to the well-being of many tribes may have led to totemism, whereby a clan within the tribe associates itself with a given animal. This animal is usually postulated as a mythic ancestor, but the clan also reveres living members of that animal. Some clans do not believe they are descended from the mythic ancestor, but that the animal is a guardian spirit. As such, killing of the clan animal is generally taboo. Members of the clan can connect with the guardian spirit through dreams and visions, sometimes induced by tobacco, mushrooms, herbs, and other means; in so doing, the individual acquires the characteristics of the spirit.[25]

The medicine man is a key link between gods and the tribe. His strictly medicinal function is only one aspect of his numerous responsibilities, which can at times involve supernatural powers. In this sense, the term "medicine" in effect refers to power. Healing is, however, central to his role. Overall, there are two types of medicine men: one is a visionary who utilises a light trance and clairvoyance, and an ecstatic who, by his perceived ability to communicate with gods and spirits, is more akin to the prototypical shaman. These roles are a product of the widespread belief that disease almost always has a supernatural cause. Some cultures also have medicine women; in a few of them (such as the Bear River Indians in California), she is thought to be more powerful

25. The use of peyote as a hallucinogenic drug to induce visions is a very recent development, dating no earlier than the 1880s.

than the medicine man. Some medicine men are transvestites (*berdache*), thus gaining the powers of both the male and the female.

All important aspects of life are celebrated by elaborate rituals. For hunter-gatherers, the beginning of the hunting season is encompassed by rites involving bones that symbolise the rebirth of the animals needed for the tribe's sustenance. Among agrarian tribes, the New Year rite reiterates the creation of the world and, hence, the renewal of crops. Among the Plains Indians, the Sun Dance, occurring in summer, is a rite of thanks to the Supreme Being for the plants and animals he provides. Puberty rites are often collective for boys, but girls (as in many cultures throughout the world) tend to be regarded as unclean during menarche.

Belief in an afterlife is well attested in most tribes, inspired by the dreams and visions of those who believe they have glimpsed the land of the dead and other phenomena associated with death. The hunting tribes have, in general, a somewhat more nebulous idea of the underworld, whereas the agrarian tribes have a fairly pronounced tripartite awareness of existence as divided between heaven, earth, and the underworld. Many tribes have envisioned two different types of soul inhabiting the body: one soul is related to life and consciousness, and the other is a "free soul" that roams outside the body in dreams. The free soul of a sick person is thought to have wandered to the land of the dead, and it is the function of the shaman to bring it back. Such journeys are regarded as treacherous, and elaborate tales have been woven of the monsters and other perils the shaman must face. Hackneyed as the idea has become, the notion of the "happy hunting grounds" is a reasonably accurate depiction of the beliefs of the Plains Indians, who envision a life of hunting, feasting, and dancing after death. There is some evidence that a moral dichotomy exists among the dead: "bad" people are not banished to a hell, but they do not attain the land of the dead at all, instead roaming the earth as ghosts. Belief in reincarnation is prevalent in many tribes. Ancestor worship is found more commonly in South American tribes rather than those in North America.

* * *

I do not pretend to have surveyed, even cursorily, all the religious traditions of the world, but only those that appear to have exercised the greatest influence on the intellectual, cultural, and social history of those nations that are of relevance to Western culture.[26] What is more, I have delayed the discussion of certain other traditions (such as those in Scandinavia, Mesoamerica, and elsewhere) because they emerged at a later date in history and should therefore be treated in their chronological sequence along with contemporary developments elsewhere. Indeed, new religions have not ceased to appear up to the present day.

But it should be apparent that a great many of these religious traditions conform to a recurring pattern: the postulation of the separation of the sky from the earth at the dawn of time; simple or elaborate creation stories regarding the emergence of life on earth, including the human race; the existence of a human soul and its fortunes in the afterlife; and so on. That these conceptions are often similar does not necessarily suggest that they are "true," but merely that they constitute similar responses by human beings at a certain stage of development as they faced phenomena—the rising and setting of the sun, the existence of the countless stars in the night sky, the rebirth of plants and crops in spring and their "death" in the fall, and especially the birth, development, and death of human beings—whose workings they could not understand or which they sought to guide or control for the sake of their own preservation. And it must be recalled that, even—or especially—at this early stage, religion was a *social* process that encompassed the entire community, infusing virtually all its members into an explicit or implied dogma or set of doctrines that governed individual and collective behaviour.

How these doctrines, and religion itself as an intellectual and cultural phenomenon, came under increasing question over the past twenty-five hundred years of human history will be the subject of the remainder of this book.

---

26. Accordingly, I have made no attempt to outline the tenets of Hinduism or of the religions of the Far East (Buddhism, Confucianism, etc.), although Confucianism developed some strikingly atheistic elements. These religions influenced Western culture only at a very late stage.

II. The Greeks

. . . perhaps one should not wonder at *anything* Greek;
the race was a super-race.

—H. P. Lovecraft

A. The Development of Greek Religion

It is difficult for many who have inherited the aesthetic legacy of Greco-Roman myth—as manifested in countless literary allusions, to say nothing of entire works of literature (Shakespeare's *Venus and Adonis,* Shelley's *Prometheus Unbound*), children's books (Hawthorne's *A Wonder Book* and *Tanglewood Tales,* Kingsley's *The Greek Heroes,* Bulfinch's *The Age of Fable*), musical compositions (Monteverdi's *L'Orfeo,* Handel's "secular oratorios" *Hercules, Semele,* and others), films (*Jason and the Argonauts, Clash of the Titans*), comic books, and other media—to grasp the fact that the Olympian gods were actually worshipped for the better part of two millennia, including for hundreds of years after Christianity had gained political supremacy in both Rome and Byzantium. But it is necessary to understand the essentials of the Greek religion, and its practice, in order to assess the proper significance of the philosophers who, for the first time in Western history, challenged the nearly universal religious conception of the origin and nature of the universe and of human society.[1]

1. In this chapter and elsewhere, I use Latinised or Anglicised versions of Greek names. Contemporary classical scholarship now prefers a more precise transliteration from the

The origin of Greek religion is, as is the case with all religious traditions of analogous antiquity, shrouded in obscurity. When we come upon the first extant texts in Greek literature—the *Iliad* and *Odyssey* of Homer—we find the Greek pantheon already in place, with well-defined characteristics and a coherent theology specifying the functions of the various gods and the nature of their interactions, individually and collectively, with the human race. They are ensconced in their home on Mt. Olympus (a mountain in Thessaly, in the northeastern corner of mainland Greece) and, in the *Iliad,* intervene at key moments in the Greeks' battle with the Trojans. Nevertheless, an examination of the manner in which the Homeric poems came to be, as well as a study of the results of many generations of archaeologists, philologists, and other scholars, allow us to have some idea of how the Olympian religion (and other, related aspects of the faith) originated and established itself in the Greek world. But what is required at the outset is a brief summary of the successive waves of peoples entering into mainland Greece as well as the islands in the Aegean Sea and the neighbouring land masses.

The Bronze Age in Greece commenced roughly at 3000 B.C.E. At this stage it cannot be stated definitively whether the inhabitants of Greece (as well as of the Aegean Islands and of the west coast of Anatolia [Turkey]) were autochthonous or came from elsewhere. By around 2200 we come upon evidence suggesting the invasion of people speaking a form of Greek (a branch of Indo-European). The existing population probably mingled with the newcomers.

Then, beginning around 2000, the Minoan culture in Crete began to exhibit rapid development, chiefly through the building of immense palaces (of which the so-called Palace of Minos at Knossos is the best-known example) and the flourishing of art and writing. At this time, the existing hieroglyphic writing gave way to what is called Linear A (still undeciphered), then to Linear B, which has been deciphered because it is in an early version of Greek. However, the formerly held belief that the Minoans developed a mastery of the seas and actually conquered mainland Greece—as suggested by the story of Theseus and the Minotaur[2]—has not been confirmed by archaeological evidence and

---

Greek (e.g., Akhaians, not Achaeans); but I follow the older convention so that non-specialists will not be confused as to what name is being referred to.

2. According to the myth, Minos, king of Knossos, exacted a tribute of seven maidens and

is now regarded as unlikely. The Minoans, in fact, appear to have been an isolated and unwarlike people. Their religious rituals were practised not in temples but in domestic shrines or in the many caves on the island, involving animal sacrifices and an expression of ecstasy through manic dancing. No specific gods or goddesses can be identified.

Following an apparent takeover of the island by people from mainland Greece around 1500, Minoan society essentially collapsed by around 1400. The attack (if it was that) was presumably launched by the so-called Mycenaean civilisation that took shape on the mainland around 1600. The term is somewhat misleading, for there is no reason to think that the city of Mycenae, on the Peloponnese, was in any way the dominant force; it is simply that some of the best-preserved landmarks come from there. The culture was marked by the erection of enormous and luxuriously decorated tombs, among them the celebrated beehive tombs, commemorating the more powerful dynasties of each city. The origin of this people is unknown. Many palace-fortresses were erected all across the mainland (including the Acropolis in Athens), suggesting a state of constant internecine warfare. Around 1200 many of these Mycenaean palace-fortresses were destroyed, perhaps as a result of an invasion from the north.

Meanwhile, in northwest Anatolia, a city that we now call Troy was settled around 3000 B.C.E. A new culture took over around 1800. The city was destroyed, possibly by earthquake, around 1300, but quickly rebuilt. What is now identified as Troy VIIa fell around 1200. It is unclear whether the Mycenaeans from the mainland attacked Troy (as recounted in the *Iliad* as the Trojan War) or whether both Mycenaean and Trojan culture fell to outside forces. Indeed, the possibility that there ever was a Trojan War—at least as pertains to Troy VIIa—is now in doubt. Dieter Hertel points out that "Greek building forms and Greek-style ceramics" appeared only after Troy VIIb2 was destroyed (by earthquake and fire), suggesting that only then did "settlement by Greeks" occur.[3]

In any event, the invasion of the Greek mainland (and perhaps

---

seven boys from the Athenians every year, who would then be sacrificed. But Theseus, one of the boys chosen in that year, battled with the Minotaur (a creature half-bull and half-man) in the Labyrinth constructed by Daedalus. Theseus killed the Minotaur and ended Minos' dominance over Athens (and, hence, mainland Greece).

3. Dieter Hertel, "The Myth of History: The Case of Troy," in Dowden and Livingstone, *A Companion to Greek Mythology* 435.

western Anatolia) by people termed the Dorians—who instituted the Doric dialect of Greek—resulted in a kind of dark age from 1200 to 800. Writing disappeared; the population declined; some cities were abandoned. Following this period, the distinctive sociopolitical unit of the city-state began to develop in the mainland, as the Greeks spread both commercially and through colonisation all through the Mediterranean, from as far east as Massilia (Marseilles) to the Near East, as well as a single colony (Naucratis) in Egypt.

We can now at last turn our attention to both Homer and Hesiod, the latter of whom flourished around 700. The Greeks themselves were unclear who was the earlier,[4] but Homer gained a precedence by virtue of the canonical status—both as literature and as the source of the Olympian religion—accorded to the *Iliad* and the *Odyssey.* It is now well known that those epic poems were transmitted orally over the course of centuries, a given bard focusing on one section of the narrative and consigning it to memory. Whether there ever was an actual person named Homer cannot now be determined. Some have maintained that the act of codifying and setting down the poems in writing occurred as early as the ninth century, but the date has now been moved forward to anywhere between 750 and 650, when writing was reintroduced to Greek society, with an alphabet borrowed from the Phoenicians. While it is evident that some elements of the epics reflect the state of society (and warfare) in the "heroic" (Mycenaean) age, other elements—notably the practice of the cremation, not the burial, of the dead—reflect more recent features.

And while Homer[5] was regarded as a kind of Bible for the Greeks (a highly misleading term, given its overtones in Christian society), I wish to turn my attention first to Hesiod as an introduction to the subject of Greek religion, since it is only there that we find a coherent and detailed "creation story" analogous to that of Genesis and other scriptures.

The *Theogony* is by design an account of the birth of the gods (whom Hesiod then paradoxically refers to as "immortal" or "deathless") and, more significant for our purpose, the fashioning of the universe. Hesiod plainly states:

---

4. Herodotus states, "Hesiod and Homer were I think 400 years older than me, no more than that" (*Histories* 2.53), which would put both at c. 830 B.C.E., far too early.

5. I use the name as a shorthand for the Homeric poems, considered collectively or individually.

> At the first Chaos came to be, but next wide-bosomed Earth, the ever-sure foundation of all . . . and dim Tartarus in the depth of the wide-pathed Earth, and Eros, fairest among the deathless gods . . . From Chaos came forth Erebus and black Night; but of Night were born Aether and Day, whom she conceived and bare from union in love with Erebus. And Earth first bare starry Heaven, equal to herself, to cover her on every side, and to be an ever-sure abiding-place for the blessed gods. . . . But afterwards she [Earth] lay with Heaven and bare deep-swirling Oceanus . . . [and] Cronos . . . (116–37)[6]

In this bewildering flurry of names, characteristic of the text, we can note certain basic features. The division of the world into three essential areas—*Ouranos* (usually translated as Heaven, although a better translation would simply be Sky), Earth, and Tartarus (the underworld)—is a common feature among the religions of the Near East, as is the generation of the universe by means of a male Sky impregnating a female Earth (Ge or Gaia). By virtue of Earth's begetting of Cronos, who was the father of Zeus, we are provided a genealogy of the Olympian gods.

We do not find an analogous creation story in Homer except in passing—in the striking "Shield of Achilles" passage in the *Iliad* (18.483–89). The passage begins: "He made the earth upon it, and the sky, and the sea's water, / and the tireless sun, and the moon waxing in her fullness, / and on it all the constellations that festoon the heavens."[7] This is highly condensed and imprecise, but it is enough to suggest an approximate parallel with the Hesiodic account.

What we otherwise find in Hesiod is a welter of personifications of natural forces: the dawn (*Eōs*), the sun (*Helios*), the moon (*Selēnē*), Night (*Theogony* 19–20), and so on. That these really are personifications or deifications rather than mere designations of the forces in question is confirmed by Hesiod's contention that Night begat (by parthenogenesis) such abstract moral conceptions as Doom (*Moros*), Fate (*Kēra*), Sleep (*Hypnos*), Death (*Thanatos*), and Woe (*Oizos*) (*Theogony* 211–14). Whether all this is a holdover of animism is unclear. It is, however, noteworthy that Hesiod also deifies rivers (the Nile, the Meander, and several others: *Theogony* 337–45), and it can be demonstrably established

6. I use the prose translation of Hugh G. Evelyn-White.

7. For both the *Iliad* and the *Odyssey* I use the translation of Richmond Lattimore.

that the Greeks worshipped rivers, seeing in them a sacred source of life.

The union of sky and earth in a *hieros gamos* (sacred marriage) is embodied in the union of the two chief Olympian gods, Zeus and Hera. It is well known that *Zeus patēr* (Zeus the father) is the incarnation of a god that was known to many Indo-European cultures, from India (Dyauspitar) to Rome (Jupiter). While he is frequently referred to by Homer as "father of gods and men," the designation (insofar as the human race is concerned) is largely symbolic. Zeus' main associations are with the sky and the weather: he is the "Cloud-Gatherer" in Homer, and his chief weapon is the thunderbolt. Hera, associated with fertility, marriage, and female concerns generally, therefore becomes a kind of earth-mother figure. None of this is to say, however, that any of the Olympian gods can simply be reduced to being a symbol or representation of natural phenomena; the Greeks clearly regarded them as individuals possessing human emotions, even if they also possessed superhuman powers as well as the prime distinguishing feature of immortality.

And yet, curiously, the other Olympian gods are not the offspring of Zeus and Hera. To the scandal of certain later thinkers and writers, Zeus begat the other Olympians by what amounts to adultery with a variety of other consorts or human women. One of the most significant of these is Apollo, who was probably not originally a Greek god (his name does not derive from Greek roots); he may have absorbed the traits of numerous local gods once the Greeks embraced him.

Zeus' brothers Poseidon and Hades (or Pluto)[8] divide the three major portions of the world, Zeus controlling the sky, Poseidon the sea, and Hades the underworld. We need not delineate the other gods of the Olympian pantheon, aside from noting that several of them—including Artemis and Athena—were probably of pre-Greek origin. The name *Athēnē* was originally given by the Mycenaeans to the Acropolis. She obviously became the patron goddess of the city of Athens, as other gods became the patrons of other cities, thereby linking the worship of the Olympians with the city government and engendering a fusion of religion, local pride, and civic patriotism. More significantly, the establishment of laws governing a city-state were often believed to be of

8. Hades is also the name of the underworld as a whole, although even the Greeks at times used the name to refer to the god of the underworld. The phrase "in Hades" (*en Haidou*) really stands for "in [the house of] Hades."

divine inspiration: the political reforms attributed to Lycurgus in Sparta and Draco in Athens were both regarded as having occurred under the aegis of Apollo. But this does not at all mean that the Greek religion should be considered theocratic in the manner of John Calvin's Geneva or the Puritan communities of seventeenth-century Massachusetts.

On two important points—the creation of human beings and the underworld—Homer and Hesiod provide intriguing information. In terms of the former, what is striking is the relative silence of both these poets on the question. In spite of his formulaic designation of Zeus as "father of gods and men," there is no suggestion in Homer that Zeus or any of the other Olympians literally created the human race or caused it to come into existence in any other fashion. Hesiod is equally silent. In the *Works and Days*—a work believed to be slightly earlier in date than the *Theogony*—he outlines the five stages of the human race (gold, silver, bronze, the age of heroes, and iron), each becoming progressively worse (although the age of heroes, which Hesiod admires, is an awkward insertion into the sequence). After telling the story of Prometheus, he states that Zeus in revenge ordered Hephaestus to fashion the woman Pandora out of earth and water (*Works and Days* 59–61) to plague humanity. But it appears that humanity is already in existence: "For ere this the tribes of men lived on earth remote and free from ills and hard toil and heavy sickness which bring the Fates upon men" (90–92). It is true that in his subsequent account of the five stages of man he specifically states that Zeus "made (*poiēsan*) a golden race of mortal men" (109–10) and also the subsequent races; but nevertheless, some race of humans apparently predated these. The *Theogony* is solely concerned with the origin of the gods and of the Olympian gods' battles with the Titans and other monsters; the human race has virtually no role to play except to provide comely damsels for Zeus to impregnate ("And Semele, daughter of Cadmus, was joined with him in love and bare him a splendid son, joyous Dionysus—a mortal woman an immortal son" [940–42]).

In terms of the underworld, Hesiod states that the god Hades is the son of Rhea and Cronos, making him the brother of Zeus. He tells the familiar story of how Hades snatched Demeter's daughter Persephone and took her to the world below, where the region is guarded by "a fearful hound" (*Theogony* 769), Cerberus. It would appear that all souls end up there, although Hesiod does not explicitly say so; one passage does state that "Hades trembled where he rules over the dead below" (*Theogony* 850).

The evidence in Homer comes from the celebrated *Nekuia* or descent into the underworld by Odysseus as chronicled in Book XI of the *Odyssey.* His motive for the trip is to consult the dead soothsayer Tiresias (10.565). Odysseus must perform some sacrifices so that the shades can gain sufficient body (and, apparently, memory) to speak to him. Homer is clear that this realm is a place for all the dead:

> . . . the souls
> of the perished dead gathered to the place, up out of Erebos,
> brides, and young unmarried men, and long-suffering elders,
> and many fighting men killed in battle . . . (11.36–39)

Odysseus meets the souls of many of the dead with whom he had been formerly acquainted, including several women; but when he meets the soul of the intrepid warrior Achilles, the latter laments:

> O shining Odysseus, never try to console me for dying.
> I would rather follow the plow as thrall to another
> man, one with no land allotted him and not much to live on,
> than be a king over all the perished dead. (11.488–91)

These are, surely, the sentiments of a warrior culture: that Achilles would prefer to be a slave than to be king of the dead is a remarkable utterance. It is not matched by anything in Hesiod. There is, however, a question as to whether this conception of the afterlife was really shared by a wide segment of the Greek populace at any time in their history.

Both Homer and Hesiod do suggest that the illustrious dead (chiefly warriors) are segregated to a separate area of Hades, variously called the Isles of the Blest (*makares*) or the Elysian Fields. In Homer the Old Man of the Sea tells Odysseus of a conversation he had with Menelaus:

> But for you, Menelaus, O fostered of Zeus, it is not the gods' will
> that you shall die and go to your end in horse-pasturing Argos,
> but the immortals will convoy you to the Elysian

> Field, and the limits of the earth, where fair-haired Rhadamanthys is, and where there is made the easiest life for mortals . . . (4.561–65)

Hesiod reports:

> But to others father Zeus the son of Crosos gave a living and an abode apart from men, and made them dwell at the ends of earth. And they live untouched by sorrow in the islands of the blessed along the shore of deep swirling Ocean, happy heroes for whom the grain-giving earth bears honey-sweet fruit . . . (*Works and Days* 167–72)

As for the well-known souls who are being punished in Hades—Tantalus, Sisyphus, and the like (11.576–600)—it is clear from the myths that they are suffering their fate not because of some general moral evil but for a specific offence to the gods, chiefly Zeus. The most famous of these is Prometheus; he is not mentioned in Homer, but Hesiod has several detailed accounts of his bringing fire to human beings and being subsequently punished by Zeus (*Works and Days* 47–59, *Theogony* 521–69).

Discussion of the underworld leads to a consideration of what some scholars call the "chthonic" gods (Dionysus, Artemis, Demeter, Persephone, and some others), some of whom were primarily gods of the earth and vegetation, others of whom were in the underworld. Artemis, the goddess of wild animals, was known in Phrygia (an area in west-central Anatolia originally populated by non-Greek-speaking peoples, although the Phrygian language is Indo-European) as Cybele, the Great Mother of the Gods, whose consort was her own son and lover, Attis (or Atys).

The origin of Dionysus is obscure. It is of some interest that his cult was chiefly conducted by women, perhaps allowing them a freedom that was largely absent in their daily lives. The cult is vividly portrayed in Euripides' play *The Bacchae* (first performed posthumously in 405 B.C.E.), depicting the wild rituals—involving women driven to madness (*mania*) by dancing, thereby becoming maenads, engaging in the consumption of wine, sexual licence, and ultimately the tearing apart and consumption of the raw flesh of wild animals (an act otherwise under a severe taboo in Greek culture)—associated with the cult. The cult probably originated in Anatolia (either Phrygia or neighbouring Lydia or in Thrace, in the northeast corner of the Greek mainland). Dionysus' association with wine really refers to all life-giving fluids, from blood to semen to the sap of plants.

The cult of Demeter, focused around the city of Eleusis in Attica, had existed since at least Mycenaean times and probably originated in Crete. Demeter, an earth-goddess, is tasked with securing the fertility of the soil. Hades is the husband of Demeter's daughter Persephone, who becomes the queen of the dead.

While some scholars believe that there is a clear distinction between the "sky-gods" (*ouranioi*) of the Olympian pantheon and the "earth-gods" (*chthonioi*) just discussed, the Greeks themselves did not seem to segregate them in this manner. However, it does appear that the latter set of gods were linked with the more ecstatic aspects of Greek worship. The notions of *ekstasis* (a standing outside of oneself) and *enthusiasmos* (the state of being "filled" with the god) are clearly associated with the cult of Dionysus and also with the evolution of the Eleusinian mysteries, suggesting a more mystical and intense expression of religious sentiment. Another element of mysticism enters in the oracles at Delphi (under the aegis of Apollo), Dodona (under the aegis of Zeus), and elsewhere. The figures of the seer (chief of whom, in Greek literature, was Tiresias, although the myth of Cassandra, daughter of Priam who was granted prophetic powers by Apollo but was fated not to be believed, is poignantly expressed in Aeschylus' *Agamemnon* and elsewhere) and the prophetess were not uncommon in Greek culture and signified the possibility of a more direct communication with a god than was generally possible through public ritual alone.

The cluster of myths surrounding Herakles appears to be an independent cycle that exhibits the emergence of the hero-cult—the deification of human beings of exceptional strength, power, or status. For there is no doubt that the Greeks believed Herakles, although the son of Zeus and the mortal woman Alcmene, to have been a human being. He is glancingly mentioned in the *Iliad,* and in the *Odyssey* Odysseus meets him in the underworld: although Herakles did suffer death (at the hands of the centaur Nessus, as recounted in Sophocles' *Trachiniae*), he was given a privileged place in Hades: "After him I was aware of powerful Herakles, / his image, that is, but he himself among the immortal / gods enjoys their festivals" (11.601–3). His achievements enabled him to gain a kind of immortality, and to that extent suggested the ability of human beings to achieve that most cherished attribute of godhead.

We must also consider the phenomenon of Orphism. Orpheus was a half-mythical figure who accompanied the Argonauts on their quest for the Golden Fleece (an event that was believed to have occurred before the Trojan War), and a substantial number of texts, mostly in verse—read and commented on by Plato—were extant in the classical period. The cult probably emerged in the sixth century B.C.E. It had an elaborate cosmogony and anthropogeny that we need not outline here; but one of its central contentions was that the body was a kind of prison for the soul, and that salvation is produced by an elaborate series of rituals involving purification of the body (abstention from meat-eating among others); the proper performance of these rituals would lead to the achievement of the soul's immortality. The Orphics also believed in the transmigration of souls and in the notion that just souls can attain bliss in the afterlife while unjust souls receive varying forms of punishment. It does not appear, however, that Orphism was widely believed in or practised by ordinary Greeks; it was more likely a belief system adopted by intellectuals of varying stripes.

It would be a crude oversimplification to assert that the Greek religion—in the absence of anything that could truly be called a scripture and a set of clearly defined religious dogmas and doctrines—focused solely or largely on ritual rather than specific moral doctrines. Greek tragedies are filled with actions (incest, failure to bury the dead properly, and so on) that clearly violate the will of the gods, so that there are any number of implicit dogmas to which the Greek people adhered. The Greek calendar teemed with festivals of all sorts in which the gods played a central role. The Olympian Games (canonically begun in 776 B.C.E.) were held under the aegis of Olympian Zeus; and these were only one of several athletic contests held in various Greek cities. What we can assert with certainty is that the Greek religion was not exclusive. As the horizons of the Greek world expanded in all directions with the establishment of trade, colonies, and other contacts with their non-Greek neighbours, they readily adopted the gods they came upon—or, rather (as Herodotus' lengthy Book II of the *Histories* attests), made attempts of varying plausibility to identify these alien gods to the members of their own pantheon.

Although there was not a well-defined priestly caste, there were priests and priestesses, some of whom worked only part-time and others for many years. The priests were chiefly responsible for tending to the many temples and sanctuaries in every city, but their chief function was performing sacrifices (although magistrates and private individuals could also perform sacrifices under certain circumstances). The sacrifice—mostly of cattle, sheep, and pigs—occupied a central role in Greek religious ceremonies. The Homeric poems are full of hecatombs (the sacrifice of a hundred oxen) preceding a battle or at other key moments. As a recent scholar has maintained, the act was meant to open "the channel of communication between man and god," their specific purpose being such things as "propitiation, thanksgiving, fulfillment of a vow, or whatever."[9]

It should not be forgotten that the Greek populace was saturated with religious sentiments and artifacts at every turn—not only in a temple (which was not used as a gathering place for ceremonies but was designed as the house of the god after whom it was named) but in such seemingly mundane aspects of life as taking a journey, welcoming a guest, and sitting down to a meal. The countless examples of Greek art that have come down to us are ovewhelmingly religious in the sense of depicting the multifarious array of gods, demigods, heroes, and narratives from what we call Greek mythology. It is, indeed, a modern art historian, not an archaeologist or scholar of religion, who reminds us that "what we call myth . . . was to the Greeks their earliest history, when gods and heroes spoke and walked with men."[10] It therefore becomes even more remarkable that something approaching secular rationalism was evolved by the Greek philosophers, becoming one of the signal contributions of Greek culture to the West.

B. The Beginnings of Greek Philosophy

The difficulty in assessing the work of the earliest Greek philosophers—those now referred to as the Presocratics, even though some of the later ones were contemporary with Socrates and in a few instances

9. Parker, *On Greek Religion* 132.
10. Boardman, *Greek Art* 275.

outlived him—is the simple one of the absence of texts. No complete text of Greek philosophy exists prior to the work of Plato in the very early fourth century B.C.E.; the apparently voluminous work of his predecessors must be gleaned through fragments quoted by a multitude of later commentators, beginning with Plato himself and carrying on through Aristotle and his disciple Theophrastus. These latter two took a particular interest in the history of previous thought on a wide variety of philosophical and scientific subjects (cosmology, biology, physics, ethics, and so on), but in numerous instances their assessments of their antecedents are coloured by their own philosophical predispositions. Some of this testimony extends far into the Christian era, or more than a millennium after some of the earliest philosophers we shall study here were active; by that time, it is certain that nearly all the work of the Presocratics had perished, surviving if at all in extracts or summaries. We do have a *Lives of the Philosophers* by Diogenes Laertius (3rd century C.E.); but, aside from the fact that he is somewhat naïve philosophically, he seems chiefly intent on portraying the lives of figures he found curious or in some cases eccentric.

The upshot of all this is that, in spite of the heroic work of legions of classical scholars over the centuries, numerous essential features of the thought of the Presocratic philosophers remain unclear or the subject of considerable controversy. We are on far surer ground when we come to Plato and Aristotle because of the preservation of a substantial number of their works, but again fall into difficulties as a result of the fragmentary nature of the work of the Epicureans, Stoics, Sceptics, and Cynics who succeeded them.

To some degree this same difficulty affects our understanding of non-philosophical Greek writers of this entire period, whom we shall also be considering in relation to their theological views. Again, prior to the fifth century B.C.E. the availability of complete texts is very slender; and even in regard to such well-known figures as the three major Greek tragic playwrights (Aeschylus, Sophocles, and Euripides), we possess only a minuscule number of the plays they are known to have written.

The overriding issue we must face, when we study the emergence of philosophical thought among the Greeks in the early sixth century B.C.E., is simply this: Why did a certain class of thinkers even attempt to seek non-theistic ways of accounting for the origin and development of the world and the universe? Essentialist assumptions about the nature of the "Greek mind" will get us nowhere; but it has to be asked why the Greeks began, haltingly and unevenly, the process of establishing a more or less secular conception of the universe when none of their predecessors or contemporaries in other cultures did so.

It is true that, from a fairly early period, the Greeks were exposed to the numerous civilisations—Egyptian, Persian, Babylonian, even the remnants of the Hittite empire—that environed them, especially in the period of their most active colonisation of both the Mediterranean Sea (specifically Sicily and lower Italy) and the western coast of Anatolia, during the eighth to sixth centuries B.C.E. It is, indeed, exactly at this juncture that the earliest Greek philosophising occurred—and occurred in the colonies established in these outlying areas rather than in mainland Greece. But the mere expansion of horizons resulting from association with foreign cultures does not seem a sufficient explanation for the flowering of philosophical thought that began in the sixth century. Throughout classical antiquity, the Phoenicians were widely regarded as the region's most diligent and successful traders; but they evolved no philosophical speculation nor even any significant literary work.

A point worth making at the outset is that the notion of the creation of the universe out of nothing—as embodied, say, in Genesis and other scriptures—is generally foreign to Greek religious and philosophical thought. The Homeric poems are entirely silent on the matter. Hesiod's *Theogony,* as we have seen, does provide an account of the origin of the universe, but it was never regarded as canonical by the Greeks, and neither it nor its author were considered to have been divinely inspired. This circumstance may have allowed early Greek thinkers to engage in speculation on the subject without incurring accusations of blasphemy or sacrilege.

It will be observed that a good many of the Presocratic philosophers (and, indeed, several who succeeded Plato and Aristotle) engaged in speculation relating to what is designated by the archaic English phrase "natural philosophy." Nature (*physis*) was highly important to them; and by this they encompassed both the nature of the universe and the nature of the human body, mind, and soul. *On Nature* (*Peri physeos*) became a sort of default title for many of the treatises written by these thinkers.

It is, of course, clear that, in probing the origin of the universe and its subsequent ramifications, these philosophers had next to nothing in the way of sophisticated instruments to confirm or refute their hypotheses. Their theorisings were largely deductive or, at best, based upon certain observations of the natural world around them, which they then attempted to apply to the universe as a whole. We need not ridicule their lack of an inductive approach; even Aristotle, who did apply empirical methods more rigorously and extensively than nearly any philosopher in Greco-Roman antiquity, made what appear to us foolish mistakes in biology, zoology, and other sciences.[11] It still remains remarkable that the Presocratics ventured as boldly and, in some cases, as perspicaciously as they did, at a time when no one else in the civilised world was doing so.

In reference to the existence of a god or gods, we will find many Presocratic thinkers referring not so much to "god" (*ho theos*) but more abstractly to "the divine" (*to theion*). In some instances it is a plausible assumption that the author has a personal god in mind; in other cases the evidence is more ambiguous. What unifies almost all thinkers who postulate the existence of divinity is the notion that it is immortal or "deathless" (*athanatos*); this is usually meant as a deliberate contrast with human beings or other animals, who even in the Homeric poems are referred to as "mortal" (*thnētos*).

C. The Ionian Tradition

Miletus, on the western coast of Anatolia, was part of the Greek province of Ionia; and because the first three philosophers for whom there is any significant evidence—Thales, Anaximander, and Anaximines—all originated from this city, they are referred to as founders of the Ionian school of philosophy. Miletus had been founded in the latter part of the second millennium B.C.E., possibly by Minoan or Mycenaean settlers from Crete. In the seventh and sixth centuries Miletus itself established colonies in the area of the Black Sea and also made forays into Egypt; it also kept in close touch with the city of Sybaris, in southern Italy. Clearly it was a city that, culturally and economically, looked both east and west.

11. Bertrand Russell famously poked fun at Aristotle by noting: "Aristotle could have avoided the mistake of thinking that women have fewer teeth than men, by the simple device of asking Mrs. Aristotle to keep her mouth open while he counted. He did not do so because he thought he knew." "An Outline of Intellectual Rubbish," in *Unpopular Essays* 103.

Thales (624?–548?) is generally acknowledged to be the first philosopher in the Western world; but, on the subject of religion, he was preceded by the poet Mimnermus (late seventh century), who declared: "From the gods we know neither good nor evil."[12] This may be nothing more than the expression of the widely held view that Greek religion was largely a matter of ritual and lacked a concrete moral agenda (in later centuries many thinkers criticised the gods themselves, especially Zeus, for behaving in a manner that, if they had been human beings, would be regarded as immoral); but Mimnermus' scepticism regarding the role of the gods in human affairs is notable.

It is uncertain whether Thales actually wrote anything; but, even considering that at that period the transmission of knowledge by oral means was far greater than it was in later Greek civilisation, it seems unlikely that the specificity of his known utterances could all have been conveyed *viva voce* in the manner of Socrates a century and a half later. In any case, his own position, in regard to the creation of the universe, is clear, if we are to believe Aristotle: "Thales . . . says that the principle is water, and for this reason declared that the earth rests on water" (*Metaphysics* 983b). What has here been translated as "principle" is the Greek word *archē*, and by the use of this term Aristotle clearly suggests a chronological priority: *archē* generally means "beginning."

Before we rashly conclude that Thales is making a significant break with the religious tradition by proposing a purely secular account of the origin of all entity, we should take note of several countervailing factors. Thales could well have been influenced by the Greek myth of Okeanos, the primal body of water that was thought to surround all other land masses; it was personified as male, and Homer declares that Okeanos is the "first parent of the gods" along with their mother, Tethys (*Iliad* 14.201). Hesiod also links Okeanos and Tethys (*Theogony* 133–36).

Accordingly, we should be careful not to maintain that Thales—or any Greek thinker prior to Democritus in the mid-fifth century B.C.E.—was advocating a "material" account of the universe. The dichotomy between "matter" and some other intangible or immaterial substance (soul, spirit, mind) was foreign to Greek thought at this time, to say nothing of the notion that matter was "dead" and required some other force to set it in

12. W. K. C. Guthrie, *A History of Greek Philosophy* 1.30.

motion. Indeed, it is likely that Thales espoused a hylozoistic conception of water: it was itself alive in some fashion; for if it were not, it could not generate the diverse phenomena of the world as we see them all around us. Thales apparently believed that water was not only alive but immortal (*athanatos*)—the chief attribute of gods as opposed to mortal human beings.

Thales's choice of water may have been influenced by his recognition of its indispensable role in the preservation of both plant and animal life. Exactly how he believed water to transform itself into other entities is not entirely clear, unless we are to assume that "living" water was the motive force. Aristotle attributes to Thales a belief in a soul (*psyche*): this property does not adhere solely or even primarily to human beings, but may perhaps exist in all entity. Aristotle specifically claims that Thales believed it to inhere in a lodestone (a naturally occurring magnet), for how else can it "make iron move" (*De Anima* 405a)?

Aristotle goes on to make the provocative statement: "Some say that soul is diffused throughout the universe; and perhaps that is what Thales meant in saying that all things are full of gods" (*De Anima* 411a7). Clearly this is a fusion of a (presumably) authentic statement of Thales and Aristotle's interpretation of it. A much later commentator, the doxographer Aetius (first or second century C.E.), makes a striking assertion on this point: "Thales declared that God is the same as mind in the universe, that the All is ensouled and full of spirits, and that a divine moving power pervades the elemental moisture. He was the first to declare that the soul by its very nature is always in motion, and indeed is self-moving."[13] It is probably safe to assume that Thales maintained that water was the primal origin of all entity, that it was alive, that it was deathless, and, by virtue of all these features, that it was divine in some fashion. And if everything came from water and remains in some sense water, then all entity is divine.

Nevertheless, Thales' break from prevailing religious thinking should not be minimised. It hardly matters that he chose water for his primal source, or that he in some manner attributed divine properties to it; the mere fact that he chose a known constituent of the visible world and refused to personify it is a landmark in Western thought. Thales is

13. Wheelright, *The Presocratics* 50. Hereafter abbreviated in the text as W.

known to have been interested in other intellectual matters, especially astronomy; one of his claims to fame was the prediction of an eclipse in 585. In this matter he may have been influenced by Babylonian astronomy, and he is also known to have travelled to Egypt.

Anaximander (610?–546?) was regarded in antiquity as a pupil of Thales, and he is known to have written several books. By this time the belief that four elements constituted all the known objects in the universe was gradually taking shape, although more generally there was a belief in a pair of dichotomies, hot/cold and wet/dry, where hot equals fire, cold equals air, wet equals water, and dry equals earth. He departed from his mentor by asserting that none of these four elements could be the *archē* of the universe, since they are all changing from one to the other. Instead, Anaximander propounded something he called "the boundless" (*to apeiron*). He elaborates upon this striking conception by attributing divinity to the boundless by virtue of its immortality; but it appears that he did not believe the boundless to be infinite in space, and he may have conceived the universe to be an enormous sphere.

In discussing Anaximander, Aristotle states: "The Unlimited [boundless] encompasses and governs all things. On this basis the Unlimited is equivalent to the Divine, since it is deathless and indestructible" (*Physica* 203b; W 55). The earth, far from resting on water as Thales believed, hangs suspended in space "because it is the same distance from all [extremities]" (W 57): so says the early Christian theologian Hippolytus (170?–235 C.E.).

At the beginning of creation, all the elements were indistinguishably melded in the boundless. Gradually there was a separation into distinct entities. Anaximander went further than Thales in proposing a natural origin to earth life, which "came-to-be from vapors raised by the sun; and man came into being from an animal other than himself, namely the fish, which in early times he resembled" (Hippolytus [W 58]). I am not certain whether, on the strength of this single quotaton, we should regard Anaximander as a pioneer of the theory of evolution, especially since Plutarch maintains that "Anaximander says that men were originally generated *in* the bodies of fishes" (W 59; my emphasis), which appears to negate the notion that human beings evolved out of fish.

It does not appear that Anaximander had any coherent view of deity aside from his belief that the boundless was divine. Cicero claims that

"It was the opinion of Anaximander that the gods come into existence and perish, rising and setting at long intervals" (*De Natura Deorum* 1.25). If this is an accurate account of the philosopher's view, it would be a remarkable repudiation of the universal Greek view that the defining characteristic of godhead was its immortality. But this opinion is not confirmed by any other ancient sources.

Anaximines (mid-sixth century) was a pupil of Anaximander. It may appear that he constitutes a regression in thinking because he returned to the belief of Thales that there is one single *archē* and that it is air. But where Anaximines made an advance is in his attempt to account for the *mechanism* by which this one substance becomes transformed into the objects we see all around us. We have seen that this point is among the weaknesses in Thales' philosophy, and Anaximander did not address it extensively either. For Anaximines, the means by which the transformations occur is the process of rarefaction and condensation. Air, in his view, is infinite; differences between objects of the known world are quantitative, not qualitative, in the sense that heavier objects have become so through greater condensation, lighter objects through greater rarefaction.

Strikingly, Anaximenes maintained that it is air "out of which proceeds whatever comes to be or has done so in the past or will exist in the future, gods also and the divine" (Hippolytus).[14] Although not explicit on the matter, it appears that he, like Anaximander, is denying immortality to the gods. Anaximenes also associated air with "soul" (*psyche*). This conception is of very old origin, reflecting the belief that *psyche* is the "breath of life." One of the few actual quotations we have from him (assuming it to be authentic) is found in Aetius: "As our souls, being air, hold us together, so breath and air embrace the entire universe" (W 60).

A very different philosophical tradition, also focused in or near Ionia, emerged in the middle of the sixth century B.C.E. This tradition was far more infused with religious conceptions—although hardly of an orthodox sort—than that of Thales and his disciples, although we also find at least one thinker whose pungent critique of orthodox religion brought him close to atheism. At the outset we shall focus on the

14. The translation is Guthrie's (*History of Greek Philosophy* 1.121). Wheelwright misleadingly translates the concluding phrase as "gods and daemons."

enigmatic figure of Pythagoras (570?–495) of Samos.

Samos is an island just off the southwestern coast of Anatolia. It was both a thriving commercial centre and a cultural and intellectual hub: in the sixth century it was the home of celebrated architects, sculptors, and writers, among them Aesop the fabulist and Anacreon, the poet of wine and drinking. Pythagoras, however, emigrated from Samos to southern Italy around 530 B.C.E., possibly to escape the tyranny of Polycrates, who had seized Samos around 540. Pythagoras settled in Croton, a colony on the toe of Italy established by the Achaeans in the late eighth century; it was such a thriving city that it itself founded colonies elsewhere, to say nothing of destroying the neighbouring city of Sybaris in 510.

Even during his lifetime, and certainly after his death, Pythagoras became almost a myth, revered by his followers as a godlike figure to whom all aspects of their thought and belief system must be attributed. Indeed, most classical authorities do not refer so much to Pythagoras as to "the Pythagoreans," so that at times it is difficult to know which views reached back to Pythagoras himself and which were fashioned or elaborated upon by his disciples. And because Pythagoreanism, like Buddhism, sought to be more a "way of life" than a set of analytically argued doctrines, it is not always clear by what course of reasoning Pythagoras or his followers came to espouse the views they did or justified their belief in them.

It is, however, safe to say that the Pythagoreans' central contentions that the soul is immortal and that it is subject to metempsychosis (the transference of the soul from human beings to animals, and vice versa) can be traced back to its founder. This focus on the soul is not a self-standing assertion but intimately connected with the metaphysics Pythagoras evolved. In short, he came to believe that the universe was a *kosmos* (a well-ordered whole), and that the study of astronomy, music, geometry, and related disciplines will allow us both to understand its basic features and to assimilate ourselves with the divine essence. This emphasis on mathematics as a key to the understanding of the universe rests upon Pythagoras' belief (according to Aristotle) that the universe, including the soul, simply *is* an arrangement of numbers:

> . . . they [the Pythagoreans] observed empirically that the properties and ratios of harmonious musical tones depend upon numbers. Since

> they found, in short, that everything else, too, in its intrinsic nature, seemed to be essentially numerical, and thus that numbers appeared to be the ultimate meaning of everything that exists, they concluded that the elements of numbers must be the elements of everything, and that the visible heavens in their entirety consist of harmony and number. (*Metaphysics* 985b)

The *kosmos* as a whole is a living god, and the soul is a fragment of that god. Hence, for Pythagoras each person's soul is a detached fragment of the universal or divine soul.

We have seen that the immortality of the soul was, after a fashion, a tenet of the Eleusinian mysteries and the Orpheus cult, in contrast to the lamentable lot of the soul in Hades as found in Homer. It is unclear to what extent Pythagoras was influenced by these religious traditions in fashioning his own view, although there is some evidence that he evolved some of his moral principles from sympathetic magic. But once he had arrived at it, the chief ethical doctrine he extrapolated from it only made sense: eating animal food is a sin, since all living things are kindred.

One other assertion by Pythagoras is of note: his contention that the earth is not the centre of the universe. W. K. C. Guthrie believes that "this idea was unparalleled in pre-Platonic thought, and called for a bold leap of the scientific imagination which proved too great for Plato himself."[15] But when Pythagoras went on to maintain that the earth revolved around a central "fire," he was not espousing the heliocentric theory: in his view, other planets and the sun itself also revolved around this fire.

But although Pythagoras' specifically religious views on the universal or divine soul may be unorthodox, he did not wholly repudiate the Olympian pantheon; indeed, he regarded Apollo as his patron deity. This may have had something to do with his notion of the universe as a *kosmos* and his mathematical/musical interests, since Apollo was the god of music and the arts generally, and was also associated with order and reason. To the extent that the Pythagorean sect (it can hardly be called anything else) was open to both men and women, it represents a rare instance of gender equality in the whole of Greek civilisation.

The life of the extraordinarily long-lived poet-philosopher

15. Guthrie, *A History of Greek Philosophy* 1.282.

Xenophanes (570?–470) superficially follows that of Pythagoras, in that he was born in Colophon, in Ionia, but was exiled to Sicily around 545, around the time of the Persian conquest of Ionia. For our purposes, the most striking of his views are embodied in two fragments about the gods:

> If oxen or lions had hands which enabled them to draw and paint pictures as men do, they would portray their gods as having bodies like their own; horses would portray them as horses, and oxen as oxen. (W 33)

> Aethiopians have gods with snub noses and black hair, Thracians have gods with gray eyes and red hair. (W 33)

This extraordinary venture into what might be called religious relativism underscores not only the persistently satirical edge in much of Xenophanes' extant writing but also his sharp criticism of conventional views of deity. Another fragment is along the same lines, albeit less pungent in its expression: "But mortals suppose that the gods have been born, that they have voices and bodies and wear clothing like men" (W 33). (The first clause is an odd assertion, since the Greeks universally believed that the defining characteristic of godhead was that it was immortal.) He boldly criticised two of the most revered figures in Greek literature—and the fount of the Greeks' knowledge of the Olympian gods: "Homer and Hesiod attributed to the gods all sorts of actions which when done by men are disreputable and deserving of blame—such lawless deeds as theft, adultery, and mutual deception" (W 33).

These various assertions might suggest at a minimum that Xenophanes' had a low view of the standard Greek conception of deity, based on a kind of rudimentary anthropology of religion whereby he understood different peoples to fashion their gods in accordance with their own outlooks, as well as an austere view of the gods that involved the repudiation of the notion that they could be morally equivalent or even inferior to human beings.

But it should be made clear that Xenophanes was not an incipient atheist. Far from it; the statement most widely attributed to him makes this abundantly clear: "God is one, supreme among gods and men, not at all like mortals in body or in mind" (W 32). It should not be assumed that Xenophanes was envisioning an immaterial god; not only was god corporeal, but he was apparently spherical and identical with the entire universe. There is, therefore, a strong likelihood that he was, like Spinoza, a pantheist.

How exactly did Xenophanes come to his views? Apart from his shrewd criticism of traditional conceptions of deity, how did he justify the positive view he espoused? It would be inaccurate to maintain that he was a mystic who believed himself divinely possessed of the secrets about the universe: he frankly espoused only the probability, rather than the demonstrable truth, of his assertions ("These things have seemed to me resemblances of what is true" [W 33]).

Xenophanes did engage in speculation—based upon some observation of visible phenomena—regarding the essential qualities of existence. He adopted the wet/dry theory of the origin of life on this planet: "Whatever comes-to-be and grows is earth and water"; "We are all sprung from earth and water" (W 33). To some extent this is a reflection of the old Greek religious view (found in Hesiod) of Mother Earth (Gaia) fertilised by Ouranos; but Xenophanes was plainly expounding his view as a natural process.

As for the often inscrutable Heraclitus of Ephesus (540?–480?), we are on less certain ground because of the owlishly oracular nature of his known utterances. His native city, in Ionia, was known for its oligarchic tendencies, even as it passed through the turmoil of being conquered first by the Lydian king Croesus (c. 560) and then by the Persians (548), who were finally ousted only when defeated by the Greeks in the early fifth century. Heraclitus, who may have come from a royal family, reveals his aristocratic and anti-democratic bias by pungent criticisms of human folly—strictures that did not exclude even the wisest of the Greeks.

Although Heraclitus believed that "the universe [is] . . . an ever-living fire" (W 71), we should not assume that he was following the path of his Ionian philosophical predecessors in coming up with his own chosen *archē* of the universe. His scorn for the mere accumulation of information is unremittinmg: "Much learning does not teach understanding, otherwise it would have taught Hesiod and Pythagoras,

Xenophanes and Hecataeus" (W 69).[16] Heraclitus believed himself to have been divinely inspired and in possession of the absolute truth. As such, he did not apparently trouble himself with justifying the daring pronouncements he made; the truth came from within the depths of his soul, and that was sufficient. In this sense Heraclitus is far more closely aligned to religion than philosophy: he is more a prophet than a rational or analytical thinker.

Indeed, his central belief—"Everything flows and nothing abides; everything gives way and nothing stays fixed" (W 70)—suggests that he believed knowledge of the visible world to be impossible, or at least futile and meaningless. Another cryptic utterance—"All things come to pass in accordance with this Logos" (W 69)—may be the key to his overall philosophy, if only we could understand precisely what he meant by Logos. This is one of several Greek terms whose exact definition is difficult to grasp to those without an understanding of Greek; and the matter is compounded by the bewilderingly numerous contexts in which Heraclitus uses the term. At its most elementary it means "word," but it can also mean an account or explanation; there are several other shades of meaning as well.

We must be absolutely clear that Heraclitus' Logos is not immaterial, by analogy with the Gospel of John; in fact, it is what manifests itself as the divine fire. In stark contrast to Pythagoras, Heraclitus believed that the universe was in a state of constant warfare: "War is both father of all and king of all" (W 71). A more wholesale repudiation of Pythagorean *kosmos* would be difficult to find. The universe has existed for eternity as "an ever-living fire" (W 71). Although attributing infinity and divinity to fire, it is surprising how infrequently (in the extant fragments) Heraclitus actually uses the term "God" (*theos*). The utterances we have are not very helpful: "To God all things are beautiful, good, and right; men, on the other hand, deem some things right and others wrong" (W 78); "God is day and night, winter and summer, war and peace, satiety and want" (W 79). The most one can say is that Heraclitus does not appear to have believed in an anthropomorphic god or any deity resembling those of the Greek pantheon.

It is also difficult to ascertain Heraclitus' view on the human soul,

16. The reference is to Hecataeus of Miletus, an early historian and geographer. See p. 131.

which he apparently believed to be "vaporized from what is moist" (W 72). There has been much debate as to whether he believed the soul to be immortal; overall, the evidence does not confirm it, although there is the cryptic and vaguely menacing utterance: "There await men after death such things as they neither expect nor have any conception of" (W 74). And what we are to make of the statement that "In Hades souls perceive by smelling" (W 73) is anyone's guess.

D. The Challenge of Parmenides

One of Xenophanes' reputed pupils was Parmenides of Elea (515?–440?), presumably when the former was a very old man. His influence is evident in the central philosophical claim of Parmenides, as we shall see presently. His residence in Elea, a city in the toe of Italy, is significant, and he is acknowledged as the founder of the Eleatic school of Greek philosophy. Elea was founded around 540 by Phocaea, a city in Ionia whose citizens, besieged by the Persians, decided to emigrate.

For now it is important to note that, like his teacher, Parmenides wrote in verse—using the hexameters that, since Homer, had been the standard metre of epic poetry. And just like Homer, he appeals to an otherwise unspecified "Goddess" to inspire him. Far more explicitly than Pythagoras and Heraclitus, Parmenides makes no secret of the divine influence upon him and his thought. In the magnificent proem of his poem he states:

> The Goddess greeted me kindly, and taking my hand in hers she spoke these words:
>
> "Welcome, my son, you who come to our abode with immortal charioteers at the reins! It is no evil fate that has set you on this road, but Right and Justice have brought you here, far away from the beaten paths of men. It is needful that you learn of all matters—both the unshaken heart of well-rounded truth and the opinions of mortals which lack true belief. For it is needful that by passing everything under review you should learn this also—how to judge of mere seeming." (W 95–96)

If it appears to our modern ears that this passage is merely "poetic licence" (analogous, perhaps, to the paean to Venus that opens the undeniably secular *De Rerum Natura* of Lucretius), it should become apparent that Parmenides is being entirely sincere and literal here. Accordingly, he is only one in a long line of thinkers or prophets who believe that some divine infusion has allowed them to perceive the truth when everyone else's vision is clouded by error and misconception.

That phrase "well-rounded truth" is the secret to Parmenides' thought. What he wishes to maintain is that the world of "mere seeming" (i.e., the world as it appears to our common and unreflective perception) is all a delusion. For him, all entity (or Being) is one, unmoving and unchanging; "not-being," as he expresses it, cannot exist. "How could What Is be something of the future? How could it come-to-be? For if it were coming-to-be, or if it were going to be in the future, in either case there would be a time when it is not. Thus coming-to-be is quenched, and . . . destruction is unthinkable" (W 97–98).

The fallacy into which Parmenides has fallen is in one sense complex and in another sense childishly elementary. Essentially, it has to do with the different senses in which the verb "to be" (or, more generally, existence and non-existence) can be understood. In effect, Parmenides is arguing about *words* rather than *things*. While it makes a perverse kind of sense to say that "not-being" does not exist and therefore the only thing that exists is entity, which must be unitary and unchanging, it ignores the plain fact that non-existence can be both a viable intellectual construct and something that actually exists in the universe—or, at any rate, cannot be said *not* to exist (in the sense that Parmenides means it) without further proof. It is as if one said that zero is "nothing" and therefore does not exist. Nevertheless, mathematicians and other scientists have found much utility in the postulation of zero in a variety of contexts. And we shall soon see that one of the chief Sophists of the later fifth century had great fun at Parmenides' expense on this very point.

To the extent that Parmenides, whose writing is both lyrical and polemical, identified certain weaknesses in his predecessors in terms of their failure to identify the *means* by which one thing becomes another (for example, how water—in the view of Thales—becomes earth, then animals and even human beings, and even the soul), his destructive criticism has validity. Specifically, Parmenides was intent on denying the very existence of anything that could be termed void, or empty space—a conception that earlier systems of Greek thought, especially that of the Pythagoreans, were blunderingly moving toward. And the forthrightness (or, from a less charitable perspective, pigheadedness) with which he flatly denied the accuracy of sense-perception must elicit our grudging admiration. "Let reason be your judge when you consider this much disputed question" (W 96), the Goddess says—but fails to note that one could go very far astray if that "reason" is based on false premises.

When he is not lambasting his predecessors (implicity, at any rate, rarely by name), he sets forth a positive account of how he conceives the universe to be. "Since there has to be limit, Being is complete on every side, like the mass of a well-rounded sphere, equally balanced in every direction from the center" (W 98). In effect, Parmenides has adapted the spherical god of Xenophanes and applied it to the universe as a whole. And yet, Parmenides must have realised that he could not wholly dispense with the bewildering array of phenomena to which our (fallacious) senses expose us—phenomena that emphatically seem to confirm the plurality and motion that he is intent on denying. In a section of his poem entitled "The Way of Opinion," as opposed to "The Way of Truth," he does engage in speculation on cosmology and other topics; indeed, this section of his poem was likely to have been far lengthier than the other: once you have asserted that Being is unitary and unchanging, there is not much more you can say about it.

Whether it is possible to harmonise these two sections of his poem, and whether we can fathom Parmenides' rationale in even putting forth his various theories regarding "The Way of Opinion," are strongly to be doubted. The most we can say is that Parmenides engages in this speculation as a means of establishing that even in this illusory realm his thinking is superior to that of his predecessors. And to some degree it is, as when he asserted that the earth is spherical and that the moon has no light of its own but reflects that of the sun; but when he maintained that the human soul is compounded of fire and earth and resides in the breast, our doubts about the value of "The Way of Opinion" are once again raised.

The Goddess tells him, "[You shall learn] how earth and sun and moon and the sky that is common to all, how the Milky Way and outermost Olympus and all the burning power of the stars arose" (W

100). The mention of Olympus suggests that he acknowledged the existence (insofar as "The Way of Opinion" allows) of the Olympian gods, a conjecture possibly confirmed by another somewhat cryptic fragment: "First of all the gods devised Eros" (W 100). How literally we are to interpret the existence of Eros is unclear; elsewhere Parmenides speaks in detail of what happens when "woman and man mix the seeds of love together" (W 100), with no mention of a divine intervention of the god of love.

Parmenides had a vigorous and combative pupil, Zeno of Elea (495?–430?), who wrote in prose and is celebrated for propounding a number of paradoxes—namely, that of Achilles and the tortoise and the flying arrow—that were meant to highlight the absurdities that other thinkers would fall into if they denied Parmenides' unchanging and unmoving Being. Another disciple, Melissus of Samos, specifically denied the existence of void even more emphatically than his teacher ("There cannot be any emptiness; for what is empty is nothing, and what is nothing cannot be" [W 115]). Interestingly enough, however, he contradicted Parmenides by asserting that Being is infinite.

Parmenides and his school are frankly of interest not on their own but because of their influence upon subsequent thinkers—both those who sought to refute them and those (most notably Plato) who adopted some of their central conceptions. Among the former, Empedocles (492?–432?) of Acragas (a city in Sicily) is of immediate interest to us. Although he came from an aristocratic family, he played a role in the transformation of his native city into a limited democracy after the overthrow of the tyrant Thrasydaeus in 480. But he was later exiled and lived out the remainder of his life in the Peloponnese.

But it is not his political activities but his philosophical speculations that are of interest to us. He is known to have written two poems, *On Nature* and *Purifications* (*Katharmoi*). One scholar, Hermann Diels, stunningly maintained that the former work was "wholly materialistic and atheistic,"[17] while the latter is transparently religious (or at least spiritual). There is strong reason to doubt the former assertion, especially since our sources are not at all clear on which fragments they are quoting come from which work.

17. Quoted in Guthrie, *History of Greek Philosophy* 2.124.

Empedocles takes account of Parmenides' challenge, even using much of his same language, in acknowledging that "From what utterly Is Not it is impossible for anything to come-to-be, and it is neither possible nor conceivable that What Is should utterly perish. For it will always be, no matter how it may be disposed of" (W 127). But Empedocles interprets this idea as simply an assertion of the ultimate indestructibility of entity—what would later be exemplified in the Latin phrase *ex nihilo nihil fit* (from nothing comes nothing); he nevertheless goes on to say that pluralism and change can and do exist, even if they do not lead to utter destruction.

For better or worse, it was Empedocles who first put forth the four elements—earth, air, fire, and water—as the ultimate constituents of the universe. Adopted by Aristotle, it remained an albatross around the necks of scientists and philosophers for the better part of two thousand years. These elements may be dissolved, but nothing actually "dies." It is of some interest to note that at times Empedocles identifies these elements with the gods from the Greek pantheon associated with them: "Hear first the four roots of all things: shining Zeus [fire], life-giving Hera [air], Aidoneus [an alternate name for Hades, hence associated with earth], and Nestis [water], who with her tears fills the springs from which mortals draw the water of life" (W 128). Once again, there is no reason to think that Empedocles was using mere poetic licence here.

But what is the motive force that leads to the bringing together and separation of these elements? It is Love and Strife. Sometimes Empedocles manifestly personifies these forces ("These two forces, Strife and Love, existed in the past and will exist in the future" [W 131]); at other times he naturally associates Love with Aphrodite, although there is no evidence that he identified Strife with Ares (god of war) or any other known Greek god.

It should not be assumed (as Diels apparently did when assuming that this account was "materialistic") that the four elements somehow consist of "dead" matter that are merely worked on by Love and Strife. In fact, it appears that Empedocles believed the elements to be sentient, immortal, and to some extent divine (presumably by virtue of their ultimate indestructibility for all the outward changes they may undergo as they enter into the composition of the entities we see all around us). In this sense Empedocles continues to adhere to the hylozoism that we saw emerging as early as Thales. Nor should we assume that Love and Strife are mere synoyms for the abstract principles of attraction and repulsion; we have already seen Empedocles distinctly personifying them, and he also posits a kind of cosmic history whereby Love and Strife will alternate for dominance in the universe.

From another perspective, it is disappointing to see Empedocles latch on to the four elements as the ultimate constituents of entity. True, Greek thought had been leading up to this conclusion for centuries; but it is evident that Empedocles engaged in nothing resembling empirical or inductive reasoning in arriving at his theory. The drawbacks of his purely deductive reasoning are painfully evident when he specifies exact measurements that in his view would lead to the creation of a given material object (e.g., one part water, two parts air, and so on). Clearly, if he had conducted even the most elementary experimentation, he would quickly have discovered that such a commingling would not produce the object in question; more generally, it is striking how he could have believed that these simple elements could produce the wondrously diverse entities we see in the world. But then, the vastly more sophisticated Aristotle made the same mistake.

Indeed, when Empedocles ventures into what might be called a rudimentary anthropology, the results are often grotesque. He maintained that "There sprang up on the earth many heads without necks, arms wandering unattached to shoulders, and eyes straying about in want of foreheads"; similarly, "Many creatures were born with faces and chests turned in different directions. There were offspring of oxen with faces of men, while on the other hand there were human offspring that had the faces of oxen" (W 134). Given the absurdity of these speculations, the fact that Empedocles in some sense anticipated Darwin's "survival of the fittest" theory can only be regarded as accidental: in his view, these maladjusted hybrid creatures eventually died out, leading to the emergence of "whole-natured forms having a due share of both water and fire" (W 135), and these survived.

Empedocles' *Purifications*—insofar as the existing fragments can be clearly identified as coming from that work—give us a multitude of reflections on religion, deity, and related subjects. He goes beyond his chief foil, Parmenides, by boldly claiming not merely that he was inspired by divine sources (such as the Goddess who expounded the cosmos for him in his other poem) but that he himself is a god: "I come among you no longer as a mortal but as an immortal god, rightly honored by all, and crowned with fillets and floral garlands" (W 143). This presumably absolves Empedocles of providing any rationale for the array of theological, ethical, and other pronouncements he makes here.

His chief focus is on the soul. This substance is divine, because it is a piece of what he appears to regard as the holy mind. The relevant fragment states: "He has no human head fitted on to his body, nor does a pair of wings branch out from his back; he has no feet, nor hairy parts. He is purely mind, holy and ineffable, flashing through the whole world with swift thoughts" (W 140). No specific subject is stated in the various clauses of this fragment, and by the rules of Greek grammar it is not possible to say whether Empedocles intends the subject of his verbs to refer to "he," "she," or "it"; but the reference to "hairy parts" (i.e., genitals) suggests a male. How this conception—if it is correct—is meant to harmonise with the previously discussed notions of Love and Strife being the motive forces of the universe is entirely obscure. Nor is the matter clarified by his further statement that Aphrodite (the personification of Love) preceded all the other gods, including Zeus (W 140). This is presumably why, at this early stage of history, "All creatures, beasts and birds alike, were tame and gentle to man, and friendly feelings were kindled everywhere" (W 140). Given this confusion as to which deity has supremacy (either temporal or otherwise) in Empedocles' thought, the view expressed by some commentators that he was a monotheist cannot be credibly maintained.

It is some advance in thought, one supposes, that Empedocles did not envision his god as anthropomorphic, although we have seen this conception already expressed in earlier thinkers. In any event, Empedocles goes on to state that the human soul, as a fragment of the divine mind, returns to it upon the dissolution of the mortal body. Indeed, this is the reason why Empedocles wrote this poem in the first place, since he maintained that with a sufficient number of "purifications" the soul would be altogether free of a confining body. Being in a physical body is, in fact, a punishment for the soul. And because Empedocles also subscribed to the doctrine of reincarnation, he is known to have advised a prohibition on the consumption of meat. It is evident that this view of the soul is a mingling of the thought of Pythagoras (reincarnation) along with the Orphic and other mystery cults that emphasised the notion of the soul's purification and eventual reconnexion with the divine.

Anaxagoras of Clazomenae (500?–428?) was slightly older than Empedocles, and no relationship between the two thinkers has been established, although it is probable that Anaxagoras was familiar with Empedocles' poems and wrote his own (prose) work, the *Physica,* in partial response to them. That treatise was written sometime after 467. He gains our attention not only for his intrinsic interest but by virtue of his spending thirty years in Athens and being the tutor of Archelaus, Pericles, and Euripides. In later life he was exiled (for a reason I shall discuss later) and spent his final years in Lampsacus, on the eastern coast of the Hellespont.

Anaxagoras rejected Empedocles' identification of the four elements as the basic constituents of matter but did adopt, after a fashion, the notion of Mind as the force that "set in order" (W 163) the rest of the cosmos. It did so by initiating a process of rotation, after which it appears that, like the god of the Deists many centuries later, it sat back and let natural causation take over. As such, Anaxagoras rejected a teleological view of the universe—a stance that predictably earned him the scorn of Plato and Aristotle. It is unclear whether we are to regard this Mind as a divine entity; at any rate, it is apparently not envisioned as material, but instead invisible and intangible.

The actual matter of the universe (and we may now call it matter, more or less in our common understanding of the term) is so constituted that "in everything there is a portion of everything else" (W 160); whatever substance predominates will define what the entity is. It is likely that Anaxagoras was led to this view—and also to the rejection of the four elements of Empedocles—by observing the process of nutrition: how does the absorption of food engender the creation of muscle and bone in the body? It can only be because each foodstuff has some small portion of muscle, bone, and the other substances making up the body, and that these substances become fused with the corresponding parts of the body upon ingestion.

Where Anaxagoras becomes, although perhaps by accident, an innovative thinker is in his conception of the formation of the universe. The universe was, in his view, at first small; but the process of rotation that Mind set in motion caused it to expand and for the stars and planets to form. Needless to say, this is an entirely fortuitous anticipation of the Big Bang theory and other elements of modern cosmology. His assertion that the stars are "fiery stones" (W 172) may have been inspired by the fall of a meteorite in Thrace in 467. Like Parmenides, he asserted that the moon's light comes from the sun.

It can be seen from the above that Anaxagoras, for better or worse, articulated—for the first time in Western history—a distinct dualism between mind and matter. And yet, to the extent that his outlook is largely secular and that he had next to nothing to say about God or the gods, he constitutes a step forward on the road to atheism. But on this issue he was quickly eclipsed by the Atomists, to whom we now turn.

In speaking of the two leading Atomists of the period, Leucippus (mid-fifth century) and Democritus (460–390?), we are hampered by a number of factors, chief of which is that Leucippus, evidently the first proponent of Atomism, wrote relatively little (he is known to have written a *Megalē Syntaxis* [usually translated as *The Great World-System*] and a treatise *On Mind*), while Democritus, although his devoted disciple, wrote prolifically on a wide array of subjects and clearly eclipsed his mentor, developing Atomism to a far greater degree of detail and subtlety than Leucippus and perhaps departing in some sense from him. Inevitably, their work exists only in fragments; in the case of Leucippus we have only a few paltry statements. Hence, in this discussion it will simplify matters if in most instances we speak of the Atomists without attempting to determine whether a given view is specifically attributed to Leucippus or to Democritus.

It is evident that the Atomists felt the need to confront the challenge of Parmenides and his denial of change and motion. The critical account is provided by Aristotle, who specifically attributes the theory to Leucippus. It is worth quoting at length:

> Leucippus believed he had a theory which would be consistent with sense-perception, in that it did not abolish coming-to-be and perishing, nor movement, nor the multiplicity of things. To that extent he accepted the testimony of appearances. On the other hand he conceded to the monists that there could not be movement within a void, that a void is not-being, and that What Is cannot ever be What Is Not. Accordingly he agrees that What Is must be a complete *plenum,*

> absolutely and continuously full; with this qualification, however, that there is not just one plenum, there are numerous plena, in fact they are unlimited in number. They move in the void—for there is a void—and by their coming together they cause coming-to-be, while by their getting loose from one another they cause perishing. (*De Generatione et Corruptione* 325a)

There are a few inaccuracies in this statement that we shall consider later. Here we can note what an elegant solution to the Parmenidean paradox the Atomists contrived. In effect, they declared that the "plenum" (the "well-rounded sphere" that Parmenides believed to be the universe) is in fact an infinite number of small particles. They are the *atomoi* (the word means "uncuttable," or indivisible). And the Atomists simply rejected Parmenides' denial of empty space (the defiant "for there is void")—not through any logical refutation, but by implicitly asserting that the assumption of void, along with the rest of their metaphysical vision, simply results in a more plausible conception of the universe than what Parmenides had imagined.

These atoms are not all of uniform shape, arrangement, or position; some are, as the Atomists charmingly maintained, endowed with hooks or other means by which atoms of various sorts are brought together to form larger units. They are, indeed, infinite in shape and infinite in number. On an individual level, however, they are without sensible qualities; only when they come together in sufficiently large units do they reveal qualities accessible to human sense-perception. And because the void is itself infinite, the motion of atoms occurs by "necessity" (*anankē*).[18] The use of this term—which was long personified by earlier writers and, in conjunction with *moira* (one's personal fate), constitutes a weighty and even baleful conception in Greek religious thought—was no doubt deliberate: here it was boldly used to designate a purely mechanical process. Specifically, the notion suggests that all events in the universe occur by the inherent nature of the individual atoms or their combinations; these events can appear as "chance" because we

18. One of the few fragments attributed specifically to Leucippus declares: "Nothing happens at random; whatever comes about is by rational necessity" (W 178), where "rational necessity" is a translation of *ek logou te kai hyp' anankēs* (literally, "by reason and by necessity").

humans are not privy to all the causes at work. In what is surely an accidental anticipation of quantum theory, the Atomists maintained that larger conglomerations of atoms reveal more regularity (as perceptible to human senses) than smaller ones.

There is some dispute as to whether the Atomists envisioned the motion of atoms to be haphazard or downward; in all likelihood the former is a more accurate description of their theory. It can be seen that this overall conception does away with the need to bring in Empedocles' twin forces of Love and Strife as the creators of motion in the universe, let alone Anaxagoras' dualism of Mind and matter. The Atomists—whether through the influence of Anaxagoras or on their own—also asserted that the intersection of atoms would result at times in a vortex-like motion that resulted in the creation of individual worlds; Democritus is on record as maintaining that "there are innumerable worlds of different sizes" (Hippolytus, *Refutatio* 1.13.2).

The Atomists ran into difficulty in explaining exactly how they came up with their theory, given that they did not (*pace* Aristotle) believe in the reliability of sense-perception, at least on the level of the individual atom. Democritus' celebrated utterance "In reality we know nothing, for truth lies in the abyss" (W 182) is one indication of this; another is a dialogue between the intellect and the senses, in which the latter expostulate with the former: "Ah, wretched intellect, you get your evidence only as we give it to you, and yet you try to overthrow us. That overthrow will be your downfall" (W 183). Democritus is even more emphatic in another passage: "It has been demonstrated more than once that we do not discover by direct perception what the nature of each thing is or is not" (W 182). It hardly need be repeated that the Atomists, like most of their predecessors and contemporaries, made no attempt at verification—certainly not through the means of instruments, which in any event didn't exist—of their theory. In the end, Democritus may simply have stated or implied that Atomism explains both the origin of the universe and more immediate phenomena better than anyone else had done.

Where Atomism in its original form gets into trouble, beyond this overriding issue of epistemology, is in the explanation of how sense-perception works. The thoroughgoing materialism of their system meant that all perception must be material, and even thought must be as well.

It is plausible enough to assert that sight, hearing, touch, and smell result from a given object giving off fine particles of itself that come into contact with our eyes, ears, nose, and hands; but material thoughts are more difficult conceptually, as are the Atomists' blundering attempts to account for hallucinations, which must somehow also be material.

Boldly, the Atomists asserted that the soul—whose atoms are distributed throughout the body and cause the body to move—is dispersed at death. (The mind is concentrated in the heart.) They denied that the gods are immortal also. For there are gods—there must be, if the images of them come to human beings in dreams and at other times. Democritus even engaged in a rudimentary anthropology of religion, maintaining (according to Sextus Empiricus) that our ideas of the gods emerged from such earthly phenomena as thunder, lightning, and eclipses, which so terrified primitive people that they attributed them to the work of gods.

Democritus is known to have engaged in all manner of research and speculation in the realms of biology, physiology, medicine, and even on such issues as language, literature, the development of culture, and music. To my mind he is unquestionably the pinnacle of Presocratic thought, and perhaps of Greek thought generally.

For all the limitations of certain aspects of the atomic theory, it constituted a breathtakingly elegant account of the origin and development of the universe along purely secular lines. The belief that Leucippus and Democritus anticipated the findings of later physical science rests largely on the fact that the physicists of early-modern Europe themselves adopted their terminology and at least some of their conceptions, especially the all-important *atom* (its first use in English, according to the *Oxford English Dictionary,* dates to 1477). Even if the Atomists could not come up with any compelling rationale for many aspects of their thought, they would eventually inspire a legion of scientists and philosophers to develop, amend, or elaborate upon their vision. But that process was held in abeyance for the better part of two millennia, until the unfortunate influence of Plato, Aristotle, and Christianity finally wore off in the later Renaissance.

In recent years some scholars have put forth a claim that one Hippon (or Hippo) (mid-fifth century B.C.E.) should be regarded as the first atheist in Greek philosophy; but the claim is more than a little dubious. Aside from the fact that we have virtually no surviving texts by this obscure writer (who was held in very low esteem by Aristotle and others), the accusation of atheism comes chiefly from a play by the comic playwright Cratinus—and, as we shall see, such claims were hurled regularly by satirical playwrights against thinkers who were anything but atheists. Scholars go on to state that Hippon maintained that the soul is material; but this view, even if it is properly attested, was by no means original to him.[19] In any case, it is a big step from this to denying the existence of the gods, for which almost no documentary evidence exists. Hippon seems to have been a popular philosopher and a bit of a rabble-rouser—a kind of Ayn Rand of the ancient world—and his general lack of profundity and influence make him little more than a footnote in Greek thought.

It may be well here to discuss a somewhat separate intellectual phenomenon that emerged around this time—the development of Greek medicine. We are here concerned with the so-called Hippocratic Corpus, a series of about fifty treatises, some of them as old as the late fifth century. They were attributed to Hippocrates of Cos (469–399),[20] but probably none of them were written by him.

The use of non-rational means to treat medicine—sympathetic magic, rituals to banish evil spirits, prayers to gods (many of whom were endowed with healing powers), and so on—is of infinite antiquity in the history of humanity and continued throughout the Greco-Roman period and on into the era of Christian domination in the West. But early Greek medicine, largely based on actual practice and seeking (not entirely successfully) to avoid philosophical presuppositions, did attempt to establish the basic principle—revolutionary in its way—that disease was a natural phenomenon and not something brought on by the gods or treatable by them.

On the Sacred Disease (c. 400), one of the earliest discussions of epilepsy in human history, opens boldly:

> I do not believe that the "Sacred Disease" is any more divine or sacred

19. Guthrie (*History of Greek Philosophy* 2.430), speaking of the roughly contemporarneous Atomists, states that "The atomists were least of all likely to depart from the consensus of their period that the soul . . . was a tenuous form of material substance."
20. Not to be confused with the mathematician Hippocrates of Chios (470?–400).

> than any other disease but, on the contrary, has specific characteristics and a definite cause. Nevertheless, because it is completely different from other diseases, it has been regarded as a divine visitation by those who, being only human, view it with ignorance and astonishment.[21]

Some of the Hippocratic treatises did, regrettably, put forth the theory of the four humours (blood, yellow bile, black bile, and phlegm) as parallel with the four elements—a doctrine that had a long and unfortunate history in Western medicine; but other treatises rejected the humours as constituting too simplistic an account of the complexities of the human body.

E. The Sophists

Before we discuss the contributions of the leading philosophers of the later fifth century, some words need to be said regarding an important sociopolitical development that had been occurring for more than a century: the ascendancy of Athens as a cultural centre of the Greek world.

We have seen how the Mycenaean culture had established itself in Athens in the second millennium B.C.E. It is possible that at this time the other major cities in Attica agreed to unite under the leadership of Athens—an event attributed to the legendary hero Theseus. As a result, Athens was ruled by an aristocracy of the leading families in the city, led by an archon (representing the civil authority) and the polemarch (representing the military authority). The archon was assisted by the advice of the Areopagus (named after the "hill of Ares" northwest of the Acropolis).

In 594, the archon Solon instituted major reforms, abolishing debt servitude and taking other actions to alleviate the plight of the poor. The military leader Pisistratus ruled Athens as a tyrant for much of the period 561–28—but this was no retrogression, as he had widespread support among the people. He was succeeded by his sons Hippias and Hipparchus. A number of democratic reforms were effected at this time, especially by Cleisthenes (archon in 510), who largely succeeded

21. Translation by G. E. R. Lloyd in *Early Greek Science: Thales to Aristotle* 54.

in overthrowing the rule of aristocratic families and their supporters and instituting a democracy (if such it can be called, given the denial of political power to women, slaves, and of course the many resident aliens [*metoikoi*] in the city) based on locale rather than tribal affiliation. By this time Athens was also becoming a prodigious commercial and military power.

The Persian Empire had, however, become a menace to the Greek city-states by the middle of the sixth century: under the reign of Darius, it defeated Croesus, king of Lydia, in 548 and took over much of the western coast of Anatolia, although the Greek cities there continued to flourish both economically and intellectually. As we have seen, it was in the Ionia of the sixth century that philosophical speculation first emerged.

By the early fifth century the Persians sought to conquer the Greek mainland. When Miletus and other Ionian cities revolted in the years 499–94, they were burnt to the ground. But the Persians suffered stunning defeats at Marathan (490) and Salamis (480) in Attica at the hands of a coalition of Greek city-states led by Athens.[22] In between these critical engagements, Darius died and Xerxes I took over; but in 479 his navy suffered a defeat at Plataea, completing the rout of Persia and establishing Athenian mastery of the sea.

Continuing Persian threats compelled Athens to establish the Delian League (478–77) with many of the cities and islands in the Aegean Sea; but with the passage of time these cities chafed at Athenian dominance, leading Athens to annex them, especially under Pericles, who held a variety of civil and military positions from the 460s until his death in 429. It was under his informal reign that Athenian democracy and culture flourished, especially with the performances of Greek tragedy in the early fifth century (as a concomitant to the Great Dionysia, a religious festival) and Pericles' encouragement of artistic expression—notably the construction of many of the prominent buildings on the Acropolis by Ictinus. It was understandable that the Greeks in general, and the Athenians in particular, having defeated a foreign foe of vastly greater numbers and apparent military power, and now witnessing the efflorescence of literature, painting, sculpture, and other arts to an

22. The battle of Thermopylae, just preceding that of Salamis in 480, was technically a defeat for the Greeks; but the valour displayed by the Greeks was immensely inspiring to them. The recent film *300* (2007) is loosely based on this battle.

unprecedented degree, gained a sense of their manifest superiority to the nations environing them.

Philosophers had been congregating at Athens from at least the middle of the fifth century. Anaxagoras, as has been mentioned, spent some thirty years of his life there. Democritus, although born in the remote city of Abdera (on the coast of Thrace), also lived in Athens for a time.[23] But it was the Sophists who made Athens the hub of a thriving culture of political, moral, and social speculation.

It should be noted that the word *sophistes* (pl. *sophistai*) did not initially have a negative connotation; it is first found, in extant Greek literature, in Pindar (early fifth century) and referred to poets, specifically in their role as moral instructors. But a certain negative connotation had been developing since at least the time of Aeschylus, and when the first avowed Sophists—Protagoras and Gorgias chief among them—emerged in the middle to late fifth century, it denoted those who provided instruction for a fee so that young men could be effective in public speaking. And while the taking of a fee was not regarded as intrinsically pernicious, their skill at arguing both sides of an argument—using all the weapons of verbal and intellectual rhetoric at their disposal—did engender in certain commentators a belief that the Sophists as a whole were merely slick talkers who sought to undermine the foundations of ethics and perhaps also of religion. It will become abundantly evident that the Sophists were not, as a result, a "school" in the sense of sharing a common set of philosophical positions; the best that could be said of them is that they generally adhered to a sceptical and empirical outlook.

A good place to begin our discussion is the treatise *On Not-Being, or On Nature* by Gorgias of Leontini (483?–376), who had established himself in Athens by 427. Its basic principles are summarised by Sextus Empiricus: "first that nothing exists, secondly that even if anything existed it could not be known by men, and thirdly that even if anything could be known by anyone it could not be communicated to anyone else" (*Against the Logicians* 1.65; W 256). It would seem that scepticism could go on further; and while it is likely that this treatise was in fact meant as a philosophical satire (clearly aimed at Parmenides, and asserting that "not-being" could, by the use of verbal gymnastics, be "proven" as

23. His strangely poignant utterance, "I came to Athens and no one knew me" (W 186), probably reflects his lack of interest in fame or notoriety among his contemporaries.

decisively as Parmenides' unmoving Being), somewhat in the manner of Voltaire, there was a more serious message that Gorgias and other Sophists were making.

It is not simply that the Sophists lacked an interest in the kind of cosmological speculation that had animated much Presocratic thought from Thales to Democritus; it was that they believed that such speculation was idle. Theories regarding the origin of the universe were intrinsically unverifiable, as evidenced by the radically different *archai* that the Sophists' various philosophical predecessors had all put forth with cocksure certainty. But their hostility to *physis*—or, rather, their pointed and multifaceted contrast of *physis* with *nomos* (law or custom)—was a defining characteristic of their thought.

The epistemological scepticism advocated by Gorgias was also a central pillar in the thought of Protagoras (490?–420?), the first and perhaps the greatest of the Sophists. His most famous utterance—"Man is the measure of all things"—was, however, radically misconstrued by Renaissance thinkers as advocating a broad humanism whereby all things should be tailored to human needs. His full utterance—"Man is the measure of all things: of things that are, that they are; of things that are not, that they are not" (W 239)—is really an expression of a radical subjectivism. Each person's view of reality is valid for that person alone; there is and can be no consensus on even basic matters relating to the nature of entity, let alone on moral or political matters. Plato (who, as we shall see, took an unusual interest in the Sophists as his immediate philosophical predecessors) attributes this conclusion to Protagoras' awareness that certain substances—food, oil, manure—are harmful to humans but not to animals or plants, or vice versa (*Protagoras* 333e–334c).

What Protagoras is maintaining, apparently, is that a given object has no intrinsic qualities; they are only attributed to the object when perceived by someone. To some degree this echoes Democritus' claim that all sensations—hot, cold, sweet, bitter, and so forth—are subjective and do not inhere in the object in question; but Protagoras went further, denying any permanent *physis* below the level of sensations.

But if this is the case, then everyone is equal to everyone else as far as intellect or wisdom is concerned; what benefit would there be for anyone to pay Sophists to make them persuasive in argument? One could perhaps adopt the cynical view that, in the wake of the radical (if, as mentioned, ultimately limited) democracy that Athens was experimenting with, a smooth tongue could be useful in persuading the populace to adopt a given policy; and, indeed, it is exactly on this point that the comic playwright Aristophanes attacked the Sophists in the *Clouds* (423), which, even though the play focuses on Socrates, clearly aims its satirical barbs at the Sophists' view that there are always two sides to any issue. Here, the Just Discourse faces off with the Unjust Discourse,[24] the former advocating justice and the rule of law, the latter denying that justice has any true existence and recommending a life of ease and pleasure.

But, while it cannot be denied that Protagoras and other Sophists did assert the relativity of values, even on the level of sense-perception, they appear to have gone on to say that, even if all beliefs are equally valid (because they represent the presumably sincere views of the given individual), not all beliefs are equally "good" (*agathos*); and that they, the Sophists—and here they seem to have used a metaphor derived from the practice of medicine—can make a person "healthier" by using the art of persuasion to inculcate sounder views.

This conception then became associated with the *physis/nomos* debate, although we find individual Sophists on both sides of that debate. While most Sophists made a break with religious tradition by denying that the body of laws that governs any given city-state is of religious origin, they differed on the validity of those laws. Protagoras believed that it was the establishment of law that allowed human beings to emerge from rude primitivism into a state of civilisation; as such, laws are sanctioned by the common consent of citizens and remain valid up to the time when the citizens collectively decide they should be altered. We will see that Socrates himself adhered to a version of this view. Other Sophists, among them Antiphon, believed that the laws of any given city-state were purely artificial and could be defied if they conflict with one's inner nature (*physis*).

We can at last approach the Sophists' attitude toward religion. It is not surprising, given the general scepticism and iconoclasm that pervade their outlook, that the Sophists criticised orthodox religion

---

24. The characters in question (*Dikaios Logos* and *Adikos Logos*) have been rendered in widely varying manners in English: some use Better/Worse, others Weaker/Stronger, and so forth. I have opted for a literal translation.

(by which they meant the Olympian pantheon) on many fronts. They followed earlier thinkers in attacking the gods for the immorality of some of their actions. Protagoras frankly espoused agnosticism as a natural concomitant to his subjectivism: "As for the gods, I have no way of knowing either that they exist or that they do not exist; nor, if they exist, of what form they are. For the obstacles to that sort of knowledge are many, including the obscurity of the matter and the brevity of human life" (W 240). Prodicus of Ceos (465?–395?) attempted a rudimentary anthropology of religion by maintaining that "The ancients considered as gods the sun and moon, rivers, springs, and in general all the things that assist our life, on account of the help they give, just as the Egyptians deify the Nile" (Sextus Empiricus, *Adversus Mathematicos* 9.18)—a crude outline of primitive animism. Several Sophists articulated the notion of the self-sufficiency of any putative deity, such as Antiphon: "For this reason he has need of nothing, nor does he expect anything from anyone, but is infinite and all-sufficient."[25]

On this issue we need to take note of several actions by the Athenian government against perceived atheists or freethinkers—the first such actions on record in Greek history. These events took place at a critical moment in the political and military history of Athens and of Greece as a whole.

The conflicts between Athens and its purported allies in the Delian League resulted in constant if sporadic warfare between the years 460 and 430. Athens' continued domination of the seas and of commerce (especially with colonies in Italy) incited Sparta and other cities to an attempt to curb its power. Sparta, a city in the Peloponnese with no access to the sea (hence no navy), had undergone extensive constitutional and military reforms, probably in the seventh century; these were attributed to the half-legendary figure of Lycurgus. The result was a society single-mindedly focused on military training for its (male) youth and the establishment of an extensive slave population, called helots, owned by the city. The clash between Athens and Sparta led to the outbreak of the Peloponnesian War, which consumed much of the period between 431 and 404 B.C.E., ultimately resulting in the defeat of Athens.

I have mentioned the exile of Anaxagoras. He was put on trial in

25. Cited in Guthrie, *A History of Greek Philosophy* 3.230.

Athens, after spending thirty years in the city, for maintaining that the sun was a "fiery stone." Exactly when this trial occurred is uncertain; some scholars place it as early as 450, but a more likely date is 433. Regardless of when it occurred, it suggests a growing intolerance on the part of the Athenian public, which always displayed a conservative hostility to those who openly defied religious orthodoxy. The charge was levelled at Anaxagoras by one Diopeithes, who argued against "those who do not acknowledge divine things or who give instruction about celestial phenomena" (Plutarch, *Pericles* 32).

It is possible that one reason for the bringing of these charges was Anaxagoras' friendship with Pericles, who spoke in his defence. The ancient sources agree that Pericles' enemies sought to tar him by linking him with a perceived atheist; indeed, the same charge was levelled at Pericles' own wife, Aspasia, although Pericles' eloquence in her defence caused her to be acquitted. Protagoras was exiled for impiety around 420 and died by drowning when the vessel taking him away from Athens was shipwrecked.

Then there is the curious case of Diagoras of Melos, an obscure figure who was habitually labelled "the atheist" by the few ancient authorities who mention him. Not much is known about him aside from the fact that he was active in the last quarter of the fifth century. The orator Lysias claimed that he was "impious in speech regarding the sacred things and celebrations in a foreign place" (6.17), and was therefore forced to flee Athens.

What appears evident—and will become more evident in our discussion of Socrates—is that accusations of atheism or impiety were abundant in Athens during the years preceding and, especially, during the Peloponnesian War. It certainly did not help that Athens was stricken with a devastating plague in 430, which carried off Pericles the following year. The political, military, and social turmoil in Athens may be sufficient to account for this seeming burst of religious intolerance, since it rarely recurred in subsequent Athenian or Greek history.

Our account of the Sophists suggests that they were a diverse but dynamic group of thinkers who boldly questioned authority (philosophical, political, moral, and social) and possibly engaged in a certain amount of satire and ridicule that did not go over very well with their contemporaries. It cannot be denied that there is a certain nihilism in the views of some of them, notably Gorgias; but, for all their disagreements with some of their philosophical predecessors, they continued a strong tendency in Greek thought that was evolving a secular and morally challenging view of the universe—a tendency that can be seen in the work of Xenophanes, Anaxagoras, and the Atomists.

But they were about to encounter formidable opposition in two thinkers whose wide influence upon subsequent Greek and Western history caused their non-theistic worldview to go into eclipse, not to be resurrected for the better part of two millennia.

F. Socrates and Plato

The difficulties in dealing with Socrates (469–399) are obvious. By design he wrote nothing, instead spending his philosophical career in face-to-face debates with colleagues and disciples. As a result, everything we know about him comes from other sources—whether it be those very disciples (of whom Plato is far and away the most significant) or hostile figures such as Aristophanes, who lampooned him mercilessly in the *Clouds*. Then there is the fact that he was compelled by the Athenian state to commit suicide, drinking hemlock in 399. As a result, he became a martyr—a martyr for intellectual integrity and for defiance of state restrictions on the pursuit of knowledge. This augmented his stature but also allowed for the accretion of myths and legends whose kernels of truth (if any) are at this point next to impossible to ascertain.

Setting aside the writings of the historian Xenophon (428?–354?), whose *Memorabilia* and *Apologia* tell us much about his mentor but which also betray his philosophical naïveté, we are obliged to base much of our knowledge of Socrates on Plato (429?–347). And the difficulty here rests precisely in the fact that his dialogues, seemingly following his tutor's method of *elenchus* (a series of questions and answers with an opponent, whereby the truth will presumably emerge), are supreme works of literary artistry and do not pretend to be literal transcripts of actual dialogues with the real figures (Protagoras, Gorgias, or Socrates himself) they put on stage. It is generally accepted that the earlier of Plato's dialogues—beginning with the *Apology of Socrates*, probably written shortly after Socrates' death—present more historically sound information on Socrates than the later dialogues, where Socrates becomes largely the mouthpiece for the enunciation of Plato's own conceptions.

What must be emphasised at the outset is the extent to which Socrates engaged in an intense debate—literally or figuratively—with the entire Sophistic movement, to which he was implacably hostile. And yet, he could hardly fail to have been influenced by some of the tendencies of Sophistic thought. For example, early in life he had been interested in natural philosophy but largely abandoned it for the study of the human soul, just as the Sophists had rejected the teachings of the Presocratic natural philosophers as incoherent, unverifiable, and mutually contradictory. This view is found in Aristotle, and Cicero reflects it acurately when he states:

> Socrates opposed them [the Sophists] and used to refute their instruction by his own subtle brand of argument. His fertile talk gave rise to a succession of accomplished thinkers, and it is claimed that then for the first time philosophy was discovered—not the philosophy of nature, which was older, but this which we are speaking of, whose subject is good and evil, and the life and manners of men. (*Brutus* 8.30–31)

This leads to Cicero's triumphant but misleading assertion that "Socrates first called philosophy down from the sky, set it in the cities and even introduced it into homes, and compelled it to consider life and morals, good and evil" (*Tusculan Disputations* 5.4.10). Clearly the Sophists also engaged in much discussion of ethics, as did several of the Presocratics, even if the latter did so somewhat sporadically or unsystematically.

It is Plato who articulates what Socrates believed to be the prime goal of life (or, at any rate, of the contemplative and moral life): "For I go about doing nothing else than urging you, young and old, not to care for your persons or your property more than the perfection of your souls" (*Apology* 30a–b).[26] This notion of the "care of the soul" became almost a cliché among Socrates' disciples. It is not entirely clear in what exact sense Socrates meant the term soul (*psyche*). It should not be assumed that he was using it in a primarily religious sense; it is more likely that he regarded the soul as the entity that governs the body's functions, and

26. I use the translation of Harold North Fowler.

chiefly its intellectual and moral functions.

It is not entirely relevant for us to pursue the details of Socrates' moral system—its assertion that virtue is knowledge, vice is ignorance, and therefore that all wrongdoing is involuntary (a view adopted by Plato but rejected by Aristotle). What is more to the point for us is to ascertain, if possible, Socrates' conception of deity and the relation of that conception to his notion of the soul.

There is no doubt that Socrates' worldview was fundamentally religious, although by no means in an orthodox manner (by the standards of the late fifth century). Early in life, if Plato is to be believed, Socrates attributed to his *daimonion* a rulership of his mind and actions. In Greek, *daimōn* (of which *daimonios* is an adjectival form, then turned into a kind of abstract noun—*to daimonion*—by Socrates and others) can at times simply be a synonym for "god" (*theos*), but it has numerous other shades of meaning. Suffice it to say that Socrates was referring to some kind of divine substance or essence that guided his behaviour:

> Perhaps it may seem strange that I go about and interfere in other people's affairs to give this advice in private, but do not venture to come before your assembly and advise the state. But the reason for this, as you have heard me say at many times and places, is that something divine and spiritual comes to me. . . . I have had this from my childhood; it is a sort of voice that comes to me, and when it comes it always holds me back from what I am thinking of doing, but never urges me forward. This it is which opposes my engaging in politics. (*Apology* 31c–d)

How exactly this *daimonion* relates to the soul is not entirely clear, but Socrates evidently believed that the human soul is in some way connected to divinity. According to Xenophon, Socrates acknowledged the existence of a supreme deity, one who "coordinates and holds together the whole cosmos"; and it is the soul that "more than anything else that is human partakes of the divine" (*Memorabilia* 4.3.13f.). This view is not entirely original either, as we have seen it in some of the other religiously inclined Presocratic philosophers. But (in Xenophon) Socrates goes on to say that this god "created man from the beginning" (*Memorabilia* 1.4.5) and, in contradiction to the rudimentary theory of evolution that some of the Presocratics had outlined, he states that the various parts of the human body are specifically designed for the purposes to which we use them.

Plato's *Apology* and *Phaedo* make it abundantly clear that Socrates believed in the immortality of the soul, as the two tracts portray the soul's wanderings after death. And yet, there are passages in the *Apology* that suggest that Socrates is something of an agnostic in the matter. He first states that "no one knows whether death, which they in their fear apprehend to be the greatest evil, may not be the greatest good" (28e), then elaborates on the idea:

> Let us consider in another way also how good reason there is to hope that [death] is a good thing. For the state of death is one of two things: either it is virtually nothingness, so that the dead has no consciousness of anything, or it is, as people say, a change and migration of the soul from this to another place. And if it is unconsciousness, like a sleep in which the sleeper does not even dream, death would be a wonderful gain. . . . But on the other hand, if death is, as it were, a change of habitation from here to some other place, and if what we are told is true, that all the dead are there, what greater blessing could there be, judges? (40c–e)

Socrates goes on to recount the many incredible souls ("Orpheus and Musaeus and Hesiod and Homer") whom he would meet and converse with, along with the great heroes of the Trojan War.

The bulk of the evidence does suggest that Socrates believes in the second of these opposing propositions. In the *Phaedo* Socrates is made to say that the soul is "most like the divine and immortal and intellectual and uniform and indissoluble and ever unchanging" (80b). Even if this dialogue has elements of Plato's own views, it is unlikely—given Plato's enormous respect for his mentor and the fact that he was writing only a short time after Socrates' death, when many other of his friends and disciples were living—that he would distort Socrates' views to the extent of putting into his mouth a view that directly contradicted his known beliefs.

And yet, what do we make of the fact that Socrates was tried and convicted on the grounds of "impiety"? The actual indictment, brought by one Meletus, is as follows: "Socrates is guilty, not honoring the gods whom the State honors, but introducing other strange divinities; and he is further guilty of corrupting the young. Penalty, death" (Diogenes Laertius 2.40). Did Socrates fail to honor the Olympian gods? For this claim, and for the whole background of the trial and conviction, we need some awareness of the political situation prevailing at the time.

Following Athens's humiliating defeat at the hands of Sparta in the Peloponnesian War, which ended in 404, a group of oligarchs called the Thirty Tyrants took over; they were led by Critias, a leading Sophist of the period and an associate of Socrates. They instituted a reign of terror against the partisans of democracy; and Socrates was known to have been sceptical of Athenian democracy, believing that politics, like other disciplines, required specialised training. Indeed, this became part of the indictment against him (see Xenophon, *Memorabilia* 1.2.9). But the tyrants were deposed in 403 and democracy was restored. In the inevitable backlash, Socrates was targeted as a proponent of tyranny and heresy. No doubt his frequent discussions of his *daimonion,* and his assertion of an unnamed "god" who governed cosmic and human affairs, was taken as an open affront to the sanctity of the Olympian godhead.

Matters were not helped by the fact that Aristophanes had pilloried Socrates in the *Clouds* as a proponent of all the worst traits of the Sophists—slickness in conducting arguments, subversion of conventional theology and morality (although Socrates' subversiveness was of a very different sort from that of the Sophists'), and so on. At one point in the play he is actually made to say that "the gods are not a coin current with us" (247–48); and the hapless Strepsiades, who has come to Socrates to assistance, states toward the end that "I was insane to cast aside the gods for Socrates" (1477).

Socrates could have chosen exile to death; but this lifelong Athenian also believed (as did Protagoras) that the laws of a city-state are sacrosanct, even the law that condemned him to death; and so he drank the hemlock and died.

It is unclear how long Plato studied with Socrates, but clearly the latter's life, teachings, and especially his death exercised a profound influence on him. But we should also be aware to what extent the Sophists—and Plato's unremitting hostility to them—fueled much of his thinking, especially in the political and religious spheres. The fact that five of his twenty-six works (twenty-five dialogues plus the

Apology of Socrates)[27] are named after, and to some extent devoted to, the Sophists—the *Protagoras*, the *Gorgias*, the *Sophist*, the *Hippias Major*, and the *Hippias Minor*[28]—is a sufficient indication that Plato regarded them as his chief philosophical opponents.

Plato's philosophy is so complex and so integrated that it is difficult to study one part of it—his religious views, which we will focus on here—in isolation. What Plato sought above all else was *certainty* and *order*, both intellectual and political. It is not surprising, therefore, that he sought to devise a philosophical system that, in his mind, established unshakable metaphysical and moral principles that could then be applied to the political sphere as an antidote to the irrational mob rule that led to Socrates' execution. In so doing, Plato adapted aspects of the thought of his philosophical predecessors to combat what he regarded as the intellectual and moral chaos wrought by the Sophists as well as such non-teleological materialists as Anaxagoras and the Atomists. This is not to deny the originality of Plato's synthesis of the materials he drew upon; but we should not be deceived into thinking that his thought emerged, as it were, from the head of Zeus without any reference to his antecedents.

From Parmenides and Heraclitus, Plato adopted the scorn of sense-perception as a viable means of attaining truth. The impressions gained from the senses inform us only of the world of "becoming"—the visible world we see around us. This world has little to do with the fixed and unchanging realm that he envisioned as the object of true knowledge. It is in reference to that realm that Plato evolved the Theory of Forms.[29] Take a physical object such as a chair. There are many different types of chairs; what allows us to understand that each one of them is a chair as opposed to something else? Well, there must be the "Form" (*idea*) of a chair that embodies the quintessence of a chair all apart from any accidental features that any actual chair may have. This Form is actually existent, not merely a mental construct, and it exists in a "place above the sky" (*hyperouranios topos: Phaedrus* 247c).

In assessing the origin of the Theory of Forms, we are once more

27. Seven letters attributed to Plato are also extant, but the authenticity of several of them is in doubt.

28. The reference is to Hippias of Elis, a younger contemporary of Protagoras.

29. The theory used to be called the Theory of Ideas, but this is an elementary error: *idea* does not mean "idea" but "form." And Plato used this term interchangeably with *eidos* ("form" or "shape"; literally, "that which is seen").

faced with the degree to which the philosophy of Plato differed from that of his mentor, Socrates. Socrates is almost exclusively the exponent of Plato's expression of this theory, even in the late dialogues, where it can be assumed that he is being largely a mouthpiece for Plato's own views. Older scholars maintained that Socrates was the exclusive inventor of the theory as a whole, and that Plato merely adopted it; but this seems unlikely, given Socrates' general lack of interest in metaphysical speculation. The most plausible view is that Socrates originated the theory in a rudimentary form, but that the extensive development of it was Plato's achievement.

Plato went on to assert that there are Forms not merely of material objects but also of abstract and moral qualities, e.g., Justice, Beauty, and so on. In this assertion he is ascribing to an objective ethics and even aesthetics that was clearly designed to combat the moral relativism that some Sophists had broached.

The realm of Forms is a world of "unchanging and harmonious order" (*Republic* 500c). But how is it to be accessed by humans? Clearly, the vehicle is the soul; and, if the Forms are themselves immortal, then the soul must be also. Here Plato is adopted the age-old Greek principle of like attracting to like; and there is the clear influence of Pythagoras as well, whose notions of an ordered universe (*kosmos*) Plato adopted, although translating it out of the visible world to the world of Forms; and Plato also adopted the Pythagorean notion of the transmigration of souls. This ties in with Plato's oft-stated notion that true knowledge is "recollection"—a remembrance of what the soul once knew in a former life.

Given that it is only philosophers—at least philosophers of a certain sort—who can attain true knowledge, it becomes inevitable that they must take a prominent place in the organisation of the state. In this manner did Plato evolve the notion of the philosopher-king. Rejecting the untidy democracy of Athens, Plato maintains that only the philosopher-king can lay down the laws of a properly functioning body politic. He made an unfortunate attempt to carry out his principles in real life when the young Dionysius II, tyrant of Syracuse, summoned him to Sicily to help set up an ideal state; but the tyrant's deficiencies of temprament caused the whole enterprise to blow up in Plato's face, and he was actually imprisoned for a time.

Plato's political views are embodied in the *Republic,* in which he describes an oligarchic system whereby a council of "guardians" have sole political power, including the power to legislate and the power to punish wrongdoers. Among these are certain poets who tell false stories about the gods, such as Homer and Hesiod. Plato's general conception of art ties in with the Theory of Forms: given that the visible world is only a weak imitation of the unchanging world of the Forms, and art is only a weak imitation of the visible world, art is doubly removed from the realm of true knowledge. Some of Plato's views were modified in a later work, the *Laws,* but its generally fascistic intent is clear.

We can at last come to Plato's views on God or the gods. His various utterances are at times difficult to harmonise into a unity, partially because they were made in different contexts in the dialogues in which they appear. Here we must turn to a later work, the *Timaeus,* written in 360. An uninitiated reader of this dialogue might find it analogous to the imaginary-world fantasy of, say, J. R. R. Tolkien, especially when Plato elaborates upon the myth of the sunken continent Atlantis. It is here that Plato introduces us to the *Dēmiourgos,* usually translated as the Craftsman. The Craftsman created the visible universe—not the world of Forms, since that is eternal and unchanging, but the world around us, which does change. But the Craftsman looked to the world of Forms as a model. He used the four elements (earth, air, fire, and water) to fashion the objects of this world; but he also created a World Soul, which infuses the objects and presumably endows them with motion, as the human soul does to the body; indeed, human souls are all fragments of the World Soul.

It is unclear whether the Craftsman is in fact equivalent to God. Probably we should not speak of "God" in Plato, since the mere use of the capital letter pushes us toward a Christian conception of the term. Even if the Craftsman is Plato's god, then there are other divine entities in his worldview—the soul as well as the stars (which are imbued with a rational soul that moves them in a circular fashion).

It might seem that Plato's overall philosophy, and in particular the Theory of Forms, would constitute about as total a rejection of the inductive and empirical method as could be imagined. But some qualifications need to be made. In his establishment of the Academy—a school situated in a park on the outskirts of Athens devoted to the hero

Academus, and established as early as 385—Plato did institute the teaching of a wide array of subjects, with the specific purpose of making pupils fit for participation in governance. Even here, however, it can be seen that the chief subjects he taught—mathematics and astronomy—were those that could bolster his own theories, either of the Forms or of the world of "becoming" (as, for example, his assigning of specific geometrical shapes to the four elements). There are also indications that Plato believed that the study of earthly phenomena is something akin to a pastime (*Timaeus* 59c–d), although this does not necessarily imply a frivolousness in the act.[30]

It may be of some interest to study Book 10 of the *Laws,* where Plato specifically addresses atheism and refutes it to his satisfaction. Here atheism is associated with a belief in the random creation of the visible entities in the universe, as outlined by Democritus and others (although no actual philosophers are mentioned). It can be seen from this that Plato's scorn of atheism is intimately tied to his belief in the ordered *kosmos* and its creation by a divine Craftsman. In Plato's resolutely teleological thinking, all motion is motion *toward* a given end, so that no other kind of motion—such as the "chance" intersection of atoms—is even conceivable. Plato also directs his ire against the proto-Deist view that, if there are gods, they care nothing about the fate of human beings. He counters this view by simply maintaining that the gods are all-powerful and benevolent.

The whole point of the *Laws* is to determine a set of laws for the colony of Magnesia, in Crete. Toward the end of Book 10, the Athenian—presumably the spokesman for Plato's views—states that it has been sufficiently proved "that the gods exist, and that they are careful [i.e., take care of humanity], and that they are wholly incapable of being seduced to transgress justice" (907b).[31] What, then, should be done about those who do not subscribe to these beliefs? They will be tried for impiety; and unless they retract their views, "imprisonment shall be imposed in every case" (908a). There are various gradations of punishment depending on the exact cause or nature of the offender's beliefs, ranging from a prison sentence of five years to death.[32] Perhaps it is just as well that Plato was

30. See Lloyd, *Early Greek Science* 71–72.
31. I use the translation of R. G. Bury.
32. Numerous other infractions are, in the *Laws,* also punishable by death.

not put in charge of setting up an actual government.

There are a number of oddities here. Plato's requirement that the people worship "the gods" would appear to refer to the Olympian pantheon, to whom Plato elsewhere explicitly denied any primacy as creators or rulers of the "real" world (i.e., the world of Forms). Evidently he regarded the continuance of this belief as socially and politically useful. But how Plato—who had expressed such outrage at the unjust accusation, trial, and execution of Socrates on this very charge of "impiety"—could then so vigorously advocate it himself in his ideal commonwealth is hard to fathom. But, as in so much of his other writing, he was convinced of the unshakable truth of his views, and he was determined to enforce those views by the force of law.

G. Atheism and Religion in Greek Literature and Art

It is insufficient to trace the development of atheistic, agnostic, or secular thought in Greece during the seventh, sixth, and fifth centuries B.C.E. without giving some attention to the non-philosophical literature of the period, at least some of which bears the influence of the dynamic views of the thinkers we have examined. But in regard to the earlier phases of this period we are faced not only with a dearth of texts—some authors celebrated in antiquity are represented by only a few fragments—but with a broader hermeneutic issue that shall concern us for the entirety of our discussion: namely, the degree to which the religious, non-religious, or anti-religious views of creative writers can be ascertained solely on the basis of their work, in the absence of reliable evidence of the views they actually espoused. This issue is particularly acute in the realm of drama, where the expression of contrary sentiments in the mouths of characters can make it exceptionally difficult to pinpoint with any accuracy whether any given opinion reflects the author's clearly held belief. Nevertheless, certain broad tendencies in the treatment of religious subjects can be observed.

A variety of epic and lyric poets—beginning with Eumelus of Corinth (late eighth century), Archilochus (early seventh century), Alcman (mid-seventh century), Terpander (mid-seventh century), and Tyrtaeus (seventh century), among others—are known as the immediate successors of Homer and Hesiod. The surviving fragments of Alcman show him particularly focused on elaborating myths about the Olympian gods. The fragments of most of the others are too paltry to allow any real insight into their religious views. The so-called Hymns of Homer are a series of poems, dating approximately from the eighth to the sixth century, paying tribute to all manner of gods, Olympian and otherwise, including Asclepius, a son of Apollo whom the Greeks regarded as a god of healing.

Sappho of Lesbos (630?–570?) is of some interest as being the only female writer of any consequence during this period (and, in fact, in nearly the entirety of classical antiquity), and it is a high tragedy that her work survives only in fragments.[33] We find in the extant corpus of her writings various odes or paeans addressed to Aphrodite, but the import of these poems—and whether such an invocation is merely conventional, or whether Aphrodite is intended as anything more than a symbol for love and/or eroticism—is an unanswerable conundrum. Elsewhere she composed a poem recounting the marriage of two (human) figures out of myth—the Trojans Hector and Andromache. One fragment—"Death is an evil. / That's what the gods think. / Or they would die"—echoes the standard belief that the gods are immortal, but again this may have been meant metaphorically as a lament on the inevitable mortality of human beings.

The one lyric poet whose work survives in bulk is Pindar (518–438). Four books of his odes are extant, written to commemorate the victors of the Olympian, Isthmian, Pythian, and Nemean games; a few other works survive in fragments. Many of the sentiments he expressed relating to the gods are transparently laudatory, as befits the genre he was working in; but in *Olympian* 1 he explicitly rejects immoral tales about the gods as unworthy of them ("For me it is impossible to call one of the blessed gods a glutton"). We have seen such a view expressed by some Presocratic philosophers, and Pindar may have been influenced by these. But his theological conservatism is betrayed in *Paean* 9, where he continues to ascribe an eclipse of the sun to the actions of the gods and goes on to

---

33. It is worth pointing out to the uninitiated that Sappho was probably not a lesbian. She married a man named Cercylas and had a child by him. Some poems addressed to women or young girls, or possibly expressing a homoerotic interest in them, presumably led to her being considered lesbian or bisexual. But the matter is hotly debated among classical scholars.

fear that the event might be a portent of war, the damaging of crops, or other deleterious actions.

It might seem that Greek tragedy, especially as practiced in the fifth century, would be inherently a religiously based phenomenon, given that it emerged out of one of the most important religious festivals in Athens, the Great Dionysia, and that the great majority of characters in the plays were either gods themselves or the children of gods;[34] but the matter is considerably more complex than what this scenario suggests. In effect, Greek tragedy as embodied in the work of the three great playwrights of the fifth century—Aeschylus, Sophocles, and Euripides—exhibits a profoundly *human* drama of domestic, psychological, and civic conflict, in which the gods (who in fact appear relatively infrequently) and other divine or semi-divine entities seem to act either as commentators on the action or as transparent symbols for the profound moral issues at stake.

Of the seven extant plays of Aeschylus (525?–456), the *Oresteia* trilogy is of consuming interest. The three plays deal with the aftermath of the Trojan War. In the first, *Agamemnon,* that great hero is killed by her perfidious wife, Clytemnestra, and her lover, Aegisthus. The act of murder, in Greek popular thought, resulted in pollution (*miasma*) that affected an individual, his or her family, or the entire community; some kind of action must be taken to relieve it. In the second play, *The Libation-Bearers,* many years have passed, and Agamemnon's children, Orestes and Electra, are now adults. Acting at the instigation of Apollo, they murder their mother and Aegisthus. This might seem to be a justified act, but in fact the crime of matricide entails further pollution, and so Orestes is pursued by the Erinyes (the Furies), female chthonic deities of vengeance. But in the final play, *The Eumenides,* an unexpected reversal takes place.

Under the aegis of Apollo and Athena, Orestes is not simply killed by the Furies but is placed on trial at the Areopagus. Athena casts the deciding vote sparing Orestes, and she also renames the Furies as the Eumenides (the Gracious Ones). What this symbolises is the establishment of the rule of law to supersede the cycle of vengeance that, as Aeschylus clearly suggests, is a holdover from primitive society. Even

---

34. The one exception in the extant literature is Aeschylus' *Persae* (performed in 472), a play explicitly designed to commemorate the Greeks' victory against the Persians at Salamis (480), in which Aeschylus himself was a combatant.

if that law is enacted under the sponsorship of the gods, the manifest implication is that it is a product of human ingenuity and constitutes a significant step forward in civilisation.

Then there is the *Prometheus Bound,* a remarkably daring work by Aeschylus—if only we could be certain that he wrote it. It was the universal opinion in antiquity that he was the author, but several leading modern scholars are doubtful of the claim. The play, if by Aeschylus, could date as early as 479; if not by him, it could be as late as 430. It was presumably the first play of a trilogy, but the other plays have been lost.

This extraordinary exhibition of the tortures undergone by Prometheus at the hands of Zeus for bringing fire to human beings portrays Zeus (who never appears on stage) as a ruthless and vengeful tyrant. Moreover, Prometheus—who in the course of the play becomes a symbol of humanity's emergence from primitivism to civilisation, and himself embodies indomitable human perseverance in the face of adversity—makes a bold prediction as to Zeus' reign: "But for Zeus I care less than naught. Let him do his will, let him hold his power for his little day—since not for long shall he bear sway over the gods" (938–40).[35] Granted, this is Prometheus' own bitter jibe at his tormentor, but the mere expression of a belief that Zeus will somehow be overthrown suggests a certain radicalism in religious expression.

Of the immense output of Sophocles (496?–406), reputed to have numbered as many as 123 plays, only seven are extant. Space forbids a detailed analysis of this complex and subtle playwright, but it should be noted that both the gods themselves and, by extention, divine elements such as prophecies and curses loom large throughout his extant work. Consider the Oedipus trilogy (*Oedipus Rex, Oedipus at Colonnus, Antigone*). The mere fact that Oedipus ends up killing his father and marrying his mother, Jocasta, is predicated upon a curse laid upon Oedipus' father, Laius, for violating the laws of hospitality—an appalling sin in Greek eyes. Oedipus himself misunderstands the (divinely inspired) oracle at Delphi that warned of his impending patricide and incest. In the *Antigone* (the first of the plays to be written, in 441), the conflict between Oedipus' daughter, Antigone, and Creon, the king of Thebes, over the burial of Antigone's brother Polynices rests upon who

35. I use the translation of Herbert Weir Smyth.

can claim divine sanction for his or her position; in the end, the prophet Tiresias maintains that Antigone's is the stance sanctioned by the gods.

When we come to the *Trachiniae* (performed sometime between 450 and 425), we find the gods in the background throughout. Herakles' hideous death—as a result of wearing the poisoned shirt that the centaur Nessus had fashioned, and which Herakles' wife Deianera had innocently given him—is explicitly declared to be a fitting punishment exacted by Zeus for Herakles' destruction of the city of Oechalia and his taking the young woman Iole as his lover. In the final lines of the play the leader of the chorus speaks to Iole: "And you, maiden, do not be left at the house. You have seen immense, shocking death, with sorrows great in number and strange. And in all of them there is nothing that is not Zeus." It is unlikely that Sophocles was asserting the actual existence of Zeus; but his work overall does seem to suggest the infusion of the divine into the most intimate features of human life.

In studying religious or anti-religious elements in fifth-century Greek tragedy our focus must inevitably be on Euripides (485?–406?), if only because of the number of his surviving plays—nineteen, including the satyr-play *Cyclops* (the only extant example of its kind)—and the fact that he is known to have been acquainted with Anaxagoras, Protagoras, and other thinkers of the time. Even in antiquity, Euripides had developed a reputation for atheism. Aristophanes has a character remark: "But now that man [Euripides] by his tragic poetry has persuaded men that there are no gods at all" (*Thesmophoriazusae* 450–51). This may be another instance of Aristophanes' comic exaggeration; it is the consensus of modern scholars that Euripides, while expressing scepticism, and even scorn, of the Greek pantheon and of the miraculous stories attributed to the gods, was not what one would today call an atheist.

The evidence for Euripides' religious scepticism is not easily interpretable. One fragment seems unambiguous on the matter: "Who is it, anyway, that says the gods exist in starry heaven? / They don't. They don't exist at all. / Anyone still willing to talk in that old-fashioned way is a moron" (fragment 286, from the lost play *Bellerophon*). But it is not clear how this utterance fits into the drama of which it is a part. Another fragment (292) is less ambiguous: "If the gods do evil, they are not gods." This, in effect, is the thrust of Euripides' surviving play *Herakles,* in which the hero Herakles is maddened by Hera and kills his own wife and children. Theseus, attempting to console Herakles after his madness has subsided and he is consumed with guilt for his actions, notes that even the gods commit adultery and other acts that would be branded as sinful. To this Herakles replies: "I don't believe gods tolerate unlawful love. / Those tales of chainings are unworthy; I never did / And never will accept them; nor that any god / Is tyrant of another. A god, if truly god, / Needs nothing. Those are poets' lamentable myths" (1341–46). The statement "A god . . . needs nothing," while probably derived from Xenophanes, constitutes a radical repudiation of the basis of Greek religion, in which the gods were believed to be pleased with the animal sacrifices and other rituals that mortals made in their honor; it is also a striking anticipation of the theology of Epicurus.

It would seem that Euripides was evolving a theology that repudiated the scandalous legends pertaining to the Greek gods as well as the notion, found in such writers as Hesiod, Pindar, and Aeschylus, that the gods were both powerful and just. Euripides has several characters express scorn of belief in oracles (*Iphigeneia in Tauris* 572–75; *Helen* 744–48). The *Bacchae* has been thought to display the viciousness of some Greek religious rituals, as Pentheus is torn apart by women (including his own mother) maddened by Dionysus. But the exact degree of Euripides' religious scepticism will always remain a matter of doubt.

Greek comic drama was a parallel development with tragedy, but we are deficient in the complete texts of what is called Old Comedy (fifth century), where the work of such writers as Eupolis and Cratinus survives only in fragments. Indeed, the only figure of Old Comedy whose work is extant in anything approaching completeness is Aristophanes (450?–385?), eleven of whose plays survive intact, along with extensive fragments of at least thirty more. The first of them was produced in 427, the last after 388.

It might seem, from an examination of the overall flamboyance and bawdiness of his work, that Aristophanes was an outspoken radical—a kind of Charles Bukowski of the ancient world—but the tenor of much of his work suggests a social, moral, and religious conservatism that may reflect the values of the general public of his time. We have already discussed the *Clouds* and its satire on Socrates and the Sophists. Its uncritical lumping of Socrates with his explicit opponents indicates something of an anti-intellectual intolerance for what Aristophanes took to be the clever verbal gymnastics of these thinkers. The *Thesmophoriazusae* (performed in 411) takes place at a sacred fertility festival for women only (the Thesmophoria, dedicated to Demeter), is a broad satire on Euripides, where the women seek revenge on the playwright for his less than flattering portrayals of them in his plays. This play appeared in the same year as *Lysistrata,* the well-known drama in which the women of Athens withhold sex from their menfolk until they agree to end the Peloponnesian War. It might seem that these plays are feminist in their outlook, but it is just as plausible that they enhance stereotypes of women as fundamentally irrational and unsuitable for participation in government. This point is emphasised in the later play *Ecclesiazusae* (392 or 391).

The writing of what we call history also emerged during the fifth century. The term *historia* originally meant something like an inquiry or course of investigation. Even if we assume that Herodotus (484?–420?) is the first historian in the West, he was preceded by several other figures who paved the way for him, including Hecataeus of Miletus (late sixth–early fifth century), who devised a map of the known world and, to accompany it, an account of his journeys around the Mediterranean and the Near East, as far as India. In another work, a mythographic account of some of the gods and their purported descendants down to his own day, Hecataeus utters what appears to be a statement of disbelief in standard accounts of the gods: "I write what I believe to be the truth, for the Greeks have many stories which, it seems to me, are absurd."

The conventional dichotomy between Herodotus and his successor, Thucydides (460?–400?)—that the former was a credulous reporter of all manner of fantastic and obviously false stories of the intrusion of the gods (or the supernatural generally) in human affais, while the latter was a steel-cold intellect who rejected *to mythōdes* (the mythic, or perhaps the made-up, element) in his account of the Peloponnesian War (1.21)—is much in need of revision, or at least of refinement. In fact, Herodotus—whose educational background is unknown, although he appears to be acquainted with Egypt (to which he devotes the entire second book of his work), the Near East, and many areas in and around mainland Greece—is far less credulous than is commonly believed. In his *Historiē* (an Ionic variant of *historia*) he frequently acts merely as a reporter taking down accounts, supernatural or otherwise, that he has heard as a result of his untiring inquiries.

This is not to say that Herodotus in any way denies that gods—whether Olympian or otherwise—exist or that they perform a critical role in human affairs. In his narrative of the history of Egypt, he lapses into the first person as he records "the accounts given me by the Egyptians and their priests" (2.142).[36] He states frankly, and evidently as his own opinion, that "before their [the priests'] time Egypt was, indeed, ruled by gods, who lived on earth amongst men" (2.144); he goes on to mention Horus and Osiris, whom he equates with Apollo and Dionysus. Herodotus' bland acceptance of supernaturalism extends well beyond the gods, as in the famous passage about the musician Arion being cast overboard and rescued by a dolphin (1.23–24).

There are some passages in Herodotus[37] that suggest an inclination to rationalise some Greek myths pertaining to the gods or the descendants of the gods and incorporate them into the historical record. Conversely, the hard-headed Thucydides, in relating the catastrophic effects of the Peloponnesian War upon the entire Greek nation, not merely the defeated Athenians, soberly states:

> Old stories of occurrences handed down by tradition, but scantily confirmed by experience, suddenly ceased to be incredible; there were earthquakes of unparalleled extent and violence; eclipses of the sun occurred with a frequency unrecorded in previous history; there were great droughts in sundry places and consequent famines, and that most calamitous and awfully fatal visitation, the plague. (1.23)[38]

This passage is perhaps exceptional in Thucydides, and some writers in late antiquity maintained that the historian was the pupil of such Sophists as Antiphon, Gorgias, and Prodicus. The celebrated Melian Dialogue (5.85–111)—in which Athens, in attempting to compel the small island of Melos to join its confederation, cynically articulates the "right makes might" trope—may well be thought of as an instance of the amoral *Realpolitik* advocated by some of the Sophists.

---

36. I use the translation of Aubrey de Sélincourt.
37. See Alan Griffiths, "Myth in History," in Dowden and Livingstone, *A Companion to Greek Mythology* 201–2.
38. I use the translation of Richard Crawley.

The other great cultural artifact that has come down to us from this general period (eighth to fifth century B.C.E.) is Greek art, chiefly in the form of architecture, sculpture, and pottery. As I have mentioned, the art that has come down to us is overwhelmingly religious in nature. During the seventh century we find scenes from Homer—as well as the separate Herakles cycle—appearing on vases executed in the Geometric style. During what is called the Archaic period of Greek art (sixth century), the only public buildings of any consequence were temples. It was at this time that the three main orders of architecture (Doric, Ionic, and Corinthian) began to take shape. *Kouroi* (naked male attendants of the gods) were widely sculpted with growing realism, perhaps pointing to an increasing humanism. The striking sculpture of a man carrying a calf on his back (c. 560), in the Athenian Acropolis, is a rare instance of non-theistic art. At this time women (whether goddesses or human beings) were almost always depicted clothed, perhaps reflecting their status as largely hidden figures in Greek society, in contrast to males, whose nudity at athletic events and elsewhere was a common sight. Only in the late sixth century do female nudes appear on vases (but not in sculptures). The red-figure vases of that period also began portraying everyday life.

The Classic age of Greek art spanned the fifth and much of the fourth centuries. At this time, a sculpture such as the so-called Critian Boy (from the Athenian Acropolis, dating to c. 480) set a new standard for anatomical accuracy and a naturalistic pose. This set the stage for the tremendous efflorescence of art of all sorts during this period, notably in such venues as the temple of Zeus at Olympia, where sculptures of Zeus, Apollo, Athena, and others could be seen. One of the most impressive, apparently, was the statue of the seated Zeus by the celebrated sculptor Phidias, a gold-and-ivory figure. It does not survive.

It was at this time that the Acropolis at Athens was reconstructed after being severely damaged during the Persian Wars. We now find the portrayal of (clothed) females reaching new heights of realism. The friezes on the Parthenon are a fascinating mix of the human and the divine—but the interior featured a forty-foot-high chryselephantine statue of Athena Parthenos by Phidias. By the late fifth century, many momental public buildings now began appearing in the Athenian agora (marketplace), and these may have been decorated with more secular art. Female nudity was still a rarity (although there is a notable sculpture of a nude adolescent daughter of Niobe that dates to c. 430), given the Greek assumption that the physical perfection of gods (and, hence, warriors and other notable human beings) was still based on the male figure.

The art of the fourth century does display some growing secularism. The female nude now comes into its own. The naked Aphrodite at Cnidus, executed by Praxiteles (c. 350), is unquestionably erotic in its design. This might also be said for the naked Hermes at Olympia (c. 340), also sculpted by Praxiteles. Portraits and busts of famous figures—ranging from statesmen to military figures to philosophers to writers—now become common. Paintings during the fifth and fourth centuries, although in very short supply, continue to emphasise mythological themes. We are given the names of several celebrated painters of the period—Polygnotus, Mikon, Zeuxis, and Apelles. Vase paintings begin reflecting domestic life, even if still in a largely mythological setting.

H. Aristotle and His Legacy

In dealing with Aristotle and the schools of thought that succeeded him we once again need to pause to assess the sociopolitical state of Greece and the Near East in the fourth, third, and second centuries.

The defeat of Athens at the end of the Peloponnesian War resulted in the end of its military and, to some degree, its political supremacy: it was forced to join the Lacedaemonian League, operated by Sparta. But otherwise Athens continued an independent existence and retained intellectual and cultural superiority in the figures of Plato, Aristotle, and others. Renewed fighting with the Persians resulted in Sparta giving up the Greek cities in Anatolia to Persia in 386. Meanwhile, other cities chafed at Spartan dominance, and Thebes under Epiminondas defeated Sparta in 371 at the battle of Leuctra. Spartan power collapsed, and the various city-states all went their own ways, engaging in constant fighting with one another.

The Greeks were constantly menaced by Persia on the east and Carthage on the west. It was at this time that Macedonia on the northern part of the mainland—not then a part of Greece, although it had long engaged in extensive trade with Greek cities, notably Athens—began to emerge into prominence, especially under Philip of Macedon (r. 360–

36). He took over much Greek territory, but his motive lay in uniting the country for its battle with Persia. Macedonia definitively defeated the Greeks at Chaeronea in 338; but Philip was assassinated two years later. His son Alexander took over, quickly conquering Phoenicia, Egypt, and then Persia (336–31).

Alexander's continuing conquests in the East, all the way to India, led to his declaring himself divine. To some degree the decision was political: many eastern peoples were accustomed to believing in the close connexion of political rulership with divinity; and Alexander (who as a boy had been tutored by Aristotle) was savvy enough to recognise that secular leadership of such an immense territory was unfeasible. But there is no doubt that he was influenced by longstanding beliefs in Greece itself that tended toward the divinisation of kings and heroes, extending back to the Mycenaean age; Alexander himself believed he was descended from Herakles. But his unexpected death in 323 resulted in the breakup of his sprawling empire.

After a generation of disputes among Alexander's successors, the region was divided into three kingdoms following the battle of Ipsus in 301: there was the Syrian (or eastern) Empire, ruled by the Seleucid dynasty; there was Egypt, ruled by the Ptolemies; and there was Macedonia (now including the whole of mainland Greece), ruled by the Antigonidae. It is at this point that the Hellenistic age commences.

With the decline of Athens as a commercial centre, Alexandria (a city at the delta of the Nile in Egypt founded by Alexander in 331) became dominant. But the Greeks were constantly endangered by outside threats, whether it be the Celts from the north, the Parthians from the east, or the emerging Romans from the west. Rome conquered Greece following the battle of Corinth in 146, definitively ending Greece's status as an independent nation.

Aristotle (384–322) was born in Stagira, in Chalcidice, a region in northwest Greece, but came to Athens in 367, enrolling in Plato's Academy and remaining there for the next twenty years, until Plato's death. Disagreements with Plato's successor, Speusippus, led him to leave the Academy and stay away from Athens for a period of twelve years; for part of this period (roughly 343–340) he was in the court of Philip of Macedon, where he acted as Alexander's tutor. In 335 he returned to Athens and established his own school, the Lyceum. Upon the death of Alexander in 323, Aristotle had to flee Athens because of the anti-Macedonian sentiment that had developed, and he died the next year in the city of Chalcis.

The difficulties in studying Aristotle are formidable. Chief among them is the fact that his extant works are, by design, not "literary" in any meaningful sense, and some may in fact be lecture notes written by him (or perhaps, in part, by others); there is doubt whether some of his major works—including the *Metaphysics*—have been assembled in the manner he would have authorised. Some of these works did not come together until centuries after his death; indeed, the extant Aristotelian corpus is derived from an edition prepared by Andronicus of Rhodes toward the end of the first century B.C.E. The other major difficulty in treating Aristotle is the dense complexity of his idiom, where he is clearly striving with varying degrees of success to craft a technical philosophical language for the many areas of thought—metaphysics, logic, the life sciences (biology, zoology, etc.), politics, ethics, aesthetics—that concerned him. There is no question that many phases of Aristotle's thought constitute the profoundest philosophical and scientific analysis of any Greco-Roman thinker whose work survives *in extenso.*

The central fact to bear in mind about Aristotle is that he was a pupil and colleague of Plato for two full decades. During this period he actually wrote dialogues in imitation of his mentor, none of which survive. Although in important particulars he departed from Plato—chiefly because he vigorously advocated and practised an empirical approach to the acquisition of knowledge, especially in those areas (biology, zoology, botany, and the like) where at the time knowledge was possible—he was exceedingly reluctant to break definitively with Plato, at least in his public remarks. In regard to Plato's central contention regarding the existence of Forms, Aristotle comes close to asserting the elementary caveat that the Forms are merely mental constructs rather than actually existing entities, but he never explicitly makes such a declaration. In effect, he simply ignores much of Plato in putting forth his own theories.

For our purposes, we will need to focus on two central issues relating to Aristotle's theology: the nature and constitution of the universe and the existence and nature of the soul. Both issues are of immense complexity—and, at times, obscurity—but the latter is somewhat easier to address than the former. We are here concerned chiefly with the short treatise *De Anima* (On the Soul).

The concept of the soul (*psyche*) in Aristotle rests upon his distinction of form and matter. A statue, for example, consists of marble; this is its matter. But its specific shape is its form. Aristotle uses this analogy to maintain that the soul is to the body as form is to matter. In effect, the soul is what distinguishes "the animate from the inanimate" (413a).[39] Even plants have souls, although they seem to be of a limited or rudimentary nature; animals certainly do. But more than this, it is the soul that establishes the *difference* between one entity and another of the same species: it is the soul that makes John Smith John Smith as opposed to Jack Robinson. "The soul is that whereby primarily we live, perceive, and have understanding" (414a). As John Herman Randall, Jr. put it, the soul is not a "thing" but "an activity or function of the living organism."[40] It is what gives the body its motion, chiefly in the areas of "nutrition, appetency, sensation, locomotion and understanding" (414a).

There was a lively controversy in the later mediaeval era, when his work was rediscovered, whether Aristotle believed the soul to be immortal or not. He seems to be somewhat cagey on the matter, but the bulk of the evidence suggests that he did not. He ridicules the Pythagorean—and, by implication, the Platonic—hypothesis of the transmigration of the soul (*De Anima* 407b), going on to say: "Those are right who regard the soul as not independent of body and yet at the same time as not itself a species of body" (414a). If it is really the soul that differentiates every living thing from every other living thing, it is difficult to imagine how it could be immortal—or, at any rate, how it could have come from outside and entered a given body, as the transmigration hypothesis advocates.

And yet, there is a part of the soul that is immortal and divine—and that is the mind. Aristotle argues that "intellect would seem to be developed in us as a self-existing substance and to be imperishable" (408b).[41] The account is full of difficulties. How does this substance become implanted in the soul in the first place? Where does it go after the death of the body? Aristotle engages in some specious argumentation

39. I use the translation of W. D. Ross.

40. John Herman Randall, Jr., *Aristotle* 64.

41. The divinity of the soul is explicitly asserted in the *Nicomachean Ethics* (1177b).

as to why, in old age, it is not the mind that decays, but apparently some other part of the soul. While Aristotle does maintain that the mind performs its intellectual functions by means of input from the senses, it is possible that this whole idea of the divine soul is a feeble gesture of reconciliation with the Platonists. Even so, Aristotle's general conception of the soul is marked by subtlety of thought and general soundness of approach.

His views on the cosmos are much more inscrutable. At a minimum we can say that the cosmology he puts forth in Book 12 of the *Metaphysics* is a substantial departure from the one found in Plato's *Timaeus;* and yet, significant traces of Platonism remain, to say nothing of certain age-old prejudices that extend back centuries in Greek thought. The chief among these is the notion that motion is indicative of life. For Aristotle, who believed that both the universe as a whole and motion within the universe are eternal, it was necessary to fashion some kind of force or entity that could generate this motion; for him this was the unmoved mover. This conception is very difficult to grasp. The critical passage is this:

> There is, then, something which is always moved with an unceasing motion, which is motion in a circle; and this is plain not in theory only but in fact. Therefore the first heavens must be eternal. There is therefore also something which moves them. And since that which is moved and moves is intermediate, there is a mover which moves without being moved, being eternal, substance, and actuality. (1072a)

Here again Aristotle has lapsed into another Greek prejudice regarding the "perfection" of circular motion. But the critical issue is why Aristotle felt the need to postulate such an entity. It does not appear as if this entity is the First Cause—a cause that is itself uncaused, lest there be an infinite regress of causation. Since Aristotle has explicitly declared the universe, motion, and also time to be eternal, he did not seem to require a First Cause, at least in a temporal sense. Randall asserts that the unmoved mover is really "an *archē,* a principle of intelligibility, a 'reason why.'"[42]

42. Randall, *Aristotle* 135.

And yet, from another perspective it does seem that Aristotle's postulation of the unmoved mover has much to do with his notions of causation. In other parts of the *Metaphysics* he advocates a fourfold breakdown of causation, as follows: 1) the formal cause; 2) the material cause; 3) the efficient cause; and 4) the final cause. In the case of, say, a statue, the formal cause is the statue itself; the material cause is the marble out of which it is made; the efficient cause is the agent that made the statue (i.e., the sculptor); and the final cause is the end or purpose for which the statue is made.

In Aristotle's resolutely teleological mind-set, the final cause is far and away the most significant. Even if the unmoved mover is not conceived as a person in the manner of a sculptor, it is nonetheless a "final cause" by virtue of its being "the object of desire": "The first mover, then, of necessity exists; and in so far as it is necessary, it is good, and in this sense a first principle" (1072a–b).

What then are we to make of a passage, later in the *Metaphysics,* that asserts the existence of as many as fifty-five unmoved movers (1074a)? It appears that this conclusion was reached as Aristotle digested the findings of the mathematician Eudoxus of Cnidus (390?–340?), who devised a mathematical system for accounting for the apparent motions of the heavenly bodies by means of a series of concentric spheres. Whether we are to regard the initial unmoved mover—the one responsible for the motion of the "first heaven" (*prōtos ouranos*), i.e., the sphere containing the fixed stars—as a kind of *primus inter pares* among the other unmoved movers is unclear.

And how this unmoved mover relates to God is also unclear. Aristotle's valorisation of intellection (recall the memorable first sentence of the *Metaphysics:* "All men by nature desire to know") has, as we have seen, already led to his assertion of a divine and immortal mind in (some) human beings; and so Aristotle concludes:

> If, then, God is always in that good state [i.e., the state of thinking] in which we sometimes are, this compels our wonder; and if in a better this compels it yet more. And God *is* in a better state. And life also belongs to God; for the actuality of thought is life, and God is that actuality; and God's essential actuality is life most good and eternal. We say therefore that God is a living being, eternal, most good, so

> that life and duration continuous and eternal belong to God; for this *is* God. (1072b)

I am not at all sure that this passage is intelligible—or, at any rate, that it truly has any bearing on the rest of Aristotle's metaphysics. This god does not actually seem to figure significantly in the rest of his philosophy, and may once more be in some sense a nod to his mentor Plato. Elsewhere he declares that all these matters, being not easily amenable to the gathering of information in the manner he generally prefers (i.e., through the senses), are filled with obscurity:

> Of these beings that are works of nature there are two kinds; those that are ungenerated and indestructible throughout all ages, and those that partake of genesis and destruction. The former are of the highest worth and are divine, but they are less open to knowledge. The evidence that might throw light on them and on all the things we long to know about them is given but scantily through the senses. (*De Partibus Animalium* 644b)

True enough! But it did not prevent Aristotle from making blandly dogmatic statements that are in themselves baffling and are not easy to reconcile with the rest of his philosophical enterprise.

Aristotle's entire theology seems to be the result of a series of deductions—rather than of an accumulation of data, which, by the very nature of things, would seem to be impossible—based upon his own theories of causation, of desire, and of what "ought" to exist if the universe is to be intelligible. But even a single flaw in his reasoning would be sufficient to cause this entire theoretical edifice to come crashing down—and, even on a charitable assessment, it must be said that there are any number of flaws in his reasoning all apart from the purely abstract and evidence-free nature of his speculations.

A brief aside can be made on Aristotle's view of the role of (conventional) religion in society. Here we turn to a notorious passage in the *Politics:*

> He [the tyrant] should always show a particular zeal in the cult of the gods. Men are less afraid of being treated unjustly by a ruler, when they

> think that he is god-fearing and pays some regard to the gods; and they are less ready to conspire against him, if they feel that the gods themselves are his friends. At the same time, the tyrant should show his zeal without falling into folly. (1314b–15a)[43]

Before one concludes that this is an appallingly Machiavellian suggestion, some context is needed. In his relentlessly empirical fashion when dealing with the subject, Aristotle is well aware that tyrants do exist in the Greek world; and he is merely advising how such a figure can best rule his domain. Aristotle makes analogous suggestions relating to the maintenance of traditional worship in regard to oligarches (1322b) and to his ideal commonwealth, a fusion of aristocracy and democracy (1331a).

From an atheist's perspective, the intellectual dominance that both Plato and Aristotle exercised over the next two thousand years of Western history is a catastrophe of the first order. Perhaps such dominance was inevitable with the political triumph of Christianity in the early fourth century C.E., but the obscurity into which their predecessors, contemporaries, and successors fell until at least the sixteenth century remains a tragedy of human thought. It may be true that Aristotle himself was not responsible for the superstitious reverence with which his work was regarded from the later Middle Ages onward, including such of his views as the doctrine of the four elements,[44] the rejection of the Atomists' void (leading to the doctrine of the impossibility of *actio in distans*), and the rejection of any sort of evolution of individual species; but the long centuries during which Plato and Aristotle were both regarded as *animae naturaliter Christianae* made a departure from their doctrines a matter of heresy. In the case of Aristotle, this is particularly regrettable because he himself, when not speculating on theology or metaphysics, was a resolute empiricist who was convinced that his own conclusions would be developed or modified by subsequent research; and there is clear evidence that Christian thinkers deliberately distorted some of his views to shoehorn them into confirmity with their dogmas,

43. I use the translation of Ernest Barker.

44. The stars in the "first heaven" are made of a fifth element, *aither*—a kind of refined air-like substance existing above the atmosphere. This idea can be traced back to remote antiquity in Greek thought and belief.

as we shall have occasion to discuss in later chapters. It has taken the work of many scholars over the past century or more to scrape away the Christian incrustations on his conceptions to reveal a persistently enquiring thinker who, for all that he was subject to unconscious bias on many fronts, did much to expand both the range of knowledge available in his time and to clarify the way in which knowledge should be established and organised.

I. Hellenistic Thought

The Hellenistic period of Greek history, literature, and philosophy is thought by some scholars to extend from the death of Alexander the Great (323 B.C.E.) all the way down to the end of the Roman Republic (31 B.C.E.); but for the purposes of this work I am choosing to regard the period as ending with the Romans' defeat of the Greeks in 146 B.C.E. To be sure, Greek philosophy continued after this date, but it did so largely under the aegis of Rome.

Once again we reach a stage where the transmission of texts is an issue. Even though some leading figures of the chief philosophical movements of the period—the Cynics, the Epicureans, the Stoics, and the Sceptics (i.e., those followers of Plato who exhibited a substantial degree of scepticism regarding the possibility of definitive knowledge)—wrote little or nothing, many of them (including, notably, Epicurus) were immensely prolific; but, at least for this Hellenistic stage as just defined, their work exists largely in fragments, sometimes extensive, sometimes otherwise. These thinkers are, for a variety of reasons (not least of which is the dominance of Christianity in the West, which embraced Plato and Aristotle), not as highly regarded as their predecessors; but we will find that their intellectual contributions—although not specifically in the area of atheism except, perhaps, in regard to the Epicureans—are impressive. In later antiquity, the Epicureans and Stoics were believed to constitute two of the four leading schools of thought, fully equal in substance and influence to the Platonists and the Aristotelians.

Even in his own day, Epicurus (341–271) and his sect (it must be called that) were accused of all manner of moral derelictions (including sexual licence) as a result of their ethical ideal of "pleasure"; more to the point, they were also believed to have disingenuously acknowledged the existence of some very curious deities as a crude cover for frank atheism. These views are wide of the mark, but they exhibit the degree to which the Epicureans were regarded as outliers both philosophically and theologically. It didn't help that even adherents such as the Roman poet Horace quipped that "you shall see me fat and sleek with good keeping, a hog of Epicurus' herd" (*Epistles* 4.15–16).[45] But Epicurus' views endured all this obloquy and could be said to have made some not insignificant contributions toward the evolution of deism, atheism, and non-theistic morality in the subsequent history of the West.

Epicurus himself was a controversial figure in antiquity. He appears to have had something of a cantankerous nature, freely abusing his predecessors and contemporaries, including those who were his own philosophical forbears. He polemically denied the very existence of the (admittedly obscure) Leucippus, and some modern classical scholars took his assertion for a fact. He was born in Samos, an island in the Aegean, the son of Athenian colonists. He first came to Athens for military service in 323—the very time when Aristotle was forced to flee the city. A few years later he went to Colophon, a city in Ionia; it was there, appropriately enough, that he studied philosophy for a decade—appropriately because, under the tutelage of Nausiphanes of Teos, he adopted the atomic theory of Leucippus and Democritus. He starting teaching his philosophy, gathering a cadre of devoted followers, including Hermarchus, his eventual successor. Returning to Athens in 306, he began giving lectures in a garden just outside the city walls, not far from Plato's Academy. Unusually for the time, his sect was open to women: a number of these were *hetairae* (courtesans), but there were also married women in the group. One of the latter actually wrote a philosophical treatise.[46]

Epicurus himself was apparently one of the most prolific philosophical writers in Greco-Roman antiquity, known as the author of hundreds of volumes, including his masterwork, *On Nature,* in thirty-seven books. The title is an obvious nod to the Presocratics. But nearly all

45. The translation is by Christopher Smart (1767).

46. One of the most distinctive followers of Epicurus was Diogenes of Oenoanda (2nd century C.E.), who was so taken with the Epicurean philosophy that he had many statements—both from Epicurus and of his own devising—carved on the outer wall of his estate. The total wordage originally came to about 25,000 words, and the extensive fragments have now been published.

this work has perished, and all we have are three long letters, a set of *Basic Doctrines,* and an array of fragments.[47] We are, however, deeply in debt to the Roman poet Lucretius (first century B.C.E.), whose magnificent quasi-epic poem *De Rerum Natura* is a nearly complete exposition of Epicurean philosophy and fills in many gaps left by the destruction of Epicurus' own writings.

The central fact we must always bear in mind about Epicurus is that, in adopting Atomist metaphysics, he took pains to amend it in light of the extensive criticisms of Plato and (especially) Aristotle, to both of whose philosophies he set himself in direct opposition; in some cases he seems to have felt that the Atomists themselves had gone astray. Many of Epicurus' deviations from Atomism were heavily criticised by earlier generations of classical scholars as clumsy and inept, but recent scholarship has vindicated a number of them, although one of his chief departures from Atomist thought remains to my mind philosophically indefensible.

Interesting and, in some senses, groundbreaking as many aspects of his thought are, we are here concerned largely with Epicurus' metaphysical and ethical stances. His epistemology—that is, his justification for how human beings have come to have knowledge of atoms and void—is a side issue that must be bypassed. His central contention is the primacy of sense-data, which are always "true"—not in the sense of being uniformly accurate reflections of reality, but in the sense that they have to be acknowledged as having arisen from some actual event or material object. It is only "opinion" (*doxa*) that sometimes results in a false interpretation of sense-data, as when someone takes the figments of a dream or hallucination for reality.

For Epicurus, who believed in both the temporal and spatial eternity of the universe, atoms and void have always existed. His assertion that the atoms always move "downward" except when encountering "blows" from other atoms has been much ridiculed, but he is clear in asserting that this downward motion is logical, not temporal; in other words, there have always been atomic compounds resulting from the "blows" of atoms.

Where Epicurus departed most significantly from Democritus is in

47. See Bailey, *Epicurus: The Extant Remains.* I cite texts from this edition, using the abbreviation B and the page number of the English text (Greek text on the facing page).

his assertion of a "swerve" of atoms. In his view,[48] atoms swerve from their "downward" motion at random intervals; if they didn't, they would never have come together into larger units. It becomes evident that Epicurus propounded this theory not merely for metaphysical reasons but for ethical ones; it was, if we are to believe a critical passage in Lucretius, his chief means of escaping from Democritean determinism and of justifying his assertion of free will in human beings:

> Again if all motion is ever linked together and a new motion ever springs from a fixed order and first-beginnings do not by swerving make some commencement of motion to break through the decrees of fate, so that cause does not follow cause from everlasting, whence have all living creatures here on earth, whence, I ask, has been wrested from the fates the power by which we go forward whither the will leads each, by which likewise we change the direction of our motions neither at a fixed time nor fixed place, but when and where the mind itself has prompted? (2.251–60)[49]

But there is a serious problem with this view. Even though the swerve might be seen as a striking but wholly accidental anticipation of quantum theory (something that, of course, takes place at the sub-atomic level), this *randomness* in the behaviour of atoms does not constitute a viable motivation for free will, even if it does establish a break in the chain of causality. What the proponents of free will want is not randomness, but a means by which human behaviour can exhibit clear choice in moral situations. Nevertheless, Epicurus clung to the swerve, since the chief motivation for his philosophical enterprise was to lay down moral codes that would free human beings from fear and superstition; and under Atomist determinism, he could not imagine how moral suasion was even conceivable. The abolition of superstition in all its forms (especially fear of retribution by the gods) was the chief motivating factor in his ethical system. This is the point Lucretius emphatically makes early on in the *De Rerum Natura,* in a line that has resonated through the ages: *Tantum*

48. It is surprisingly difficult to find, among the extant fragments, any explicit statement on the swerve by Epicurus. We are therefore obliged to believe that Lucretius' lengthy discussion of the subject is an accurate reflection of Epucurus' views.

49. I use the prose translation of H. A. J. Munro (1864), with some revisions of my own.

religio potuit suadere malorum (1.101: "So great the evils which religion could prompt!").

Epicurus' conception of the human soul goes far in this direction. The soul is material—that is, it is wholly composed of atoms. Although it is scattered throughout the body, intermixed with other atoms, the soul can conceptually be regarded as of two sorts: a rational sort (*dianoia* [mind]; in Latin, *animus*) and an irrational sort (*psyche* [soul]; in Latin, *anima*). Because it is evident that the mind or soul is affected by the body, decaying as it decays, it was clear to Epicurus that the soul atoms must disperse on the death of the body. His outlook is as emphatic a repudiation of life after death as any devised in human thought; but to him this was one of its chief virtues. He was well aware that many people are plagued with a fear of death; to this he responds resoundingly, "Death is nothing to us" (B 85). This is because, when we are alive, death is not present; when we do die, our consciousness dies with it, therefore there is no reason to fear that we shall be aware of our own non-existence. The conclusion of the third book of Lucretius' *De Rerum Natura* is an extraordinarily poignant exposition of this idea. At one point the soul upbraids the weak human for bemoaning his inevitable death:

> "Now no more shall your house admit you with glad welcome, not an excellent wife and sweet children run to be the first to snatch kisses and touch your heart with a silent joy. No more may you be prosperous in thy doings, a safeguard to your own people. One evil day has taken from you, luckless man, all the many prizes of life." This do men say; but add not thereto, "and now no longer does any craving for these things come upon you either." For if they could rightly perceive this in thought and follow up the thought in words, they would release themselves from great distress and apprehension of mind. (3.894–903)

In asserting that human beings are (or should be) exclusively motivated by "pleasure" (*hēdonē*), he exposed himself—sometimes deliberately—to widespread misapprehension, both in antiquity and in later centuries. He divided "pleasures" into two sorts: first, what he called "katastematic" pleasures, which one scholar has defined as "pleasure deriving from a well-balanced and steady state of the moving atoms in a sensitive organ";[50] second, kinetic pleasures, which are those that we are more commonly inclined to regard as pleasures—those of eating, sex, and so on. Epicurus believed the former were far more to be prized than the latter; indeed, once the former are attained, the latter are, strictly speaking, supernumerary. This is because the aim of pleasure is not stimulation or repletion but *ataraxia*—a word difficult to render into English, but perhaps best translated as "untroubledness." The greatest pleasure, in effect, is the absence of pain. And "absence of pain" must be interpreted as applying both to the body and, especially, to the mind (i.e., freedom from fear, worry, apprehension, and unreasoning cares). Epicurus was particularly keen on distinguishing his views from those of Aristippus, the grandson and namesake of a younger companion of Socrates who founded the Cyrenaic school of philosophy, which indeed advocated the pursuit of sensual pleasures as the sole aim of life.

But Epicurus at times engaged in polemics on this critical point that often led to misunderstanding. For example, he declared that "The beginning and the root of all good is the pleasure of the stomach" (B 135). This notorious view ultimately led to the use of the term "epicure" for someone devoted to the consumption of exquisitely prepared foods; but what Epicurus meant is that the satisfaction of bodily pains engendered by hunger and thirst played a critical role in the attainment of *ataraxia:* "The flesh cries out to be saved from hunger, thirst and cold. For if a man possess this safety and hope to possess it, he might rival even Zeus in happiness" (B 111). Elsewhere, Epicurus is emphatic that immoderate sexuality is not equivalent to pleasure: "When, therefore, we maintain that pleasure is the end, we do not mean the pleasures of profligates and those that consist in sensuality, as is supposed by some who are either ignorant or disagree with us or do not understand" (B 89).

The relevance of all this to Epicurus' conception of deity will soon become apparent. Let us first outline what attributes and behaviours Epicurus attributed to the gods. They themselves are material, consisting of particularly fine atoms; they are also changeless and immortal. There are, indeed, innumerable gods, including those of the Greek pantheon; they dwell in the "spaces between the stars" (in Latin, *intermundia*), at peace with themselves; but they do not concern themselves a whit in

50. J. M. Rist, *Epicurus: An Introduction* 102.

human affairs. This is because, as changeless creatures who perfectly embody Epicurus' ideal of *ataraxia,* they cannot be bothered with an imperfect and perishable species such as ourselves. Although the gods have always existed, they certainly did not create the universe; how could they, since it is so imperfect? In the imperishable words of Lucretius, *tanta stat praedita culpa* (5.199: "[the world] stands endowed with so many flaws"). But it is not that the gods don't do anything, as Cicero claimed (*De Natura Deorum* 1.102). They talk to one another, establishing strong bonds of friendship (a point of particular importance to Epicurus' conception of the good life for human beings). They do not sleep, but they do rest on occasion.

If it be asked how Epicurus knows so much about these gods, it must frankly be admitted that his answers are unsatisfactory. He claims that because all people believe in gods, there must be some justification for such a belief. This may seem like a bizarre instance of the fallacious "argument from consensus," but in truth it is based on Epicurus' assertion that all sense-data is "true" in some sense. Since people do in fact "see" gods of various sorts in their dreams and at other times, there must be gods out there, even if they do not correspond to the false "opinions" that many people hold about these entities.

The question of whether Epicurus conceived his gods to be anthromorphic is surprisingly difficult to answer. It is striking that there is not a single word in the extant fragments of Epicurus himself to justify the view that he imagined the gods as anthropomorphic, and there may be some evidence to the contrary. Let us turn to Epicurus' own surviving statements on the gods. One utterance seems to be of enormous importance in this context:

> For gods there are, since the knowledge of them is by clear vision. But they are not such as the many believe them to be: for indeed they [the many] do not consistently portray them as they believe them to be. And the impious man is not he who denies the gods of the many, but he who attaches to the gods the beliefs of the many. For the statements of the many about the gods are not conceptions derived from sensation, but false suppositions . . . (B 83, 85)

A passage in Lucretius suggests anthromorphism (5.1169–78), but he is clearly referring to the false gods of "the many." Epicurus probably believed that we see images of the gods in our minds in human form; but this is also how the many see the gods. These images must be *interpreted* by means of analogy and inference; otherwise the images of Juno and Minerva that we oftentimes see in dreams would have to be accepted as real. The gods, then, must not be "such as the many believe them to be"; but what exactly are they? Epicurus seems not to have had any fixed notions on this point; all his extant remarks about the gods merely stress their tranquillity and lack of concern for human beings. It is likely that this very ambiguity in Epicurus' doctrine led later Epicureans to elaborate Epicurean theology in a way not intended by Epicurus. There is, for example, no question that Philodemus (an Epicurean of the first century B.C.E.) declared the gods to be anthropomorphic, going even so far as to state that the gods must speak Greek, since Greek is the only language fit for philosophical discourse.[51]

There is indeed a question as to whether Epicurus' conception of the gods was just a dodge to avoid an accusation of (and prosecution for) impiety. There is nothing in the extant evidence to justify this uncharitable view. It is true that Epicurus brought further obloquy upon himself when he maintained that it is acceptable to participate in the religious ceremonies of one's nation, even if these ceremonies embody false beliefs about the gods. Epicurus would have maintained that this does not amount to hypocrisy, because one can use these moments to contemplate the perfection of the (true) gods. And yet, we remain surprised when we learn that Epicurus himself was once a participant in the Eleusinian mysteries—certainly one of the darker and more mystical of Greek religious practices, and one certainly not tending toward the attainment of *ataraxia*.

Overall, there is no denying that Epicurus was bold and forthright in denying many central and widely held beliefs regarding the gods. As J. M. Rist puts it, "There is, then, according to Epicurus, no such thing as divine providence, no teleological order in the world, since all apparent design is the result of the chance union of atoms, and there is no divine

51. This question would no doubt be settled if we had Epicurus' *Peri theōn* (On the Gods; see Diogenes Laertius 10.27), but it does not survive. On this general issue see the appendix ("Are Epicurus' Gods Anthropomorphic?") in my paper "Cicero's Criticism of Epicurean Theology," in *Classical Papers* 239–43.

retribution."[52] Epicurus also denied the divinity of the "heavenly bodies," in a direct rebuke of his predecessors Plato and Aristotle. As such, it can well be maintained that, for all his apparently sincere claims about the nature of his deities, his worldview is admirably sane and realistic and overwhelmingly secular.

The Cynics and the Stoics both rejected nearly the totality of the Epicurean worldview, and all three sects engaged in much abuse of one another in their writings. I have delayed discussion of the Cynics until now—even though its founder, Diogenes of Sinope (412?–323) was not only a generation older than Aristotle but a younger contemporary of Plato—because their philosophy, if it really is a philosophy and not merely an attitude or way of life, significantly influenced Stoic ethics at certain key points.

Both the Cynics and the Stoics had a vested interest in tracing their lineage back to Socrates, by means of a tendentious philosophical genealogy they promoted, whereby Antisthenes (446?–366?), a disciple of Socrates, was thought to have been a mentor to Diogenes, who in turn was (in fact) the tutor of Crates of Thebes (368?–288?), who in turn taught the founder of the Stoic movement, Zeno of Citium (335–263). Several features of this genealogy, especially the first link, are either exaggerated or entirely false. The assertion that Antisthenes—who did display some personal characteristics later associated with the Cynics—was Diogenes' tutor falls to the ground when we discover that the latter only came to Athens in 340, twenty-six years after Antisthenes' death.

As for Diogenes himself, a number of amusing anecdotes about him emerged both during his lifetime and afterward—as when he went about during the daytime carrying a lit lantern, looking for an honest man; or when, being asked by Alexander if he could do anything for Diogenes, the latter replied, "You can get out of my sunlight." These and other anecdotes, some of which may well be true or at least may have originated with Diogenes himself, point to a certain level of brash showmanship in his temperament. And his wide use of *parrhēsia* (outspokenness), frequently descending to abuse or ridicule, makes him come across at times like an ancient Don Rickles.

The Cynics expressed total disdain for many standard aspects of

52. *Epicurus: An Introduction* 148.

philosophy, including metaphysics, logic, rhetoric, and the like. As such, it is difficult to determine the exact bases of their ethical system, which focused largely on "living according to Nature" (however that may be defined). For Diogenes, this meant living outdoors in a bathtub with only a staff for walking and what is usually translated as a "wallet" (which might better be regarded as a knapsack) for his few provisions; a bland acceptance of doing all manner of things, from eating to having sex, in public; and even refusing (although no doubt with a certain deadpan humour) to condemn incest or cannibalism on moral grounds. After all, he reasoned, certain other nations engage in these practices—an implicit acknowledgement of the relativity of values, at least on a societal level. All these things were purportedly derived from the example of Socrates, whose asceticism and questioning of conventional morality Diogenes claimed to be following. It is what presumaby led Plato, in a much-repeated comment, to declare that Diogenes was "Socrates gone mad."

The very word Cynic (*kynikos*) means "doglike," referring to the supposed shamelessness of that animal in its public actions. A late commentator on Aristotle spells out four reasons for the term, one of which is: "they make a cult of *adiaphoria* [indifference] and, like dogs, eat and make love in public, go barefoot, and sleep in tubs and at crossroads."[53] This commentator also stresses the "shamelessness" (*anaideia*) of the dog, a trait the Cynics relished. The aggressive *autarkeia* (self-sufficiency) of the Cynics, instanced chiefly in their lack of interest in personal possessions (many of them went begging throughout the cities of Greece), was a leading hallmark of the movement. Indeed, Diogenes Laertius attributes to Diogenes the statement that "it was the privilege of the gods to need nothing and of godlike men to want but little" (6.105). It is not easy to extract a genuine theological stance from this solitary utterance.

Some of this will be of relevance when we consider the ethics of the Stoics.[54] As for their cosmogony, it at times seems as if it was devised for the express purpose of contradicting the Epicureans at every turn. The three leading philosophers of the early Stoic movement—Zeno, Cleanthes of Assos (331–232), and Chrysippus of Soli (280?–205?)—

53. A scholium on Aristotle, quoted in Dudley, *A History of Cynicism* 5.

54. The word Stoic (in Greek, *Stōikos*) is derived from the Stoa Poikilē, the painted colonnade in Athens where Zeno lectured.

were separated by a generation from one another, and they appear to have established the basic principles of Stoic metaphysics. Their works, however, are even more poorly preserved than those of Epicurus, and we are often reliant upon later commentators, many of them hostile to the movement, for the details of their views.

The Stoics asserted that the cosmos was a kind of Parmenidean plenum, with no void in it, although they maintained that void existed outside the plenum. (They frequently used the analogy of fish swimming in water as a means of accounting for motion without relying on the void.) The cosmos is spherical; it is alive; it is endowed with a soul (*psyche*) and reason. Indeed, the Stoics identified reason (*logos*) with one of the two principles in the cosmos: it is the active agent and is to be identified with God, Nature, and fate; matter (*hyle*) is the passive principle. It is important to note that both of these principles were regarded as material, as was the soul; in that sense, the Stoics and Epicureans were in agreement. Even the Stoic god was material.

For the Stoics, the principle of reason pervades everything, including ourselves; in other words, the two principles are only logically separable. They believed the cosmos to be eternal, but subject to periodic destruction by fire, which they denoted by the term *ekpyrosis*. There are considerable problems with this view, but we need not go into their details. Somehow, after the *ekpyrosis* the Stoic god refashions the universe into a cosmos again. It is not entirely clear why the early Stoics even felt the need to put forth the *ekypyrosis,* and later Stoics largely rejected the notion.

It is of some interest to note the arguments the Stoics used to justify belief in God—or, at least, their god. As these arguments would be used ad infinitum in later Christian apologetics, it is worth paying some attention to them now to see how easily they can be refuted.

Their first argument is the argument from consensus: everyone has some idea of deity, therefore a deity must exist. The fallacy here is simply in believing that truth can be determined by a vote of the majority. There was a time in the West when belief in witchcraft was nearly universal; but that does not establish the reality of witches (i.e., human beings—usually female—with supernatural powers). The earth is round; even if every person on earth believed the earth to be flat, the earth would still be round. And the consensus argument rapidly loses its force even on its own terms when a substantial proportion of people disbelieve in, or have doubts about, the existence of God.

The second argument is the argument defending providence on the basis of the mere existence of divination. It would appear that the Stoics did not question whether the seers and oracles they appealed to had actually come up with demonstrably accurate predictions—or whether (as with modern "psychic" readers) the prophecies were so deliberately vague and ambiguous that they could be deemed "true" in a multiplicity of circumstances.

The third argument is the argument from design: the cosmos is so beautiful, and so pefectly fitted for life (especially human life), that a god must have designed it. This view took quite a bit longer to overthrow: it had to wait until Darwin. At times it almost seems as if the Stoics were appealing to aesthetics in stressing the beauty of the cosmos; but in Greek thought the notion goes back at least to Pythagoras and continued to have a powerful hold on the beliefs of philosophers, artists, and ordinary people for many centuries.

The Stoics also made an unwise attempt to embody their arguments in easily refuted syllogisms, for example:

> First Premise: A man may reasonably honour the gods.
>
> Second Premise: Those who are non-existent a man may not reasonably honour.
>
> Conclusion: Therefore the gods exist.[55]

Note how the syllogism rigs the game by slipping in "reasonably" in that first premise, although that is the very point at issue. Without that single word, the whole syllogism collapses.

There is, indeed, some confusion about the very nature of the Stoic god; at a minimum, the Stoics seem to have had a very elastic conception of the god's essence and properties. The god is at once Nature, fate, providence (*pronoia*), and the "creative fire" (*pyr technikon*) that engenders the *ekpyrosis*. How all these properties could subsist in a single entity is not easy to fathom. What is more, even though the Stoics emphatically rejected the Olympian gods, they attempted to bridge the gulf between

55. Cited in Keimpe Algra, "Stoic Theology," in Inwood, *The Cambridge Companion to the Stoics* 163.

their own monotheism with the prevailing polytheism of the Greek populace. Here is Diogenes Laertius' account of the Stoic theory:

> The deity, they say, is a living being, immortal, rational, perfect or intelligent in happiness, admitting nothing evil [in him], taking providential care of the world and all that therein is, but he is not of human shape. He is, however, the artificer of the universe and, as it were, the father of all, both in general and in that particular part of him which is all-pervading, and which is called many names according to its various powers. (7.147)[56]

In this manner, as Diogenes goes on to say, the Stoics can acknowledge the quasi-reality of Zeus: "Zeus [exists] in so far as he is the cause of life or pervades all life." (This is something of a pun, relying on a variant spelling of Zeus [*Zēn*] to make it seem related to the verb "to live" [*zēn*].) Other gods of the Greek pantheon are accounted for in a similar manner. How convincing any of this is—and, in particular, how such a concatenation of properties can inhere in a single entity—is a matter of doubt. There is extant a *Hymn to Zeus* written by Cleanthes (who seems to have been the most religiously inclined of the three early founders of Stoicism) that is undeniably sincere in its piety and stresses the identification of god and fate. A late commentator attributes to the Stoics the view that providence should be identified with the "will of Zeus."[57]

The Stoic notion that God is equivalent to providence and fate leads to the age-old dilemma of the problem of evil: how can bad things happen when God (a) created the cosmos, and (b) designed it for the benefit of humanity? Without going into details, it appears that the Stoics conceived their god as having limited powers. Then there is the curious Stoic view regarding demons (*daimones*). Diogenes Laertius maintains: "Also they [the Stoics] hold that there are daemons who are in sympathy with mankind and watch over human affairs" (7.151). How seriously we are to take this assertion is unclear.[58]

56. I use the translation of R. D. Hicks.
57. Cited in Algra 168.
58. Plutarch (*Of Isis and Osiris* 260e), writing centuries after the fact, has a contrary view, noting that Chrysippus was one of several philosophers who maintained a belief that bad

We can now come to the matter of the Stoic conception of the soul. For the Stoics, each individual human soul, although a fragment of the divine soul that governs the cosmos, is capable of growth and development. In childhood the soul is chiefly focused on a selfish (or, perhaps more neutrally, self-centred) attainment of basic needs—food, shelter, and the like. Gradually, the soul (at least the soul of the philosopher or other "good" people) will entertain a wider ideal of harmony (*homologia*), leading to what the Stoics believed to be the true and sole aim of the good life: the pursuit of virtue for its own sake. The Stoics could be frustratingly vague (unless this is a result of the faulty or incomplete transmission of texts) on what "virtue" actually consists of. But at this point the Stoics engaged in some deliberate paradoxes to get their point across. They identified virtue with reason, hence asserted (analogously with Socrates and Plato) that all fools are insane. And because the key to "virtue" is one's mental state rather than the virtuous act being performed, they maintained that in merely thinking of committing a crime one has already committed it.

Where the Stoics gain some interest is the manner in which they harmonise their belief in causal determinism with a certain element of free will. In effect, the Stoics, by rejecting fatalism, adopted (and may have been the first in Western history to adopt) a "soft" determinism, whereby the soul is capable of choice within a broadly deterministic system. Moral choice is a product of our individual characters, which are an integral feature of causation; hence free will of a sort is preserved. Chrysippus did go on to acknowledge that our characters are themselves the result of antecedent causes (i.e., our growth from infancy to adulthood). To be frank, this is a happier solution to the overall problem of determinism vs. free will than what the Epicureans evolved.

The question of whether the soul, in the Stoic view, is immortal—whether, in other words, there can be anything that can meaningfully be termed survival of personality after death—is a vexed question. They asserted (plausibly) that the soul must be material, since it is inconceivable how an immaterial substance could act on, and be acted upon, a material entity such as the human body; but at a minimum, those Stoics who maintained the reality of the world-destroying *ekpyrosis* would surely

---

things may happen because of *daimones*. But it seems an error to attribute such a view to Chrysippus or any of the early Stoics.

have acknowledged that the soul cannot be immortal beyond the lifespan of the current incarnation of the cosmos. A late source, Eusebius (265–335 C.E.), specifically states that the Stoics claimed the soul survived the destruction of the body; but Diogenes Laertius notes: "Cleanthes indeed holds that all souls continue to exist until the general conflagration [*ekpyrosis*]; but Chrysippus says that only the souls of the wise do so" (7.157). Again, it is not clear how seriously we are to take this prejudice against fools. Given how emphatic the Stoics were about the complex intertwining of the (material) body and the (material) soul, it is difficult to envision a circumstance in which survival of personality could be said to occur after death.

There is no need to go into further details about Stoic ethical teaching, interesting as they are; the Stoics clearly worked out their ethical principles in considerable detail, although in some cases they seem to have engaged in a kind of double-talk that could lead to ambiguity. Their repeated assertions that we must live "according to Nature" is an echo of Cynic teaching; but in both sects there is an ambiguity as to what that phrase actually means, and whether "Nature" refers to the natural world or stands in contrast to social convention. Crates the Cynic was one of Zeno's tutors, and his influence shows in Zeno's categorisation of such phenomena as health, property, wealth, and even slavery as "good, bad, or indifferent"; Zeno went on to deem certain things "preferable" or "not preferable"—i.e., helpful but not essential to the good life, and therefore to be disregarded by the person who pursues virtue. It is this attitude that, filtering down into subsequent Western history, led to the use of "stoicism" in the contemporary sense of the term.

I have gone into the details of Stoic ideas of God in such detail not because it had any bearing on the development of atheism, but because the Stoics exercised a marked influence (far more so than the proto-secularist Epicureans) upon subsequent thought in antiquity and thereafter. Indeed, it must be said that, like Plato and Aristotle, the Stoics come across as anticipating many features of Christian metaphysics and theology; and, in light of that obvious fact, it is surprising that their work was not better preserved by later generations. Chrysippus alone is known to have written more than 700 volumes, but none of them survive except in fragments.

As noted, the other major philosophical schools during this period continued to function, but they are of little interest to our specific enquiry. Aristotle's successor was the notable thinker Theophrastus (371?–287?), who was hugely prolific and did sound work in chronicling and analysing earlier Greek thought, especially the Presocratics. Several of his works survive intact, but they do not reveal any significant departure from Aristotle. After him, the Lyceum largely went into decline.

In the Academy, Plato was succeeded by Speusippus, Xenocrates, Polemo, and others. But under Arcesilaus (318?–242), who became head of the Academy around 268, the school took a radically sceptical turn, returning to the doubt of the certainty of human knowledge purportedly espoused by Socrates. This tendency culminated with Carneades of Cyrene (213–128). But it is difficult to imagine—and, in any case, no evidence exists to substantiate the view—that even these thinkers departed significantly from Plato's theological conceptions; the best that can be said is that they merely ignored or downplayed them. Their chief interest was simply in maintaining that the attainment of knowledge is inherently problematical.

As mentioned, the Cynics appear to have paid virtually no attention to metaphysics, hence their theological views span a wide spectrum, from atheism to fairly orthodox reverence to the Olympian gods. Among the former is the shadowy figure of Theodorus, a Cynic thinker from the late fourth century who, coming to Athens from Cyrene (a Greek colony in what is now Libya) around 310, was designated an "atheist" and came close to being prosecuted for impiety. Diogenes Laertius maintains that Theodorus "utterly rejected the current belief [*doxai*] in the gods" (2.98), which leads one to think that he simply denied the existence of the Olympian gods. He wrote a book called *On the Gods,* and Diogenes (who had read the book and found it "not contemptible") absurdly states that "From that book, they say, Epicurus borrowed most of what he wrote on the subject" (2.98).

Conversely, there was Cercidas of Megalopolis, a Cynic philosopher and poet (he invented the meliambic metre) of the later third century, who wrote a long diatribe bitterly condemning God for taking no interest in suffering humanity.[59] But elsewhere Cercidas claimed to look forward to meeting Pythagoras, Homer, and other notables after his death, so he

59. Quoted in Dudley, *A History of Cynicism* 79.

can hardly be considered an atheist or even an agnostic.

And we cannot bypass Euhemerus of Messene, who was in the service of Cassander, one of the successors of Alexander, and later (after 297) came to Alexandria. He wrote a work of utopian fiction entitled *Sacred Scripture* (*Hiera Anagraphē*), in which he maintained that he ventured to a group of islands in the Indian Ocean and came upon monuments devoted to Ouranos, Cronus, and Zeus; and so he concluded that these "gods" were in fact heroes who had been deified. The adjective "euhemeristic" derives from this conception, although the actual import of Euhemerus' work (which survives only in fragmentary quotations from later writers) is open to interpretation. For all that he could be putting forth a rudimentary "natural history of religion," his meaning could simply be that there is no clear line of demarcation between hero and god—a notion convenient to the Ptolemies, who envisioned themselves on the path to imminent deification.

The question has frequently been asked why the Hellenistic philosophers were so concerned with the moral status of the individual person in what appears to be a hostile or indifferent society. More than a century ago, Eduard Zeller suggested that the radical alteration in the political fortunes of the Greeks—the abrupt shift from a once-vibrant city-state to a succession of occasionally oppressive monarchies beginning with Alexander—impelled philosophers to turn inward, away from bold speculations about the universe that characterised Greek philosophy from Thales to Aristotle and more toward the fate of the hapless individual engulfed in a society that was becoming increasingly precarious, with ever-present threats of being sold into slavery or of being the victim either of intolerant tyrants or unruly mobs, or of the threat of poverty through a widening gulf between rich and poor. This view is easily caricatured, but there seems to be more than a grain of truth in it.

Diogenes actually wrote a treatise called the *Republic,* but it is not clear what views it propounded. When he observed that he was a "citizen of the world" (*kosmopolitēs*), he may have been the first to use the term; but his meaning was largely negative, in that he claimed independence of the laws and customs of any given city-state, and his recorded behaviour emphatically confirms his scorn of the restrictions on personal liberties that many city-states still expected its citizens to observe.

Epicurus was relentless in his suggestion that the securing of political office, or political engagement of any sort, is inevitably accompanied by mental perturbation that is antithetical to the attainment of *ataraxia.* (Recent history seems to offer confirmation of this view.) One of Epicurus' most famous utterances was: "Live unknown" (B 139).[60] The Stoics were less hostile to involvement with politics. Zeno wrote a *Republic* early in his career; its contents are also not well known, but it does appear that he advocated a more positive view of cosmopolitanism than the Cynics. Plutarch reports that the treatise asserted that "we should regard all humans as our fellow citizens and local residents, and there should be one way of life and order, like that of a herd grazing together and nurtured by a common pasture" (*De Alexandri Magni Fortuna aut Virtute* 329a–b). Elsewhere the Stoics recommended participating in the normal range of social activities (marrying, having children, and so on) and of political life, as these offer a fertile field for the exercise of virtue. Later Stoics, after all, included at least one Roman emperor in their number.

And yet, the shift that Zeller proposed is undeniably real. The contrast with Aristotle's confident statement "Man is by nature a political animal" (*Politics* 1253a) is clear, especially when we realise that by *politikon zōon* ("political animal") Aristotle meant "an inhabitant of the *polis,*" i.e., the city. In his view, a man (and it is always a man, never a woman) would be intimately involved in the affairs of his native city, whether as an actual governing figure or as a participant of Athenian democracy. This option was largely removed with the emergence of Alexander and the monarchs who succeeded him.

J. Hellenistic Science, Literature, and Art

Important developments in Greek science occurred during the Hellenistic period, although a number of them are of little relevance to our enquiry. This was the period when the library and museum of Alexandria came to prominence. It was here that Euclid wrote his celebrated *Elements* (c. 300), establishing for all time the principles of geometry. His work, of course, was not wholly original; rather, it was a synthesis of the work of earlier mathematicians, including Eudoxus of Cnidus and Hippocrates

60. A literal translation of the phrase *lathe biōsas* would be something like: "In the act of living, escape [people's] attention."

of Chios. Eratosthenes (276?–195?) applied mathematics to the study of geography, producing the first detailed map of the world and arriving at a tolerably accurate figure for the circumference of the earth.

The astronomer and mathematician Aristarchus of Samos (310?–230?) was apparently the first scientist in the West to put forth the heliocentric theory. Prior to him, it was axiomatically assumed that the earth was the centre of the universe and also that the "fixed" stars (including the sun) were unmoving; indeed, Aristarchus himself adhered to the latter view. Eudoxus of Cnidus (408?–355?) had devised an elaborate system of concentric spheres that was exceedingly cumbersome, and Aristarchus' model is far simpler and more economical. But it was not widely accepted in antiquity. The great mathematician Archimedes of Syracuse (287?–212?) rejected it on scientific grounds, as did other leading figures.

There is some doubt as to whether the religiously minded Stoic Cleanthes rejected the heliocentric theory on religious grounds.[61] But it is undeniable that Cleanthes wrote a treatise against Aristarchus, and it is also not in doubt that the heliocentric theory conflicted with the long-held Greek view—traceable back at least to Hesiod—that the earth was a sacred object and therefore fittingly at the centre of the universe. But the objections to Aristarchus by mathematicians and astronomers rested chiefly on their inability to conceive how the earth could rotate on its axis without causing us, and every other entity on its surface, to fly off into space. This set the stage for Ptolemy's theory of epicycles, which we shall discuss in the next chapter. Here, however, we can note that the astronomer Hipparchus of Nicaea (190?–120?) did conjecture that the "fixed" stars may not in fact be fixed. But our source (Pliny the Elder's *Natural History* 2.24.95) suggests that Hipparchus was by no means secular in his outlook, as Pliny praises him for demonstrating "the kinship of man with the stars, and prov[ing] that our souls are part of the heavens."

Turning to the creative literature of the period, we are once again met with the inadequate transmission of texts. This applies in particular

61. The controversy rests on the accuracy of the text of Plutarch's *De Facie Quae in Orbe Lunae Apparet* 923a, where Plutarch appears to state that Cleanthes believed Aristarchus should be tried for impiety for propounding the heliocentric theory. But this may be the result of an editor's alteration of the text.

to the dramatist Menander (342?–290?), the most significant figure of the New Comedy that succeeded the great tragic and comic playwrights of the fifth century. Our knowledge of the more than 100 plays he wrote has recently been augmented by the transcription of numerous papyri containing fragments of his work, or in one instance nearly an entire play (*Dyskolos* [The Grouch]); but our overall assessment of him must remain provisional.

Nevertheless, it is clear that he embodies one of the chief features of Hellenistic literature—the portrayal of ordinary people in ordinary domestic circumstances, rather than an exclusive focus on gods, heroes, and other legendary figures. This feature alone might to some extent signify a waning belief in the Olympian gods, but such a conclusion should not be pressed too far. In the New Comedy of which Menander was the leading proponent, plays focused on domestic conflicts, a fusion of tragic and comic elements (but predominantly the latter), and an almost invariable conclusion leading to the marriage of the chief male and female protagonists. This largely formulaic schema makes the plays resemble our TV sitcoms.

Menander came from a wealthy Athenian family and may have been acquainted with Epicurus in his early adulthood; he was also a disciple of Theophrastus. It is notoriously difficult, given the fragmentary nature of his work, to identify any coherent attitude on his part toward religion or deity, especially given the truism (applicable to all dramatists) that the sentiments of a given character cannot be unthinkingly attributed to the author in the absence of external evidence. Hence, when in one fragment a character prays to Night, Aphrodite, and Apollo for help in his love life,[62] it is difficult to fathom any implied belief in these deities by the author. It may be of some interest that the *Dyskolos* features a prologue by the rural god Pan. Although the worship of the god can be traced to no earlier than the early fifth century, there is some evidence that he became a deity of increasing interest in the Hellenistic period. But in Menander's play the god's presence merely functions as a device to get the plot moving, and the rest of the action features only human actors.

Turning to poetry, we are faced with two prominent poets associated with what came to be regarded as the Alexandrian school: Callimachus

62. Quoted in Gutzwiller, *A Guide to Hellenistic Literature* 55.

(310?–240?) and Apollonius of Rhodes (first half of the third century). To some degree these poets embody an idiom that, in its allusiveness and learned references to their poetic predecessors, brings the Modernist poets of the twentieth century to mind; clearly they were feeling the weight of the accumulated cultural heritage of their literary forbears stretching back to Homer and Hesiod, and they sought to make frequent tips of the hat to their predecessors in a manner that can make their poetry seem at times overly refined and recherché. But what effect this stance had in regard to their religious beliefs is difficult to determine.

No doubt Callimachus—a prolific and encyclopaedic literary figure who was employed in the library of Alexandria and did landmark work in cataloguing its immense holdings—took pride in his erudition and sophistication; but it is easy to exaggerate the degree to which his appeals to gods, demigods, and heroes in his poetry are merely a literary device. One of his major works, the *Aetia* (Origins), survives only in extensive fragments. Its various poems, seeking to recount the origins of various myths and legends, frequently evoke the Muses and other deities. It is difficult for a modern reader to imagine Callimachus expressing any naïve belief in these gods; no doubt we are decidedly in the realm of I. A. Richards's "aesthetic belief."

But we should not categorically assume Callimachus' disbelief as an established fact. While it is true that many of the poems in the *Aetia* quickly depart from myth and legend and focus on historical events (mostly after the Trojan War), such as the colonisation of Sicily and even the early history of Rome, it is difficult to ascertain any explicit attitude on the author's part as to the reality of the gods. The degree to which his poetry was meant to be read in the privacy of one's study, rather than publicly declaimed, may have been exaggerated by scholars of an earlier generation—and the utterance of openly blasphemous or heretical sentiments in the public sphere could easily have led to prosecutions for impiety, as had happened on numerous occasions in the past.

What is not in doubt is that a number of poems, both in the *Aetia* and in the *Hymns* (several of which survive intact), are designed to curry favour with the Greco-Egyptian rulers of the time, Ptolemy II Philadelphus (r. 283–46) and Ptolemy III Euergetes (r. 246–22). The well-known poem of the "Lock of Berenice" (one of the *Aitia*, surviving only as a fragment) was consciously designed as a tribute to the latter pharaoh's wife, Berenice; the astronomer Conon of Samos conveniently found in the sky a constellation that is now named Berenice's Hair (Coma Berenices). An earlier poem, the "Apotheosis of Arsinoe," commemorates the deceased wife of the earlier Ptolemy.

The six surviving *Hymns* are addressed to Zeus, Apollo, Artemis, Athena, Demeter, and the island of Delos (sacred to Apollo). It is difficult to determine any lack of sincerity by the author in his evocations to and accounts of these deities. But in the *Hecale,* a "little epic" (*epyllion*) of about 1000 lines, the nominal subject—the Athenian hero Theseus—is overshadowed by an old woman, Hecale, who provides him shelter for a night. Once again, the Alexandrian focus on ordinary characters may signal a shift of emphasis away from the godlike and toward the human.

The *Argonautica* of Apollonius of Rhodes—who was born in Alexandria, studied or worked with Callimachus, was a librarian at Alexandria, and may or may not have moved to the Aegean island of Rhodes later in life—was long thought to be a counterweight to Callimachean "refinement" (*leptotēs*) in its return to the form of the Homeric epic; but, for all that the *Argonautica* does indeed violate Callimachus' strictures (anticipating those of Edgar Allan Poe two millennia later) against the long poem ("big book, big evil" is an utterance frequently attributed to him), more recent scholarship on this nearly 6000-line poem sees it largely in line with the Callimachean aesthetic. It is the only surviving epic poem of this period.

The *Argonautica* tells the story of Jason and the Argonauts as they venture to Colchis (a remote area on the coast of the Black Sea, in present-day Georgia). This event purportedly took place before the Trojan War, although that does not mean that the legend itself predates that of the Trojan War. The progress of the epic is of some interest. No doubt the entire journey of the *Argo* is made under the aegis of the gods; the poem opens with an invocation to Apollo, and at a later point the Argonauts avoid disaster (at the Clashing Rocks—i.e., the Straits of Messina) with the aid of Athena. But it is of some interest to note that Herakles, who is the leading hero on board the ship, is left behind at the end of Book 1—perhaps a signal that the work is being written on the human scale. Many commentators have noted that Jason himself is far from a heroic figure; as leader of the expedition, he exhibits the traits of a good manager rather than of a superhuman warrior.

In Book 3 we are treated to what can only be regarded as a seriocomic episode wherein three leading goddesses on Olympus—Hera, Athena, and Aphrodite—put their heads together to determine the best way to help Jason and his cohorts. When Hera suggests to Aphrodite that she send her "boy" (Eros) to cause Medea (the daughter of Aeetes, king of Colchis) to fall in love with Jason, so that together they could secure the golden fleece, Aphrodite replies:

> "But ladies . . . he [Eros] is far more likely to obey you than me. There is no reverence in him, but faced by you he might display some spark of decent feeling. He certainly pays no attention to me: he defies me and always does the opposite of what I say. In fact I am so worn out by his naughtiness that I have half a mind to break his bow and wicked arrows in his very sight, remembering how he threatened me with them in one of his moods. He said, 'If you don't keep your hands off me while I can still control my temper, you can blame yourself for the consequences.'" (3.90–99)[63]

This sounds more like the mother of some wayward teenager in Menander than the all-powerful goddess of love. Nevertheless, Aphrodite does what Hera asks; Eros causes Medea to fall in love with Jason, and she subsequently uses her witchcraft to fateful effect. It is true that Medea is a supernatural figure—or, at any rate, by virtue of her status as priestess of the temple of Hecate, capable of manipulating supernatural forces—but her sorcery is portrayed more as a kind of horrific set-piece (as, indeed, it is in Euripides' *Medea*, which ends in a hideous account of her killing her husband and children) than something stemming directly from the gods.

The connexion of Aratus of Soloi (315?–240) to philosophy and religion is far more pronounced than that of Callimachus or Apollonius. His *Phaenomena*, on astronomy and weather signs, was immensely popular throughout antiquity, as several Latin authors including Cicero produced translations of it. Aratus, born in a city in Cicilia (on the southern coast of what is now Turkey), came to Athens and is known to have studied with Zeno the Stoic as well as other philosophers. In the early 270s he accepted an invitation by Antigonus II Gonatas of

63. I use the prose translation of E. V. Rieu.

Macedonia (r. 276–39) to be a court poet. There is now some doubt as to whether Antigonus specifically asked Aratus to versify a prose treatise by Eudoxus of Cnidus, but at any rate he wrote the *Phaenomena* under the Macedonian monarch's aegis.

The proem to the work appears to reflect some elements of Stoic teaching:

> From Zeus let us begin; him do we mortals never leave unnamed; full of Zeus are all the streets and all the market-places of men; full is the sea and the havens thereof; always we all have need of Zeus. For we are also his offspring; and he in his kindness unto men giveth favourable signs and wakeneth the people to work, reminding them of livelihood. He tells what time the soil is best for the labour of the ox and for the mattock, and what time the seasons are favourable both for the planting of trees and for casting all manner of seeds. For himself it was who set the signs in heaven, and marked out the constellations, and for the year devised what stars chiefly should give men right signs of the seasons, to the end that all things might grow unfailingly. (1–13)[64]

This passage—if we assume "Zeus" to be a metonymy for the otherwise unnamed Stoic god—appears to reflect basic Stoic metaphysics: the creation of the world (including humanity) by the god, the arrangement of the cosmos for the benefit of human beings, and other elements. In this sense the proem bears an approximate resemblance to Cleanthes' *Hymn to Zeus.*

But the poem overall may not be quite the mechanical echo of Stoic doctrine that it has been assumed to be. As one scholar has recently put it, "Aratus' universe is compatible with the Stoic universe, but it is not described in Stoic terms."[65] His descriptions of the constellations (both north and south of the ecliptic), the various Zodiacal signs, and other celestial phenomena seem designed merely to bring out their aesthetic beauty; in effect, they serve as fodder for his poetic versatility. And in his account of weather signs, he explicitly states that human beings are on their own in determining their significance ("Not yet do we mortals

64. I use the translation of A. W. and G. R. Mair.

65. Katharine Volk, "Aratus," in Clauss and Cuypers, *A Companion to Hellenistic Literature* 204.

know all from Zeus, but much remains hidden" [769–70]). The first part of the *Phaenomena* was used as a school textbook on astronomy for centuries.

We now come to the last major poet of the Hellenistic era to be studied here, Theocritus (300?–250?), a Sicilian about whom very little is known, aside from the fact that he made his way to Alexandria during the reign of Ptolemy II Philadelphus. What we do know is that he became the founder of the bucolic or pastoral poem, a genre of tremendous popularity extending into the twentieth century. While it might appear that his *Idylls*—thirty of which survive intact, although a few of these may be spurious—are the very essence of frivolous irreality, dealing with the laments of shepherds about their love life and other troubles, there is more going on in his work than merely an exercise in poetic fantasy.

As with other Hellenistic poets, Theocritus plays off of his literary predecessors, notably Homer and Pindar; and like his contemporaries, he focuses on the lives of ordinary people—as in *Idyll* 15, a realistic portrayal of two housewives attending a religious festival (the Adoneia, or the festival of Adonis) at the court of Ptolemy II. Their qvetching about their husbands and other domestic matters make for wryly amusing reading, and there does not appear to be a great deal of religious sentiment among the women: one is only struck with religious fervour because she is taken with the beauty of a statue of a seated Adonis in the temple.

And what do we make of *Idyll* 7? Here the protagonist, on the way to a harvest-home, encounters a celebrated piper and singer, Lycidas. The entire poem plays upon the ancient topos of human encounters with disguised deities—but the text implies that Lycidas may be nothing more than a smelly goatherd. *Idyll* 1, in which the shepherd Thyrsis sings a song commemorating the death of Daphnis, a mythical cowherd, describes Daphnis being visited by Hermes, Priapus, Pan, and Aphrodite in his dying hour—but this may signify nothing more than Daphnis' closeness to Nature.

A number of Theocritus' poems on mystic or religious subjects are transparently meant to heap praise on Ptolemy and his circle, playing upon the fact that "in Egypt the Ptolemies continued the Egyptian practice of regarding the ruler as a son of god."[66] So no particular religious

66. Anthony W. Bulloch, "Hymns and Encomia," in Clauss and Cuypers, *A Companion to Hellenistic Literature* 175.

feeling on the author's part need be read into these works.

The implicit lampooning of the gods—or, more specifically, of the treatment of gods in the now storied work of Homer and Hesiod—that we have detected in some of the poetry of this period becomes explicit in the *Batrachomyomachia* (Battle of the Frogs and Mice), a hilarious parody of Homer that was probably written in the Hellenistic era. This was probably one of numerous parodies written at this time.

In the several millennia covered by this chapter—and in particular in the period between the sixth and the second centuries B.C.E.—we have seen a broad dichotomy between two sets of thinkers: first, a slow, halting, but none the less striking attempt (notably by Empedocles, Anaxagoras, and the Atomists) to put forth a "natural" origin of the universe or to question the nature or divinity of the Olympian gods (Xenophanes), and a countervailing tendency by philosophers, several of whom believed themselves to have been divinely inspired (Pythagoras, Heraclitus), to fuse natural philosophy with religion, even if that religion departed widely from that prevailing in Greece in their time. Needless to say, none of the thinkers in question fit neatly into either of these schemas. The emergence of Socrates, Plato, and Aristotle lent substantial weight to the latter tendency; and, in spite of the strikingly secular vision of the Epicureans, the Stoics made it the centrepiece of their philosophy.

Other writers displayed some independence from religious orthodoxy, but none of them—nor, indeed, any of the major philosophers dealt with here—could be said to be "atheists" in any meaningful sense of the term. At most, they provided a nucleus of philosophical and scientific thought that would later flower into full-fledged atheism—but only after many centuries of intellectual, social, and political dominance in the West by the Judaeo-Christian tradition.

Hellenistic art shows some tendencies toward secularism. The goddess Tyche was a "new" goddess whose worship seems to have begun during this period. Her name signifies "luck," "chance," or "good fortune," and may be another indicator of the precariousness of ordinary life in this era. A well-known sculpture of her by Eutyclides survives in a copy; she was the city goddess of Antioch. Aside from the immense temples that were constructed at this time, other grand structures of a more secular purpose were built—most prominently amphitheatres for theatrical events, as well as clock towers and lighthouses (including the famous Pharos at Alexandria, one of the seven wonders of the ancient world).

Expressions of intense emotion begin appearing in sculptures, enhancing their realism and evoking strong reactions in viewers. Notable among these is the statue of Laocoon and his sons being attacked by snakes. The story of course goes back to the Trojan War (Laocoon is a priest of Troy, and the serpents were sent by Apollo), but the expression of horrified anguish on all the human figures is unforgettable. Female nudes are commonly depicted, as in the Venus de Milo (the surviving statue is a second century B.C.E. version of a sculpture executed in the fourth century). Busts of human figures become more expressive and lifelike, although the artists of the Roman period carried this technique to still greater heights.

III. The Romans

The gods having vanished and Christ not yet having come,
there was, from Cicero to Marcus Aurelius, a unique moment
when only man existed.

—Gustave Flaubert

A. The Romans and the Etruscans

Our analysis of the philosophical currents in Latin literature must be conducted in a very different manner from our investigation of Greek thought. It is not merely that there is (even accounting for vagaries of transmission) far less Latin literature than Greek; it is that Roman philosophers are relatively few in number and are generally followers of some of the leading schools of Greek thought. This applies mosst notably to Lucretius (an Epicurean) and Seneca the Younger (a Stoic). The only other thinker writing in Latin who is of any note, Cicero, is chiefly a chronicler or summariser of the philosophical currents of his time, exhibiting little in the way of original thought.

And yet, these thinkers are of value in a different way: Lucretius in particular, through the dynamism of his expression of many facets of Epicurean thought (some of which are not found in the extant works of Epicurus himself or his immediate followers), as well as the exquisite lyricism of his poetry, became a vital transmitter of Epicurean philosophy in the Renaissance and later, constituting a key counterweight to Christian thinking; Cicero's and Seneca's works were similarly of immense influence during the revival of learning. Later philosophical writing in the Roman world (Epictetus, Marcus Aurelius, and a few others) is in Greek, but it too is of value and substance.

What is more, a wide array of Latin writing that is not strictly philosophical—whether it be epic or lyric poetry, satire (in which the Romans could be said to be pioneers), drama (both tragic and comic), history, letters, and even treatises on farming or other mundane subjects—betrays the authors' views on religion and philosophy in a way that is of consuming interest in gauging the extent to which the Greco-Roman pantheon and other religious or anti-religious tendencies were accepted, at least by the intelligentsia, and perhaps even by the wider populace. In this chapter I shall study much of this literature, in both Greek and Latin, produced in the Roman Republic and Empire down to about 500 C.E., or just after the fall of Rome to the Goths. Our first concern, however, is to sketch an outline of early Roman history and the development of its religion, especially its fusion with the Greek religion of the period.

The founding of Rome was canonically dated to what amounts to 753 B.C.E. The establishment of the city was explicitly attributed to divine (or at least supernatural) forces. The Roman historian Livy, whose 142-book chronicle (titled *Ab Urbe Condita* [From the Founding of the City]) became the authoritative account of early Roman history, explicitly endorses supernaturalism at the very outset of his work. In a passage probably written around 29–27 B.C.E., he states:

> Events before Rome was born or thought of have come to us in old tales with more of the charm of poetry than of a sound historical record, and such traditions I propose neither to affirm nor refute. There is no reason, I feel, to object when antiquity draws no hard line between the human and the supernatural:[1] it adds dignity to the past, and, if any nation deserves the privilege of claiming a divine ancestry, that nation is our own. (Preface 6–7)[2]

Some years earlier, Cicero said much the same thing in a broader sense:

1. The Latin text reads *divinis* (i.e., divine matters).

2. For Livy, Books 1–5 and 21–30, I use the translation of Aubrey de Sélincourt. For Books 31–45, I use other translators as specified in notes.

> . . . and yet it is not in numbers that we are superior to the Spaniards, nor in personal strength to the Gauls, nor in cunning to the Carthaginians, nor in arts to the Greeks, nor in the natural acuteness which seems to be implanted in the people of this land and country, to the Italian and Latin tribes; but it is in piety and religion, and this especial wisdom of perceiving that all things are governed and managed by the divine power of the immortal gods, that we have been and are superior to all other countries and nations. (*De Responso Haruspicarum* 19)[3]

These comments embody that strong fusion of historicmindedness, national pride, and religiosity that is so typical of even the most educated of Roman writers and thinkers.

The tale, as Livy tells it in Book 1 of his history, begins with Aeneas. In the *Iliad* he is glancingly mentioned as a Trojan hero, and he is featured in the Homeric *Hymn to Aphrodite,* in which Zeus impels the mortal man Anchises to fall in love with Aphrodite; she gives birth to Aeneas. Livy states that, after the Trojan war, Aeneas ventured out of Troy to Italy, where he was eventually given Lavinia, the daughter of a local chieftain, Latinus, for his wife. His son Ascanius was born to her. Turnus, a leader of another tribe, the Rutili, who had been engaged to Lavinia, went to war against Aeneas' men; significantly, Turnus appealed to Mezentius, an Etruscan king, for assistance. But the Trojans (now calling themselves Latins) defeated the combined forces of the Rutuli and the Etruscans. Aeneas died soon thereafter, and Ascanius founded the city of Alba Longa (about 20 miles southeast of Rome).

Several generations later, the Vestal Virgin Rhea (or Ilia) Silvia was raped by Mars (by her own testimony) and gave birth to twins, Romulus and Remus. The king of that time, Amulius (Rhea Silvia's uncle), ordered them to be drowned in the Tiber, but a she-wolf came to rescue them and suckled them. Later they were taken in by the king's herdsman, Faustulus, and his wife, Larentia. When they grew up, they wished to found a city on the spot where they were left to die—but they quarrelled, and Remus was killed. Rome was therefore named after Romulus.

Among other acts, Romulus established the Roman Senate, naming 100 of the leading citizens to fill it. Needing women to increase the population, Romulus held a festival and had his men seize young Sabine

3. I use the translation of C. D. Yonge. The oration was delivered in 56 B.C.E.

women (the Sabines were a tribe—now referred to as the Umbro-Sabellians—to the east of Rome, occupying a broad stretch of Italy along the Adriatic). This "rape of the Sabines" did not go unpunished; the Sabine forces attacked and momentarily took the citadel at Rome. But the Sabine women intervened and made peace between their new husbands and their old tribe; in the process the Romans essentially annexed Sabine territory. Soon thereafter, Romulus disappeared in a cloud during a storm and was never seen again.

Numa Pompilius (a Sabine) was now appointed king. He effected numerous religious reforms, including installing a permanent priest of Jupiter and establishing the cult of the Vestal Virgins, importing it from Alba Longa. He also created the office of pontifex, a member of the chief college of priests. Several more kings added extensively to Roman territory in the succeeding decades.

In Etruria (a wide area of central Italy), Lucumo, a high-born exile from Corinth, and his wife Tanaquil left the city of Tarquinii and made their way to Rome. He interpreted a supernatural incident with an eagle—which snatched up the cap he was wearing and then returned it to his head—as an omen. He renamed himself L. Tarquinius Priscus (Tarquin the Elder).[4] He won popularity among the masses and was elected as the new king (c. 600 B.C.E.). His successor, Servius Tullius, also an Etruscan, married Tarquin's daughter. Tarquin was killed (c. 570) by men hired by the sons of the previous king, Ancus Marcius. Servius took over as king.

Tarquin's son, L. Tarquinius Superbus (Tarquin the Proud), and his brother Arruns's wife Tullia (the daughter of Servius) killed their respective spouses and married each other. Tarquin boldly occupied the king's chair in front of the Senate House, heaping abuse on Servius. Tarquin then had Servius killed (c. 530) and took over the kingship. He became a ruthless autocrat, killing many senators and ruling on his own authority. But he also completed the magnificent temple of Jupiter Optimus Maximus (Jupiter Best and Greatest) on the Capitoline hill—not to mention the all-important Cloaca Maxima, the main sewer for

4. The convention among classical scholars is to supply the *praenomen* of a Latin name only by an abbreviation, since there are only a limited number of names for (male) Romans, as follows: C. = Gaius; Cn. = Gnaeus; L. = Lucius; M. = Marcus; P. = Publius; Q. = Quintus; T. = Titus.

the city of Rome. When his son, Sextus Tarquinius, raped Lucretia, L. Junius Brutus resolved to rid Rome of all the Tarquins, and did so. They were sent into exile and left for Caere (in Etruria) around 510. The monarchy was overthrown, and there would be no more kings in Rome.

It need hardly be stated that substantial portions of this account are pure fiction. In numerous instances, scholars have identified Greek myths that clearly served as the basis for the more spectacular or supernatural elements in this narrative. The suckling of Romulus and Remus by a she-wolf, for example, is probably adapted from the legend of Neleus and Pelias, sons of Poseudon who were suckled by a bitch and a mare. And yet, the whole account, beginning with Aeneas, is likely to have been of fairly early origin. The Greek historian Dionysius of Halicarnassus (60 B.C.E.–7 C.E.), writing contemporaneously with Livy and probably independently of him, tells substantially the same story. Among his sources was the *Origines* of L. Porcius Cato (234–149 B.C.E.), probably written in the early second century. The work does not survive. Livy himself cites another early historian, Q. Fabius Pictor (fl. c. 200 B.C.E.), from whom he may have derived some of his material.

And yet, it would be an error to discard this entire account as fictitious or mythical. It is worth examining what archaeology and other modern disciplines have to say about the founding of Rome, and the settlement of the Italian peninsla in general. Our enquiry will focus on the eternal conundrum of the Etruscans.

Iron Age Italy was populated by numerous ethnic or linguistic groups largely independent of one another. They are now referred to as the Appenine culture, the Terramara culture, the Villanovan culture, and so on. These people spoke a variety of non-Indo-European languages. A proto-Latin language was probably spoken in southwest Italy in the early first millennium B.C.E., gradually spreading northeast. Moreover, an infiltration of peoples from the north (the area of the Danube) or the eastern Mediterranean may have occurred. This does not necessarily suggest any sort of "conquest"; the legend of Aeneas coming from Troy to Italy may reflect such a migration. In the eighth century we find ethnic groups called the Umbrians, the Sabines, the Samnites, and others.

The Etruscans (also referred to in ancient sources as the Tyrrhenians, since their territory extended along a large swath of land in Italy bordering the Tyrrhenian Sea) were established by no later than the eighth century.

The overriding question is about their origins: were they indigenous or did they come from elsewhere? The question appears to be unanswerable in any definitive way, and scholars have taken radically different positions on the issue. The case for migration (from Asia Minor or the Aegean Islands) is usually made by appealing to linguistic similarities between their language and those in the purported areas of their origin; but these similarities could be merely a matter of cultural borrowing, since the Etruscans clearly engaged in trade with a wide array of peoples from an early date.[5] Similar problems plague theories conjecturing a northern or an autochthonous origin of the Etruscans. At best we can say that the Etruscans as a linguistic-ethnic group took shape in Italy, whatever their ultimate source. We are on safer ground in saying that there may be some connexion between the Etruscans and the Villanovan culture, since both practised cremation.

It was inevitable that the Etruscans would come into contact—and conflict—with the Greek colonies in Sicily and southern Italy, ranging from Cumae (near Naples) to Syracuse and many others. In some instances they established trade relations; but in the sixth and fifth centuries the Etruscans teamed up with the Carthaginians in north Africa (who, let us recall, were Phoenician in origin) in battles against the Greeks. But the Etruscan naval power declined in the fifth century, and they lost a battle at Cumae to the Syracusans in 474.

Etruscan control of Rome and Latium (the region around Rome), as reflected in the Roman historical myths about the Tarquins, is confirmed by archaeology. In the north, however, the Etruscans were crushed by an invasion of the Celts in the fifth century. Their influence upon Roman life extended in numerous directions—from their adoption of the Greek alphabet to their distinctive tripartite nomenclature (the praenomen [corresponding to our given or first name], the nomen [reflecting the *gens* or clan name], and the cognomen [reflecting the family name]). It is likely that their political system did indeed feature a king in its early stages, later transitioning to republican rule that was essentially aristocratic in essence.

The importance of the Etruscans from our perspective rests upon their dominant influence in transmitting the Greek pantheon, and perhaps

5. It is worth noting that surviving Etruscan artwork frequently depicts Aeneas—a point that may enhance the notion of their migration from the eastern Mediterranean.

other elements of the Greek religion, to the nascent Roman culture. The Etruscans' initial conception of deity appears to have been a somewhat vague sense of a divine entity manifesting itself in multifarious ways in the natural world; but under the influence of the Greek colonies, a more concrete polytheism and anthropomorphism gradually supervened. This can be seen in the number of Etruscan gods who were linked with Greek counterparts and were then taken over by the Romans:

Greek	*Etruscan*	*Roman*
Zeus	Tin or Tinia	Jupiter
Hera	Uni	Juno
Athene	Menerva	Minerva
Hephaistos	Sethlans	Vulcan
Hermes	Turms	Mercury
Aphrodite	Turan	Venus
Ares	Maris	Mars

Other Greek gods, such as Apollo, were absorbed directly by the Romans, while they renamed Poseidon as Neptune, Demeter as Ceres, and Dionysus/Bacchus as Liber, among others. Needless to say, the fusing of the Roman gods with their Greek counterparts was not always seamless: Mars, for example, was originally an agricultural god, but when he took the place of Ares he became the god of war. (The Romans also worshipped Bellona, a goddess of war.) Faunus was a god of the Italian countryside—a personification of the *Fauni,* who were conceived as goatlike creatures living in remote places. Faunus was eventually identified with the Greek Pan.

Other elements of Etruscan religion that were taken over by the Romans were *haruspicina* (the ascertaining of the divine will through inspection of animal entrails); a sixteen-fold division of the sky, each controlled by a given deity, including those from the underworld; divination by various means, including by the interpretation of lightning; and so on. Some of the more elaborate religious beliefs and practices of the Etruscans probably evolved toward the end of Etruscan rule, when domination by priests was at its height.

Tombs in the shape of houses with furniture, clothes, jewellery, and food for the dead clearly suggest a belief in the bodily continuance of life in the afterlife. How exactly this is to be reconciled with the practice of cremation is unclear. Possibly under Greek influence, the presence of the dead in a Hades-like realm was postulated. Other entities were also thought to exist there, including Vanth (the goddess of fate) and Charun (a demon who has some relation to the Greek Charon). It was believed that every living person, no matter how illustrious, ended up in the realm of the dead. At a late stage of the Etruscans' history, there was some suggestion of a kind of salvation for the dead—generated, not by a morally upright life, but by rituals and incantations.

Exactly how we are to gauge Etruscan political domination of Rome during the purported time of the kings (Tarquin the Elder, Servius Tullius, and Tarquin the Proud) remains unclear. In the period 625–600 there probably was some kind of Etruscan infiltration of Rome, but this may have been merely by settlers rather than by armed conquest. By 575 the Etruscans had replaced the early nature-religion of the Romans with the Greek pantheon. The date of c. 510 for the expulsion of the Tarquins may have been an adaptation of Athenian history and the overthrow of the tyrants by Cleisthenes around that time; but since the Romans retained a list of consuls—the pair of magistrates who led the government after the expulsion of the kings—since at least 507 B.C.E., there is a strong likelihood that some sort of transition from monarchy to a more democratic (or aristocratic) rule occurred at this time.

The Etruscans, who do not seem to have had a literature aside from books of religious rites (which are mentioned in Greek and Roman sources, and some of which appears to have been in verse) and some historical chronicles, wrote in a non-Indo-European language that has only been partially deciphered. As such, they will remain an eternal mystery, but their influence on the subsequent development of Rome is manifest.

B. Roman Politics and Religion to the End of the Republic

The end of the regal period (assuming there was such a period) ushered in an era in Roman politics that is generally referred to as the Republic, although at the outset a hereditary aristocracy was still firmly in control. It is true that the annual election of two consuls as chief magistrates was in the hands of the people, but their election had to be ratified by the Senate. As such, it was the Senate that gained power by being a permanent body in contrast to the rapidly changing consuls, who were forbidden from holding office more than once.

But in the first half of the fifth century, a social rebellion now called the Conflict of the Orders took place in Rome, whereby the leading families (the patricians) were forced to yield some power to the rest of the populace (called the plebeians) to the extent of allowing the establishment of an office called the tribune of the plebs to protect the plebeians' interests. It should not be assumed that the plebeians were entirely at the lower end, economically or socially, of the populace; some of them were wealthy businessmen who simply were not members of the old-time aristocracy.

In a landmark development, the patricians yielded on another point: the writing and publication of the Twelve Tables, a detailed legal code that bound magistrates and judges. It was passed around 450; and, although for the most part it merely codified customary practices in regard to private transactions, it at least allowed the law to be known to those who had the literacy and other skills to read and interpret it. The plebeians continued to win more and more concessions from the patricians, and by 287 they had become dominant both politically and economically. But the wars that consumed Rome over the next two hundred years gave power back to the Senate to some degree, as it was now filled with ex-magistrates (including some plebeians) who had expertise in law and governance.

Those wars were not necessarily a product of Roman agression; in some instances the Romans defended themselves against attacks from their neighbours, either in Italy or elsewhere. Indeed, Rome itself was sacked by the Celts from Gaul around 390, although the Romans quickly retook the city. But the end result was an unsystematic but seemingly inexorable accretion of power and territory across the Mediterranean. By the end of the fourth century, Rome had become dominant in most of Italy; but, after fending off Pyrrhus, the ruler of Epirus (a province in western Greece) in the Pyrrhic War (280–75), the Romans had to face the much more significant threat of the Carthaginians. This led to the first (264–41) and second (218–201) Punic War.[6]

This conflict was an inevitable result of Roman expansion and the tenacity of Carthaginian control of northern Africa and the waters of the Mediterranean around it. The Second Punic War was particularly traumatic for the Romans. Not only did their army suffer humiliating defeats at Lake Trasimene (217) and Cannae (216) at the hands of Hannibal, but that formidable Carthaginian general ravaged southern Italy for years. But at last the tide turned in favour of the Romans, and the Roman general P. Scipio Cornelius Africanus defeated Hannibal in the Battle of Zama (now in Tunisia) in 202; the Carthaginians sued for peace the next year.

Roman conquest continued apace. During the Second Punic War, much of the Iberian peninsula (Spain) was secured. Macedon and the rest of Greece was annexed by 146.[7] After the conclusion of the three Mithridatic Wars (89–63), against Mithridates, ruler of Pontus, much of Asia Minor fell under Roman control. Julius Caesar conquered Gaul by 50. (He made forays into Britain in 55 and 54, although he made little attempt to subdue the island.)

These seemingly unending conflicts had the effect of investing enormous power and prestige upon the army, and in particular upon the leaders of the army. In the last century of the Common Era, these generals became an unpredictable element that could defy the central government for their own ends. The general C. Marius (157?–86) reorganised the army as a professional force, so that it was no longer one of citizen soldiers. His struggles with L. Cornelius Sulla (138–78) were a product of the ongoing rivalry between forces allied to the Senate (now called the *optimates,* with Sulla as their leader) and those associated with the plebeians (now called the *populares,* who looked to Marius). Sulla made the unprecedented move of twice marching on Rome with his army (in 88 and 82); after the latter event the Senate appointed him a dictator to reform the constitution. But his reforms did not endure very long after his voluntary retirement in 79.

It is now clear that Sulla's actions set a precedent for Julius Caesar's analogous "crossing of the Rubicon" in 49. Caesar (100–44) had gained

6. The name derives from the Latin term for the Phoenicians, *Poeni.*

7. At the conclusion of the Third Punic War (149–46), the entire city of Carthage was razed. But a century later Julius Caesar established a "Roman Carthage" on the site.

enormous prestige with his conquest of Gaul, and he was disinclined to disband his army as ordered by the Senate. In spite of the fact that his clan (the Julii) were among the most ancient patricians in Rome, he took the side of the *populares;* Pompey (Cn. Pompeius Magnus, 106–48) led the senatorial faction. There is no need to enter into the immensely complex circumstances surrounding the Civil War, but the upshot was that Caesar defeated Pompey at Pharsalus (in Greece) in 48 and was appointed dictator. The Senate now swung to his side, showering honours upon him. But a faction in the Senate, angered by Caesar's apparent desire to become king (the term *rex* still evoked visceral reactions in many Romans five hundred years after the expulsion of the Tarquins) and led by D. Junius Brutus Albinus, assassinated him on the Ides of March of 44 at the Senate.

This hardly put an end to the Civil War. Caesar's adopted son, Octavius (C. Octavius, 63 B.C.E.–14 C.E.) sought to avenge Caesar's murder. Once again, the complexities of the next decade and a half need not be gone into, but in one of the climactic battles of world history Octavius defeated the combined forces of Mark Antony and the Egyptian queen Cleopatra at the Battle of Actium (31 B.C.E.), thereby essentially putting an end to the Roman Republic.

The history of Roman religion during this five-century period is difficult to specify; for by the time any substantial written records survive (no earlier than the mid- to late third century B.C.E.), religion as both a state institution and a matter of private worship was in full flower. The manner in which the Romans adopted the Greek pantheon and other religious elements is of a piece with their own genius for administration and lawmaking. Just as political governance was put into the hands of a multitude of officials (consuls, praetors, aediles, and so forth) who efficiently managed both the city of Rome and its increasingly far-flung empire, so was Roman religion managed by a wide array of priestly officials.

The Romans believed that religion was, essentially, a kind of contract whereby human beings would worship the gods in return for good will (or, at the very least, absence of harm) from them. The very word *religio* derives from the verb *religare* (to bind), referring specifically to a binding obligation. As such, it is understandable that numerous functionaries had to serve as intermediaries between the people and their deities. Hence we have a college of priests (led by the pontifex maximus), augurs (reflecting the importance Romans placed on divination, or the ascertaining of the will of the gods), quindecimvirs (a board of priests tasked with the proper performance of religious rituals), and numerous other positions. We have already seen that the Vestal Virgins—a body that tended a sacred flame symbolising Vesta, the goddess of the hearth—appeared very early in the history of Rome.

The determination of the will of the gods was especially important in warfare. As Valerie M. Warrior notes, "At every stage of any military undertaking, from beginning to end, the gods' favor had to be maintained by the correct performance of various rituals, especially the taking of auspices. Success was attributed to the favor of the gods, whereas defeat was the result of a failure to gain that favor."[8] A convenient strategy for avoiding the acknowledgement that the "gods' favor" may be illusory! In any event, it is in warfare that priests called the *fetiales* came into prominence. Dionysius of Halicarnassus, who was puzzled by this specifically Roman feature of their religion, explains:

> It is their duty to take care that the Romans do not enter upon an unjust war against any city in alliance with them, and if others begin the violation of treaties against them, to go as ambassadors and first make formal demand for justice, and then, if the others refuse to comply with their demands, to sanction war. . . . They are also to take cognizance of the crimes committed against ambassadors, to take care that treaties are religiously observed, to make peace, and if they find that peace has been made otherwise than is prescribed by the holy laws, to set it aside; and to inquire into and expiate the transgressions of the generals in so far as they relate to oaths and treaties . . . (*Roman Antiquities* 2.72)[9]

This creates the impression that the fetiales' function was more political or diplomatic than religious; but the overall discussion of their function in the ancient sources does point to a largely religious purpose.

Vesta is only one of several "household gods" who presided over individual families. Of greatest note here are the Lares and Penates,

8. Warrior, *Roman Religion* 56.
9. I use the translation of Earnest Cary.

who presided over the family and the pantry, respectively, and who were worshipped at shrines in the house. Ancestor worship was practised at the Parentalia and the Feralia (18–21 February), honouring the dead. These were among numerous festivals filling the Roman calendar; many of them were devoted to gods, but there were festivals of other sorts as well, among them the Matralia (relating to women, especially in regard to childbirth) and the Saturnalia—nominally a feast devoted to the god Saturn (the father of Jupiter, Neptune, and others) but chiefly associated with the winter solstice.

Elements of a popular religion among the Romans can be detected as well. The efficacy of magic, incantations, potions, and so on was widely credited, and they appeared at a quite early stage in Roman social history. The Twelve Tables enacted punishments against those "who shall have enchanted signing evil spell[s]" and those who ha[ve] enchanted crops away" (Table VIII).[10] Remarkably, the otherwise staid farmer-philosopher-historian L. Porcius Cato (Cato the Elder) soberly informs us that dislocations can be cured in the following manner:

> Any kind of dislocation may be cured by the following charm: Take a green reed four or five feet long and split it down the middle, and let two men hold it to your hips. Begin to chant: "motas uaeta daries dardares astataries dissunapiter" and continue until they meet. Brandish a knife over them, and when the reeds meet so that one touches the other, grasp with the hand and cut right and left. If the pieces are applied to the dislocation or the fracture, it will heal. And none the less chant every day, and, in the case of a dislocation, in this manner, if you wish: "huat haut haut istasis tarsis ardannabou dannaustra." (*De Agri Cultura* 160)[11]

We learn that astrologers had become so popular that they were expelled from Rome in 139 B.C.E.

The attainment of an empire, even during the period when the Republic was in effect, inevitably engendered encounters between the Romans and those peoples who differed from them in religious belief and ritual. As with the Greeks and their relatively short-lived empire,

10. I use the translation of E. H. Warmington (*Remains of Old Latin* 3).

11. I use the translation of William Davis Hooper (rev. Harrison Boyd Ash).

the Romans generally allowed foreign groups or nations to continue practicising their religion, so long as it did not jeopardise the political security of those regions that had come under their administrative control. In the process, Roman religion itself underwent certain modifications. This occurred quite early on in its history. In 433 B.C.E., during an outbreak of the plague, the Romans formally devoted a temple to Apollo in his capacity as healer. Much later, in 292, the Greek god of healing, Asklepios, was brought to Rome under the name Aesculapius.

Remarkably, in 217, during the Second Punic War, the Romans attempted to co-opt the Carthaginian goddess Astarte under the name Venus Erycina (Venus of Eryx). Eryx was a city in Sicily that had become Hellenised in the fifth century B.C.E. It subsequently came under Carthaginian control, and a still-extant temple there was worshipped by the Greeks, Carthaginians, and Romans. But the Romans also erected a temple to Venus Erycina in Rome itself, on the Capitoline Hill—"the first known example of a foreign deity to be brought inside the *pomerium* [the sacred boundary of the city of Rome]."[12]

Even more remarkably, the Romans felt the need to introduce the Phrygian goddess Cybele (as the Magna Mater—the "Great Mother" of the gods) into Rome in 205, fulfilling a prophecy of the Sibylline Books (a collection of oracles frequently consulted by priests, magistrates, and others) that only in this manner could a foreign foe that had invaded Italy be defeated. The orgiastic nature of this cult was highly unsuitable to the staid Romans of the period, but the ravages of the Carthaginians seemingly left them with no other option.

But once the Carthaginians had been defeated, matters returned to a semblance of normality. In 186 the Senate issued its momentous *Senatus Consultum de Bacchanalibus* (Decree of the Senate Regarding the Bacchanalian Rites). The text of this decree is still extant. It does not specifically ban the worship of Bacchus (Dionysus), but merely restricts the manner in which it can be conducted. Livy provides an overcoloured portrait of the scandalous nature of these rites prior to the decree:

> There were initiatory rites which at first were imparted to a few, then began to be generally known among men and women. To the religious

12. Warrior, *Roman Religion* 82.

> element in them were added the delights of wine and feasts, that the minds of a large number might be attracted. When wine had inflamed their minds, and night and the mingling of males with females, youth with age, had destroyed every sentiment of modesty, all varieties of corruption first began to be practised, since each one had at hand the pleasure answering to that to which his nature was more inclined. There was not one form of vice alone, the promiscuous matings of free men and women, but perjured witnesses, forged seals and wills and evidence, all issued from this same workshop: likewise poisonings and secret murders, so that at times not even the bodies were found for burial. (39.8)[13]

It can be seen from this that, at least in Livy's judgment, the rites were both intrinsically immoral and productive of criminal behaviour.

The Egyptian god Isis was brought to Rome in the early first century B.C.E. The turmoil of the Civil War period resulted in both the demolition of some of the shrines and also in the construction of new temples to Isis and also to Serapis. Cleopatra's participation in what amounted to an attempt to overthrow Rome resulted in the banning of Egyptian cults from Rome; even so, Isis made a comeback in the mid-first century C.E. The treatment of the Jews under Roman rule will be considered in a separate section.

The Romans did not evolve their own creation story, and there is not even a great deal of evidence that they accepted the account of the creation of the world as found, say, in Hesiod. In regard to the afterlife, the early Italians appeared to believe in a realm in which the undifferentiated spirits of the dead, called *Manes,* dwelt. Funerary inscriptions throughout the Republic and Empire are dedicated *Dis Manibus* (to the sacred spirits of the dead); sometimes the abbreviation D. M. is used. At a later stage, ancestor worship can be identified in the reverence of the *di parentes* (the sanctified spirits of dead family members). Ghosts (*umbrae*) or restless spirits (*lemures*) were widely believed in. Once the influence of Greek religion manifested itself, the Romans adopted the Greek vision of the underworld, with Dis serving as the equivalent of Pluto/Hades, Proserpina the equivalent of Persephone, and so on.

There is a legitimate question as to how fervently or sincerely the

13. I use the translation of Evan T. Sage.

Roman people believed in the Greco-Roman pantheon, either in the dawn of their civilisation or as it was crumbling during the fourth and fifth centuries C.E. Some hints of the answer may be found in the sections to follow; but the tenacity with which many citizens clung to the pagan faith even when, after Christianity became the state religion in the fourth century C.E., probably points to more than the inveterate tendency of individuals to adhere to beliefs and practices with which they are familiar. The writings of even the most eminent, sophisticated, and perhaps most sceptical Roman writers are littered with references to the Greco-Roman gods and myths, in a way that leads one to assume that they would be readily accepted by their readers and axiomatically believed.

C. Religion in Early Roman Literature

The Romans themselves acknowledged one Livius Andronicus (284?–204? B.C.E.) as the first significant literary figure who wrote in Latin. His appearance in the early to mid-third century may seem rather late in the history of Rome. Indeed, some historians of the nineteenth century conjectured the existence of an extensive array of poetic literature dating to as far back as the fifth century, which was somehow lost or actively suppressed by later figures; but little evidence for any such body of work exists. But some rudimentary verse forms in Latin, such as those in the primitive Saturnian metre, fragments of hymns, and the so-called Fescennine verses—songs sung during harvest time, weddings, and religious festivals—laid the groundwork for the Latin poetic idiom that flourished from the third century onward.

Livius himself is of little interest to us. He was probably a native of Greece who was brought to Rome as a young slave, and later freed. His major work—a translation or paraphrase of the *Odyssey* in Saturnian verse—is extant only in fragments, as are the works of nearly all the authors discussed in this section. He also wrote what he called *Saturae* (medleys accompanied by the flute) and wrote and acted in the first Roman comedy and tragedy (c. 240). Most of the tragedies he wrote were on subjects out of Greek mythology. He also wrote hymns celebrating Roman victories during the Punic Wars.

It is these two elements—the significant, indeed overwhelming, influence of Greek literature and culture and the impetus that the Punic Wars, in some fashion, gave to Latin literature—that characterise the work of the several writers who followed Livius. Two of them—Naevius and Ennius—are of some interest in the context of the development of Roman religion and, to a lesser extent, Roman secularism.

Cn. Naevius (270?–201?) was a plebeian from Rome who began producing plays around 235. We will consider these presently, but for now our interest resides in his epic poem, *Bellum Poenicum* (The Punic War), written chiefly in his old age, in Saturnian metre. The book, in at least seven books, deals only with the First Punic War, even though it was apparently written at a time when the Second Punic War was winding down. What is important here is that Naevius very likely expounded on much of the fabulous history of the founding of Rome—the departure of Aeneas from Troy, his arrival in Italy, the birth of Romulus and Remus, Numa Pompilius, and so on. His treatment of the First Punic War (in which he had served) appears to be largely shorn of mythological or supernatural elements.

Q. Ennius (239–169), although about two generations later than Livius, was regarded as the true founder of Latin literature. He was raised in a southern Italian district where Greek was widely spoken, and he was fluent in both Greek and Latin. His *Annales,* in eighteen books, tells in even greater detail the history of Rome from Aeneas down to his own day; it is probable that he published individual books, or batches of books, successively over many years. From the extant fragments we can tell that he too began his account with the sack of Troy, the marriage of Venus and Anchises, Aeneas' arrival to Italy, and so on, all the way down to the Tarquins.

At a minimum, it is clear that this account of the origin of Rome dates to at least the third century B.C.E. How much earlier it can be traced is a matter of debate. The first historian to take an interest in the rise of Rome, the Greek historian Timaeus of Tauromenium (350?–160?), wrote extensively about both Rome and Carthage. It is he who probably chronicled not only Aeneas' journey to Italy—a purported event that can be traced as far back as the sixth century B.C.E.—but also his voyage to Carthage, although there is debate as to whether he expounded upon the romance between Aeneas and Dido, queen of Carthage, so memorably portrayed in Book IV of Virgil's *Aeneid.* There is no textual evidence that Naevius included such a discussion; but the mere fact that he felt compelled to speak of Aeneas and Roman "prehistory" at all in what was ostensibly a factual (if poetically enhanced) account of the First Punic War suggests that he made this connexion as a means of accounting (as Virgil certainly did) for the enmity of Rome and Carthage in his own time. Aeneas' abandonment of Dido and her subsequent suicide would, by this theory, be the ultimate *casus belli* that led to the Punic Wars.

There is no reference to Dido and Aeneas in Ennius' *Annales.* This poem is essentially an epic glorifying the greatness and destiny of Rome; the mingling of historical fable (Aeneas, Romulus, and so on) and contemporary history serves that end. But the execution of this agenda reveals occasional awkwardnesses. It is one thing to portray a council of the Olympian gods during which they decide upon the deification of Romulus after his death (W 23);[14] it is an altogether different—and grotesque—matter to exhibit Jupiter and Juno sanctioning the Romans' defeat of Carthage in the Second Punic War (W 109).

But in other works Ennius reveals considerably greater religious scepticism. He wrote a didactic poem, *Epicharmus,* on the little-known Greek playwright and philosopher Epicharmus of Kos (550?–460?), in the course of which Ennius presents a natural origin of the universe by means of the four elements (W 411); more strikingly, he equates Jupiter with *aer* ("who is wind and clouds, and afterwards moisture; out of wetness he becomes cold, and after that wind, and air once again" [W 415]) and Juno with earth.

And what of the fact that Ennius wrote a *Euhemerus, sive Sacra Historia* (Euhemerus, or The Holy History), translating or paraphrasing the work of Euhemerus of Messene, who demythologised the gods as illustrious human beings who, because of their significant contributions to human development, were deified? Virtually all the quotations we have from this work come from the Christian writer Lactantius (250?–325? C.E.), who records Ennius' descriptions of the birth of Jupiter, Juno, and the other gods of the Greco-Roman pantheon and—what particularly exercised the pious Lactantius—the *death* of Jupiter of old age on Crete:

---

14. Henceforth I cite passages from early Roman authors as found in Warmington's *Remains of Old Latin* by the abbreviation W and a page number. I also use his translations throughout.

> When he was sunk in the depths of old age, he parted with his life in Crete, and went away to join the gods; and the Curetes and his sons tended and decked his corpse. His tomb exists in Crete in the town of Cnossus (a city which Vesta is said to have set up) and on the tomb is written in archaic Greek letters ZAN KPONOY, that is, in Latin, Jupiter Son of Saturn. (W 429)

It is difficult to know to what extent the sentiments expressed in the *Euhemerus* reflect Ennius' own views as opposed to those of the author he was translating or paraphrasing; but the mere fact that he chose to write such a work must suggest some sympathy with the iconoclastic views of the Greek philosopher. One final clue may be found in a fragment of the tragedy *Telamo* (on the Greek hero Telamon, who accompanied Jason and the Argonauts and was also involved in the Trojan War). One fragment states (in a speech of the title character): "For my part I have always said, will say, / There is a race of gods in heaven; and yet / They take no thought, it seems, how fares mankind; / for if they did care, it would go well with well-doers, but this, as things are, is not to be seen" (W 339, 341). This seems Epicurean, but in fact Epicurus did not attribute the gods' indifference to human affairs to this rationale, which suggests a wrestling with the "problem of evil"—a problem that even polytheism has difficulty contending with. But as this play is probably a translation or adaptation from a Greek original, and as the context of Telamon's remark is unclear, it is unwise to place too much emphasis on it.

I have mentioned that Livius Andronicus wrote the first known tragedy in Rome. Ennius wrote numerous tragedies, as did Naevius, Ennius' nephew, M. Pacuvius (220?–130?), and L. Accius (170–85?); but as no Roman tragedies prior to those of Seneca the Younger in the first century C.E. survive in their entirety, it is difficult to gauge their thrust and import. Overwhelmingly, they are on Greek mythological subjects. One of the few substantial fragments we have is from an unknown play by Pacuvius, where he ruminates on the nature of Chance (*Fortuna*):

> Dame Fortune, some philosophers maintain,
> Is witless, sightless, brutish; they declare
> That on a rolling ball of stone she stands;

> . . .
>
> But there are
> Other philosophers who against all this
> Deny that there is any goddess Fortune,
> Saying it is Chance Medley rules the world.
> That this is more like unto truth, in fact
> Practice doth teach us by the experience;
> Orestes thus, who one time was a king,
> Was one time made a beggar. (W 319)

I am not sure how much is to be made of this, aside from the obvious fact (which we shall see in other instances as well) that elementary philosophical conceptions and debates of this sort—is Fortuna an actual goddess or merely a convenience term for a concatenation of chance events?—were common even among the general populace of Rome. The deification of Fortuna (the Latin equivalent of the Greek Tyche) is one more indication of the pervasive influence of Greek culture on Rome at this time.

Of Roman comedy during this period, much more can be said. Naevius, most of whose dramatic work took the form of comedies, pioneered the *fabula praetexta* (plays on Roman historical subjects) as well as the *fabula togata* (plays on contemporary subjects), including one in which he sharply attacked the conqueror of Hannibal, Scipio Africanus—an act that caused Naevius to be imprisoned for a time. But most of the comedies written by Roman playwrights of this era are overwhelmingly in the form of the *fabula palliata* (plays on Greek historical and mythological subjects). And it is here that we encounter the first complete texts of a work of Latin literature, in the plays of Plautus.

Of the more than 100 plays written by T. Maccius Plautus (250?–184), twenty-one exist in complete or nearly complete form; and they provide a fascinating window into Roman popular culture. Plautus came from Umbria, and his first plays were probably written around 210; most of the surviving ones appear to date to the last decade of his life, after the Second Punic War was concluded. He was thoroughly versed in Greek, and his plays (as with the majority of others written down to the end of the Republic) were adaptations of the Greek New Comedy of

Menander and others. But in Plautus there is a liveliness, a vigorous use of racy language, and an overall exuberance (as exhibited in his manifest fondness for food, sex, and general good humour) that are clearly his own, for all that most of his characters and settings are Greek. There are, moreover, abundant examples of Roman life, customs, and language in his plays.

Our interest focuses on two plays in particular. The first is the *Mostellaria.* This play is generally translated as *The Haunted House* (from *mostellum,* a diminutive of *monstrum*); perhaps a more accurate, if clumsy, rendition would be "A Place Where a Strange Entity Appears to Exist." Of course, there is no ghost in the play; rather, the ghost is a fabrication by the clever slave Tranio as a means of distracting Theopropides, the father of the wastrel Philolaches, from becoming aware that his son has frittered away a great deal of money by purchasing the freedom of a fetching female slave and giving a succession of lavish parties. Tranio makes no secret of the fact that his purpose is to "frighten his [Philolaches'] father" (421).[15] The plan is to assert that the house has become haunted because its former owner had killed his guest—an appalling crime in Greco-Roman civilisation and one, therefore, that could plausibly (among the credulous, at any rate) engender the kind of haunting that Tranio is attempting to put over. What is more, Tranio maintains that the guest was actually buried in the house. This, in the slave's words, is what the spirit of the murdered guest told Philolaches:

> "Diapontius am I, a guest from o'er the sea. Here do I abide, this house is the abode allotted to me. For Orcus [a god of the underworld] hath denied me entrance into Acheron, I having been cut off before my time. I trusted, and I was betrayed. Here was I murdered by my accursed host, for the sake of gold, and in this very house did he give me secret, unhallowed burial. Hence with you now! Accursed is this house, 'tis a defiled abode!" (497–504)

All this sounds plausible enough, but the charade collapses very quickly.

The "haunted house" element in the *Mostellaria* comprises a small element of the plot, but to the extent that it is the catalyst for the

15. I use the translation of Paul Nixon.

entire scenario it can be considered significant enough. The fear that Theopropides—in spite of his initial scepticism of the ghost's appearance to Philolaches in a dream (his repeated queries, "In his sleep?" [*in somnis?*] suggest that he is initially inclined to interpret the dream merely as a dream and not as a spectral occurrence)—occasionally exhibits is meant to suggest nothing more than his own credulousness. The manner in which the ghostly phenomena are made the butt of jest suggests a degree of scepticism in even the more uncultivated members of his audience that argues for a substantial level of doubt among the Roman public as a whole as to the reality of supernatural phenomena.

Still more interesting, from our perspective, is the *Amphitryo* (probably staged around 195). The very premise of the play is a satire on some of the central conceptions of Greco-Roman religion—specifically, the role of Zeus (Jupiter) as "father of gods and men" and, as recorded in numerous myths, his inveterate penchant for bedding down with human women to produce demigods or heroes by them. In this case, Plautus addresses the well-known story of Zeus' seduction of Alcmene and the resultant birth of Herakles. In the prologue, Mercury outrageously refers to Jupiter as an "adulterer" (135: *moechus*) as he is lying with Alcmena in the guise of her husband, Amphitryon, who is off fighting the wars. The result is that Alcmena is pregnant with twins—one by her true husband, the other (Hercules) by Jupiter. Mercury himself is disguised as Amphitryon's slave, Sosia. The use of twins or doubles was very common in both Greek and Roman comedy (and is at the crux of Plautus' celebrated play *Menaechmi*), but having a pair of gods as the doubles of mortals is not at all usual.

Mercury, noticing that both Sosia and Amphitryon are about to return, now plans for various delaying tactics so that his father, Jupiter, can have a little more time for cuddling. When he presents himself to Sosia and claims to be the real Sosia, all manner of confusion occurs. When Amphitryon shows up and learns from his wife that she had been in bed with someone claiming to be her husband, he at once suspects her of infidelity, to which she responds with justifiable outrage. Toward the end of the play Jupiter appears in person, soothing things over between husband and wife and then ascending into the sky. The nurse Bromia had previously announced the miraculous birth of twins. Hercules is never mentioned by name in the play, but the audience would not be in any doubt that he was one of the twins.

The buffoonery of the *Amphitryo*—even though, exceptionally, Plautus himself (through Mercury) refers to it as a "tragi-comedy" (59: *tragicomoedia*)—is perhaps just on this side of impiety. After all, he is recounting a standard Greek myth, and Zeus/Jupiter's penchant for dalliance with comely human females was one of his best-known attributes. Let us recall that some Greek philosophers had expressed doubt of the veracity of Greek myths precisely because they articulated a morality among the gods that would be regarded as unseemly if applied to human beings. But Plautus (whether he based his play on a Greek original or not) found in the scenario only the possibility of good-natured ribbing directed at the king of the gods.

One other play is of some interest. *Rudens* (The Rope) begins with a prologue from Arcturus, who identifies himself both as a star and a god. He states that Jupiter has sent him and others down to earth to gauge the moral actions of human beings and report back to Jupiter, who will somehow punish them. But the actual course of the play—which involves a young woman, Palaestra, who was sold into slavery as a child and is now on the verge of becoming a prostitute at the hands of a pimp, Labrax, but is ultimately rescued and reunited with her father, Daemones—is on a purely human level, with no intervention of the gods of any kind. True, Palaestra herself at one point blames the gods for her plight:

> Is it really the will of God that I should be cast on a strange shore in this pitiable plight and frightened so? Oh dear, oh dear! Am I to think that I was born for this? Is this my reward for trying my best to do right? Why, I can suffer this and not think it suffering, if I have sinned against a parent or against the gods. But if I have been careful as could be not to do so, then, gods, you are treating me unfittingly, unfairly, unjustly. For how will the guilty be marked out by you now, if this is the way you honour the innocent? (187–96)

But this seems a largely conventional lament over the injustice of her fate, as does Daemones' later attribution of a prophetic dream to the gods (594–95) and his thanking the gods for answering his prayers (1191f.).

It is true enough, as Anna Clark has asserted, that "the wide range of ways in which gods are engaged with in the comedies [of Plautus], from being embedded in everyday vocabulary to specific appeals for divine aid," points to the fact that "Divinities and the divine were integral to the context and content of much of the work of Plautus in particular."[16] But the rollicking irreverence with which Plautus treats these elements suggests, at a minimum, a liberality in what was permissible in works of this sort. After all, these plays appeared as part of public festivals or athletic contests, all devoted to a specific god or set of gods; and while the lampooning of gods or other aspects of Roman religion was not as flamboyant as that of, say, Aristophanes, it does not in any way suggest an intolerant piety whereby such depictions would be considered blasphemous or sacrilegious.

The other dramatist whose plays are extant—Terence (P. Terentius Afer, 185?–159?)—is of little interest in this context. Aside from the fact that his six surviving plays are all adapted from Greek originals, they exhibit few traces of scepticism regarding divine matters. Terence gains importance entirely from a literary perspective, in that he wrote in a pure and elegant Latin diction that, while considerably less entertaining than the rambunctiousness of Plautus, presented a model for the artful use of Latin for literary purposes. In this sense he is a kind of Roman Jane Austen.

One other author who can be profitably studied here, although he is a frustratingly obscure figure in Latin literature, is C. Lucilius (d. 103 B.C.E.). The dates of his birth are wildly divergent, ranging from 180 to 148, and his work survives only in extensive fragments. His strictly literary significance resides in his invention of Roman satire. The word *satura* originally referred to a medley, as in *lanx satura* (a bowl of different kinds of fruit). We have seen that Livius Andronicus wrote *Saturae* of this sort. Initially Lucilius—who wrote at least thirty books of satires—wrote in various metres, but he eventually settled upon the hexameter (the metre of epic poetry) for the bulk of his satirical work.

Lucilius' satires are not entirely of the kind that we now associate with the term, although he did gain a reputation in antiquity for biting wit and personal attacks. While some of the extant fragments do point to a certain pungency of expression (the hallmark of later satirists such

16. Anna Clark, "Gods and Roman Comedy," in Dinter, *The Cambridge Companion to Roman Comedy* 228.

as Persius and, preeminently, Juvenal), other satires are of a milder sort, setting an example that Horace followed in his own writings, some of which were directly modelled upon Lucilius' examples. Some of his books of satires are on a single topic (e.g., sexual relations, women, even orthography); others broach a wide array of subjects.

Book XV of his satires is of some interest to us in that it apparently focused on philosophical issues and exhibits knowledge of prevailing Cynic and Stoic thought. One fragment in particular ridicules a man who is taken in by images of the gods:

> As for scarecrows and witches, which our Fauns and Numa Pompiliuses established—he trembles at them, and thinks them all-important. As baby children believe that all bronze statues are alive and are men, so these [superstitious adults] think the fictions of dreams are real, and believe that bronze statues have a living heart inside. These things are a painters' gallery, nothing real, all make-believe. (W 167)

This is perhaps not much to go on in pointing to Lucilius' scorn of religion; but it is worth adding that another substantial fragment, in which he offers moral advice to one Albinus, is wholly secular in its outlook: "virtue is knowing what is right and useful and honourable for a man" (W 393).

D. Philosophy in Early Rome

The Romans, with their genius for warfare and for political and military administration, as well as their adherence to the simple ideals of the farmer-citizen, did not take naturally to philosophical speculation; but they could hardly avoid exposure to the philosophical and religious (and anti-religious) theories emanating from the Greeks. A canonical moment in Roman civilisation was the arrival in 155 B.C.E. of three Greek philosophers to Rome—Carneades (an Academician), Diogenes of Babylon (a Stoic), and Critolaus (a Peripatetic). The purpose of their visit was to lobby the Roman Senate to intercede in a political dispute in Greece; but when they began giving lectures to the public, a furore resulted. Carneades in particular elicited outrage among the philosophically naïve Romans by arguing for one side of an argument on one day and the polar opposite the next day. This was something that had brought disrepute to philosophers since the days of the Sophists, but Carneades was intent on showing how any philosophical question can be cogently debated from multiple and at time antipodal perspectives, with the result that a resigned scepticism may be the only viable stance. It is of some note that Epicurean philosophers were not represented in the trio of philosophers. Two of them came the following year, but were promptly exiled by the Senate.

It was at this very time that a philosophical circle had grown around the figure of P. Cornelius Scipio Africanus Aemilianus (185–129; generally referred to as Scipio Aemilianus), the adoptive grandson of Scipio Africanus and a significant military and political figure in his own right. Among his colleagues was C. Laelius, whom Lucilius referred to as *Sapiens* (the Wise) and whom Cicero regarded as the first home-grown Roman philosopher. No writings of his survive.

At the moment, however, our attention can turn to a Greek member of the Scipionic circle—the historian Polybius (200?–118?). He had attained some prominence in his native Megalopolis; but when the Romans defeated Perseus of Macedon in 167, Polybius was one of a thousand noblemen who were taken to Rome as hostages. His learning quickly endeared him to Scipio Aemilianus and other intellectuals, and even after his release in 150 he remained in Rome, where he undertook a massive history of Rome from 264 to 146. Of the forty volumes he wrote, only the first five survive intact, with extensive fragments of the remainder.

What the *Histories* reveal is, in the first place, a notably scientific attitude toward the writing of history and, concomitantly, a strikingly secular attitude that entirely dispenses with the intervention of gods and other supernatural forces in human life. There is, for example, no evidence that Polybius accepted the fantastic early history of Rome—Aeneas, Romulus, and so on. It is true that his purpose was not to write a history *ab urbe condita;* but he had numerous opportunities to discuss these matters, and he refused to do so. There is even some (negative) evidence that he denied the divinity of the entire Greco-Roman pantheon. In any case, nothing in the surviving text suggests his belief in the Olympian gods. A lengthy passage (6.6–7) on the origin of morality among human beings—a preface to his description of the Roman constitution—is likewise wholly secular, anticipating the anthropologists of the eighteenth and nineteenth centuries who speculated on the "natural" origins of human society and government.

As a contrast to the liberal, and possibly irreligious, figures in the Scipionic circle we have the formidable presence of L. Porcius Cato (234–149), variously called Cato the Elder or Cato the Censor. As a representative of the dour, inflexible Roman of the old school, he is easily caricatured. He gained stature during the Second Punic War when, in military campaigns against Hannibal, he thundered, *Delenda est Carthago* ("Carthage must be destroyed"). (He would not live to see the actual destruction of the city in 146.) It is true that he was also vehemently opposed to the infusion of Greek culture into Rome, which he believed to be a corrupting influence on Roman morality and political culture. But it should be remembered that, as a result of the conquests Rome had made throughout the Mediterranean, Rome itself was becoming both thoroughly cosmopolitan and overflowing with wealth and luxury, and a certain moral laxity may actually have occurred.

The only extant work by Cato is the *De Agri Cultura* (on farming and related subjects). We would very much like to have his *Origines,* a seven-volume history of Rome from its founding to his own day. It is, however, likely to have reiterated the now canonical stories of Rome's origins under supernatural auspices. Cato heard the Greek philosophers of 155, and (as recounted in Plutarch's biography) he lobbied for them to be escorted out of the city. They were, in his judgment, dangerous subversives, from both a moral and a political perspective. But his fulminations went for naught, and Greek culture continued to infiltrate Rome.

One of the most significant figures of this period is Panaetius of Rhodes (185?–110?), a pupil of Diogenes of Babylon and one of the leading Stoic philosophers of his day. Coming to Rome around 146, he remained there until at least 129. Following the death of Scipio Aemilianus, he returned to Athens, where he had studied before coming to Rome. He and his own pupil, Posidonius (135?–51?), made major reforms in Stoic teaching, specifically regarding the soul. As a result, they are referred to as members of the Middle Stoa, in contrast to the Old Stoa of Cleanthes, Zeno, and Chrysippus. But because their work exists only in fragments, there is considerable difficulty in characterising the specifics of their views and their philosophical justification for them.

Because Panaetius and Posidonius, in consonance with earlier Stoic thinkers, regarded their philosophy as all of a piece, some examination of their metaphysics is essential to the understanding of their ethics and theology. Most notably, Panaetius denied or, at the very least, doubted the Stoic *ekpyrosis* (the periodic destruction of the universe by fire) and asserted the absolute eternity of the universe. It is possible that he was influenced in this view by the scepticism of Carneades. Once *ekpyrosis* is taken out of the equation, the human soul must be regarded as either entirely mortal or entirely immortal; and since Panaetius presumably maintained the standard Stoic doctrine of the material nature of the soul, he was compelled to believe in its mortality. The soul, like the body, can feel pain and fall into disease, hence must be mortal (see Cicero, *Tusculan Disputations* 1.79–80).

The end result of Panaetius' reforms is a focus on the moral condition of human beings in society (and, indirectly, government). Whereas the Old Stoa had a tendency to dismiss the concerns of the "striver after virtue" and focus only on the "wise man," Panaetius actively sought to smooth down some of the harsher aspects of Stoic ethics and make them more accessible to a popular audience—or, at least, to the burgeoning Roman intellectual and political class to whom they were apparently directed.

Posidonius was a widely travelled polymath who wrote on an impressive number of subjects, ranging from physics to astronomy to botany to anthropology and much else besides. But he reversed some of Panaetius' innovations by reasserting a belief in divination (which his teacher had overtly denied), and he reaffirmed Old Stoic teaching that the cosmos is governed by reason and providence.

It is clearly in the constitution of the soul that Posidonius makes his clearest break with Stoic tradition. Although Diogenes Laertius (7.157) states that Posidonius agreed with Zeno and Antipater in regarding the soul as *pneuma enthermon* (warm breath), Galen notes Posidonius' belief in various "powers" (*dynameis*) of the soul, and elsewhere labels the powers as appetitive, passionate, and rational (fr. 32). It is obvious that Posidonius is reverting to a Platonic theory here, but its motivation is not simply Posidonius' fondness for Plato, frequently noted in the tradition; rather, this division of the soul appears to have been derived from what Posidonius believed to be flaws in Chrysippus' account of the soul.

Posidonius' central query was how evil comes to be in the human being. Excessive emotions (*pathē*) cannot, according to Posidonius, be accounted for by the Old Stoic notion of the unitary soul, which recognised only rational powers in the soul: animals and children are given to such *pathē* as anger, and yet no Stoic would attribute rationality to them. If it were the case that we are impelled toward the good as soon as we are born, then evil must be some external force. But evil does not come from without, having no root (*riza*) in our own souls; on the contrary, there is a *sperma* of evil in us. Hence Posidonius stressed the need for teaching (by Stoics, one imagines) to inculcate good behaviour and elminate the seeds of evil.

On the vexed question of the immortality of the soul as envisioned by Posidonius, the sources do not provide any coherent answer, and it remains unclear whether he followed his teacher Panaetius in denying immortality. The extant fragments also fail to clarify whether either thinker retained the Old Stoic view of god. What can be said about Posidonius, however, is that, as a result of his wide-ranging studies in a number of disciplines, he apparently developed a kind of empiricist approach to the acquisition of knowledge that may have bled over into his understanding of human psychology and related areas.

E. Lucretius: The Exponent of Epicureanism

And now we come to Lucretius (T. Lucretius Carus, 99?–55? B.C.E.), the first authentically great literary figure in Rome (at least, among those whose work has survived roughly intact) and, perhaps, the only writer of classical Latin who exhibited philosophical acuity analogous to that of the greatest of Greek thinkers. His philosophic epic, *De Rerum Natura,* which exhaustively expounds the Epicurean philosophy, comes to us in six books, although it is possible that we lack a bit of the ending and perhaps some earlier sections.

It is therefore a tragedy that we know so little about him. Hundreds of years after his presumable death, the Christian writer Jerome wrote a one-paragraph biography that is probably nothing but a tissue of lies and errors—and is apparently an attempt (frequent in antiquity) to extrapolate biographical data from the author's literary work. Hence Jerome makes the ludicrous assertion that Lucretius "was driven mad by a love-philtre, after he had written several books in the intervals of insanity."[17] To write a work as philosophically cogent as *De Rerum Natura* would be quite an achievement even for one not struggling with intermittent insanity. The bit about the love-potion is obviously an allusion to Lucretius' warnings about sexual excess in Book 4 of his poem. Jerome goes on to say that "Cicero subsequently corrected these books" and that "Lucretius died by his own hand in the forty-fourth year of his life." Both of these assertions are overwhelmingly likely to be false.

The note about Cicero relates to the fact that Cicero is the one person among Lucretius' contemporaries who (as far as the extant literature is concerned) mentions him. In a letter to his brother Quintus dating to February 50, he writes: "The poems of Lucretius are as you say—with many flashes of genius, yet very technical" (2.9.4).[18] One suspects that, in the absence of this documentary evidence, there might be all manner of speculation as to whether Lucretius actually existed or—along the lines of the Shakespeare/Bacon controversy—whether he wrote the work attributed to him. But the *De Rerum Natura* manifestly influenced the subsequent Latin poetic tradition (Virgil, Horace, Ovid, and Manilius, among others, were clearly affected by it), although its influence on the Greco-Roman philosophical tradition up to the fall of Rome is less certain.

The poem opens resoundingly—and, perhaps, problematically:

> Aeneadum genetrix, hominum divumque voluptas,
> alma Venus, caeli subter labentia signa
> quae mare navigerum, quae terras frugiferentis
> copncelebras, per te quoniam genius omne animantum
> concipitur visitque exortum lumina solis. (1.1–5)

> Mother of the Aeneadae, delight of men and gods, nurturing Venus, who beneath the gliding signs of heaven fillest with thy presence the ship-carrying sea, the corn-bearing lands, since through thee every kind of living thing is conceived, rises up, and beholds the light of the sun.[19]

17. Quoted in Hadzsits, *Lucretius and His Influence* 5.
18. I use the translation of Evelyn S. Shuckburgh.
19. As before, I use the prose translation of H. A. J. Munro (1864), with some revisions of

This is problematic because it simultaneously invokes both the central principle of Epicurean philosophy, *hēdonē* (Latin *voluptas* ["delight" in the above passage], placed strategically at the end of the first line), and the actual goddess Venus. Generations of scholars have tortured themselves about this thunderous opening, but two points can be made.

There is no doubt that Lucretius is faithfully echoing orthodox Epicurean teaching on all the subjects he treats in his poem. The reverence with which Epicurus was held by both his immediate disciples and later followers (a reverence that, as we shall see presently, Lucretius unequivocally echoes), militates against any radical departure from the founder's principles. But let us recall that, contrary to hostile critics, Epicurus did acknowledge the existence of gods of some sort, and even sanctioned the worship of the Olympian pantheon, so long as this does not involve any degrading superstition. David Sedley has proposed that Lucretius is consciously harking back to Empedocles, whose poem *On Nature* opened with an invocation to Aphrodite as one of the two forces (Love and Strife) he maintained were the moving forces in the universe.[20] There is something to be said for this view (Empedocles was indeed a notable predecessor of Lucretius as a philosopher-poet), but there must surely be more going on here than that.

The very first word, *Aeneadum* ("the offspring of Aeneas"), cannot be accounted for by an appeal to the Greek philosopher. What Lucretius is maintaining is some minimal degree of independence from Epicurus—in other words, he will be a *Roman* writing for a Roman audience. To the extent that he is thereby acknowledging the myth that Rome was ultimately founded by a son of Venus, he appears to be sanctioning a belief he could not actually have accepted; but it is possible that through this exquisite evocation (literarily analogous to every other epic poet's evocation of a god, goddess, or muse to inspire his song) he hopes to lead his Roman audience from the conventional gods and myths to the reality of the Epicurean philosophy.

In any case, the *De Rerum Natura* is a thorough-going exposition of Epicurean doctrine, beginning with the theory of atoms and void (Books 1 and 2) and proceeding to the mortality of the soul (Book 3), sense-perception (Book 4), the origin of life on earth (Book 5), and

---

my own.

20. See Sedley, *Lucretius and the Transformation of Greek Wisdom* 22.

celestial phenomena (Book 6). Much of this material would not seem very amenable to elegant poetic treatment; and it is one of Lucretius' great accomplishments that he has both evolved a Latin philosophical language to treat these difficult subjects[21] and expressed it in some of the most gorgeous poetry in the entire corpus of extant Latin literature, his ringing hexameters (the standard metre of epic poetry) laced with archaism and also infused with his own passion for conveying the teachings of Epicurus to as wide an audience as possible.

For Lucretius' overall purpose is not an abstract portrayal of a philosophical system but the manifestly moral goal of banishing the fear of death and of vengeful gods from the human mind, so that it can attain the *ataraxia* (*tranquillitas* in Latin) that was the goal of Epicurus' teaching. In regard to the first, I have already noted how Lucretius lambastes the unphilosophical man who laments his lot after death, but fails to recognise that he will lack any consciousness to perceive such a fate. His treatment of the gods—both the "true" Epicurean gods and the false gods of conventional religion—deserves more exhaustive discussion.

We are, however, faced with the difficulty that such a discussion is largely absent from the *De Rerum Natura.* After a brief exposition of the nature of the Epicurean gods (5.146–54), Lucretius states, "All which I will prove to you later in copious argument" (155). But he never does so. This may be one indication that Lucretius never put the finishing touches on his poem prior to his death; but perhaps an alternative view could be asserted, and this relates to his compelling account of the origin of life—especially of human life—on earth, which fills much of the end of Book 5.

This passage has evoked extensive discussion among scholars as to whether Lucretius is a "primitivist" or a "progressivist"—that is, does he vaunt primitive people on the basis of their simplicity and general absence of religion, or does he (in anticipation of Thomas Hobbes) condemn them as crude, uncivilised, and ignorant? A more nuanced view suggests that the passage in question (specifically *De Rerum Natura* 5.821–1457) articulates not two, but *three* stages of human society.[22] It

21. Sedley has made a convincing case that Lucretius' chief text was Epicurus' 37-book *Peri Physeos* (On Nature) rather than the highly compressed *Kyriae Doxai* (Basic Doctrines) or any other surviving works.

22. For a more detailed account of this theory, see "The Three Stages of Man in Lucretius" in

is apparent that Lucretius' overall purpose in outlining the history of humanity is (a) to present a "natural" origin and development of human life and society, dispensing either with a Platonic lawgiver or (as in his account of the discovery of fire) with a godlike figure out of Greek myth such as Prometheus. But if this were Lucretius' only purpose, then there would have been no need for him to make such sharp and frequent comments upon the moral virtues and failings of his various stages of humanity. There is manifestly a second purpose—perhaps subordinate to the major one just outlined—and this is to show the proper way of life for human beings.

The primitive stage of life (beginning at 5.925) is full of woe and misery, and there is little justification for thinking that Lucretius found this stage preferable to others, in spite of its absence of religious belief. Primitive people are frequently compared to beasts; they are ignorant of agriculture; their food is "rough" (*durus*) and fit for the wretched; they did not know of fire, lacked clothing, and lacked the social contract; their love was uncontrolled, they suffered horrible deaths at the hands of beasts, and they lacked medicine to cure their ills. But in contrast we find many admirable traits in primitive people: their bodies were stronger and larger than ours, they were less affected by the elements, and their wants were simple. Although they sometimes died of starvation, there was no organised warfare to compare with modern times. Most importantly, they lacked the empty fear that the sun might not rise in the morning. This total lack of superstition by savages (in opposition, it hardly need be said, to the modern anthropologist's view of primitive peoples) forms a telling contrast to the religiosity that developed during the third or political stage of man.

The second stage is heralded by the discovery of many of the advantages of life that the first stage lacked: people now live in houses, they have clothing, they have discovered fire, they have learned friendship (a critical element in Epicurean ethics), which leads to the formation of the social contract; they have discovered love, which leads to marriage and the propagation of children; they have learned to pity the weak, and, of course, have discovered language. Here we can see a step-by-

---

my *Classical Papers*. Nichols (*Epicurean Political Philosophy* 122f.) does articulate the three stages, using the terms "primitive," "pre-political," and "political." Although my views differ significantly from his, I shall adopt his terms here.

step reversal of all the negative aspects of primitive man. The notable discovery of agriculture (and also music) leads to a paean to the beauties and pleaures of the rustic countryside, which have endured to Lucretius' own day (5.1370–78). E. J. Kenney has plausibly maintained that this is very probably a description of the Italian countryside as actually seen by Lucretius.[23]

As we advance to the third or political stage, we find that everything has gone wrong. This stage is typified not merely by the building of cities (*urbis* 1108) and citadels to protect kings, but by a restlessness that may be an example of the *cupido* (greed) so condemned at the close of the sixth book. Contemporary people are beset by boredom in spite of their lavish houses and the gold that they have only now discovered. The worst, however, is yet to come. Religion now raises her head for the first time:

> And now what cause has spread over great nations the worship of the divinities of the gods and filled towns with altars and led to the performance of stated sacred rites, rites now in fashion on solemn occasions and in solemn places, from which even now is implanted in mortals a shuddering awe which raises new temples of the gods over the whole earth and prompts men to crowd them on festive days, all this is not so difficult to explain in words. (5.1161–68)

The emergence of religion is attributed to the false inferences of the mind as depicted in Book 4, especially a passage on the deceptive quality of dreams (4.453–68). Another cause of religious belief was failure to understand the workings of the heavens. All this leads to a bitter condemnation of humanity:

> O hapless race of men, when that they charged the gods with such acts and coupled with them bitter wrath! What groanings did they then beget for themselves, what wounds for us, what tears for our children's children! No act is it of piety to be often seen with veiled head to turn to a stone and approach every altar and fall prostrate on the ground and spread out the palms before the statues of the gods and sprinkle the altars with much blood of beasts and link vow on to vow, but rather

23. Kenney, *Lucretius* 34–35.

to be able to look on all things with a mind at peace. (5.1194–203)

It is here that Lucretius' morality, theology, and anthropology unite. It is, of course, unlikely that he was departing notably from Epicurean teaching on this subject, although it is unfortunate that Epicurus' own anthropological theories are among the poorest preserved passages among his extant fragments. But even if Lucretius is not propounding anything truly new here, there are abundant evidences that he is drawing upon his Roman heritage to present an Epicurean outlook suitable for his native audience.

Whether there is anything problematical about Lucretius' increasingly ardent paeans to his mentor, culminating in the assertion that Epicurus was himself a god (5.8), is unclear. This occurs in the proem to Book 5, where he appeals to his patron, C. Memmius (a praetor in 58), to compare Epicurus' achievements with those of other benefactors of humanity. The passage may be no more than poetic exaggeration or an excess of enthusiasm, although there is some evidence that Epicurus was in fact regarded as a deity by his own followers.

But the glory of the *De Rerum Natura* lies in its seamless melding of philosophical profundity and the loftiest poetic expression yet known in Latin literature. Its immediate influence upon the Greco-Roman philosophical tradition may have been relatively slight, given that Epicureans were not popular in an empire that increasingly favoured Stoic thinking; but his exhaustive exposition of Epicurean thought proved immensely influential in the Renaissance and afterward, given that by then Epicurus' own writings had largely disappeared, leaving the *De Rerum Natura* the chief means by which his doctrines could be understood. And in that task of elucidation Lucretius has performed his task impeccably.

Lucretius' almost exact contemporary, Catullus (C. Valerius Catullus, 84?–54? B.C.E.), is a poet of a very different order, but he too raised Latin poetry to heights of aesthetic expression never seen before. In the chronicling of his love affair with a married woman, Lesbia (probably to be identified with Clodia, wife of the proconsul Q. Caecilius Metellus Celer), he utilises an explicitness (at times extending into obscenity) and an emotional openness that give his poetry a very modern cast. These poems manifestly have little in the way of religious import; if anything, they indicate that religious scruples counted for little where Catullus' sexual behaviour was concerned. Any reference to the gods in these poems seems purely formulaic:

> Oh ye great gods! if you can pity feel,
> If e'er to dying wretch your aid was given,
> See me in agony before you kneel,
> To beg this curse may from me far be driven. (76.17–20)[24]

A hymn to Diana (34) is a pretty little poem to the virgin goddess, but does not seem imbued with genuine religious feeling. Numerous other poems about the gods (including a charming retelling of the myth of Ariadne and Theseus [64], a poem on Berenice's hair [66], and so on) seem more like exercises in poetic expression or even translation, as some of them are adapted from Catullus' Greek mentor, Callimachus.

Much more can be said about the famous Attis poem (63). Written in a strange metre for which there is no parallel in the entirety of extant Latin poetry, it tells the grim tale of how Attis, son and lover of the great mother of the gods, Cybele, was driven to frenzy by love for her and sliced off his own testicles with a flint. The poem was written not long after Catullus visited Phrygria (c. 57), where he might have seen the rites devoted to Cybele in person. There is every reason to believe that this poem is a warning on the dangers of religious fanaticism. The protagonist is likely to have been, as Sir James George Frazer observed long ago, not the legendary Attis, "but one of his ordinary priests, who bore the name and imitated the sufferings of his god."[25] It is of some interest that Lucretius devotes a passage to Cybele (*De Rerum Natura* 2.600–660), although the likelihood of influence one way or the other is remote. Whatever the import of the poem, we can all agree that, because of its unusual metre and subject-matter, it remains (as W. Y. Sellar wrote) "the most remarkable poetical creation in the Latin language."[26]

Then there is Catullus' poignant poem on the death of his brother. It is difficult to find any reference to an afterlife in this brief elegy; indeed, the expression "silent ashes" (*mutam . . . cinerem:* 101.4) suggests the

24. I use the translation of Theodore Martin.
25. Frazer, *The Golden Bough* 5.270n.
26. See Sellar, *Roman Poets of the Republic* 461.

very reverse. Its heartrending final line, *atque in perpetuum, frater, ave atque vale* ("And in perpetuity, my brother, hail and farewell")[27] raises a question as to what the exact signification of *in perpetuum* might be. I read it as an expression of the eternity of Catullus' grief rather than any allusion to his brother's continued existence after death.

F. Cicero: Sceptical Critic of Epicureans and Stoics

In discussing philosophical or religious thought during the first century B.C.E., there is no escaping the dominant presence of Cicero (M. Tullius Cicero, 106–43). The significant position he occuped during the last decades of the Republic, and the high regard in which his philosophical writing—in spite of its largely derivative nature—was held for the next millennium and a half or more require that he and his work be discussed in detail.

Philosophy remained a consuming interest for Cicero from his earliest years. In 88 he came under the influence of Philo of Larissa, an Academician, and through Philo he absorbed the scepticism of Carneades. Posidonius and other Stoic philosophers also left an impression on Cicero, but through the whole of his life he heaped scorn upon the Epicureans.

But from 81 onward, it was political activity that chiefly defined Cicero's life and career. As a lawyer, he argued numerous private and public cases; many of his orations are extant. He held numerous offices during the turbulent years from 75 to 62, attaining the lofty rank of consul in 63. It was at this time that he helped to foil a plot by Catiline (L. Sergius Catilina) to overthrow the government—and his four orations on the subject augmented his already formidable reputation as a public speaker, even if they incline toward an unseemly bombast and self-aggrandisement. Without going into the fearsome complexities of his involvement in the Civil War, we can simply say that Cicero chose to side with the senatorial faction against Julius Caesar; and although he had no direct hand in Caesar's assassination in 44, his falling out with Mark Antony and Octavian resulted in his being declared an enemy of the state. He was captured while attempting to flee from his villa in

27. This is my literal translation.

Formiae and summarily executed.

Cicero's high reputation as a prose stylist has resulted in the preservation of a wide array of his writings, from orations to treatises on rhetoric and even to an extensive corpus of letters. His numerous philosophical writings were largely written during the period of his enforced exile or political quiescence (46–43 B.C.E.). Even more than Lucretius, his treatises established a Latin philosophical vocabulary that was used by Western thinkers for the next millennium and a half or more, and it is largely through these works that the doctrines of Plato, the Stoics, and the Epicureans were transmitted to thinkers in the Middle Ages and Renaissance.

Our chief concern will be with the *De Natura Deorum* (On the Nature of the Gods), written in 45. The structure of this three-book work is straightforward: in Book 1, C. Velleius (a senator) articulates the Epicurean theology and is pungently rebutted from the Academic (sceptic) perspective by C. Aurelius Cotta, another senator who became consul in 75. Book 2 is an elaborate exposition of Stoic theology by Q. Lucilius Balbus (of whom little is known), with Book 3 constituting a rebuttal of that position by Cotta.

It becomes plain that Cicero's hostility to the entire Epicurean system results in a weak and distorted presentation of Epicurus' theories on the gods. Incredibly, he does not seem to have drawn upon Lucretius at all in this work (or in any other of his philosophical treatises), even though it is hard to imagine him not being impressed with the strength of that poet's arguments. But we can see from an early stage where Cicero's own predilections lie. Speaking in his own voice, he declares that, if we accept the Epicurean view that the gods have no concern for human beings and are in no way involved in human affairs, "how can we show devotion to the gods, or have a sense of the holy or of religious obligation? All such chaste and scrupulous acknowledgement of the divine power is pointless unless the gods take notice of it, and unless the immortal gods make some acknowledgement to the human race" (1.3).[28] Cotta articulates an analogous criticism: "Piety means giving the gods their due; but what religious law can we follow, when humans and gods have no common bond? Religious observance is expertise in divine worship, but I fail to

28. I use the translation of P. G. Walsh.

understand why the gods should be worshipped if we neither obtain nor anticipate any blessing from them" (1.116). This comes dangerously close to a transactional view of deity: if human beings can't derive any benefit from the gods, what's the point of worshipping them?

Cotta goes out of his way to attack other elements of Epicurean philosophy, even those that have only a tangential relation to theology. He flatly denies the existence of atoms (1.65); if atoms existed, that would render the gods mortal, "for what is formed from atoms came into being at some time" (1.68). Cotta also evokes much merriment at the notion of the supposed Epicurean theory of the anthropomorphism of the gods; but we have seen that the evidence that Epicurus himself advocated such a theory is highly debatable, even if later Epicureans (among them Philodemus [110?–40?]) undoubtedly did so. Using a kind of rudimentary anthropology, he notes that "Egyptians, Syrians, and virtually all the uncivilized world do not envisage gods in this way; you can observe that they maintain more passionate beliefs in the divinity of certain animals than we manifest in our most hallowed shrines and statues of the gods" (1.81).

But on two points Cotta's criticism against Epicurus ends up *proving too much*—that is, it presents arguments against the idea of godhead altogether, not merely the Epicurean gods. This was no doubt unintentional, for in other texts (for which see below) he makes clear his own belief in deities of some sort. But in taking on Epicurus' contention that belief in the gods is justifed by the argument from consensus, Cotta simply denies its force:

> You advanced, as a sufficiently compelling proof for us to acknowledge the existence of gods, that persons of all communities and nations believe it to be so. But this argument is not merely unsubstantial in itself, but also untrue. To begin with, what is the source of your knowledge of the beliefs of nations? My own opinion is that many races are so monstrously barbarous that they entertain no suspicion that gods exist. (1.62)

He goes on to note that Diagoras, as well as one Theodorus of Cyrene (fl. c. 340 B.C.E.), openly advocated atheism (1.63), and that Protagoras had expressed grave uncertainty as to whether gods existed or not. (Cicero in his own voice had made this same assertion at the very beginning of his treatise [1.2].) As I have already argued, a single exception to the "argument from consensus" causes that argument to collapse.

Even more strikingly, Cotta openly asserts that belief in gods may have been culturally induced:

> To begin with, was anyone ever so blind in his survey of realities as not to see that these human shapes have been ascribed to the gods for one of two possible reasons? Either some strategy of philosophers sought to divert more easily the minds of the unsophisticated from debased living towards observance of the gods; or superstition ensured that statues were furnished for men to worship in the belief that they were addressing the gods themselves. Poets, painters, sculptors have nurtured these attitudes, because it was not easy to preserve the impression that gods were active and creative if they were represented by non-human shapes. (1.77)

This may well be the first extant instance of such an argument. It is true that Cotta's remarks are specifically directed toward the anthropomorphism of the gods, but the criticism has wider force than this.

Cotta concludes with the definitive statement that Epicurus, "in refusing to allow the gods to accord help and favour to men, has wholly uprooted religion from human hearts" (1.121), and he repeats a statement attributed to Posidonius' treatise *On the Nature of the Gods* that Epicurus was a closet atheist "and that the statements which he made affirming the immortal gods were made to avert popular odium" (1.123). It is a view that had a long history in Western thought.

Cicero's treatment of Stoic theology is considerably more extended—and charitable—than his account of the Epicurean view, but Cotta's criticisms in Book 3 are no less destructive. After examining many of the Stoic arguments in support of a deity, Cotta remarks, "So your explanation up to this point, Balbus, does not convince me that gods exist. In fact, I believe that they do, but Stoics do not prove it" (3.15). Cicero's criticisms appear to be based on the work of Carneades and prove to be quite devastating. Stoic assertions that the regularity of the motion of the heavenly bodies is a sign of divinity is countered by the assertion that this regularity is the product of nature, not of God (3.23–24). In any event, if the sun, moon, and stars are divine, why wouldn't other celestial or meteorological phenomena—the rainbow, clouds, storms, and so on—be similarly divine (3.51.f)? Regrettably, Cotta's criticisms of the key Stoic claims that the universe is governed by divine providence and that the gods do concern themselves with human affairs, and indeed that they have arranged all entity for the benefit of humanity, are lost; but he perhaps unwittingly follows Lucretius (although in fact the argument is self-evident) when he states, "what benefit, I ask, can be observed in mice or cockroaches or snakes, all of them troublesome and destructive to the human race?" (3.65). And Cotta strikingly anticipates David Hume and others by maintaining that the Stoics will have to give up one of their two contentions about God: either God is not omnipotent, or he is not benevolent:

> Either God wishes to remove evils and cannot, or he can do so and is unwilling, or he has neither the will nor the power, or he has both the will and the power. If he has the will but not the power, he is a weakling, and this is not characteristic of God. If he has the power but not the will, he is grudging, and this is a trait equally foreign to God. If he has neither the will nor the power, he is both grudging and weak, and is therefore not divine. If he has both the will and the power (and this is the sole circumstance appropriate to God), what is the source of evils, or why does God not dispel them? (3.65)

Once again, Cicero seems unaware that this criticism undermines belief in a deity altogether. So too does Cotta's relentless expression of the "problem of evil": if (as Stoics contend) human beings are endowed with reason, why are a distressing number of them also endowed with malice? Why do bad things happen to good people, and why do bad people prosper? Cotta concludes, "there is certainly no divine governance in the universe, in so far as it is directed towards men, if no distinction is made in it between persons who are good and those who are evil" (3.85).

After all this, Cicero's own equivocal statement, at the very end of the treatise, that "in my eyes Balbus' case seemed to come more closely to a semblance of the truth" (3.95), doesn't amount to much.

The treatise *De Divinatione* (On Divination), written in 44, is—as

J. P. F. Wynne has established[29]—a follow-up to *De Natura Deorum* and must be read in conjunction with it. There is no need to examine its arguments in detail. Book 1 exhibits Cicero's brother Quintus arguing in support of the truth of divination from a Stoic perspective (necessarily so, since the Stoics' views on fate and on divine providence compelled a belief in the possibility of predicting the future by such means), while in Book 2 Cicero himself articulates strong arguments against divination. But it is to the conclusion of the work that our interest extends, for Cicero attempts to make a distinction between religion and superstition as a justification for his condemnation of divination (which he believes to be a facet of the latter):

> But I want it distinctly understood that the destruction of superstition does not mean the destruction of religion. For I consider it the part of wisdom to preserve the institutions of our forefathers by retaining their sacred rites and ceremonies. Furthermore, the celestial order and the beauty of the universe compel me to confess that there is some excellent and eternal Being, who deserves the respect and homage of men. (2.148)[30]

This all sounds straightforward; but the difficulty comes in how one can make such distinctions in any given religion. Cicero was fully aware that divination and other "superstitious" elements were endemic to Roman religion, as he himself notes in condemning the interpretation of dreams, soothsaying, astrology, omens (bolts of lightning, etc.), and the like (2.149). Cicero is, inevitably, facing the age-old problem of "purifying" religion of such irrational elements, but cannot face the dilemma of whether anything substantive is left at the end of the process. And his assertion about the "celestial order and the beauty of the universe" (*pulchritudo mundi ordoque rerum caelestium*) justifying belief in God is a curious backtracking from the refutation of exactly such a view in *De Natura Deorum.*

Cicero acknowledges that he himself is an Academician (*De Natura Deorum* 1.11), and he recognises that one of the hallmarks of the (current) Academician methodology is to withhold judgment on

29. See Wynne, *Cicero on the Philosophy of Religion*, esp. chs. 4–6.
30. I use the translation of William Armistead Falconer.

matters that have evoked so many varied opinions by philosophers (1.1). If, however, we are to ascertain Cicero's own views on certain key questions regarding gods, the soul, and the afterlife, we do not have far to go. *Tusculan Disputations,* written in 45, is a treatise whose purpose Cicero asserts is the dispelling of the fear of death. It need hardly be said that he does not adopt the Epicurean view that the soul is mortal and that therefore there is no consciousness to perceive the fact of one's non-existence. Instead, he adopts a fusion of Stoic and Platonic views in his conception of the soul, asserting that it is made up of "ignited air" (1.18; an adaptation of the *pneuma enthermon* of the Stoic Panaetius) but going on to indulge in a flight of fancy in which he depicts the soul rising up into "the heavenly regions" (1.21). This conception is vastly elaborated upon in another work, the *Somnium Scipionis* (The Dream of Scipio), a part of the otherwise fragmentary work *De Republica,* which in manifestly Platonic terms envisions a universe made up of nine celestial spheres, describes the music of the spheres, and so on.

In both these works, Cicero argues that the soul is both eternal and divine (or part of the divine). His argument relies on Pythagoras' and Plato's contentions on the acquisition of knowledge. He is amazed at the very existence of such a thing as memory and cannot imagine how it functions except by a belief in metempsychosis. But if this were the case (i.e., if knowledge, and hence memory of that knowledge, is derived from the soul's acquisition of information in a past life), would that not lead to an infinite regress? But this is what Cicero apparently believes:

> Believe me, then, you are a god—if indeed a god is the force that lives and feels in us, that remembers and foresees, that rules, governs, and moves the body over which it presides, even as the supreme deity yonder rules this world. And as nothing sort of an eternal deity quickens the world which has an element of mortality in it, so an eternal spirit quickens your brittle frame. (*Somnium Scipionis* 10)[31]

But once again, in some of his criticisms Cicero unwittingly undermines both this position and the entire belief in the existence of a soul. In criticising the Epicureans, he pointedly asks where the soul is in

---

31. I use the translation of James A. Kleist.

the body: "I would ask those who say that they cannot understand the soul without the body, to consider what they understand the soul to be in the body" (*Tusc. Disp.* 1.22).[32] Exactly! The problem is that this criticism applies as well to the Stoics, who also asserted that the soul is material—and also failed to come up with an answer as to where exactly in the body the soul might reside. The logical conclusion to this deficiency is stated bluntly by Cicero: "It must be borne in mind that if we are incapable of understanding the nature of what we have never seen, we can form no idea of God himself and of the divine soul which has no body" (*Tusc. Disp.* 1.22). Cicero goes on to make the standard arguments that, without belief in an afterlife, people will have no incentive to do anything; they shall certainly not seek "death with glory" (1.49).

That comment may point to Cicero's overall theological purpose. His criticism of Epicurus rested upon many bases, but chief of them is his utter distaste for Epicurus' quietist perspective, embodied in the pungent aphorism, "Live unknown." For a man who spent the great majority of his life in the public sphere, and who (if we are charitable) did not pursue public honours merely for self-aggrandisement but passionately believed in the ability of the state (both in its military and its political aspects) to benefit the people, such a view would be anathema. This outlook coloured the totality of his ethical and theological views. In the *De Finibus* (On Moral Ends) he scorns Epicurus' reduction of the standard virtues (honour, courage, and so on) to pleasure: "Believe me . . . we are born for higher and nobler things" (2.113).[33] It is significant that, in the *Somnium Scipionis,* he states plainly that "all those who save, aid, or extend their country have a definite place set apart for them in Heaven, where they may enjoy eternal life and happiness" (4). And later: "Life spent in the service of one's country is a direct passport to Heaven" (5). Similarly, in *De Natura Deorum* Cicero states bluntly: "Rome never could have achieved such greatness without the supreme benevolence of the immortal gods" (3.6).

It is therefore scarcely a surprise that in *De Legibus* (On the Laws), his approximate counterpart to Plato's *Laws,* Cicero wishes to found a nation's laws on the basic principle that human beings were created by a higher power that itself created the universe; therefore, laws must be

32. I use the translation of Andrew P. Peabody.
33. I use the translation of Raphael Woolf.

founded upon religious belief. The only mercy is that the laws Cicero actually proposes do not as a rule exact dire punishments for violations of religious or moral principles.

There is some reason to believe that the works of Cicero, like those of Plato and Aristotle before him, were preserved to such an extent precisely because Christian thinkers saw in him yet another *anima naturaliter Christiana.* The *Somnium Scipionis* was, indeed, preserved because the fifth-century writer Macrobius wrote a Neoplatonic commentary on it. But Cicero's theological views also reflect the beliefs of many of the intellectual, military, and political leaders of the Roman Republic (and, to a lesser extent, the Empire) in its tight fusion of history, religion, the state, and the morality that is required for their maintenance.

G. The Augustan Age

Octavius' defeat of his opponents at Actium led to the Senate bestowing upon him the titles *Princeps* and *Augustus.* Both were terms full of heavy and complex symbolism, signifying his dominance in the government. *Princeps* simply means "first," but it essentially indicated his superiority to the Senate; *Augustus* (meaning, approximately, "the revered one") was a term that had significant religious overtones. But, although he also adopted the name Caesar to signify his connexion to the ancient Julian line, he wisely resisted taking on the trappings of kingship that had led to Julius Caesar's assassination. He also accepted the title of *pontifex maximus* (an office that Julius Caesar had held), but only after the current holder, M. Aemilianus Lepidus (89–12 B.C.E.), died.

In the military front, Augustus had much work to do. During his reign, the Romans added extensively to their already vast empire, including extensive portions of central and eastern Europe (the provinces of Dalmatia, Raetia, Pannonia, Noricum, and others), the entirety of Asia Minor (Galacia, Cappadocia), Egypt, Mauretania (the northern coast of western Africa), and others.

But Augustus recognised that relieving the political and social chaos in Rome and Italy were among his chief priorities. He may have engaged in the fiction of "restoring" the Republic by allowing consulships and other offices to be held by others, but it is not likely that many were deceived. Caesar himself was responding to increasing calls for authoritarian rule to stem the turmoil of the Civil War; it is simply that Augustus handled the matter more deftly.

And religion was a central means by which he did so. He rebuilt many temples and filled many priesthoods that had been left empty during the later years of the Civil War. He consciously advocated the notion of a new golden age of Roman greatness, simultaneously promoting the worship of both Apollo (in his healing functions as well as in his role as the god of peace and civilisation) and Mars (as god of "just" wars and as the father of Romulus—where once again we see the fusion of religion, history, and nationalism). The yearning for a new age is poignantly etched in the fourth eclogue of Virgil, published between 44 and 38 B.C.E. Expressing a hope that borders on wishful thinking, it speaks of a boy who will transform the world:

> Justice returns, returns old Saturn's reign,
> With a new breed of men sent down from heaven.
> Only do thou, at the boy's birth in whom
> The iron shall cease, the golden race arise,
> Befriend him, chaste Lucina; 'tis thine own
> Apollo reigns.[34]

Augustus laid the groundwork for his subsequent deification. In 29 he ordered Julius Caesar to be regarded as divine; subsequently he referred to himself as *Divi filius* ("son of the god"). Augustus well knew that, as we have seen, the deification of human beings—especially kings and other important heads of state or military figures—was a widespread tendency in the cultures of the eastern Mediterranean, so his suggestion that he be declared a god after his death was relatively uncontroversial. The Senate made the decree soon after Augustus' death, also decreeing the construction of a Temple of Augustus in Rome; but that structure was not completed for several decades.

Not entirely by design, the reign of Augustus coincided with the greatest flowering of Latin literature in the history of Rome. While several of the major figures—Virgil (P. Vergilius Maro, 70–19 B.C.E.), Horace (Q. Horatius Flaccus, 65–8 B.C.E.), Livy (T. Livius, 59? B.C.E.–17?

34. I use the translation of J. B. Greenough.

C.E.), and Ovid (P. Ovidius Naso, 43 B.C.E.–17? C.E.)—were born during the latter stages of the Republic, they all contributed to the spiritual and aesthetic renewal that Augustus hoped to foster.

Of Virgil, much may be said. He was born near Mantua, in Cisalpine Gaul. A long biographical tradition asserts that he lost his family farm as a result of appropriations of land made by Octavian following the Battle of Philippi (42 B.C.E.), in which the assassins of Julius Caesar were defeated; that he appealed to Octavian for the restoration of his property; and that, when Octavian relented, Virgil delivered an encomium to him as a "god" in the first eclogue (1.6–10). But this entire attempt to draw biographical information from works of poetry has now come under severe criticism, and there is little evidence that any of it occurred.

What we do know is that, after publishing the *Eclogues* (a group of ten short pastoral poems modelled upon those of Theocritus, although with abundant details about Italian country life) around 38 B.C.E., Virgil went on to write four *Georgics*—lengthy poems chiefly about agriculture (planting of crops, tending of livestock, and so on), infused with poignant philosophical reflections about the relation of human beings to the soil. These poems were written under the patronage of C. Clinias Maecenas (70–8 B.C.E.), a well-known equestrian and friend of Octavian who did much to foster poetry in the Augustan age. The *Georgics* were written chiefly between 37 and 29 B.C.E.

Virgil's work on his national epic, the *Aeneid,* occupied the remainder of his life. This composition—the greatest poem ever written in Rome and one of the hallmarks of world literature—was left in a slightly incomplete state upon the poet's death, but its twelve books chronicle with exquisite power and emotive force the flight of Aeneas from Troy after its overthrow by the Greeks, his visit to the Carthaginian queen Dido, and his abandonment of her as he goes on to Italy and lays the groundwork for the founding of Rome.

Scholars have long ago discarded the view that Virgil in the *Aeneid* was serving as some sort of propaganda minister for the Emperor Augustus. Indeed, we may find that the ultimate message of the poem is the very opposite of the triumphalism embodied in Book 6, where the shade of Anchises (Aeneas' father) articulates a noble and idealistic vision of Rome's future greatness.

The poem opens resoundingly:

Of arms I sing, and of the man who first
From Trojan shores beneath the ban of fate
To Italy and coasts Lavinian came,
Much tossed about on land and ocean he
By violence of the gods above, to sate
Relentless Juno's ever-rankling ire,
In war, too, much enduring, till what time
A city he might found him, and bear safe
His gods to Latium, whence the Latin race,
And Alba's sires, and lofty-towering Rome. (1.1–7)[35]

This, essentially, is the "plot" of the *Aeneid.* That pregnant phrase *fato profugus* (1.2; literally, "banished by fate") may be the most significant in the entire poem; for Virgil depicts Aeneas as repeatedly heeding, or being compelled to heed, the call of fate (stemming ultimately from the gods) to depart from his defeated homeland, attain a new homeland, and defend it against the local tribes already occupying it.

Every phase of this process is worth detailed study, but we can only touch upon a few highlights. The searing depiction of the Greek defeat of Troy—chiefly by the use of the Trojan horse—in Books 1 and 2 features countless elements of the gods' intervention in the human drama. Juno's wrath against the Trojans is balanced by Jupiter's consoling words to Venus (Aeneas' mother) regarding Rome's future glory:

"Then wars shall cease, the rugged times grow mild;
Hoar Faith, and Vesta, and Quirinus [= Romulus] then
Yoked with his brother Remus, shall give laws;
Grim-knot with bolts of iron, War's temple-gates
Shut fast shall be, while hellish Rage within
High on a grisly pile of arms, his hands
Brass-bound behind him with a hundred knots,
Shall roar terrific from blood-boltered mouth." (1.291–96)

That image of "hellish Rage" (*Furor impius*) being held at bay is worth keeping in one's memory.

35. I use the translation of James Rhoades. The lines numbers are those of the Latin text.

Aeneas is, indeed, *pius*—a descriptive applied to him on dozens of occasions throughout the poem. The term is so pregnant with meaning that it is difficult to specify all its ramifications. As Cyril Bailey wrote long ago:

> The root idea of *pius* and *pietas* seems to be harmony or conformity with the will of the gods, or, as the established State-religion puts it, conformity to the *ius divinum* [divine law]. . . . But from the outset—and certainly in Virgil's use—it is more than this, for it implies not only right action but also a right relation of man to god; it has a moral and even spiritual implication as well as a formal content.[36]

And when Venus, restraining her son from killing Helen, to whom Aeneas attributes chief responsibility for the destruction of his city, she allows him a horrific glimpse of the Olympian gods as the ultimate authors of Troy's downfall (2.604f.). Aeneas now realises he must leave Troy; but, although he manages to carry his father Anchises on his back, he loses track of his wife Creusa. Searching frantically for her, he encounters her ghost, who urges him to proceed on to Italy.

The poignant encounter with Dido (whom Venus fired with love of him) is the central episode whereby Aeneas must put aside personal considerations in order to fulfil his goal of founding Rome. But Virgil etches Dido's unrequited love with imperishable plangency, and her suicide is only the first of several instances whereby Virgil portrays the human costs inextricably tied with Aeneas' fated mission.

It is when, with the aid of the Cumaean Sibyl, Aeneas descends to the underworld in Book 6 to speak to the shade of his father (Anchises had died in Sicily, before Aeneas' forces reach Italy), that we hear of his prophecy of Rome's future greatness. These underworld scenes are largely based on Greek myth (chiefly Book 11 of the *Odyssey*), but we also find hideous personifications of human ills:

> Fronting the portal, even in Orcus' jaws,
> Grief and avenging Cares have made their bed;
> And pale Diseases house, and dolorous Eld,

36. Bailey, *Religion in Virgil* 79–80.

And Fear and Famine, counsellor of crime,
And loathly Want, shapes terrible to view,
And Death and Travail, and, Death's own brother, Sleep,
And the soul's guilty jous, and murderous War
Full on the threshold, and the iron cells
Of the Eumenides, and mad Discord, who
With blood-stained fillet wreaths her snaky locks. (6.273–81)

Aeneas sees the shade of Dido, but she refuses to speak to him. But in another area of the underworld Aeneas sees the famous war-dead. He soon comes upon Anchises, whom he tries to embrace, but his hands "closed upon nothing" (6.701). Anchises shows Aeneas visions of the future:

Lo! 'neath his [Romulus'] auspices yon glorious Rome
Shall bound, my son, her empire with the world,
Her pride with heaven, and with encircling wall
Clasp to her single heart the sevenfold hills,
Blest in a breed of heroes . . . (6.781–84)

Included in these visions is one of very recent date:

Here is Caesar [i.e. Augustus], there
The whole line of Iulus, that shall pass
One day beneath the mighty pole of heaven.
This, this the man so oft foretold to thee,
Caesar Augustus, a god's son,[37] who shall
The golden age rebuild through Latian fields
Once ruled by Saturn . . . (6.789–94)

The tableau culminates in the most famous lines in the poem:

"Others the breathing brass shall softlier mould,
I doubt not, draw the lineaments of life
From marble, at the bar plead better, trace
With rod the courses of the sky, or tell

37. This phrase (*divi genus* in Latin) alludes to the deification of Julius Caesar.

> The rise of stars: remember, Roman, thou,
> To rule the nations as their master: these
> Thine arts shall be, to engraft the law of peace,[38]
> Forbear the conquered, and war down the proud." (6.847–53)

If the *Aeneid* ended at Book 6, there would be a much stronger case that Virgil is merely engaging in a propagandistic effort to vaunt the military might of the Roman Empire (and the passage above undeniably etches Rome's keen sense of inferiority to the Greeks in matters of art, science, and other realms); but there are six more books of the *Aeneid,* and they paint a very different portrait of the morality of Rome's conquests.

Those six books (7–12) are not as intrinsically compelling as what went before, as they are chiefly chronicles of Aeneas' attempts to subdue the Italian tribes who continue to rebel against his dominance. The text focuses on Turnus, himself "goddess-born" (6.90) by virtue of being the son of the nymph Venilia (not quite as lofty, to be sure, as being the son of Venus), the grandson of Faunus (whom we have noted as an important Italian god of the countryside), and the brother of the nymph Juturna. Turnus' enmity against the Trojan is augmented by the fact that Latinus, king of Latium, has taken his daughter away from Turnus and bestowed her upon Aeneas; she will essentially become the mother of the Roman people. Turnus and his allies wage ferocious battle against Aeneas' forces; but, in a dramatic single combat between the two warriors, Aeneas subdues Turnus. Turnus begs Aeneas for mercy. Aeneas is inclined to grant it; but when he sees the belt of Pallas (a friend of his whom Turnus had killed) on his foe's person, he is inflamed with rage:

> So saying, with fiery force he plunged the steel
> Full in his bosom. Then the warrior's limbs
> Grow chilled and slackened, and the spirit flies
> Moaning indignant to the shades below. (12.950–52)

That is the end of the epic. A more chilling conclusion—and one less conducive to a view of Virgil as a pompom-waving spokesman for the

38. The difficulty of this phrase (*pacique imponere morem*) is compounded by the fact that some texts read *pacisque*. Putnam (*Poetry of the Aeneid* 193) translates it as "impose the tradition of peace."

Roman Empire—would be difficult to imagine. Is this final scene not an utter repudiation of the idealistic words of Anchises ("Forbear the conquered, and war down the proud")? That last line was used earlier, when the Amazon Camilla, battling for the Italians, is killed in a cowardly fashion by Arruns, who is then promptly killed by an acolyte of Diana. The repetition of the line at this critical juncture forces a most unwelcome comparison between Aeneas and the contemptible Arruns. And the whole scenario, involving as it does the killing of a suppliant, is similarly a subversion of the oft-repeated descriptive *pius* applied to the hero of the *Aeneid*.

Perhaps it is going too far to say that this problematical ending overturns the entire thrust of the epic as a paean to the glories of past and future Rome; but at the very least we can agree with Michael C. J. Putnam in stating: "The tragedy of the destruction of Turnus and his world does much to negate any romantic notion of the *Aeneid* as an ideal vision of the greatness of Augustan Rome, and it negates, too, the image of Virgil as its poet-laureate, preaching moderation, mercy, and a certain humility which such a far-reaching accomplishment as that of Augusus could well bear."[39]

This extended discussion of the overall thrust of the *Aeneid* may seem incidental to our concerns; but, given the tightly woven nexus of nationalism, morality, and worship that we have seen as characteristic of Roman religion, the grave doubt that Virgil casts upon Rome's ultimate mission in the world necessarily casts doubt on Roman leaders' axiomatic assumption that the immortal gods are favouring their acquisition of an empire. It is now time to turn to the difficult question of what Virgil's own religious and philosophical views might have been.

It must be declared at the outset that any precise answer to this question is all but impossible. Virgil is a poet, not a philosopher, and there is nothing approaching a systematic or consistent philosophy in his treatment of any of the subjects he deals with in his poetry, whether it be the pastoral life, agriculture, or the grandeur of Rome. We have very little reliable information on Virgil's own philosophical training. A poem in the so-called *Appendix Vergiliana* (a series of nine poems or groups of poems that were attributed to Virgil in antiquity but are almost certainly

39. Putnam, *Poetry of the* Aeneid 192.

not by him) states in the first person that he is going to study with the Epicurean philosopher Siro; but there is no independent confirmation of this. Virgil was certainly familiar with Lucretius' *De Rerum Natura,* as any number of passages in his work confirm; the noble line *felix qui potuiit rerum cognoscere causes* ("Happy he who was able to know the causes of things": *Georgics* 2.490) not only alludes to Lucretius but is written as a pastiche of Lucretius' poetic idiom.[40] But to what extent the content of the *De Rerum Natura* affected Virgil is in serious doubt.

Perhaps the best we can do is to focus on the notion of "fate" in the *Aeneid,* which some scholars have seen as betraying a Stoic influence. The terms *fatum* (pl. *fata*), *Parcae* (the three goddesses—analogous to the Greek Moirai—called the Fates), and *fortuna* (fortune, chance) occur well over a hundred times in the *Aeneid,* but it is no easy task to systematise their wide and varying usage. It is worth noting that, in contrast to the Greek *ananke* (necessity) or *moira* (fate), *fatum* is derived from the verb *fari* (to speak), evidently referring to the spoken decree of either a god (notably Jupiter) or of a prophet or seer.

We have seen that Aeneas' entire mission is performed under the aegis of *fatum:* he was forced to leave Troy by fate (*fato profugus* ["banished by fate"], 1.2); he abandoned Dido because he recognises the fate has tied his hands (4.240f.); and so on. At the end of the epic, Juno admits that fate is against her in her support of Turnus and the Italians against Aeneas. Addressing Juturna, she states:

"So far
As Fortune seemed to suffer, Fate allow
Good hap to Latium, I have guarded well
Thy town and Turnus: now I see him rush
Ill-matched upon his fate, and lo! the hour
Of destiny draws near, and force malign." (147–50)[41]

It is plausible enough to assume that this repeated use of fate necessarily

40. Cf. *nec poterant quibus id fieret cognoscere causes* (*De Retum Natura* 5.1185), a line that occurs in the course of Lucretius' discussion that the origin of religious belief lies in human beings' inability to understand natural causation.

41. The translation does not quite make clear how all the terms in question—*Fortuna* (147), *Parcae* (147), and *fatis* (149)—are used.

implies a belief in a predetermined future that can be foretold and cannot be overturned. It is also the case that *fata* (especially in the phrase *fata deum*, used frequently in the text) means something like "the decrees of the gods," and specifically the father of gods and men, Jupiter.

But it remains unclear to what extent—if any—Virgil actually subscribed to this (possibly Stoic) conception. Just as his audience would have expected a recounting of the largely mythical history of the settlement of Rome, with the gods intervening at every critical moment, so too would that audience have expected to see Aeneas fulfil his *fatum* (here "destiny") by means of actions that led him inexorably from Troy through Carthage to Italy.

As for Virgil's treatment of the underworld, we can note some significant differences between Book 11 of the *Odyssey*. Virgil outlines several distinct regions—one for those who have died a violent death, were killed in war, and so on; another where the souls of people who have committed evils are judged by Minos and suffer various punishments; and Elysium, where the souls of the blessed reside. Virgil places a much greater emphasis on such moral distinctions than Homer does—something that may reflect popular theology as well as the influence of Pythagoreanism, Orphism, and other movements, which were all tending in this direction. A passage on souls drinking from the river Lethe to wipe away memories of their past life (6.703f.) unquestionably puts forth the theory of metempsychosis.

A curious passage (6.724–51) in Anchises' speech lays out a sort of cosmogony in which it is claimed that "spirit" (*spiritus* 726) and "mind" (*mens* 726) are diffused through the universe. Human beings are infused with a "fiery force" (*igneus . . . vigor* 730) originating in the heavens; nevertheless, our bodies corrupt the soul, leading to moral evils. After death, souls pay a punishment for their past evils and are purified. A few souls gain the bliss of Elysium; most return to new bodies on earth. The suggestion is that these latter are the ones who will become some of the illustrious Romans of the future. It is not at all clear what we are to make of this farrago of Stoicism, Pythagoreanism, Platonism, and popular theology—all expressed in an idiom that unmistakably evokes the *De Rerum Natura* of the Epicurean Lucretius.

But I repeat that it is impossible to attribute any of these conceptions—metempsychosis, the "world-soul," the role of fate in human affairs—to Virgil. The best we can do is to state that throughout his work Virgil exhibits a nostalgic fondness for the Italian countryside, where he presumably spent his youth and adolescence, and an interest—not necessarily a belief—in the old Italian deities of the soil (Faunus, Pales, Silvanus, etc.) that the rural population probably still believed in and worshipped.

Virgil's overall portrayal of the early history of Rome accords well enough with that found in Livy.[42] Of his immense *Ab Urbe Condita,* written in 142 books and probably occupying at least forty years of his life, we have Books 1–10 (from the origins to 292 B.C.E.) and Books 21–45 (from the Second Punic war [beginning in 218] to 167). Livy carried his history all the way down to about 9 B.C.E., but the content of the missing books is known only through summaries or abridgements by other hands.

I have already quoted a passage from the opening of Livy's history sanctioning the mingling of "divine" and human matters in his accounts of the entire period covered by his work; in spite of this, recent scholars have attempted to maintain that significant scepticism enters into Livy's accounts of specifically religious or supernatural phenomena—a scepticism that is thought to have been widely shared by the educated classes of his day. But the evidence for such contentions is highly problematical.

There is, indeed, evidence of a certain element of scepticism in some of Livy's accounts of both early Rome and of later periods; but what conclusions we are to draw from this is unclear, and there is no reason to think that Livy was engaging in a repudiation of the divine element in human affairs. Oftentimes he adopts a strategy whereby multiple "explanations" of strange or supernatural phenomena are offered, and it is doubtful whether we are to regard these as mutually exclusive. To choose only one example among many: at the end of his account of the suckling of Romulus and Remus by a she-wolf, after which the twins were taken up by a herdsman named Faustulus and then nursed by his

42. It also approximates the account found in the early books of the *Roman Antiquities* of Livy's almost exact contemporary, Dionysius of Halicarnassus (60? B.C.E.–7 C.E.), the most significant Greek historian after Polybius who was interested in Roman affairs and whose work has come down to us. Dionysius, however, does not cite Aeneas' visit to Dido in Carthage.

wife Larentia, Livy writes: "Some think that the origin of this fable was the fact that Larentia was a common whore and was called Wolf by the shepherds" (1.4.7). This certainly sounds like a "demythologising" of the Romulus legend, but Livy simply leaves the matter at that and proceeds with his history.

For a much later period, Livy makes a telling comment:

> I am well aware that, through the same disregard of religion which has led men into the present prevailing opinion, of the gods never giving portents of any future events, no prodigies are now either reported to government or recorded in histories. But for my part, while I am writing the transactions of ancient times, my sentiments, I know not how, become antique; and I feel a kind of religious awe, which compels me to consider that events which the men of those days, renowned for wisdom, judged deserving of the attention of the state and of public expiation, must certainly be worthy of a place in my history. (43.13.1–2)

At the most elementary level, this passage points to a conservative tendency in Livy in which his own unwavering belief in the Roman religion—and the multifarious rituals that accompany it—leads him to a querulous whine that disbelief of some sort is spreading. This is one of several passages in works of this period that historians have pointed to as testifying to a radical scepticism among the Roman intelligentsia (which included figures at the highest levels of the government) in regard to religion in general and the role of the gods in human affairs in particular. And, to be sure, there are other passages one can cite, such as Cicero's dismay that auspices (the religious rite whereby the sanction of the gods is sought for any crucial action, especially in going to war) are no longer believed in:

> . . . the most important activities of the state, including the wars that ensure its safety, are conducted without taking the auspices. We no longer take them when crossing rivers, or witnessing flashing spear-points, or when men are summoned for call-up (and that is why soldiers no longer make their wills when geared for battle; our commanders begin their military operations only when dispensing

> with the auspices). (*De Natura Deorum* 2.9)

But these words are placed in the mouth of the Stoic Balbus, who has a vested interest in affirming the integral role of gods in human life, a central tenet of Stoicism. Elsewhere Cicero, in dismissing the idea that the general public has a uniform fear of death, writes:

> When I think of these things I cannot help often marvelling at the absurdity of some philosophers, who admire the study of natural science, and render thanks with expressions of joy to its first discoverer and teacher, reverencing him as a god, because they have been freed by him from the severest tyranny, from unceasing terror, from fear by day and by night. From what terror? From what fear? What old woman is so far demented as to fear what you perhaps might have dreaded, if you had been entirely ignorant of natural science? (*Tusc. Disp.* 1.48)

But this polemic is clearly directed at the Epicureans whom he despised; and Cicero himself is in no doubt as to the existence of the soul (he ridicules those who deny it) and that it will survive the death of the body. Overall, it hardly needs to be emphasised that no philosophical sect in Rome, not even the Epicureans, actually denied the existence of the gods, even if their intervention in human affairs (especially in remote periods of the past where verification is difficult) was a matter of controversy.

Livy's position might be further clarified by a remark he makes in regard to a prodigy in the year 208: "at Cumae (superstition sees the finger of God even in trivialities) mice had gnawed the gold in the temple at Jupiter" (27.23.2). What the translator here has rendered as "superstition" is in the Latin text *prava religio* (degraded religion). The mere use of such a phrase suggests Livy's belief in a *religio* that is not *prava*. This is clearly the case at 39.16.6, where the phrase is used again—in the context of the Senate's condemnation of the Bacchanalian rites in 186. Livy is consistent in criticising religions or religious practices originating in foreign lands, with their potential to corrupt the Roman religion in which he obviously believes.

Livy, indeed, is a voluminous chronicler of prodigies (*prodigia*)—lightning strikes on temples, stones falling from the sky, mutant animals being born, and so on. At times he rattles off so many of them in succession that he begins sounding like a Charles Fort of the ancient world. At a minimum, his citation of such phenomena—usually without specific comment, and certainly without any notable expression of scepticism—suggests a tentative belief in them, or at least an absence of disbelief. But once again, we may be in a situation where Livy is consciously or unconsciously reflecting the beliefs of his perceived audience. The numerous bizarre events that purportedly occurred around the time of Julius Caesar's assassination became a byword in Roman culture, both among the populace and among the intelligentsia; and the dominant philosophical sect in Rome, the Stoics, were hardly in a position to deny their significance.

In the end, we can agree with Jason P. Davies's assessment of Livy's religious outlook:

> The intentionality of the gods is intrinsic to their nature, as they are constructed in Livy's account; for the historian evoking cult practice, they *are* a will that permeats all human existence, and their will has a 'plan' in so far as specific events are willed, often under the explicit aegis of *fatum*. [But] whatever the gods do for men, there is scope and responsibility for those men also.[43]

What Livy was seeking was that all-important *pax deorum* ("the peace of the gods"—or, more specifically, peace engendered *by* the gods) that the Romans saw as both the cause and the effect of their own political and military might. It hardly need be pointed out that an obvious circular argument was utilised in this conception: Rome's successes were attributed to the help or favour of the gods, while their relatively few defeats were caused by insufficient piety or a failure to follow the (not very clear) strictures of the gods in regard to public and private behaviour.

As for Horace, we are once again on slippery territory. His life is of some relevance to his literary ouput. Born in southern Italy, he was (by his own testimony) son of a freedman—that is, a man who was taken into slavery, although the precise circumstances are not known, but who later gained his freedom and raised his son as a free-born Roman, spending lavishly on his education, which included some period of study

43. Davies, *Rome's Religious History* 100.

in Athens. Unfortunately, Horace ended up taking the "wrong" side in the Civil War—at least to the extent of joining an army led by Caesar's chief assassin, Brutus. When this force was defeated at the Battle of Philippi in 42, Horace was among many who were granted amnesty by Octavian. But upon his return to Italy he found that his family estate had been confiscated by army veterans, rendering him impoverished. He managed to get a minor position in the government—a position that supported him until, in 33, he was granted his famous Sabine farm by Maecenas, the patron of Virgil.

The relatively small body of work for which Horace is known is peculiar in the sense that the titles that have been bestowed upon various bodies of it are not the ones Horace himself used. What we call his *Satires* he called *Sermones* (talks); what we call his *Odes,* by far his most notable accomplishment, he referred to as *Carmina* (songs). In addition, he wrote a slender book of *Epodes* (poetry in iambic metre) and two books of *Epistles.* The chronology of these works is fairly clear: the two books of *Satires* appeared in 35/34 and 30; the book of *Epodes* in 30; the first three books of *Odes* in 23; the two books of *Epistles* in 20/19 and 11; the *Carmen Saeculare* in 17; the fourth book of *Odes* in 13 (or 11); the *Ars Poetica* in 10, 9, or 8.

The nature of this material is highly diverse. The *Satires* are referred to as such because, although many of them are indeed "talks" between various interlocutors (most amusingly, between Horace and an inveterate bore), they are generally satirical in tone, although of a relatively mild sort characteristic of some of the work of their model, Lucilius. The *Epodes* are a pendant to the satires in being tartly abusive to their subjects. The *Epistles* also follow the satires in general tone and atmosphere. But with the *Odes* we are in a different world altogether. These exquisite gems—the highest expression of lyric poetry in all extant Latin literature—are among the world's great contributions to literature, fully justifying Horace's own boast that they constitute a "monument more durable than brass" (3.30.1).[44] The *Ars Poetica* is literary criticism in verse, while we shall discuss the *Carmen Saeculare* in its place.

The *Satires* and *Epistles* provide some of the most vibrant and apparently realistic accounts of daily life in Rome that comes down to us,

44. I use the translation of Lord Dunsany.

not unlike the plays of Plautus. But what strikes us from the perspective of religion is the near-total absence of religion. Consider, for example, the moral advice that Horace offers in *Epistles* 1.2: amidst the strictures against the accumulation of money, warnings to keep bad emotions (envy, anger, and so forth) in check, and the pungent adjuration "dare to be wise" (*sapere aude* 40), we find not one word about pietry toward the gods or devotion to religious ritual. When Horace does refer to historical or mythological exempla, he cites only human figures (Paris, Nestor, and other figures in the Trojan War).

On the few occasions where religion does figure in these books, it is presented unfavourably. *Satires* 2.3 is a long catalogue of human folly, in which religious mania is cited. Presenting the words of one Stertinus (apparently a voluminous Stoic philosopher), Horace writes:

> "'O Jupiter, who givest and takest away sore afflictions,' cries the mother of a child that for five long months has been ill abed, 'if the quartan chills leave my child, then on the morning of the day on which thou appointest a fast, he shall stand naked in the Tiber.' Should chance or the doctor raise the sick lad up from his peril, his crazy mother will kill him by planting him on the cold bank and bringing back his fever. What is the malady that has stricken her mind? Fear of the gods." (2.3.288–95)[45]

We have already noted that Horace at one point whimsically refers to himself as a follower of Epicurus (*Epistles* 1.4.16); but Stoic influence is evident in the frequent citations of Chrysippus, the standard Stoic view (embraced in *Satires* 2.3) that moral evil is equivalent to folly and (in *Satires* 2.7) that only the wise are free. But Horace pointedly neglects to include any discussions of Stoic theology, specifically the notion of a god who designed all things for the benefit of human beings.

An early satire (1.3) gives a somewhat crude account of the development of life on earth, whereby a primitive war of all against all gradually led to the growth of civilisation. One passage is of interest:

> Between right and wrong Nature can draw no such distinction as

45. For the *Satires* and *Epistles* I use the translation of H. Rushton Fairclough.

> between things gainful and harmful, what is to be sought and what is to be shunned; nor will Reason ever prove this, that the sin is one and the same to cut young cabbages in a neighbour's garden and to steal by night the sacred emblems of the gods. (1.3.113–17)

The amorality of Nature—and the notion that "justice was born of the fear of injustice" (1.3.111)—is of note, as is the clear rejection of the Stoic view that all "sins" are equal. Whether that final reference to sacrilege somehow testifies to Horace's religious beliefs is doubtful; he was citing that specific example as a particularly heinous "sin" as envisioned by the commonality of people.

But the *Odes* present a very different picture. I do not refer merely to the numerous hymns to the gods: Mercury (1.10, 3.11), Venus (1.30, 3.26, 4.1), Apollo (1.31, 4.6), Bacchus (2.19, 3.25), and Diana (3.22); there is also a striking ode (1.34) in which Horace professes to a renunciation of science and a renewal of his belief in the gods:

> Little and seldom to the gods I gave
> Due worship once, a wanderer in the ways
> Of crazy science. Now my sails I have
> Turned round to sail the course of earlier days. (1.34.1–4)

How seriously are we to take this—and how seriously are we to take the numerous odes that speak of the terrors of the underworld? In speaking of the narrowness of his escape from death from a falling tree, he states:

> How near I saw Proserpina's domain,
> And Æacus upon his judgement-seat,
> And regions trodden by just spirits' feet . . . (2.13.21–23)

But when Sappho and other dead lyric poets sing their songs in the world below,

> What wonder, when the hundred-headed beast
> His dark ears droops, enchanted by that air,
> And serpents, interwoven with the hair
> Of the Eumenides, from pain have ceased. (2.13.33–36)

Perhaps all this is nothing more than stock imagery of the Roman hell, as well as a flamboyant paean to the exquisite poetry of Horace's predecessors. But the frequency with which such imagery appears must give us pause—and, if in any way sincere (or, at a minimum, if it was meant to evoke a sharp response from his audience—which, let it be noted, was the intellectual elite and not the common people), then it would presumably put the lie to Cicero's comment, quoted earlier, that only old women are terrified by the spectre of the underworld.

We might conjecture that the horrors of the Civil War and its aftermath have impelled Horace to be gravely troubled about the fate of the Roman people—physically, morally, and religiously. *Odes* 1.2 is a plangent appeal to Augustus—and also the gods—to put an end to civil strife. Is Augustus, then, to be our semi-divine saviour? It would appear so. He is in fact second only to Jupiter himself (1.12.51–52). Elsewhere he is directly compared to Jupiter by virtue of what Horace believed to be his future conquests at opposite ends of the Roman Empire:

By thundering of Jupiter we know
    He reigns in Heaven, and we shall see clear
Augustus, by the Britons' overthrow
    And Persians hordes', a god amongst us here. (3.5.1–4)

Analogously, Augustus will be regarded as a god by conquered nations (4.5). Such passages may strike us as distastefully obsequious, but they probably reflect a widespread belief that Augustus' military conquests, his bringing relative stability to the Roman world, and his regeneration of Roman religion constituted immense boons after the turmoil of the last days of the Republic.

The theme is broadened in some of the *Odes*. In addressing the Roman directly, Horace notes:

Roman, though guiltless, thou must expiate
    Thy fathers' sins until thou build'st again
The temples, and the statues, desecrate
    With sooty smoke, and every fallen fane.

Thou reign'st because the gods are over thee,

From them all policies and all success.
The gods neglected gave to Italy,
Sorrowfull country, many a distress. (3.6.1–8)

This is only one more example, if one were needed, of how tightly even intellectuals such as Horace saw religion as the nexus for Roman military and political achievement. It therefore seems uncharitable to assume, with V. G. Kiernan, that the poem presents a "shallow, evasive explanation of Rome's misfortunes as due to neglect of public prayer."[46]

As for the *Carmen Saeculare*—it is obviously not a "secular song," but rather one that was commissioned by Augustus to be sung at the *Ludi Saeculares,* the games that mark the end of one century (*saeculum*) and the beginning of the next. Augustus reinstituted the games in 17 B.C.E.[47] Horace's poem is largely a paean to Diana and Apollo, the latter a stand-in for Augustus himself, who erected a temple to Apollo on the Palatine Hill in Rome. We are once more treated to the mythological history of Rome—the Trojan War, Aeneas' divine origin ("Anchises' son and Venus'"), and so on. One would not expect anything else from the circumstances of its composition and performance.

Ovid is the only one of the major poets of the Augustan Age who had no experience of the Republic, even in its dying stages. Born in 43 at Sulmo, in central Italy, he made a name for himself by writing of some of the most exquisite (and, at times, erotic and even obscene) poetry of his or any other era. From the 20s to about 2 C.E. he wrote such works as the *Ars Amatoria* (The Art of Love), the *Amores* (Loves), the *Remedia Amoris* (The Cure for Love), and the *Heroides* (The Heroines: love letters in verse written by women out of Greco-Roman myth to men). Then, as he wrote in a pungent phrase, he was exiled by Augustus for a "poem and a mistake" (*carmen et error: Tristia* 2.207). It is unclear what exactly happened; some scholars have maintained that it had something to do with the disgrace of Augustus' granddaughter Julia, who was exiled at the same time (8 C.E.) for adultery. In any event, Ovid spent the remaining nine years of his life in the remote town of Tomi, a city now in Romania on the Black Sea. He did not help his cause with posterity by writing several works—the *Tristia* (Sorrows) and the *Epistulae ex Ponto* (Letters

46. Kiernan, *Horace: Poetics and Politics* 81.
47. Lord Dunsany properly translates the title as "The Song of a Hundred Years."

from Pontus)—where he engages in lugubrious self-pity over his unjust fate. Before his exile, he produced the two works—the *Metamorphoses* and the *Fasti* (an account of the Roman religious calendar)—that are of greatest relevance to us.

The difficulties involved in pinpointing Ovid's religious beliefs are formidable, chiefly because his work from beginning to end is filled with humour, satire, irony, and a general flippancy that make it nearly impossible to know when Ovid is being sincere or when he is merely making a joke. At the very beginning of the *Ars Amatoria* he heaps scorn on the conventional poet's claim to inspiration from the gods:

> I boast no aid the Delphian god [Apollo] affords,
> Nor auspice from the flight of chattering birds,
> Nor Clio, nor her sisters have I seen,
> As Hesiod saw them on the shady green. (1.25–28)[48]

But then he reverses himself by asserting a different source of inspiration: "Experience makes my work a truth so tried, / You may believe; and Venus be my guide" (1.29–30).

A striking line later in the poem—"'Tis for our interest the gods should be" (1.637 [*Expedit esse deos, et, ut expedit, esse putemus;* literally, "It is convenient for the gods to exist; and, because it is convenient, let us believe that they do")—which would seem to be a striking approximation of what Voltaire said seventeen centuries later. But in context, the passage comes in the course of Ovid's deadpan instruction on how seduction should be practised: if acknowledging the gods will help you to take a girl to bed, well, then go for it.

We now turn to the *Metamorphoses,* Ovid's greatest and most influential work—one that inspired countless poets, artists, and others in all manner of ways from the Renaissance onward. This fifteen-book epic (written in iambic hexameter, not elegiac couplets) is nominally incomplete, but what we have is extensive enough—a kaleidoscopic catalogue of "transformations" (Daphne turning into a tree to escape the clutches of Apollo, for example) culled from the bountiful stores of Greco-Roman myth. The opening of the poem propounds a not very

48. I use the translation of Anne Mahony. The line numbers refer to the Latin text.

coherent cosmogony whereby the primal Chaos (the memorable phrase *rudis indigestaque moles* [1.7: "a rude and undeveloped mass"])[49] was brought to some sort of order by "God . . . and nature" (1.21: *deus et . . . natura*). What god? Ovid doesn't know; it was some god or other (1.32: *quisquis fuit ille deorum*). The entire passage reads like a parody of Hesiod (the opening of the *Theogony*) in the "cosmic" poetic idiom of Lucretius (who pointedly contrasted *natura* with the false "gods" who were to be banished by the philosophy of Epicurus).

The account goes on to tell how this god separated the land from the waters, harnessed the winds, and created various animals. At some point the god determined that a "holier animal" (1.76: *sanctius . . . animal*) needed to come into being; but Ovid can't decide whether it was this god or Prometheus who created the human race. We are then treated to a standard account of the four ages of man (gold, silver, brass, and iron), pretty much out of Hesiod; humanity becomes increasingly corrupt, until Jupiter decides that it has all been a mistake and sends a flood to wipe out the human race—well, not quite: Deucalion and Pyrrha are conveniently around to regenerate the race. All this, of course, does bear a certain resemblance to the creation story in Genesis, and its very existence at the outset of Ovid's poem may have had something to do with its preservation in Christian culture.[50]

Surely the rest of the book cannot possibly have provided any comfort to Christians; for it is an unending succession of bad behaviour—usually of a sexual nature—by the gods as practised upon human beings. As Julia Dyson Hejduk remarks, "The Olympians in the *Metamorphoses* are an unsavory lot, lustful, duplicitous, vengeful, petty, and, in short, having no redeeming features whatever."[51] This is not entirely the case: there is the touching tale of Baucis and Philemon, an elderly married couple who take Jupiter and Mercury (disguised as peasants) into their humble home and, as a reward, are turned into intertwining trees upon their death. But overall the gods do not present a picture of moral uprightness. And yet, this "disrespectful" treatment of the gods by Ovid does not

49. I use the translation of Brookes More.

50. One translator from the nineteenth century, John Benson Rose, soberly commented: "The lore treated upon by Ovid appears to have been derived from our Holy Scriptures, or to have been deduced from the same fount they arose from." *The Metamorphoses of Ovid* (London: Whitaker & Co., 1866), 2n.

51. Julia Dyson Hejduk, "Ovid and Religion," in Knox, *A Companion to Ovid* 51.

necessarily signal religious scepticism on his part. All apart from the question of whether the wit, irony, and humour that Ovid brings to all these accounts can allow for any conjecture as to his own beliefs, such treatments had a long history in Greco-Roman culture. We have seen that as early as the sixth century B.C.E. various writers found the lascivious or otherwise immoral acts of the gods (immoral, that is, if the same acts had been committed by human beings) distasteful; and Ovid may simply be making explicit the implicit sexual undertones of many of the myths he writes about. Indeed, he perhaps chose these specific myths for that very reason.

If we turn to the end of the book, we are no closer to resolving the quandary. Here Ovid presents a compressed account of Roman history, including all the standard mythological trappings from Aeneas on down and culminating in the apotheosis of Julius Caesar and the anticipation of the apotheosis of Augustus. Venus pleads with Jupiter not to allow the assassination of Caesar to happen; Jupiter says he is unable to "change the fixed decrees of Fate" (15.807: *insuperabile fatum*); but he assures her that Augustus will avenge Caesar's death, conquer many lands, and regenerate the Roman people. Upon his death he will ascend to the sky, taking his place with Vesta, Quirinus (the name of the deified Romulus), and others.

Once again, in spite of a certain nobility and grandeur in its expression, there is no reason to believe that this concluding passage of the *Metamorphoses* expresses Ovid's "real" views. To be sure, there is the clear influence of Virgil's *Aeneid* on certain portions of it, although that does not negate the possibility of a certain element of parody in Ovid's borrowings.

As for the *Fasti,* there is not the slightest reason to think that Ovid wrote this long poem (of which we apparently have only half the text: he himself notes that it was in twelve books, but we have only six, covering only the first six months of the Roman calendar as revised by Julius Caesar) out of any sincere religious feeling. As was typical of this sex-obsessed author, the *Fasti* allowed Ovid to write lubricious tales relaing to the various festivals throughout the calendar—although, it would appear, a fair amount of sexual activity actually went on at these events. Otherwise, I am not sure we can derive much from this poem, although Sir James George Frazer found it of such interest as a mine of information for Roman religious rituals that he published a five-volume edition of it (with translation and commentary) in 1929.

A few words—very few—should be devoted to M. Manilius, about whom almost nothing is known; his *Astronomica* was probably written between 10 and 15 C.E. This five-book poem, in spite of its title, is a windy account of astrology—specifically, an outline of the constellations, zodiacal signs, and so forth, and their influence on human life. It is obvious that Manilius wrote with Lucretius in mind—not in an attempt to imitate him (aside from lame efforts to duplicate his poetic idiom), but to refute him at every turn from his orthodox Stoic perspective. Hence we have a feeble venture into an anthropology of the human race (1.66f.) intended to counteract the account in Book 5 of the *De Rerum Natura.*

At the very outset, Manilius makes his agenda clear by maintaining that "Deeper knowledtge of heaven was first granted to earth by the gift of the gods" (1.25–26).[52] He offers an eclectic view of the origin of the universe, alternately offering atomist, Heraclitean, and other irreconcilable conjectures before asserting the veracity of the Stoic view of the cosmos, echoing its standard assertions of divine governance and the four elements:

> This fabric which forms the body of the boundless universe, together with its members composed of nature's diverse elements, air and fire, earth and level sea, is ruled by the force of a divine spirit; by sacred dispensation the deity brings harmony and governs with hidden purpose, arranging mutual bonds between all parts, so that each may furnish and receive another's strength and that the whole may stand fast in kinship despite its variety of forms. (1.247–54)

Elsewhere he asserts that the god Mercury was the founder of "this great and holy science" (1.30) and that the gods are the guardians of the zodiacal signs (2.433–52).

The Stoics were obliged to believe in astrology as a result of their dogmas regarding the creation and/or rulership of the earth by a god (or gods) who designed the entire cosmos for the benefit of humanity. As such, the heavenly bodies must play some role in human affairs, and it is

52. I use the translation of G. P. Goold.

Manilius' task to elucidate what that role is—which he does at tedious length. There is evidence that his book had some minimal influence on the poetry and philosophy of the succeeding century, but after that the work disappeared from sight until rescued in the later Renaissance.

H. Rome, Britain, and the Jews

The two centuries following the death of Augustus saw the Roman Empire achieve its widest territorial extent, especially under the reigns of Tiberius (r. 14–37), Caligula (r. 37–41), Claudius (r. 41–54), Nero (r. 54–68), Vespasian (r. 69–79), Domitian (r. 81–96), Trajan (r. 98–117), Hadrian (r. 117–38), Antoninus Pius (r. 138–61), and Marcus Aurelius (r. 161–80). Several of these emperors have gained notoriety as epitomes of moral and political corruption, but (with the exception of Caligula) probably unjustly, as they were tarred by the prejudice of the otherwise notable historian Tacitus and of that irresponsible gossip-monger, Suetonius.

All the emperors of this period, with the exception of Caligula and Nero, were duly deified. It was the belief of the Roman government that the figure of a deified emperor was one of the few unifying factors that could knit together the diverse population it now governed. There is some evidence to suggest that the intelligentsia—and even the emperors themselves—regarded the whole tactic with a certain scepticism. The celebrated passage in which Suetonius records Vespasian, on his deathbed, uttering the words *Vae, puto deus fio* (*Vespasian* 23.4: "Dammit, I think I'm becoming a god") certainly points in that direction, even if the utterance is apocryphal. And then there is the exquisite satire *Apocolocyntosis Divi Claudii*, almost certainly written by Seneca the Younger shortly after Claudius' death. Amidst all the torrent of abuse about Claudius' physical shortcomings (he apparently walked with a limp, had poor hearing, and sometimes spoke incoherently) and some aspects of his political, legal, and military actions, the piece ultimately focuses on the contention that Claudius is unworthy of deification. The neologism *apocolocyntosis* is manifestly a pun on *apotheosis*, and the word is generally believed to be derived from *kolonynthē* (pumpkin), hence a recent translation renders the title as "The Pumpkinification of Claudius."

Seneca puts these words into the mouth of the two-headed god

Janus: "Once it was a great thing to become a god; now you have turned our reputation into a farce" (*Apoc.* 9).[53] Later the Deified Augustus is made to say: "So long as you make such gods [as Claudius], no one will believe that you are gods" (*Apoc.* 11). Are these remarks to be interpreted as actual denunciations of the very principle of deification? Such a view can hardly be upheld. The whole tenor of Seneca's remarks points only to the fact that it is ridiculous to make Claudius (and such like him) a god. Augustus' position in the heavenly pantheon is never questioned by Seneca; indeed, the very fact that Augustus himself thrusts Claudius out of heaven and down to the underworld shows that Seneca was certainly not criticising deification per se.

The expansion of the empire continued apace under the successors of Augustus. Britain (into which Julius Caesar had made a foray in 55 B.C.E.) was subjugated in 44 C.E., but the subsequent rebellion led by Boudicca required eight years to quell; the job was finally completed in 61. Trajan annexed Dacia (in eastern Europe) in 101 and Mesopotamia in 111. The empire reached its maximum extent under Hadrian in 117.

While it is true that the Romans had already begun securing an empire as early as the third century B.C.E., it was only in the first century C.E. that they had to confront the issue of religious differences among the diverse peoples they governed. While it is a commonplace to say that the Romans did not interfere with the religious practices of the people under their rule, there are two noteworthy exceptions: the Druids and the Jews.

I have noted that the Druids were the priests among the Celtic peoples. Some scholars have disputed this characterisation, but it is unclear what else we can call them given the evidence at our disposal: whether they were priests or seers or sages, they occupied a distinct place in Celtic society in both Gaul and Britain. Caesar expelled many of them from Gaul during his eight-year campaign (58–50); he may well have exaggerated their political importance in his account of them in the *Bellum Gallicum* (Gallic War) as justification for his brutal suppression of them and of the Gauls generally.

Augustus and subsequent emperors took various measures to restrict Druid influence and practices; Suetonius, indeed, remarks that in 54 "The religious rites of the Druids, solemnized with such horrid cruelties,

53. I use the translation of Apostolos N. Athanassakis.

which had only been forbidden the citizens of Rome during the reign of Augustus, he [Claudius] utterly abolished from the Gauls" (*Claudius* 25). I have noted that the practice of human sacrifice by the Druids rests upon fairly sound evidence; but it has been observed that the Romans were not especially dainty themselves—especially at this juncture—in terms of blood-sports and other activities, so why did they react so viscerally to the Druid menace?

It could be argued that the Romans used human sacrifice as an excuse to wipe out the Druids in both Gaul and Britain. For reasons not entirely clear the Druids had developed a ferociously anti-Roman stance; and that is something the Romans could not tolerate, because it engendered *political* instability in the provinces under their control. The Romans strove mightily to import both the imperial cult and the worship of the standard Roman gods to Britain. An enormous temple to Claudius was built at Camulodunum (Colchester); it was completed in 60. Much of the temple (and the town) were destroyed by the Boudiccan rebels, but the temple was later rebuilt. There were other temples in other Roman cities, and the Romans sought to identify local gods with their own; hence, the Celtic god Sulis, based in Bath (Aquae Sulis), was fused with Minerva. Mars consolidated the numerous war gods of various Celtic tribes.

In general, however, it could simply be the case that the conflict of Romans and Celts/Druids was emblematic of the incompatibility of the two cultures, and that the Romans could not allow the Celts to remain an independent force that refused emperor-worship or the worship of the Roman pantheon; they saw no option but to take forceful measures to suppress the threat.

Much the same, on an even grander scale, could be said of Rome's relations with the Jews. There were Jews in Rome as early as 139 B.C.E. It was at that time that the Hasmonean dynasty (140–63) had taken control of Palestine, although there is some evidence of integration with neighbouring Greek-speaking and -settled regions, as the greater use of the Greek language in documents and inscriptions and the use of bilingual coinage indicate. Strict religionists among the Jewish people objected to this practice, but they were ruthlessly suppressed. The Jews gradually expanded their territory to rule the whole of Palestine up to the Jordan river, including regions controlled by related groups such as the

Idumaeans, the Galileans, and so on; these groups gradually converted to Judaism.

A war over succession broke out in 69, leading the Roman general Pompey (Cn. Pompeius Magnus) to arrive in the region in 65. Over the next several years the Romans annexed Judea, Syria, and portions of nearby Pontus and Bithynia. But a civil war among the Jews continued down to about 40, exacerbated by an invasion of the Parthians. The Roman Senate named Herod (74–4? B.C.E.), an Idumaean, as king of Judea in 47. It is true that aspects of his rule provoked much loathing of him among the Jews, especially a siege of Jerusalem he undertook in 37. But overall, the Romans bent over backwards to accommodate Jewish religious principles, exempting them from participating in many aspects of Roman civil and religious life and also allowing the Jews to practise their own religion largely unmolested. This dispensation continued under the Principate, although Tiberius did exile Jews from Rome for excessive proselytising.

Herod, for his part, rebuilt the temple in Jerusalem, making it one of the largest structures in the Roman world. As a result, there was an immense influx of Jewish pilgrims to the temple, resulting in a substantial increase of wealth in the region—but also an increase in sectarianism. Three sects gained prominence at this time: the Sadducees, the Pharisees, and the Essenes. The Sadducees accepted the legal authority only of the Torah, while the Pharisees looked to other sources as well. Interestingly, the Sadducees rejected the survival of the soul after death, the bodily resurrection of the dead, and the moral distinction of souls in the afterlife; the Pharisees and Essenes accepted these doctrines. The Essenes tended toward extreme asceticism, and there was a distinct element of apocalypticism in their thinking: "they lived in permanent expectation of the imminence of the final apocalyptic battle between the forces of good and evil, which would result in the restoration of God's kingdom on earth."[54] These sects seem to have become increasingly radicalised by the end of the first century B.C.E., their chief *bête noire* being Roman overlordship.

In 4 B.C.E. Augustus split Herod's kingdom into three parts: 1) Samaria, Judea, and Idumaea; 2) Galilee; and 3) the northeastern (non-

54. Schwartz, *The Ancient Jews from Alexander to Muhammad* 68.

Jewish) part of the kingdom. There is debate about how violent and turbulent the region was under subsequent prefects and procurators. What is not in doubt is that conflicts between Jews and Greeks broke out in the 60s, with atrocities on both sides. A purported incident of blasphemy by a Greek at the Jewish synagogue at Caesarea (a largely Greek city) triggered the Jewish revolt of 66. Many of the details of the revolt come down to us from the *Jewish War* of Flavius Josephus (37–100?), who was head of the Jewish forces in Galilee.

It is difficult to deny that the exclusivity of the Jewish religion had something to do with the revolt. For all that the Romans by and large did not interfere with the religious practices of the regions they controlled, they did expect the peoples in question to acknowledge the validity of the Roman pantheon and of the emperor cult, since these were so intimately connected with Roman rule. And whereas both Romans and other cultures could (and did) identify their gods with the Greco-Roman pantheon (however contrived and fanciful these identifications may have been), this option was not available to Jews. And in a battle between Jews and Greeks, the Romans would, for obvious cultural reasons, take the side of the Greeks.

In 67, the Roman general Vespasian arrived in the region with 60,000 troops. Many Jews fled to Jerusalem. Vespasian abruptly left the area in 69 to become emperor (following the turbulent "year of the four emperors," 68–69), leaving his son Titus to lead the army. Titus laid siege to Jerusalem in 70; after four months the city capitulated. The Romans burned the temple and razed the city. Out of an estimated Jewish population of about 300,000 to 500,000, nearly 100,000 were sold into slavery or otherwise displaced. The religious freedoms the Jews had received were now taken away; Judea became just another Roman province, forced to obey the rules that Romans enforced throughout their far-flung empire. The Torah was no longer regarded as having legal authority. A final siege at Masada in 74 purportedly resulted in the mass suicide of the Jewish forces there, although archaeological evidence does not appear to corroborate such an event and some scholars reject its veracity.

There was a further revolt some fifty years later, after the emperor Hadrian established the city of Aelia Capitolina on the site of Jerusalem. This led to the so-called Bar Kokhba revolt (132–35), which was ruthlessly crushed by the Romans. The whole province was devasted and was renamed Syria Palaestina.

It was only at this time, apparently, that rabbis came into prominence in Jewish society. At the time the term referred to men who had become authorities in the Torah and Jewish laws, and hence were authorised to teach it and also to act as judges. There is considerable controversy over exactly how much power and influence the rabbis had. Some scholars believe that they essentially gained control of the Jewish legal system directly after the Jewish revolt of 66–70, but the bulk of the evidence renders that view unlikely. We in fact know very little of Jewish political and social life during the two centuries following the Bar Kokhba revolt; but it is unlikely that the rabbis would have gained the authority they had in the mediaeval period as early as the decades after 70, nor is there much evidence that Jewish communities were self-contained and impervious to Roman rule. In fact, Jews were definitely ruled by the Roman governor of Judaea/Palaestina and other local (non-Jewish) authorities.

Some scholars maintain that the rabbis emerged out of the Pharisees, but this conjecture has little to support it. In all likelihood they grew out of low-level judges and priests in the pre-70 period. They did not gain significant prominence until the second or third century, when the Mishnah (a consolidation of the Oral Torah) was set down around 200. Its compiler, Judah I, is referred to as the first of the Jewish patriarchs, but his legal powers were probably not extensive. In effect, until the takeover of the Roman government by Christianity in the early fourth century, the Jews were largely under Roman control.

I. Seneca: Eclectic Stoic

The Golden Age of the Augustan Era gave way to the Silver Age of the first and second centuries C.E. The diverse group of writers who flourished during this period included one authentic philosophical mind (Seneca the Younger) and a host of poets, satirists, and historians who left a distinctive mark on Roman literature; indeed, it could be said that Roman literature (i.e., literature written in Latin) largely came to an end at this time, with only a small number of prominent names in the third, fourth, and fifth centuries.

Of Seneca (L. Annaeus Seneca 4? B.C.E.–65 C.E.) much can be said, but only a relatively small portion of his work is of direct relevance to the study of his religious views. His philosophical writings—not to mention his eight surviving tragedies—are of significant interest, but our assessment of them may be coloured by an awareness of the numerous problematical incidents in his own life. Born in Corduba (in Romanised Spain) of a father who was a noted rhetorician (some of whose works survive), he was brought to Rome as a child by his family. He entered the Senate in the reign of Caligula but was banished to Corsica during the years 41–48 by Claudius because he had committed adultery with one of Caligula's sisters. Agrippina—another sister of Caligula, with whom Seneca may also have had an affair—was now married to Claudius (her uncle), and she brought Seneca back to Rome to tutor her son, who would become the emperor Nero. He became Nero's official "friend" (*amicus principis*) upon Nero's ascension to the throne in 54.

Agrippina was intent on becoming a dominant force in her son's reign, essentially wishing to be a sort of co-ruler with him. There is little doubt that, when Nero had his mother murdered in 59, Seneca was somehow involved. He also became fabulously wealthy through Nero's patronage. Seneca, however, clearly realised that the unstable Nero was a danger to himself and others, and he attempted to withdraw from the emperor's court in 62. It was during this period that many of his essays were written. Seneca was implicated in a plot by C. Calpurnius Piso to kill Nero in 65, and Nero ordered him to commit suicide—which he did, although it took repeated efforts to do so. In this act Seneca was both following the example of the doctrinaire Stoic Cato the Younger—who killed himself in 46 B.C.E. when he recognised that Julius Caesar would in effect become the dictator of Rome—but also of his own philosophical precepts, which repeatedly stressed the Stoic notion that the wise man must live well and die well.

There is, I suppose, some question of the sincerity of Seneca's writings—or, rather, of their relation to the turbulent events of his life. Is he merely a hypocrite in, say, advocating poverty while he himself lived in the lap of luxury? Do his strictures on maintaining Stoic *apatheia* (lack of [bad] emotions) ring hollow when he himself appears to have indulged in carnality, backstabbing, and even murder? Such a facile repudiation of the value of Seneca's philosophy fails to take account of the bizarre and perilous situation in which he found himself in the courts of several of the most problematical emperors in Roman history; and it would be more prudent to assess his philosophical writings on their own terms for whatever value they may have, all apart from the question of whether Seneca himself did or did not live up to his own advice.

Among the bountiful array of Seneca's philosophical works—from essays on various key topics in Stoic thought (*De Ira* [On Anger], *De Brevitate Vitae* [On the Shortness of Life], *De Clementia* [On Mercy], etc.) to a succession of "consolations" to selected individuals to assuage their grief over the loss of loved ones—the capstones are his *Epistulae Morales* (Moral Epistles), written to a C. Lucilius, and *Naturales Quaestiones* ("Natural Questions"—i.e., queries on natural phenomena). The *Epistulae* embody the rhetorical flourish that characterises his entire work, while the at times ponderous *Naturales Quaestiones* shows Seneca wrestling with the complex issue of how Stoic moral principles can be harmonised with an understanding of the seeming indifference or even hostility of the natural world toward human life and security.

What we do not find in Seneca's extant writing, however, is a detailed—or even a cursory—discussion of theological principles. It is a truism that Seneca's entire corpus is focused relentlessly on questions of morality and behaviour (both public and private); in this he is largely in congruence with the entire trend of Roman philosophy, which (with the shining exception of Lucretius) chose not to engage in "natural philosophy" or issues relating to metaphysics; but it cannot be assumed that Seneca's silence on theological matters means that he merely subscribed unthinkingly to standard Stoic teaching on the subject, especially since that teaching had itself undergone some significant changes since the days of Zeno and Chrysippus in the third century B.C.E. Indeed, Seneca reveals himself to be a surprisingly eclectic philosopher, drawing upon the thought of contemporary Platonists, Aristotelians, and even Epicureans (generally considered the arch-rivals of the Stoics) in the enunciation of his views. His celebrated comment about Epicurus—"'Epicurus,' you reply, 'uttered these words; what are you doing with another's property?' Any truth, I maintain, is my own property" (*Ep.* 12.10–11)—is representative of his seeking what he believed to be the truth from all sources.

There is some reason to think that Seneca was also affected by a resurgence of Cynicism in the Roman Empire. In the second century B.C.E., Panaetius had striven to eliminate Cynic influence upon Stoicism, but the school continued to be of interest to philosophers of the time, although its true revival dated to the second century C.E. Seneca's advocacy of the benefits of poverty, however much it failed to conform to his personal circumstances, may well be derived from the Cynics.

Seneca's views on the soul may be worth investigating before we examine his views of the (Stoic) god. On the physical constitution of the soul Seneca says little—perhaps in accordance with his general distaste for metaphysics and logic, and his preoccupation with moral exhortation. In *Ep.* 50.6 Seneca declares explicitly: "For what else is the soul than air in a certain state?"[55] The important *Ep.* 92, however, speaks of the parts of the soul along the lines established by Posidonius, and introduces the notion of rational and irrational parts or faculties in the soul: "in the soul there are certain parts which minister to us, enabling us to move and to sustain life, bestowed upon us just for the sake of the primary part of us. In this primary part there is something irrational, and something rational." Later Seneca remarks: "The irrational part of the soul is twofold: the one part is spirited, ambitious, uncontrolled; the other is lowly, sluggish, and devoted to pleasure" (*Ep.* 92.8). This is exactly the Posidonian distinction (taken over from Plato and Aristotle) of the passionate and appetitive parts or faculties of the soul. But the subsequent portions of *Ep.* 92 contrast not the rational and irrational parts of the soul, but the soul and the body: "no man is free who is a slave to his body" (92.33).

Seneca's remarks as to the immortality of the soul are studiously ambiguous, and no clear picture emerges. We know that Panaetius doubted or denied even limited survival of the soul after death, and that Posidonius may have followed him; and there are times when Seneca seems to express similar doubts. It is true that in the *Consolatio ad Marciam* he paints a picture of the souls of great Romans (the Scipios, the Catos, Marcia's father Cremutius Cordus) as inhabiting the celestial abode (25.1–2), and even hints at some sort of purification; but the genre of the *consolatio* may have inclined him to utter such opinions. Indeed, in the *Consolatio ad Polybium* Seneca presents Polybius debating whether

55. I use the translation of Richard M. Gummere.

souls in fact survive the body: "If the dead retain no feeling whatever, my brother has escaped from all the troubles of life" (9.2).[56] Elsewhere, however, Seneca seems more certain of the soul's survival: "death … merely interrupts life, but does not steal it away" (*Ep.* 36.10, where some sort of reincarnation—after the destruction of the world by *ekpyrosis?*—is envisaged). Of one thing Seneca is certain: the soul (or at least the rational part of it) is a piece of the divine: "Reason … is nothing else than a portion of the divine spirit set in a human body" (*Ep.* 66.12). His most extensive discussion of the subject appears in another letter:

> Just as fire cannot be crushed out, since it will escape round the edges of the body which overwhelms it; just as the air cannot be damaged by lashes and blows, or even cut into, but flows back about the object to which it gives place; similarly the soul, which consists of the subtlest particles, cannot be arrested or destroyed inside the body, but, by virtue of its delicate substance, it will rather escape through the very object by which it is being crushed. Just as lightning, no matter how widely it strikes and flashes, makes its return through a narrow opening, so the soul, which is still subtler than fire, has a way of escape through any part of the body. We therefore come to this question—whether the soul can be immortal. But be sure of this: if the soul survives the body after the body is crushed, that soul can in no wise by crushed out, precisely because it does not perish; for the rule of immortality never admits of exceptions, and nothing can harm that which is everlasting. (*Ep.* 57.8)

The reasoning here, however, is very poor: aside from repeated use of analogies that do not seem at all valid or relevant (however much they conform to the standard Stoic doctrine of the soul as material and as a "heated fire" [*pneuma enthermon*]), that concluding remark is merely an exercise in circular reasoning: Seneca has already assumed the immortality of the soul, whereupon its resistance to being crushed or harmed is an inevitable consequence. But even here it is not at all clear that Seneca envisions any kind of *personal* immortality, as opposed to merely the return of a given human soul to the divine substance (presumably God)

56. I use the translation of Aubrey Stewart.

of which it is a part.

Seneca also runs into difficulties when, while seeking to defend the standard Stoic view that the universe was created for the benefit of human beings, he must contend with the obvious fact that bad things happen to human beings of all stripes, independently of their moral status. In the *Naturales Quaestiones* he attempts to establish that the study of nature will inevitably lead one to the divine—but he does so by the awkward means of investigating meteorological phenomena (storms, floods, earthquakes, etc.). Aside from curiously noting that the human race will one day be destroyed by a flood (*N.Q.* 3.27f.), Seneca maintains that earthquakes must simply be accepted as part of the natural order of things. This is not a very satisfactory answer from the Stoic point of view (or any other point of view that rests upon the notion of a benevolent and/or omnipotent god).

Seneca wrestles further with the question—venturing clearly into the "problem of evil"—in the short treatise *De Providentia* (On Providence), which enunciates the Stoic conception of a providence (*pronoia* in Greek) that presumably has human welfare at heart. This treatise is also addressed to Lucilius, but it is similarly unsatisfactory. Here Seneca simply evades or ignores the central Stoic tenet that the universe was created for the benefit of humanity, asserting instead that God has thrown various natural disasters at us as a means of testing our fortitude:

> God bears a fatherly mind towards good men, and loves them in a manly spirit. "Let them," says He, "be exercised by labours, sufferings, and losses, so that they may gather true strength." . . . Do you wonder that God, who so loves the good, who would have them attain the highest goodness and prominence, should appoint fortune to be their adversary? I should not be surprised if the gods [*sic*][57] sometimes experience a wish to behold great men struggling with some misfortune. (1.2.6–7)[58]

This is not very reassuring to the presumably wide array of people who

57. The Latin text does not actually cite the noun "gods" (*dei*); but they are implied in the use of a plural verb (*capiunt*).
58. I use the translation of John W. Basore.

are not "good men" (i.e., the Stoic wise man), who are presumably of no account in this formulation. And when Seneca goes on to state that the "evils" he is discussing aren't really evils at all, we know he has descended into equivocation and doublespeak.

Given that many of Seneca's views on the soul/body dualism, the nature of providence, and the attributes of God are in conformity with Christian teaching, it should come as no surprise that he too, like other ancient philosophers, was seen as *anima naturaliter Christiana,* although it remains unclear to what extent his writings directly influenced Christian metaphysical and moral principles. Some centuries after Seneca's death, a body of letters between him and the apostle Paul (still extant) came to light. These documents are almost certainly spurious, their composition probably triggered by the fact that Paul's life dates (5?–67? C.E.) were almost exactly identical with Seneca's. This body of fourteen letters was probably fabricated in the fourth century. They are entirely contentless, largely consisting of mutual flattery and passing references to events in Rome during the 50s and 60s.

J. Literature During the First and Second Centuries C.E.

The question of how the Silver Age of Latin literature differs from the Golden Age is beyond the scope of this volume, but some discussion may be necessary in order to understand the manner of expression the authors of the first century C.E. adopted, both as poets and prose writers. It is commonly asserted that the dawn of the imperial era resulted in a lack of freedom for artists of all sorts, as if this somehow explains the at times dense, convoluted, and obscure writing we find in several of the writers of this period. While there is evidence that the emperors did inhibit free speech to some degree (especially in regard to what could be said about themselves and the members of their court), and while this may account for some of the unseemly effusiveness toward imperial patronage that a few authors exhibited, a more compelling elucidation of the overall tenor of Silver Age literature can be made by noting (a) the rise of rhetorical training in the schools of the period, and (b) a general sense of the "anxiety of influence," as authors of both prose and verse became increasingly aware of the immense heritage of Greco-Roman literature that had preceded them, leading them to strike out in different directions (while nonetheless being markedly influenced by the very authors whose influence they attempted to evade) and to engage in writing that, like the Modernists of early twentieth-century Europe, is quite difficult to absorb even on the level of metre and syntax, let alone in its conceptual foci.

A notable case in point is the poet Lucan (M. Annaeus Lucanus, 39–65 C.E.), the nephew of Seneca. Born in Spain (Hispania Baetica), he came to Rome and at first enjoyed the favour of Nero; but, when he wrote abusive poems about the emperor, Nero understandably became displeased. Lucan's involvement in the Pisonian conspiracy of 65 resulted in a death sentence, and he committed suicide well before his twenty-sixth birthday.

His sole surviving work, the *De Bello Civili* (On the Civil War; sometimes erroneously as the *Pharsalia*),[59] appears to be unfinished. The work begins with Caesar's crossing of the Rubicon in 49 B.C.E., but tenth and final extant book is considerably shorter than its predecessors and ends abruptly with Caesar dallying with Cleopatra in Egypt after Pharsalus. Lucan probably intended to write at least twelve books (in imitation of Virgil's *Aeneid*) and bring his account to the death of Caesar in 44.

If the overall structure of the *De Bello Civili* is difficult to ascertain, Lucan's attitude toward the gods, and toward religion in general, is still more so. It is a standard assertion that Lucan effected an alteration in the tradition of epic poetry in that he eschewed the direct intervention of the gods in the affairs he narrates; but there is substantial doubt as to whether this decision is in any way indicative of religious scepticism. In the first place, the intrusion of the gods in historical events of relative recency would have seemed absurd to many of his readers;[60] and in the second place, the gods are in fact not absent, manifesting themselves in numerous other contexts. And we must always be aware that Lucan, as a creative artist (even one who seems given to flamboyant bombast and

---

59. This title is derived from the passing phrase *Pharsalia nostra* (9.985; "Our [i.e., my] Pharsalia"), interpreted by many authorities over the centuries as meaning "my poem entitled *Pharsalia*." But in context the phrase clearly refers to the battle of Pharsalus as fought by Julius Caesar and as told by Lucan. In any event, the battle is featured only in Book 7, and the work covers a considerably broader historical period than that.

60. A similar motive may have led Naevius to downplay the role of the gods in his epic poem on the Punic War, as previously discussed.

a frequent straining for effect), cannot automatically be said to endorse the views he places in the mouths of his characters or even in that of his third-person narrator.

As such, it is virtually impossible to discern a coherent theological message in the *De Bello Civili.* It is true that Lucan, as a pupil of the Stoic philosopher L. Annaeus Cornutus, occasionally expresses Stoic doctrine throughout his poem; but his epic seems largely motivated by furious hatred of Caesar as the chief figure in the downfall of Roman "freedom" and the establishment of the imperial regime. (This motif could also not have sat well with his former patron, the emperor Nero.) Astrological references are scattered from the beginning to the end of the work, in accordance with Stoic belief in the practice. Lucan also reflects orthodox Stoic principles in asserting that "It may be that a large part of the whole divine element is embedded in the world to rule it" (5.93–94),[61] although the faint scepticism (*Forsan* [perhaps]) is curious, and the remark is made in the context of a priestess's prophecies.

One supposes we can dismiss the frequent appearances of ghosts—Sulla, Marius, and others—as merely nods to epic convention, not to mention the supernatural events surrounding Caesar's crossing of the Rubicon and such things as a witch's vivid appeal to the gods of the underworld (6.685f.). A dream in which Pompey sees and talks with his deceased wife Julia (formerly in the Elysian Fields, but now in Hades), is evidently to be regarded as a real event, as her ghost was sent to him by the shades of the dead (3.36).

Perhaps the most extensive passage relating to the gods occurs in Book 7, in the very midst of Lucan's account of the battle of Pharsalus:

> Why did we [Romans] enjoy a period of lawful government, or years named after the consuls? Fortunate are the Arabs and Medes and Eastern nations, whom destiny has kept continuously under tyrants. Of all the nations that endure tyranny our lot is the worst, because we blush for our slavery. In very truth there are no gods who govern mankind: though we say falsely that Jupiter reigns, blind chance sweeps the world along. . . . Man's destiny has never been watched over by any god. Yet for this disaster we have revenge, so far as gods may give

61. I use the translation of J. D. Duff.

> satisfaction to mortals: civil war shall make dead Caesars the peers of gods above; and Rome shall deck out dead men with thunderbolts and haloes and constellations, and in the temples of the gods shall swear by ghosts. (7.440–59)

There seem to be some strikingly anti-theist sentiments here; but the context of the passage must be carefully considered. The thrust is overridingly political, as a lament for the loss of Roman freedom; and it is difficult to take seriously the cynical (or despairing) utterance that "there are no gods who govern mankind" (*Sunt nobis nulla profecto / Numina*), since the Olympian gods are abundantly in evidence elsewhere—indeed, in an earlier passage it is clear that both Jupiter and Neptune are attacking Caesar's fleet (5.86f.), a notable exception to Lucan's supposed banishment of the gods from active participation in the events he is narrating. And the final lines of the passage refer with sardonic bitterness to the establishment of the imperial cult as a virtual replacement of the Olympian gods.

This passage must be read in light of an earlier tableau where Caesar orders a sacred grove in Greece to be cut down. Lucan asks incredulously whether the gods would or would not punish such an appalling desecration? Evidently not: "But Fortune often guards the guilty, and the gods must reserve their wrath for the unlucky" (3.448–49). Without expressing any notable scepticism, Lucan is appalled that the tyrant Caesar escapes divine wrath in this manner.

Lucan records in a more orthodox Stoic manner how, after his death, Pompey's soul ascended to heaven (9.1f.). And he finds in Cato the Younger (who, let us recall, was a dogmatic Stoic) the perfect mouthpiece for both the demise of Roman freedom and the religious piety that Lucan (or, at any rate, his narrator) believes a morally upright person should exhibit: "Assuredly you have ever lived your life in accordance with divine law, and you are a follower after God" (9.556–57). Cato himself goes on to say that "We men are all inseparable from the gods, and, even if the oracle be dumb, all our actions are predetermined by Heaven. The gods have no need to speak; for the Creator told us once for all at our birth whatever we are permitted to know" (9.573–76).

And yet, Lucan at times appears to vaunt either fate (usually expressed in the plural, *fata*) or chance (variously expressed as *Fortuna, fors,* or *casus*) as the true motivating factor in human affairs—a factor perhaps greater than the gods themselves. In a curious passage at the beginning of Book 2, a concatenation of forces—"heaven's wrath" (*irae deum* 2.1), the universe (*mundus* 2.2), Nature (*natura* 2.3), and Jupiter (*rector Olympi* 2.4)—are all evoked to proclaim the onset of the civil war. Lucan goes on to say:

> Whether the author of the universe (*parens rerum*), when the fire [i.e., the Stoic *ekpyrosis*] gave place and he first took in hand the shapeless realm of raw matter, established the chain of causes for all eternity, and bound himself as well by universal law, and portioned out the universe, which endures the ages prescribed for it, by a fixed line of destiny (*Fatorum*); or whether nothing is ordained and Fortune, moving at random, brings round the cycle of events, and chance (*fors*) is master of mankind—in either case, let thy purpose, whatever it be, be sudden; let the mind of man be blind to coming doom; he fears, but leave him hope. (2.7–15)

Whether the universe is ruled by the fixed laws of destiny (which may or may not include a creator god) or whether everything is blind chance doesn't seem to matter. If any passage indicates Lucan's fundamental lack of interest in philosophical or theological matters, so long as he can use either the gods or Fortune as elements in his lurid and overcoloured account of the events that led to Rome's purported transformation from freedom to slavery, this must be it.

Lucan was not the only epic poet of the era; and while the epics of Statius, Silius Italicus, and Valerius Flaccus are no longer held in quite the low esteem that they once were, none of these works are of great relevance to our study. Statius (P. Papinius Statius, 45?–96 c.e.) largely sought safety in Greek mythological motifs in his work, which survives in abundance, although he did write a (non-extant) work on Domitian's wars in Germany. What do survive are the *Thebaid,* the *Achilleid,* and the *Silvae.* The *Thebaid,* in its account of the war between the brothers Eteocles and Polynices (sons of Oedipus) for the throne of Thebes, has been seen as an indirect reflection of the Roman civil war that put an end to the Republic; and to the extent that the gods who appear in the work are more allegorical than anthropomorphic, we can see some hint of originality on the author's part. The *Achilleid* exists in an unfinished state, only one and a half books having been written before the poet's death. This biographical portrayal of Achilles' actions during the Trojan war and elsewhere is—aside from the necessary presence of his mother, the sea nymph Thetis—largely shorn of supernatural or divine figures.

The *Silvae* is a volume of occasional poetry in various metres on random domestic subjects. Its reputation (and that of Statius overall) has not fared well because of what appear to be fawning obsequiousness to the emperor Domitian; and even if we are to believe the assertions of recent scholars that such passages present a covertly subversive criticism of the autocratic tendencies of the Roman imperial court and aristocracy, the work as a whole has little relevance to our enquiry.

Valerius Flaccus (fl. c. 80 C.E.) similarly retreated to a Greek theme in his *Argonautica.* While it cannot be said to be anything like an exact copy of the epic of Apollonius of Rhodes, there is little originality in the work, and Flaccus is content to tread familiar ground in his portrayals of both the human and divine figures in the story of Jason, Medea, and the golden fleece.

The *Punica* of Silius Italicus (Tiberius Catius Asconius Silius Italicus, 26?–101?) is the longest surviving epic poem in classical Latin, but has few other virtues—if indeed its length is a virtue. It relates the events of the Second Punic War in seventeen books totalling some 12,000 lines; and although his work bears the manifest influence of Livy (in historical details), Varro (in geography), and Lucan himself, he abandoned Lucan's eschewing of divine interference in human affairs and was happy to feature Jupiter, Juno, Venus, and all the rest of the pantheon at key moments.

It is of some note that much of the writing of this period is sharply satirical in nature, whether it be the languid cynicism of Petronius, the frequently prurient obscenity of Martial, or the hectoring moral condemnations of Persius and Juvenal. Whether such a tendency was inspired by the decadence of the age (the well-chronicled luxuriousness of the wealthy class, the corruption—ranging from incest to adultery to actual murder—of the imperial court, the ongoing social and moral corrosion endemic to a slave-owning society, and so on), or whether the authors simply chose to utilise their gifts of rhetoric, wit, and pungent outrage to lambaste their contempories is not entirely clear; but the result is a series of works that have painted a lurid picture of the multitudinous degeneracy of the sprawling megalopolis that Rome had undeniably become.

Of the *Satyricon* of Petronius (C. Petronius Arbiter, 27?–66 C.E.) it is difficult to speak with precision, given that what has come down to us is a small fraction of the entire work, which may have been as much as five to ten times as long. Whether we are to regard the title as deriving from *satura* (satire or medley) or *satyros* (satyr) or both is unclear; in any event, what we have is a sprawling and not particularly coherent text that traces the activities of a young Greek freedman, Encolpius, and some of his companions (the boy Giton; another young man, Ascyltos) as they roam the Greek and Roman world for no clear purpose. The central surviving tableau is the *Cena Trimalchionis* (Trimalchio's Dinner), a broadly satirical glimpse at the appalling flamboyance and vulgarity (in numerous senses of the term) of the *nouveau riche* host and his obsequious dinner companions. As a slice of life (at least of a certain segment of it), it is unmatched in Latin literature for vividness and deadpan drollery.

Whether any genuine attitude toward religion can be derived from the text as we have it is gravely open to doubt. Trimalchio himself is mercilessly ridiculed for his belief in astrology, the ridiculous errors he makes in rattling off common Greco-Roman myths, and other examples of his general ignorance and absence of refined culture. It is of little significance that, when a lugubrious Trimalchio makes ostentatious preparations for his own funeral, he axiomatically assumes life after death (71).

Later, Encolpius laments the decline of philosophy and religion (88), but this is part of a general (and formulaic) whine about the general decline of society, one that is probably intended to poke fun at Encolpius himself. Another character, Lichas, a ship captain, tells a woman, "Tryphaena, I believe you admit that the Gods in Heaven take some trouble about men's affairs" (106).[62] But Encolpius later blames both the gods and *fortuna* (114) for the wreck of the ship they are on. In reciting a long poem on the civil war, Encolpius puts these words in the mouth of Dis, the ruler of the underworld: "Disposer of life in

62. I use the translation of Michael Heseltine (rev. E. H. Warmington).

earth and heaven, Chance (*Fors*), always angry against power too firmly seated, everlasting lover of change and quick forsaker of conquests, dost thou not feel thy spirit crushed under the weight of Rome, and that thou canst not further raise up the mass that is doomed to fall?" After all this, the passing mention of Epicurus as the "father of truth" (*pater veri:* 132) doesn't amount to much. Indeed, this mention is more than a little problematical, since Encolpius goes on to vaunt Epicurus for his advocacy of sexual pleasure—the very thing he strove to deny in his definition of pleasure.

In some poems that may or may not have been part of the *Satyricon,* we find Petronius (or some narrator) asserting that "It was fear first created gods in the world" (3.1), and later that it is not gods who send dreams (31.1–3). But these random remarks do not amount to anything approaching a philosophy, a theology, or an expression of scepticism. There is little evidence that Petronius had much interest in these subjects; his manifest aim was to provide amusement, and in that goal he was eminently successful.

The satirist Persius (A. Persius Flaccus, 34–62) was yet another writer of the Neronian era who died young, although in his case it was not through forced suicide but apparently through some kind of stomach ailment. What is left is a small book of six satires plainly written under Stoic principles; Persius was another pupil of the philosopher Cornutus. His poems are crabbed, dense, and at times obscure, but they are fired with loathing of the decadence he saw all around him. In this sense (as well as in the apparent purity of the life he led) he is the antipodal opposite of the languid Petronius, who relished his title of *arbiter elegantiae* (arbiter of elegance) as a member of the imperial court. There is little religious speculation in Persius' work. His second satire is a long harangue on foolish prayers to the gods. The targets of the satire are prayers that are unworthy of the gods (e.g., prayers for riches, advantageous marriages for one's children, and so forth); there is no trace of any scepticism regarding the value of prayer in itself. Indeed, the satire concludes:

> Nay rather let us offer to the gods what the blear-eyed progeny of the great Messala [a degenerate aristocrat] cannot give out of his lordly salver:—a heart rightly attuned towards God and man; a mind pure in

> its inner depths, and a soul steeped in nobleness and honour. Give me these to offer in the temples, and a handful of grits shall win my prayer for me! (2.71–75)[63]

The fifth satire, addressed to Cornutus, expounds on the standard Stoic topos that all people except the Stoic wise man are slaves.

There is surprisingly little of relevance to us in the bountiful work of Martial (M. Valerius Martialis, 38?–104?), author of fourteen books of epigrams and some other work. He was born in Spain (Hispania Tarraconensus) and came to Rome around 63. He began publishing in 80, and his first book of epigrams appeared in 84. These works—written in a variety of metres but generally short, pointed, and full of barbed satire against all manner of individuals or issues that caught Martial's interest—made him famous, but he remained impoverished (by his own testimony) and dependent on the financial assistance of various patrons, including the emperor Domitian. Indeed, he actually refers to that emperor as a "master and god" (5.8.1), and elsewhere he virtually vaunts Domitian above the Olympian gods themselves (9.3).

The most notable characteristic of Martial's work is, however, an exuberant and unabashed obscenity that relishes the sexual irregularities of the various individuals upon whom he focuses.[64] To the extent that this is an indication of an apparent disregard for the stern morality of the old-time Roman culture and, by implication, an equal disregard for any disapproval or punishment that might be meted out by gods or human beings for such actions, we may find a highly indirect implication of religious indifference among the segment of the populace with whom Martial concerns himself. But that is just about all that we can ascertain in this context from his otherwise engaging work.

With Juvenal (D. Junius Juvenalis, 55?–140?) we are on very different ground. This last and greatest of Roman verse satirists—and one of the towering figures of Latin and world literature—is the author of sixteen satires (the last one incomplete or fragmentary) that were published in five books beginning around 100 and proceeding to the end of his life.

---

63. I use the translation of G. G. Ramsay.

64. There are probably more instances in Martial of the verb "to fuck" (*futuare*) than in any extant author in Latin literature, to say nothing of obscene terms referring to other sex acts and the men and women who perform them.

Unlike Horace, he adopted a mordant tone of bitter condemnation of the vices and moral deficiencies he claimed to see all around him, and his work is grimly effective even if we assume his portrayals are exaggerated or overcoloured. Although we must deprecate the sixth satire (a 661-line work published separately as his second book), against women, as exhibiting vicious misogyny, and although some of his other work betrays occasional signs of racial or ethnic prejudice, his third satire (on the moral collapse of Rome) and the heavily philosophical tenth satire, among others, have been immensely influential.

Virtually nothing is known of Juvenal's life, and attempts by ancient commentators to reconstruct it on the basis of his writings must be regarded as implausible or at best speculative. He was evidently born in the Italian city of Aquinum. At some point in his life he was exiled for insulting an actor who was popular at the imperial court; at this time he apparently went to Egypt (the subject of his fifteenth satire). He was acquainted with Martial, who mentions him in several poems.

There is much room for speculation as to Juvenal's philosophical and religious orientation.[65] Over the centuries scholars have labelled him a Cynic, a Stoic, and even an Epicurean; but he himself, in a late satire, expounds what might be called a declaration of independence from any single school of philosophy: "And now hear what consolations can be offered on the other side by one who has not embraced the doctrines either of the Cynics, or of the Stoics—who only differ from the Cynics by a shirt—nor yet reverenced Epicurus, so proud of the growing slips in his tiny garden" (13.120–23).[66] And yet, these three schools were in accord on many points relating to ethics (which is virtually Juvenal's sole concern when discussing philosophical issues), so it may not much matter what sect Juvenal consciously allied himself with. If anything, he reveals more Stoic tendencies than any other; and the conjectures of some scholars that he had a late conversion to Epicureanism cannot be plausibly maintained. It is, however, undeniable that Juvenal was influenced by Lucretius, whose poetry he clearly admired; but he seems largely to have rejected Epicurean metaphysical and ethical principles, especially as relating to the doctrine of *voluptas*.

In his religious views, Juvenal scarcely accepts the Roman pantheon

65. See, in general, my "Juvenal and Ancient Philosophy," in *Classical Papers* 273–307.
66. I use the translation of G. G. Ramsay.

in a conventional way—note his ridicule of Calvinus' naïveté concerning the gods:

> Tell me, you old gentleman . . . do you know nothing of the charm of other people's money? Are you ignorant of how the world laughs at your simplicity when you demand of any man that he shall not perjure himself, and believe that some divinity is to be found in temples or in altars red with blood? (13.33–37)

It is true that this remark is directly followed by: "Primitive men lived thus in the olden days, before Saturn laid down his diadem and fled, betaking himself to the rustic sickle; in the days when Juno was a little maid, and Jupiter still a private gentleman in the caves of Ida" (1.38–41); but the sardonic tone suggests that he is hardly a devout believer in the Olympian gods. Conversely, we must not regard too seriously his disbelief in the underworld—"That there are such things as Manes, and kingdoms below ground, and punt-poles, and Stygian pools black with frogs, and all those thousands crossing over in a single bark—these things not even boys believe, except such as have not yet had their penny bath" (2.149–52)—not only because this is a wicked parody of Propertius, but because such disbelief had been common among the intelligentsia since Cicero's time.

But if Juvenal has no real belief in Jupiter, he evidently feels that Roman religious rites ought to be preserved. On the positive side we note his glowing description of the sacrifice of a lamb for Corvinus (12.1–9), while on the negative side must be observed Juvenal's censure of the Egyptians for their worship of outlandish gods ("In one part cats are worshipped, in another a river fish, in another whole townships venerate a dog; none adore Diana" [15.7–8]) and his loathing of Roman women's base prayers to the gods (6.390–92). Indeed, Juvenal's attitude toward foreign gods is an unusually hostile one, and is perhaps a reflection or adoption of popular sentiment.

In conjunction with this belief, however, is a scorn for religious intolerance—the brunt of his attacks upon both the Jews and the Egyptians. In the fourteenth satire the former are satirised not only for their exclusivity but for their refusal to accept Roman authority: "Having been wont to flout the laws of Rome, they learn and practise and revere the Jewish law, and all that Moses handed down in his secret tome, forbidding to point the way to any not worshipping the same rites, and conducting none but the circumscribed to the desired fountain" (14.100–104). The Egyptians are treated no more kindly, as Juvenal recounts a vicious battle between the denizens of Ombi and Tentyra: "Each people is filled with fury against the other because each hates its neighbours' gods, deeming that none can be held as deities save its own" (15.35–38).

If Juvenal recognises any sort of divinity, it is Fortuna. Fortuna was often associated with fate (hence Juvenal's ironic reference, through the mouth of Naevolus, "Man is ruled by destiny" [*fata regnunt homines* 9.32]—a reference that is clearly intended to satirise Naevolus through his own inane utterances), and it was a very real force to the Stoics: almost no page of Seneca lacks a mention of Fortuna. Pliny the Elder (*Natural History* 2.22) tells us that the goddess was "deemed volatile and indeed by most men blind as well [= *casus* or Chance], wayward, inconstant, uncertain, fickle in her favours and favouring the unworthy."[67] Juvenal certainly accords her great power: "If Fortune so choose, you will become a Consul from being a rhetor; if again she so wills, you will become a rhetor from being a Consul" (7.197–98). But in the end it is merely a product of human folly: "Thou wouldst have no divinity, O Fortune, if we had but wisdom; it is we that make a goddess of thee, and place thee in the skies" (10.365–66). Wisdom is the conqueror of Fortune (13.20)—a Stoic notion.

The fifteenth satire reveals a dawning monotheism that may be both Cynic in source and representative of his own time; and its sharp distinction between animals and human beings is unmistakably Stoic:

> When Nature gave tears to man, she proclaimed that he was tender-hearted; and tenderness is the best qality in man. . . . It is this that separates us from the dumb herd; and it is for this that we alone have had allotted to us a nature worthy of reverence, capable of divine things, fit to acquire and practise the arts of life, and that we have drawn on high that gift of feeling which is lacking to the beasts that grovel with eyes upon the ground. To them in the beginning of the world our common maker (*communis conditor*) gave only life; to us he

67. I use the translation of H. Rackham.

> gave souls as well, that fellow-feeling might bid us ask or proffer aid . . . (15.131–50)

But Juvenal can't resist concluding this plangent passage with barbed cynicism: "But in these days there is more amity among serpents than among men" (15.159).

Juvenal's theology is, in spite of connexions with Stoic and Cynic theory, more that of the average educated Roman than one founded upon any true philosophical system. The distinction is not always an easy one, for Stoic religious theory tended in the Roman Empire to merge gradually with traditional belief—hence, of course, its great popularity among the Romans. Juvenal is typical of his time not merely in his disbelief in the traditional gods, not merely in his scorn of emperor-worship (cf. 4.71, 6.115), but in a gradual tendency toward monotheism that would make all the easier the eventual Roman conversion to the Christian faith. But in the final analysis Juvenal finds little divinity in the world. One wonders whether he found solace even in his largely secular recommendation of "a sound mind in a sound body" (*mens sana in corpore sano* 10.356).

The only Roman historian of any consequence during this period is Tacitus (P. Cornelius Tacitus, 56?–120?). He was born of an equestrian family, probably in Gaul or northern Italy, and came to Rome as a young man. He married the daughter of the celebrated general Cn. Julius Agricola, the conqueror of Britain, and wrote a flattering biography of him. Ascending the ranks of the Roman political hierarchy, he gained some experience as an administrator in various provinces before settling down to write his two major works, the *Histories* and the *Annals*.

The *Annals* cover the period 14–68 C.E., while the *Histories* cover the period 69–96. Both works survive in incomplete form, but there is enough of them for us to gain a thorough idea of Tacitus' formidable skills as an historian and rhetorician. In a sense he is the Roman Thucycides, a cold, cynical observer of Roman political and social decline, as compared to Livy, the garrulous Roman Herodotus. Oddly enough, the *Histories* were written first; it is conceivable that, in writing this work, Tacitus realised that the woes he perceived in the political life of his time had roots in the succession of emperors following Augustus, so that he felt the need to study the earlier period in detail. Whatever the case, the result is a searing—if at times tendentious—account that emphasises the misdeeds of the emperors (especially Caligula, Claudius, and Domitian) and the general degeneracy of the Roman people as a whole.

Tacitus has long been assumed by scholars to be a religious sceptic, but there is reason to doubt this characterisation. Even a passing comment about the gods' indifference to the fate of human beings ("so impartially indifferent is heaven to examples of virtue and vice" [*Annals* 16.33.1])[68] acknowledges the existence of the gods. There is no real evidence that Tacitus doubted the validity of the imperial cult; at best, there are some indications that, in his view, the Senate was not up to the task of making a sound judgment as to which emperor deserved deification and which did not. This itself is part of Tacitus' oft-expressed accusation that the Senate had lapsed into gross sycophancy in regard to the emperors.

At the opening of Book 4 of the *Annals,* chronicling the period 23–28 C.E., Tacitus expounds on the ascension of L. Aelius Sejanus, a Roman soldier who won the favour of Tiberius and for the next eight years exercised all but unlimited power in the court. Remarkably, the otherwise sober Tacitus declares that Sejanus' rise was not due to his own skills; "it was rather from heaven's wrath against Rome, to whose welfare his elevation and his fall were alike disastrous" (*Annals* 4.1.1.). The *Histories* opens with the turbulent period of the "year of the four emperors" (68–69), and Tacitus is explicit in stating that the gods were intimately involved in the outcome:

> Besides the manifold vicissitudes of human affairs, there were prodigies in heaven and earth, the warning voices of the thunder, and other intimations of the future, auspicious or gloomy, doubtful or not to be mistaken. Never surely did more terrible calamities of the Roman People, or evidence more conclusive, prove that the Gods take no thought for our happiness, but only for our punishment. (*Histories* 1.3.2)

Whether that final comment is intended straightforwardly or sardonically, it is clear that Tacitus, like Livy before him, finds validity in at least some "prodigies" as signs of impending doom or catastrophe. As

68. I use the translation of Alfred John Church and William Jackson Brodribb. The Latin text reads *deum* ("gods") for "heaven."

Jason P. Davies states, "Tacitus has no doubt that prodigies indicate the wrath of the gods, and that Rome suffered from that wrath increasingly during the first century, and he shows great skill in incorporating them into his narrative."[69]

During this same turbulent period, Tacitus is appalled by the burning of the temple of Jupiter on the Capitoline Hill on 19 December 69, at a time when Vespasian was ousting his rivals and establishing himself as emperor. Tacitus flamboyantly states that "This was the most deplorable and disgraceful event that had happened to the Commonwealth of Rome since the foundation of the city" (*Histories* 3.72.1). The gods are explicitly recognised here ("Heaven [was] ready to be propitious, had our vices only allowed"). This whole conception may connect with Tacitus' frequently expressed hostility to foreign religious customs. Egyptians, for example, are pointedly criticised for their superstitiousness (*Histories* 1.11.1), while the Germans are ridiculed for the "barbarous altars" (*Annals* 1.61.3) where Roman officers were immolated during the staggering defeat of the Roman army, led by P. Quinctilius Varus, at the hands of Arminius and his tribes at the battle of the Teutoberg Forest (9 C.E.).

And yet, Tacitus openly expresses doubt as to whether it is fate, chance, or the gods who are ultimately responsible for the miseries suffered by the human race. In his most extended discussion of the subject (*Annals* 6.22), he begins: "When I hear of these and like occurrences, I suspend my judgment on the question whether it is fate and unchangeable necessity or chance which governs the revolutions of human affairs." He goes on to wonder whether certain philosophers are right in thinking that "heaven does not concern itself with the beginning or the end of our life, or, in short, with mankind at all" (the reference is obviously to the Epicureans), or whether there is any truth in astrology ("others, on the contrary, believe that, though there is a harmony between fate and events, yet it is not dependent on wandering stars"). Tacitus comes to no conclusion on these fraught issues.

Tacitus' friend Pliny the Younger (61?–113) is of interest from a very different perspective. Having inherited the estate of his uncle, Pliny the Elder (for whom see section L), he became a lawyer, then a government functionary, rising to the rank of consul in 100. In 111 he became Emperor

69. Davies, *Rome's Religious History* 222.

Trajan's representative to the province of Bithynia and Pontus (in what is now the northern coast of Turkey). His ten books of letters—the first nine books of which are addressed to various correspondents, with the tenth book consisting of official correspondence between himself and Trajan—were carefully selected and edited by himself, and therefore lack some of the spontaneity of Cicero's letters; but they nonetheless reveal a distinctive personality.

Pliny evinced virtually no interest in philosophy, although in an early letter (1.12) he speaks of the death of a philosopher of his acquaintance, Corellius Rufus. This letter itself, aside from a formulaic utterance that "the gods answered his prayer"[70] (i.e., to die), is instructive in revealing the uniform secularism of Pliny's outlook. Neither in this letter nor in any others (and there are several), in which he offers consolation to correspondents regarding deaths of loved ones, does Pliny utter a word about the afterlife, not even any such anodyne comments such as "he/she has gone to a better place." It is particularly striking that, in a relatively lengthy passage regarding the death of a fourteen-year-old girl, he is entirely silent about her survival after death (5.16). A remark regarding one Verginius Rufus, who had recently died—"For he lives and will live for ever" (2.1)—is, in context, merely a suggestion that he will live in the memories of those who knew him. An adjuration to one Valerius Maximus to "Respect the gods" (8.24) refers to the fact that Valerius is going to Greece as some sort of administrator and is "set to order the constitution of free cities"; hence Pliny's comment is largely prudential, as a means of placating Greek citizens by not disturbing their religious views.

This attitude is the more remarkable in that Pliny himself held several religious posts—but many of these appear to have been largely honorific titles that were bestowed upon him for his services to the (secular) state. For example, he became an augur in 103 and wrote about it in a letter (4.8); but in this letter he makes no reference to his own religious beliefs, merely taking pride in the fact that the office had formerly been held by Cicero and that he was replacing Julius Frontinus, the author of numerous technical treatises (some still surviving), whom Pliny regards as "one of our greatest citizens."

70. I use the translation of Betty Radice.

The one instance where Pliny reveals some sort of vaguely religious—or, perhaps more precisely, superstitious—sentiment is in his celebrated letter to Licinius Sura (7.27) about a supposed haunted house in Athens that he heard about. The house had a bad reputation, as on occasion the clanking of chains could be heard, followed by "the spectre of an old man, emaciated and filthy, with a long flowing beard and hair on end, wearing fetters on his legs and shaking the chains on his wrists." This actually led some occupants of the house to perish in fear, whereupon the house was deserted and lay empty. A philosopher, Athenodorus, comes to Athens and decides to spend a night there. He too hears the clanking; then the ghost appears. But being a philosopher, Athenodorus is not frightened. The ghost leads him into the courtyard of the house, then vanishes. The next day Athenodorus brings city officials to the place and—predictably enough—the bones of the "ghost" are discovered, "twisted round with chains." Pliny is inclined to accept the story.

Otherwise, Pliny reveals as thoroughly secular an outlook as can be found in Latin literature outside of Lucretius. This is not in any way to say that he is an atheist; but he may be representative of a wider class of urbane, educated Romans who had largely dispensed with religion except insofar as it figured in official government functions. Pliny's interests are wholly secular, ranging from a devotion to Greek and Roman oratory, the particulars of his house in Laurentum, the various legal cases he prosecuted, and even chatty gossip about the pleasures of fishing in Lake Como. In many ways he reveals a strikingly modern perspective on religion, society, and politics.

K. Greek and Latin Literature and Philosophy in the Later Empire

Other writers during this period (first and second centuries C.E.), whether they be avowed philosophers or writers of other sorts (novelists, satirists, historians, and so on), are worth studying on a number of levels, chiefly to underscore a tendency we have already been noting—the extent to which Stoicism (involving, crucially, an increasing tendency toward monotheism) had become the de facto religious and philosophical outlook of educated Romans. And yet, other writers point to the persistence of Epicureanism as a counterweight to Stoicism and other religiously inclined philosophies as well as a recrudescence of Platonism that would ultimately lead to the movement called Neoplatonism (for which see the next chapter). Five authors, four of whom wrote in Greek, shall be studied here.

The Stoic philosopher Epictetus (50?–135?) was a slave in the court of Nero but gained his freedom around 68. Having studied with the philosopher Musonius Rufus, he began teaching philosophy—first in Rome, then (when Domitian exiled the philosophers in 93) in Greece. A copious body of work bearing his name has come down to us, but its provenance is to some degree dubious: his extant writings, the *Discourses* (four out of eight books of which survive) and the *Enchiridion* (Handbook), were set down by his pupil Arrian, who claimed to have recorded Epictetus' lectures word-for-word. No one, however, seriously doubts that what we have is indeed a reasonably faithful record of Epictetus' teaching, since it presents a fairly consistent account of his beliefs and principles.

Epictetus' thinking is resolutely religious and monotheistic. "We are all primarily begotten of God, and . . . God is the father of men as well as of gods," he states early on in the *Discourses* (1.3.).[71] But does he ever question the very existence of god (or the gods)? In one discourse (1.12) he claims he will do so, but he refuses to engage in a truly searching enquiry into the matter. "Concerning gods there are some who say that the divine does not so much as exist; and others, that it exists, indeed, but is inactive and indifferent, and takes forethought for nothing" (1.12.1). The second group is the Epicureans, but the very existence of a group of apparently open or avowed atheists is of interest, unless Epictetus is merely setting up a hypothetical straw man he intends to knock down. And although he claims that "We must, therefore, first of all enquire about each of these statements, to see whether it is sound or not sound. For if gods do not exist, how can it be an end to follow the gods?" (1.12.4–5), his subsequent discussion simply fails to grapple with the issue.

We may perhaps have to infer his stance from other passages, such as his apparent contention that a belief in providence rests upon the argument from design (1.6). In a later discourse, we learn that "when someone asked him [Epictetus] how a man could be convinced that each thing which he does is under the eye of God" (1.14.1), Epictetus

71. I use the translation of W. A. Oldfather.

replied: "How else comes it that so regularly, as if from God's command, when He bids the plants flower, they flower, when He bids them put forth shoots, they put them forth, [etc.]" (1.14.3). This is an elementary instance of begging the question, since the contention that God does do these things is the very point at issue.

Also in question is how exactly we are to ascertain the will of God as a gauge of our own actions—and this too is something Epictetus never clarifies. Throughout his works he is keen that people "must cease to blame God or man" (3.22.13) for their own troubles. Well and good; but this gets us no closer to how we are to "follow God" without some clear and explicit formula for so doing. Evidently Epictetus believed in a sort of free will in spite of his belief in providence; but we have seen other Stoic philosophers fumbling toward what I have called a "soft determinism," and Epictetus' writings may constitute only the most explicit assertion of this view.

Epictetus subscribes to other standard Stoic doctrines, such as the unbridgeable gulf between human beings and animals; the latter exist merely for the sake of the former:

> Each of the animals God constitutes, one to be eaten, another to serve in farming, another to produce cheese, and yet another for some other similar use; to perform these functions what need have they to understand external impressions and to be able to differentiate between them? But God has brought man into the world to be a spectator of Himself and of His Works, and not merely a spectator, but also an interpreter. (1.6.18)

We are also evidently endowed with an innate concept of good and evil (2.11.3). This faculty is perhaps related to the notion that God is in us ("you are a being of primary importance; you are a fragment of God; you have within you a part of Him" [2.8.11); but in that case, why do moral failings even exist? And why would we need a teacher like Epictetus to exhort us to do good rather than evil?

With Marcus Aurelius (121–180; emperor, 161–80), Stoic philosophy reached the very heights of Roman political life. His *Meditations,* extant in twelve relatively short books, were written in the course of his military campaigns, chiefly in the 170s. This may account for their scattershot nature, whereby they leap from one topic to the next without much coherence and at times consist of nothing but quotations from previous thinkers.

Marcus is just as convinced as Epictetus and other Stoics of the existence of God—but, it appears, chiefly because the alternative is too repugnant to contemplate. "If indeed there are no Gods, or if they do not concern themselves with the affairs of men, what boots it for me to live in a Universe empty of Gods, or empty of Providence?" (2.11).[72] Although Marcus uses "God" and "gods" interchangeably, he later clarifies that there is in fact only "one God immanent in all things" (7.9). Only at the very end of his *Meditations* does he take up the critical issue of whether gods exist at all and how we are to know of their existence:

> If any ask, *Where hast thou seen the Gods or how hast thou satisfied thyself of their existence that thou art so devout a worshipper?* I answer: In the first place, they are even visible to the eyes. In the next, I have not seen my own soul either, yet I honour it. So then from the continual proofs of their power I am assured that Gods also exist and I reverence them. (12.28)

This is not likely to convince a sceptic. That phrase about the gods being "visible to the eyes" is a nod to the Stoic belief that the stars were divine. And as for the invisibility of the soul—it would probably have been unreasonable to expect someone like Marcus to question whether the soul really exists, since such a proposition would have been virtually inconceivable to the entire Greco-Roman intellectual community. In the end, Marcus dismisses the idea that the gods "take counsel about nothing at all" as an "impious belief" (6.44) and is done with the issue.

And yet, much of what Marcus lays out in his *Meditations* would make for a sound secular ethic, and many of his recommendations for thought and behaviour have little relation to theology ("Firstly, eschew action that is aimless and has no objective. Secondly, take as the only goal of conduct what is to the common interest" [12.20]). Strikingly, Marcus denies the immortality of the soul of even "good men" (12.5). It is true that this passage is crippled by the fatal Stoic fallacy of living "in

72. I use the translation of C. R. Haines.

conformity with Nature" (a largely meaningless formulation—or, rather, one with such a multiplicity of meanings that it becomes useless as a guide to conduct) and the more generally religious notion that "the Gods [are] infinitely good and just," so that "they could not have overlooked anything being wrongly or irrationally neglected in their thorough Ordering of the Universe"; but the stance is nonetheless noteworthy.

Some of the most interesting, and iconoclastic, religious speculation is found in authors who are not self-proclaimed philosophers. The writers of this period had, as I have suggested, received exhaustive rhetorical training, and that included at least a superficial awareness of the chief philosophical schools then current in Rome and elsewhere. That several authors are not shy about poking ribald fun at the Olympian gods is yet one more sign of weakening belief in them among the intelligentsia.

The life of Plutarch (L. Mestrius Plutarchus, 46–120?) almost exactly matched that of Epictetus in terms of chronology, but his output was quite different. A greater quantity of writing by Plutarch has come down to us than any other writer in classical antiquity; but this is, in his case, a somewhat dubious distinction. Chiefly, the Christians who curated the writings of ancient authors found much use in his *Parallel Lives* (a series of biographies of statesmen, writers, and other notables in whom Plutarch found intriguing parallels between Greek and Roman figures he dealt with, although in many instances the parallels are highly artificial) and in his *Moralia,* an extensive series of essays on all manner of subjects, many of which appear to echo Christian doctrine in spite of the fact that Plutarch professed himself a follower of Plato. A systematic reading of Plutarch's bountiful output cannot dispel the impression that he simply wasn't very bright, and that much of his work is the tiresome and contentless work of a windbag.

The difficulty in studying Plutarch's work is that its chronological progression is in many instances impossible to ascertain, so that it becomes problematical to speak of any development in his outlook from his early works to his later ones. His life may be of some interest in this regard. Born in Chaeronea, near Delphi, he studied philosophy under one Ammonius (who is sometimes referred to as a Peripatetic [i.e., a follower of Aristotle], but who apparently was also a Platonist) as a young man. He then became a priest at the Temple of Apollo at Delphi; he served this function for at least the last thirty years of his life, and "it is most likely that all the *Lives* were written when Plutarch was a priest at Delphi."[73] Many features of his thought are elucidated once we understand the deep religiosity that was manifestly a central feature of Plutarch's character.

His consistent and often-expressed hostility to the Epicureans is of note. In what is likely to be an early work, *De Superstitione* (On Superstition),[74] Plutarch sees superstition and atheism as opposite poles that both reflect "the stream of ignorance and of misconception about the Gods" (164e).[75] And yet, atheism is marginally superior to superstition in certain particulars. Atheism leads people to "disbelief in the Divine . . . ; its object in not acknowledging Gods is that it may not fear them" (165b), which is a plain reference to Epicureans. It is of some interest to observe that Plutarch essentially equates Epicureanism and atheism, here and elsewhere, even though that sect itself was vociferous in denying such an identification. But superstition is worse because, although such people believe in gods, they also believe (reprehensibly) "that they are grievous and hurtful" (165b). The superstitious cannot escape their fears even in death, because they populate the afterlife with "the apprehension of undying ills" (166f). The superstitious are, in fact, more impious than atheists themselves: "Is the man who recognizes no Gods a profane person, and does not he, who takes them for such beings as the superstitious think, hold a far more profane creed?" (169f). The superstitious in fact hate the gods, and their pernicious beliefs have led to such horrors as the sacrifice of infants to gods.

All this sounds promising from our perspective, but it is by no means clear to what extent Plutarch upheld such sane views in the rest of his career (if in fact *De Superstitione* is an early work). A series of three interrelated works, *De Defectu Oraculorum* (On the Cessation of Oracles), *De Pythiae Oraculis* (On the Pythian Responses), and *De E apud Delphos* (On the E at Delphi), are all resolutely determined to shield the oracular utterances at Delphi and elsewhere from scepticism, notably by Epicureans. The first is of greatest interest to us. Here the text features two different accounts as to why there has been a decline in the efficacy of oracles: Cleombrotus opines that the *daimones* who convey the

73. Brenk, *In Mist Apparelled* 185.
74. It is customary to cite Plutarch's works by Latin titles.
75. I use the translation of A. O. Prickard.

divine intentions to oracles have gone to another world, while Lamprias (Plutarch's brother) states that the *pneuma* (air or wind) that engenders the prophetic spirit of oracles has dissipated. Between these two theories there is not a great deal for the rational person to choose from, even if the latter is by a very long stretch a pseudo-scientific doctrine whereas the former is, in spite of Cleombrotus' long-winded attempts to justify it on scientific or philosophical grounds, pure fantasy. The other two texts concern even more recondite points that need not concern us.

The notion of *daimones* is widespread in Plutarch's diverse writings, and he apparently concludes (as Lamprias does in *De Defectu*) that these are souls who have been stripped of the bodies they occupied and now wander free. In his view, human souls always possessed the prophetic faculty, but it manifests itself only in dreams or at the time of death. There are also hints of a belief in metempsychosis in Plutarch; we find it suggested in both the *De Esu Carnium* (On the Eating of Flesh), where he rejects the eating of animal flesh, and also in *De Sera Numinis Vindicta* (On the Delay in Divine Punishment).

That dialogue, however, is of greater interest in demonstrating Plutarch's extreme incompetence in arguing against the proposition (put forth, naturally, by an Epicurean) that "the slowness [of divine vengeance] takes away all assurance of a Providence" (549b). Here he actually cites the age-old maxim "The mills of the Gods grind slowly" (548d–e), but the actual arguments he puts forth are comical in their ineffectiveness. First he compares divine justice to medicine: "By his [God's] punishment he corrects a few, by the slowness of his punishment he helps and admonishes many" (551c). He notes that some tyrants came to power by wicked means but governed well (but what about those tyrants who didn't?). He asserts that "wickedness as it grows breeds its own pain and punishment" (554a); this notion rests upon the comforting belief that the wicked will ultimately feel a sense of remorse for their bad deeds—but what of the many who never do? And yet, Plutarch asserts against all evidence that "the soul of *every* bad man" (556a; my emphasis) feels remorse.

Plutarch ventures further into fatuity—and, it can safely be said, moral evil—by lame attempts to refute the Epicureans' belief that punishing the descendants of evildoers is unjust. In his view, such punishments are merely the mirror-image of the honour given to the descendants of noble families. He regards evil as a literal contagion, concluding: "An offspring is never separated from its begetter" (559d). After a long and tortured discussion, Plutarch finally admits that "If a good son be born of a bad sire . . . he is relieved from the penalty of race" (562f). It is at this point that he at last explores the notion of punishment after death. Elsewhere he had stated that no one now seriously believes in the standard torments of the afterlife in Hades;[76] here he maintains that souls go through a "purgation and chastisement" (565c) that ultimately leads to metempsychosis. But he also indulges in a grotesque fantasy of the numerous hideous punishments that await bad souls:

> And there were lakes lying side by side, one of boiling gold, one of lead, exceeding cold, and one of iron, which was rough. Over these stood daemons, as it might be smiths, with tongs, picking up by turns the souls of those whose wickedness came of greed and grasping, and plunging them in. When they had become all fiery and transparent in the burning gold, they were thrust into the bath of lead; and when frozen till they became hard as hailstones, they were shifted on to the iron, and there they became hideously black, and were broken up and crushed, so hard and brittle were they, and their shapes were chanaged. Then they were conveyed, just as they were, back to the gold, enduring dire pains in the transition. (567c–d)

With this kind of horror supposedly awaiting the wicked in the afterlife, one would think the fates of Sisyphus, Tantalus, and the like would be minimally preferable.

In sum, Plutarch is an amateur philosopher (and biographer) whose fusion of Platonism, Stoicism, and other doctrines was entirely put to the service of defending divination, omens, portents, and especially God or the gods as he conceived them. It is no wonder he was music to the ears of the mediaeval Christians who diligently preserved his work for posterity.

Lucian of Samosata (120?–180?) is of exceptional interest for his multifarious array of literary works, many of which contain pungent criticisms of religion. Born in the capital of the kingdom of Commagene

76. See Brenk 24f.

(now in south-central Turkey), he travelled widely throughout the Roman Empire as a teacher of rhetoric. More than seventy of his works are extant, many of them dialogues; and their bountiful use of satire, parody, repartee, and general ribaldry makes him something of a Greek Voltaire, although generally without the Frenchman's intellectual heft.

A fair number of his works merely present lampoons on the Greco-Roman gods, "demythologising" them (and also the human heroes with whom they are frequently associated) and presenting them as ordinary human beings with the mundane foibles we all share. Hence, in *The Judging of the Goddesses* (*Dearum Judicium*),[77] a recounting of the ancient myth of Paris, the Trojan hero who was tasked with the unenviable job of determining whether Aphrodite, Hera, or Athena is the most beautiful goddess, Paris himself is presented as something of a country bumpkin, and his request to see each of the goddesses naked is laced with lascivious overtones. *The Assembly of the Gods* (*Deorum Concilium*) uses largely the same shtick, where Momus (a personification of "blame") makes all manner of objections to the deities who now crowd around Olympus, including Dionysus, who is only half-human and who has brought in other unsavoury figures such as Pan, Silenus, the satyrs, and so on. "So," Momus concludes, "can we be surprised that humans despise us when they see such ridiculous, misshapen gods?" (5).[78] It is of some interest to note that this dialogue glancingly mentions the Christians (see the next chapter) as well as Mithras, a god associated with Zoroastrianism but who had become popular in the Roman Empire, especially among soldiers, in the early centuries C.E. Momus derisively notes that this god doesn't even speak Greek (9)—and what are we to make of the half-animal gods of Egypt? (10).

Very much the same methodologically is the well-known *Dialogues of the Gods* (*Dialogi Deorum*). Some of the jokes are rather funny. Relating the tale of how Athena was born full-grown (complete with a suit of armour) from the head of Zeus, Hephaestus comments: "I am no longer surprised that you suffered such a cruel headache" (8).[79] Herakles refers to Asklepios as a "quack doctor" (13). Hermes and Apollo, dismissing Hephaestus as a mere blacksmith, can't believe how he managed to win

77. As with Plutarch, it is customary to cite Lucian's works by Latin titles.
78. I use the translation of M. D. Macleod.
79. I use the translation of William Tooke.

the transcendently lovely Aphrodite for a wife.

Other works by Lucian exhibit a somewhat greater level of philosophical sophistication. It is clear that he was generally conversant with the leading philosophical movements of his day—Platonism, Stoicism, Cynicism, and especially Epicureanism, with which last he seems to have had the greatest sympathy. One of his most pungent dialogues, from a religious perspective, is *Zeus Cross-Examined* (*Juppiter Confutatus*), where a Cyniscus (a derogratory term for a Cynic philosopher) hauls Zeus up before an imaginary courtroom and subjects him to a severe tonguelashing. What, Cyniscus demands, is the distinction between Fate (or the Fates), Destiny, and Fortune? "Do the Fates also control you Gods? . . . Why do men sacrifice to *you,* and bring hecatombs, and pray for good at *your* hands?"[80] Zeus blusters for a time, calling Cyniscus a sophist "who would deny us all concern in human affairs" (the Epicurean position). Later Zeus finally declares, "The Fates work *through us*"; but Cyniscus is not satisfied, turning the tables on Zeus and saying that the gods are in fact the Fates' "tools" and "instruments."

The criticism becomes even more searching. Why do Zeus' thunderbolts bypass criminals and hit trees or stones to no purpose? And this leads to the most uncomfortable question of all:

> Well, I suppose I must not ask you all (Providence and Destiny and you) why honest Phocion died in utter poverty and destitution, like Aristides before him, while those two unwhipped puppies, Callias and Alcibiades, and the ruffian Midias, and that Aeginetan libertine Charops, who starved his own mother to death, were all rolling in money? nor again why Socrates was handed over to the Eleven instead of Meletus? nor yet why the effeminate Sardanapalus was a king, and one high-minded Persian after another went to the cross for refusing to countenance his doings? I say nothing of our own days, in which villains and money-grubbers prosper, and honest men are oppressed with want and sickness and a thousand distresses, and can hardly call their souls their own?

80. I use the translation of H. W. Fowler and F. G. Fowler (also for *Juppiter Tragoedus* and *Alexander*). The emphasis in the English translation is of course not found as such in the Greek, but it is a plausible approximation of the sense of the Greek text.

In other words, why do the bad prosper, and why do bad things happen to good people? When Zeus lamely points to the "punishments [that] await the evil-doers after death," Cyniscus scoffs: "Whether there is such a place as Hades, I shall be able to satisfy myself when I die."

Even more intellectually challenging is *Zeus the Tragedian* (*Zeus Tragoedus*). Here Zeus summons a council of the gods because a debate has just occurred between the Stoic Timocles and the Epicurean Damis over the role of gods and providence in human affairs; the debate was not completed, and Zeus is fearful that Damis will prevail when it resumes. After all, Damis had maintained that "we did not concern ourselves in thought or action with human affairs, and [he] practically denied our existence" (a comment that once again suggests that Epicureanism had, in certain circles, become tantamount to atheism). Zeus is worried that Damis' views were "far the more popular," and there would be very bad results if he won the debate:

> You now know the occasion of this meeting—no light one, ye Gods, if you reflect how entirely our dignity, our revenue, our honour, depend on mankind. If they should accept as true either our absolute non-existence or, short of that, our indifference to them, farewell to our earthly sacrifices, attributes, honours; we shall sit starving and ineffectual in Heaven; our beloved feasts and assemblies, games and sacrifices, vigils and processions—all will be no more.

Zeus disdains the crude strategy of Poseidon (who just wants Zeus to kill Damis with a thunderbolt) and of Herakles (who is prepared to bring down the Portico where the debate is being held). But he has to deal with the annoying Momus, who now says, "Did your interest in mankind ever carry you so far as to sift the good from the bad?"

When the debate resumes, Damis systematically destroys a number of the pillars of Timocles' arguments in defence of the gods and providence, denying that the regularity of nature suggests design ("You beg the question; whether the effects *are* produced by Providence is just what is not yet proved. Your description of nature I accept; it does not follow that there is definite design in it; it is not impossible that things now similar and homogeneous have developed from widely different origins"), and also the argument from consensus, where Damis points out that the conceptions of the gods held by different cultures (Scythians, Ethiopians, Egyptians, and so on) are so radically different that it becomes absurd to maintain that these could all refer to the same kind of deity. And when Timocles offers a ridiculous syllogism ("If there are altars, there are Gods: there are altars; therefore, there are Gods"), Damis just laughs.

Zeus the Tragedian displays impressive philosophical knowledge and a notable ability to destroy opposing arguments; and the manifest sympathy extended here, as elsewhere in Lucian, to the Epicurean stance suggests that, if he accepted any philosophy as his own, it was this one.

But Lucian's most exhaustive screed on religion may be *Alexander*, a diatribe against a particularly corrupt and self-serving prophet who gained surprising sway in the Greco-Roman world. Alexander of Abonuteichos was a philosopher who apparently had some medical training, and he used it to good advantage when setting himself up as the interpreter of oracular utterances emanating from a snake-god he himself invented, Glycon. In Lucian's account, Alexander fashioned a snake-head out of linen and other materials so that it could open its mouth. There was more chicanery involved in how he looked into questions put to the oracle (he came up with a way to undo the wax seals on the packets containing the questions, and then he sealed them up again). Alexander became fabulously wealthy, but suffered attacks from opponents (especially the Epicureans) as a bogus prophet; he replied by claiming that "Pontus was overrun with atheists and Christians," and that these people should be stoned. This probably means that atheists (i.e., Epicureans) and Christians were hostile to him, not that Christians themselves were atheists. Alexander's influence reached all the way to the imperial court, where he was embraced by Rutilianus (P. Mummius Sisenna Rutilianus), a leading Roman senator of the period, whom Lucian accuses of "religious mania."

There is perhaps nothing philosophically significant in *Alexander*, although his allegiance to Epicurus is even more pronounced here than elsewhere: that thinker had "alone had imparted true insight into the good." Some have believed that Lucian's screed is a bit overzealous, but C. P. Jones makes a good case that Alexander really was a highly regarded (and dangerous) figure whose religious deceptions were well worth lambasting.[81]

Other works are of lesser interest but flesh out Lucian's overall view of religion. *On Mourning* (*De Luctu*) sharply ridicules the fear of death, the lurid pictures of the underworld as portrayed by poets and others, and the ludicrously elaborate rituals undertaken to prepare corpses for burial. *Charon* underscores the inevitability of death and the need of human beings to face that realisation. *On Sacrifices* (*De Sacrificiis*) criticises the very idea of making sacrifices to the gods, as if the gods have any need to be flattered by human beings. Overall, Lucian's work is a bracing antidote to the increasing religiosity of the entire period, by philosophers, politicians, and the general public; but he was a relatively solitary figure in holding out for the cause of reason and scepticism.

The most significant Latin author of this period is Apuleius (125?–180?).[82] Born in the town of Madauros, in the Roman province of Numidia (North Africa), he was the son of a local magistrate, and his family was apparently quite wealthy. He studied philosophy and rhetoric in Carthage and Athens and became a Platonist. His subsequent travels throughout the Empire resulted in the loss of much of his fortune. He remedied that by marrying a wealthy widow, Pudentilla; but this caused Apuleius some additional problems, as one of her sons accused him of casting a spell over her so that she would marry him. The case was actually brought to court, and Apuleius wrote his *Apologia* in defence of himself. The verdict in the case is not known with certainty, but he would presumably not have published the work if he had been found guilty. His novel, the *Metamorphoses,* is probably (but not certainly) a late work written in the 170s.

The central fact that must be borne in mind when considering Apuleius as both a philosopher and a novelist is that he was aligned with a movement—beginning as early as the reign of Nero and extending into the early third centiry C.E.—called the Second Sophistic; indeed, he could be considered the most prominent member of this movement who wrote in Latin, since most of the other writers associated with it (Dio Chrysostom, Aelius Aristides, Herodes Atticus, and perhaps Lucian)

81. See Jones, *Culture and Society in Lucian*, ch. 12.

82. There is no justification for using the praenomen Lucius, which is plainly derived from the name of the central character in his novel, the *Metamorphoses*. And there is similarly no reason to follow Augustine in referring to that work as *The Golden Ass*.

wrote in Greek. The movement led to a revival of displays of public speaking, with rhetorical flourishes and exhibitions of learning; in spite of its name, philosophy (whether deriving from the Sophists or any other sect) was not stressed, although it could be a feature of the rhetorical virtuosity its exponents sought to portray. With this backdrop in mind, let us consider the actual philosophical writings of Apuleius that have come down to us (a small fraction of what he apparently wrote).

Our chief focus will be on *De Deo Socratis* (On Socrates' God), an outline of Plato's philosophy with a special emphasis on the *daimōn* that Socrates frequently claimed as an internal voice that guided his moral decisions. In this work as elsewhere, Apuleius makes no secret of his theism. He speaks unequivocally of "the gods of heaven of whom we apprehend some visually, while others we study intellectually" (1.2).[83] The first branch of this statement apparently refers to the sun, moon, and other heavenly objects that the Platonists (and others) regarded as divine; the second apparently refers to the Olympian gods, although strangely he maintains that these gods can only be "seen" by the mind, since they are uncorporeal (2.6f.) and live "at the highest level of ether, far removed from human contact" (3.2). These gods, "by their innate perfection, [are] supremely blessed" (3.3); their "father" (otherwise unspecified, although possibly to be identified with Plato's demiurge) is the "ruler and creator of all things" (3.4).

If this sounds unnervingly close to Epicurus' belief that the gods do exist but have no concern for human affairs, that is no accident; for there are clear traces of the influence of Lucretius—both linguistically and intellectually—throughout Apuleius' corpus of writings. Indeed, in *De Deo Socratis* he implicitly criticises poets (and those who believe their assertions) that the gods are directly involved in vengeance against mortals who sin against them or are pleased by human beings' worship of them:

> But all these billows and storms are far removed from the tranquillity of the heavenly gods, since all the heavenly ones forever enjoy the same state of mind in an eternal invariability. This state of theirs is never driven from its limits into either pain or pleasure, and nothing diverts it from its everlasting course into any sudden state . . . (12.3–4)

83. I use the translation of Christopher P. Jones.

If Lucretius had written in prose, he would have said much the same thing; and Apuleius consciously employs the Epicurean philosophical vocabulary of tranquillity (*tranquillitate*), pain (*dolorem*), pleasure (*voluptatem*), and so on to get his point across.

But, of course, Apuleius proclaims himself a Platonist; and so he is compelled to postulate the *daimones* as intermediaries between the gods and human beings to "carry both our desires and our good deeds to the gods" (6.3). This was, as we have seen, a view that one of Plutarch's interlocutors in *De Defectu Oraculorum* propounded, although it appears that Plutarch himself rejected it; but Apuleius goes on to echo Plutarch in asserting that another class of *daimones* consists of "the human soul that has renounced its body after doing its years of service in life" (15.5), a view Plutarch appears to endorse. The text culminates in a mingling of Platonism, Stoicism, Cynicism, Pythagoreanism, and some further bits of Epicureanism, pointing to the syncretism of philosophical and religious views that was common during this period.

To what extent Apuleius actually accepted any of the views he propounds, or whether he is simply seeking to display his learning while playing with philosophical concepts, is unknown. When we turn to the *Apologia,* we find other points of interest. In defending himself against the accusation that he used magic to win over his wife, he maintains (not entirely plausibly) that he is really defending all philosophy; this is because philosophers of the past were accused of witchcraft or even atheism merely for seeking to understand natural phenomena. Here he rattles off a familiar list of names—Anaxagoras, Democritus, and Epicurus—as those who were unjustly accused of "denying the gods' existence" (27.1). But Apuleius' true sympathies lie with the more religiously inclined thinkers—Empedocles, Plato, and so on, who devoted "particular study to universal providence and greatly honor the gods" (27.2).

Nowhere in his treatise—which was probably an enhanced version of the defence he delivered in court—does Apuleius explicitly condemn magic as false or the product of superstition. Possibly he was being merely prudent, tacitly acknowledging the widespread belief in magic even among the intellectual class; but when he states that magic "is an art pleasing to the immortal gods" (26.1), one begins to wonder. The substance of Apuleius' defence is not that magic does not exist but merely that he did not practise it in wooing Pudentilla. Indeed, he attempts to turn the tables on his accuser (not Pudentilla's son, who was underage, but an uncle, Aemilianus, who brought the charge on his son's behalf) of impiety and even "defiance of religion" (*divini contumaciam* 56.8) because Aemilianus does not make the customary sacrifices or tributes to the gods that would be expected of someone of his social standing.

When we turn to the *Metamorphoses,* we are in a different world altogether—although its own rhetorical flourishes should be borne in mind when attempting to decipher its philosophical or religious thrust. Such a task is always a tricky one when analysing a work of fiction. Classical scholars of the past seemed inclined to exhibit a certain naïve belief that certain elements in the work could be read as transparent reflections of Apuleius' actual views or as testimonials to his personal religious outlook; but I trust we are now aware that such a text must be interpreted in light of its own internal coherence as a creative work in which the pronouncements of its protagonist cannot be attributed to the author in any straightforward manner.

The story should be familiar to many readers as a result of the work's popularity in the West since at least the Renaissance. In its eleven books, it tells of one Lucius who comes to Thessaly (notorious throughout antiquity as a haven for witches) and finds that his friend Milo's wife Pamphile is a witch with supernatural powers. Lucius actually sees her turn into a bird after rubbing her naked body with some ointment; but when her maidservant, Fotis (with whom Lucius carries on a sexual affair at odd moments), does the same to Lucius, he turns into an ass. Fotis has used the wrong ointment. The rest of the novel deals with Lucius' seriocomic attempts to return to human form (he needs to eat roses in order to accomplish that goal) while being snatched away by thieves, brutalised by a cruel little boy, and so on and so forth. It is all hugely entertaining and has a surprisingly modern feel to it.

For all the foreboding accounts of the powers of witchcraft exhibited by Pamphile (one character says: "Verily, she is a magician, and of divine might, which hath power to bring down the sky, to bear up the earth, to turn the waters into hills and the hills into running waters, to call up the terrestrial spirits into the air, and to pull the gods out of the heavens, to extinguish the planets, and to lighten the very darkness of hell" [1.8][84]—a formidable woman, indeed!), the novel is chiefly just a literary entertainment—albeit one of a high order, and of a virtually unprecedented type in extant Latin literature. It is worth pointing out that the basic plot was taken from an extant Greek work, *Lucius, or the Ass,* attributed to Lucian but almost certainly not by him. But the manner in which Apuleius works out the complex and meandering plot is surely his own.

One crucial element that does not appear in *Lucius* is Lucius' conversion, in the eleventh book, to Isis-worship. It is here that scholars of a prior day assumed that Apuleius intended to suggest that he himself had become a devotee of Isis. The claim strikes me as preposterous, or at the very least unwarranted. There is no documentary evidence of such a conversion in Apuleius' extant nonfictional work. It is true that, at one point toward the end, Lucius (the first-person narrator) refers to himself as a "man of Madaura" (*Madaurensem* 11.27); but this reference has plausibly been explained by S. J. Harrison as a metafictional allusion.[85] It is also true that another Platonist, Plutarch, wrote a treatise called *De Iside et Osiride* (On Isis and Osiris), which at a minimum indicates some interest among the intellectual class (and possibly a certain segment of the Greco-Roman public) in the Egyptian gods; but Harrison has gone on to make a detailed case that this entire account of Lucius' conversion is a parody, although even he notes (not convincingly, to my mind) that it is still remotely possible that Apuleius himself was initiated into the Isis-cult as a "feature of elite intellectual life."[86] While Apuleius elsewhere states that "I have been initiated into many mysteries in Greece" (*Apologia* 55.8), this is still a far cry from becoming a devotee of what was still regarded as the fundamentally foreign cult of Isis. In effect, what Apuleius is striving do in this eleventh book of the *Metamorphoses* is (a) to display his own learning as evidenced by his detailed account of what is involved in becoming a worshipper of Isis, and (b) to poke fun at the gullibility of Lucius as he swallows increasingly ludicrous practices as part of his initiation.

Scholars are divided on whether there are Platonic elements in the

84. I use the charming Elizabethan translation of William Adlington (1566) as revised by S. Gaselee.
85. See Harrison, *Apuleius: A Latin Sophist* 231.
86. Harrison 243.

Metamorphoses. Some point to the lengthy (and beautiful) account of Cupid and Psyche (which fills the entirety of the fifth book and large portions of the fourth and sixth) as a Platonic exhibition of the union of love (Cupid) and the soul (Psyche); but this may also be simply an exhibition of Apuleius' learning rather than (as has been argued) a condemnation of the sexual irregularities Lucius exhibits in other parts of the narrative.

Whatever the case, it is difficult to argue that Apuleius was a religious sceptic; but if the end of the *Metamorphoses* is indeed intended parodically, then we can say that he at least displayed some scorn of the foreign importations of gods that Rome was seeing during this period—a point that Apuleius makes clear by his sharp criticism of the corrupt priests of the "Syrian goddess" in Books 8 and 9 of the *Metamorphoses.* Whether his passing mention in this same work of a woman who was "a despiser of all the gods whom others did honour, one that affirmed that she had instead of our sure religion an only god by herself" (9.14), is a reference to a Christian, as some scholars have maintained, must remain unverified.

L. Greek and Roman Science

There is, in effect, no such thing as Roman science. We have, to be sure, any number of extant treatises in Latin on technical matters: M. Terentius Varro's *De Lingua Latina* (On the Latin Language); Vitruvius Pollio's *De Architectura* (On Architecture); Columella's *De Re Rustica* (On Agriculture); Celsus' *De Medicina* (On Medicine); works on rhetoric and oratory by Seneca the Elder, Quintilian, and Fronto; and Frontinus' *De Re Militari* (On Military Affairs).[87] But none of these qualify as "science" in the conventional sense of the term. Even the one work that may qualify—the *Historia Naturalis* (Natural History) of Pliny the Elder (C. Plinius Secundus, 23?–79 C.E.)—is the work of a self-confessed amateur, albeit an unusually diligent and indefatigable one.

The text survives in a whopping thirty-seven books, one of the

87. M. Terentius Varro (116–27 B.C.E.); M. Vitruvius Pollio (80?–15? B.C.E.); L. Junius Columella (4–70 C.E.); A. Cornelius Celsus (25? B.C.E.–50 C.E.); L. Annaeus Seneca (54? B.C.E.–39 C.E.); M. Fabius Quintilianus (35?–100); M. Cornelius Fronto (100?–166?); Sextus Julius Frontinus (30–104).

longest single works to come down to us from the Greco-Roman world. Its scope is impressively wide: astronomy, meteorology, geography, ethngraphy, anthropology, zoology, botany, pharmaclogy, mineralogy, and other topics are discussed in detail. But Pliny was not a pioneer or original researcher in any of these disciplines; he was simply a tireless collector of information (and, in some cases, misinformation) by other hands. He manifestly intended his work to be a broad investigation of natural phenomena fit for the educated Roman, with an emphasis on the practical uses to which his vast and sprawling assemblage of data could be put.

Insofar as Pliny has an overarching philosophical or theological view, he inclines toward pantheism. He may, indeed, be the first pantheist since the Presocratic Xenophanes, and probably the only Roman who can be so categorised. But the designation must be regarded as tentative, since Pliny's views can only be ascertained by a collation of many remarks made in passing throughout his work.

The one instance where Pliny outlines his theology is at the opening of Book 2. Here he is frank in declaring the "world" (*mundum*)—by which he means the universe—to be "a deity" (*numen*).[88] It is "eternal, without bounds, neither created, nor subject, at any time, to destruction" (2.1). This view is to some degree derived from Plato (whose *Timaeus* exercised a marked influence on Pliny), Aristotle, and the Stoics, although the contention that the universe is not subject to destruction is a clear denial of the Stoic belief in *ekpyrosis.* He does, however, subscribe to the Stoic belief (although it was of course embraced by others) in the four elements, making the remarkable statement that "I do not find that any one has doubted that there are four elements" (2.4).

When it comes to a characterisation of God, Pliny is clearer on what he denies than on what he asserts. He rejects the deification of abstract moral qualities (Hope, Honour, and so on), as well as Fortune, which the Stoics in particular (as well, perhaps, as popular theology) had increasingly deified in an apparent attempt to account for the vagaries of life in a world beset by natural and human-made disasters. He is scornful of the various myths about the Olympian gods, thinking that their adulterous dallyings are disgraceful. But he does not reject

88. I use the translation of John Bostock and H. T. Riley.

the Olympian pantheon altogether;[89] instead, he contorts himself into a backhanded acknowledgement of their existence, as well as that of the deified emperors. (His work is dedicated to Vespasian, as an obsequious prefatory note to Book 2 attests.) Putting forth the claim that "to assist man is to be a God" (*deus est mortali iuvare mortalem*), he finds himself justified in believing that Jupiter, Mercury, and the other Olympians "have reference to certain natural phenomena"; similarly, the emperors also assisted humanity, and so were properly deified: "This was the ancient mode of remunerating those who deserved it, to regard them as god" (2.5). But at the end of this long disquisition, Pliny comes forth with the startling assertion: "But it is ridiculous to suppose that the great head of things, whatever it be, pays any regard to human affairs" (2.5)—which is pure Epicureanism.

If any sense can be made of this farrago of seemingly conflicting theories, it is that *deus* is equivalent to *Natura*. This must be the sense of Pliny's belief, expressed at the very outset of his disquisition on deity: "For whatever God be, if there be any other God, and wherever he exists, he is all sense, all hearing, all life, all mind, and all within himself" (2.5). The "other" god is presumably the god (or gods) postulated by humanity distinct from Nature—and it is this latter conception with which Pliny takes exception.

While rejecting astrology (thereby breaking from prevailing Stoic opinion), and also magic and superstition as unworthy of man's dignity as an intellectual being, Pliny acknowledges that human beings share the faculty of "reason" (*ratio*) with the divine mind; but that *ratio* can be perverted to bad ends. This is orthodox Stoic doctrine, but Pliny departs from the Stoics in regard to the radical distinction they established between human beings and animals (who, in their view, lacked *ratio*). Pliny is fascinated by the animal world, right down to insects and other tiny creatures; and even though he cannot bring himself to declare that these creatures possess reason, they may in his view possess other qualities similar (but inferior) to human reason, art, memory, and so on. It is, after all, Nature that has created these entities, so there must be some justification for their very existence.

This common creation of man and animals may have led to Pliny's

89. *Contra* Beagon, *Roman Nature* 33.

remarkable rejection of traditional belief in the afterlife—a stance that again places him in alignment with the Epicureans and in opposition to nearly every other philosophical tradition in the ancient world. In a striking passage in Book 7, he rejects both the survival of the soul after death and any theories of transmigration. At one point Pliny appears to deny the very existence of the soul:

> For what is the actual substance of the soul, when taken by itself? Of what material does it consist? Where is the seat of its thoughts? How is it to see, or hear, or how to touch? And then, of what use is it, or what can it avail, if it has not these faculties? Where, too, is its residence, and what vast multitudes of these souls and spirits must there be after the lapse of so many ages? (7.56)

Pliny concludes with a high disdain reminiscent of Lucretius:

> But all these are the mere figments of childish ravings, and of that mortality which is so anxious never to cease to exist. . . . Out upon it! What downright madness is it to suppose that life is to recommence after death! or indeed, what repose are we ever to enjoy when we have been once born, if the soul is to retain its consciousness in heaven, and the shades of the dead in the infernal regions? This pleasing delusion, and this credulity, quite cancel that chief good of human nature, death, and, as it were, double the misery of him who is about to die, by anxiety as to what is to happen to him after it. (7.56)

Pliny died as he lived—as a scholar and researcher. He was stationed with a fleet near when Mt. Vesuvius erupted, and the vessel he was on was pelted with some hot rocks and cinders. Pliny wished to explore the phenomenon more closely, but he apparently died—either of a heart attack or from inhaling toxic fumes. His nephew, Pliny the Younger, wrote a poignant letter to Tacitus (6.16) about the event; and in a follow-up letter he reveals some insight on what everyday Romans may have thought of the catastrophe: "Many besought the aid of the gods, but still more imagined there were no gods left, and that the universe was plunged into eternal darkness for evermore" (6.20).

The actual scientists of this period wrote in Greek. Two can be singled out: Ptolemy and Galen. Ptolemy (Claudius Ptolemaeus, 100?–170?) lived in or near Alexandria, in Egypt, and wrote the *Almagest*—the Arabic rendering of the Greek title *Mathēmatikē Syntaxis* (Mathematical Treatise), which G. E. R. Lloyd has referred to as "the most comprehensive astronomical treatise that has come down to us from antiquity."[90] And yet, there is some question as to how much original research the treatise embodies. Its celebrated assertions—that the earth is a sphere and is at rest in the centre of the universe; the stars and planets proceed in a circular motion—are largely derived from Aristotle and other metaphysicians and astronomers, particularly Hipparchus in the second-century B.C.E. And although Ptolemy refreshingly dispenses with the study of theology because of its utter obscurity, he still betrays the influence of religious thinking in assuming that circular motion is "perfect," and therefore must be attributed to the heavenly bodies. And his elaborate devising of cycles and epicycles was merely intended to "save the appearances": to account for the apparent motions of the stars and planets on the unquestioned assumption that the geocentric theory must be true. The fact that this treatise proved to be so influential is merely a result of the utter collapse of anything that can be called science in the West from this point until the early Renaissance.

The fundamentally religious basis of Ptolemy's outlook is exhibited in another work, the *Tetrabiblos,* which sought to justify the validity of astrology and also sought to provide a plausible framework for divination. Somewhat more valuable is a geographical work, the *Geographikē Hyphēgēsis* (Guide to Drawing the Earth), although this work is heavily dependent upon the research of an older contemporary, Marinus of Tyre.

Galen (Aelius [or Claudius] Galenus, 129–216?) is the leading medical authority in the Greco-Roman world, working six or seven centuries after the pioneering work of Hippocrates of Cos. As a resident of Pergamon (now in Turkey), Galen was exposed to much scientific and philosophical speculation from a number of different schools. In pursuing medicine, he travelled widely, then came to Rome in 162, eventually entering the imperial court and becoming the personal physician of Marcus Aurelius, Commodus, and other emperors. He was therefore present during the hideous plague that spread throughout the

90. Lloyd, *Greek Science After Aristotle* 113.

Roman Empire from 165 onward; it may have killed millions over the next several years, and Marcus Aurelius himself perished of it in 180. Accounts of the plague in Galen's writings indicate that it was probably smallpox.

Galen is the author or attributed author of an immense number of works in Greek; some of his writings exist only in Arabic translations. The theoretical foundations of his medical work do not represent much of an advance on his predecessor, Hippocrates: he accepted the theory of the four elements (although he refers to them more generally as hot, cold, wet, and dry, and he attempted to bring quantitative analysis to these qualities), and he expanded upon the Hippocratic theory of the "humours" that determine both the physical and psychological features of the human being.

Where Galen's work gains importance is in his pioneering work on anatomy. He gained renown in antiquity for his surgical skill, even though he had to battle against the Roman prohibition against the dissection of human corpses, instituted in 150. His research established the distinction between veins and arteries; he did landmark work in identifying the function of the spine and its role in the central nervous system; and he performed experiments that led to an awareness of the differing capacities of the brain and the heart.

But in his overall philosophy he adhered to a religious conception of the universe. His tripartite division of the soul follows Plato, and he expressed belief in astrology—although there has been debate among scholars as to how (or whether) this belief influenced his medical work.

* * *

The Romans perennially exhibited an inferiority complex to the Greeks in terms of their literature, art, and general culture; but they justifiably boasted of their preeminence in military might and the administration of their far-flung empire. There is no doubt that the Roman religion, whose primitive rudiments were significantly and permanently altered by Greek religion (through the mediation of the Etruscans), became far more intimately enmeshed in their political and military culture than what obtained in the Greek city-states; and, because the Romans never truly evolved their own philosophical outlook but largely inherited essential principles from Greek thought (chiefly the Stoics, the Epicureans, and, in the early centuries of the Empire, Plato), it becomes difficult to find a Roman thinker of truly independent thought, especially in the critical issue of the validity of religion.

Were there any atheists in the entire history of Rome covered by this chapter? Perhaps not; but secularism did seem to gain an increasing share of adherents among the intellectual class (including the political class), if Pliny's letters are any indication. Lucretius and other Epicureans constantly had to fend off accusations (as Epicurus himself did) that they were closet atheists. The advent of the imperial cult—the deification of deceased emperors—probably enhanced secularism: the cult took increasing precedence over the Olympian gods, but in so doing it rendered the whole concept of deification implausible among a wide class of philosophers, writers, and statesmen, many of whom were personally acquainted with the emperors and exhibited understandable scepticism as to their becoming a god. And there is some evidence that the emperors themselves expressed wry doubts on the issue.

The turbulence of the post–Civil War period—the period following the triumph of Octavian over his rivals and the establishment of the Empire in the late first century B.C.E.—engendered a multifarious array of salvific religions that attracted adherents hoping to make sense of the political and military turmoil all around them. It is now time to turn to one of these religions—a religion that began in an obscure corner of the Roman world and, by a series of historical accidents, ultimately gained supremacy in the West. It was a development no one living in the early years of the first century C.E. could have predicted.

IV. The Triumph of Christianity

Christianity remains today the greatest misfortune of humanity.

—Friedrich Nietzsche

The prevalence of Christianity in the West can scarcely be overstated. From our most common epithets ("Goddamnit!" "Go to hell!"), to such given names (formerly termed "Christian" names) as Theodora ("gift of God"), Christopher (literally, "carrier of Christ"—i.e., someone who has taken Jesus into his heart), Jesús (in Spanish-speaking nations), and the innumerable variants of Mary throughout European culture, to such widely used expressions derived from the Bible as "turn the other cheek" and "a thief in the night," Western civilisation is saturated with Christian elements: its art, literature, music, and general culture are incomprehensible without reference to the Christian dogmas underlying them. In prior centuries the entire political, legal, and social apparatus of many nations was explicitly and rigidly based on Christian doctrine as it evolved in the first few centuries C.E., and it has taken an heroic effort by philosophers, scholars, activists, and politicians to eliminate or minimise Christian influence in these realms—a far from completed goal, as the ongoing establishment of the Anglican Church in England and many other now archaic holdovers of Christian dominance attest.

How did an apparent variant of Judaism emerge in the Near East and, by the early fourth century C.E., become the state religion of the waning but still immensely powerful Roman Empire? It is a long and tangled tale, and every aspect of the story—the existence and teachings of a person named Jesus, the dissemination of these teachings among non-Jews, and the ultimate triumph of Christianity when it was adopted by the Emperor Constantine—is now increasingly in doubt, as a result of searching enquiries by legions of scholars over the past several centuries.

A. Was There a Jesus?

The basic events in the life of Jesus, as recounted in the three synoptic gospels of the New Testament (Mark, Matthew, and Luke), are well known to nearly everyone in the West, even those who profess disbelief in Christianity:

- Jesus was born in Bethlehem, about six miles south of Jerusalem. He was the product of the impregnation of his mother, Mary, by the Holy Spirit (formerly termed the Holy Ghost); this occurred just after her marriage to Joseph.
- Because King Herod of Judea feared the emergence of a "king of the Jews" who would replace him, he ordered the killing of all infants in the area (the "slaughter of the innocents"); but Jesus' family fled to Egypt and then settled in Nazareth (Mary's hometown).
- At the age of thirty, Jesus was baptised by John the Baptist.
- Jesus began preaching in the area, particularly Galilee, where he delivered the Sermon on the Mount and also performed various miracles (walking on water, the miraculous feeding of his followers with a small quantity of loaves and fishes, healing the deaf and the mute, and raising the dead).
- Jesus made his way to Jerusalem (about 70 miles south of Galilee), where he was so offended by the moneychangers in the Temple that he uprooted them and caused them to flee.
- This and other events led him to be arrested by the Jewish authorities. Before he was tried, he held a Last Supper with his twelve apostles. He was betrayed by one of them, Judas, to the Roman authorities.
- Jesus was tried by the Sanhedrin and condemned for declaring himself the "Son of God." The Sanhedrin had no authority to punish

him, so he was brought before the prefect[1] of Judaea, Pontius Pilate, who found no reason to punish Jesus; but he later yielded to the vociferous crowd of Jews demanding Jesus' execution and sentenced him to be crucified.

- Jesus was hung on the cross and died. His body was taken by Joseph of Arimathea, who placed it in his own tomb. Three days later several people saw Jesus resurrected in the flesh; the tomb was found to be empty.
- The resurrected Jesus was taken up to heaven and now sits at the right hand of God, to be judge of the living and the dead. He has fulfilled his mission: the salvation of the human race through his own death.

It is, however, a disconcerting fact that every one of these "events" is poorly attested and many of them almost certainly never occurred. Indeed, the possibility that there never was a Jesus Christ is one that must seriously be considered.

It is customary, especially among Christian apologists, to assert that such a view is "extreme" and animated purely by atheistic hostility to Christianity and a fervent desire to bring the entire religion down. Let us set aside the unlikelihood that any course of reasoning, however well argued, could ever bring down a religion so entrenched in the West and elsewhere as Christianity; what the proponents of Christianity fail to note—or, in many instances, deliberately set out to obfuscate—is the extraordinarily feeble support for Jesus' existence in non-Christian sources, and *a fortiori* for the basic events of his life and death.[2] And if it be argued that a movement so immense and all-encompassing as Christianity, which in a matter of three centuries took over the Roman Empire both religiously and politically and over the next millennium and a half dominated the religious, political, social, and cultural discourse of the West, had to be based upon at least a core element of "truth" in regard

1. The office was later termed procurator, but only after Pilate's administration (26–36 C.E.); nevertheless, Pilate himself is sometimes referred to as the procurator of Judaea.
2. My chief sources for this discussion are Doherty (*The Jesus Puzzle*) and Price (*Deconstructing Jesus*). The latter, while not explicitly denying the historicity of Jesus, does state at the outset that it is "practically impossible and ill-advised" (12) to construct an account of his life. A later work, *The Incredible Shrinking Son of Man* (2003), firmly embraces the Christ myth theory.

to its founder, one can counter that we have already seen instances where obviously mythological figures from Greco-Roman antiquity (Hercules, Aeneas, etc.) were assumed to be real and for whom elaborate accounts of their life were written and accepted as veridical. Even in our own day, quasi-religious movements based on pure fiction—and, in some cases, deliberate fabrication—have gained an alarmingly wide circulation and belief.[3]

It is well known that, in the first century and a half of the Common Era, mentions of Jesus or Christians in extant pagan literature are vanishingly few. It is surely remarkable that the Jesus movement—if there was one—could have escaped the attention of the first several Roman emperors, for whom Palestine was a critical region, bordering as it did on the Persian Empire and other constant threats to the Roman imperium; and the Jewish rebellion of 66–70 did indeed require an extensive focus on the native population in that area. And yet, there is no mention of Jesus or Christians in Seneca or Martial or Juvenal. Pliny the Younger does mention them in letters to Trajan dating to c. 112, which we shall consider presently. But what we are left with is a celebrated passage in Tacitus' *Annals,* dating to c. 115, discussing Nero's persecution of Christians, whom he sought to blame for the fire that engulfed Rome in 64. Tacitus writes that Nero attempted to propitiate the gods by carrying out various vigils, banquets, and so on; but all in vain:

> But all human efforts, all the lavish gifts of the emperor, and the propitiations of the gods, did not banish the sinister belief that the conflagration was the result of an order. Consequently, to get rid of the report, Nero fastened the guilt and inflicted the most exquisite tortures on a class hated for their abominations, called Christians by the populace. Christus, from whom the name had its origin, suffered the extreme penalty during the reign of Tiberius at the hands of one of our procurators, Pontius Pilatus, and a most mischievous superstition (*exitiabilis superstitio*), thus checked for the moment, again broke out not only in Judaea, the first source of the evil, but even in Rome, where all things hideous and shameful from every part of the world find their centre and become popular. (15.44)

3. I refer of course to phenomena ranging from UFOs to QAnon.

This seems to constitute some sort of validation of the life and death of an actual Jesus, but it is plain that Tacitus is merely relying on hearsay (possibly from Christians who by this time were already present in Rome); the notion that Tacitus had some kind of documentary evidence of Jesus' execution under Pilate, or that there could ever have been any such evidence, is little short of fantastic.

Otherwise, all we have in pagan sources is a passing mention in Suetonius' life of Claudius, probably written c. 120: "Since the Jews constantly made disturbances at the instigation of Chrestus [*sic*], he expelled them from Rome" (25.4). It is not clear that Suetonius is even referring here to Jesus, since Chrestus is a variant of Christos, both meaning "the anointed one" (i.e., the Jewish Messiah), and there may have been several such figures active in Rome at the time.

What about Jewish sources? There is, incredibly, nothing about Jesus or Christians in the extensive work of Philo of Alexandria (20? B.C.E.–50? C.E.), whose life dates exceed those of Jesus' purported dates on either side and who lived and worked not far from where Jesus is supposed to have been active. Talmudic sources (none earlier than the end of the first century) are bafflingly wide of the mark in regard to the "facts" of Jesus' life and death.

What Christian scholars have latched on to for centuries is the work of Flavius Josephus, who wrote the *Jewish War* and *Jewish Antiquities.* There are two passages in the latter (written c. 93–94, or at least two generations after the supposed death of Jesus) that mention Jesus, but there is strong reason to believe that they are partially or entirely forgeries. The first passage is so celebrated that it has been deemed the *Testimonium Flavianum:*

> Now there was about this time Jesus, a wise man, if it be lawful to call him a man; for he was a doer of wonderful works, a teacher of such men as receive truth with pleasure. He drew over to him both many of the Jews and many of the Gentiles. He was [the] Christ. And when Pilate, at the suggestion of the principal men amongst us, had condemned him to the cross, those that loved him at the first did not forsake him; for he appeared to them alive again the third day; as the divine prophets had foretold these and ten thousand other wonderful

> things concerning him. And the tribe of Christians, so named from him, are not extinct to this day. (18.3.3)[4]

Even Christian commentators acknowledge that at least a few phrases in this passage are obviously spurious: as a pious Jew Josephus would never have acknowledged Jesus as something other than a man, since Judaism regarded the concept of human beings turning into gods as blasphemous. But the entire passage does not fit well in the course of the discussion in *Jewish Antiquities:* Josephus is writing of the actions Pilate took to suppress a Jewish revolt in Judaea, and the passage disturbs an otherwise unbroken account of the tribulations of the Jews both in Judaea and in Rome. The fact that the *Testimonium Flavianum* is not cited by any Christian apologists for the better part of two centuries—at a time when there were mutual polemics by pagans and Christians against each other—is highly anomalous. The first mention we have is in Eusebius (260?–339?).[5] Moreover, given that Josephus repeatedly condemns other would-be messiahs as contributing to the Jews' downfall at the hands of the Romans, the relatively neutral or even praiseworthy tone of the *Testimonium,* even when it is purged of its obviously spurious phrases, is inexplicable.

The other passage relates to the Sanhedrin, the court of elders in Judaism. We are told that Ananus (d. 68), one of the leaders of the Jewish revolt of 66–70, "assembled the sanhedrin of judges, and brought before them the brother of Jesus, who was called Christ, whose name was James, and some others. And when he had formed an accusation against them as breakers of the law, he delivered them to be stoned" (20.9.1). There are numerous reasons for believing that the insertion of Jesus' name and description ("who was called Christ" [*tou legomenou Christou*]) is spurious, since the wording matches that of Matt. 1:16 and John 4:25.

Before we consider Christian sources for the life and death of Jesus, it is worth giving some preliminary attention to the purported events of his life. Let us first examine Jesus' very name (Jeshua in Hebrew). The name simply means "Yahweh saves." What a convenient name for

4. I use the translation of William Whiston.

5. Doherty (*Jesus Puzzle* 209) thinks Eusebius himself might have been the author of the passage.

the person who will be humanity's saviour! It is as if a barrel-maker were named Cooper ("cooper" being the now archaic English word for a barrel-maker). Indeed, there is evidence that the name Jesus was a pre-existing term for a saviour-god, as indeed is implied in Paul's letter to the Philippians: "Therefore God raised him to the heights and bestowed on him the name above all names, that at the name of Jesus every knee should bow" (2:9–10).[6]

It is well known that Jesus' supernatural birth (by means of the Holy Spirit) is not found in the gospel of Mark, the earliest of the gospels; indeed, he fails to mention Mary as the mother of Jesus at all.[7] The assertion that Jesus was born in Bethlehem (even though Mary was a resident of Nazareth, many miles away) appears to have been fashioned by the gospel writers as a means of linking Jesus to David and therefore seeing in him the fulfilment of prophecies that a Messiah would emerge from the ancestry of David and rescue the Jewish people from oppression. It is perhaps a small point that Jesus' birth is not likely to have happened in the year 1 C.E. The various gospels are maddeningly imprecise on the matter, and the best that scholars have been able to establish is that his purported birth occurred between 6 B.C.E. and 4 C.E.

Herod's slaughter of the innocents almost certainly did not occur. Firstly, it appears to be a recycling of the Old Testament story of Pharaoh's attempt to kill the infant Moses because of his concern that he would overthrow him.[8] Jesus' family's fleeing to Egypt had a similar import, providing another link to Moses. Secondly, a slaughter of this extent would surely have come to the attention of Roman authorities, but there is not the faintest record of it in any non-Christian historical sources of the period. Thirdly, the story fits into a well-known mytheme of a current ruler seeking to eliminate a young rival (usually an infant) but failing and being in fact superseded by him. Even in Greek myth we

6. See Price, *Deconstructing Jesus* 84f.

7. How exactly Mary became pregnant by the Holy Spirit is also a perennial mystery. A recent Christian scholar defines the Holy Spirit as follows: "It is the function of the [Holy] Spirit to maintain, strengthen and, where need be, restore the unity of Being with the beings [*sic*], a unity which is constantly threatened" (Macquarrie, *Principles of Christian Theology* 201). How such an entity could have impregnated a human woman is not easily understandable. Zeus' powers of impregnation when he became a shower of gold is no less explicable—but of course no one believes that.

8. See Crossan, *Jesus: A Revolutionary Biography* 11f.

have seen that Kronos, the father of Zeus, sought to kill his son because of prophecies that Zeus would become king of the gods. Romulus and Remus had to be whisked away as infants and hidden because King Amulius wanted them dead.

It is peculiar that we know exactly nothing about Jesus' life between his infancy and the age of thirty. Surely, if he had existed—and had attracted as many followers and disciples as we are told he did, including supposed members of his own family (such as his brother James), who presumably supplied the gospel writers with their recollections—we should have at least an inkling of what Jesus did in the first three decades of his life. But the record is perplexingly empty.

Jesus' baptism by John the Baptist is also problematical. The account is found only in the gospels; Josephus mentions John the Baptist on numerous occasions but not his baptism of Jesus. There are, indeed, striking parallels between the supernatural birth and the religious mission of John the Baptist and those of Jesus, as recounted in the early chapters of Luke; and one suspects that some sort of reduplication of mythic elements has occurred. Other elements of Jesus' purported life will be discussed once we examine the Christian sources for them.

What we know of Jesus' life and ministry is found in two quite discrete bodies of work in what is now the New Testament: the letters of Paul and the four gospels (especially the three synoptic gospels—Mark, Matthew, and Luke). Our understanding of the relation of these two groups of texts has, over the centuries, been clouded by Christian apologists' unquestioned assumption that they are referring to the same events in the same manner, when in fact their treatment of those events is highly dissimilar. In effect, what we have are two substantially different traditions: the letters of Paul and other documents constitute the Jerusalem tradition, while the gospels and other texts constitute the Galilean tradition.

Of the twenty-two "epistles" included in the New Testament [hereafter NT], thirteen are explicitly stated to have been written by Paul, but only seven are believed to have been actually written by him: Romans, 1 and 2 Corinthians, Galatians, 1 Thessalonians, Philippians, and Philemon. These were probably written between 49 and 62; the others (including the other nine, which are attributed to other authors) are dated anywhere from the 60s to as late as 130.

The first problem that confronts us is the unfortunate placement of these letters after the four gospels, suggesting that the former were written after the latter when in fact the reverse is the case. More significantly, the picture of Jesus and the Jesus movement that emerges from these letters is radically different from that found in the gospels.

By his own testimony, Paul began life as a vicious persecutor of Christians on behalf of Jewish authorities. At some point he converted to faith in Jesus; but the dramatic manner of this conversion, as recounted in Acts of the Apostles—"While he was still on the road and nearing Damascus, suddenly a light from the sky flashed all around him" (9:3), with the voice of Jesus saying, "I am Jesus, whom you are persecuting" (9:5)—is almost certainly a fabrication. It is not mentioned by Paul himself and is implicitly contradicted by him, since he declares that he went to Damascus only after he had already been converted (Gal. 1:17).

But that is a small point. Far more significant is the fact that nowhere does Paul speak explicitly of Jesus as a person who was or became a human being on earth; nowhere does he refer to Jesus as the Messiah; nowhere does he mention any "miracles" associated with Jesus; nowhere does he mention Jesus in Jerusalem; nowhere does he cite a Last Supper with disciples, or the betrayal of Jesus by Judas.

These are astonishing departures from the picture of Jesus as portrayed in the gospels as one who was brought down to earth to save humanity from the burden of sin, who was crucified by Pilate (never mentioned by Paul), and so on. Instead, the picture of Jesus that emerges in Paul's authentic letters is of a figure who is as old as God who has only now (i.e., in Paul's lifetime—indeed, by Paul's own agency as Jesus' only true "apostle") been "revealed" as humanity's saviour. In the scenario outlined by Paul, Jesus "operates entirely on a spiritual plane,"[9] and there was no need for him to have descended to the earth to fulfil his mission as humanity's saviour.

Indeed, there is considerable evidence in the letters to Paul, or those written roughly contemporaneously with him, that such a descent to the earthly plane never occurred. 2 Timothy (probably written between 90 and 140) states that the salvation effected by Jesus had occurred "from all eternity" and is only now being "disclosed" to the world (1:9–10).[10]

9. Doherty, *The Jesus Puzzle* 92.

10. The NEB's translation of the latter phrase—"now at length disclosed by the appearance

This is also the thrust of Ephesians 3:9–11. The anonymous Epistle to the Hebrews (a quite early document, possibly dating to c. 63) essentially gives the game away by stating: "If he [Jesus] had been on earth, he would not even have been a priest" (8:4).[11]

What of Galatians, where Paul states that "God sent his Son, born of a woman, born under the law, to buy freedom for those who were under the law" (4:4)? Aside from the fact that the phrase is probably an allusion to the celebrated "prophecy" in Isaiah ("A young woman is with child, and she will give birth to a son and call him Immanuel" [4:14]), the sense of the passage is that God has made *everyone* into his "sons" by sending the "Spirit of his Son" (4:6) into our hearts.

This brings up a related matter. Paul, who was no doubt intimately acquainted with the Hebrew Bible, makes clear references to it in his discussions of Jesus. When he says, "Christ died for our sins, in accordance with the scriptures" (1 Cor. 15:3), he cannot of course be referring to the Christian scriptures (i.e., the NT), which did not yet exist; he is referring to the Hebrew Bible, specifically Isaiah ("Yet it was our afflictions he was bearing, our pain he endured" [53:4]). And Paul's subsequent comment that "he was buried; that he was raised to life on the third day, in accordance with the scriptures" (1 Cor. 15:4) is manifestly an allusion to Hosea ("after two days he [the Lord] will revive us, on the third day he will raise us to live in his presence" [6:2]).

Before we consider two of the most controversial aspects of Jesus' life—the "miracles" associated with his ministry and his death (and subsequent resurrection)—we must examine the Galilean tradition embodied in the three synoptic gospels and certain other documents. For many centuries Christians believed that all four gospels constituted independent sources for the life of Jesus, drawing upon first-hand eyewitness accounts; but that view has been shattered by a more searching examination of the manner in which the relevant documents came to be

---

on earth of our Saviour Jesus Christ"—is blatantly tendentious in that the words "on earth" do not appear in the Greek text.

11. The translation in NEB is: "If he were on earth, he would not be a priest at all." But Doherty (*Jesus Puzzle* 310f.) strongly argues that "The writer says nothing which shows any cognizance of the fact that Jesus *had* been on earth, recently; that it was on earth where an important part of his sacrifice, the shedding of his blood, had occurred." Even if the NEB translation is used, the construction of the phrase as a contrary-to-fact condition clearly implies the absence of Jesus' presence on earth.

written. The synoptic gospels were probably written toward the end of the first century. Mark was almost certainly written first, perhaps as early as 65–75 or as late as 85–90. Matthew and Luke are heavily reliant upon Mark, dating to at least a decade later, and more likely to the period 100–120. The gospel of John, radically different in tone from the other three although in other ways reliant upon them, probably dates to between 90 and 110. What is more, at least certain portions of all four gospels were probably added at a later date. All scholars agree that the last several verses of Mark (16:9–20) constitute such a later addition, as does the prologue to John (1:1–4). There is considerable evidence that individual phrases or sentences in the gospels may have been inserted into the text as much as a century or more after the date of their initial composition.

Furthermore, Matthew and Luke are now believed to have been founded upon a conjectural document called Q (standing for the German word *Quelle,* "source"). The Q document—which itself has several layers—never speaks of Jesus going to Jerusalem, nor cites his death or resurrection. What is called Q1 largely consists of a series of sayings that closely resemble Jewish wisdom collections such as Proverbs; it also includes Jesus' well-known parables. Many of these sayings—especially those relating to the moral virtues of the poor, hatred of the rich, and so on—appear to reflect the beliefs of a disadvantaged class in Galilee, dating perhaps to the 20s or 30s, expressing dissatisfaction at the rapid urbanisation and radical increase of the inequality of wealth in the region. Moreover, they are almost entirely devoid of historical or personal context; in other words, they are very likely the product, not of a single individual, but of a group or movement. Their attribution to someone named Jesus apparently occurred at a later date. It is worth noting that a document called the *Didache* ("Teaching")—a sort of church manual probably dating to the first or second century—features many saying similar to those in Q1, but does not assign them to Jesus.

It is worth emphasising that a number of the sayings clearly reflect Cynic philosophical tropes. Cynicism was experiencing a revival of interest in the Greco-Roman world, as exemplified in heavy borrowings from Cynic thought in the work of Seneca and Epictetus. Some of the most well-known utterances placed in the mouth of Jesus—"Blessed are the poor, for theirs is the kingdom of God"; "I say to you, love your enemies"; "If someone slaps you on the cheek, offer him the other also"—have striking parallels in Cynic aphorisms.[12] And, just as these utterances were assigned to Jesus by the Q community, so did many of the Cynic statements become formulaically attributed to the founder of the school, Diogenes of Sinope, although it is highly unlikely that he actually uttered any significant number of them. This manner of attribution was widely practised in antiquity, especially among the Jews, as such documents as the Wisdom of Solomon and the Proverbs of King David attest.

The layer of Q known as Q2 is of a radically different sort. It is here that we find the blood-and-thunder apocalypticism that features fulminations against a sin-ridden human race and prophecies about the end of the world. How could such a radically different sort of utterance be the product of a single mind? And why, again, are these statements in no way tied to the purported events of Jesus' life, such as the Last Supper or his death and resurrection? If these things had happened to an historical Jesus, how is it that the Q community (and hence the Q2 document) exhibits no awareness of them? The Q2 material appears to be the product of some group (probably not the same as that which produced Q1) encountering a foreign group with which it was in conflict and which it condemned to perdition as a means of gaining at least a rhetorical revenge upon it.

There is evidence that the Q2 sayings were originally attributed to a personified Wisdom (*Sophia*) (see Luke 11:49). At some later date they were transferred to Jesus, who (several generations after his purported life and death) was envisioned as the saviour of the Jews. In addition, some scholars detect a further layer of Q, called Q3, composed after the Jewish War of 66–70, in which certain stories were explicitly (and for the first time) declared to have applied to Jesus. These include such things as Jesus' temptation by Satan, certain stories of miraculous healing, and the like. It is worth pointing out that the entire Q document has almost no resemblance to anything in the letters of Paul.

The first person to bring all this together was Mark.[13] Although it is unlikely that Mark had direct access to the Q document, his gospel

12. See Price, *Deconstructing Jesus* 151–60.

13. In spite of many Christian scholars' ingenious attempts to tease out biographies of the four writers of the gospels, it is next to impossible to say anything definitive about their lives; and the names affixed to them are purely conventional.

does include certain elements that indirectly relate to Q—specifically, the placement of Jesus in Galilee, certain apocalyptic utterances, and a development of the association of the Q3 material to Jesus. All the evidence points to Mark as the inventor of the story of Jesus coming to Jerusalem, undergoing death and resurrection, and therefore becoming a messiah or saviour.

What was his rationale in doing so? If the community associated with Mark had been exposed to both the Galilean and Jerusalem traditions, it may have occurred to someone to combine the two or to create an earthly messiah by drawing elements from the OT. This is not to say that Mark invented the material out of whole cloth, nor that he was being deliberately deceptive in fabricating a Jesus—or, rather, in attributing to Jesus the multifarious and at times self-contradictory statements put in his mouth or the events of his purported life. Instead, what Mark was doing was practising the age-old Jewish technique of *midrash*—a method of scriptural interpretation whereby, in certain contexts, earlier texts are reconfigured to suit the needs of the present. And what texts did Mark have at his disposal? What else but the Hebrew Bible? At a later date, Mark's text was read by Matthew and Luke. They felt that Mark had left out the Q material (which by this time had been definitively attributed to Jesus), and so they put it in.

But Mark fails to cite many of the standard events in Jesus' life—including, incredibly, his very birth by Mary and the Holy Spirit. This was a detail supplied by Matthew; and it is well known that his quotation of what he believed to be a prophecy from the OT ("A virgin will conceive and bear a son, and he shall be called Emmanuel" [Isaiah 7:14]) is a mistranslation of the Hebrew word *almah* ("young woman"), which the Greek translation of the OT (the Septuagint)[14] renders as *parthenos,* which could either mean "virgin" or "young woman" (i.e., one who is recently married but not yet pregnant); Matthew clearly took it in the former sense. As John Dominic Crossan states, "Somebody went seeking in the Old Testament for a text that could be interpreted as prophesying a virginal conception, even if such was never its original meaning."[15]

It is now time to turn to Jesus' so-called miracles. The literal

14. The first five books of the Hebrew Bible were translated into Greek around the mid-3rd century B.C.E.; the remaining books no later than the mid-first century C.E.
15. Crossan, *Jesus: A Revolutionary Biography* 18.

historicity of many or most of these events have long been rejected even by Christian scholars, and they became a source of acute embarrassment as science and rationalism made progress in the West. But it can now be seen that they were almost entirely taken directly from stories in the OT, with minimal revisions or alterations. Jesus' walking on water bears striking similarities to Moses' parting of the Red Sea; his miraculous feeding of his followers is drawn from similar feeding miracles in the OT (1 Kings 17:10–16; 2 Kings 4:42–44); his raising of the dead draws upon a similar act by Elijah (1 Kings 17:17–24) and Elisha (2 Kings 418–37). In other words, Jesus is being portrayed as a new kind of Moses or Elijah.

As for the passion story (Jesus' accusation by his Jewish opponents, his betrayal by Judas, his crucifixion, and his subsequent resurrection), Earl Doherty remarks: "Virtually every detail of the Gospel passion story can be shown to have a parallel in scripture" (i.e., the OT).[16] It follows a well-known myth pattern whereby a righteous person is falsely accused, puts his trust in God, undergoes a trial and suffering, and then is miraculously saved by God and raised to a high level either in the land of the living or in heaven. Certain elements are manifestly borrowed from the OT. Jesus' entry into Jerusalem on a colt is adapted from Zechariah 9:9 ("See, your king is coming to you, his cause won, his victory gained, humble and mounted on a donkey, on a colt, the foal of a donkey"). Note that whereas Mark (11:5f.) speaks of a colt, Matthew (21:1–5) mentions both a donkey and her foal, failing to understand that the Zechariah passage is referring to a single animal, not two separate ones.

Jesus' overturning of the tables at the Temple—the ostensible reason given for why he was arrested and tried—is widely recognised by New Testament scholars as fictitious. Firstly, the Temple complex was enormous, and the idea of a single individual creating the kind of havoc Jesus is supposed to have created is ludicrous. Secondly, the whole incident seems stitched together from a succession of passages in the OT (e.g., Malachi 3:1, Hosea 9:15, Zechariah 14:21). Jesus himself is made to quote Isaiah 56:7 ("my house will be called a house of prayer for all nations") and Jeremiah 7:11 ("Do you regard this house which bears my name as a bandits' cave?") at Matt. 11:17. Judas' betrayal has echoes

16. Doherty, *The Jesus Puzzle* 244–45.

in various OT texts; specifically, the 30 pieces of silver he is supposed to have received echoes Zecharaiah 11:12 ("Then they weighed out my wages, thirty silver pieces").

The question of whether there ever were any apostles as depicted in the gospels is now severely in question. The assumption that there were twelve of them appears to be an attempt to link them up with the twelve tribes of Israel in the OT; other documents—such as the Gospel of Thomas (discovered in 1945 and believed to date to the late first or early second century)—supply a different number. Indeed, Luke 10:1 gives a radically different figure ("After this the Lord appointed a further seventy-two and sent them on ahead in pairs to every town and place he himself intended to visit"). And the very idea of a Last Supper, while found both in Paul (1 Cor. 11:23–26) and in the gospels (although with significantly differing details), appears to have been retrojected back to Jesus from traditions beginning later in the first century.

Numerous other details can be seen to be derived from OT passages: Jesus' statement at the Last Supper, "This is my blood of the covenant" (Mark 14:24 = Exodus 24:8); Jesus' silence at his trial (= Ps. 39:9 et al.); Pilate's washing of his hands of Jesus' blood (= Deut. 21:6–8); Jesus' scourging (= Isaiah 50:6–7 et al.); Jesus being jeered at the cross (= Ps. 22:7–8); the centurion's awed utterance, "Truly, this man was the Son of God" (= "Fools that we were . . . he is one of the Sons of God" [Wisdom of Solomon 5:4–5]).

As for the crucifixion itself, the NT is frustratingly vague on when it actually took place. Pontius Pilate was prefect of Judaea in the years 26–36, but there is no clear indication in any documents as to the year in which the crucifixion occurred. It is true that it is cited a few times in Paul's letters; but those citations are entirely devoid of any historical context: no mention of it taking place in Jerusalem, no mention of the role of Herod Antipas (the tetrarch of Galilee and Perea [4 B.C.E.–39 C.E.]) or of Pontius Pilate, and so on and so forth. In Paul it appears to be an entirely spiritual event—for what else could it be, given that Paul's Jesus is a purely spiritual entity? The critical passage is in 1 Corinthians: "None of the powers that rule the world has known that wisdom; if they had, they would not have crucified the Lord of glory" (2:8). Many scholars now conclude that this passage is more naturally read as referring to Jesus' death at the hands of the demons who, in Paul's view, rule the earth; in other words, that the time is fast approaching when their rulership of the earth is coming to an end with the imminent advent of the "kingdom of God." A later reference to Jesus on the cross ("For he has cancelled the bond which was outstanding against us with its legal demands; he has set it aside, nailing it to the cross. There he disarmed the cosmic powers and authorities and made a public spectacle of them, leading them as captives in his triumphal procession" [Colos. 2:14–15]) makes it a wholly spiritual event; and Paul clearly speaks of crucifixion as a kind of metaphor when he states, "Those who belong to Christ Jesus have crucified the old nature with its passions and desires" (Gal. 5:24).

It is only in the gospels that the crucifixion becomes a literal event on earth; but the details differ significantly from one gospel to the other. It is, strikingly, only in John that we find the grisly mention of the nails that pierced Jesus' hands and feet; but this seems manifestly to be derived from certain OT passages (e.g. "They have bound me hand and foot" [Ps. 22:16]; "Then they will look on me, on him whom they have pierced" [Zech. 12:10]).

We now come to the famous "empty tomb" story.[17] This too seems to be a tissue of fabrications and borrowings from the OT. Mark appears to have invented the characters of Mary Magdalene, Mary (mother of Jesus and James), and Salome; there is no evidence that such women existed. Once the story was cited in Mark's gospel, it was elaborated with an increasing (and unlikely) number of details by Matthew and Luke. Jesus' rising from the tomb on the third day is a manifest adaptation of Hosea 6:1–2 ("Come, let us return to the Lord. He has torn us, but he will heal us, he has wonded us, but he will bind up our wounds; after two days he will revive us, and on the third day he will raise us to live in his presence"). Matthew adds the detail (not found in other accounts) of guards at the tomb. And note that Paul states that Jesus exhibited himself to a whopping five hundred people (1 Cor. 15:6); possibly the later gospel writers found this to be implausible, so they reduced the number of those who saw Jesus to only a few.

Paul is so insistent on Jesus' rising from the dead because he feels it is required to convince his followers that they too will rise from the dead and ascend to heaven; this is surely the meaning of his statement that

17. For searching criticisms of the historicity of the account from a number of perspectives, see Price and Lowder, *The Empty Tomb*.

"Christ was raised to life—the firstfruits of the harvest of the dead" (1 Cor. 15:20). In other words, Paul never believed in a *second* coming of Jesus; his resurrection from the dead was the *first* and only coming that would occur, because the "kingdom of God" was in his view imminent. Indeed, Paul plainly declares that if Jesus' resurrection did not occur, then the entire system of Christianity must be regarded as false: "If there is no resurrection, then Christ was not raised; and if Christ was not raised, then our gospel is null and void, and so too is your faith" (1 Cor. 15:14). It was the gospel writers who—perhaps because they recognised to their dismay that Jesus' death did not in fact result (now several generations after its supposed occurrence) in the advent of the kingdom of God—felt that they had to invent a second coming at some point in the future.

Even what Christians have for millennia assumed is the signature function of Jesus' life and death, the Atonement—i.e., his acting as the "saviour" of the human race—has its origins in the OT. (Exactly what Jesus was atoning for will be discussed later.) It is worth pointing out again that the Q document says nothing about this aspect of Jesus' life. The issue does emerge in Paul's letters; indeed, there is reason to believe that Paul, if he did not actually invent the Atonement, made clever use of it as a means of persuading Gentiles (pagans and non-Jews) to latch on to the faith without being born into it or having to practice all the various dietary and other regulations in the OT (including circumcision).[18] Numerous other cults in antiquity speak of the death and resurrection of a saviour-god, ranging from Aleyan Baal to Osiris to Attis to Dionysus. As early as Leviticus we have an atonement ceremony whereby Aaron

> is to bring forward the live goat. Laying both his hands on its head he must confess over it all the iniquities of the Israelites and all their acts of rebellion, that is all their sins; he is to lay his hands on the head of the goat and send it away into the wilderness in the charge of a man who is waiting ready. The goat will carry all their iniquities upon iself into some barren waste, where the man will release it, there in the wilderness. (16:20–22)

How is this not identical to John's celebrated report of what John the

18. See Price, *Deconstructing Jesus* 76f.

Baptist said when he saw Jesus: "There is the Lamb of God . . . who takes away the sin of the world" (1:29)? But whereas the goat was not actually killed (although in a previous ceremony a different goat was, along with a bull [Lev. 16:6–16]), and its salvific function apparently applied only to the Israelites, Jesus' sacrifice applies to the entire population of the world.

The upshot of this entire discussion is that every single "event" in the purported life of Jesus was taken from various texts in the OT, where their implications and ramifications were at times radically different; then, by a rather perverse process of reversal, the various authors of the NT pointed to these very passages as "proof" that they constituted "prophecies" of the emergence of an historical Jesus as saviour of mankind. This inescapable conclusion leads to the high probability that there never was a Jesus—that he was invented at some point in the mid-first century C.E. as various Jewish sects, chafing under Roman rule, envisioned a messiah for themselves who would swiftly deliver them from their oppression. Both Paul and the gospel writers, in their very different ways, latched onto this imaginary figure; but whereas Paul conceived of him as a purely spiritual entity, the gospel writers and others chose to believe in his literal existence.

Those who cling to the belief in Jesus' actual existence must nonetheless confront the alarming reality that it is at this point simply impossible to have any firm knowledge on any of the details of his life or, more relevantly, on what he actually believed. The texts on which his purported views are set down are so full of conflicting and contradictory doctrines, deriving from multiple sources over decades or centuries and mashed together in a not entirely competent way, that the doctrines he espoused become all but unascertainable. Even those scholars who cannot bring themselves to give up the possibility of an historical Jesus are forced to admit: "With so few reliable early sources no one can recreate a historical Jesus with any confidence."[19] The multiplicity of viewpoints recorded in the gospels and other materials has led to two millennia of schisms, "heresies," and modifications as successive generations of Christian theologians cherry-pick the sentiments they favour and declare them—as opposed to others of an antipodally different sort—the "real" views of Jesus. We shall soon see that the actual working out of a

---

19. Freeman, *A New History of Early Christianity* 30.

more or less coherent set of "Christian doctrines" was a largely political process effected by Christian emperors and high-ranking religious officials as a means of dispensing with embarrassing dogmas (which in many cases had just as much scriptural support as the ones they vaunted) and unifying Christians against ongoing political, military, and doctrinal threats.

There is some reason to question whether the issue of Jesus' actual existence is of any relevance today: surely no significant number of Christians are likely to accept that he never existed, and the dogmas associated with him—and with other Christian leaders over the past two millennia—will probably not stand or fall even if it were possible to establish definitively that there never was a Jesus. But at least some thoughtful Christians have maintained that the reality of Jesus—and especially of his death and resurrection—are vital to the *authority* of the doctrines they profess. As the Catholic writer Russell Kirk (1918–1994) put it:

> The Resurrection lacking, what we call Christianity would be a mere congeries of moral exhortations, at best; and exhortations founded upon no more authority than the occasional utterances of an obscure man whose hints of divinity and half-veiled claims of power to judge the quick and the dead might be regarded as manifestations of delusions of grandeur. . . . Without the Resurrection, which prefigures our own resurrection and life everlasting, one might as well turn again to the gods of the Greeks, or to Epictetus, Marcus Aurelius, and Seneca.[20]

B. The Spread of Christianity

The dissemination of Christianity throughout the Empire took place with surprising speed, expanding well beyond its origins in the Near East. Already by the end of the first century C.E.—as exhibited in such documents as the apocryphal 1 Clement (c. 96) and the letters of Ignatius (early second century), patriarch of Antioch—we find evidence of an increasingly elaborate church hierarchy and the establishment of *episkopoi* (bishops) as leaders of various Christian communities.

20. Quoted in Buckley, *Nearer, My God* 124.

The spread of Christianity was substantially enhanced by the political, social, financial, and military turmoil that engulfed the Roman Empire in the course of the second, third, and fourth centuries. Following the death of Marcus Aurelius in 180, the Empire was plagued by a succession of emperors—Commodus (180–92), Caracalla (211–17), Elagabalus (218–22)—who were manifestly unfit for their role and were assassinated by rivals or by their own household troops. A brief civil war (193–97) led to a half-century of anarchy beginning in 235, where many emperors were murdered by the Praetorian Guards or other army officers.

During this entire period, incursions into the Roman Empire by neighbouring tribes were a constant threat. Septimius Severus (r. 193–211), one of the few efficient emperors of the time, managed to suppress the Parthians in the East, but failed to subdue the Caledonians in Scotland. By this point the army had essentially become a frontier militia, and a great many natives served in its ranks. This and other factors led to Caracalla's momentous edict granting citizenship to all free men in the Empire, although this process had been underway among his predecessors. Severus Alexander (r. 222–35) restored some stability to the Empire by battling the emerging Alamanni and Goths in Germany; but during the chaos of 235–85 such tribes as the Goths, the Franks, and the Saxons all invaded the frontiers of the Empire. The Emperor Claudius Gothicus defeated the Goths on both land and sea in 269; Probus (r. 276–82) repelled the Alamanni and Franks in their attempts to invade Gaul.

Some emperors attempted to salvage Roman religion or lead it into different directions, with only middling success. Elagabalus was a priest of Baal who wished to spread the worship of the sun-god Elah-Gabal; but his murder curtailed the plans. Aurelian (r. 270–75) sought to introduce a cult of the sun as a unifying influence to tie all the various cults of the Empire together: how far he succeeded is debatable, but this very action to some extent underscored the increasing monotheism of the era.

The chaos of the third century led to more persecution of Christians—especially under the emperors Decius (250–51) and Valerian (257)—although it remained sporadic and unsystematic. Ironically, Caracalla's granting of Roman citizenship to all male members of the far-flung Empire actually enhanced opportunities for persecution, since citizenship necessarily entailed religious duties that Christians could not or would not fulfil. Hence, Decius demanded that every citizen must sacrifice to the pagan gods. Jews were exempted, but not Christians. However, it was relatively easy to purchase a certificate (*libellus*) testifying that one had made such a sacrifice. The emperor Galienus rescinded this order in 261.

In 284 a Danubian officer named Diocles proclaimed himself emperor, naming himself Diocletian (C. Aurelius Valerius Diocletianus). He defeated a rival emperor in the West in 285. During his twenty-year reign he came to recognise that the emperor must move about the Empire leading the army, and he therefore made the imperial court mobile; he named Maximian (M. Aurelius Valerius Maximianus) as his Caesar (later Augustus). Maximian led armies in the Rhine, Gaul, and elsewhere, while Diocletian focused on Bithynia, Egypt, and other points in the east. In 293 he named two more officers to share imperial power, giving them the title of Caesar. Thus the tetrarchy—a system whereby an emperor and his underling governed the western and eastern portions of the Empire—was born.

With the advent of Diocletian, persecution was renewed. His motives were clearly a facet of his goal of restoring stability to an empire racked by a half-century of civil war. He did so, in part, by exalting the religious status of the tetrarchs. In this attempt he came just short of declaring that the emperors were either themselves living gods and that they ruled by some sort of divine right: by bestowing upon the emperors the cognomen Jovius and the Caesars the cognomen Herculius, he consciously associated them with two of the most powerful and revered figures in the Olympian pantheon. One of his Caesars, the superstitious Galerius, persuaded Diocletian to undertake a widespread persecution of Christians, entailing the burning of their scriptures, destruction of their churches, and legal and political penalties for avowed Christians. At a later date some priests were actually put to death. When, in 304, Diocletian proclaimed that all citizens must sacrifice to the gods, many Christians willingly subjected themselves to martyrdom.

In 305, Diocletian and Maximian abdicated. Persecution eased, especially in the West, after this date, but it did not fully abate until Galerius's death in 311. Remarkably, a few days before his death he wrote a document that has come to be called the Palinode of Galerius, which for the first time explicitly extended toleration to the Christian sect, albeit with an important proviso: "Wherefore in accordance with this our indulgence it will be their duty to pray to their god for our safety and for that of the State and for their own, so that on every side the State may be preserved unharmed and that they themselves may live in their own homes free from care."[21] In effect, Galerius—who believed that the illness that led to his death was some kind of curse from the god of the Christians—was co-opting the Christians in the attempt to preserve the Roman state, a task formerly restricted to pagans whose proper worship of the Greco-Roman pantheon was thought to ensure the rulership of Rome over its immense conquered territory.

But all was not well for the Christians, at least in the short term. One of the Caesars, Maximin, revealed himself very hostile to Christianity. Not only did he attempt (in manoeuvres that anticipated the reign of Julian a half-century later) to revive pagan religion in a number of ways, he reinstated Christian persecution, especially in the East. But this only set the stage for a battle between Constantine (a bastard son of one of the Caesars, Constantius) and his Caesar, Licinius (whom Galerius had wished to succeed him), and Maximin and Maxentius, culminating in the Battle of the Milvian Bridge, some miles north of Rome, in 312.

There is a great deal of tendentious fantasising regarding that battle, or more specifically regarding Constantine's supposed conversion to Christianity prior to it. In fact, there was no conversion at this time. What is likely is that Constantine—who had formerly avowed belief in Sol Invictus (the Unconquered Sun) and had claimed to have seen a vision of Apollo in 310—had a dream in which he saw the chi-rho symbol, which he interpreted as an omen from the Christian god, and he accordingly had the symbol painted on the shields or helmets of his soldiers. Eusebius' contention that Constantine saw a cross in the sky with the words *Hoc signo victor eris* ("you will be the victor by this sign") appears to be his own invention, or possibly this was something that Constantine himself declared many years later. Constantine may well have been influenced by Galerius' contention that he had been cursed by the Christian god; Constantine clearly subscribed to a belief in omens, and his victory at the battle conformed to a centuries-old tradition of (pagan) Roman generals who attributed their triumphs to the (pagan)

21. Quoted in Browder, *The Age of Constantine and Julian* 20.

gods from whom omens had been sought.

Furthermore, Constantine's reign (312–37) did not signal any attempt to suppress pagan religion; he could hardly have done so, since paganism still dominated the populace, especially in the West. When he undertook to complete the temple of Venus and Roma in the Roman Forum, he made sure to include a depiction of him making a pagan sacrifice; and he continued to pay tribute to Sol Invictus. While it is clear that Constantine subscribed to some kind of monotheism, he was deliberately vague on the identity of the god he was acknowledging.

The edict of Milan in 313, issued jointly by Constantine and Licinius, again explicitly articulates toleration for Christians; but it also sanctions pagan worship:

> . . . Christians should be given full liberty to follow the religion of their choice, so that all that is divine in the celestial seat may be appeased and propitious towards us and towards those under our authority. This is why we thought that, with a wholesome and just purpose, we should embark upon this policy of not refusing to anyone the opportunity of devoting himself either to the cult of the Christians or to whatever religion he feels is most suited to him, so that the highest divinity, whom we freely worship, may in all things bestow upon us his customary favour and goodwill.[22]

If the Christians, when they gained full control of the political and legal machinery of the Empire, had adopted this sane attitude, the history of Western civilisation would have been very different.

But we should not be fooled about Constantine's fundamental predilections: his preference for the Christians was unmistakable, as evidenced by his extensive building of Christian churches throughout the Empire. And yet, in contrast to later Christian propaganda, when Constantine began construction of the Christian church of Sancta Sophia in Constantinople he made sure to include hundreds of statues—most of them pillaged from all over the Empire—of the pagan gods. He also built numerous temples to these gods, including even the foreboding Cybele, as well as his favoured sun god. But while such actions bespeak

22. Quoted in Brower 28.

a concern not to alienate the pagan citizens of the Empire, other actions of Constantine betray his inclinations. He decreed that certain civil litigation (including the freeing of slaves) be entrusted to a bishop instead of the secular courts—an initial but ultimately ominous foreshadowing of the Christian takeover of the legal system during the Middle Ages. To make up for a shortfall in the treasury (which had been depleted largely because of his prodigal generosity to Christians), he stripped gold and other valuable items from pagan temples; he also exempted certain Christians from the payment of taxes. But Constantine also exhibited annoyance at the continuing schisms and doctrinal disputes afflicting the Christian church; as we shall see presently, he at times sought to resolve these disputes by fiat, since his knowledge of or interest in the actual bases of the disputes was probably minimal. He himself was baptisted only on his deathbed in 337.

In the course of the third century, both the Senate and many executive offices become largely moribund. Emperors became autocrats, ruling as long as their armies supported them. Inflation was rampant as a result of the constant devaluation of the currency. Tax collection was placed in the hands of local landowners, who sometimes found it difficult to collect taxes from citizens. This led Constantine to make the landowners a hereditary class, forbidding them to leave their residences. Other workers also became hereditary, ushering in the era of serfdom long before the official commencement of the Middle Ages.

After Constantine, more civil wars followed, as his sons Constantius II, Constantine II, and Constans battled for various parts of the Empire. Constans issued an edict in 341 (which he claimed was merely a renewal of an edict of Constantine himself) condemning pagan religion; this led to the destruction of some pagan temples by Christians. A Christian theologian, Firmicus Maternus, wrote a polemic, *On the Error of the Profane Religions* (346/7), likening paganism to worship of the Devil and recommending actual persecution of pagans. In 356 Constantius issued edicts demanding the shutting of pagan temples, the confiscation of the property of pagans, and even the death penalty for pagans; but, because the provincial governors and their administrations throughout the Empire were still largely pagan, enforcement of these edicts was spotty at best.

The elevation of Julian—a half-brother of Constantine and a cousin of Constantius II—to the throne in 361 resulted in a radical change of direction in Rome's attitude toward the Christians. As the last pagan emperor, Julian sought both to revive the Olympian religion—or, at any rate, what it had become at this time—and to suppress Christianity; but his reign lasted only a little longer than two years, and his death in 363 signalled the ultimate triumph of Christianity and the doom of paganism.

Julian had been instructed in the Christian scriptures but also had access to an enormous library of pagan literature. He gained a passion for Greek literature and culture from his early tutor, the eunuch Mardonius; and he was also influenced by the lectures of Libanius (314?–392?), a Greek teacher of rhetoric, as well as by Maximus of Ephesus, who inculcated in Julian the mystical practice of theurgy, a movement growing out of Neoplatonism that stressed the role of divination and oracles in human affairs. As such, Julian was anything but an atheist; indeed, he became initiated in such cults as those of Mithras, Cybele, and the Eleusinian mysteries.

Julian's campaign to overthrow Christianity and reinstitute paganism was broad-based, encompassing legal reforms as well as reforms pertaining to the conduct of religious affairs. He rescinded Constantius' edict confiscating the property of pagan temples. Sensing that paganism's lack of a hierarchical organistion was a cause of weakness, he urged the appointment of a high priest in each province of the Empire and made sure that these men were morally worthy of the role, not mere politicians or aristocrats to whom the office had been bestowed as an honorific or sinecure. In imitation of the Christians, these priests were asked to institute charities to assist the poor.

In his attempt to develop a coherent pagan theology, Julian urged the melding of Neoplatonism with the ongoing tendency toward monotheism as embodied, for example, in the cult of Sol Invictus. He assisted in the growth of pagan cities and exacted financial penalties upon those that were largely Christian. One of his most controversial manoeuvres was to ban Christian teachers from instructing their pupils in pagan literature and philosophy. As we shall see, such Christian theologians as Clement of Alexandria and Origen relied heavily on pagan thought as a necessary foundation for Christian culture, and the withdrawal of such instruction would—as Christian officials rightly recognised—have deleterious effects on their pupils' future functioning within Greco-Roman society. But, in essence, Julian was merely calling out Christian teachers as the hypocrites they were: while condemning pagan thought as the product of grave religious error, they used that same thought (especially that of Plato) as a means of undermining paganism. As he wrote pungently in a letter written in 362:

> A man who praises what he knows is worthless and promotes what he privately condemns is a hypocrite, a cheater, a seducer, a peddler of wrothless goods.... Did not the gods bestow all learning on the likes of Homer, Hesiod, Demosthenes, Herodotus, Thucycides, Isocrates, Lysias? And did not these same men think themselves inspired by Hermes or one of the Muses? How terrible that the men who have the duty to expound these writers revile the gods whom these writers loved![23]

Julian, however, refused to enact or condone the actual killing of Christians—which paradoxically led Gregory of Nazianzus to complain that Julian was denying Christians the blessings of martyrdom!

Julian's death, while leading the Roman army in a war against the Persians, brought an end to these efforts. Probably his goal of overthrowing Christianity at this late date was futile from the start, since Christians had by this time infiltrated all levels of society, government, and the military; it is, however, impossible to state with certainty what would have happened if a succession of pagan emperors had carried on the campaign. But all the emperors following him were Christians, and his reforms were quickly negated.

Theodosius I (r. 379–95) did much to foster the establishment of Christianity throughout the Empire as well as settling doctrinal disputes among the Christians; he also made strong efforts to suppress paganism, going so far as to allow Christian monks to ravage pagan shrines. Indeed, his own actions unleashed so much violence against the perceived opponents of Christianity that he was forced to issue an edict prohibiting Christians from "laying violent hands on Jews and pagans who are living quietly and attempting nothing disorderly or contrary to law."[24]

23. R. Joseph Hoffmann, ed. and tr., *Julian's Against the Galileans* 148–49.
24. Cited in Freeman, *A New History of Early Christianity* 267.

C. The Evolution of Christian Doctrine

Christianity is the first (but not the last) of the major religions of the world that is based upon an existing written scripture—that is, the Hebrew Bible (which Christians deemed the Old Testament [hereafter abbreviated OT]). It is worth examining how the OT and the New Testament (hereafter abbreviated NT) came together as a single scripture called the Bible: the process was long and convoluted and not completed until 367. The early Christian theologian Tatian (120?–180?) is among the first to reveal familiarity with all four of the canonical gospels: he weaved them together into a single narrative, the *Diatesseron,* that was meant to smooth away the differences and contradictions in the four texts. But, as previously mentioned, we know of two dozen other "gospels" that were ultimately discarded or suppressed by successive generations of theologians and church councils.

Then there is the vexed issue of why and how the OT was regarded as a kind of vast preface to the NT. (The OT, even excluding the Apocrypha, is in terms of text about four times the size of the NT.) Indeed, given that Paul himself declared that the doctrines associated with Jesus formed a "new covenant" (2 Cor. 3:6) that essentially superseded the OT, there is reason to wonder why and how the two bodies of scriptures were fused in the first place. While it is true that, as C. K. Barrett maintains, many NT texts "make it clear that their authors regarded the Old Testament as an authoritative body of literature which claimed the attention and obedience of Christians,"[25] there was no uniformity of opinion regarding the nature of the relation of the OT and the NT. A succession of Christian theologians from the second to the fifth century—Justin Martyr (100?–165?), Irenaeus (130?–202?), Clement of Alexandria (150?–215?), Tertullian (Q. Septimius Florence Tertullianus, 155?–220?), Origen of Alexandria (184?–253?), Lactantius (L. Caelius Firmianus Lactantius, 250?–325?), Augustine of Hippo (354–430)—gradually latched on to the notion that the OT, because of its purportedly accurate "prophecies" of the coming of Christ, must

25. C. K. Barrett, "The Interpretation of the Old Testament in the New," in Ackroyd and Evans, *The Cambridge History of the Bible* 377.

therefore be regarded as a necessary adjunct to the NT; and, in a classic case of circular logic, both the OT and the NT were as a result regarded as divinely inspired.[26] (These scriptures speak the truth about God and Jesus because they were divinely inspired by God.)[27] And, of course, the scriptures themselves make such claims (e.g., 2 Timothy 3:16), but that hardly counts as evidence.

In one crucial instance, however, the use of purportedly veridical prophecies as a "proof" of their divine inspiration produced extremely awkward results. The increasing apocalypticism prevalent in Jewish thought in the first centuries B.C.E. and C.E.—evidenced in the work of Josephus—led to a certain embarrassment when the followers of Jesus were forced to confront the startling fact that he did not (in the purported words of John the Baptist) "overwhelm you [i.e., Jesus' enemies] with the Holy Spirit and with fire" (Matt. 3:11; cf. Luke 3:16). Jesus' apparent death—however temporary it may have been—seemed to leave his supporters in the same boat they were in before, still oppressed by the Romans and other foes.

And what of the prophecies placed in his mouth about his imminent return in the Second Coming? The statements occur in all three of the synoptic gospels: "He said to them, 'Truly I tell you: there are some of those standing here who will not taste death before they have seen the kingdom of God come with power'" (Mark 9:1); "Truly I tell you: there are some of those standing here who will not taste death before they have seen the Son of Man coming in his kingdom" (Matt. 16:28); "In truth I tell you: there are some of those standing here who will not taste death befoe they have seen the kingdom of God" (Luke 9:27). When, after the passage of two or three generations after Jesus' supposed crucifixion and no Second Coming seemed to be happening, some Christians expressed doubt and dismay. Already by the mid-50s, when Paul presumably wrote 1 Thessalonians, he is saying, "About dates and times, my friends, you yourselves know perfectly well that the day of the Lord comes like a thief in the night" (5:1–2)—although this need not be a reference to a Second Coming, in which Paul apparently did not believe. But the conception

26. The Jewish theologian Philo had already maintained—without any reference to the NT—that Moses had written the Pentateuch "under God's guidance" (*De Vita Mos.* 1.1).

27. Cf. Augustine: "I cannot question Moses, whose words were true because you [i.e., God], the Truth, filled him with yourself" (*Confessions* 11.1).

is repeated by the author of 2 Peter (probably written c. 150), where he repeats the lamentation, "What has happened to his promised coming?" (3:4), and replies with the manifest sophism, "in the Lord's sight one day is like a thousand years and a thousand years like one day" (3:8), and therefore "the day of the Lord will come like a thief" (3:10).

By the second or third century, when the Second Coming and Last Judgment still seemed nowhere in sight, theologians began efforts to explain it away—either by putting it off to the far future (in contradiction to the plain words of the gospels) or by interpreting it other than literally. Irenaeus still believed that the kingdom of God was imminent, but later theologians asserted that this kingdom would be a kind of spiritual or internal matter, seizing upon a passage in Luke for the assertion.[28]

The fusion of the OT and NT was effected, it would seem, partly as a result of controversies that emerged in the mid-second century, chiefly associated with Marcion of Sinope (85?–160?). Marcion displayed some affinities with Gnosticism, a mystical sect that regarded the material world as a product of an evil demiurge; knowledge of the actual supreme deity of the universe relied upon some kind of spiritual insight (*gnosis*) available only to the lucky few. Marcion went on to proclaim that the material world was created by the the Jewish god Yahweh, and that Jesus (a spirit, not a man-god) was put on earth to free humanity from Jewish law. Marcion had joined the Christian church in Rome in 138 but was thrown out in 144; he later founded his own church in Asia Minor.

But Marcion's chief function was to assemble what was perhaps the first "canon" of Christian documents. He understandably rejected the OT as merely a chronicle of the evil god Yahweh, whom he blamed for killing Jesus, and he also denied that Jesus' emergence was foretold in the OT. Vaunting Paul as the only "apostle" who understood Jesus' message, he gathered some of the letters of Paul (with whom he had a clear affinity in his advocacy of a spiritual and not a human Jesus) and an abridged or rewritten version of Luke. This led the orthodox Christian church to compile its own canon, consisting of the four gospels and thirteen letters attributed to Paul. But more significantly, it is likely that the Acts of the Apostles was written at this time (not earlier, as many Christian scholars

---

28. "The Pharisees asked him, 'When will the kingdom of God come?' He answered, 'You cannot tell by observation when the kingdom of God comes. You cannot say, 'Look, here it is,' or 'There it is!' For the kingdom of God is among you!" (Luke 17:20–21).

have maintained) as a means of counteracting the Marcionite movement and also of bridging the broadening gulf between Pauline Christians and those who adhered to the view of an historical Jesus whose life is chronicled in the gospels. As such, it cannot be plausibly maintained that the Acts provides a glimpse of early Christianity during Jesus' purported lifetime. Indeed, the very idea of "apostles" was probably invented in Acts as a counterweight to the Gnostics' claim about Paul as the only legitimate apostle of Jesus.

Although Justin Martyr is the first extant Christian author to quote extensively from the gospels,[29] it was Irenaeus who first deemed the four gospels canonical; but he did so on curious grounds, namely that the gospels correspond to the four winds, the four points of the compass, and other natural phenomena. Augustine drew parallels between the four gospels and the four rivers of Paradise (*De Civitate Dei* [On the City of God] 13.21).[30]

And yet, even the combined OT and NT said relatively little about certain fundamental questions relating to God and human beings. The scriptures were either narratives (purportedly veridical and historical) or were homilies or tracts urging supporters toward faith and toward the adherence of certain moral codes. The failure of the scriptures to define the precise parameters of the religion they were broaching left the field open for two millennia of theologians to fill in the gaps in the texts, to tease out their "true" meaning, or to cherry-pick those portions of the texts that would validate the interpretations they were putting forth. The central issue of how exactly God is to be conceived—and, consequently, what relation Jesus bears to God—was the subject of centuries of dispute.

It would appear that Justin Martyr was the first to claim that the Christian god, as an unbegotten entity, was the first cause upon which all other causes depend. He did not, however, apparently believe in a *creatio ex nihilo* (creation from nothing); that is, in his view God fashioned the cosmos by taking hold of formless matter. But whether that matter was pre-existing or co-existing with God was an unresolved issue: some theologians believed that, if God had actually created matter *ex nihilo,* then God would be responsible for the evil that is so plainly prevalent in

29. See J. N. Birdsall, "The New Testament Text," in Ackroyd and Evans, *The Cambridge History of the Bible* 337.

30. Hereafter referred to in the text as *CD*.

the world. Irenaeus—who repeatedly denigrated the OT but nonetheless wished to preserve it in scripture because of its inclusion of a creator-god—believed that God must be the creator of the universe and that that creation was "good" (in contrast to Marcion). Irenaeus rejected the notion of a god subordinate to God (as in Marcion's demiurge) because he believed God to be omniscent, omnipotent, and all-provident. Irenaeus went on to maintain that God is the only thing that *is,* ontologically speaking; everything else is in the process of becoming (or of dying). By this means, he believed that he had "saved" God from being responsible for the evil in the world. How that comports with the other attributes he fastened onto God is unclear. Clement of Alexandria, who did believe in a *creatio ex nihilo,* also asserted that whatever is evil in the world cannot be blamed on God—but this appears to be coming dangerously close to the argument that God could not have prevented bad things from happening.

Justin became the first known "subordinationist" in that he maintained that, as the *logos* or word of God, Jesus is God's first-born; and while (in some fashion) Jesus is also God, he is "second to him in number, but one with him in essence."[31] As such, Jesus was evidently "born" or "created" before anything else in the universe. Origen followed him in this, but he maintained that, while Jesus was "begotten" by God, he was nonetheless as eternal and incorporeal as God. This general issue—associated in some senses with the baffling doctrine of the Trinity—plagued theologians, emperors, and church councils for centuries. The focus of the controversy was the figure of Arius (250?–336), a Cyrenaic priest who lent his name to what was ultimately deemed the heresy of Arianism.

Arius, following Origen, bluntly declared that Jesus was not created coevally with God; his rival, Alexander (bishop of Alexandria), asserted the opposite. This dispute caused mayhem throughout the Empire. In the epochal Council of Nicaea, held in 325 in a city in Bithynia not far from Constantinople, Constantine summoned as many as 250 bishops to resolve the dispute. Constantine himself advocated a solution whereby Jesus was declared to be *homoousios* (of the same substance) as God. The bishops ultimately accepted this opaque formulation and condemned

31. Osborn, *Justin Martyr* 28.

Arius, who was then excommunicated. And yet, the council still maintained somehow that Jesus was "begotten" of God. It is important to note that the Nicene creed, as initially formulated, makes no mention of the Trinity.

Constantine's precise motives in summoning the council and attempting to resolve this and other internal disputes are not entirely clear, but it is evident that he found such controversies annoying and generally harmful to the sociopolitical unity he was attempting to establish in the Empire. His efforts were, however, largely in vain. Under the influence of his own son Constantius, some bishops in 359 rejected the *homoousios* doctrine, decreeing that Jesus was only "like" (*homoios*) the Father. Thus emerged the notorious "dispute over an iota"—the distinction between *homoousios* and *homoiousios*. After the turmoil of Julian's brief reign subsided and the Christians were back in charge, Athanasius, the new and dogmatic bishop of Alexandria, doubled down on the Nicene creed, viciously attacking his opponents and branding them all as Arians whether or not they actually ascribed to Arius' views.

It was Basil of Caesarea who, in *On the Holy Spirit* (375), officially enunciated the doctrine of the Trinity. Irenaeus had articulated the doctrine two centuries previously, managing to maintain both that God is one and also that God is Father, Son, and the Holy Spirit (formerly termed the Holy Ghost). As one sympathetic commentator has wryly noted, Irenaeus "does not seem to have been too much troubled by the problems that arise when the two statements are brought together as an answer to one question about the nature of God."[32] Origen, for his part, claimed to find evidence of the Trinity in the OT.

After Basil's screed, the Emperor Theodosius in 381 issued an edict declaring that the Trinity must be believed, and severe penalties were inflicted upon its deniers. In that year a new version of the Nicene creed was issued, citing the Holy Spirit but not explicitly mentioning the Trinity. One scholar has proposed that Theodosius' support of this doctrine may have been inspired by his desire to minimise what was seen as Jesus' rebellious nature (especially his advocacy of the poor, as plainly recorded in scripture) by making him a divine figure equal to God; as a result, the Trinity became a tool to keep the masses in order.[33] Certainly,

32. Minns, *Irenaeus: An Introduction* 31.
33. See Freeman, *A New History of Early Christianity* 252–53.

no new evidence could possibly have led to this revision of Christian dogma.

Paul is by all measures the chief evangelist in early Christianity: he made the crucial decision to spread the faith outside of the Jewish communities of the Near East and focus on the conversion of Gentiles. This created an immediate conflict with those who wished to restrict Jesus' teachings to Jews; as a result, we have such contradictory statements in scripture as "Do not suppose that I have come to abolish the law and the prophets; I did not come to abolish, but to complete" (Matt. 5:17) and "for Christ is the end of the law and brings righteousness for everyone who has faith" (Rom. 10:4). The gospels of Matthew and Mark generally took the anti-Pauline approach, while the gospel of John largely sided with Paul; Luke and the Acts of the Apostles attempted to effect a reconciliation of the two—but, as will be seen presently, it did so under very different political and doctrinal circumstances.

This debate about the proper way to spread the gospel later extended to the relation between Christian and pagan, and specifically to the role of pagan texts as either nurturing or undermining Christian teaching. Theologians took antipodal views on this question. Both Irenaeus and Clement of Alexandria, bred on pagan Greek literature, found much value in those texts. Clement maintained that pagan philosophy (especially his idol Plato) was a useful preparation for becoming a Christian. He was one of several Christian theologians who believed that it is reason, not merely unquestioning belief, that facilitated acceptance of Christianity. Origen likewise believed that education in pagan philosophy (excluding, of course, the Epicureans) leads inexorably to Christianity. Lactantius followed suit; his *Institutiones Divinae* (Divine Institutes), a kind of primer of Christian faith, "set out to demonstrate that sources from classical poetry and philosophy to mythology and oracular literature all testified to what Lactantius saw as the basic claims of Christianity."[34]

In this debate Tertullian would seem to stand resolutely on the other side. His celebrated (and much misquoted) utterances, *Credo quia absurdum* and *Certum est, quia impossibile* (I believe because it is absurd; It is certain, because it is impossible: *De Carne Christi* 5.4), were made specifically in reference to Jesus' death and resurrection from the dead.

34. Digeser, *The Making of a Christian Empire* 11.

For many centuries it was believed that Tertullian was asserting that the issue is inexplicable by ordinary reason and must simply be accepted on faith. The view of scholars today, however, is that this interpretation is a distortion of Tertullian's overall theology, which did indeed stress the role of reason in the absorption of Christianity. And yet, Tertullian did reveal a hostility toward pagan learning, as expressed in another famous comment: "What has Athens to do with Jerusalem, or the Academy with the Church?" (*De Praescriptione* 7).

A related issue is how Christianity, especially once it gained legal and political dominance in the Roman Empire, was to deal with the many different religions beyond paganism throughout the Mediterranean. As early as the mid-second century, Justin Martyr happily embraced the pagan accusation that Christians were "atheists"—so they were, he contended, precisely because they denied the existence of the Olympian gods. Some theologians developed the view that those gods were not merely false, they were actually demons.

At the same time, early Christians were eager to absorb or co-opt elements from other religions to foster their own. One of the most notable instances of this is their response to the cult of Mithras, a god created in Persia under the guise of the Zoroastrian deity Mithra. During the first several centuries of the Roman Empire, the Mithras cult spread widely, especially among soldiers; it involved an elaborate set of rituals that had some resemblance to the Eleusinian mysteries. There were also—and this was the point that troubled Christian leaders—striking similarities with Christianity. As one scholar attests, "The cult's belief in an eternal struggle between the powers of light and darkness—reflecting its Iranian origins—had much in common with Christian perspectives, and it would have appeared an attractive alternative to many waverers in Christian ranks, particularly among those serving in the army."[35] Although Mithraism was probably never a serious rival to Christianity except in certain limited locales, Christians made efforts to subsume it into its own religion—not least by applying the date of Mithras's birthday (December 25) to Jesus.

Christian antisemitism begins with the earliest known Christian documents—namely, the letters of Paul. Paul himself (born Saul) was

35. Rankin, *Tertullian and the Church* 24.

a Jew, but the vigorous efforts he took to spread the Christian gospel outside of the Jewish community bespeaks a tension with his ethnic compatriots. Several of Paul's letters (including 2 Corinthians and Galatians) emphatically declare the supersession of the OT (the "law" of Moses) by Christian teaching. But it should be noted that the passage in 1 Thessalonians where Paul accuses the Jews of killing Jesus ("You [Jews who converted to Christianity] have been treated by your own countrymen as they were treated by the Jews, who killed the Lord Jesus and the prophets and drove us out" [2:14–15]) is now widely regarded as an interpolation, since this same letter also speaks of the destruction of Jerusalem, which occurred after Paul's death.[36] Whatever the case, this passage constitutes the first extant mention of Jews as responsible for Jesus' death. The gospel of Matthew pungently recounts how the Jews were thirsting for Jesus' blood: "With one voice the people cried, 'His blood be on us and on our children'" (27:25), a peculiar utterance in which Jews appear to be condemning themselves to punishment for their role in Jesus' demise.

Christian theologians of the second century frequently denied that the Jews were the chosen people. We find this statement as early as the *Epistle of Barnabas* (usually dated to c. 90–130). Justin Martyr maintained that it was Christians, not Jews, who were the chosen people. Justin and others were responding to vigorous and at times abusive opposition by Jews to the new faith, which they regarded as an illegitimate splinter-religion advocated by what was, at the outset, a relatively small group of renegade Jews.

Marcion's contention that the god of the Jews, Yahweh, was in fact an evil demiurge who produced the physical world should be noted. He explicitly denied that the OT prophesied the coming of Jesus, going on to say that it was the Jewish god Yahweh who killed Jesus. And yet, it was precisely the desire to preserve the predictive value of the OT prophecies that led Irenaeus and others to condemn Marcion and others for their denial of the OT as an indispensable component of the Bible. At the same time, Irenaeus followed Paul in denying that the uniting of these two bodies of work meant that Christians must follow Mosaic law, although he did maintain that the Decalogue must be observed for

36. See Doherty, *The Jesus Puzzle* 14–15.

salvation.[37] Irenaeus went on to condemn Jews for believing that they can know God directly without the revelation provided by Jesus; and he was emphatic in asserting that the Jews, by killing Jesus and the apostles, had deprived themselves of eternal life.

Ambrose (339?–397), bishop of Milan, exhibited vicious prejudice against Jews, refusing to intervene when a mob of Christians burned down a synagogue in Callinicum (now Raqqa, in Syria) in 388. As one of the teachers of Augustine, he presumably influenced the latter's condemnation of the Jews for refusing to accept what he believed to be the obvious prophecies of Jesus' coming in the OT (see *CD* 17.18–19).

The loathing of the physical body—and, concomitantly, the horror of what was perceived to be unbridled or unregulated sex as well as the disdain of women as temptresses who must be subjugated—that has been a prevalent feature of Christianity for many centuries also began with Paul. The passages one could cite on this subject are innumerable: "So put to death those parts of you which belong to the earth—fornication, indecency, lust, evil desires, and the ruthless greed which is nothing less than idolatry" (Colossians 3:5); "you must have nothing to do with those who are sexually immoral" (1 Cor. 5:9); "Make no mistake: no fornicator or idolator, no adulterer or sexual pervert . . . will possess the kingdom of God" (1 Cor. 6:9–10). This attitude meshes with Paul's assertion of a purely spiritual Jesus in whom the taint of physical humanity was entirely absent. Paul reluctantly acknowledges that the sexual instinct is so strong in human beings that it cannot be suppressed altogether, even though it is clear he would prefer it to be; the only solution he can come up with, grudgingly, is Christian marriage.

Paul's comments on marriage—especially the notorious remark "for it is better to marry than to burn" (1 Cor. 7:9)—are well known. The King James version is ambiguous: does it mean that Paul was saying it is better to marry than to commit fornication or adultery and therefore consign oneself to burning in eternal damnation? Evidently not, as the NEB translation makes clear: "It is better to be married than burn with desire." Paul goes on to decree a ban on divorce (1 Cor. 7:10).

But Paul's views on these subjects would not have gained such wide currency—indeed, become orthodox church doctrine for many

37. Minns, *Irenaeus* 98f.

centuries—if later theologians, laypersons, and even emperors did not find them consonant with their own prejudices. Tertullian, for example, reveals hostility to adulterers, fornicators, and even those who marry a second time, even though Paul had sanctioned a woman's remarrying—"provided the marriage is within the Lord's fellowship" (1 Cor. 7:39)—if her husband dies.

But it was Augustine, plagued by his own perceived lustfulness in youth, who definitively stamped early Christianity as implacably hostile to sexual activity outside—and sometimes even within—the parameters of marriage. Augustine was so horrified at his sexual laxity in youth—in his early adulthood he lived with his mistress and had a child with her—that he fled to the opposite extreme. He could not condemn his own addiction to the sins of the flesh with sufficient outrage: "Love and lust together seethed within me. In my tender youth they swept me away over the precipice of my body's appetites and plunged me in the whirlpool of sin. More and more I angered you [God], unawares. For I had been deafened by the clank of my chains, the fetters of the death which was my due to punish the pride in my soul" (*Conf.* 2.2).[38] And later: "I was bound down by this disease of the flesh. Its deadly pleasures were a chain that I dragged along with me, yet I was afraid to be freed from it" (*Conf.* 6.12). Upon his conversion to his fanatical brand of Christianity, he adopted an asceticism that took the form not only of absention from sex, but even from food; food becomes a "medicine" (*Conf.* 10.31) to be taken only when the desire for food and drink become so insistent as to be painful.

To the extent that early Christian thinkers expressed a loathing for sex and the physical body, they similarly expressed doubt as to the place of women in society. The role of the Judaeo-Christian religion in fostering misogyny is a fraught question, and it certainly cannot be said that the Greco-Roman culture treated women with anything approaching legal, moral, social, or political equality; but certain features of the Jewish and Christian religions were significant in making prejudice against women a permanent element in Western culture. The very fact that Eve was, in the account in Genesis, created out of Adam's rib made her inferior to him metaphysically and therefore subservient to him. Several well-

38. I use the translation of R. S. Pine-Coffin.

known scriptural verses endorse such a view. The tenth commandment—"Do not covet your neighbour's household: you must not covet your neighbour's wife, his slave, his slave-girl, his ox, his donkey, or anything that belongs to him" (Exod. 20:17)—makes it abundantly clear that (a) the commandment is addressed only to men, and (b) the man's wife is his property (perhaps his most valued property, but nevertheless his property). Paul outlines in some detail the respective duties of husband and wife, noting: "Wives, be subject to your husbands as though to the Lord; for the man is the head of the woman, just as Christ is the head of the church" (Eph. 522–23).[39] Augustine enshrined this lesser role for women by observing that woman is the "weaker part of that human alliance" (*CD* 14.11).[40] Indeed, this was the reason why, in his view, the serpent chose her as the instrument of Adam's temptation.

Throughout the three or four centuries during which Christian doctrine was being hammered out, a variety of schisms and heresies[41] emerged. Early Christian historians—such as Eusebius (260?–340?), author of the influential *Historia Ecclesiastica* (Church History)—tendentiously asserted that the initial unity of Christian doctrine was subsequently shattered by a succession of heretics whose views required ruthless suppression in order to preserve the purity of the faith; but we have already seen that such heresies and schisms were present at the very founding of the religion in the mid-first century C.E.

Although it was Ignatius of Antioch (d. 140?) who appears to have initiated the meaning of *haeresis* (a Greek word that originally meant just a "choice") in the pejorative sense of a religious doctrine contrary to orthodoxy, the notion was an inevitable concomitant to the idea of a scripture (and, hence, the doctrines believed to derive from it) that was divinely inspired. Justin Martyr followed Ignatius' example, writing a non-extant treatise "against all heresies." Irenaeus' *Adversus Haereses* (Against the Heresies) does survive, and it attacked Gnosticism, Marcion, and many others. Clement of Alexandria also condemned heresies, but

39. What is here translated as "be subject" appears in KJV as "submit."

40. I use the translation of Marcus Dods (Books 5, 6, 7, and 8 translated by J. J. Smith; Books 4, 17, and 18 by George Wilson).

41. A schism is defined as a split within the church that does not necessarily involve major disputes in doctrine; a heresy is a split that does involve a major doctrinal dispute, during which the view in question is deemed out of bounds by whatever group professes to represent orthodox teaching.

often resorted to fallacious analogies in doing so: a "true" doctrine can be distinguished from a "false" doctrine in the same way that a real piece of fruit can be distinguished from one made of wax. But this of course begs the question in assuming that there is a "true" doctrine that can somehow be verified empirically instead of being merely the doctrine that the official church has adopted by fiat.

The issue of apostolic succession, broached by Acts, was brought into play chiefly to combat heresy. The doctrine was expounded in the document now referred to as 1 Clement (probably dating to c. 96). It was then seized by Irenaeus, who traced the apostolic line back to Peter (or Simon Peter), one of Jesus' apostles who notoriously denied his association with Jesus on three separate occasions around the time of the latter's crucifixion. Nonetheless, theologians seized upon him as an early leader of the church, appealing to Jesus' purported statement to him, "And I say to you: you are Peter, the Rock; and on this rock I will build my church" (Matt. 16:19)—a punning reference to his name (the Greek word for rock is *petros*).

Irenaeus felt that "tradition"—extending well beyond scripture and covering the orthodox interpretation of scripture—was a crucial means to refute heresy. His main antagonists, once again, were the Gnostics, who were claiming that their view of scrupture was validated by the "secret" knowledge (*gnosis*) they derived from the apostles. Irenaeus denied that there was any such secret knowledge. He went on to declare that the mere fact that a bishop (*episkopos*) was in office and was succeeded by his replacement guaranteed the orthodoxy of the doctrines they preached; and he made a list of the bishops of the central sees in the Empire (Rome, Alexandria, Antioch, and Constantinople); Peter was designated the first "bishop of Rome," and later bishops—subsequently called popes—were traced in an unending succession back to him.

One of the hermeneutical tools utilised by Christian theologians of this period was an increasing use of a symbolic or allegorical interpretation of scripture, although they may have found in Philo a similar practice in interpreting the Hebrew Bible. Irenaeus interpreted the biblical verses about God fashioning humans "in our own image and likeness" (Gen. 1:26) as meaning that human beings are endowed with both a material body and a spirit. There is no reason to think that the author(s) of Genesis had such a view in mind. Irenaeus also interpreted

Adam as both a literal, material individual (also Eve, who is theologically subordinate to him because she emerged from his rib, something Irenaeus apparently believed actually happened) and as a kind of parallel to Jesus. He asserted that Adam was generated "from the untilled and still virgin earth" (*Adv. Haer.* 3.21.10), thereby standing as a parallel to Jesus, who was born of the virgin Mary. Contrarily, Adam's disobedience in eating the apple was seen in contrast to Jesus' obedience in allowing himself to be crucified. Clement of Alexandria wrote analogously that Adam, the primal man who was "led astray by lusts" (*Protrepticus* 11.111.1), would be redeemed by another man, Jesus Christ. He interpreted the "image and likeness" phrase from Genesis as meaning that human beings were endowed with reason and freedom of choice. Augustine, as we shall see, emphatically endorses the view that Adam and Eve must have been real individuals; their existence as such is central to his entire eschatology.

Origen claimed that the OT prophecies purportedly fulfilled by Jesus testify to the Bible's divine inspiration; but those prophecies must be interpreted allegorically. Some passages, in his view, are deliberately presented as "impossibilities" to impel the intelligent reader toward a more symbolic interpretation. Which passages those are, Origen neglects to specify. This brings into clear focus the methodological problem with an allegorical or symbolic interpretation of scripture: it is obviously resorted to (and it continues to be right down to the present day) largely as a means of evading certain embarrassing or obviously untrue statements that would otherwise make any reasonable person believe that scripture is in error. Given that no theologian has ever articulated a coherent formula as to which portions of scripture are to be interpreted literally and which allegorically, there is nothing to stop someone from interpreting, say, Jesus' resurrection from the dead allegorically—but this is one of many doctrines that Christians insist on interpreting literally, merely to preserve the essence of their dogma.

We have already cited the Arian heresy, although that was a relatively late development in the history of early Christianity. An earlier heresy was Montanism, associated with the shadowy figure of Montanus, who lived in the mid-second century and felt he had a direct pipeline to the Holy Spirit for the prophecies he uttered, chief of which was that the New Jerusalem (the belief that a new city would be erected around the rebuilt third temple, cited in the OT) would be built not in Palestine but in Phrygia (which happened to be Montanus' place of origin). Like many other heretics, he could appeal selectively to scripture to justify his views. Tertullian was an adherent of Montanism for a time.

A more formidable heresy was Manichaeism. The Persian prophet Mani (d. 276) believed himself to be the Holy Spirit and established the sect around himself. His chief contention (derived in part from his absorption of Zoroastrianism) was that there was a cosmic struggle between good and evil in the cosmos, with two equal powers, God and the Devil, battling for supremacy and humanity caught in the middle. Mani was of course not a Christian, although he did acknowledge the divinity of Jesus after a fashion. But his denial of the omnipotence of God—and the numerous points of resemblance between Manichaeism and Gnosticism—caused the sect, which spread widely in the third and fourth centuries, to be condemned as heretical by both Roman authorities (beginning with Diocletian in 296) and the Christian church, culminating in Theodosius I's edict in 382 decreeing death to Manichaean monks.

D. Heaven, Hell, and the Devil

What was the precise nature of Jesus Christ's salvific mission? What, in other words, was he sent down to earth to save? The answer is not self-evident, and in attempting to provide an answer Christian theologians became entangled in all manner of paradoxes and internal contradictions. There was general agreement among theologians and church leaders that some kind of "sin" in the human race necessitated God's extraordinary act of sending himself (in the guise of Jesus) down to earth to be crucified in order to effect humanity's salvation; but what exact sin was involved? Paul seemed to be clear on the matter: "It was through one man that sin entered the world, and through sin death, and thus death pervaded the whole human race, inasmuch as all have sinned" (Rom. 5:12). The reference seems unambiguously to refer to Adam, whose sin involved disobedience to God and, as a consequence, the entry into human life of the additional sin of carnal lust. Given the general hostility to the body exhibited by many Christian theologians of the first four centuries C.E., such an interpretation is unsurprising; and it culminates in Augustine's notion of original sin. But this notion is itself intimately tied to conceptions of free will, God's grace, baptism, the problem of evil, and ultimately the role of heaven and hell in ensuring the rewards granted to the "good" and the proper punishment of the "wicked."

The free will argument cannot, of course, be specifically found in scripture, but it was assumed by many theologians to be a necessary inference from the events chronicled in the Bible from the time of Adam onward. Justin Martyr advocated free will in opposition to Stoic notions of fate, as well as the determinism that Marcion was propounding. For him, free will is deeply connected with salvation: God is giving us a chance to repent so that we can be ready to go to heaven at the Last Judgment. In a sense, this is one more attempt to explain away the awkward fact that the Last Judgment hasn't actually arrived in spite of Jesus' plain words that it should have done so long ago. Accordingly, Justin denied even the Stoics' "soft determinism": in his view, any sort of determinism would mean that human beings are absolved from moral responsibility for their beliefs and actions.

For Irenaeus and others, human free will was in effect a means of partially absolving God—whom he conceived to be omnipotent, omniscient, and benevolent—of responsibility in the evils that plainly exist in the world. For him, the existence of evil (and our ability to choose or reject it) will make us appreciate the good all the more. Clement of Alexandria states this doctrine explicitly. One scholar sums up his views on the subject: "Whatever is evil cannot be blamed upon God."[42] Origen, in his fervent desire to preserve the essential benevolence of creation, saw in both human reason and human free will the means for us to embrace God willingly.

What such a stance leads to, of course, is the issue of the problem of evil. There is no denying that the problem of evil as conventionally construed—why bad things happen to good people and why bad people appear to prosper in the world (however "good" and "bad" are to be defined)—is a problem of religion's own making. In a world without God, the problem of evil falls away, as a natural product of the imperfections of the individual and of human society, the inability of laws to restrain "bad" behaviour in every instance, and so on. Even in a polytheistic cosmos the problem is dissipated, if we assume that different

42. Osborn, *Clement of Alexandria* 48.

gods have different powers that allow for "good" people to suffer and for "evil" people to go unpunished (although the pagan philosophers do not seem to have made any such arguments). But the issue is uniquely problematical for the Christian religion, which wishes simultaneously to maintain the omnipotence, omniscience, and benevolence of a solitary God. Free will, as we have seen, is in part an attempt to address the problem, but it does not seem to account for "natural" evils (hurricanes, tornadoes, and the like). Augustine at one point discusses natural evils, contending that they are in fact good "when used in conformity with their qualities and design," whatever that means; but he goes on to say that at times their "utility" is "hidden." Just so! Indeed, after wrestling with the issue to no especial purpose Augustine simply throws up his hands:

> For we do not know by what judgment of God this good man is poor and that bad man rich; why he who, in our opinion, ought to suffer acutely for his abandoned life enjoys himself, while sorrow pursues him whose praiseworthy life leads us to suppose he should be happy; why the innocent man is dismissed from the bar not only unavenged, but even condemned, being either wronged by the iniquity of the judge, or overwhelmed by false evidence, while his guilty adversary, on the other hand, is not only discharged with impunity, but even has his claims admitted; why the ungodly enjoys good health, while the godly pines in sickness . . . (*CD* 20.2)

There is a good deal more to this, but Augustine simply concludes with a shrug, "His [God's] ways are past finding out" (*CD* 20.2)—a sentiment that would echo down the centuries in multiple iterations by perplexed Christian theologians. Augustine is desperately trying to preserve both human free will and the "goodness" of God, but at the risk of seeming heartless and indifferent to the incalculable amount of suffering (human, animal, and even vegetable) in the world. As Walter Kaufmann keenly points out in regard to the entire free will argument:

> Those who believe in God because their experience of life and the facts of nature prove his exitence must have led sheltered lives and closed their hearts to the voice of their brothers' blood. . . . The deepest

> difference between religions is not that between polytheism and monotheism. . . . Even the difference between theism and athiem is not nearly so profound as that between those who feel and those who do not feel their brothers' torments.[43]

It is worth noting that Augustine's clinging to free will and rejection of "fate" were strongly influenced by his peculiar assumption that a belief in fate was equivalent to the belief in astrology: "we demonstrate that the name of fate, as it is wont to be used by those who speak of fate, meaning thereby the position of the stars at the time of each one's conception or birth, is an unmeaning word, for astrology itself is a delusion" (*CD* 5.9). How so acute a thinker as Augustine could not envision determinism to be valid on other grounds is a mystery.

Whether it was inevitable that the free will doctrine led to the doctrine of original sin—the notion that the "sin of Adam" was so severe that it infected all subsequent human beings from infancy onward, necessitating, firstly, infant baptism and, secondly, the Jesus' salvific mission—is now an unanswerable question; suffice it to say that the doctrine was in large part fueled by Augustine's dour, bleak vision of a humanity so mired in sin that only such extraordinary measures are required to relieve it. His *Confessions,* written between 397 and 400, is certainly unlike any other work in the whole of classical antiquity—a poignant, searing, but also horrifying tract that reveals him to be in such a state of mental distress (tantamount to mental illness) over his own corrupt nature that he is compelled to fly to the other extreme of religious mania. In this tract, addressed directly to God, he testifies how he was raised in a nominally Christian household, instructed chiefly by his devout mother, Monica, although his father Patricius was considerably less pious. But his religiosity was initially at a fairly low ebb. It was his reading of Cicero's *Hortensius* that inspired in him a love of wisdom; but later he rejected pagan learning for the all-encompassing doctrines of the Christian scriptures.

For Augustine, God is a sort of moral dictator: "all must yield to God" (*Conf.* 3.8). He is also committed to the doctrine of God's foreknowledge of all events in the future, including human free will: "In His [God's] supreme will resides the power which acts upon the will of

43. Kuafmann, *The Faith of a Heretic* 180.

all created spirits" (*CD* 5.9). But Augustine somehow convinces himself that this foreknowledge does not essentially negate the free will he is so intent on preserving.

Augustine is convinced that it was Adam—whom he conceived as an actually existing person, as his entire argument hinges on it—who, both by his disobedience and the lust which he subsequently exhibited in his sexual relations with Eve in propagating the human race, introduced the taint of sin in humanity. How can this be? He explains in a lengthy passage in *De Civitate Dei:*

> For God, the author of natures, not of vices, created man upright; but man, being of his own will corrupted, and justly condemned, begot corrupted and condemned children. For we all were in that one man, since we all were in that one man who fell into sin by the woman who was made from him before the sin. For not yet was the particular form created and distributed to us, in which we as individuals were to live, but already the seminal nature was there from which we were to be propagated; and this being vitiated by sin, and bound by the chain of death, and justly condemned, man could not be born of man in any other state. And thus, from the bad use of free will, there originated the whole train of evil, which, with its concatenation of miseries, convoys the human race from its depraved origin, as from a corrupt root, on to the destruction of the second death, which has no end, those only being excepted who are freed by the grace of God. (*CD* 13.14)

That first sentence points to another bizarre doctrine of Augustine's: evidently God is somehow not responsible for the "wicked" acts or beliefs in humanity. Augustine elsewhere wrote that "wicked souls are not from Him, being contrary to nature, which is from Him" (*CD* 5.9). But surely this is tantamount to denying God's omnipotence. In any event, it can be seen from this passage how intimately Augustine's theology leads him to fuse free will, hatred of the body (and of the body's natural desires), and the need for supernatural salvation to redeem a corrupt humanity.

The doctrine leads to the appalling notion that infants are born corrupt and will be consigned to hell unless they are baptised within a few days of their birth.[44] "God ordained that infants should begin the world as the young beasts begin it, since their parents had fallen to the level of the beasts in the fashion of their life and death" (*CD* 13.3). What Augustine means is that, because the conceiving of children is the product of carnal lust, the infant itself must be in a state of sin prior to baptism. Even this is only a temporary reprieve, for these human beings may also end up in hell by acts and deeds in their subsequent life. Augustine evolved the doctrine in battles with Pelagius (348–418), a British monk who maintained that Adam's sin applied only to himself and that infants were not born in sin. Augustine waged furious polemics against Pelagius and his followers. The doctrine of the Pelagians was declared a heresy in the Council of Carthage in 418.

The end result was that the moral sorting out of human lives had to wait until the afterlife. This is an easy argument to make, because it is irrefutable by evidence: the good shall wind up in heaven and the bad in hell. But this very formulation—at least as Augustine and other early Christian theologians made it—is itself highly problematical and paradoxical. The whole issue of the origin of heaven and hell in the Judaeo-Christian tradition is a complex one, and it elicited vociferous debates among theologians for centuries; but, sadly, once again Augustine's view ultimately prevailed in the early Christian tradition.

The critical issue is whether heaven and hell are destinations for bodies and/or souls by means of some kind of *moral* calculus. We have seen that the Greco-Roman tradition by and large assumed that *everyone* ended up in Hades, regardless of their actions in life; some thinkers and religious sub-groups did envision a separation of the "good" and the "wicked," but it was by no means the dominant view. The Jewish hell, Sheol, was similarly the locus for all souls, except in certain later documents in the OT. Certain texts unmistakably point to central features in what became Christian orthodoxy, specifically the eternal punishment of the wicked by fire; both of these elements are neatly summed up in the memorable statement in what is termed Trito-Isaiah: "As they go out they will see the corpses of those who rebelled against me, where the devouring worm

44. Augustine appears to have been inspired in part by Ps. 51:5 ("From my birth I have been evil, sinful from the time my mother conceived me"). Many commentators have noted that Augustine claimed that unbaptised infants were "limbs of Satan," but I have not been able to ascertain whether this is a genuine quotation from his work.

never dies, and the fire is not quenched" (Isa. 66:24). The notion of a Last Judgment can be found in Daniel: "many of those who sleep in the dust of the earth will awake, some to everlasting life and some to the reproach of eternal abhorrence" (12:2).

Paul is unclear as to the role of hell in his eschatology. He believed that those who accept Christ as their saviour will live everlastingly; those who don't will simply be annihilated: that, for him, was punishment enough. He is similarly silent as regards any sort of *eternal* punishment of the wicked; indeed, he seems to hold out the possibility that everyone potentially can be the recipient of God's grace ("For as through the disobedience of one man many were made sinners, so through the obedience of one man many will be made righteous" [Rom. 5:19]).

The gospel of John follows Paul in many particulars, notably in the doctrine that everyone who embraces Jesus will be granted eternal life. This is surely the import of the celebrated statement (placed in the mouth of Jesus): "God so loved the world that he gave his only Son, that *everyone* [my emphasis] who has faith in him may not perish but have eternal life" (3:16)—although, as with Paul, this is also an expression of the view that the gospel must be preached outside of the Jewish community.

The other gospels, however, unambiguously refer to eternal punishment for the wicked. In Matthew, Jesus is made to say, "A curse is on you; go from my sight to the eternal fire that is ready for the devil and his angels" (25:41). An earlier passage in Matthew (5:21f.) clearly articulates consignment to hell for general moral failings, not merely for the failure to acknowledge Jesus as saviour. A number of texts refer to Hades or to Gehenna—the latter being the rendering in the Septuagint of the Hebrew Ge-Hinnom, a ravine outside of Jerusalem where sacrifices to Moloch were made. It would seem that these two realms (if they are distinct) are intermediate locales for the wicked before the Last Judgment.

The mention of the Devil in Matthew is of interest; for more on this redoubtable entity, we must turn to the document known as the Revelation of John, which became the last book of the Bible. The document probably dates to the very late first century; and while Christians long believed that the "John" who proclaims himself its author was identical to the author of the gospel of John, most scholars now reject such an identification. John claims that the words he is setting down were dictated to him by the apparently resurrected Jesus.

Revelation is, indeed, a very strange text, and its lurid imagery calls out for some kind of symbolic or allegorical interpretation, although how (and on what basis) such an interpretation could plausibly be made is seriously in question. In any event, it is here that we find the well-known scenario whereby Satan and his angels "were thrown down to earth" (12:9), i.e., out of heaven; those who receive the mark of the beast (whatever that is) will be "tormented in sulphurous flames in the sight of the holy angels and the Lamb" (14:10). Later Satan will be thrown down into a pit for a thousand years. Christians will come to life and go up to be with Jesus in heaven. After the thousand years, Satan will be freed, but after a battle he will suffer eternal torment (20:10). Then the dead will be judged; the evil will join Satan in the "lake of fire" (20:14).

The notion of "bad" angels rebelling against God and being thrown out of heaven first appears in the Hebrew document known as 1 Enoch (of which the relevant portions are thought to date to the third century B.C.E.).[45] Then there is the celebrated passage in Isaiah: "Bright morning star, how you have fallen from heaven, thrown to earth, prostrate among the nations!" (14:12). This entity attempts to regain heaven, but "Instead you are brought down to Sheol, into the depths of the abyss" (14:15). Here the personage in question is the king of Babylon; but in the Christian tradition, beginning with Origen, this was believed to be an allusion to the Devil, and in the Vulgate he appears as Lucifer ("light-bringer"), the Roman name for the planet Venus.

As for Satan, we have seen that the term *sātān* appears in the OT, generally as a common noun (meaning "adversary") and a few times as a proper noun. In the Septuagint the term was translated as *diabolos* ("slanderer"), which then appeared in Latin as *diabolus.* It should, however, be emphasised that in scripture the Devil is not in hell but on earth; indeed, the work of the Devil and his minions is said to account for the evil deeds of human beings, and thereby becomes yet another means of partially absolving God of responsibility for these deeds—but, again, at the risk of compromising his omnipotence.

Then there is the shadowy figure of the Antichrist. This creature is not mentioned in Revelation but in certain late letters in the NT, namely 1 and 2 John. One passage merely fastens the label on any disbeliever in

45. The notion is also found in 2 Peter (2:4), but this is now believed to postdate Revelation.

Jesus: "Anyone who denies that Jesus is the Christ is nothing but a liar, He is the antichrist, for he denies both the Father and the Son" (1 John 2:22). Other passages are of similar import. Early Christian theologians attempt to determine the nature of this entity; but his role in Christian eschatology was largely an invention of the mediaeval period.

Various apocryphal texts in early Christianity discuss hell extensively. The *Apocalypse of Peter* (first half of the second century) presents lurid pictures of the torments of hell—and, perhaps for the first time, the punishments are crudely designed to fit the crimes (e.g., "blasphemers hang by their tongues, suspended over a lake of burning mire").[46] The *Apocalypse of Paul* (late fourth century) depicts Paul witnessing the machinery of post-mortem justice in both heaven and hell.

Among formal theologians, Justin Martyr, influenced by the Jewish and Platonic traditions, envisioned God as having created angels to have oversight over human beings; but some angels "fell" because they had had intercourse with human women. The result was a race of demons who have enslaved the human race. Some of these are the gods worshipped by the pagans. Jesus therefore becomes necessary to defeat these demons definitively.

The question of who would be saved, and in what manner, tormented generations of early Christian theologians. Would everyone be saved, or only a select few? Clement of Alexandria appeared inclined toward the doctrine of universal salvation. Because of his intellectualist stance (his belief that God's greatest gift to human beings is reason, which will allow us to choose the salvation and immortality that God is laying open for us), he maintained that salvation was theoretically open to everyone as long as they harnessed both intellect and faith toward belief in the Christian god. "How could he [God] be saviour and lord if he were not saviour and lord of all?" he asks plangently (*Stromateis* 7.2.7.6).

But it was Origen who unequivocally came down on the side of universal salvation. For him, some souls will have to undergo a period of burning (which he interprets as a kind of purification) before attaining to God. Evidently this is the ultimate origin of the notion of Purgatory, although the doctrine was not codified until well into the mediaeval period. Origen was even more emphatic than Clement in asserting that

46. Bernstein, *The Formation of Hell* 285.

all rational beings will eventually reunite with God. He extended this principle even to demons. Whether he went so far as to assert that even the Devil would ultimately be received in heaven is a matter of debate.

Origen's views were much debated in the course of the third and fourth centuries. It was Augustine, however, who set himself in stern opposition to such a liberal stance. He acknowledged that certain "tender-hearted Christians" (*CD* 21.17) had propounded the universal salvation idea; but his own bleak vision of humanity—the vision that led him to incline toward Manichaeism for nearly a decade—could not countenance such leniency toward the wicked. Indeed, the "great majority" (*CD* 13.23) will experience what he calls a second death (i.e., the consignment of the wicked to hell; the first death being what we would ordinarily call death, the separation of body and soul). Such a position requires a certain amount of fancy footwork to evade the obvious meaning of the celebrated scriptural verse "As in Adam all die, so in Christ *all* [my emphasis] will be brought to life" (1 Cor. 15:22). But Augustine could appeal to other verses that tell a very different story, as we have already seen. And he is insistent on the eternity of punishment, dwelling at great length over the precise manner in which human bodies (for it is bodies, not just souls, who are consigned to hell) can suffer burning *eternally* and yet not be entirely consumed (*CD* 21.10).

The means by which, according to Augustine, the few shall achieve salvation is a fusion of human free will and the grace of God. There are some difficulties in this notion, although it is perhaps too much to admit, with J. B. Bury, that Augustine's theory, "while it professed to admit the freedom of the will, really annulled it."[47] What led Bury to such a view was Augustine's resolute determination that "good works" (i.e., beneficent actions in life) are of no benefit in the attainment of salvation. Once again, he was apparently driven to this view by his dark vision of an unregenerate humanity:

> The more enjoyment man found in God, the greater was his wickedness in abandoning Him; and he who destroyed in himself a good which might have been eternal, became worthy of eternal evil. Hence the whole mass of the human race is condemned; for he who at first gave

47. Bury, *History of the Later Roman Empire* 1.360.

> entrance to sin has been punished with all his posterity who were in him as in a root, so that no one is exempt from this just and due punishment, unless delivered by mercy and undeserved grace; and the human race is so apportioned that in some is displayed the efficacy of merciful grace, in the rest the efficacy of just retribution. (*CD* 21.12)

This passage shows how intimately connected are the notions of original sin, humanity's fundamental corruption, and eternal punishment in Augustine's thought. In other words, a small number of humans will be subject to God's *mercy* (by being transported to eternal life in heaven) while everyone else will be subject to God's *justice* (by being condemned to eternal perdition). God's "undeserved grace"—what later came to be called predestination—is our only hope of salvation, because it testifies to *God's* free will and freedom of action. Evidently God has some magical insight as to which human beings have the capacity for faith and will actualise that capacity.

We need not go into the controversy as to whether the resurrection of human beings at the Last Judgment will be a bodily resurrection or merely a resurrection of the soul. Origen did not believe in a resurrection of the body; Tertullian declared that the resurrection of the flesh must be accepted as orthodoxy. Here, as elsewhere, Augustine's view prevailed. He was emphatic in asserting a bodily resurrection of both the good and the wicked. Peculiarly, he maintained that the bodies of the good will not be *immediately* resurrected (even though the soul survives the "first death" of the body), because this would in some manner undermine faith—perhaps by leading the faithful to commit suicide to reach heaven that much sooner (*CD* 13.4).

It is certainly unfortunate that, at least in the short term, the dour view of Augustine prevailed to become Christian orthodoxy. His conception of the world was so bleak that he envisioned our life on earth as a kind of hell: "Our infancy, indeed, introducing us to this life not with laughter but with tears, seems unconsciously to predict the ills we are to encounter" (*CD* 21.14). This pessimism, bordering on misanthropy, is also evident in his celebrated account in the *Confessions* of his stealing some pears as an youth, and the bitter recriminations he inflicted upon himself. What many of us would conclude to be an instance of adolescent mischievousness, or at worst a case of social maladjustment, is viewed by Augustine as an instance of cosmic sin that must be atoned for by repeated self-flagellation. If it is maintained that such a view of Augustine is an anachronistic importing of our own secularism into a very different time, it can be countered that, as we have seen from the letters of Pliny the Younger, a secular outlook of exactly this sort was adopted by an educated pagan centuries before Augustine, and it is unlikely that he was alone in that outlook.

Indeed, it need hardly be stated that the tortuous arguments of Christian theologians during this time (and, in fact, in the centuries to follow) are fatally vitiated by the unquestioned assumption of the "truth" of scripture, so that all they can do is to undertake increasingly fanciful rhetorical gymnastics to preserve its "truth" without any reference to the realities of the external world. These latter were frequently condemned as the falsehoods that non-Christian Greek philosophers wasted their time expounding. Augustine is unusually explicit in the valuelessness of anything that could be called scientific enquiry, referring to it as "a different kind of temptation" against which we must be constantly on guard: "This futile curiosity masquerades under the name of science and learning" (*Conf.* 10.35).

Indeed, it could be said of theology in general and Christian theology in particular that it was about as evidence-free an undertaking as any purportedly intellectual undertaking could possibly be. There were not—and by the very nature of things could not be—any real-world "facts" that could be brought to bear in solving such conundrums as the nature of Jesus in relation to God, the resurrection of human bodies at the Last Judgment, the fate of bodies or souls in heaven or hell, or many other issues on which theologians disputed with such fervour. All they could do was pluck fragments of scripture (themselves often so opaque that they could legitimately afford fodder for many differing interpretations) as they engaged in increasingly arid speculation to justify their views. In the profoundest sense, all theology is not really philosophy, and it is certainly not science; it is merely commentary. It is about words rather than things. This problem was exacerbated by the fact that the doctrines emerging from theological argument served as the basis for political and legal policies of Christian nations for many centuries—and we shall have occasion to trace the results of those policies in subsequent chapters of this book.

E. The Pagan Response

Persecution of Christians by Roman authorities was in large part sporadic and incited by local uproars. As I have mentioned, Suetonius' citation of the devotees of "Chrestus" in the reign of Claudius (r. 41–54) seems anomalously early as a reference to Christians, and most scholars now assume that it referred to one of numerous would-be Messiahs among Jews who may have attracted a following. The NT is full of warnings of such individuals. The following is placed in Jesus' mouth: "If anyone says to you then, 'Look, here is the Messiah,' or 'There he is,' do not believe it. Impostors will come claiming to be messiahs or prophets, and they will produce great signs and wonders to mislead, if possible, even God's chosen" (Matt. 24:23–24). Jesus does not explain how one is to distinguish between the pretenders and the real McCoy (namely, himself).

Nero's singling out Christians as responsible for the devastating fire in Rome in 64 was—if Tacitus is to be believed—merely a scapegoating of a sect that was already loathed by the general populace, hence made a convenient target. If nothing else, Tacitus' brief passage suggests that Christians were definitely established in Rome by this point. We hear little more on persecution of Christians until the early second century, when Pliny the Younger, in his role as the emperor's representative to the province of Bithynia and Pontus (110–13), wrote some revealing letters to Trajan on what to do with the Christians in his remote province (the northern coast of Turkey). It is evident that Pliny was reluctant to take harsh actions against Christians—unless they persisted in avowing their faith and, accordingly, in refusing to participate in the customary rituals of the imperial cult. It is of interest that Pliny spoke with a number of individuals who had renounced Christianity and "reviled the name of Christ"; these individuals "all did reverence to your statue and the images of the gods in the same way as the others" (10.96.6). He notes plaintively that stopping the spread of the movement may now be difficult: "It is not only the towns, but villages and rural districts too which are infected through contact with this wretched cult" (10.96.9). In his brief reply Trajan largely endorses Pliny's cautious policy, and that is all we hear of the matter.

What is clear is that the unspecified "punishment" that Pliny has inflicted upon those who confess themselves Christian is entirely based on their refusal to participate in the ceremonies that Roman emperors insisted upon as a unifying force for their diverse and widely spread empire. It is a delicate point whether such conformity should be regarded as chiefly political or chiefly religious; but the fact that Romans generally did not interfere in the strictly religious actions or beliefs of other sects suggests a somewhat greater emphasis on the former point.

It was only in the later second century that we find pagan philosophers actually wrestling with Christianity in regard to both its religious tenets and its place within the political and social fabric of the Empire. The first notable figure is one Celsus, whose attack on Christianity (the *Alethēs Logos* [True Discourse]) is preserved in extensive extracts by Origen (184?–253?) in his treatise *Contra Celsum.* It is, therefore, unfortunate that do not know anything about Celsus. There were two philosophers of that name, in the reigns of Nero and of Hadrian, but this seems too early for our author. Origen refers to him as an Epicurean, and many scholars have believed that he is therefore to be identified with the Celsus cited in Lucian's *Alexander;* but Origen's own treatise makes it quite clear that Celsus was a Platonist. Some believe that Origen branded Celsus as an Epicurean merely as a general term of abuse, since it was widely believed that Epicureans were one step away from actual atheism. Celsus' endorsement of the efficacy of magic (he accuses Jesus of being a magician, having learned the art from his early years in Egypt) makes it clear that he cannot be the Celsus of Lucian's *Alexander.* As such, the dating of his treatise to c. 177–80 is highly conjectural.

In any event, Celsus' treatise, insofar as it can be reconstructed in Origen's text, is a bracing one, although much of its criticism tends to be captious, carping, and even abusive. But its central point is one that remains unanswered and unanswerable. In relating the various pillars of Christian thought (the virgin birth of Jesus, his death and resurrection, and so on), Celsus notes:

> One ought first to follow reason as a guide before accepting any belief; since anyone who believes without testing a doctrine is certain to be deceived.... Christian teachers ... do not want to give or to receive reasons for what they believe. Their favorite expressions are "Do not ask questions, just believe!" and "Your faith will save you!" "The wisdom

> of this world," they say, "is evil; to be simple is to be good."[48]

In effect, faith is a chimera and unworthy of the rational person; it will inevitably lead to error, because one cannot justify what one believes. It is, incidentally, the same argument as was used by Lucian in the satirical piece *Peregrinus,* in which a charlatan named Peregrinus, living in Palestine, was initially accepted as a god by credulous Christians and made a fair amount of money from them.

Much of Celsus' argument is founded in the *undistinctiveness* of Christian doctrine; that is, the assertions of Christians in regard to Jesus and other points can be found in other religions, so what reason is there to believe that the Christians are right and these other religions wrong? The prophecies in the Old Testament, which Christians aver relate specifically to Jesus, could apply to "a thousand others besides Jesus" (64). Later he states: "It is easy for the Christians to use the books of the Jews to their advantage, since anyone can prove anything from so-called prophecy" (106). How can we distinguish the "miracles" of Jesus from those of a magician? And other figures in history or myth have claimed to have risen from the dead (Celsus cites Zalmoxis, a servant of Pythagoras, Pythagoras himself, Orpheus, Herakles, Theseus, and several others). The Christians criticise Greek gods as human beings who were later deified—but isn't that exactly what they are saying about Jesus himself?

Celsus rejects the notion of a general resurrection of the flesh—but his view is chiefly based on the Greco-Roman belief that only the soul survives the body; it may also reflect Platonists' scorn of the body as a substance unworthy of attention. Indeed, it was standard pagan doctrine that God did not create material bodies at all: only the human soul is, as philsophers of many different stripes attested, a fragment of the divine.

Celsus lambastes the anti-intellectualism of Christians, even of the "more intelligent" (72) Christians who seek to defend their faith by logic:

> Their injunctions are like this: "Let no one educated, no one wise, no one sensible draw near. For these abilities are thought to be evils. But as for anyone ignorant, anyone stupid, anyone uneducated, let him come

48. I use the translation of R. Joseph Hoffmann in *Celsus: On the True Doctrine* 54. Subsequent citations will occur in the text.

> boldly." By the fact that they themselves admit that these people are worthy of their god, they show that they want and are able to convince only the foolish, dishonorable and stupid, and only slaves, women and little children. (72–73)

He finds it deeply troubling that Christians have "concocted an absolutely offensive doctrine of everlasting punishments and rewards" (70); indeed, they use the fear of hell as a weapon of conversion, just as they indoctrinate their young into dogmatic theology. Jews and Christians share the view that "God is vindinctive and repentant" (78), and they argue over who are the true chosen people. In this there is an implicit criticism of both sects for believing they have the exclusive "truth" about godhead—a point that is particularly awkward, since they don't agree on the nature of that godhead. Celsus reveals a clear awareness of the multiplicity of gods accepted by cultures around the Mediterranean, from the Arabians to the Egyptians to the Scythians, all of whose conceptions of god are antipodally different and contradictory.

Coming to certain elements of Judaeo-Christian doctrine, Celsus finds paradoxes in the conception of Satan, ridicules the Garden of Eden story, and has great fun with the idea of an anthropomorphic god: "Their absurd doctrines even contain reference to God walking about in the garden he created for man; and they speak of him being angry, jealous, moved to repentance, sorry, sleepy—in short, as being in every respect more a man than a God" (103). But Celsus' criticisms are directed from a specifically Platonist perspective ("God has neither hands, mouth, nor voice, nor any characteristics of which we know . . . God resembles no form known to us" [103]).

Celsus' final argument is that Christianity is not only false but politically dangerous. The Christians' refusal to swear by the emperor jeopardises the state:

> If everyone were to adopt the Christian's attitude, moreover, there would be no rule of law: the legitimate authority would be abandoned; earthly things would return to chaos and come into the hands of the lawless and savage barbarians; and nothing further would be heard of Christian worship or of wisdom, anywhere in the world. (124)

Celsus is maintaining that the very existence of Christians in the midst of the Empire would become problematic if the Roman religion upon which (in his view) the Empire continues to function were to fall.

Celsus' tract may or may not have been written at a time when persecution of Christians by the Roman state became severe and widespread for the first time, in the reign of Marcus Aurelius. But it should by now be evident that this persecution was chiefly political, in that Christians were believed to be a threat to the stability of the Roman state because of their refusal to participate in the imperial cult. Jews had been exempted from the cult, but their numbers were smaller and the antiquity of the Jewish religion had impressed the Romans; the new cult of Christianity, spreading with alarming rapidity throughout the Empire, engendered no such sympathy.

Porphyry—the name given to the philosopher Basileus of Tyre (234–305) by his tutor, the rhetorician Longinus—is, or at any rate was believed by Christian theologians themselves to be, a much more formidable opponent than Celsus. That is no doubt why his work survives only in fragments, mostly quoted by his opponents in wide-ranging attempts to refute it. He wrote a treatise, *Against the Christians,* in fifteen books; it probably dates anywhere between 270 and 300. Condemnations of the work began as early as the reign of Constantine and continued into the mid-fifth century. Porphyry repeatedly sought to tease out contradictions in the NT, even if some of these were trivial or captious; for example, he notes a three-hour time difference between the date of Jesus' crucifixion in Mark (15:25) and John (19:14).

More significantly, Porphyry condemned the notion that the way of salvation was possible only with Jesus. He may have been among the first to raise the awkward question of what is to be done with pre-Christian pagans who unquestionably led moral and distinguished lives. In tackling the vexed issue of the allegorisation of certain passages in both the OT and the NT as practised by a number of Christian thinkers, he maintained that these passages were not in fact ambiguous but merely embarrassing to Christians in that they related obviously false statements that Christians were seeking to explain away. A Christian critic accused Porphyry of doing the same with the text of Homer; but this is merely a *tu quoque* argument.

Then there is the obscure figure Macarius Magnes, a Christian philosopher of the early fourth century who wrote a fictional dialogue between a pagan and a Christian, *Apocriticos*. It is believed that many of the statements of the pagan in this dialogue (which was first published only in 1876) are taken from Porphyry. His broad-based criticism of many features of the NT is impressive. The obscurity of a number of the NT texts is, in his view, an indication that their appeal is not to reason but to irrationality. The resurrection of Jesus is ridiculed because Jesus did not reveal himself to "men of note" such as Pontius Pilate or Herod Antipas—the very ones who had purportedly condemned him to death—but only to a few obscure women. Like many other pagans, he finds the general resurrection of the dead ludicrous: "the question . . . is one full of silliness."[49] The eucharist, if taken literally (as indeed it is by devout Christians), is repulsive; the pagan likens it to the numerous Greco-Roman stories of cannibal feasts, such as that of Thyestes.

The one extant treatise in Latin that embodies a pagan response to Christianity is found in the *Octavius* of M. Minucius Felix (d. 250?), about whom almost nothing is known. It appears that Minucius was a Roman lawyer who converted to Christianity, and his treatise presents a dialogue between Caecilius, a pagan, and Octavius, a Christian convert, with Minucius acting as a somewhat biased moderator. Caecilius makes a strong argument for scepticism—not merely scepticism regarding Christianity, but about the very existence of gods of any sort, although it is not entirely clear that that was his intention. (It is unlikely that the interlocutors are actual individuals of the period.)

Caecilius begins by expounding what is essentially an atomist theory of the universe, although he presents it merely as a hypothesis; but he pungently notes that, if such a conception is true, "what room is there for a God as the artificer?" (5.7).[50] He then goes on to articulate already familiar arguments against the existence of gods—at least those who are envisioned to be benevolent toward humanity: natural disasters affect both the innocent and the guilty; vice often prospers. As a result, "the truth of a divine government is hidden in uncertainty and withheld from us" (5.13). Therefore, it is best to adhere to the religion of our ancestors. Caecilius here recounts an anthropology of religion that underscores the

49. Quoted in Cook, *The Interpretation of the New Testament in Greco-Roman Paganism* 241.

50. I use the translation of Sir David Dalrymple.

degree to which human beings largely remain in the faith of their region and upbringing:

> Hence we see, that in every empire and province and city men have their national and peculiar rites as to things sacred, and that they worship such gods as are of their own community. Thus the inhabitants of Eleusis worship Ceres; the Epidaurians, Æsculapius; the Chaldeans, Belus; the Syriabs, Astarte; the people of Tauris, Diana; and the Gauls, Mercury; while the Romans pay their adoration to all divinities whatsoever. (6.1)

Indeed, Rome became all-powerful precisely because it embraced the gods of all the regions it encountered. Caecilius does lash out against philosophical atheists (he mentions Theodorus of Cyrene and Diagoras of Melos), "who, by averring that there are no gods, took away the whole of that sacred awe which is necessary to the government of mankind" (8.2)—but this is standard Roman doctrine that faith in the Olympian gods is a necessary adjunct to the political and military might of the Empire.

In regard to the Christians, Caecilius attacks them for sexual impropriety and for their secrecy (unlike the Jews, who worship their god openly). Their conception of God is incoherent and self-contradictory; the notion of the resurrection of the flesh is nonsensical; and Caecilius is offended by the arrogance of Christians who assert that they alone will be svaed, while others will receive "everlasting punishment" (11.5). But he pungently asks: why does this god, whose benevolence toward his own followers you profess so ardently, allow you to suffer through persecution? "Hence he is weak or he is unjust" (12.2)—anticipating David Hume's argument by a millennium and a half. Caecilius concludes with a renewed emphasis on scepticism in regard to deity:

> And thus, in my judgment, things doubtful ought to be left in their present state of uncertainty; nor, while so many and so eminent persons hesitate, ought we precipitately and hardily to pronounce a definitive sentence, lest on the one hand the dotage of superstition should be introduced, or on the other, all religion overthrown. (13.5)

After a brief interval, Octavius now takes over, occupying nearly two-thirds of the entire treatise; but his defence of Christianity is, to put it mildly, peculiar. His most extensive argument comprises not an advocacy of the specific tenets of Christianity but of natural religion. For Octavius, there must be a "divine intelligence"—and he puts forth the argument from design at considerable length, emphasising the regularity of celestial motions, the seasons, and so on. "Above all, the comeliness of our own form acknowledges God as its artificer" (17.11)—a statement that may or may not reflect the biblical "Let us make human beings in our image, after our likeness" (Gen. 1:26), but which in any case is not likely to convince the sceptic. Octavius completely ignores the argument *against* design that Caecilius made in putting forth the problem of natural disasters.

A number of points in Octavius' speech brings Stoicism to mind, as when he states that "Of a superintending Providence there can be no doubt" (18.5); but he goes on to say that there cannot be a multiplicity of gods, since they would all be battling against one another. And yet, he here lapses into inadvertent agnosticism by suggesting that God is esentially unknowable: "He is invisible, because too bright for mortal eye; he cannot be felt, because too pure for mortal touch; neither can his attributes be justly estimated, for he is beyond our senses, infinite, immense, and known in his perfection to himself alone" (18.5). At this point it would seem that Octavius' only recourse would be to appeal to faith, as so many Christians have done; but he is determined to make what he believes to be a reasoned case for belief.

Several of Octavius' assertions have the embarassing feature of backfiring against the very religion he is defending. Condemning the stories about the Olympian gods as "the fables of dotards" (20.4), he goes on to say: "We learn those fables and delusions from rude and ignorant parents" (24.1). But do not Christians learn their faith from their own parents also? Octavius criticises Homer for showing gods intervening in human affairs—but surely it is a central principle of Christianity that God (through Jesus) made exactly such an intervention.

While Octavius attempts to refute Caecilius' slanders against Christian communities of his day, his entire account says nothing of the life, death, and salvific function of Jesus or any of the other central tenets of Christianity as then understood. Predictably, however, this tendentious treatise depicts Caecilius quickly becoming convinced by Octavius' arguments and converting to Christianity himself.

The Emperor Julian, in addition to taking the political and other measures previously outlined, wrote a stirring treatise *Against the Galileans.* As with Celsus, large fragments of the work survive as a result of their being quoted in the Christian theologian Cyril of Alexandria's attack on Julian, *Pro Christiana Religione* (c. 429–41). It need hardly be stated that Julian was writing from anything but an atheistic perspective; his own philosophical or religious views tended toward Neoplatonism, a mystical philosophy chiefly developed by Plotinus (204?–270). Julian emphasises the connexion when he compares the creation story in Genesis unfavourably with that found in Plato's *Timaeus,* which he asserts is a "nobler" conception.[51] And although he declares bluntly that it is the Christians views that "are on trial" (91), a certain proportion of Julian's remarks are addressed to the god of the OT. That deity's assertion that "I am a jealous god" is, to Julian, an expression of immorality: "Now if a man is jealous or covetous you consider him immoral; but if it is God—you call the attribute divine" (110). This is a clever rhetorical turnabout, as numerous Christians (and, in fact, pagans as well) had claimed that the actions of the Olympian gods, if committed by human beings, would be considered flagrantly immoral. Along the same lines, Julian believes that the Garden of Eden story is as ludicrous as any number of Greek myths about the gods.

For Julian, the Ten Commandments are merely commonplace moral axioms that any society would adopt for the purpose of self-preservation. Julian in fact comes close to asserting a kind of relativistic or anthropological view of the development of society, maintaining that "civil and moral laws were established by those in whom civilized instincts were dominant above other instincts" (103). But the OT's attempt to address the issue, in its tale of the Tower of Babel, is simply preposterous.

Like Celsus, Julian ridicules the Christians for believing that the "prophecies" in the OT predicted the advent of Jesus; this assumption is, in his view, highly tendentious, a result of choosing passages that seem to fit Jesus but in fact don't really fit him very well at all. Moreover, the

51. I use the translation in Hoffman, *Julian's Against the Galileans* 96. Further page citations will occur in the text.

OT makes it clear that there is only one supreme god; how can this be reconciled with the very idea of a Jesus? This is an implicit assertion that the doctrine of the Trinity is incomprehensible nonsense.

What scientific developments have the Christians fostered? None that Julian can see. The Greeks, Babylonians, Egyptians, and Phoenicians all had a role in the development of mathematics, geometry, astronomy, and other sciences, but the contributions of Christians to these subjects is a nullity. The Christians also have no one equal to Alexander or Caesar or Asclepius: "Now consider whether we are not superior to you in every single one of these things—in art, wisdom, intelligence—not regarding whether we are speaking of the useful arts or the imitative arts whose end is beauty: Statuary, painting, household management, healing from Asclepius" (122). Julian's point is to underscore the persistent strain of anti-intellectualism found in many of the Christian theologians of the period—and it is a point that Renaissance thinkers picked up on during the revival of classical learning.

More purely literary figures in the Roman Empire continued to write in the wake of the increasing Christianisation of culture, society, and government. Ammianus Marcellinus (330?–400?), the last of the great Roman historians, wrote a history whose extant portions cover the period 353–378 (constituting books 14–31); it is, indeed, from him that we gain a substantial proportion of our knowledge of the reign of the Emperor Julian. As a native Greek speaker who wrote in Latin, he identified closely with traditional Greco-Roman culture. He seems to have made a conscious choice simply to ignore Christianity during the era he is writing about: he makes passing references to the unseemly ambition and power-grabs of Christian bishops in Rome, but that is about all. Conversely, Ammianus is relatively charitable toward other "foreign" religions in Rome—even those of the Egyptians and (surprisingly) the Druids, as well as the Magi of Persia.

In poetry, we have the touching *Pervigilum Veneris* (The Vigil of [or for] Venus), a poem of uncertain authorship and date, but which was probably written in the fourth or fifth century. It is a curious piece that evokes the wonders of the natural world in a proto-Romantic manner; one scholar has referred to its "secular piety."[52] Ausonius (D.

52. Albrecht, *A History of Roman Literature* 2.1311.

Magnus Ausonius, 310?–395?) was still doggedly writing poems about the Olympian gods, the Greco-Roman underworld, and so on among a copious output. Claudian (Claudius Claudianus, 370?–404?) was also a prolific poet whose *Panegyricus dictus Probino et Olybrio* (a paean to the Olympian gods) was widely read. The *De Bello Gildonico* mingles recent history with a backdrop of the gods, somewhat in the manner of such early poets as Ennius and Naevius. He was prominent enough to earn the enmity of both Augustine and Orosius (*Adversus Paganos*) as an "obstinate" pagan.

In contrast, Prudentius (Aurelius Prudentius Clemens, 348–413?) was the first notable Christian poet, and he chose to engage in attacks upon Christian heretics in such works as the *Apotheosis,* which chastised those who expressed doubts about the Trinity and the divinity of Jesus. The *Contra Symmachum*—a polemic against the pagan orator Symmachus (Q. Aurelius Symmachus, 345?–402)—focuses on the controversial removal of the Altar of Victory from the Senate House by the emperor Constantius II in 357. It was restored by Julian, but then removed by the emperor Gratian in 382. At the time the fate of the altar was believed to be a symbol of the demise of paganism in Rome. Prudentius, in attacking Symmachus, goes on to attack polytheism in general. In the *Psychomachia,* an allegorical poem, Prudentius sets up a conflict between such personified virtues as hope and chastity and their evil counterparts, pride, avarice, and so on; and in the process he essentially links Christian virtue to the former and paganism to the latter. The poem was widely read throughout the mediaeval era.

F. The Consolidation of Christian Rule

By the end of Theodosius' reign in 395, most of the heresies that had plagued the Catholic church had been suppressed. In the course of the fifth century the church waxed both immensely powerful and immensely wealthy; individual bishops acquired fabulous wealth and lived in palatial mansions or villas on large stretches of property.

There was, however—in consonance with the lingering Christian hatred of the body and bodily functions—a countervailing tendency toward extreme asceticism. Monasticism began to flourish at this time. A pioneer was Anthony (c. 300), followed by Jerome (author of the

Vulgate—the Latin translation of the Bible, issued between 392 and 406), Basil, and Martin of Tours, who brought monasticism to Gaul in the 360s. Jerome's letters reveal a loathing of the body and of sexual activity that exceeds even Augustine's. He was particularly insistent on female virginity, maintaining that Mary somehow remained a virgin even when conceiving Jesus and giving birth to him.

But the proliferation of mendicant monks—to say nothing of their fanaticism, as exemplified in their destruction of pagan temples and even their murder of pagans—became a problem for the civil authorities, so efforts were made to bring the monastic communities more strictly under the control of the church. Celibacy for priests was introduced in 384, but was widely practised only in the West.

The Roman Empire in the fifth and sixth centuries faced repeated incursions from foreign powers—whether it be the resurgent Persian Empire in the east or various German "barbarians" in the north and west. These latter tribes had been encroaching upon Roman territory since at least the late second century, chiefly as a result of a lack of food and a disinclination for a settled agricultural life. The Goths, migrating to the Black Sea, divided into the Visigoths and Ostrogoths. In the western German regions, many tribes had been invited by the Romans to settle within the borders of the Empire, simply because the Roman army was insufficient to combat them; many soldiers in the area were already taken from the ranks of the barbarians. The Huns took over large stretches of southern Russia, as they themselves were pushed west by Chinese peoples. Many of these tribes had been converted to Christianity prior to their incursions into the Roman Empire, initially through the efforts of one Ulfilas (311?–383), a Cappadocian Greek bishop who translated the Bible into Gothic; but by some quirk of circumstance the Goths adopted Arianism and clung to it long after it had been declared a heresy by the orthodox Christian church.

After the death of Theodosius, a general named Stilicho (of Vandal origin) gained supremacy, essentially ruling over the young emperor Honorius (r. 393–423) in the West. The Visigoths (already settled by Theodosius in Moesia), led by Alaric, invaded Greece, and the Huns invaded Syria. But in 400 the German tribes were defeated in their attempt to invade the Eastern Empire. Alaric made incursions into Italy in 401 and 403, but was repelled by Stilicho; but these invasions led

Honorius to move his court from Rome to Ravenna, which became the de facto capital of the West for many years. Alaric's continuing attacks led to his sack of Rome in 409, but after his death the next year the Visigoths withdrew from Italy and occupied Gaul. Franks and Burgundians now emerge into history, taking control of large stretches of Gaul. Honorius was obliged to accept them as "federates" (*foederati*) of the Empire.

Honorius' celebrated declaration to the Romans in Britain in 408 that they were now on their own in defending their land from invasions by the Picts, Scots, and Saxons was probably not as dramatic a move as is often portrayed, and he probably continued to lend assistance to the province for some years. In Gaul, Theodoric I (grandson of Alaric) took over rulership of the Visigoths in 418, and his struggles with Rome culminated in 430 with Rome's offer of a treaty that ceded much land to the Visigoths. In 429 the Vandals, led by Gaiseric, teamed up with the Alans to take over North Africa, which they did while committing dreadful atrocities upon the local populations. The Romans, meanwhile, were forced to unite with the Huns to battle the Burgundians in Gaul; the latter's defeat in 436 was the basis of the Niebelungenlied. The Vandals, meanwhile, adhering rigidly to their Arian Christianity, banished other Christian sects in the parts of Africa they controlled.

Emperor Theodosius II (r. 408–50) was now forced to deal with the Huns, led by Attila. In the 440s Attila came close to besieging Constantinople, and in 452 he invaded Italy, but then abruptly withdrew. Apparently plague was decimating his troops. He himself died in 454, and his empire quickly fell apart. The next year, Vandals under Gaiseric entered Rome, ransacking the city for two weeks before returning to Africa. Repeated efforts by the Romans to oust the Visigoths from Africa over the next several years failed.

Visigothic rule in Gaul and Spain expanded under the rulership of Euric (r. 466–84); but the Franks (under Clovis, a Catholic), followed by the Burgundians, later captured much of Gaul. By this time the Roman army in the West was largely made up of German troops, and they now began unprecedentedly demanding plots of land *in Italy.* They ultimately appealed to Odoacer, who overthrew the young emperor Romulus Augustulus in 476 to become "king" of Italy. It would be misleading to regard this date as constituting any sort of "fall of the Western Empire": Odoacer had agreed to protect Italy as leader of the army under the eastern emperor Zeno (r. 474–91).

The Ostrogoths, now led by Theodoric the Great (r. 471–526), gained strength in the Danube region. Zeno came to terms with him, even adopting him as a son. But Theodoric continued battling the Roman forces, forcing Zeno to make further concessions to him. Zeno persuaded Theodoric to wage war against Odoacer in Italy, ultimately leading to the latter's surrender in 493. Theodoric essentially gained control of Italy, but he was in effect a viceroy, subordinate to the emperor. He later took over Spain. Meanwhile, incursions by the Bulgarians (formerly the Huns) into Illyricum forced the eastern emperor Anastasius I (r. 491–518) to build a "Long Wall" west of Constantinople.

The accession of Justinian I (r. 527–65) constituted the Roman Empire's swan song. He was determined to win back as much territory as he could, essentially seeking to restore the Empire as it existed under Constantine, the first Christian emperor; but in this effort he achieved only indifferent success at great cost. In addition, his increasing autocracy resulted in a substantial loss of freedom for citizens throughout the Empire, and the machinations of his ruthless wife Theodora, who sometimes worked against him, caused repeated difficulties.

Many of Justinian's military campaigns were led by his general Belisarius. But the latter had little success in the two wars against Persia (527–32, 540–45), which resulted in the fall of Antioch and other Roman losses. The attempt to oust the Vandals from Africa was more of a success, although the Romans were obliged to unite with the Ostrogoths in the effort. They ultimately prevailed in 548. In Italy, dynastic troubles among the Ostrogothic leaders led Justinian to invade. Horrible atrocities were committed during the years of battle: Belisarius took Rome but was besieged by the Ostrogoth Witigis (537–38), during which Rome's aqueducts were destroyed; when the Ostrogoths seized Milan in 539, they slaughtered all the male inhabitants—as many as 300,000. Belisarius was ultimately able to take Ravenna and banish the Ostrogoths to the area north of the Po river. But a new Gothic king, Totila, recaptured some of the land in central and southern Italy in 541–43. Totila besieged Rome on two occasions, but was finally defeated in 552 by a new Roman general, Narses. The Romans also annihilated the Franks in the battle of Capua in 555. By 562 the Romans had regained control of the entirety of Italy.

The Bulgarians boldly crossed the Danube in the 530s and threatened Greece in 540. Later, Justinian set two branches of the Huns, the Kotigurs and the Utigurs, against each other to keep them in check in southern Russia. And when the Lombards and Gepids became active in central Europe, Justinian took the side of the Lombards, who then defeated the Gepids in 552. To guard against incursions in the area of Constantinople, Justinian built hundreds of forts in Thrace, Macedonia, Greece, and elsewhere; but these were not entirely successful in keeping the barbarians at bay.

In the religious movements of these centuries, the dominant thrust was the resoluteness with which both emperors and Christian leaders suppressed both paganism and any sects deemed heretical in order to present a uniform, orthodox brand of what came to be called Catholic Christianity. The efforts were not always successful and often led to bloodshed. There were, indeed, repeated rhetorical battles as to whether the misfortunes suffered by the inhabitants of the Roman Empire during this period was a result of the persistence of pagan belief or of the abandonment of it. The pagan historians Eunapius and Zosimus went further, actually blaming Christianity for the catastrophes of the fourth and fifth centuries. Augustine's *City of God* was written in part to combat this view. The Senate in Rome long remained a bastion of paganism, and during Alaric's invasion of the city in the early fifth century the Senate attempted to resume pagan ceremonies—but could find no one to perform them publicly. In a notorious incident, Cyril, patriarch of Alexandria (412–44), in the midst of a ruthless campaign to persecute pagans and Jews, contrived the death of the pagan philosopher Hypatia in 415.

Meanwhile, continuing controversies among the Christians themselves did not help matters. When Theodosius II nominated Nestorius to be patriarch of Constantinople in 428, a furore broke out over his disputes with Cyril as to how the divine and human aspects of Jesus intermingled. This was in effect a contination of the *homoousios/homoioousios* theory, with Nestorius stressing Jesus' human side and Cyril his divine side. This led to Nestorius' condemnation at the Council of Ephesus (431), but the controversy continued. At a new council at Ephesus (449), the position of Cyril was reinstated, but at the council of Chalcedon (451) a compromise was effected, in which it was somehow determined that Jesus had two inseparable natures, human and divine—a doctrine still maintained by the Catholic church. Actual riots occurred over this notion, and as a result the Monophysites (who asserted that Jesus had only one "nature"—i.e., the divine one) emerged as a powerful force in Christian theology, ultimately forming the Coptic church in Egypt.

Justinian was forthright, and ruthless, in his desire to see Catholic Christianity prevail over paganism and heresy. When the church of St. Sophia was partially destroyed by fire in a revolt in the early 530s, he spared no expense in rebuilding it (532–37), making it one of the most magnificent structures in the ancient world. Other churches were also rebuilt after 532. Otherwise, Justinian was intent on fusing the church and the state more intimately than before, with himself at the head of both. He arranged for bishops to become increasingly involved in civil administration, sometimes in place of provincial governors. Justinian even took an interest in the rules governing monastic institutions, on the grounds that their collective prayers assisted the state and the military. In effect, this was not so different from figures from republican and imperial Rome who sought the sanction of the gods when going into battle.

Justinian's desire to wipe out paganism, especially among the educated classes and those who instructed the young, was unremitting. These pagan instructors were now barred from teaching on any subject. Persecution quickly followed, with torture, imprisonment, and even some executions of holdouts. Many of those under threat of punishment pretended to convert to Christianity. In an epochal moment, schools in Athens—which had flourished since the days of Socrates and Plato in the late fifth century B.C.E.—were shut down in 529. Pagan temples were destroyed in Asia Minor and Egypt.

But Justinian also instituted systematic attempts to crush heresy within the Christian church. Heretics were deprived of citizenship; they could not inherit property or bear witness in court against the orthodox; other penalties were also decreed. Jews and Samaritans were also subject to these laws. The death penalty was enforced on Manichaeans and those converts to Christianity who had lapsed in their faith. Justinian also had to deal with the flaring up of the Monophysite controversy, resulting in many priests and bishops being expelled or imprisoned. The controversy was settled, after a fashion, by the fiat of Leontius of Byzantium, but his solution (which need not be gone into, as it is incomprehensible to the mere layman) did not satisfy everyone. Justinian attempted to settle the matter himself (even though his own wife, Theodora, was inclined toward Monophysitism and strove to support those who advocated it) through the summoning of various church councils and synods, but to little effect; so he resorted to persecution of Monophysites.

Another problem was the unexpected resurgence of interest in Origen's liberal doctrines on salvation, when some theologians of the early sixth century adopted it (or a distorted version of it) under the influence of Neoplatonism. Justinian was not about to stand for that, and in 543 he issued an edict condemning Origenism and ordering the destruction of his books. In this and other actions, Justinian established the principle that the emperor has the authority to dictate doctrine by edicts that are binding on the church and its followers.

Justinian's celebrated legal code—an extensive revision of earlier codes reaching all the way back to the Twelve Tables—was a landmark in legal history, in that it remained for many centuries the foundation of European law. Our chief interest is in the revision of the laws pertaining to divorce, which were heavily affected by Christian doctrine. That doctrine, of course, outlawed divorce altogether, although certain NT texts perhaps inadvertently allowed for some wiggle room on the matter (see, e.g., Matt. 5:32: "If a man divorces his wife for any cause other than unchastity he involves her in adultery; and whoever marries her commits adultery"; cf. Mark 10:2–12). Recognising that banning divorce entirely was unfeasible, Justinian's law code prohibited divorce by mutual consent, formerly allowed under Roman law; but an outcry from the populace forced Justin II to restore it in 566. Overall, Justinian made divorce much more difficult than before without abolishing it altogether. It is unsurprising that a husband could divorce his wife for adultery but his wife could not if the husband committed adultery.

In his reforms of criminal law, Justinian (as well as his predecessor, Theodosius II) were probably led by Christian influence to decree harsh penalties for adultery, ranging from deportion to remote islands to the relegation of an offending wife to a convent. Incest, understandably, was also subject to severe penalties; and the death penalty was exacted for the abduction of women for "immoral" purposes. Sodomy and other sexual irregularities were also punishable by death.

During these turbulent centuries, it is understandable that literature would not flourish in any copious or vibrant manner. Much of this literature, especially among (pagan) historians, is lost. What we do have is the copious work of Procopius (500?–565?), who wrote an orthodox *History of the Wars* dealing with the wars against the Persians, Vandals, and Ostrogoths, as well as a remarkable treatise, the *Secret History*, which Procopius kept as a closely guarded secret because of its vicious and at times scurrilous portrayal of Justinian, his wife Theodora, and others. At one point he asserts that the emperor and his consort were demons. And although there is probably no reason to doubt that Procopius was a Christian of some sort, at one point in the *History of the Wars* he lapses into what may well be an unintentional agnoticism. In discussing the theological controversies of the period, he writes: "As for the points in dispute, although I know them well, I shall by no means make mention of them; for I consider it a sort of insane folly to investigate the nature of God, enquiring of what sort it is. For man cannot, I think, apprehend even human affairs with accuracy, much less those things which pertain to the nature of God" (5.3.6–7).[53] This may be nothing more than the reluctance—customary at this time—of historians to engage in church matters, but it is nonetheless a striking utterance.

The curious *Christian Cosmography* of Cosmas (written in 545–50) gives some indication of how low the pursuit of pure science had fallen, to say nothing of the dominance of the Christian outlook in every phase of intellectual enquiry. Cosmas wrote his treatise to refute the pagan view that the earth is round; it is, he contends, a flat rectangle. Moreover, the sun is smaller than the earth, and angels guide the movements of the stars. While some parts of the treatise are based on Cosmas' own travels, it is largely an attempt to infer a geography and cosmology from scripture.

The one literary work that may merit our attention is the celebrated *De Consolatione Philosophiae* (On the Consolation of Philosophy) by Boethius (Anicius Manlius Severinus Boethius, 477?–524), a text that was immensely popular throughout the Middle Ages and Renaissance. The peculiar thing, however, is its near-total absence of specifically Christian doctrine. There is little doubt that Boethius was a devout

53. I use the translation of H. B. Dewing.

Christian, as his so-called *Opuscula Sacra* (treatises on the Trinity, the Catholic faith, and other subjects) attest. The *Consolation* was written at a critical time in Boethius' life: a senator in Rome, he was imprisoned in 523 (presumably on orders of Theodoric) on an accusation of treason. Although attempts were made to free him or lessen his sentence, he was executed the following year.

The basic thrust of the *Consolation* is how the philosopher can maintain tranquillity, equilibrium, and even happiness while being buffeted by misfortune. The framework of the piece is the appearance of the goddess Philosophy to Boethius in prison and their subsequent dialogue (chiefly a monologue by Philosophy, with Boethius quickly agreeing to virtually everything she says), interspersed with rather unfortunate bits of doggerel. It is true that, at the outset, Boethius asserts the role of God in the universe, but this is largely an argument against the "randomness of chance events" and the assertion of a "divine reason" (1.6).[54] And this passage is immediately followed by a long disquisition on *fortuna* (2.1f.), in defining which Boethius seems to waver between fate, chance, good luck, and happiness. The poetic interludes exclusively refer to the pagan gods and heroes.

It is only in Book 4 that Boethius comes close to Christian teaching in his discussion of the problem of evil. But the treatise remains remarkably general, not to say unconvincing. By a series of verbal gymnastics Boethius manages to persuade himself that "the good are powerful, but the evil weak" (4.2)—indeed, that "evil men . . . do not exist" (4.2)! There follows a laborious passage on why God seems to allow the good to suffer and the bad to prosper, ending in what seems like an unwitting agnosticism: "For it is not allowed to a man either to comprehend with his natural powers or to express in words all the devices of the work of God" (4.6). A discussion of God's foreknowledge (5.3f.) probably owes something to Augustine. But most remarkable of all, there is not one sentence devoted to the afterlife, which Christian thinkers had already used extensively as an antidote to the woes of the good on earth.

The development of Christian art during the early centuries C.E. is of some interest. Christians gradually overcame their distaste for "graven images" and other forms of representation by seeing Christian art as a

54. I use the translation of S. J. Tester.

mode of education and even of conversion. As wealthy Romans became Christians, they commissioned art that, although Christian in substance, remained strongly classical in style. It is noteworthy that the cross did not become a dominant Christian symbol until the fourth century C.E., after Constantine's supposed vision in the sky prior to the Battle of the Milvian Bridge. Prior to that, the fish (*ichthus* in Greek) was the central Christian symbol—an acronym meaning "Jesus Christ Son of God, Saviour."

Christian architecture in the fourth and subsequent centuries gradually rejected the model of the Roman temple and adapted that of the secular basilica with its long, rectangular hall lined on either side with columns. The need to accommodate increasing numbers of congregants and pilgrims resulted in a new design embodied in the Church of the Holy Sepulchre in Jerusalem (mid-fourth century), in which the circular design of the Christian mausoleum (frequently used to house relicts of saints or martyrs) was superimposed on the basilica, as in the Basilica of St. Peter in Rome (completed in 333). The classical style, however, persisted in fifth-century churches in Rome, Ravenna, Milan, and elsewhere.

The difficulties Christians faced in the first two or three centuries C.E.—a succession of schisms and heresies, persecution by Roman officials—stemmed in large part from their claim that their religion embodied the exclusive truth about the nature of deity and entity. The Greco-Roman religion, which made no such explicit claim, welcomed most of the other religions it encountered throughout the Mediterranean over the centuries, even if many of its efforts to syncretise these religions with its own were clumsy and makeshift. Judaism also embraced claims to exclusivity, but because Jews by and large did not engage in proselytising, the Romans tended to leave them in peace; the antiquity of Judaism also impressed the Romans, who granted the Jews a grudging respect for devotion to what they called the *mos maiorum* (the ways of our forefathers).

It is disheartening, but hardly surprising, that once Christianity became the dominant political and legal force in the Roman Empire, it at once began persecuting its opponents with relish. What else can one do if one is convinced that one has the truth and everyone else is wrong?

Non-Christians were, therefore, not merely misguided but under the aegis of Satan. Christianity and Judaism are also dubiously distinguished for linking morality to their religion; the Greeks and Romans generally left moral argument in the hands of philosophers. But, as Nietzsche long ago wrote, when moral principles (or, indeed, any principles) are explicitly attributed to a god, it becomes exceptionally difficult to modify or overturn them when they are found to be unsatisfactory, inadequate, or outmoded; the problem is compounded when it is assumed that the god in question is omnipotent, omniscient, and infallible, and that the scriptures outlining these principles were written under his inspiration.[55] It is a problem Christianity continues to wrestle with to the present day.

55. Cf. the Emperor Julian: "As God is eternal it follows that his ordinances are unchanging" (Hoffman, *Julian's Against the Galileans* 107).

V. The Mediaeval Era

Mediaevalism, with its saints and martyrs, its love of self-torture, its wild passion for wounding itself, its gashing with knives, and its whipping with rods—Mediaevalism is real Christianity, and the mediaeval Christ is the real Christ.

—Oscar Wilde

It is well known that the term Middle Ages (of which "mediaeval" is simply the Latin-derived equivalent) is a pejorative term invented during the Renaissance to denote an era that was believed to have been engulfed in ignorance, superstitition, and the (not coincidental) prevalence of the Christian church over virtually all aspects of political, social, legal, and cultural life; and yet, it is not clear that an adequate substitute can be found. To be sure, the people of the mediaeval era, insofar as their views can be ascertained, believed themselves to constitute a continuation of either the Roman Empire in both the West and the East (the latter now termed the Byzantine Empire). But the culture that operated in Europe from the seventh to the fifteenth century ultimately developed into a radically different civilisation from that of pagan antiquity—not only as a result of the dominance of Christianity and the fragility of a society where ignorance, poverty, and political instability were endemic, but also because a new and aggressively dynamic religion evolved in the East to challenge both the military might and the intellectual and religious culture of Europe.

A. The Emergence and Spread of Islam

The emergence of Islam in the early to mid-seventh century was an epochal event—one that ultimately led to the dissemination of the new faith over at least four continents (to one of which it gave the name we now use: Africa, from the Arabic Ifraqiya), so that by the twentieth century it would rival (and, in the future, perhaps surpass) Christianity in the number of its adherents. And like Christianity, but to an even greater degree, it was based on a pre-existing scripture—if we regard the combined OT and NT as a single document.

In Islam's foundational text, the Quran,[1] it is stated that the prophet Muhammad received the words of Allah (the Arabic word for "god") from a series of encounters with the angel Gabriel, who dictated the text to him. But since Muhammad was unable to read or write, he himself dictated the text to scribes over the course of years or perhaps decades. It should be emphasised that Muslims believe that the text of the Quran embodies the actual words of Allah.

The evidence for the existence of Muhammad ibn Abd Allah (570?–632) is not as firm as one would like, but there is no compelling reason to doubt that he did in fact exist at approximately the time given by his life dates. And yet, in a disturbing analogy with Jesus, next to nothing is known of the first forty years of his life aside from his presumed birth in Mecca, then a relatively small town in Arabia. At this time the Arabian continent was populated by a number of tribes, many of them of the nomadic *bedu* (Bedouin in English) culture, whose pre-Islamic religious inclinations are not at all clear aside from hints of local animism. Muhammad's tribe, the Quaraysh, presided over the Kaaba stone (at that time the focus of the cult of the god Hubal). There are, indeed, traces in the Quran that Muhammad sought to replace the worship of Hubal, as well as that of three female deities, with the all-encompassing monotheism of Allah.

Even this rudimentary account tells us much about the origins of Islam in Arabia. The region was on the borderland of the Byzantine Empire on the west and the Sasanian Empire (Iran) on the east; its populace was a mix of nomadic tribes along with Christians, Jews,

1. In rendering Arabic names and terms I follow the practice of Esposito, *The Oxford History of Islam,* in omitting certain diacritical marks.

Zoroastrians, and other sects. For all Muhammad's illiteracy, it is plain that he must have absorbed some of these religious traditions in early life: the Quran's theology is fundamentally based on biblical doctrines regarding the existence a solitary creator-god, the existence of Adam and Eve as the originators of the human race, and an eschatology that explicitly cites a Day of Judgment and a division of human souls on moral principles, the good attaining paradise and the wicked consigned to a hell presided over by a Satan figure named (once) in the Quran (2:32) as Eblis. Satan is mentioned by name elsewhere (2:34, 7:19), and he is reported to have tempted Adam and Eve and was accordingly expelled from paradise. Mentions of Abraham, Moses, David, and many others from the OT are frequent; less frequent are citations from the NT, although the Quran does acknowledge Jesus as a prophet and wonder-worker. Where Jews and Christians erred, in Muhammad's view, was in the attribution of godlike qualities to Jesus, which caused Christianity in particular to lapse into an unwitting polytheism. As a necessary corollary, Muhammad rejected the doctrine of the Trinity. He also believed that Jesus did not die by crucifixion. Judaism went astray in declaring Ezra the son of God, as Christians had done with Jesus. All this leads to the grotesque assertion in the Quran (3:60) that, because in Muhammad's view Abraham was the first human being to reject idolatry and accept the one true god, "Abraham was neither Jew nor Christian; but he was sound in the faith, a Muslim; and not one of those who add gods to God."[2]

Muhammad maintained that the visitations from Gabriel (a figure cited in both the OT [the late books of Daniel and Ezekiel] and in the NT as the angel who came to Zacharias, the father of John the Baptist, to signal that his elderly wife Elizabeth would become pregnant and bear a child [Luke 1:10–20]) began as early as 610, but in all likelihood the Quran did not begin to be set down until Muhammad—ostracised by his tribe (which adhered to some form of polytheism)—moved in 622 to Yathrib (about 250 miles north of Mecca), subsequently renamed Medina ("the Prophet's city"). Warfare between the two cities broke out, leading to an uneasy truce in 628. Muhammad returned to Mecca in 630, taking over the city; by the time of his death in 632, his forces

2. I use the translation of the Quran by J. M. Rodwell.

controlled the whole of western Arabia.

The Quran was canonically assembled in the reign of the third successor to Muhammad, Uthman ibn Affan (r. 644–56). There is no compelling reason to doubt this assertion, and some extant fragments of the Quran do date to the seventh century.

After Muhammad's death, Islam spread rapidly through the military actions of his ever-growing cadre of disciples. His father-in-law Abu Bakr took over leadership of the sect after Muhammad's death and became a caliph ("successor"). By 634 all Arabia was under Islamic control, and by 642 conquests had occurred in Syria, Palestine, Mesopotamia, Egypt, and elsewhere. Muslims captured Jerusalem in 636; it had become a sacred place because of its numerous ties to events in Muhammad's life. Some land in Iraq and Iran was taken over from the Sasanians by the mid-650s. It was at this time that the concept of *jihad* ("militant efforts to combat evil and spread Muhammad's message")[3] emerged, underscoring the fusion of politics, militarism, and religion that has almost always defined Islam. And yet, in its early centuries Islam made little effort to interfere with the religious beliefs of the regions it conquered, so long as those beliefs were of a monotheistic sort. It frequently extended toleration specifically to Jews and Christians, who like Muslims were "people of the Book."

Dissatisfaction with the caliph Uthman led to his assassination in 656, leading to the onset of the First Civil War (656–61). It was at this time that the faith split into its two most critical factions. The *shiat Ali* (the party of Ali), or Shiites, asserted that Ali ibn Abi Talib, Muhammad's cousin and son-in-law, was the only true heir to Muhammad, and that the three caliphs who had succeeded Muhammad were usurpers. The Shiites maintained that only by direct descent from the Prophet could Islam attain legitimacy. But in the short term it was the opposing Ummayad caliphate (661–750) that prevailed, emerging out of the Second Civil War (680–92) in control of the faith and embodying the dominant sect, the Sunnis, who ascribed to the *sunna*—the doctrines embodied in both the Quran and the *hadith,* or accounts of the Prophet's deeds and sayings that were recorded in six books compiled between the ninth and eleventh centuries. Each body of work was regarded as an authoritative text that

3. Fred M. Donner, "Muhammad and the Caliphate," in Esposito, *Oxford History of Islam* 13.

must guide Sunni Muslims' beliefs and actions.

The caliphate continued to expand even after the Ummayads, based in Damascus, gave way to the Abbasid caliphs (750–1258). The latter established a new capital, Baghdad, in 762. Muslims ousted the Byzantines in Carthage and elsewhere in North Africa; there were extensive incursions into Spain, as Muslims overran the Visigoths in that region; they even reached into France as far as the Loire before being defeated by Charles Martel in 732.

But by the mid-tenth century the Abbasid caliphate was in decline, as power had slipped from the central government into the hands of the military. Individual tribes gained prominence on the local level. Among these were the Seljuk Turks, whose leaders called themselves sultans (secular Islamic monarchs). Provincial governors gained substantial autonomy; Spain, for example, became a virtually independent region under the self-styuled caliph Abd al-Rahman III (891–961). There was, however, much fighting among individual cities, which allowed Christians to make gains in the area (Toledo fell out of Muslim control in 1085).

In Egypt, the Copts (Monophysite Christians) became the dominant population in spite of Muslim rule; by the late tenth century the country was all but autonomous. A Kurdish officer, Saladin (1137–1193), took control of Egypt in 1169 and later expanded his domain into Syria and Mesopotamia. Islam spread to the sub-Saharan regions of Niger, Sudan, and elsewhere. In Iran, which also became largely independent of the caliphate by the late ninth century, a succession of Muslim dynasties finally yielded to the Seljuk Turks, which expanded both into Anatolia (Turkey) and far to the east, facilitating the spread of Sunni Islam into India. It was the Seljuk Turks who initially established schools (*madrasas*) to foster the dissemination of Sunni Islam.

Some attention should be paid to slavery in the early centuries of Islam. The institution was endemic, but limited in extent. However, slave trading was widespread, as Muslims imported black slaves to cultivate sugar cane fields in Mesopotama in the seventh and eighth centuries; slavery then spread to Egypt and elsewhere. From at least the seventh century, Muslims had been seizing and trading slaves from Nubia (Ethiopia) and, by the mid-eighth century, from Sudan. The trans-Saharan slave trade developed at the same time, reaching a peak between the years 900–1400, a period in which at least 3.4 million slaves were sold.

B. The Basic Principles of Islam

The specifics of Islamic doctrine vary depending on the sect to which a devotee subscribes. Certain principles are universal among all Muslims, such as the notion that God created the universe *ex nihilo;* the Quran goes on to assert that Allah is continually at work in keeping the universe and everything in it operating (16:8f.). Also extant from the very beginning of Islam is the emphasis on human beings as *creatures*—entities created by God and hence subordinate to him. The very word *Islam* means "surrender" or "submission"—i.e., submission of one's own will to the will of God. Such submission leads, theoretically, to humility and other beneficial moral beliefs. God is constantly keeping a kind of balance sheet on every human being, for the time when humans will face God at the Day of Judgment for consignment to heaven or hell.

And yet, the doctrinal disputes that were present almost from the beginning led, by the early eighth century, to the development of the *sunna* (the word means "path"), whereby a "harmonious community" (*jama'a*) was sought that would minimise internal conflicts among the various sects. These Sunnis deprecated conflicts among Muslims, believing that battles should only be waged against "infidels"—by whom they specifically designated those who rejected monotheism. As such, the Sunnis evolved the five pillars of Islam, as embodied in a document called the Hadith of Gabriel:

1. the proclamation that there is no god but Allah and that Muhammad is the messenger of Allah;
2. the necessity of praying five times a day to the Great Mosque in Mecca;
3. the payment of a yearly tithe to some representative of the Islamic state, usually amounting to approximately 2.5% of one's liquid assets;
4. the observation of the festival of Ramadan, which stipulates a month-long fast;
5. the yearly pilgrimage to Mecca.

In addition, there are six pillars of the faith:

1. belief in Allah;
2. belief in Allah's angels;
3. belief in Allah's revealed books (which include the Psalms of David, the NT, and other texts);
4. belief in Allah's messengers (not only Muhammad but also, on a lesser level, Jesus, John the Baptist, and others);
5. belief in the Day of Judgment;
6. belief in Allah's foreknowledge.

In most Islamic communities, from an early period, politics, law, and religion were fused. In Islam, all law is regarded as of divine origin because it derives from pronouncements in the Quran; but many of its specifics come from the *sunna. Shariah* is the global concept of sacred law; *fiqh* is the interpretation of the law in individual cases. This distinction roughly corresponds to the Islamic belief that law is a fusion of divine revelation and human reason. Shariah also extends into the sphere of moral values. In practice there is a fivefold range of behaviours: obligatory, recommended, permissible, reprehensible, and forbidden.

The splintering of Islam into Sunnis and Shiites rested not merely on disagreement as to the line of succession stemming from Muhammad; the Shiites evolved the notion that the imam (Islamic leader) must be a descendant of Ali, and his pronouncements were regarded as divine; Sunnis rejected such a claim, restricting divine status only to the Quran and the *hadith.* For Shiites, this means that the imam is both a political and a religious leader, in contrast to the caliph, who ruled over both believers and non-believers. But the Abbasid caliphs, adhering to Sunnism, made their own claim to legitimacy by appealing to the roots of Islam, maintaining that it was Abbas (i.e., al-Abbas ibn Abd al-Muttalib [566?–653], Muhammad's uncle) who was the source of the caliphate. Shiites understandably rejected this interpretation and were persecuted.

The Shiites, however, hindered their own cause by splitting into a number of sects and factions. The major split occurred between the Imami (Twelvers)—a quietist group that asserted that, as an infant, the twelfth imam went into hiding in 874 and that upon his return he would lead all Muslims in preparation for the Day of Judgment—and the Ismailis, a more activist sect that believed that the imam was still present even if hidden. The Ismailis gained power in Yemen, North Africa, Egypt, and elsewhere. Yet another Shiite sect, the Fatimids, established a capital city, Cairo, in Egypt, in the late tenth century.

The Kharijites were a more militant sect, appealing to those verses in the Quran that call for battling unbelievers (e.g., 4:76). They accordingly formed their own communities apart from the Umayyad caliphate. In the ninth century yet another sect, Sufism, emerged. It constituted a kind of fundamentalist movement that decreed the total submission of the ego to God and the rejection of contemporary rationalistic elaborations of Islamic theology (for which see the next section) and a return to what it believed to be the doctrines advocated by Muhammad. To the Sufis, strict observance of Islamic law was the only sure path to faith. In some senses the Sufis were combating such movements as the Qadarites, which sought to establish greater freedom of the will for human beings while nonetheless maintaining the central principle of God's all-encompassing power over creation.

C. Politics, Society, and the Church in Mediaeval Europe

It is impossible to understand the power exercised by the Catholic Church in Europe from the seventh to the fifteenth century without an awareness of the social, political, and cultural developments that resulted from the "fall" of the Roman Empire in the West and the gradual weakening of the Byzantine Empire in the East. The decline of trade in the West (chiefly focused on luxury goods designed for consumption by the church and wealthy noblemen) and of urban life led to the proliferation of "domains" operated by noblemen (counts) who ruled over tenants living in villages. Government was radically decentralised, as each domain became largely self-sufficient—economically, socially, and legally. This system was a natural development of the stipulation in the later Roman Empire whereby both landowners and tenants were obliged to remain on their property and never leave it. Now, however, the land did not belong to the tenant but to the nobleman or the church. This was the institution of serfdom. Serfs were obliged to ensure that their descendants also remain on the land in perpetuity. Slavery also existed, and the distinction between serfs and actual slaves was minimal. Meanwhile, a king's army consisted of vassals—soldiers who have taken an oath of loyalty to the king. Many vassals themselves owned property, and the more important vassals became counts who themselves had vassals. This was the feudal system. Both serfdom and feudalism originated for the sake of protection in the absence of a strong central government. The king therefore lost power to the counts, especially once the bequeathal of their lands to their (male) offspring became an accepted practice.

The Catholic church's role in this system was ubiquitous and multifaceted. In a world where belief in Christianity was all but universal, it was assumed that these social conditions were ordained by God. Monasteries emerged as the chief source of the church's power. They gained large plots of land, with many tenants to cultivate them. The church was also one of the major slave-owning institutions in the mediaeval era, chiefly by virtue of the extensive lands it owned. A church decree of 743 stated that Christian slaves could not be sold to pagans; but Jews and pagans were regularly sold to Christians, including the clergy.

By the early eighth century, the see of Rome was attempting to claim primacy over all Christendom, since several of the other major sees—Antioch, Jerusalem, and Alexandria—had fallen to the Muslims. The perilousness and fragility of life made many believe that they were living in the sixth or penultimate age of Christianity, and that the second coming of Jesus was imminent.

The iconic coronation of Charlemagne on Christmas Day 800 by Pope Leo III symbolised the intertwining of church and state in Europe; it initiated the Holy Roman Empire. The event was, however, the culmination of the Franks' centuries-long struggle to gain control of Roman Gaul. Charlemagne's father, Pepin the Short (r. 751–68), had overthrown the Merovingian dynasty and sought legitimacy from the pope. Charlemagne, becoming king of the Franks in 768, had ousted the Lombards in 774 at the behest of Pope Hadrian. Among the figures in Charlemagne's court at Aix-la-Chapelle (Aachen) was Alcuin (735?–810), an English deacon who promulgated the study of ancient literature--exclusively in Latin, since knowledge of Greek had lapsed in the West. By this time Christian theologians had subsumed the history of Greece and Rome within Christian history. To be sure, Alcuin and others deprecated the ancient writers for their paganism, but they nevertheless copied manuscripts of their work and therefore assisted in the preservation of their texts. They established the Bible as well as the Church Fathers as authoritative texts—but also found in these documents clues that secular authority must be obeyed, because the king had been chosen by God (and, now, had been anointed by religious authorities). The tensions between the church and kings would fuel many of the difficulties the church would face in the remaining centuries of the mediaeval era.

In 910, Duke William I of Aquitaine founded the Abbey of Cluny in central France. He made it entirely independent of secular authority, unlike most other churches, which were still under the control of lay noblemen. Cluniac orders spread across Europe. By the turn of the millennium, the papacy felt the need for significant reforms. Many parish priests, especially in rural areas, openly had wives or concubines, with no awareness that they were violating canon law. Oftentimes these priests would bequeath their positions to their offspring. Their educational attainments were generally low. Accordingly, the papacy made efforts to outlaw simony (the purchase of ecclesiastical offices) and to enforce a celibate priesthood. Both simony and a married priesthood were condemned by Pope Leo IX (1049–54), but the campaign against married priests was not completed until the Second Lateran Council of 1139.

But Leo's main purpose was to make the papacy independent of secular rule—chiefly as a way of resisting such rulers' attempts to place pliant clerics in positions of authority. But his emphasis on papal authority had the effect of engendering a break with the eastern wing of the church—a break initiated by his insistence that the Byzantine churches use Latin in the churches in southern Italy. This led to the first Great Schism in 1054, whereby Michael I Cerularius, patriarch of Constantinople, parted ways with the see of Rome.

Leo's campaign was taken up by Pope Gregory VII (1073–85), one of the most dominant and controversial popes of the mediaeval era. He decreed immense powers to the pope—including, remarkably, the power to depose emperors and the infallibility of the Roman church. When Henry IV (Holy Roman Emperor, 1084–1105) attempted to install his chosen candidate as archbishop of Milan, Gregory excommunicated him and deposed him twice (1076 and 1080). But Gregory's opponents claimed he had not been properly appointed pope and chose Clement III as his replacement. Henry's army occupied Rome in 1084; Gregory fled and died a year later. But his cause would be taken up later by Pope Urban II (1088–99).

D. Interaction of Christians and Muslims

As early as the mid-seventh century, Islam came to the attention of Christian theologians. John of Damascus, although he initially referred to Muhammad as the Antichrist, later moderated his views and sought some sort of dialogue between the two religions; not entirely surprisingly, he was condemned in a synod in 754 for being too "Saracen-minded."[4] For the next several centuries, Christians paid little attention to Islam, some regarding it either as a Christian heresy or as a pagan superstition. But it is uncanny how many of the same theological issues cropped up in Islam and Christianity during the mediaeval period—to say nothing of political and military encounters between the two religions throughout Europe, the Mediterranean, and the Near East.

The theological contortions in which Islamic theologians engaged from as early as the late seventh century were, as with Christianity, a result of the simultaneous attribution to God of the traits of omnipotence, omniscience, and benevolence. In essence, Islam was simply unable to harmonise these traits—or, at any rate, unable to make a plausible account of the existence of either natural or human evil. The Quran itself ties itself in knots on the issue, especially in its treatment of Eblis/Satan. It is of interest to note that God banished Satan from paradise *prior* to his temptation of Adam and Eve; his banishment is explicitly attributed to his failure to prostrate himself before God as all other creatures were doing (7:10–12). There was, accordingly, a persistent tradition in Islam toward Manichaeism: Satan was regarded as an all-but-equal antagonist of God. Islam did, however, eschew the concept of original sin, declaring that everyone has the opportunity to accept God's direction and attain paradise.

One of the most vexing problems in early Islamic theology was

4. "Saracen" was a term used by Christians to denote Muslims of Arabic, Persian, and Turkic origin.

the dispute between free will and predestination; and it is here that the problem of evil becomes most acute, as it does in Christianity. Those who advocated predestination maintained that, at the very outset of creation, God had already decided who would be consigned to hell or to paradise. Theologians associated with Jahm ibn Safwan (696–745) came close to embracing a kind of religious determinism that denies humans the power to perform any acts independent of God's will. And yet, how this doctrine—in light of the plain fact that human beings do commit "evil" acts (however these may be defined)—can be squared with the notion that "It was intrinsic to God that He could not generate anything but the best"[5] is not at all clear.

The issue seemed to be settled, in an unusual manner, by Ahmad ibn Hanbal (780–855), who openly acknowledged that humanity's evil deeds originate with God. Evidently, Hanbal was so intent on preserving God's omnipotence and power of predestination that he was willing to subvert God's benevolence (although in his mind he did not believe he was doing so). Other theologians attempted to establish some kind of middle ground between predestination and free will, although their arguments do not escape the paradoxes inherent in such an accommodation.

The theologian Abu l-Hasan al-Ashari (874?–936) doubled down on the issue of God's omnipotence, maintaining that all "created" entities are entirely dependent on God, right down to their material attributes. It is possible that al-Ashari was inclined toward this view in opposition to a series of "rationalising" philosophers who in his view were diluting both the omnipotence and the personal nature of God. Jahm ibn Safwan, for example, was embarrassed at the Quran's mention of God's "hands," "face," and other anthropomorphic attributes and therefore engaged in an allegorising tactic, asserting that these attributes are not to be taken literally. In his view they are merely indications that God is everywhere and is also a single indivisible entity. But this stance makes it problematical how anyone (including Muhammad) could ever have had a direct experience of God. The philosopher Abu al-Kindi (801?–873) went further in making God an abstract force, claiming that the universe was the work of a single homogeneous cause that could be equated with the God of the Quran. But such a view (possibly influenced by

5. Nagel, *The History of Islamic Theology* 115.

his studies of Greek philosophy) reduced God to a kind of "first cause" and not a personal creator, and also implicitly rendered unnecessary the revelation embodied in the Quran. Al-Kindi went so far as to suggest that philosophical knowledge could replace revelation altogether. His work was developed by Abu Nasr al-Farabi (870?–951?), who explicitly identified God with a first cause.

Ibn Sina (980?–1037; known in the West as Avicenna) derived much of his thought from al-Farabi, articulating a "proof" of the existence of God that has been called the "necessary existent"—i.e., an entity that *must* exist in order to create other entities in the universe, which are only contingent. We shall see that, in the West, Anselm came up with an approximately similar argument; but all such arguments appear to rely on mere juggling of words, and that is exactly the criticism that another Islamic theologian, Ibn Rushd (1126–1198; known in the West as Averroes), made. He declared that the existence of God must be established by an appeal to the external world, especially since it is difficult to identify an abstract entity with the specific, personal nature of the god Allah as described in the Quran.

As we have seen, al-Ashar was opposed to this entire line of thinking, and his disciples—called Asharites—condemned Avicenna and others because their belief that philosophical logic could validate Islamic doctrines was "irreconcilable with the Quranic concept of God's unlimited power and inscrutable ways."[6] In particular, the theologian Abu Hamid al-Ghazali (1058–1111), an Asharite, declared that any philosophers who asserted the eternity of the world (which implicitly denied God's creation of it) and denied the bodily resurrection of the dead on the Day of Judgment should be declared heretics. Al-Ghazali went on to maintain that since philosophers have not proved the immortality of the soul or the bodily resurrection of the dead, all we can do is rely on scripture for these key doctrines. Averroes, who was profoundly influenced by Aristotle and wrote many commentaries on his work, attempted to rebut many of the Asharites' contentions in his attempt to harmonise religion and philosophy. He interpreted certain passages in the Quran as suggesting that the universe did in fact exist from eternity but that its *form* did not—in other words, that God created

6. Majid Fakhry, "Philosophy and Theology from the Eighth Century C.E. to the Present," in Esposito, *Oxford History of Islam* 282.

the forms we know. He claimed that no text in the Quran could be found stating that God was ever "alone" or that he ever created the universe *ex nihilo.*

Many of these same controversies emerged among Christian philosophers and theologians of the early mediaeval era. As early as the ninth century, Christian thinkers became anxious to "prove" the existence of God by philosophical reasoning rather than merely by revelation, although there was also a countervailing tendency to regard such philosophical proofs as illegitimate. Consider the curious case of John Scotus Erigena (800?–877?), who seems to have believed that philosophy's exclusive goal was to facilitate understanding of scripture. Many of his more peculiar views—strongly influenced by Neoplatonism—rested upon the unproven and unprovable assumptions that God is simultaneously infinite, immaterial, and benevolent. This led Erigena to believe that God was not comprehensible even to himself, let alone to us mere mortals. It is not only human beings but the entire universe that has "fallen" as a result of original sin.

Then there is Anselm (1033?–1109), a devotee of Augustine. His claim to fame is the creation of an "ontological proof" of the existence of God. It runs as follows. God is the being "than which none greater can be thought." If it be asserted that this is a conception that only exists in the human brain, Anselm counters that such an entity must exist in reality, because there will always be some greater conception of God that the brain can envision.

This is the kind of "proof" that gives both philosophy and theology a deservedly bad name. In essence, Anselm is playing tricks with words—although some philosophically naïve Christian historians right down to the present day seem to find his "proof" a marvel of subtle reasoning.[7] Refutations of it are in fact easy to come by. Firstly, it becomes painfully obvious that Anselm has begun with a presupposition that the God he is envisioning must exist, chiefly in order to salvage the value and authority of scripture. Secondly, his conception of God is a dubious one, since it is eminently possible to imagine gods who are not "greater than can be thought," but who are of limited powers (as most of the Greco-Roman

7. Anselm was able to "devise a rigorous, logical, revelation-free proof for the existence of God, one with which philosophers and theologians are wrestling a millennium after his death." Madigan, *Medieval Christianity* 260.

gods were). But doesn't Anselm's proof apply to the Christian god? We have already seen that the simultaneous attribution of omnipotence, omniscence, and benevolence to God is highly problematical and results in insuperable difficulties and paradoxes that have not been resolved to this day.

But there are two overriding objections to Anselm's proof. One is that it conjures up an entity out of thin air without even the attempt to find it in the external world. This was precisely the criticism of Averroes. Even more significantly, this abstract "god of the philosophers" does not bear the faintest resemblance to the personal, all-loving god of the Bible, so it would seem unlikely to convince anyone who is not already committed to belief in God or inspire anyone to worship such an entity.

The main interactions of Muslims and Christians in the Middle Ages were, of course, the Crusades. Just as the Muslims took advantage of the weakening of the Byzantine Empire to capture Jerusalem and the surrounding area in 636, so did Christian forces temporarily wrest Jerusalem away from the Muslims more than four centuries later at a time when their own empire was teetering in various parts of Europe. It was, in fact, in the course of a fleeting revival that the Byzantine emperor Alexios I Komnenos (r. 1081–1118), after the Byzantines had earlier taken much of Anatolia from the Seljuk Turks, appealed to Pope Urban II for assistance. It was at this time that Christian leaders conveniently adopted the belief that the Holy Land "belonged" to Christians and that Muslim control of it was illegitimate. Exactly why God allowed the Muslims to exercise such control for nearly half a millennium was never explained. In any event, in response to a council summoned at Clermont in 1095 asking for merecenaries to aid Byzantium, tens of thousands responded; the clergy throughout Europe took up the cause. This hastily assembled army did manage to retake Antioch and then Jerusalem on 15 July 1099—an event that was seen as a sign of divine favour. The Holy Land was thereupon parcelled out among various European leaders. All this was a boon to the church, which had been seeking to harness people's emotions to the defeat of the "heathen" throughout Europe and the Near East. Needless to say, many joined the Crusades to escape the harsh economic conditions at home and, concomitantly, to gain whatever booty they could pilfer from the lands they conquered.

The capture of Jerusalem was, however, relatively short-lived.

Tensions developed between the Crusaders and the Byzantine church, and the Muslims regrouped under the leadership of Saladin, who took back Jerusalem in 1187. There does not seem to have been any talk of God's divine plan among Christian thinkers at this time. Several subsequent crusades sought to regain the iconic city. The third crusade led to a truce with Saladin in 1192 that left Jerusalem in his hands. The fourth crusade (begun in 1198) ended up focusing on Constantinople as a means of ensuring Catholic control over the city. Christians took control of the city in 1204, initiating the so-called Latin Empire (1204–61). But Christians hurt their cause by carrying off huge amounts of booty. The remaining crusades (there were a total of six of them) accomplished little, and Jerusalem was never retaken.

The deleterious effects of the Crusades were manifold. They were the true triggers of the overt and sustained hostility between Christians and Muslims that has persisted down to the present day. In places where the two religious groups coexisted, each attempted to develop its own laws and live as a separate community. Paradoxically, the Crusades also gave an increased impetus to the antisemitism latent in Christianity from its origins. Why this would have been so, given the explicit goal of the Crusaders to "liberate" Jerusalem, is not entirely clear. In some inexplicable fashion Jews were identified with Muslims as enemies of the (Christian) god—and, inevitably, their role as "killers of Christ" was once again emphasised. It may well be that these were merely covers for greed and envy—that is, the resentment that Christian communities in Europe felt at the dominance of Jewish moneylenders. But this very circumstance was itself the product of a different sort of antisemitism whereby the mediaeval guilds openly excluded Jews from participating in other occupations. And greed—or the desire to free themselves from debts owed to Jews—does not fully explain why so many Christians conducted a series of pogroms throughout Europe beginning in the late eleventh century, even extending into England a century later.

It was at this time that the "blood libel" (the belief that Jews committed ritual torture and murder of Christian children) emerged as a powerful force motivating antisemitism. It appears that Christians had forgotten that, centuries earlier, the Romans had accused the adherents of the new faith of cannibalism when they heard of the nature and function of the eucharist. In fact, Jews were accused of stealing and polluting the communion wafer so that it would bleed. In essence, this canard was a fabricated re-enactment of the crucifixion and also, in the minds of Christians, a testament to the truth of scripture.

At the Fourth Lateran Council (1215), called by Pope Innocent III, a number of canons severely restricting the liberties of Jews were enacted. Later, marriage and sexual relations between Jews and Christians were prohibited; violators were subject to the death penalty. There were repeated attempts to expel Jews from European countries beginning as early as 1096.

E. Muslim and Christian Science and Philosophy

The one positive force in the interaction of Muslims and Christians in the Middle Ages was the rediscovery of some of the notable works of classical thought. Greek philosophical and theological texts were initially transmitted to the Islamic world when the Muslims captured Alexandria in 641. It was then that the works of Aristotle, the Neoplatonist Porphyry, and others were translated—first into Syriac, then into Arabic. This activity advanced in the early ninth century under the influence of the Abbasid caliph al-Mamum (r. 813–33). Almost from the beginning of Islam, efforts were made to separate scientific enquiry from religious doctrine. As Ahmad Dallal has noted, "In many ways science in the Muslim world was a secular enterprise, and religion neither made an enemy of science nor championed its cause to the extreme."[8]

Muslim scientists and philosophers made good use of translated Greek material. But it should not be assumed that this material directly inspired Arabic scientific progress; the translation of Greek scientific work functioned concurrently with original Arabic research. This was particularly true in the realm of medicine, where Greek medical texts (notably the works of Galen) were translated and original treatises composed as early as the eighth century. It is true that many Arabic writers assumed Galen's theory of the four humours; but others developed medical practices based on actual diagnosis and observation. Chief among these was Abu Bakr al-Razi (864?–925?), a Persian physician

8. Ahmad Dallal, "Science Medicine, and Technology: The Making of a Scientific Culture," in Esposito, *Oxford History of Islam* 213.

who conducted controlled experiments to gauge the relative efficacy of various treatments. Abu al-Qasim al-Zahrawi (936–1013) was a pioneer in surgery. Avicenna wrote the most exhaustive book on the theory of medicine up to the seventeenth century. Ibn al-Nafis (1213–1288) made striking advances in the study of the circulation of the blood, in spite of the Islamic prohibition against dissection.

Astronomy was extensively pursued, as was astrology; but many astronomers condemned astrology as a false science. Some Indian and Persian astronomical works were translated into Arabic in the late eighth century, and the discovery of Ptolemy's *Almagest* in the early ninth century proved immensely influential. While many Arabic treatises were mere summaries of or commentaries on Ptolemy, others sought to verify or correct his observations. Arabic astronomers made extensive use of mathematics (including trigonometry) in conjunction with observations. Among the most notable of these was Abu al-Biruni (973–1050?), a mathematical astronomer who pioneered empirical observation over metaphysical theorising. It was al-Biruni who proposed that planets proceed in an elliptical and not circular rotation. No Arabic astronomer, however, is known to have questioned the geocentric theory.

In pure mathematics, Arabs adapted the Hindu numerical system (i.e., the use of nine digits plus zero) and passed it on to the West. Arabs essentially invented algebra (the very word is Arabic) in the early ninth century. Progress was made in optics, and Ibn al-Haytham (965?–1940?) discovered the role of light in allowing vision to occur—a problem that, as we have seen, stumped the Greek Atomists among others.

The work of Aristotle and other Greek philosophers began filtering back into the West in the late eleventh century, when Christians retook Sicily and portions of Spain from the Muslims. Since knowledge of Greek had largely been lost in the Latin West, the works appeared in Arabic translations and were translated from Arabic into Latin; later, the original Greek texts were rediscovered. One of the most prolific translators of these texts—including the work of Aristotle, Archimedes, Euclid, and most notably Ptolemy's *Almagest*—was Gerard of Cremona (1114–1187); his translations of medical and astronomical treatises were particularly influential.

There was, in Europe, extensive scientific investigation during the mediaeval era, but relatively little of it challenged the dominant

Christian worldview. But to the extent that it laid the groundwork for the revolutionary findings of the Renaissance, it is worth at least brief mention. For example, the Venerable Bede (672–735), the English monk best known for the *Historia Ecclesiastica Gentis Anglorum* (Ecclesiastical History of the English People), wrote a substantial number of scientific treatises that were widely read during the Middle Ages. In his *De Rerum Natura* (presumably a deliberate echo of Lucretius' celebrated work expounding the Epicurean philosophy) he stated that the earth was a sphere rather than a cylinder or disk. Gerbert d'Aurillac (945?–1003), who became Pope Sylvester II (999–1003), may have been the first in the West to use Hindu-Arabic numerals—work that was carried on by the Italian mathematician Fibonacci (Leonardo Bonacci, 1170?–1250?).

Robert Grosseteste (1168?–1253) is a figure of some interest. Although an English clergyman (Bishop of Lincoln), he used his study of Aristotle to propound new theories of causation, even proposing a theory of verification and falsification in the investigation of natural phenomena—an approach that would ultimately bear fruit with the advent of empiricism several centuries later. His own experimental work chiefly focused on light and optics, with mathematics as a foundation. He parted with Aristotle in believing the heavenly bodies to be constituted, not of aether, but of the four elements—an advance of sorts. But he did not doubt God's creation of the universe and criticised those who questioned the biblical account of creation; nor did he doubt the validity of Ptolemaic astronomy.

Peter of Albano (1250–1313?) was apparently the first European to maintain that the "fixed" stars are not in fact fixed but move through space. But he may have done so only because he believed these bodies to be guided by cosmic spirits of some sort. He was later accused of being a magician. Albertus Magnus (Albert the Great, 1200?–1280) was a pioneer in the realms of biology, botany, and other areas. Like Aquinas, he sought to fuse Aristotle with Christianity, always deferring to the latter in instances where the two conflicted.

Albertus's pupil, the English philosopher and polymath Roger Bacon (1214?–1292), has long exercised a fascination in the West, chiefly on account of his apparent prediction of technological advancements many centuries before their advent; the science fiction writer James Blish wrote an historical novel, *Doctor Mirabilis* (1964), depicting Bacon as a pioneering theoretical scientist who anticipated not only Newton but even Einstein. It is true that, in a letter written around 1250, *De Mirabile Potestate Artis et Naturae* (On the Incredible Power of Magic and Nature), he conjectures the future discovery of self-propelling ships, flying machines, and automobiles, while in the *Opus Maius* (1267; Greater Work) he envisions more realistic inventions such as the telescope, the microscope, and gunpowder; but, although he did landmark work in optics, the calendar, and other areas (influenced to some degree by Albertus as well as by Grosseteste), his theological views were relatively conventional. To the extent that he criticised the theologians of his day, he did so because he believed they were insufficiently educated in the sciences. Bacon did propose that the foundations of knowledge should be based on "experimental science" (*scientia experimentalis*—the title of a section of *Opus Maius*); but he still regarded theology as the "mistress" of the sciences, "to which the remaining sciences are vitally necessary and without which [theology] cannot reach its end."[9] It is only through all these sciences that we can know about creation, and hence, by a corollary that Bacon believed to be inevitable, the Creator.

More relevant to our purposes is the work of Jean Buridan (1295?–1358?), a French philosopher whose extensive work in mathematics and physics allowed him to develop the concept of *impetus*—the notion that a body that has been impelled by some force does not require constant contact with that force to continue its motion, in contrast to the Aristotelian view. This anticipation of one of the Newtonian laws of motion had in fact been developed in a rudimentary form as far back as the work of John Philoponus (490?–570?), a Christian theologian who expounded his theory in a commentary on Aristotle's *Physics*. But Buridan developed the idea in considerably greater detail, in the course of which he even approached Newtonian conceptions of inertia and gravity. He then applied this principle to the heavenly bodies: "For it could be said that God, in creating the world, set each celestial orb in motion . . . and, in setting them in motion, he gave them an impetus capable of keeping them in motion without there being any need of his moving them any more."[10] This is, of course, an early form of Deism, although it would be more than three centuries before the doctrine was

9. Quoted in Clegg, *The First Scientist* 120.
10. Quoted in Freely, *Before Galileo* 164.

elaborated by philosophers of the seventeenth century.

Buridan toyed with the idea that the sun is the centre of the universe; and his disciple, Nicole Oresme (1320?–1382), conjectured that the earth might rotate on its axis. But ultimately he rejected both of these radical ideas because they were contrary to the Christian doctrine that God had established the earth as a fixed object around which the universe revolves.

We cannot leave this period without addressing the work of Moses ben Maimon (1138–1204), known as Maimonides, the greatest Jewish philosopher of religion before Spinoza. Born in Cordoba, he and his family were compelled by Muslim incursions to flee Spain for Morocco and then Egypt, where he remained for the bulk of his life. He ultimately gained a reputation as a leading rabbinic authority in the Muslim world. As such, Maimonides took a somewhat more lenient view of Islam than of Christianity; it is only the latter that is idolatrous and otherwise heretical. But Christianity had some virtues as a result of its adoption of the Hebrew Bible as part of its canonical scripture.

Maimonides is known for two major works, the *Mishneh Torah,* a massive revision and clarification of *halakhah* (Jewish law), written in 1168–77, and the *Guide of the Perplexed,* a series of letters written in Arabic and completed in 1191. An earlier work, the *Commentary on the Mishnah* (written 1166–68), established thirteen basic tenets that Jews must believe if they are not to be regarded as heretics or apostates. This was a revolutionary step in Judaism, since "the sages of the Talmud never formulated principles of faith. Membership in the community was determined primarily by reference to norms of conduct that manifest loyalty to the *halakhah,* and a fair degree of diversity was allowed with respect to matters of opinion and belief."[11]

What led Maimonides to take this step? His immersion in the thought of Aristotle led me to believe that the immortality of the soul could only be achieved by understanding the truth about the universe (as embodied in his tenets), not merely by observance of the actions sanctioned by the Torah.

The *Mishneh Torah* is an attempt to cut through the innumerable debates over the *halakhah* in Talmudic literature and also to establish

11. Halbertal, *Maimonides: Life and Thought* 136–37.

a theological foundation for the laws Mainonides lays down. Here, he "proves" the existence of an eternally existing god by appealing to the constant revolutions of something he calls the "Sphere" (evidently, the universe conceived spherically), which requires some cause to move it. The universe is therefore also eternal. In this formulation there is an implicit rejection of the miracles of the HB that, for Maimonides, would constitute a disruption in the chain of causation—but in so doing, the doctrine also appears, radically, to reject God's intervention in the history of the Jews as recounted in the Pentateuch. Maimonides also denied the efficacy of magic, divination, sorcery, and astrology. Not surprisingly, later commentators criticised him for this stance. He replied to some of these criticisms in the *Letter on Astrology*.

The *Guide of the Perplexed* is the culmination of Maimonides' religious theorisings. It is directed at a relatively small audience of educated Jews who are nonetheless "perplexed" by possible tensions beween traditional doctrines of Judaism and the findings of contemporary philosophy and science. In this work (as in its predecessor), Maimonides broaches the notion of "true" beliefs (which only a philosopher can understand) and "necessary and useful" beliefs (which may be false but are needed to preserve social cohesion). This anticipation of Voltaire and other Enlightenment philosophers is striking, as Maimonides rejects such notions as the corporeality and anthropomorphism of God as well as the very notion of a personal god who will dole out rewards to the good and punishments to the wicked. Maimonides insisted that such beliefs are necessary in order that the ignorant masses not fall into atheism (and, hence, bad behaviour); they are incapable of understanding the "true" god of the philosophers, so must be kept in line by these myths.

The problem with such a view is that it requires Maimonides to reinterpret every single passage in the HB pointing to these mythical attributes of God as allegorical or metaphorical—solely on the basis of his own presuppositions of the nature of deity. Maimonides goes farther, saying that any language that implies that God has a multiplicity of attributes must also be considered metaphorical (on the presupposition that God must be conceived as a unity). His belief in a transcendent god separate from his creation required him to reinterpret still more passages that suggested otherwise.

Maimonides devotes many chapters in the *Guide* to the question of whether God created the world *ex nihilo* or whether the world has existed for eternity. After wrestling with the issue, he appears to side with the *ex nihilo* theory (in contrast to his assertion in the *Commentary on the Mishnah*)—but he may have done so to preserve other essential elements of Judaism, such as revelation, prophecy, reward and punishment, and miracles, which all depend on God's will and not his mere existence. In asserting, however, that God has a "will," he conveniently maintains that it is in no way analogous to human will, and therefore it cannot be used as an argument against God's perfection and unity.

In dealing with the problem of evil, Maimonides essentially states that evil does not exist. He was not the first to do so and would not be the last. But at least he did not blame the victims for the evils (natural or human-generated) that befell them, nor did he believe that there will be a reckoning in the afterlife. Maimonides adopted the weak argument that the evils faced by human beings are the inevitable concomitants of human life and that they represent "privations" of their opposites—for example, illness is just the absence of health. But he is apparently unaware that such a stance does not justify the view that evils don't exist—such privations can be very real to the sufferer; more significantly, this doctrine surely makes a mockery of divine omnipotence.

In the end, Maimonides failed in eliminating disputes over the *halakhah,* which flourished with redoubled force in the centuries after his death; and he also failed in his attempt to allegorise away the literal meaning of the HB. His significance rests in his being one of the first thinkers in the West to wrestle with the intractable conflict between the advance of knowledge and a literal acceptance of scripture—a conflict that would only grow when learning and science revived during the Renaissance.

F. The Rise of Scholasticism

By the mid-eleventh century in Europe, population and trade were increasing. There was increased cultivation of land and a greater diversity of crops grown on those lands. Benedictine and Cistercian monasteries began to till land that had lain fallow for centuries. Noblemen enticed their tenants to work the land by granting them greater freedoms. Large villages became the focus of life for many. Goods once more arrived from the Far East, the Indies, and the Levant. Flanders and Italy became the most important trade centres. In the absence of a strong central government, many of the cities in these regions became largely self-governing, devising their own laws. The cities became fiercely independent, seeing others as rivals; battles frequently broke out among them for political and commercial supremacy.

For centuries after the "fall" of the Roman Empire, monasteries had a monopoly on education; understandably, the focus of education was largely or exclusively on scripture, the Church Fathers, and related subjects. Pagan authors were read only in extracts and only to enhance proficiency in Latin. But the revitalisation of cities led to an increased demand for learning of all sorts. It is unsurprising that some monasteries became hostile to the presence of students who were not engaged in religious education; this happened especially at the schools run by the Abbey of Cluny. The Cistercians came to believe that the "urban schools" that had been established in cities were hotbeds of religious scepticism. Nevertheless, some schools developed a reputation for excellence in certain areas. These schools were still under the control of local churches or cathedrals, and theology was widely taught; but so were other subjects.

The university as an institution developed from these cathedral schools. Among the most prominent during this time were the University of Paris (founded in 1150; later known as the Sorbonne) and the University of Oxford (founded no later than 1096); Cambridge was founded in 1209. The term *universitas* was the Latin word for guild, and these institutions constituted a guild of instructors on a wide range of subjects. Instruction was exclusively in Latin, the international language of scholarship. The emergence of these institutions led to the development of that branch of Christian theology called scholasticism.

The term scholasticism, used to designate some of the central figures of Christian philosophy and theology during the twelfth to fourteenth centuries, simply indicates that these scholars emerged out of the environment of the burgeoning university culture that was being fostered throughout Europe. One of the earliest such figures—whom some historians regard as "pre-scholastic"—was Peter Abelard (1079?–1142), whose extraordinary life—involving his open love affair with an unmarried young woman, Héloise, whom he was tutoring and with whom he had an illegitimate child—is perhaps a bit more interesting than his philosophical contributions, which rest on the treatise *Sic et Non* (For and Against), whose intent was to present arguments for and against the central theological issues of the period. To the extent that he rejected original sin and parted company with Augustine on several other crucial points, and posed the question "Should one believe in God?" as one of the 168 topics for philosophical debate, he may have minimally fostered scepticism; but there is no reason to believe that he in any way intended to inculcate doubt about the existence of the Christian god. Nevertheless, the doctrinaire Catholic Bernard de Clairvaux prosecuted Abelard for heresy in 1141, forcing him to retire to the Abbey of Cluny, where he soon died.

The *Sentences* (*Sententiae*) of Peter Lombard (1096?–1160), published in four books between 1155 and 1158, was a comprehensive summary of Christian doctrine that remained a standard textbook for centuries. In the course of time, scholars began to lecture on the *Sentences* rather than on scripture itself, since Lombard was a strictly orthodox theologian whose treatise had become authoritative. One of those who did so was Thomas Aquinas.

Aquinas (1224?–1273) was born near Naples[12] and became a Dominican friar around 1242.[13] He studied with Albertus Magnus and began teaching at the University of Paris in 1256. His major works are the *Summa contra Gentiles* (approximately translated as "Summary of Arguments against Unbelievers") and *Summa Theologiae* (Summary of Theology). His thought was deeply influenced by his lifelong studies of Aristotle; indeed, a substantial part of his intellectual mission was to utilise Aristotelian principles for the support of Christian dogmas.

Aquinas began with the premise that the Bible is the word of God, and that therefore all philosophy must be subordinate to scripture and must be exercised to elucidate the self-evident truth of revelation—specifically on such points as the existence of God, the role of Jesus Christ as saviour, and other key Catholic doctrines. Such a presupposition vitiates nearly the entirety of his work, since it is apparent that the imposing edifice of

12. The town was Aquino, hence the name Aquinas ("of Aquino") is not a surname. Many scholars therefore refer to him as Thomas and make an adjective or other derivatives of his given name (Thomist, etc.).

13. The Dominicans (founded in 1216 and initially led by Dominic of Guzman [1170–1221]) and the Franciscans (founded in 1209 by Francis of Assisi [1181?–1226]) were two important orders within the Catholic church during the later mediaeval era.

his philosophical argument is exclusively directed toward establishing what he has already come to believe is the truth. And while Aquinas claims to be prepared to acknowledge the theoretical possibility that God does not exist, he quickly dismisses the idea with the childish insult from the OT, "The impious fool says in his heart, 'There is no God'" (Ps. 14:1).

Aquinas became celebrated—and, apparently, continues to be celebrated—for five proofs—or "ways" (*viae*), as he called them—of the existence of God, based as he believed on pure reason without appeal to scriptural revelation. These proofs are as follows:

1. There must be something that causes motion but does not itself move. This is God.
2. There must be some entity that initiates causation upon other entities but is not itself caused, otherwise there would be an infinite regress. This is God as First Cause.
3. If there are perishable things, there must be something that is imperishable and is the cause of the perishable things. This is God.
4. There are degrees of perfection in things; therefore, there must be some supremely perfect thing, i.e., God.
5. The order and regularity of nature necessitates the existence of a god who created these features in the natural world.

Inexplicably, many Catholic intellectuals still regard these proofs as cogent and, indeed, conclusive proofs of the existence of God (or, at least, of some sort of god); but their refutation is not difficult. The first is an adaptation of Aristotle's Prime Mover and is subject to all the difficulties in that conception. It could, for example, be postulated that there are an infinite number of Prime Movers that produce motion in every single entity in the universe. This may be a cumbersome scenario, but from a logical perspective it is no less sound than the Aristotelian/Thomist conception; indeed, Aristotle himself, as we have seen, postulated dozens of other prime movers subsidiary to the chief Prime Mover. This same criticism applies to the First Cause argument, which many philosophers now regard as a uniquely bad argument. In any event, the Big Bang has essentially negated this proof. There are those who have thought that the Big Bang is itself a sort of god; but if there are any who wish to worship the Big Bang, they are free to do so.

The third and fourth proofs rest upon arbitrary assumptions that are not justified by our experience of nature. The strong probability that every object in the universe will perish at some point—or be reduced to its component atoms—does not in any way necessitate the postulation of a being that does not perish. Similarly, the idea of "perfection" is a purely abstract one based upon our conceptions of what is or is not perfect, and the belief that there is any object attaining utter perfection (even on the assumption that there can be such a thing as degrees of perfection) is entirely gratuitous. The fifth proof would seem to be a more compelling argument *against* the existence of God than the converse, since the order and regularity of nature would appear to suggest that the universe is governed by natural principles that do not require the intervention of a creator. On the earthly scale, the theory of evolution definitively destroyed the derivative argument that the "argument from design" (e.g., the apparent adaptation of the human hand for grasping) is a testimonial to a god or creator who fashioned us in this manner.

The irony is that many of these proofs are, in spite of Aquinas's own belief that he was appealing to nature and hence practising what would now be called a sort of empiricism, precisely the sort of ontological proofs that he himself criticised in rejecting Anselm's proof: there he claimed that verbal juggling is insufficient to justify belief in God, and that the existence or presence of God must be found in the external world. But his own proofs rely to a dangerous degree on exactly such verbal (or conceptual) juggling.

Even though, at one point, Aquinas states that "we cannot know what god is, but only what he is not" (Part I, Question 3), we should not be misled into thinking that he is lapsing into some sort of agnosticism. He is quite convinced that he can demonstrate that God is simple (i.e., not composite), that he cannot change, and that he is "good" (but this is simply a reiteration of his notion of God's "perfection"). But this of course raises the issue of the problem of evil—i.e., why the bad prosper and the good suffer. Aquinas, largely following Augustine, endorses the view that evil is simply a deficiency of the good (*privatio boni*)—there is no such thing, in his mind, as pure evil, not even in the Devil. Natural evil happens when one thing, being what it is (i.e., being "good" because it is fulfilling its own nature), causes something bad to happen to somebody or something else. This would, I imagine, be cold comfort to those who have perished from earthquakes, tornadoes, and other such "natural" evils. Aquinas appears to acknowledge that God is in some sense the "cause" of natural evil; but he weasels out of attributing to God the causation and results of moral evil, or the evil that human beings cause by virtue of their own moral deficiency. In some incomprehensible manner the human beings who perpetrate such evils are the true "causes" of them; and for all that God himself is the "cause" of the very existence of human beings, he is somehow exempt from responsibility in these moral evils. How does this square with Aquinas's assertion of God's omnipotence and omniscience? If "God is almighty because he can do everything that is absolutely possible,"[14] then surely it would have been possible for God to have at least mitigated the appalling amount of both natural and moral evil in the world. But Aquinas somehow manages to believe both in God's foreknowledge of all actions in the universe (i.e., predestination) and in the preservation of an Augustinian form of human free will. We are, it appears, free but are not "independent of God's causal operation."[15]

Having to his satisfaction established that there is a god who created the universe, it is a matter of relative simplicity for him to swallow all the other central features of Christian revelation. He accepts, with some modifications, Augustinian original sin, and therefore requires Jesus Christ to relieve it. And the bulk of *Summa Theologiae* is devoted to a laborious explication of how pretty much everything in the New Testament is philosophically sound and does not depend on revelation for belief.

Aquinas pontificated on all manner of other subjects about which he knew little. He unquestioningly adopted the Aristotelian doctrine of the four elements, incorporating them within a hierarchy of beings in the universe: after God came the angels, followed by human beings, animals, plants, and the four elements. Aquinas also evolved the notion of "natural law," which Catholic theologians still adopt. This is the idea that certain tendencies in human thought and action are "natural" because they purportedly conform to or exemplify "the basic inclinations of our nature. Since the natural tendency of our will is toward the good,

14. Cited in Davies, *The Thought of Thomas Aquinas* 123.
15. Davies 176.

the most general prescription of the natural law is: Do good and avoid evil."[16] It does not appear that Aquinas, or those who follow him on this point, are prepared to admit that many of these "natural" tendencies are the result of social or cultural conditioning and vary widely from culture to culture and from one historical era to the other.

The starry-eyed adoration with which Aquinas is still regarded by many Catholic theologians is a dismaying sign of their philosophical naïveté and of their desperation to seize upon any argument, however fallacious, that would allow them to retain belief in their scripture. But the severe judgment of Bertrand Russell—for all the howls of protest it has evoked—remains today as incisive an indictment of Aquinas's failings as a philosopher and theologian as when it was written nearly seventy years ago:

> There is little of the true philosophic spirit in Aquinas. He does not, like the Platonic Socrates, set out to follow wherever the argument may lead. He is not engaged in an inquiry, the result of which it is impossible to know in advance. Before he begins to philosophize, he already knows the truth; it is declared in the Catholic faith. If he can find apparently rational arguments for some parts of the faith, so much the better; if he cannot, he need only fall back on revelation. The finding of arguments for a conclusion given in advance is not philosophy, but special pleading. I cannot, therefore, feel that he deserves to be put on a level with the best philosophers either of Greece or of modern times.[17]

Incredibly, Aquinas did not escape posthumous censure himself. His doctrines were attacked from many directions, leading to the condemnation of some of his doctrines in 1277. The chief impetus for this condemnation was the resurgence of Averroeism in the universities at this time. The central figure in this movement was Siger of Brabant (1240?–1284), who boldly asserted—in line with Aristotle and Averroes—that the universe had existed from eternity (and also, strangely enough, that the human race had existed from eternity), defying those many Islamic and Christian theologians who believed that such a conception was in direct contravention to scripture (both the Bible and the Quran), as it

16. Maurer, *Medieval Philosophy* 188.
17. Russell, *A History of Western Philosophy* 463.

would negate God's creation of the universe. In 1323, however, fifty years after his death, Aquinas's views were rehabilitated; he was canonised by the Catholic church and became a saint.

The English philosopher William of Ockham (1287?–1347), a Franciscn monk, presented a much stronger case against Thomism and the church in general, although once again it is highly unlikely that that was his goal. But in denying that theology is a science at all (since it relies on faith and authority rather than on the accumulation of empirical data), and in asserting that many proofs of the existence of God cannot be definitively "proven" but can only be deemed "reasonable" (specifically in regard to the doctrine of the Prime Mover or First Cause), William may have laid the groundwork for more searching investigations of the soundness of Christian theology. His celebrated "razor"—the principle that explanations of phenomena must be as simple as possible, with all extraneous elements cut away as with a razor—is certainly a valid tool of philosophical logic; but it is doubtful whether he would have been pleased that, with the passing of centuries, God himself would become the greatest casualty of Ockham's razor.

Perhaps even more radical than William of Ockham was Nicholas of Autrecourt (1299?–1369), a French philosopher who cast severe doubt on Aristotle's doctrines and also maintained that the existence of God cannot be proven by natural reason. His ultimate solution was, startlingly, to adopt a version of Democritean atomism. Predictably, his views were condemned as heretical by Pope Clement VI in 1346. It is, however, unclear to what extent—if any—Nicholas's thought affected philosophers in the Renaissance and subsequent eras.

G. Christian Heresy and Its Consequences

It is a singular irony that Pope Gregory VII's insistence upon papal authority directly resulted in the proliferation of "heresies" in the later eleventh and twelfth centuries. Henry of Lausanne (d. 1148?), a monk initially connected with the Abbey of Cluny, may be as close to a religious sceptic as one could hope for during this period. Not only did he reject original sin and the efficacy of baptism and prayer, but he rejected the ordained priesthood and even advocated the elimination of the eucharist. Of course, from his perspective he was only returning to the Christianity of the New Testament; but he constituted an obvious danger to the church establishment, and so he was in effect condemned in 1120.

A more dangerous force, from the church's point of view, was the emergence of the Albigensians (or Cathars) in the mid-twelfth century. This group quickly attracted adherents in France, Germany, Italy, and elsewhere, among both lower-class and upper-class citizens. Their goal, apparently, was to escape the "problem of evil" by asserting that creation itself was evil: it was fashioned by Satan, who also entrapped angels into the bodies of Adam and Eve and enticed them to engage in debauchery. Some extreme Cathars believed that the world was created by an independent force of evil. God had created his own wholly good parallel universe. As a result, our (bad) universe is the equivalent of hell. But eventually we would be released and enter the (good) universe by becoming "perfect" (*perfecti*) through study and training.

These tenets may have been partially derived from the Bogomils, a radical sect in Bulgaria. Both were clearly inclined toward Manichaeism. And in spite of their anticlericalism, the Cathars developed the rudiments of a church hierarchy of their own, with bishops, deacons, and other officials.

Another sect, the Waldensians, were the followers of Peter Waldo (1140?–1205?), a wealthy merchant from Lyons who, inspired by a fifth-century saint, Alexius, gave away all his property (after providing for his wife and daughters) and embraced poverty. But he became a danger to the church when he began preaching on his own, for this act threatened the church's monopoly on preaching. During the Third Lateran Council (1179), Pope Alexander III, although expressing some sympathy for the Waldensians, endorsed a prohibition against lay preaching. Waldo signed a document repudiating his heterodox views on many issues, but the Waldensians continued to believe in their right to preach and were excommunicated in Lyons. They went elsewhere and continued to preach into the fourteenth century. They gradually developed increasingly heretical views, fueled by a loathing of what they took to be a corrupt priesthood in the Catholic church. As a result, the church referred to the Waldensians as "the synagogue of Satan."[18]

18. Madigan, *Medieval Christianity* 196.

This was precisely the time when Pope Innocent III (1198–216) was renewing Leo IX's quest to maintain church unity and to assert papal supremacy throughout Christendom. Innocent ordered the confiscation of the property of those found guilty of heresy, although the actual confiscation was carried out by the secular authorities. Both the church and the state had a vested interest in suppressing heresy, since it was regarded as a rebellion against the divine authority of the church and as treason against the state. But when Philip II of France (r. 1180–223) refused to act against the Cathars, Innocent gathered an army—led by Simon de Montfort, 5th Earl of Leicester—to wage an "Albigensian Crusade" (i.e., a crusade against the Cathars or Albigensians) in 1209; as a result, many Cathars (but also some Catholics) were killed and the movement was largely suppressed.

It was the threat of the Cathars that led to the establishment of the Papal Inquisition. The roots of that body can be traced to Pope Lucius III's bull *Ad Abolendum* (1184), in which bishops were asked to conduct an examination (*inquisitio*) into accused heretics. The priesthood initially had little appetite or interest in such a pursuit, but the emergence of the Cathars and Waldensians lent urgency to the issue. Pope Gregory IX (1227–41) established the Inquisition in 1231–32, to be conducted largely by Dominican friars, although some Franciscan friars were also involved. At the outset, inquisitors had no coercive powers to gather evidence or compel testimony. When an accused heretic did appear before the court, he/she had no legal counsel—not surprisingly, since few lawyers were willing to sustain the reputational damage of representing even an accused heretic, let alone one who would later be convicted. Efforts were made to dismiss or prohibit testimony by the accused's enemies. The power to compel testimony of witnesses by torture was granted in 1252; it became more frequent and severe with the passage of time. Punishment mostly took the form of public penance. But many Cathars refused to recant and willingly endured torture and death. Only a small percentage of the convicted faced death by burning; incarceration was the more common punishment. After the Cathars and Waldensians were largely suppressed, the Inquisition turned its attention to sorercers and other kinds of heretics.

Innocent's battles with these heretical movements—to say nothing of his ability to appoint his own chosen candidate, Frederick II, as Holy

Roman Emperor (r. 1220–50)—rendered him the most significant political leader in Europe. The triumph of papal supremacy seemed to have been achieved. The papacy gained power by presiding over litigation on a wide variety of subjects, with canon law becoming the tool of enforcement. Papal legatees worked at the local level, ousting the authority of bishops. But this centralisation of power in the papacy led to corruption. By the thirteenth century the papacy increased its collection of taxes from the citzenry, including a tax on the local clergy. There were widespread complaints that the popes were engaging in a kind of extortion. What seemed, therefore, to be the high water-mark for the papacy would in a century or two lead to ruptures that would severely and permanently damage its standing.

More broad-based accusations of heresy were directed against those who were thought to believe in and worship the Devil. There were lively debates among Christian theologians in the twelfth and thirteenth centuries as to the exact place and function of the Devil and his fallen angels. Peter Lombard's *Sentences* maintained that these baleful entities dwell in the air just below heaven; but Lombard could not determine whether the Devil was or was not bound in hell after he had been conquered by Jesus. Aquinas believed that Satan and his angels existed in the "gloomy" air around the earth for the purpose of tempting human beings. And yet, there was a persistent tension, even a paradox, in Christian thought regarding Satan, fallen angels, and demons, who, for all their apparent evil, could also be considered "agents" of God because they "execute[d] the divine justice on the wicked."[19] To that extent, these infernal entities were part of God's plan and could not be regarded as purely evil. Similarly, there was some confusion as to how they could continue to function on earth even after their supposed "defeat" by Jesus.

There was a related debate as to the role of the Devil in relation to the thousand-year reign of Christ, during which Satan is presumably confined in some sort of pit, in the words of Revelation. But was this millennium to be in the future or had it already occurred? Augustine believed the latter. But, especially at the turn of the second millennium C.E., the belief became prevalent that the three-year interval that would follow the millennium and precede the Last Judgment was imminent,

19. Almond, *The Devil* 66.

and it was at this time that the concept of the Antichrist—also mentioned fleetingly in Revelation and elsewhere—came to the fore. There was some confusion as to where and in what form the Antichrist would emerge. A figure named Adso (910?–992), abbot of Montier-en-Der, wrote a biography of the Antichrist in which he maintained that the entity would be a Jewish man whom the Devil had entered while in his mother's womb. He would come to Jerusalem, rebuild the temple, and recovert the Jews (who had been converted to Christianity by the never-dying prophets Enoch and Elijah). After three and a half years, the Antichrist would be killed—either by Jews or by the archangel Michael.

Those who believed that the millennium was still in the future developed a different eschatology. For these theologians, the period of the Antichrist would *precede* the thousand years. Some postulated that this would occur in the year 1260; when this year came and went with no apparent advent of the Antichrist, they moved it to 1320–40. Alas, that period passed with no Antichrist in sight. A number of theologians did not hesitate to brand their opponents—up to and including the reigning pope—as the Antichrist.

The infusion of Greek/Arabic philosophical, theological, and scientific texts into the West encouraged interest in both "natural" magic (astrology, alchemy, and so on) and "demonic" magic (necromancy). It was at this time that Simon Magus—a shadowy figure cited sporadically in scripture (e.g., Acs 8:9–24), who was thought to have attempted to buy his way into the Apostles, thereby lending his name to the crime of simony—became the prototype of the Devil-inspired magician. As early as Augustine, all magic was attributed to demonic influence; the point was elaborated upon by Isidore of Seville in the treatise *De Magis*, dating to 636.

It is unsurprising that the massive outbreak of bubonic plague known as the Black Death (1346–53) resulted in a corresponding increase in superstition and persecution (especially of Jews, who were killed en masse in 1348–49 throughout Europe after having been accused of poisoning wells). It is not at all surprising that the ravages of the Black Death augmented Christians' terrors of death (and the consignment of their souls to hell at the Last Judgment).

The Inquisition played its role in sniffing out heretics who believed they were inspired by the Devil to perform feats of magic, benevolent or malevolent as the case may be. There is little doubt that many individuals seriously believed they were possessed by Satan: the accounts of such self-admissions are too numerous to be entirely accounted for merely as the result of false confessions engendered by torture. What that signifies, of course, is these hapless people's thorough indoctrination into Christian doctrine.[20] It was Pope Eugenius IV (1431–47) who first declared that sorcerers had formed a church contrary to the Christian church, and therefore were ripe for eradication. Around this time an anonymous treatise, *Errors of the Cathars,* proposed the existence of an actual cult of Devil worshippers, with such familiar imagery—later to be applied to suspected witches—as the broomstick, the "familiar" (an animal, usually a black cat, who accompanied the sorceror), and so on. The extensive persecution of witches occurred at a somewhat later period, so discussion of it will be included in subsequent chapters.

H. Troubles in Church and State

The papacy's attempts to exert its authority over secular powers in Europe, beginning in the eleventh century, encountered a series of obstacles in the course of the thirteenth and fourteenth centuries. This was precisely the time when kings were beginning to create a stronger central government in many parts of Europe: the rise of an educated bureaucracy resulted in greater efficiency in the running of the government, including tax collection; national and legal systems were taking shape. Occasionally, as in England, when a king was thought to overstep his legal boundaries the nobility reacted—in this case forcing King John to sign Magna Carta (1215), specifying the relative rights of kings and nobles. In France an opposite tendency, toward an absolutist monarchy, occurred with Louis VI (r. 1108–37) and subsequent kings. In Germany and Italy, the Holy Roman emperors entered a period of weaknesss and turmoil (1077–152), allowing nobles to gain more power. Frederick Barbarossa (r. 1155–90) attempted to rein in the independent cities in Italy; but they countered by forming the Lombard League to defeat him in 1176.

20. The most celebrated victim of a heresy accusation was Joan of Arc (1412–1431), but her trial, conviction, and execution by an English-leaning bishop, Pierre Cauchon, was manifestly the result of complex political machinations during the Hundred Years War (1337–1453) between the English and the French.

Frederick was forced to sign the Treaty of Constance (1183) validating the cities' independence.

The figure of Frederick II of Hohenstaufen (Holy Roman Emperor, 1220–50) is of some interest from our perspective. Aside from encouraging science, vernacular love poetry, and other secular elements, he appeared to be inclined toward religious scepticism and possibly even unbelief. It is of course preposterous to think that he was in any way an atheist; indeed, it appears that his "rationalism" extended largely to doubt of Catholic philosophers' justifications of orthodox dogma. But for his pains he was excommunicated in 1227, although this was brought on by his failure to lead a crusade to recapture Jerusalem. The next year he sought to make amends with the church by going to the Holy Land, where he won back Jerusalem from the Muslims in 1229 by negotiation. But Muslims ousted both Christians and Jews from Jerusalem in 1244.

In the thirteenth century, especially in England, France, and Spain (where the Muslims were slowly being ejected by Christian forces beginning in the late twelfth century), a gradual sense of national unity was developing. This phenomenon—although far from what it is today, since many people's loyalties remained largely local—created a nascent sense of secular identity in tension with the universalising tendency of the papacy.

It was at this time that Boniface VIII became pope (1294–303). The papacy's earlier decrees that the clergy be taxed (chiefly to fund the Crusades) had led secular powers in England and France to expect these revenues to fund the government. But when war broke out between these nations in 1294, clergy in both countries objected to the taxation demands. In 1296 Boniface issued a bull prohibiting the kings from levying taxes without papal approval; but he had no means of enforcing his dictum, so he was forced to modify it. Later, however, in 1302, he issued a bull essentially claiming the papacy's superiority over secular leaders. The measure was directed at Philip IV of France (r. 1285–304). Philip countered by declaring that Boniface was not the real pope; he actually tried to kidnap Boniface, but failed. Nevertheless, Boniface died soon thereafter. His bull became in effect a dead letter. What this conflict demonstrated to many was that "The temporal power of the popes seemed the chief obstacle in the contemporary world to terrestrial peace and concord."[21]

In the wake of the dispute, Pope Clement V (1305–14), aside from repudiating Boniface's bull, took up residence in Avignon, in southeastern France, becoming for all practical purposes a French puppet. For nearly a century popes maintained their primary residence there, where an elaborate and costly "Palais des Papes" was built. At last, Pope Gregory XI (1370–78) ended the so-called "Babylonian Captivity" and agreed to return to Rome (he died before he could do so); but the papacy's reputational damage was severe. When Pope Urban VI (1378–89) was elected by means of popular pressure, the second Great Schism (1378–417) began. Cardinals objected to his irregular election and chose another candidate, Clement VII (1378–94), in his stead; he went to live in Avignon. European nations split between supporting the Roman popes and the Avignon popes. At last, the Council of Constance (1414–18) resolved the schism by asserting its authority even above that of the popes; all the popes (there were now three of them) were deposed. Later popes condemned the notion that church councils could be superior to popes; indeed, a bull by Pius II, dating to 1460, grotesquely asserted the papacy's "primacy over the whole world."[22] But in fact, by this time national churches were gaining power at the expense of the papacy.

It was exactly at this time that several other "heresies" distracted the papacy's attention. Among the most dangerous, from the church's perspective, was that of John Wyclif (1331?–1384), an English theologian and professor at Oxford who propounded a number of daring ideas:

1. church property is not owned by clerics or even by the pope, but by God, hence could under certain circumstances be seized by the secular powers;
2. monastic life is a "private religion" that has illegitimately segregated itself from the communal life of the church;
3. morality among church leaders at all levels has woefully declined from the time of the apostles (Wyclif came down especially hard on the accumulation of wealth by clerics, including popes);
4. the only head of the church is Jesus Christ, not the pope or any of the church hierarchy; hence the church ought not to exercise any

21. Keen, *The Pelican History of Medieval Europe* 219.
22. Quoted in Madigan 385.

secular authority;
5. the power of a morally bad pope is essentially nil.

And yet, it was another issue on which Wyclif held heterodox views—the eucharist—that caused him to lose the support he had from church leaders who otherwise backed him. In essence, Wyclif denied the whole doctrine of transubstantiation—the notion that the bread and wine given at communion constitutes the actual body and blood of Christ, as in standard Catholic doctrine. He maintained that the eucharist served only a symbolic function. Wyclif also sponsored the translation of the Bible into Middle English, although it is unclear how much he himself contributed to this text, which appeared piecemeal over the period 1382–95.

It is not surprising that Wyclif's views provoked ire in the church hierarchy. Many of his stances were condemned by a synod called in 1382 by the Archbishop of Canterbury, and it was later forbidden to read or own any of his books. But his influence spread both during and after his lifetime. His ideas most profoundly affected Bohemia, where a movement to purify Christianity had already been under way, led by the charismatic Jan Hus (1372?–1415). Although Hus rejected Wyclif's teachings on the eucharist, he followed his English predecessor's principles in many other regards. It may well be that the Hussites' dominant concern was a protest against the prevalence of German-speaking figures in both their church and the university at Prague—a cause in which the government at Prague lent support to the Hussites. But the church hierarchy complained to the pope, who excommunicated Hus in 1411; he was later imprisoned and then burned at the stake.

I. Mediaeval Literature

French was the first major language in Europe that saw the emergence of a vibrant vernacular literature. Some texts date to as early as the ninth century, but literary activity began in earnest in the twelfth century. In the standard breakdown of the development of the French language, early Old French was written until about 1100, later Old French from 1100 to 1300, and Middle French from 1300 to 1500.

The *Chanson de Roland* (Song of Roland) exists in seven different versions, the most celebrated of which is the so-called Oxford *Roland,* the manuscript of which is at the Bodleian Library and dates to around 1100. It was probably sung orally. Roland is depicted as Charlemagne's nephew who, having been betrayed by his stepfather, was killed at the battle of Roncevaux (778) by the Saracens. The Oxford version is much more ambiguous in its moral portrayal of both Christians and Saracens, whereas later versions unequivocally depict the Saracens as cartoon villains and the Christians as saints. This is one of several extant *chansons de geste,* depicting heroic adventures of royal and noble figures.

It was French writers who first made extensive use of the Arthurian myth, which has extensive if at times circumscribed connexions with Christianity. The legend of a Dark Age king of England named Arthur can be traced to some writings as early as the sixth century, but it entered literature definitively with the English historian Geoffrey of Monmouth's *Historia Regum Britanniae* (History of the Kings of Britain), which dates to c. 1130; it derived some of its information on Arthur from an earlier work, the *Historia Brittonum* (History of the Britons), purportedly written by one Nennius in the early ninth century.

This legendry was embodied in literature in various works by Chrétien de Troyes (late twelfth century). The bulk of Arthurian myth focuses on the warrior-culture of the period in which it is set (fifth or sixth century), fused with the traditions of noble knights and courtly love that emerged in the later mediaeval era. Hence, the figure of Lancelot (in Chrétien's epic poem of that title) is morally and religiously ambiguous for his seduction of Arthur's wife, Queen Guenevere; but she is also morally blameworthy: "The devil entered her," Chrétien writes.[23]

It is in the legend of the Holy Grail that Christian elements emerge most strongly in the Arthurian story. In what is called the Old French Vulgate Cycle (poems written in the period 1220–40), the Grail becomes a metonymy for the conversion of Britain to Christianity. It is portrayed as a dish or bowl whose first owner was Joseph of Arimathea, establishing a tie to Jesus Christ. Chrétien's *Perceval* portrays that knight from Arthur's court as pursuing his search for the Grail, but later tradition bestows that honour to Lancelot's son Galahad, because of his sinless nature. In these accounts, religious faith becomes equivalent to sexual abstinence.

23. See Peggy McCracken, "The Old French Vulgate Cycle," in Gaunt and Kay, *The Cambridge Companion to Medieval French Literature* 44.

Le Roman de la Rose (The Romance of the Rose) is a composite work: the first 4000 lines were written by Guillaume de Lorris around 1230; the remaining 18,000 lines were written by Jean de Meun around 1275. The two sections are radically discordant in tone and subject-matter, especially in its treatment of its central subject—love. Guillaume's portion presents some relations to Christian theology and morality, especially in its portrayal of the central female character Rose's need to defend her chastity as constituting the highest Christian good; but it also features both Cupid and Venus as allegorical figures plainly representing carnal love. This aspect of the story is extensively elaborated upon by Jean's section, which is largely a satire that even includes some parodies of the Bible. The poem concludes with what one scholar has called "the most explicit allegorical rape scene in the history of literature."[24] *Le Roman de la Rose* was, by mediaeval standards, a bestseller, with more than 300 manuscripts of it surviving; in English translation (*The Romaunt of the Rose*) it exercised a significant influence upon mediaeval English literature.

The whole topos of courtly love and seduction was treated by a wide array of *fabliaux* (fables), mostly in verse and frequently featuring highly eroticised and even obscene elements with little regard for Christian morality. These *fabliaux,* dating to as early as 1150 and continuing on until about 1400, were generally sung by *jongleurs* in northeast France; their generally earthy nature has been described by critics as among the earliest instances of literary realism in European vernacular literature.

One of the poets most strongly influenced by *Le Roman de la Rose* was Guillaume de Machaut (1304?–1377), who wrote numerous poems of courtly love. In the *Confort d'amy* (Comfort of the Soul) Guillaume draws upon the Bible for moral lessons; but in the *Prologue* to his collected works, written late in life, he has Nature stating frankly: "I, Nature, by whom all is created . . . come before you, Guillaume, whom I created specially so that by you would be created new and pleasing poems about love."[25] How seriously we are to regard this repudiation of God as the creator of the universe is debatable; elsewhere in his corpus God is indeed frequently invoked.

24. Steinberg, *Reading the Middle Ages* 83.

25. Deborah McGrady, "Guillaume de Machaut," in Gaunt and Kay, *The Cambridge Companion to Medieval French Literature* 115.

Christine de Pizan (1363?–1431?) is of some note not only because she is one of the earliest and most notable female writers of French vernacular literature but because some facets of her work strongly question the place of women in a Christian society. She was married at the age of fifteen, but her husband died in 1390, forcing her to take up writing to support her children and her mother. *L'Épistre de Othéa a Hector* (Epistle of Othea to Hector) elaborates upon the characters in the Trojan War (she adhered to the notion that France had been founded by descendants of the Trojans) and is saturated with Greek and Roman mythology. This circumstance in itself need not suggest any sort of disbelief in Christianity, since Greco-Roman myth had long ago been (uneasily) incorporated into the Christian account of history; but other of her works reveal her strong criticism of clerics who condemned women as vile and evil, thereby expressing scepticism about the "curse of Eve" that had long led Christians of all stripes to justify prejudice against women.

The most significant French poet of the late mediaeval period was François Villon (1431?–1463?), whose unorthodox life—including the murder of a man in Paris and his involvement in the robbery of gold coins from the Collège de Navarre, leading to his banishment and early death—overshadows his scintillating poetic work, embodied in a late collection, *Le Testament* (1461). Without going into details, it can be stated that at least some of his poems present, if not an actual parody of Christianity, at least a use of Christian doctrine in an ironic and irreverent manner.

The emergence of Italian vernacular literature occurred at a somewhat later period. Among the first instances of it is the poetry of Francis of Assisi (1182–1226). The thirteenth century saw the development of love and lyric poetry inspired by French and (especially) Provençal models. The sonnet form was invented by Giacomo da Lentini (fl. 1233–45). Much poetry written during this period seems overwhelmingly secular, although some verse by Guittone d'Arezzo (1230?–1294) is on religious themes. In prose, much religious writing (sermons, moral tracts, and the like) is extent, but so are accounts of romantic adventures, Arthurian legendry, and other more secular work.

It is, however, in the figure of Dante Alighieri (1265–1321) that we reach an early apotheosis of Italian literary expression that resulted in the production of an epochal work of religious literature, the *Commedia,*[26] whose influence continues to be felt down to the present day. Dante was a Florentine politician who was exiled to northern Italy in 1301. This event, as well as his infatuation with a married woman whom he called Beatrice (probably to be identified with Bice Portinari [1266–1290]), were the guiding impulses that fueled much of his literary work. Dante himself was married (as was Bice) and fathered three or four children, and it appears that Beatrice's early death led him to further study of theology and philosophy.

La Vita Nuova (1294), a mix of prose and verse, speaks of his love for Beatrice. Here she is entirely spiritualised, and Dante's writing about her reveals the probable influence of the Song of Solomon as well as of the numerous saints' lives (hagiographies) that were already a widely practised literary genre. For Dante, Beatrice has become a kind of saint. He maintains that, after her death, he saw her in a vision and suggests that she will inspire him to write the *Commedia.* (It is possible that this section of *La Vita Nuova* was added later, after he had written the *Commedia.*)

Although Dante did write poems on courtly love with little religious feeling, the *Commedia*—written between the years 1306 and 1318 and apparently conceived as a unity—so far outshines his other work that he has largely been defined by it. This poetic trilogy, in which a figure pointedly called Dante is led through Hell, Purgatory, and Paradise, certainly impresses us as the work of a supreme literary artist—one who evolved a complex verse form (*terza rima*) and utilised it in a way that places him (like Homer, Virgil, Shakespeare, and Goethe) at the pinnacle of his language's poetic idiom, but who also expounded a religion and philosophy that is by turns bizarre, cruel, sophistical, and mired in the same paradoxes and internal contradictions besetting the work of earlier Christian thinkers.

The *Inferno* begins with Dante meeting Virgil, the Roman poet, who has been sent by Beatrice to lead him out of his intellectual and religious perplexity by showing him the three regions of the afterlife. (Virgil cannot take him to Paradise because "I was a rebel to His law"

26. The title *La Divina Commedia* (The Divine Comedy) was coined by Boccaccio and added to the title in 1555.

[*Inf.* 1.125],[27] i.e., he was not a baptised Christian.) There is little doubt as to why Dante chose Virgil as his guide to Hell and Purgatory: he himself acknowledges that "Thou art my master and my author" (*Inf.* 1.85), and many passages of his text—including, above all, the very trip to Hell, echoing Aeneas' descent to the underworld in the sixth book of the *Aeneid*—bear the literary influence of the Roman poet. But far beyond this, Virgil had already come to be regarded as a quasi-Christian figure by virtue of his supposed prediction of Jesus' birth in the fourth *Eclogue.*

Virgil takes him on a long journey through the nine cicles of Hell. The first is Limbo, where pagan figures as Socrates, Plato, Aristotle, and (somewhat surprisingly) the Atomist philosopher Democritus are to be found; they are consigned here because, although they led worthy lives and wrote in a way that in some senses anticipated Christianity, they too did not receive Christian baptism. (It is noteworthy that Epicurus, who was widely regarded as something close to an atheist—especially because of his denial of the soul's survival of the body after death—is relegated to the sixth circle of Hell.) As the journey continues, Dante catches sight of all manner of sinners—among them emperors, popes, and cardinals—in the various circles of Hell. The eighth and ninth circles are subdivided into what Dante calls Malebolge (literally, "evil pouches"). Muhammad is in the ninth circle, because he and others were "sowers of scandal and schism" (*Inf.* 28.35).

Finally, at the very bottom of the ninth circle, is Satan. He is endowed with three heads, each of a different colour: "With six eyes he was weeping and over three chins dripped tears and boody foam. In each mouth he crushed a sinner with his teeth as with a heckle and thus he kept three of them in pain; to him in front the biting was nothing to the clawing, for sometimes the back was left all striped of skin" (*Inf.* 34.53–57). The three unfortunate individuals Satan is chewing on are Judas, Brutus, and Cassius.

The trip to Purgatory—a lofty mountain—is a trifle tedious, as it chronicles a number of figures who in various ways are striving to purify themselves of their sins and thereby attain Paradise. We do find an area for upbaptised infants, in accordance with Augustine's views on the

27. I use the translation of John D. Sinclair but cite the *Commedia* by the line numbers of the Italian text.

matter. Toward the summit of the mountain Virgil discreetly withdraws and Beatrice appears. In a curiously petty chastisement, Beatrice criticises Dante for forgetting all about her after her death and marrying someone else (*Purg.* 30.124f.).

Nonetheless, she leads him to Paradise, where there are ten different regions, aligned to the planets of the solar system and the "fixed stars." We find here various pettifogging disquisitions on theology. Toward the end Dante sees St Peter, then the Virgin Mary and other women (mostly from the OT). The work ends with a prayer to the Virgin Mary by St Bernard, the twelfth-century abbot of Clairvaux.

The chief point we must stress in what would otherwise be a farrago of lurid imagery, monotonous repetition, and tiresome theology is Dante's devotion to the ancient (and specifically the Roman) world. For him, pagan Rome led directly to the Papacy; and for all that the *Commedia* is laced with anticlericalism, he never questions the rightness and inevitability of the Christian dispensation. His reverence for Rome is the reason why Brutus and Cassius, the murderers of Julius Caesar, are two of the three worst sinners in Hell. It is also why Ulysses and Diomedes—the chief figures involved in the treachery of the Trojan horse, which led to the downfall of Troy (and therefore the departure of Aeneas from Troy to found Rome)—are consigned to a deep level of Hell. The Holy Roman Empire is and must be a bulwark against the forces of evil, whether they are embodied in false religions such as Islam or impious popes and other figures who are damaging the church from within. It is perhaps no accident that Dante began the *Inferno* only two years after the popes took up residence in Avignon: for someone like Dante, this development might well have seemed akin to blasphemy, as an intolerable insult both to the dignity of the church and to the majesty of Rome.

Indeed, much of Dante's anticlericalism is fueled by his belief—expounded in his treatise, *De Monarchia* (1312–13)—that the church should not be a temporal power at all: it should not hold property, have jurisdiction of the courts, or in other ways participate in governance. (It is unsurprising, therefore, that the church declared *De Monarchia* heretical in 1329.) This is by no means to say that Dante advocated some kind of separation of church and state; for him, the state itself is a sacred institution, and all history is sacred history.

And yet, at times Dante's nearly idolatrous passion for ancient literature betrays him into something close to heresy. The *Paradiso* opens with a florid appeal to Apollo—clearly the Greek god, not merely a symbol for the sun or anything else:

> O good Apollo, for the last labour make me such a vessel of thy power as thou requirest for the gift of thy loved laurel. . . . Come into my breast and breathe there as when thou drewest Marsyas from the scabbard of his limbs. O power divine, grant me so much of thyself that I may show forth the shadow of the blessed kingdom imprinted in my brain thou shalt see me come to my chosen tree and crown myself then with those leaves of which the theme and thou will make me worthy. (*Par.* 1.13–27)

This seems far more than a routine plea for poetic inspiration. And what of the fact that, in the ecstatic realms of Paradise, Dante sees the Greek gods (including Jupiter) cavorting joyously (*Par.* 22.139f.)?[28]

Otherwise, Dante is tolerably orthodox in his Christianity. Of course, his portrayals of the various regions of Hell, Purgatory, and Paradise are his own invention, although much of the lurid imagery is taken from Revelation. And his placement of worthy pagans in Limbo is a merciful break from Christian tradition. But he appears to sanction the belief in an actual Adam who, "condemning himself, condemned all his progeny" (*Par.* 7.27). Jesus is the absolver of sin; indeed, humanity could never have redeemed itself without such assistance.

What, then, is the overall "message" or thrust of the *Commedia?* In the opinion of one scholar,

> God is love: there can be little doubt that this realization lies at the heart of Dante's *Commedia.* It is from divine love—'l'amor divino'—that creation issues (*Inferno* 1.39–40), and it is in and as that love that Dante's journey famously ends: 'l'amor che move il sole e l'altre stelle' [love that moves the sun and other stars] (*Paradiso* 33.143–145).[29]

---

28. All this makes one question Peter S. Hawkins's blithe assertion that "it is the Christian God, rather than the muse of Virgil and Ovid, who ultimately inspires" Dante (*Dante's Testaments* 73).

29. Montemaggi, *Reading Dante's* Commedia *as Theology* 31.

All this sounds unexceptionable, but one has to wonder whether the "divine vengeance" cited in the *Paradiso* is entirely a product of God's love for his creation and his creatures. While it would be untrue and unfair to say that Dante—either the poet or the persona—takes delight in the increasingly harsh punishments doled out to the lamentable inhabitants of Hell, it is undeniable that in at least a few instances Dante does engage in a sort of schadenfreude, especially when he speaks of individuals he was actually acquainted with and whom he seems to relish portraying as suffering torments in the various levels of Hell. There is also a curiously parochial aspect to Dante's entire cosmogony, peopled so often with Italians of his own generation or in the decades preceding his; this has a tendency to subvert the purported universality of Dante's message.

Whatever the case, it can easily be argued that Dante's portrayal of the afterlife—especially of Hell—has, along with that in Milton's *Paradise Lost,* coloured our own view of that baleful realm far more vividly than the fleeting passages found in scripture. No doubt this is a testament to Dante's powers as a literary artist; but in the same degree it is an acknowledgement of the obsessions that led him to create such a terrifying locale in the first place.

When we move on to Giovanni Boccaccio (1313–1375), we are in an entirely different world—at least if we consider his main work, the *Decameron.* An illegitimate child born in Tuscany, Boccaccio alternated between Florence and Naples for much of his life. While in the latter city (1327–41) he initially helped his father in the banking business, but became increasingly attracted to literature—Latin, Greek, and Italian, as well as French and Provençal. His first work dates to 1334. These early works, written in verse, focus on love, sex, and romance in a way that clearly betrays the influence of Ovid but also features a Christian substructure. Some of them, such as the *Ameto* and the *Amorosa Visione* (Vision of Love), are elaborate Christian allegories. The *Ameto* is, on the surface, a tale of the loves of seven nymphs, but each of them stands for one of the seven virtues. The *Amorosa Visione* appears to contrast sacred and profane love, with the palm nominally handed to the former; but the emphasis is so strongly on sensual love that sacred love appears to fall by the wayside. The influence of Dante on both works is pronounced.

Up to this point we would not suspect that Boccaccio is in any way different from other creative writers in the mediaeval era, where Christian influence was overwhelming; but signs of religious rebellion begin to appear in the *Elegia di Madonna Fiammetta* (1343), which focuses on a woman, Fiammetta, who engages in an adulterous relationship with a Florentine merchant, Panfilo, but is ultimately abandoned by him. The dissection of her psychological state is singular, and it has been compared to *Madame Bovary* or *Anna Karenina.* The idea of Christian or sacred love seems entirely absent, and the emphasis is wholly on Fiammetta's feelings of betrayal, jealousy, and torment.

The *Decameron* (written 1348–53) presents yet another side of Boccaccio's genius—this one focusing on a relentless and occasionally malicious satire on religion. The framework of this long prose text—seven women and three men are fleeing the plague in Florence and head to a villa outside the city, telling a total of 100 tales divided into ten books—is initially grim, and the prologue to the first day is as realistic an account of the Black Death (in which many of Boccaccio's friends died) as has come down to us. But the tone shifts radically to one of lighthearted buffoonery, with religion often the butt of jest.

The ridicule gets underway in the very first tale, where a notoriously sinful notary, Ser Ciappelletto, falling ill and close to death, seeks absolution in spite of his corrupt nature. As he blithely states, "In my lifetime I have committed so many sins against God that if I commit another on my deathbed it can make no difference" (1:1).[30] He brazenly lies about himself to a foolish friar, who grants him extreme unction—and later becomes Saint Ciapelletto!

The next tale (1:2) speaks of a Christian who has a Jewish friend, Abraham. Abraham goes to Rome and finds the clergy there utterly corrupt—but converts to Christianity anyway, because he comes to believe that the constant advance of the Christian religion in spite of the manifest flaws of its leaders must indicate that it is supernaturally blessed by the Holy Spirit.

Throughout the rest of the book, religious satire pops up sporadically but pungently. The sexual derelictions of priests, friars, canons, and other church officials are relentlessly exposed. Perhaps the nastiest of the lot is

30. I use the translation of Richard Aldington (first published in 1930). I identify the various stories by day and tale, with a colon separating them; hence, 1:1 is the first tale of the first day.

3:10, where a hermit shows a young woman how to "put the devil in hell" (that is, how to place his penis into her vagina). As a result, this phrase becomes a proverb. In 3:8, an abbot lusts after a man's wife and states that her husband must go to Purgatory to cure himself of his inveterate jealousy. He thereby dallies with the wife for ten months; and even when the husband (who has been put to sleep with a magic potion) awakes and returns to his wife, she continues her relations with the abbot.

In 4:2, a friar tricks a married woman into thinking he is the angel Gabriel, and so he takes her to bed. In 7:3, a friar sleeps with a woman whose child is the friar's god-daughter; when the husband shows up, the friar gets out of the jam by claiming he is treating the child for worms. In 8:2, a canon falls in love with a widow, but she refuses to sleep with him. She tricks him into sleeping with an ugly maidservant, and he is caught by the widow's brothers, who bring his bishop to the house. A late tale, 9:2, shows that female religious figures are not exempt from sexual desire. A nun falls in love with a young man; the abbess catches them in the nun's room, but she herself is having an affair with a priest.

The *Decameron* focuses on other issues aside from the sexual irregularities of the clergy. Their general lack of intelligence is frequently noted, as in 3:3, where "a trick [is] played by a fair woman on a stupid friar": she uses him to gain access to her lover. 1:6 is a send-up of the Inquisition; 1:7 is a satire on the greed among the monks of the Abbey of Cluny; 2:1 is a satire on "miraculous" cures from saints' relics.

While it is certainly not the case that the majority of the 100 tales in the *Decameron* poke fun at religion, the fact that such a significant number of them do—in a manner that would seem to evoke Gore Vidal rather than the religion-soaked Middle Ages—is striking. It is not at all clear what led Boccaccio in this direction, but if the whole of the *Decameron* is considered, it could be said that its dominant theme—the primacy of Nature and Fortune (fate, luck, chance)—compels Boccaccio to condemn the chastity advocated by Christian doctrine is entirely unworkable. Nature, for him, is largely equivalent to the sexual impulse, and its ubiquity renders the Christian insistence on celibacy for priests, nuns, and other figures profoundly unnatural. Indeed, in the one instance (5:8) where Boccaccio speaks of the afterlife, a woman who refused to give herself to her lover is consigned to hell. What Boccaccio is doing, in essence, is nothing less than the advocacy of a moral revolution: "What is substituted for the moral order bequeathed by the Church, is a new morality that stems from the lay world and is based on a juxtaposition of the realistic needs of an open mercantile society with the lay ideals of love and friendship inherited from the old courtly culture and the classical world."[31]

It is widely believed that few of the tales in the *Decameron* are original in their broadest themes; but their sources have in many instances not been found. The French *fabliaux* may have been one source for the bawdy and anticlerical stories, but the grounding of many tales in the contemporary Italy known to the author suggests that many aspects of them are based on his observation.

The tone of light-hearted satire is something new in Boccaccio's work—and, indeed, it is the first and last instance of it in his overall corpus. His subsequent writing is serious and scholarly, and chiefly written in Latin. He wrote two works about Dante: the first, a short biography, is a kind of hagiography of the author, but does not discuss the theology of the *Commedia* to any great extent; the other, a commentary on the *Commedia* (Boccaccio died after having completed only a discussion of the first sixteen cantos of the *Inferno*), adopts an allegorical interpretation of the work, but its chief focus is on its value as poetry, not as an embodiment of theological "truth." There is some indication that Boccaccio came to regret, and even to repudiate, the anticlericalism of the *Decameron* in later life;[32] but as his most popular and enduring work, it stands as a nearly unprecedented nose-thumbing of many of the cherished pieties that animated the mediaeval era.

The third great Italian writer of the period, Petrarch (Francesco Petrarca, 1304–1374), occupies a middle ground between Dante and Boccaccio in terms of his religious outlook. While he himself held various minor religious positions during his life, including that of canon, he was also the poet laureate of Rome and a champion of what came to be called humanism. His knowledge of pagan literature and mythology was exhaustive, even though there is little reason to doubt that his thought remained essentially Christian.

Indeed, there is something schizophrenic in Petrarch's output. In

31. Serafini-Sauli, *Giovanni Boccaccio* 84.

32. In 1559 the work was placed on the Index; later it was removed, and an expurgated text was presented whereby clerics were simply replaced by lay figures.

his numerous essays and treatises, many of them written in Latin, he is unequivocally Christian in outlook and doctrine. Such works as *Secretum Meum* (1347–53; My Secret) and *De Otio Religioso* (On Religious Leisure) rely heavily on the teaching of Augustine and other Christian writers;[33] but the works for which he is best known—namely, his poetry—paint a very different picture.

In the *Canzoniere*—a cycle of 366 poems, mostly sonnets, written over a long period, from 1327 to 1368—Petrarch presents a searingly personal exhibition of his fluctuating psychological state as he ruminates over his unrequited love for a woman he names Laura, whom he purportedly met in 1327 and who died in 1348. Unlike Dante's Beatrice, Laura is a flesh-and-blood woman whom Petrarch almost never speaks of in a spiritual manner. No one can maintain that these exquisite instances of lyric poetry are in any way atheistic or even agnostic; but some of the sentiments they betray—or, rather, the manner in which they are expressed—are surprising. In poem 16 Petrarch compares a pious old man's pilgrimage to Rome to see images of Jesus to his own hope of seeing Laura. This poem is one of several where religious imagery is made to serve secular purposes. It is true that, once Laura dies, Petrarch writes a number of poems expressing the hope and expectation that he will see her in heaven; but the impression the reader is ultimately left with us the inexpressible grief he feels at her departure ("I weep and sing and carry on as though / nothing has changed. She whom I adored / has left me here behind in familiar woe"),[34] so that their eventual reunion in the beyond is cold comfort indeed.

J. Mediaeval Art and Music

Christian art and architecture of the early mediaeval period constituted a fusion of the artistic style of the German "barbarians" and their successors—with their extensive use of geometrical figures, animals, or human-animal hybrids—with Christian images and symbols. And yet, Charlemagne's palace complex at Aix-la-Chapelle relied heavily on classical Roman models—perhaps not surprisingly, since he himself

33. For which see Lee, *Petrarch and St. Augustine*.
34. I use the translation of David R. Slavitt (2012).

promoted his rulership as a *renovatio Romani imperii* (renewal of the Roman empire). Nevertheless, Christian elements were widespread there, as in the Palatine Chapel. Churches and monasteries outside of Rome revealed greater originality of design: the cloister now appeared as an architectural form. Some monastery complexes were so elaborate that they were in effect miniature cities. It was here that lavish illuminated manuscripts began to be produced—including the exquisite Lindisfarne Gospels (early eighth century) and, even more impressively, the Book of Kells (late eighth–early ninth century) in Ireland, which reveals Byzantine influence. A revolution in script—the institution of the "Carolingian minuscule"—stimulated the copying of classical and Christian manuscripts. But the extent to which Christianity dominated art of all sorts is evident even in what appear to be secular portrayals of nature, where Christian imagery and allegory were incorporated at every level.

In the Byzantine Empire, the iconoclastic movement—fueled by Monophysites who believed that any depiction of Jesus Christ as anthropomorphic was blasphemous—resulted in the destruction of many works of art in the eighth and early ninth centuries. In 843 the Council of Constantinople ended the controversy, and thereafter emperors undertook to restore churches and other structures. Byzantine political and artistic influence extended into eastern Europe and Russia in the tenth and eleventh centuries (as in the Cathedral of St. Sophia in Kyev), and also in Venice and elsewhere in Italy.

Feudalism led to the development of some forms of secular architecture, such as the fortified castle with stone towers, crenellated battlements, and so on—clearly the utilitarian result of the need for defence. This period—the eleventh and twelfth centuries—was the heyday of Romanesque art. The term was coined in the nineteenth century to designate mediaeval art heavily reliant on Roman architectural forms, as is evident in many churches in Italy and France, where such elements as Corinthian capitals were used. The Normans brought Romanesque art to England, as in the Cathedral of Durham (1093–133).

Gothic art, initiated in the mid-twelfth century, began in France. This term, like Romanesque, was also initially pejorative—coined to denote the "barbarian" (and, implicitly, heavily Christian) art and architecture that the rational era of the eighteenth century had presumably repudiated.

In France, the increasing prosperity of cities and the increasing power of the monarchy, as well as the growth of universities, led to the creation of more imposing edifices, both religious and secular. Rib vaulting, pointed arches, and stained glass began to be used in churches. Chartres Cathedral (1134–220) is the epitome of early Gothic. The Gothic style then spread throughout Europe. The high towers and vaulting created a sense of lightness and space in contrast to the heaviness of Romanesque. But all these elements were still in strict consonance with Christian doctrine; the increasing use of windows to let in light into churches was seen as a concrete embodiment of Jesus Christ as the "light of the world." Church architecture was explicitly designed to cast the viewer's eye upward to the heavens, as in Notre Dame in Paris (1163–200). In England, Canterbury Cathedral was rebuilt beginning in 1174.

Pictorial art was revolutionised by Giotto di Bondone (1277?–1337), with his deft use of perspective, realism, and other features; but his subject-matter remained overwhelmingly religious. Art in general remained didactic and Christian. Secular architecture did make some strides in the later Gothic period (mid-fourteenth to mid-fifteenth centuries), when lavish public buildings for government use were erected. Private homes were more elaborately furnished. But the most impressive buildings of the era remained religious—the Chapel of King's College, Cambridge (1446–515), Westminster Abbey (the current building's construction began in 1245 and was not completed until the late fourteenth century), and others.

Western music is another immense area where, in the early mediaeval period, Christianity dominated. I have said little about Greco-Roman music because its exact nature and components remain a source of debate, and because so few examples of it survive. There is evidence, however, that the early Christians rejected Greco-Roman cultural norms in regard to music, eschewing public spectacles featuring music or musical competitions. Early Christian church music may have followed Jewish practices in synagogues, especially in the close relationship between liturgy and musical performance. Jewish psalm-singing was adapted to Christian hymns; in some instances, popular song tunes were used. A number of different chants were developed, the most significant being the Ambrosian (canonically associated with Ambrose, bishop of Milan [374–97], although it is unlikely that he himself set it down).

Pope Gregory the Great (590–604) extensively reformed both the liturgy and the chant, leading to the establishment of a uniform repertoire used throughout Roman churches in the West. As with the Ambrosian chant, it is unlikely that Gregory was directly responsible for the establishment of Gregorian chant—a series of melodies that remained in use for close to a thousand years. Music outside the church did exist, but we know almost nothing of its nature. Much of it may have been either suppressed or incorporated into the church service.

From as early as Boethius' *De Institutione Musica* (On the Principles of Music) in the early sixth century, music was seen not as an instance of abstract aesthetic expression (or appreciation) but as a means of leading the soul to the divine—an idea that has its roots in Plato and the Greek conception of the "music of the spheres." Music was almost exclusively vocal, and instrumental music was deprecated because it was not directly conducive to Christian instruction. The Ordinary of the Mass (that is, the five sections that are invariable parts of the service—Kyrie, Gloria, Credo, Sanctus, and Agnus Dei) was established at a very early stage, perhaps the sixth or seventh century; so was the text of the Magnificat ("My soul doth magnify the Lord," taken from Luke 1:46–55), derived from Byzantine ritual.

What secular music existed in the mediaeval era took the form of popular songs, such as the Goliard songs of the eleventh and twelfth centuries, which treated of women, wine, and other subjects with a satirical flair. These were in Latin. Songs using vernacular texts appear in the *chansons de geste,* which were sung by roving bards or minstrels, either individually or in groups. This led to the emergence of troubadours or trouvères, the latter of whom flourished in Provence and wrote in Provençal. From there they spread to other parts of France. Some of them composed songs for aristocratic audiences. Love and seduction were the dominant motifs, although moral and political commentary was also offered. These musicians worked in tandem with the "courtly love" ideal of the period. In Germany the *Minnesinger* (singer of love songs) emerged in the twelfth century. But these love songs were often tinged with religious themes. A later development was the *Meistersinger* (master singer)—a guild of middle-class artisans who performed both in secular settings and in churches.

In the eleventh century, written compositions—stimulated by the development of a uniform musical notation—emerged, slowly replacing the improvisation that had dominated musical performance up to this point. Two of the earliest composers of note, Léonin (1135–1201) and Pérotin (1160–1230), were both associated with Notre Dame. They wrote exclusively sacred music. Both employed *polyphony,* the increasing use of harmony and independent musical lines as opposed to the *monophony* (unison singing) of prior eras. Pérotin wrote pieces for three or four voices, which came to be called motets; thousands were composed during the thirteenth century, mostly by anonymous composers. Some of these were on secular themes using vernacular languages.

In the fourteenth century, secular music outpaced sacred music, and the leading composer of the period—Guillaume de Machaut (1304?–1377)—wrote both monophonic and polyphonic music. And yet, Guillaume's most celebrated work is the *Messe de Notre Dame,* the first major setting of the Ordinary of the Mass—and one composed as a unity rather than as a random collection of the five sections of the Mass. But sacred music by him and others was in decline because of the turmoil in the church at this time and the church's own fulminations about the increasingly elaborate musical settings of sacred texts.

In Italy in the fourteenth century there was no tradition of polyphonic music, but the madrigal now emerged as a dominant form of secular song, usually on romantic or pastoral themes. Other forms also flourished. Francesco Landini (1325–1397) gained celebrity by composing *ballate* (songs to accompany dancing). Incredibly, no sacred music by him is extant.

K. Norse Mythology

The Scandinavian nations emerge into history chiefly during the Viking Age (793–1066), when Norsemen from the areas later designated by Denmark, Norway, and Sweden began their ventures by sea into Europe and North America. Although they made incursions into France, Germany, and elsewhere, their territorial gains proved evanescent. The celebrated voyage of Leif Erikson to Newfoundland (Vinland) and other areas in North America around 1000 C.E. also proved short-lived, although a colony in Greenland survived for some five hundred years.

It is difficult to know when the mythology of the Scandinavian countries became fully formed, but it probably did not occur until the first several centuries C.E. Artifacts in the region, including rock carvings and carvings on reindoor horn, date to as early as 6000 B.C.E. In the Neolithic period, great meglithic tombs for the illustrious dead have been found. Evidence indicates the worship of an Earth Mother, both as a fertility goddess and as a patron of the dead, receiving the dead back into her womb. By the Bronze Age, use of burial mounds began. Grave goods were common, including weapons as well as depictions of axe-wielding figures. The axe was probably associated with a sky-god who was thought to control the weather. This god was also accompanied by a ship or wagon traversing the heavens, thereby connecting him with the sun.

Full-fledged Norse myth is embodied in a number of texts, both in prose and in verse. Two scholars of the mediaeval era, Saxo Grammaticus (1150?–1220?) and Snorri Sturluson (1179–1241), assembled the various myths and legends into the *Prose Edda* and other texts. There is also a *Poetic Edda* that was discovered in the seventeenth century. These texts, supplemented by archaeological and other sources, allow for a fairly complete account of Norse myth.

The Norse creation myth begins with the notion of a World Tree (Yggdrasil), which connects the realms of the gods (Asgard), giants, and the dead. The World Serpent is at the foot of the tree, surrounding the earth. Midgard (Middle Earth), the dwelling-place of the human race, was created around the tree. The world was created from a nothingness (named Ginnungagap) that nonetheless bore within itself the potential for life. The melding of fire and ice led to the creation of the giant Ymir, from whom the other giants and also human beings emerged; mountains, the sea, and other natural features were also fashioned out of Ymir. Ymir was killed by Odin and his brothers Vili and Ve to engender the first humans (Ask and Embla). Our world is, however, also populated by dwarves, elves, and monsters of various sorts (dragons, snakes, and so on) possessing supernatural powers.

At first, Odin was the supreme god of Norse myth. He emerged as a god of death and battle who welcomed warriors who had died on the battlefield. Peat bogs in Scandinavia, dating from the first to the sixth century C.E., have revealed booty (including human remains) that were evidently meant as a tribute to Odin. The warrior-culture of the ancient

Scandinavians is embodied in the figures of the Berserks—warriors who believed themselves under the protection of Odin and who therefore fought with frenzy on the battlefield, wearing skins of bears or wolves. There is also evidence that eagles, ravens, and other animals associated with the gods were venerated.

The Valkyries were initially "fierce female spirits attendant on the war-god, delighting in blood and carnage and devouring corpses on the battlefield."[35] Only later did they become maidens riding on horseback and escorting fallen warriors to the Norse afterlife, Valhalla. It is possible that Valhalla may have been underground rather than in the sky. In any event, it was a fitting place for the warriors: daily battles took place, in which the dead were resurrected in the morning to begin battles anew. The feasts held in Valhalla may have been inspired by awareness of the feasts among Celtic and German warriors elsewhere in Europe.

The one-eyed god Balder is a significant figure in relation to Odin. He is in fact the son of Odin and Frigg, and at some future date will be inadvertently killed by his brother Hoder. Odin, with his knowledge of the future, knows that Balder's death foretells the fall of the gods at Ragnarok. The death of Balder will trigger warfare among human beings and the coming of a great cold (engendered by the wolf Fenrir's breaking of his bonds and devouring the sun). The World Serpent will emerge, generating a flood. Many of the gods will perish, but the World Tree will survive, and it will engender a new earth, sun, and other elements that will begin creation anew.

Odin has some characteristics of a sky-god, as he is traditionally accompanied by an eagle and a raven. But over time he gave place to Thor, who emerged as the Scandinavian thunder god. Thor is usually depicted anthropomorphically, but with various supernatural accoutrements, especially his famous hammer. Numerous accounts of Thor's battles with giants are extant; some of these appear to mythologise the power of lightning to wreak havoc on earth or the sound of thunder in the sky. Both the hammer and the axe (also associated with Thor) are symbols of the thunderbolt. While most of the Norse gods were worshipped in the open air, with feasting and animal sacrifices, Thor was also worshipped in the home, as he came to symbolise the fertility of crops and the well-

35. Davidson, *Scandinavian Mythology* 40.

being of the family unit.

Among the other significant gods of the Norse pantheon are Freyr and his twin sister Freyja, the offspring of Njord. This points to a division of the gods into a group known as the Aesir (including Odin, Thor, and others) and another group called the Vanir (Njord and his offspring). Freyr is chiefly a fertility god, although also associated with the sun. Njord is chiefly associated with the sea, fishing, and so forth. Freyja is connected with the Valkyries and with the underworld. She is also a mother goddess and presided over childbirth. Freyja is at the heart of divination ceremonies presided over by a *völva* (seeress), who behaved something like a spiritualistic medium.

One of the most intriguing of the Norse gods is Loki, a trickster who occupies an ambivalent position in regard to the other deities, sometimes aiding them and sometimes hindering or deceiving them. It is he who has created numerous monsters and demons (including the World Serpent and Hel, the goddess who took over control of the underworld after the fading of Odin). Loki is also a shapeshifter.

With the advent of Christianity in Scandinavia, Norse and Christian elements frequently became intermingled. Odin was sometimes regarded as a form of the devil, as was Freyr. Some goddesses were depicted as hideous trolls. Thor came to be considered the chief antagonist of Jesus Christ. Some citizens, including those in wealthy families, were tortured or killed for refusing the abandon the pagan faith.

L. Religion, Society, and Literature in Great Britain

Because of its geographical isolation, England and Ireland remained to some degree separate from continental Europe in its religious, social, and political development during the mediaeval era, although some notable features—such as feudalism and serfdom—did exist roughly along European lines. The Romano-British culture had fallen into decay by the time the Anglo-Saxons invaded from Germany in the mid-fifth century. Bede's classic formulation of the tribes that invaded—"Angles, Saxons, and Jutes"—presumably refers to the Angles (from Angeln, a region in northern Germany), Saxons (from lower Saxony), and Jutes (from the Jutland peninsula of what is now Denmark). It is unlikely, however, that these groups were clearly distinct—or, at any rate, remained distinct once they came to England.

The German tribes brought over from their native land some sort of fertility cult associated with the Norse religion. A number of heathen practices apparently endured for centuries—among them the belief that their script (in the form of runes) had magical properties, and that supernatural creatures of all sorts existed. Anglo-Saxon kings—each of whom ruled a greater or lesser portion of the island—from an early period claimed descent from Odin (rendered as Woden in Old English).

The introduction of Christianity to Great Britain is canonically dated to 597, when Pope Gregory the Great sent a mission, led by one Augustine (who became the first Archbishop of Canterbury) to convert the Anglo-Saxons.[36] Not surprisingly, the gods of the Anglo-Saxons were quickly deemed to be devils by Christian converts, and the Anglo-Saxon kings now claimed authority to rule by the grace of God. Heathen practices were still being condemned by the church a century or more after the introduction of Christianity, suggesting their continued prevalence among some segments of the population. Some of the Anglo-Saxon kings refused to convert to the new faith. By the late seventh century, the church had established dioceses all over the island, and closer ties to the Roman church were effected. Many churches—more, proportionately, than on the Continent—were built across England, as were monasteries. As early as the late seventh century, English missionaries ventured to Europe to convert the heathen, often returning to their place of origin, Germany.

The church was involved in legal proceedings from an early period. Witchcraft persecutions were already in evidence at this time, sometimes resulting in death. But the church generally deprecated the death penalty—only because it wished to offer offenders the opportunity to repent and save their souls. Family law (i.e., laws pertaining to marriage, divorce, incest, and other such issues) was of course under the complete purview of the church. The church nominally prohibited divorce, but it was widely practised—and was, on the whole, quite liberal as regards the status of the former wife. A kind of community property law was in

36. The conversion of Ireland to Christianity had occurred at an earlier period, when St. Patrick (390?–461?) was taken to the island by Irish pirates at the age of sixteen. He later declared himself a priest, then a bishop. St. Columba (d. 597) established a monastery on the island of Iona and converted the Picts of Scotland.

effect. Overall, "Ecclesiastical blessing was not necessary to the legality of the marriage, although the Church advocated it."[37]

The Danish invasion of England (865–78) resulted in the ceding of large portions of eastern England to the Danes, who were heathen. They destroyed many churches and monasteries and put a halt to Christian expansion in the island for a century or more. But the Danes gradually converted to Christianity.

The Norman invasion of England, culminating in the definitive defeat of the Anglo-Saxons at the Battle of Hastings in 1066, resulted in the establishment of a Norman aristocracy that ruled the Anglo-Saxon populace. The Normans came from various regions in northern France, led by the Duke of Normany, who became William I (the Conqueror). William united the island under one crown for the first time, although the process took some decades. He decreed the building of castles throughout England—a tangible sign of the Normans' victory.

As an autocrat, William I was intent on gaining control of the English church, wresting it away from the pope. Although this process lapsed among his successors, he laid the groundwork for a nationalised church. The issue took on a grim aspect when Thomas à Becket (1119?–1170), archbishop of Canterbury, engaged in disputes with King Henry II (r. 1154–89) over the relative powers of church and state; as a result, Henry contrived his assassination. Nonetheless, the church flourished in other ways during this period, especially in the proliferation of monasteries, which often received generous financial support from tithes and other sources.

The Hundred Years' War with France (1337–1453), for all that it featured notable English victories at Crécy (1346), Poitiers (1356), and Agincourt (1415), ultimately resulted in the loss of all French territory (except Calais) controlled by England. During this period, the English exhibited an even greater desire to vaunt the national church over the papacy; various acts of Parliament (established in a rudimentary form in the early thirteenth century) promoted this view, especially in regard to the financial exactions made by the papacy upon the people.

At the same time, the English government was determined to wipe out the one home-grown heretical movement, the Lollards. There

37. Whitelock, *The Beginnings of English Society* 152.

is considerable confusion and controversy over the precise nature and extent of the Lollards' influence upon English religion and society during the late fourteenth and early fifteenth centuries, and especially on the question of how (or whether) they were following the doctrines of John Wyclif. It can in any event be stated that the various terms (Lollard, Loller, Lollardy) denoting them were devised by church figures opposed to them, as it generally signified an ignorant or uneducated person who was unfamiliar with the Latin language and stuck to vernacular English. And yet, as an important recent study has pointed out,[38] none of these terms appear in the documents emerging out of the Blackfriars Council of 1382, summoned by William Courtenay, Archbishop of Canterbury (1381–96), whose purpose was to condemn the central doctrines that Wyclif had advocated. The terms only emerged later in the decade and were then embraced by the Lollards themselves. The chief focus of the council was to suppress the unlicenced preaching of laymen (and laywomen), since that practice—even more than Wyclif's repudiation of the Real Presence in the sacrament—challenged church authority.

A more dramatic step was taken in 1401 by the passage by Parliament of *De heretico comburendo,* which allowed the burning of heretics for the two central crimes attributed to Wyclif and the Lollards: denial of transubstantiation and lay preaching. Under the leadership of Thomas Arundel, Archbishop of Canterbury (1396–1414), and his successor, Henry Chichele (1414–43), several heretics were in fact burned, most prominently Sir John Oldcastle in 1417.

For all the attempts to suppress it, Lollardy persisted in some fashion all the way up to the Reformation. Indeed, there is some reason to see in Wyclif and the Lollards an anticipation of the principles that fueled England's split with the Roman Catholic church in the sixteenth century.

The literature of England during the entire mediaeval period may seem to offer few hints of the development of anything approaching religious scepticism, even if we set aside Wyclif and the Lollards (who, for all their iconoclasm and anticlericalism, were fervent believers in what they took to be scriptural Christianity). As one scholar, Richard Newhauser, has noted, "The bulk of extant Middle English literature is made up of a wide variety of religious works."[39] What Newhauser

38. Cole, *Literature and Heresy in the Age of Chaucer.*

39. Richard Newhauser, "Religious Writing: Hagiography, *Pastoralia,* Devotional and

asserts for Middle English (roughly the period from 1100 to 1500) could also apply to Old English or Anglo-Saxon (c. 550–1100).

Beowulf is the chief literary document of the Anglo-Saxon period, although many questions regarding it—notably the date of its composition (anywhere from the eighth to the early eleventh century) and its author—remain the subject of heated scholarly debate. What we can say with some degree of certainty is that the surface story—the battle between Beowulf (a hero of the Geats, a tribe occupying southern Sweden) with the monsters Grendel, Grendel's mother, and a dragon—does not seem inherently Christian, even though Grendel is described as a "fiend out of hell" (l. 101)[40] and is said to be a descendant of Cain. The dragon mortally wounds Beowulf, who is then burned on a pyre.

The uneasy mingling of a pagan backdrop and Christian elements is typical of the poem, and has engendered disputes as to whether such elements are integral to the poem or were perhaps added later by Christian scribes. The nod to Cain and other features of the Genesis story is not the only Christian reference, and allusions to hell and the Last Judgment are present as well, although Jesus Christ is not mentioned. It is, however, undeniable that the poem strongly reflects the warrior culture of the Anglo-Saxons prior to their conversion to Christianity.

With the Norman invasion, English literature took on a French or generally European cast. Many texts were translated from French, Latin, and other languages, although they often incorporated much original material. They were written both in prose and poetry; many adhered to the chivalric code. The subject-matter reached back to pagan Greece and Rome, some claiming to be historical accounts even when they included elements of fantasy and the supernatural. Lyric poetry emerged in the late twelfth century; it was largely religious and may have been used for didactic purposes. But there are hints of a secular appreciation of nature, love, and other elements.

William Langland's *Piers Plowman* (mid- to late fourteenth century) is of some interest. Nothing is known of its author, and the poem exists in three versions, each one longer than the last. Presented as a dream (in accordance with much other mediaeval writing), it offers occasionally

---

Contemplative Works," in Scanlon, *The Cambridge Companion to Medieval English Literature 1100–1500* 37.

40. I use the modern English verse translation (1914) of John R. Clark Hall.

searing criticisms of contemporary lapses in religious and moral rectitude. But it concludes with a condensed version of the Gospels and Revelation, so it could hardly be said that Langland embodies scepticism to any appreciable degree.

Quite a bit more to our interest is the work of Geoffrey Chaucer (1340?–1400). His wide travels throughout Europe may have inclined him to absorb European literature; he seems to have been particularly influenced by the Latin and Italian literature of the period. *The Book of the Duchess* is adapted from Ovid's *Metamorphoses; The House of Fame* from Virgil's *Aeneid; Troilus and Criseyde* from Boccaccio; *The Legend of Good Women* draws heavily upon classical sources. But it is in the *Canterbury Tales* (begun in the 1380s and left unfinished at the time of his death) that is most indicative of his attitude toward the Christian religion.

There is no denying that some segments of the work reflect sincere and devout faith in Christian doctrine. "The Second Nun's Tale" is a reverent treatment of the story of St. Cecilia, a Roman martyr of the second century; the tale lays bare the persecution of Christians during the reign of Marcus Aurelius. "The Prioress's Tale" is a supernatural narrative of a Christian boy who is killed by Jews but still manages to sing, even though his throat is cut. The tale is marred by ugly antisemitism. In neither of these stories, nor in several others that faithfully reflect orthodox Christian teaching, have scholars been able to argue convincingly that Chaucer's intent is satirical or parodic.

"The Man of Law's Tale" is a meandering account of a woman, Constance (the name is significant), who is first pressured to marry a Syrian sultan (on the proviso that he convert to Christianity), then makes her way to England, where she marries a local king, Alla, but is then banished by Alla's mother and is almost raped aboard a ship, but finally returns to Rome and is eventually reunited with Alla and her son Maurice. There might be some hint of comedy in Constance's continual buffeting by fate (much more extreme than in the account of "patient Griselda" in "The Clerk's Tale"), but even here it is difficult to perceive what the parodic intent would have been.

On the other hand, there are any number of tales that present severe criticisms of individual churchmen and, more broadly, some phases of Christian doctrine as practised in Chaucer's time. "The Pardoner's Tale" is a prime example, whereby the Pardoner (a church official who absolves people of their sins—for money) convicts himself of greed ("I preche of no thyng but for coveityse" [424]);[41] and while the tale he recounts condemns gluttony, drunkenness, gambling, perjury, murder, and other sins, he makes sure to add unctuously: "Myn hooly pardoun yow alle warice" (906; i.e., my pardon will free you from all this).

"The Friar's Tale" recounts how an archdeacon is determined to punish fornication and lechery in his district, and so he hires a "summoner" (an official associated with an ecclesiastical court, tasked with summoning those who were accused of religious crimes) to entrap individuals by means of bribery and blackmail. If this wasn't bad enough, the summoner goes on to meet the Devil, who—when the summoner unjustly accuses a woman of adultery—carries him off to hell, where (as the Friar pungently notes) "somonours han hir heritage" (1641; i.e., have their special area).

"The Summoner's Tale" is a direct rebuttal to "The Friar's Tale" by a summoner, who makes frequent jibes about friars' inclinations toward mendicancy. And while the tale begins with a sober retelling of the seven deadly sins, it descends into scatalogical humour by a lengthy disquisition on farting. In these two tales, neither friars nor summoners come off very well.

And we can hardly overlook the bawdy "Wife of Bath's Tale," where a woman frankly admits to having had five husbands and wants at least one more; after all, wasn't it Paul who said, "Bet is to be wedded than to brynne" (Prologue, 52)? She takes pride in using her body to keep her husbands in line. The sexual frankness of the story has a very modern feel to it.

As noted, much of *The Canterbury Tales*, like Chaucer's other works, was adapted from other sources, ranging from Ovid to Boccaccio, but the vibrancy and rollicking good humour we find throughout the text are surely Chaucer's own. It is remarkable that he wrote his work at precisely the time when England was embroiled in the Lollard controversy, with accusations of heresy abounding; and while nothing in the book can be said to be strictly heretical, let alone sceptical of the fundamental truth of Christianity, the pungent and satirical expressions of anticlericalism are a further suggestion that doubts about the efficacy

41. I use the line numbers in F. N. Robinson's edition of *The Works of Geoffrey Chaucer.*

of Roman Catholicism—and the corruption that the intertwining of church and state could engender—were becoming widespread among the intellectual class.

About a century later, Sir Thomas Malory (1415?–1471) wrote *Le Morte Darthur.* The religious environment in England during the fifteenth century was highlighted by the appearance of a range of Christian mystics, whether it be Julian of Norwich (1343–1416), an anchoress (i.e., a woman who has withdrawn from secular society to devote her life to prayer) and author of *Revelations of Divine Love,* or Margery Kempe (1373?–1438?), whose *Book of Margery Kempe* recounts her trips to the Holy Land and her intense commitment to celibacy (although she was married) and personal devotion to God. In Europe, a similar movement was underway, embodied in the work of Thomas à Kempis (1380?–1471), the German author of *De Imitatione Christi* (c. 1418–27; On the Imitation of Christ), featuring a call for personal communion with God without the need of clergy or even church attendance, and a disregard for the niceties of theological conundrums. This movement, along with Lollardy and the increasing nationalisation of the English church, pointed in the direction of the break with Rome in the sixteenth century.

This development may not be of direct relevance to Malory, but it provides an intriguing backdrop in which to consider the religious (or secular) implications of *Le Morte Darthur.* We must, however, face the fact that two substantially different texts of the work now exist—the version published by William Caxton in 1485 and the so-called Winchester Manuscript, discovered in 1934, which presents the chapters in different order and contains numerous other textual differences. It is unclear which text is closer to Malory's intentions.

Whatever the case, the volume is undeniably the most vivid retelling of the Arthurian legend in English literature, and the basic outlines of the story are widely familiar: the emergence of King Arthur as the head of a group of knights (the Round Table); their frequent battles with various foes, both natural and supernatural; the adultery committed by Arthur's wife, Guinevere, when she sleeps with the greatest of the knights, Lancelot; and—most centrally for our purposes—the overt religiosity of the quest for the Holy Grail by Lancelot, Galahad (Lancelot's son), and others. The book concludes with the death of Arthur, Lancelot, and other knights. John Boorman's 1981 film *Excalibur* is a vibrant retelling of the legend, largely based on Malory.

The degree to which Malory wished to present a secular or religious account of the Arthuriad has been the subject of much scholarly debate in recent years. It would probably be best to conclude with K. S. Whetter that "the *Morte* is, at the very least, both secular *and* Christian."[42] But, as Whetter himself goes on to argue, the emphasis should perhaps be on the secular side.

While it is true that the knightly ideal that Malory exhaustively chronicles is itself based upon the principle of defending the church, it is significant that the *Morte* itself never asserts such a principle anywhere in the text. The assumption by Christian-inclined critics, including C. S. Lewis, that the downfall of Arthur and the Round Table is due to the various sins committed by them—Arthur's incestuous union with Morgawse (wife of King Lot) as well as Lancelot's affair with Guinevere, among other events—is not as straightforward as it seems. It is true that Morgawse gives birth to Mordred, who ultimately wounds Arthur mortally at the end of the epic; but Arthur's death is presented by Malory as a noble if tragic death, a symbol for the end of an heroic era.

Lancelot is the most equivocal figure in the *Morte,* especially in his role in the pursuit of the Holy Grail (which Malory refers to as the Sankgreal). In this regard it is worth comparing Malory's text with his chief source, the thirteenth-century French work *Queste de Saint Greal.* Whetter frankly asserts that Malory's "Tale of the Sankgreal is far more secular than its source."[43] It is true that Malory repeats the standard account of the Grail—that it was brought to England by Joseph of Arimathea, and that it has miraculous healing powers; it is also true that Lancelot, when he comes upon the Grail, is supernaturally prevented from seizing it (see Book XVII, ch. 15), leaving it to the sinless Galahad to do so. But some countervailing arguments may be brought forward.

The text presents the notion of fellowship as the chief virtue of the knightly ideal, not devotion to God or the church. Lancelot's miraculous healing of King Urry (Book XIX, ch. 12) by a prayer to the Trinity ("Thou

42. K. S. Whetter, "Malory's Secular Arthuriad," in Hanks and Jesmok, *Malory and Christianity* 162.
43. Whetter 159.

blessed Father, Son, and Holy Ghost, I beseech thee of thy mercy . . .")[44] and by the laying on of hands would seem to be an emphatic instance of God's grace; but, as Elizabeth Archibald declares, it can also be seen as "a final celebration of the Round Table fellowship."[45] Note that this incident occurs *after* his adulterous union with Guinevere; nonetheless, he is declared to be the greatest of knights, and, after the demise of the Round Table, he is borne up to heaven by angels upon his death (Book XXI, ch. 12).

Malory's status in regard to Christianity will remain a debated issue. Suffice it to say that *Le Morte Darthur* is anything but a text that uniformly or unequivocally sanctions Christian doctrine, especially as it avowedly portrays events in what every reader must have known was a pre-Christian England.

44. I use a modernised text edited by John Matthews.
45. Elizabeth Archibald, "Malory's Ideal of Fellowship," *Review of English Studies* n.s. 43 (1992): 326.

VI. The Renaissance

> In some respects, Italians of the Renaissance . . . had still the reverence for authority that medieval philosophers had, but they substituted the authority of the ancients for that of the Chruch.
>
> —Bertrand Russell

Two events in the 1450s—the invention of printing and the Ottoman Turks' conquest of Constantinople—in their disparate ways signalled a new age in the making. The German Johannes Gutenberg (1400?–1468) had begun working on his invention—a movable-type printing press—as early as 1440 and perfected it around 1450. His Bible—set up in type in 1452 and published in 1455—was not the first item to roll off his press; indeed, he was noted for many other types of printed material, including broadsheets, flyers, and the like. He issued an encyclopaedia, the *Catholicon,* in 1460. The true innovation of Gutenberg's invention was not the printing process iself but the mass-production of reading matter in identical copies. Printing spread rapidly into France, Italy, and England (where William Caxton established his press in 1476), although in Germany itself the continued use of difficult-to-read Fraktur type has been seen as emblematic of the region's resistance to Renaissance humanism.

What printing did, in essence, was to destroy the church's control of literary, religious, and other texts. It had had a monopoly on the distribution of reading matter by virtue of the copying of works by monks. Now, texts were broadly available to the middle class. (Interestingly, wealthy or aristocratic patrons initially scorned printed books, preferring handwritten manuscripts.) Even if early printed works remained predominantly religious, their widespread absorption by lay readers foreshadowed the demise of the church as the focus of culture and literacy. Other publishers—such as Aldus Manutius in Venice and Guillaume Budé in Paris—made a point of publishing sound, accurate editions of Greco-Roman literary and philosophical texts, thereby fostering Renaissance thinkers' burgeoning interest in these works. Desiderius Erasmus and Martin Luther, in the early sixteenth century, became among the earliest intellectual figures to make adept use of printing to disseminate their views outside of the church or the university environment.

The Turkish invasion of Europe was a phenomenon of a very different order, signifying the political and military turmoil that engulfed the region in the later fifteenth and early sixteenth centuries. The Ottoman Turks[1] had gained a toehold in Europe as early as 1354, when they had taken Gallipoli. They systematically acquired much of the Balkan region by the end of the fourteenth century. But in Turkey itself they suffered defeat at the hands of Timur (Tamerlane) in 1402. Mehmed II (r. 1451–81) captured Constantinople in 1453, sending shock waves throughout Europe. He renamed the city Istanbul, seeking to repopulate it not only with Muslums but also with Christians, Jews, and others. Mehmed took Athens, Serbia, Bosnia, and other territory by 1479. Syria and Egypt fell to the Ottmans by 1517. Suleiman the Magnificent (r. 1520–66) battled the Habsburg dynasty in many areas of Europe; he came close to sacking Vienna in 1529 and again in 1532, but failed; he did capture parts of Hungary in the 1540s, making Transylvania a vassal state; and he took portions of Greece away from Venice in 1537–40, also making gains in North Africa.

The effect of these victories by a Muslim power created in Europeans a sense of instability and panic that may well have fed into the Reformation of the early sixteenth century. At a time when military conquest by Christians was seen as a vindication of their religion, these defeats caused many to question the wisdom and authority of the leaders

1. The name is not an ethnic designation, but derives from the name of its founder, Osman or Othman I (d. 1326).

(both ecclesiastical and political) in whom they had placed their trust. As Renaissance humanists exhibited the intellectual and cultural glories of the pre-Christian civilisation of Greece and Rome, the educated class (still a tiny proportion of the general public) had reason to question whether the Christian god was as all-powerful as scripture claimed he was.

A. The Emergence of Humanism

The very term Renaissance (like Middle Ages or "the mediaeval era") has long been the subject of controversy among historians. The popular conception of the Renaissance is largely based upon the pioneering work of the Swiss historian Jakob Burckhardt, author of *Die Cultur der Renaissance in Italien* (1860), translated into English in 1878 as *The Civilisation of the Renaissance in Italy*. What Burckhardt professed, according to this conception, was that the mediaeval era was a period of ignorance and barbarism, and that the sudden flourishing of "humanism" in Italy in the early fifteenth century led to a rebirth of individualism and a renunciation of religious belief, thereby ushering in the modern age of science and secularism.

But this view is itself a simple-minded caricature of Burckhardt's enormously complex thesis. And while it is true that the basic principle was propounded by secularists of the eighteenth, nineteenth, and early twentieth centuries as a justification for their own renunciation of religious belief (or, more broadly, their advocacy of the separation of church and state), the countervailing view—that the very term Middle Ages is pejorative (as suggesting an unsatisfactory interlude between two periods of enlightenment, Greco-Roman classicism and the Renaissance) and that there were any number of "renaissances" during the Middle Ages, so that the transition to the Renaissance was gradual and not clear-cut—while having much validity, was itself pushed to extremes by those who had a vested interest in promoting the mediaeval era as an era where Christianity (and especially Catholicism) was thought to have been universal and unchallenged. This view—advanced by such non-scholarly figures as G. K. Chesterton, Hilaire Belloc, Arthur Machen, T. S. Eliot, and others—is itself a tendentious rewriting of history. There really was a pretty significant difference—politically, economically, intellectually, artistically, and culturally—between 1400 and 1500; and even if overt atheism was still vanishingly rare, both the literary and the scientific advances of the Renaissance laid the groundwork for the flourishing of religious scepticism in the centuries that followed.

It is notoriously difficult to define what "humanism" is in the context of the early fifteenth century in Italy. The phrase *studia humanitatis*—generally translated (inaccurately) as "the study of the humanities"[2]—was frequently used by thinkers of that age; but no one now maintains that humanism was a "philosophy" in any coherent sense. It should be noted, however, that the humanists themselves by and large believed that the movement they embodied marked a distinct and historic break from the era that preceded it; and there is every reason to think that they were right in so thinking.

The Renaissance took hold at various times in the various nations or regions of Europe, and first manifested itself in Italy in the early fifteenth century. Petrarch was a significant forerunner in his comprehensive knowledge of ancient (Latin) literature and in his belief that he was a pioneer in looking back to Greece and Rome for literary and philosophic inspiration and in deeming the intervening period a "dark age." There may have been a certain national pride involved here, since many humanists specifically pointed to republican Rome for inspiration; and they were therefore seeking a rebirth (*rinascimento*) of the culture that produced it.

This rebirth took place amidst a chaos in which the major cities of Italy—Venice, Milan, Florence, Naples (then a dependency of Aragon), and the Papal States (separate from but associated with the Holy Roman Empire) all fought for economic, political, and military supremacy. In 1434 Florence came under the control of the Medici family, which maintained its dominance continuously until 1494, engendering an era of commercial prosperity as well as a spectacular efflorence of art and architecture.

It was in Florence that Renaissance humanism flourished for a century following the death of Petrarch in 1374. Scholasticism had never taken firm root in Italy overall, and Florence had no university until 1349; and it remained a republic when many other Italian cities fell under the sway of despots. This factor enhanced Florentine intellectuals'

2. The problem lies in the fact that *studia* is plural while *humanitatis* is singular, so that a literal (but probably misleading) translation would be "studies in humanity."

belief that they were reviving the traditions of republican Rome.

It may seem paradoxical that the Renaissance humanists' thirst for classical literature could foster a new intellectual era; but their absorption of Greek and Latin texts was anything but an antiquarian exercise. What is more, the rediscovery of these texts went far beyond those that, as no one now denies, were widely read in the mediaeval era. Whereas such writers as Cicero, Virgil, and Ovid had always maintained their popularity, and Aristotle maintained his standing as "the Philosopher" (a status that would endure until the seventeenth century), the Renaissance now found other authors of consuming interest—the Greek tragic playwrights, the satirists Juvenal and Persius, the philosopher and dramatist Seneca the Younger, and many others. The reading of these texts—in complete form rather than in the extracts or *sententiae* that had been dominant in the mediaeval period—led not merely to a broader understanding of the authors in question and a renewed appreciation of their literary greatness, but to a gradual awareness that the mediaeval era's belief that Greco-Roman culture was a natural prelude to Christianity was untenable. This critical realisation laid the groundwork for the flourishing of Renaissance culture throughout Europe.

Among the pioneers in this literary research were Luigi Marsili (1342–1394) and Coluccio Salutati (1331–1406), the latter of whom worked with both Greek and Latin texts. These pursuits, far from being purely academic, were designed to focus on such issues as rhetoric, poetry (to be read for the ethical values it contained), moral philosophy, and public speaking, for the purpose of preparing younger members (invariably male) of aristocratic families for civic leadership. In this scenario, logic and metaphysics of the scholastic sort were deemed less useful. But it was Leonardo Bruni of Arezzo (1370–1444) who propounded a radically revisionist account of ancient history whereby both Athenian democracy and republican Rome were seen as pinnacles of civilisation because (so he believed) they advocated freedom of thought, whereas the Roman Empire (which mediaevalists such as Dante saw as a necessary step toward the establishment of Christianity) was seen as a retrogression. He made good use of texts by Aristotle (the *Ethics* and the *Politics*) and others to promote his notion of civic humanism.

Other Italian humanists diligently sought out ancient texts beyond those well known to the mediaeval era. Many Greek texts were translated into Latin, since Greek was still a rare acquirement even among the intelligentsia. Lorenzo Valla (1407–1457) made a profound study of the history and development of classical Latin; he subjected the work of Roman historians to critical scrunity; and, in a pioneering development, he applied his literary and philological skills to Christian texts. It was he who exposed the Donation of Constantine (a document purportedly written by the Emperor Constantine and which granted political authority over the entirety of "Christendom" to an early pope) as a crude forgery, thereby destroying a central pillar in the papacy's claim of supremacy over secular rulers. Predictably, however, popes continued to cite the document as genuine for several more centuries.

Although most humanists were devout and few doubted the overall truth of Christian revelation, their movement gained a reputation for scepticism, even heresy. The mere fact that many clerics objected to such intensive study of pagan literature as inherently anti-Christian is the surest sign that humanists were evolving a new way of thinking and not merely continuing mediaeval interest in Greco-Roman literature. Pope Paul II (1471–84) accused humanists in the papal curia of impiety, although this may have been a mask for other concerns.

Marsilio Ficino (1433–1499) was a significant figure in the revival of Platonism and Neoplatonism in the Renaissance. It may not be immediately evident how such a stance had any value in promoting humanism, much less secularism, since Plato's worldview (to say nothing of that of such Neoplatonists as Plotinus) was religious from beginning to end. But Ficino's advocacy of these doctrines played some role in questioning the dominance of Aristotle as a philosophical and scientific authority (Ficino objected to Aristotle because he believed the Greek thinker denied the immortality of the soul). More generally, Ficino's work resulted in a sort of spiritualised Christianity that downplayed specific doctrines and sought to eliminate the crude supernaturalism that he correctly believed his audience of intellectual elites could no longer accept.

What particularly exercised Christian thinkers was the humanists' presentation of a more optimistic view of human nature, as an antidote to the mediaeval view (stemming from Augustine an embodied in Pope Innocent III's *De Miseria Humanis Conditionae* [On the Misery of the Human Condition], written in the 1194–95 and enjoying popularity for centuries) that humanity was irredeemably corrupt and sinful. Valla wrote a treatise, *De Voluptate* (1431; On Pleasure) that accurately portrayed and defended the Epicurean view of pleasure as freedom from pain, thereby justifying the pursuit of rational pleasure as an inherent good. (Let us recall that Dante had placed Epicurus in one of the lower circles of hell.) A later essay on the subject—*De Dignitate et Excellentia Hominis* (On the Dignity and Excellence of Man; written 1452–53) by Giannozzo Manetti (1396–1459)— was a direct response to Innocent III's treatise. Without in any way repudiating Christian revelation, Manetti flatly denies original sin, waxes eloquent on the manifold pleasures of human life on earth (including sexual fulfilment), and suggests that God's artistic craftsmanship of the human body is reflected by both religious and secular artists.

Another significant advance initiated by the humanists was a reform of education. The emphasis away from the philosophical abstractions of mediaeval metaphysics and toward a more practical focus on the development of literary and rhetorical skills underpinned by moral engagement created a general sense among the intelligentsia that a purely Christian instruction was insufficient to the needs of the time. The revision of educational practice culminated in the work of Erasmus. In his various pedagogical works he frankly recommended a secular education and rejected the idea of religious schools—points that had been made in rudimentary form by humanists over the past century.

The writings of Giovanni Pico della Mirandola (1563–1594) have often been taken as a compact summary of Italian humanism; but anyone who has actually read his work—even the supposed humanist manifesto *On the Dignity of Man* (1486)—could not possibly lend any credence to such a view, if by that we mean that he is propounding anything approaching secular individualism. Pico's philosophy was a bizarre mishmash of Platonism (derived in part from Ficino), the more mystical elements of other Greek philosophers (Pythagoras and the Hermetic/Orphic tradition, which he believed to be of vast antiquity), and Christian revelation, with the Jewish Kabbalah thrown in for good measure. What his essay on the dignity of man actually asserts is that human beings literally and symbolically stand between God and the natural world, being comprised in equal portions of angels, the heavenly bodies, and earthly bodies. This led him to the view that human beings are singular among earthly creatures in being able to choose their own "nature," for good or ill. To this extent, Pico joins the humanists in a relatively optimistic view of human nature and its potential for secular achievement. In the opinion of one scholar, "His view of human nature seems to leave no need at all for the action of divine grace, no need for a crucified and resurrected Saviour: it seems totally Pelagian."[3] Other aspects of his work—notably his belief that every religion or philosophy has some grain of truth in it—had the unintended effect of demoting Christianity from its position as the sole arbiter of truth. This predictably led to a charge of heresy against Pico in 1487.

By 1500, humanist scholars were ensconced in all the major universities of Europe (including England), although there were frequent clashes with older generations of scholars who continued to cling to scholasticism. The sixteenth century saw the emergence of a cadre of classical scholars in France—Guillaume Budé (1467–1540), Robert Estienne (1503–1559), and Joseph Justus Scaliger (1540–1609), and Isaac Casaubon (1559–1614)—who are still revered by classicists for their pioneering work in textual and historical studies. And while it is true that no humanist of the fifteenth or sixteenth century ranks among the leading philosophers of the West, several of them questioned the reverence with which the philosophy and science of Aristotle was regarded, thereby preparing the groundwork for the overthrow of "the Philosopher" in the seventeenth century as the ramifications of a new science began to be understood.

It is often stated that Renaissance humanism never produced a philosopher of the highest stature, and that is essentially true; even Erasmus (for whom see the next section) does not qualify. However, from our perspective Pietro Pomponazzi (1462–1525) holds some interest. He was one of the leading figures of what came to be called the Padua school, a group of thinkers associated with the University of Padua. Pomponazzi, a physician, wrote a pioneering work in Latin, *De Immortalitate Animae* (1516; On the Immortality of the Soul), who employed his studies of Aristotle (he had lectured on the *De Anima* when he was a professor at Ferrara) to come close to denying the immortality of the soul. He did not do so explicitly, maintaining that since such a

3. Nauert, *Humanism and the Culture of Renaissance Europe* 76.

claim is made in scripture, it must be true; but it is fairly evident that Pomponazzi was using this as a convenient cover for the claim that the soul's immortality cannot be established by human reason. It does not appear, however, that his treatise was widely influential.

Probably the keenest thinker of the period was Niccolò Machiavelli (1469–1527); and although his work is significantly influenced by humanism and the revival of learning, it is restricted to political philosophy. The standard caricature of him—derived from an ahistorical reading of *Il principe* (The Prince; written c. 1513, published 1532)—as an amoral cynic who advocated ruthless manipulation in the sphere of politics is very wide of the mark, and much of his writing is a product of the political and military turmoil Italy was facing during his life. His *Discorsi* (Discourses; written 1517, published 1531), under the guise of a commentary on the first ten books of Livy's history of Rome, speaks out randomly against the corruption of the papacy (Book I, ch. 12). And his novella *Belfagor arcidiavolo* (written 1518–27; Belfagor the Archdevil) is a wicked satire on religion (and also marriage and women), dealing with a demon who comes up from hell, marries a woman who proves to be an irrepressible spendthrift, and ultimately returns to the safety of the underworld.

There is a furious debate among scholars as to the relation of Machiavelli's work to religion in general and Christianity in particular, ranging from those who believe Machiavelli was essentially Christian in his outlook (even if he also appealed to historical examples from classical antiquity and also cherry-picked those aspects of Christian doctrine he favoured) to those who argue that Machiavelli was openly anti-Christian—morally, politically, socially, and militarily.[4] It is probably safest to take a stand between these polar opposites, although perhaps with a slightly greater emphasis on the latter.

There is no denying that Machiavelli's chief objective was to defend the Florentine republic (especially after its ousting of the Medicis in 1494) and to vaunt its political system by appealing to the Roman republic whose origins nearly two millennia earlier Machiavelli—thoroughly versed in the work of both Greek and Roman historians—

4. For these varying perspectives see Viroli, *Machiavelli's God* and Parsons, *Machiavelli's Gospel*. I generally follow Parsons, although I refrain from condemning Machiavelli for "blasphemy" (183) as Parsons does.

traced in his *Discourses.* There is also little doubt that he scorned the meekness, humility, and implied pacifism that many have taken to be central to Christian morality. His scorn of the papacy from multiple perspectives is based on these central principles.

In the seminal chapter 6 of *The Prince,* Machiavelli speaks of four "princes" who by force of arms secured powerful kingdoms: Moses, Cyrus, Romulus, and Theseus. It is worth noting that the latter three of these stand outside the Judaeo-Christian tradition, and that Jesus himself is absent from the list. This is because Jesus, unlike Moses, did not gain his "kingdom" by force of arms, as Moses and the others did; the suggestion—never explicitly articulated—is that such a kingdom will ultimately fail, as it is unable to defend itself from attack by its opponents. (Machiavelli could well have had the Muslim incursions into Europe in mind here.)

The case of Girolamo Savonarola (1452–1498) is for Machiavelli a telling example of the bad things that can happen if religion is unsupported by military might. Savonarola gained power after the Medicis' overthrow and established himself as a Christian fanatic hostile to secular culture and keen on establishing Florence as a kind of new Jerusalem. In the ensuing turmoil, which included his excommunication by Pope Alexander VI, Savonarola was overthrown and executed in 1498.

In his discussion of "ecclesiastical principalities" (*The Prince,* ch. 11), Machiavelli presents an account of the papacy entirely shorn of any reverence for its status as the cynosure of Christian doctrine, examining it purely from the perspective of power politics. The papacy, in his view, has been so corrupted by "bad" popes that what few "good" ones there are can hardly prosper. The very moral qualities that are thought to be essential to Christianity—mercy, meekness, and charity—are impossible to maintain so long as the papacy is a political and military entity. Any attempt by the papacy to preserve these virtues will inevitably lead to its military defeat, and so the popes themselves are obliged to set them aside, becoming hypocrites in the process.

Machiavelli's Christian critics were especially enraged by his bland suggestion that a prince should be prepared to profess belief in the religion of the state he governs even if he doesn't believe in it himself. Chapter 18 of *The Prince* seems emphatic on the point:

> Thus it is well [for the prince] to seem merciful, faithful, humane, sincere, religious, and also to be so; but you must have the mind so disposed that when it is needful to be otherwise you may be able to change to the opposite qualities. And it must be understood that a prince, and especially a new prince, cannot observe all those things which are considered good in men, being often obliged, in order to maintain the state, to act against faith, against charity, against humanity, and against religion.

It is perhaps impossible to deny that Machiavelli is sanctioning a certain level of hypocrisy and duplicity in this passage; but his overriding concern for "maintain[ing] the state" meant that a prince might have occasion to act in this manner when faced with hostile princes equally ruthless or duplicitous.

In none of these discussions, however, can we see anything approaching atheism or even religious scepticism; and yet, Machiavelli quickly became a byword not only for political sleight-of-hand but also for freethinking. Such views were understandably articulated by conservative Catholics in the course of the Counter-Reformation of the later sixteenth century. The Spanish theologian Pedro de Ribadeneira (1527–1611), in his *Tratado de la religion* (1595),[5] an avowed rebuttal to *The Prince,* states flamboyantly that Machiavelli "attribute[s] Moses' laws and victories, not to God, who was guiding him, but to his own valor and power. . . . [Machiavelli and his followers] go so far as to deny (although not in so many words . . .) that there is a God or that He exercises providence over states!"[6] This claim had been made a few decades earlier—not by a Catholic but by a French Huguenot, Innocent Gentillet (1535–1588), who in 1576 published a treatise that also accused Machiavelli of atheism.

B. Erasmus, Luther, and the Reformation

It is in the context of Renaissance humanism that we must regard the

5. The full title is *Tratado de la religión y virtudes que debe tener el principe cristiano para gubernar y conservar sus estados* (Treatise on the religion and virtues that a Christian prince ought to have for governing and preserving his nation).
6. Quoted in Higuera, *Eros and Empire* 143.

revolutionary work of the two leading intellectual and religious figures of the early sixteenth century: Desiderius Erasmus (1466?–1536) and Martin Luther (1483–1546). Erasmus, born in Rotterdam, was already a revered figure throughout Europe by the time the young Martin Luther promulgated his celebrated *Ninety-five Theses* on 31 October 1517,[7] and their interrelations over the next two decades did much to determine the manner in which the Reformation proceeded.

Their largely intellectual activities occurred against the backdrop of an incredibly complex series of political, diplomatic, and military actions conducted by the leading European powers (France, Spain, England, the Holy Roman Empire), with a flurry of dynastic marriages that resulted in oftentimes temporary alliances, engendering a constant jockeying for power and influence across the face of Europe. Religion—in particular, the Catholic-Protestant divide as it emerged in the early sixteenth century—played a role, but it was only one of many factors at play.

In France, the Valois dynasty took control of the monarchy in 1328. After the Hunded Years War, Louis XI (r. 1461–83) was keen on suppressing rebellious nobles throughout his kingdom and had some success. He sought to establish an absolute monarchy, subjugating the Estates-General (a legislative assembly comprising the clergy, the nobility, and commoners); but his successor, Charles VIII (r. 1483–98), was forced to backtrack somewhat in this effort. Francis I (r. 1515–47), although forced to relinquish his territories in Italy in 1526, continued a push toward absolutism, bringing the church under his control. He was initially sympathetic to some elements of the Reformation, but later cracked down harshly on reformers—a policy his successor, Henry II (r. 1547–59), continued, as he set up the *chambre ardente* (burning court) to try heretics.

The Holy Roman Empire controlled a large amount of territory in Europe, mostly in Germany and portions of what is now France; ironically, as we have seen, it did not control Rome itself, which was part of the Papal States. Even in Germany, however, government was largely decentralised, as power rested in the hands of Electors of the various major regions (Saxony, Hanover, etc.). Germany was, at this time, a loose federation of principalities.

7. The widely held belief that he nailed this document to the door of All Saints' Church in Wittenberg is apparently a myth.

In Spain, Ferdinand II of Aragon and Isabella of Castile united in 1479 to rule the Spanish peninsula. But the region had significant divisions in population, and various regions asserted an element of independence. Even so, Ferdinand and Isabella became the leading Catholic monarchs of Europe. In 1478 they received papal blessing to set up the Spanish Inquisition (for which see section E). The monarchs also finally defeated the Moors by the conquest of Granada in 1492, thereby freeing the last remaining territory in Spain from Muslim control.

The Holy Roman Emperor Charles V took over rulership of Spain as Charles I (r. 1516–56), also ruling the Netherlands and parts of Austria. His successor, Philip II (r. 1556–98), became the leader of the Counter-Reformation. He also seized Portugal in 1580.

Against the backdrop of all this turmoil, Erasmus gained prominence—surprisingly so, as he was the illegitimate son of a priest and his paramour. There is no question of his piety and devotion to the Christian religion, given his upbringing and temperament. His early years, spent among the Brethren of the Common Life, which focused on the study of the Bible and a rejection of scholasticism, led to his taking up residence at an Augustinian monastery (1487–92). And yet, this was exactly where Erasmus became a thoroughgoing humanist, chiefly from his voluminous reading. In 1492 he became an ordained priest.

Visits to England beginning in 1499 made Erasmus aware of English scholars' focus on studying the NT from an historical perspective shorn of the theologising of the scholastics. Erasmus himself wished to study the NT, but realised that he needed to learn Greek in order to do so properly. With great effort he managed it. A treatise he wrote at this time, the *Enchiridion Militis Christiani* (1503; Handbook for the Christian Soldier), outlines many of the stances he maintained throughout his life: the emphasis on knowledge as a central basis for Christian faith; avoidance of the logic-chopping of mediaeval scholastics; and a reliance on the writings of the early Church Fathers as more reliable guides to Christian doctrine than later thinkers. There was little new in this tract, and the text remained essentially Catholic in its overall outlook and prescriptions; it would therefore be misleading to characterise it (as some scholars have done) as some sort of anticipation of Luther's thought. It was widely read throughout the sixteenth and seventeenth centuries.

It was in Louvain, where he settled in 1502, that Erasmus came upon Lorenzo Valla's unpublished *Annotations on the New Testament,* a work he had written around 1450. For Erasmus it was a revelation in its close readng of the biblical text and keen historical analysis. Inspired by this work (which he arranged for publication), Erasmus edited a corrected version of the Vulgate of Jerome (1505). It was at this time that he developed the notion that promoting humanism as well as the *philosophia Christi* (philosophy of Christ) could somehow proceed in tandem. What exactly the philosophy of Christ signified is not always clear in Erasmus's writings. Its basic principles were "the restoration of the authority of the Gospels over that of theology and tradition"[8] and, more broadly, a faith based on the infusion of human values into Christian belief.

In 1516 Erasmus issued a Latin translation (with Greek text) of the Greek NT—the first time that the latter was published. For all that Erasmus used inferior manuscripts as the basis of the Greek text, the edition was a landmark—but it was not free of controversy. The Vulgate itself had by this time become a kind of holy scripture in its own right, and any alteration of it was seen as heretical. Even though an encouraging letter from Pope Leo X (1513–21) provided Erasmus some cover, the Catholic church ultimately refused to sanction the text, and the Council of Trent (1545–63) reauthorised the Vulgate.

It was a year after the publication of this edition that Martin Luther burst upon the scene. His connexions to humanism have perhaps been exaggerated; while he may have been influenced by some aspects of Christian humanism, especially as to the importance of a thorough familiarity with the text of the Bible as opposed to scholastic interpretations of it, his temperament and doctrines are far out of step with those of the dominant humanists of the period, especially his sometime friend Erasmus.

Like Erasmus, he received a thorough religious education. Born in Saxony, he joined the Augustinian Friars, who had helped to found the University of Wittenberg in 1502. He became an ordained priest in 1501, then studied theology at Wittenberg. With Augustine, he came to believe that "man is too corrupted by sin to do anything truly righteous in the sight of God."[9] It is immediately evident that this assertion stands

8. Faludy, *Erasmus* 157–58.
9. Tracy, *Europe's Reformations* 49.

in stark contrast to the generally optimistic views of the humanists, especially Pico and Erasmus. As a result of this stance, Luther was obliged to accept the ubiquity of God's grace as well as predestination, with a concomitant rejection of free will.

The immediate impetus of the *Ninety-five Theses* was Pope Leo's doling out of indulgences (a penance required of sinners to reduce their guilt in the afterlife, often satisfied by the donation of money to the church) to raise funds for the rebuilding of St Peter's. Protestant historians have seized upon this practice as a cudgel with which to beat the Catholic church, but there is reason to doubt how widespread the practice was; Luther's ire was largely directed at one Johann Tetzel, a Dominican friar in Germany who did indeed dole out indulgences frequently and perhaps corruptly.

Whatever the case, the theses spread widely, thanks to their wide dissemination through the printing press. Clearly Luther had touched a nerve in those who objected to Rome's domination of Christian doctrine. For his part, Luther emphasised *sola scriptura* ("only scripture"), i.e., the contention that scripture is the sole authority in determining doctrine, as well as *sola fide* ("by faith alone"), i.e., that salvation is possible only through faith, not through good works (of which indulgences were, in his view, a part) or any other means. He relied chiefly on a passage from one of Paul's letters ("For I am not ashamed of the gospel. It is the saving power of God for everyone who has faith—the Jew first, but the Greek also—because in it the righteousness of God is seen at work, beginning in faith and ending in faith" [Rom. 1:16–17]), although other texts of a very different purport could be cited on this tortured question. Soon Luther was denying the infallibility of church councils, and then asserted that the throne of St Peter's was occupied by the Antichrist!

Erasmus appears at the outset to have been generally approving of the *Ninety-five Theses.* Luther got in touch with Erasmus by no later than March 1519, speaking warmly to him in correspondence but privately criticising him for emphasising the human over the divine. For his part, Erasmus correctedly determined that Luther was both intolerant and impetuous. Their views were antithetical in many ways, and they came to symbolise "the whole conflict between humanism and Reformation."[10]

10. Faludy, *Erasmus* 176.

In fact, Erasmus's programme of moderate reform seemed to be making strides within the Catholic church before Luther blew it up with his fanaticism and dogmatism, which triggered a parallel reaction on the part of Catholic authorities.

A papal bull of 15 June 1520 demanded that Luther recant his major doctrines (which by now included a rejection of transubstantiation and the pope's spiritual authority over Christians); Luther scornfully burned the bull. Erasmus attempted to act as intermediary, but he was becoming more and more disenchanted with Luther, who was now advocating violence against popes and cardinals. A second bull, issued on 3 January 1521, excommunicated him. Inspired by Erasmus, who had urged the publication of the Bible into the vernaclar languages, Luther (who was well versed in Greek and Hebrew) published his German translation of the NT in 1522; he then translated the OT from Hebrew in 1526. By this time Luther had gained some significant followers, notably Philip Melanchthon (1497–1560) and, in Zürich, Huldrych Zwingli (1484–1531), although they differed with him on certain points.

But Erasmus was no longer a colleague or friend. He was appalled at Luther's refusal to condemn the murder of some 100,000 people during the Peasants' War in Germany: Luther had trotted out the old "Render unto Caesar the things that are Caesar's" canard, even though the leaders of the peasants looked to his own writings in partial support of their complaints of mistreatment by their noble masters. Erasmus was also offended by a scurrilous pamphlet against him written by some of Luther's colleagues. And so Erasmus wrote a pamphlet rejecting Luther's denial of free will, to which the latter responded by calling Erasmus an "atheist"[11] and an Epicurean. (Insofar as Epicurus similarly affirmed the doctrine of free will, Luther was correct in the accusation, even though it was clearly meant to prejudice Erasmus in the eyes of Christians, who had long believed Epicureans to be closet atheists.)

But, as the split between Catholics and Protestants continued to widen, Erasmus stuck to his moderate platform by arguing for religious coexistence for all the various sects of Christianity. But his own adopted city of Basle, where he had been living since 1521, had now become implacably hostile to Catholics, and he decided to leave, settling in

11. Tracy 66.

Freiberg, Austria. He returned to scholarship, preparing editions of nearly all the early Church Fathers. But he must have recognised on his deathbed that his hope of effecting some kind of peace among the ever-increasing Christian sects was hopeless.

C. The Spread of Reformation Theology

In the decades following Luther's manifesto, successive church councils attempted to resolve disputes between Lutherans and Catholics; but by 1541, it was evident that these attempts had failed, largely due to intransigence on both sides. The Council of Trent emphatically endorsed the Catholic stance on the central issues of the debate (confession, transubstantiation, the role of the priesthood, and so on) against what it saw as Lutheran heresy. Emperor Charles V sought to beat German princes into submission, but after many bloody battles he was forced to sign the Peace of Augsburg (1555), in which Protestants were essentially granted the right to practise their religion, although individual princes and other authorities could dictate which religions were sanctioned in their principalities. Protestantism continued to grow in Germany, Austria, and elsewhere. But even before Luther's death in 1546, Protestants were fracturing into discrete and mutually hostile sects.

One of these new sects was the Anabaptists, who, although they had antecedents in the mediaeval era, emerged in the wake of Luther's break from Rome. They quickly gained a following in Switzerland, the Netherlands, northern Germany, Austria, and elsewhere. They rejected the doctrine of infant baptism, since they maintained that baptism could only be offered to one who requested it in full understanding of what it means to assert faith in Jesus Christ. They pointed out that "Nowhere in the scriptures was there an example of infant baptism. Rather, in the Gospels and the Acts of the Apostles only adults were baptized, and only after confession of faith."[12] This doctrine (like Luther's *sola scriptura*) eliminated the need for priests to ensure salvation, hence was anathema to a Catholic church intent on maintaining its spiritual control over the people. The church ferociously persecuted them for the better part of the

12. B. Emmet McLaughlin, "The Radical Reformation," in Hsia, *The Cambridge History of Christianity* 47.

next century and a half.

The case of one of Luther's supports, John Calvin (1509–1564), is instructive. Born in Picardy in northern France, he received a thorough religious training as a youth but became a lawyer rather than a priest. It was during Calvin's stay in Basle, beginning in 1535, that he became a full convert to Luther's programme of reform. The very next year he published his most famous treatise, *Christianae Religionis Institutio* (1536; Institutes of the Christian Religion), a catechism of Christian doctrine for adults. The first edition was only of modest size; the third edition of 1559 is five times as large and presents a comprehensive summary of Calvin's theology.

It was in 1536 that Calvin first settled in Geneva. In the early sixteenth century the city was not part of the Swiss Confederacy; it was nominally a "free" city but in fact was under the effective control of the Dukes of Savoy. It threw off this yoke in the 1520s. Calvin's initial stay in the city—as a "reader" of Holy Scripture—was marred by theological disputes, and he was expelled in 1538. In 1541 he was asked to return, and it was at this point that he systematically undertook to realise his goals for church and secular governance.

Calvin's theology rested upon the assumption that God had established a fixed order of nature to which human beings had no choice but to conform—the antipodal opposite of the human freedom proposed by the humanist Pico della Mirandola. With Luther, he believed that all human nature was fatally tainted by sin; reason was an insufficient tool to lead us to virtue. Only the grace of God and the guidance of the Holy Spirit can do that. But, in some fashion, God has implanted in us a dim sense of right and wrong. Since God had, in Calvin's view, established "laws" for human behaviour (embodied in the Decalogue and other passages in scripture), obedience to them must be absolute; any deviation from them signals an abandonment of God. Hence the need for a civil/religious governing authority that must practise constant vigilance in guarding against such deviations.

This is exactly the authority that Calvin instituted in Geneva. The citizenry were to be overseen by elders or presbyters who, along with pastors, formed a Consistory. Such a body was not Calvin's invention, but Calvin was unique in his intimate fusing of using the Consistory to fuse the functions of church and state. Essentially, Calvin established a theocracy that examined the minutest details of people's lives and was constantly on the lookout for moral or religious "sins." The Consistory could and did hand down punishments up to and including the death penalty for all manner of derelictions: "those who slandered the government and even Calvin himself . . ., witches, 'plague mongerers,' heretics, conspirators, murderers, and hardened criminals."[13] In particular, the Consistory asserted its right to carry out the weighty penalty of excommunication without the consultation or approval of the local magistrates.

The most notorious instance of Calvin punishing a religious rebel was the case of Michael Servetus, although the matter is not quite as straightforward as it appears. Servetus had already been sentenced to death for heresy in the city of Vienne, but had escaped from prison and come to Geneva. When he asserted some doubts as to the precise meaning and application of the doctrine of the Trinity, Calvin felt the need to act. In a subsequent trial he testified that Servetus was an atheist for denying the orthodox doctrine of the Trinity; this testimony, along with Servetus' previous conviction for heresy, led the magistrates to carry out a death sentence on him in 1553. It is true that the magistrates were reluctant to do so (in part for a very secular reason: it might harm trade relations with France), but in their minds Calvin's testimony left them no choice.

The standard portrayal of John Calvin as a heartless theocrat intent on ruthlessly rooting out heresy may well be something of a caricature; but there is no denying that he was an inflexible dogmatist in whose mind it was unimaginable that the Christian revelation could possibly be untrue or even that it could be viably questioned; as such, his punitive approach to religious heterodoxy must be regarded as akin to fascism. His passion for order—or, more precisely, his terror of disorder on the level of both belief and social organisation—led him to impose his vision on the citizens of Geneva. Calvin did institute significant social reforms, from assistance to the poor to establishment of schools and colleges; but Geneva remained Calvinist (although with a substantial Catholic population) until well into the eighteenth century.

It was inevitable that the remarkably rapid spread of the reformed

---

13. Alexander Canoczy, "Calvin's Life" (tr. David L. Foxgrover and James Schmitt), in McKim, *The Cambridge Companion to John Calvin* 17.

sects would be regarded by the Catholic church as an existential threat, and it was equally inevitable that the church would push back hard to reclaim its rights. And so the Counter-Reformation was born. The term is regarded as prejudicial to Catholics, and here it will be used strictly to refer to Catholic attempts to counteract Protestant theology and the dissemination of its doctrines. Ignatius of Loyola (1491–1556) led the campaign. A Spanish Catholic priest, he founded the Society of Jesus (the Jesuits) in 1540 as a means of promulgating a scholarly foundations of Catholic faith. To the extent that he endorsed classical learning in the schools he established, he could be considered a disciple of the humanists; but the Jesuit programme was fallacious at its very core in that it utilised all the philosophical and rhetorical modes of classical thought to justify the unquestioned presupposition of the truth of Catholic doctrine. There was no attempt at an open-minded or sceptical approach to scripture or Christian belief.

There is, in any case, some question as to how effective the Counter-Reformation actually was. It is true that Spain and Italy remained largely Catholic (due in part to the actions of the Inquisitions in these countries, for which see section E); but Lutheranism reached Denmark (then combined with Norway) and Sweden no later than the 1530s. Catholic bishops' extensive wealth and properties were seized by the crown in both of these nations. Most of Austria became Lutheran by 1550. Jesuits, however, did infiltrate Austrian universities and churches in the later sixteenth century, supported by influential princes, some of whom even banned the practice of Lutheranism in certain cities. Various monarchs managed to effect the re-Catholicisation of Austria by the early to mid-seventeenth century.

D. England's Break with the Papacy

At the culmination of the Wars of the Roses in England (the century-long struggle among two aristocratic families, York and Lancaster, both of them branches of the House of Plantagenet), Henry Tudor—a man from a Welsh line who, through a series of historical accidents, had come to be recognised as the heir to the throne on the Lancaster side—defeated the Yorkist Richard III at the Battle of Bosworth on 22 August 1485, initiating the reign of the Tudors. He married Elizabeth of York to put a definitive end to the struggle.

Henry VII's reign (1485–1509) was relatively placid, although at the outset he was occupied in suppressing a variety of internal insurrections, both by aristocrats and by commoners. He ruled largely by seeking the advice of a small number of counsellors—a group that ultimately came to be called the Privy Council. The Star Chamber came into being in 1487 at the head of the judicial system, supervising the work of the justices of the peace. Parliament was rendered largely supernumerary, as Henry summoned it with decreasing frequency.

Henry VII made no significant alterations in English religious practice, which was still firmly Catholic; but that could not be said of his son and successor, Henry VIII (r. 1509–47). His marriage to Catherine of Aragon (his brother Arthur's widow) in 1510 cemented an alliance with Spain as a bulwark against French aggression. Only one of her five children survived, and that was a female—Mary (b. 1516). At this time the clergy still had an iron grip on educational facilities, and they also enjoyed other advantages, such as being largely exempt from criminal laws (hence the phrase "benefit of clergy"). But the "higher" clergy—bishops and other leaders of the church—were dependent on the king for their positions (and, accordingly, their substantial wealth). Thomas Wolsey, Henry VIII's leading advisor during the first two decades of his reign, was an ordained priest who later garnered many other clerical titles and became a cardinal in 1515; he was also immensely wealthy. In effect, he became head of the English church.

At the outset of his reign, Henry showed no particular sympathy toward the anti-Catholic movements roiling the Continent; indeed, he had written a tract against Martin Luther, the *Assertio Septem Sacramentorum* (1521; Defence of the Seven Sacraments), leading Pope Leo X to declare Henry the *Defensor Fidei* (Defender of the Faith). But Henry, his counsellors, and the nation as a whole became increasingly concerned about his succession. The need for a male heir was seen as paramount, since England had never been governed by a regnant queen.[14] Henry began lobbying the pope for an annulment of his marriage as early as 1527. The request was, in fact, not regarded as unreasonable, and Pope Clement VII (1523–34) was inclined to grant it; but he was under the

14. An Empress Matilda (or Maude) unsuccessfully claimed the crown for several months in 1141 during the turbulent reign of King Stephen (r. 1135–53).

thumb of the Holy Roman Emperor Charles V (r. 1519–56), a nephew of Catherine of Aragon. But when, in that year, Charles sacked Rome and seized the pope, Protestants in Europe reacted in horror, envisioning a new "Babylonian captivity." The pope made peace with Charles, but Henry's annulment now seemed out of the question.

In a series of four epochal sessions (1529–32), Parliament enacted severe restrictions on the clergy as well as measures to separate the English clergy from the papacy. No formal break with Rome occurred at this time; but Henry's mistress, Anne Boleyn, was now pregnant, and there was a need to ensure that her child was legitimate and could therefore ascend to the throne if necessary. Henry and Anne were married secretly in January 1533. A fifth parliamentary session (February–April 1533) passed laws permitting the Archbishop of Canterbury (Thomas Cranmer) to annul Henry's marriage; this occurred on May 23. On June 1, Anne Boleyn was crowned queen of England, and her first and only child, Elizabeth, was born on September 7.

The pope declared the marriage invalid; Cranmer and others were excommunicated, followed by Henry. It was in 1533–34 that England's ties with the papacy were definitively severed, and the Church of England became an independent entity. Henry, as king, was the head of the church, and leading figures in the church were compelled to swear an oath of loyalty to the king. These and other measures were facilitated by Thomas Cromwell, who had emerged as a leading advisor to Henry and had a strong anticlerical bent. Indeed, it becomes apparent that England's break with Rome in no way signalled an embrace of Lutheranism, to say nothing of the even more radical reforms of Calvin and others. In the aftermath of the split, Lutheran books were burned and a small number of "heretics" (those opposed to Rome in matters of doctrine) were burned, including about two dozen Anabaptists in 1535.

On the opposite side, Sir Thomas More (1478–1535), Henry's Lord Chancellor (1529–32), was violently opposed to any deviations from Catholic doctrine and from papal supremacy. He therefore refused to take the Succession Oath, avowing loyalty to whatever children were born of Henry's second marriage. He was tried and found guilty of treason and beheaded on July 6, 1535.

It was Cromwell who led the campaign to dissolve the monasteries. These institutions had become fabulously wealthy, and they were understandably hotbeds of Catholic resistance; so they had to go. The state claimed objects of value in the monasteries; the property was largely transferred to private hands. Cromwell deserves credit for supporting a new authorised translation of the Bible into English—the so-called Coverdale Bible, compiled by Myles Coverdale and published in 1535; it was itself based on William Tyndale's translation of the NT (printed in complete form in 1526). The Coverdale Bible was revised in 1539 and was deemed the Great Bible.

The matter of the succession was still uncertain. With two daughters (one of whom was a Catholic), there was bound to be trouble. So Anne Boleyn had to go, and after her execution on trumped-up charges Henry married Jane Seymour, who died giving birth to a son, Edward, on October 12, 1537. Upon Henry's death in 1547, Edward—only nine years and three months old—was nominally king, but a council ruled in his stead, headed by the Duke of Somerset. Furious battles broke out as to whether church services should be a "Mass" or a "Communion"; a raucous press, having discovered the power of the printed word to sway minds and hearts, joined in the struggle. In 1549 Cranmer issued the *Book of Common Prayer* (usually referred to simply as the Prayer Book), with revisions in 1553 and 1559. It remains to this day the central pillar of the Anglican Church. In 1553 there followed the Forty-Two Articles. These various documents laid out the fundamental features of the Church of England: the Catholic Mass was essentially eliminated, although confession and other Catholic elements were preserved; all service books aside from the Prayer Book were ordered destroyed; altars were abolished. But, as earlier, not everyone was happy with these changes—not so much because they violated Catholic doctrine as because people were reluctant to give up rituals to which they had become accustomed. A rebellion broke out in Cornwall and Devon in 1549–50 and was violently put down, with hundreds being executed. The Second Act of Uniformity in 1552 stipulated various punishments for failure to attend church services.

As Edward VI fell ill, efforts were made to prevent Mary from becoming queen. But she managed to get the crown upon her half-brother's death in 1553. She immediately brought Catholicism back to England. It is arguable, however, that she would not have been so relatively successful if there had not been a substantial number of citizens who wanted it. Many Protestants fled to France, Germany, and Switzerland. Parliament acquiesced to Mary's demands, rescinding many of the laws on religion that it had recently passed. But Parliament refused to recognise the pope as head of the church, and Mary had to capitulate on this point.

Over Parliament's objections, Mary married Prince Philip of Spain (later Philip II, r. 1556–98) in 1554, since—in spite of her advanced age—she saw the need to produce an heir so that England would not revert to Protestantism under Elizabeth. That plan came to naught, however, as she bore no children. Many others protested even more strongly to Mary's reign and the return to Catholicism. Sir Thomas Wyatt led an army of 4000 men from Kent to London, but was forced to surrender when he reached the city. Many of his supporters were executed. This initiated a period of persecution against non-Catholics that—in spite of the comparatively small numbers who were killed (about 300 people were burned, 60 of them women)—permanently coloured the English imagination, fastening the label "Bloody Mary" on the monarch and instituting a prejudice against Catholics that lasted for centuries. Some years later, the more noteworthy of those who perished in Mary's reign were glorified in John Foxe's *Book of Martyrs* (1563).

Mary's early death on November 17, 1558 ushered in the reign of Elizabeth. No one could have predicted that she would sit on the throne for the next forty-five years, presiding not only over the permanent establishment of the Church of England but also over the greatest flowering of English literature in history. There were, of course, immediate concerns about who would succeed her, since the English were still unused to being governed by a female monarch. Henry II of France proclaimed Mary Stuart (queen of Scotland [1542–67] and wife of the French Dauphin, Francis) as queen of England by virtue of her being the granddaughter of Henry VIII's sister Margaret; but Pope Pius IV (1559–65) was reluctant to go along, chiefly because his alliance with the Habsburgs made France his political enemy.

For her part, Elizabeth deliberately kept clerics out of her Privy Council, and her leading advisor, Sir William Cecil (later Lord Burghley), was a firm Protestant. She had Parliament declare her the "Supreme Governor" (not the "Supreme Head," a small but significant distinction) of the church, and she of course restored the use of the Prayer

Book. Many bishops refused to swear the Oath of Supremacy and were removed; lesser clergy tended to go along. The Presbyterian John Knox attempted to stir up trouble in Scotland in 1559, and Cecil essentially purchased Scottish loyalty with the Treaty of Edinburgh (1560), which ensured that the French would not meddle in Scottish affairs.

Like her father, Elizabeth chose to steer a middle ground between Catholicism and the Reformed movements on the Continent, in terms of both doctrine and liturgy. She initiated a significant Convocation in 1563, where among other important matters the Forty-Two Articles were revised as the now canonical Thirty-Nine Articles, still utilised by the Church of England. It decreed explicitly that the clergy can marry (reversing Mary's reinstitution of clerical celibacy), and it also asserted that "the body of Christ is given, taken, and eaten in the Supper only after an heavenly and spiritual manner" (Article 28)—a significant deviation from Catholic understanding of the nature of the eucharist. Concurrently, Parliament passed an act enhancing punishments on those who refused to take the Oath of Supremacy. It also decreed the translation of the Bible into Welsh (the NT was translated in 1567; the entire Bible was translated in 1588).

But the matter of succession would not go away. Elizabeth was reluctant to marry, especially a foreigner, since that would have necessitated (in accordance with the custom of the era) that she relinquish much of her power and authority to her husband. And what to do about Mary Stuart? Through her own blunders, Mary was deposed from the Scottish throne in 1567, in part through her ill-advised marriage to Lord Robert Darnley. Around this time the Duke of Norfolk and others engaged in a movement to put Mary on the English throne, but they failed. She was imprisoned in England in 1568.

Meanwhile, the papacy had not given up hope of luring Elizabeth back into the fold. The sticking point was papal supremacy. Successive popes attempted to entice her to send delegates to the ongoing Council of Trent, which would in effect signal that Elizabeth had relinquished her role as head of the English church; but she refused. And yet, there was no systematic persecution of Catholics during the first decade of her reign, for all that there were persistent rumours that "Roman Catholic powers had formed a league to depose the queen of England."[15] All this led at last to Elizabeth's excommunication in 1570, which allowed anyone to depose her. But the move came to nothing, either at home or overseas. Once again, political and dynastic elements played a role. Philip II of Spain preferred a "heretic" on the English throne rather than Mary Stuart with her French sympathies. Indeed, where action was taken by Elizabeth against Catholics, it was against those who were intriguing with the French to overthrow her. Parliament passed a much tougher law against Catholics in 1563—but (in a curious parallel with classical Rome's persecution of Christians) its focus was on Catholics' failure to take the Oath of Supremacy. Even so, Elizabeth was reluctant to carry out the measure in its full severity.

Let it not be thought, however, that Elizabeth was inclining toward any sort of "toleration" of the Catholic religion, or heterodox religions in general. In a letter dating to September 24, 1563, in response to the plea of Ferdinand I (Holy Roman Emperor, 1556–64), she made it clear that

> to found churches expressly for diverse rites, besides being openly repugnant to the enactments of our supreme Parliament, would be but to graft religion upon religion, to the distraction of good men's minds, the fostering of the zeal of the factious, the sorry blending of the functions of church and state, and the utter confounding of all things human and divine in this our now peaceful state . . .[16]

The Convocation of 1563 also saw the emergence of a group of radical Protestants who would later be called Puritans. They were initially constituted from the Protestant exiles during Mary's reign, and upon their return to England they adopted many of John Calvin's measures, including predestination (they of course axiomatically assumed that they were among the "elect" who would find their way to heaven). Exactly how they reconciled predestination with their own ardent evangelicalism—since they explicitly denied that "good works" could have any bearing on God's choosing who will reach heaven and who will be consigned to hell—is not clear. But evangelical they certainly were: they maintained that the Church of England was insufficiently "Reformed"; they rejected

15. Haugaard, *Elizabeth and the English Reformation* 308.
16. Cited in Haugaard 324.

the Prayer Book as too "popish"; they despised the power of bishops, endorsing instead Scottish Presbyterianism. In essence, the Puritans wanted God and the church to be the sole focus of human life. The movement at once took hold in the universities, and it sought still harsher punishments against Catholics, since the papacy was now deemed the Antichrist.

But they faced an enemy in Elizabeth, who, while no friend of Catholics, was in no way inclined to let Puritan fanatics cause instability in her realm. Catholics, however, continued to cause trouble. Most notably, in 1580 Edmund Campion, a Catholic Jesuit, instituted an aggressive proselytising campaign, but this only led to greater repression of Catholics under an act passed by Parliament in 1581. Campion himself was convicted of high treason (again, a political and not religious offence) and hanged. But the queen also took actions against Puritans, naming the anti-Puritan John Whitgift as Archbishop of Canterbury (1583–1604).

It was Elizabeth's overriding desire to maintain the stability of the state that led her at last to execute Mary Stuart on February 8, 1587, since Mary had repeatedly become entangled in attempts to overthrow the queen. But Elizabeth had bigger fish to fry. Spain's increasing power (it had annexed Portugal and had established numerous colonies in the New World) led Elizabeth to ally herself with the Low Countries in their struggle against their Spanish overlords. This led to the spectacular and unexpected defeat of the Spanish Armada at the hands of the English navy, led by Sir Francis Drake, in 1588. This did not end the war in the Low Countries, but did establish England as a major naval power.

Toward the end of Elizabeth's reign, the theologian Richard Hooker (1554–1600) wrote *Of the Laws of Ecclesiastical Polity* (1593–97). This immensely influential work steers a middle ground between Catholicism and Puritanism, as his monarch did; indeed, if anything he condemns the latter far more forcefully than the former. And although he does draw upon some aspects of Aquinas's thought in regard to abstract issues such as "natural law," he endorses Elizabeth's role as "Supreme Governor," the use of the Prayer Book, and the authority of bishops (tempered by "reason") in matters of doctrine and church governance. Hooker's treatise significantly influenced the development of Anglicanism in the following century.

Some further words should be said about John Knox (1514?–1572). Ordained as a Catholic priest in Edinburgh in 1536, he became inclined toward Reformation principles in the 1540s. But with Scotland firmly Catholic at the time and an ally of France, Knox found little traction for his views; indeed, he was imprisoned for a time aboard a French galley. A lengthy stay in England (1549–54) made him familiar with the Prayer Book, but he was forced to go abroad upon Mary's accession. In Geneva he met John Calvin, and he returned to Scotland after Elizabeth took the throne. By 1560 he had effected the Scots Confession, which enshrined reformed practices in Scotland and banished the mass. He and others worked on a *Book of Discipline* (1561), the rule book for the reformed church.

The Catholic Mary Stuart arrived in Scotland that year, and Knox proved a constant thorn in her side for years, until her exile in 1568. Although Knox died a few years later, his work ultimately led to the establishment of Presbyterianism in Scotland in 1689.

E. Toleration and Inquisition

Even during the turmoil of the early sixteenth century, when emotions ran high and Catholics and Protestants at every level were battling for both political control and for the hearts and minds of their followers, a nascent movement toward religious toleration emerged. Even John Calvin initially advocated some minimal form of toleration, although once he gained control of Geneva he quickly changed course and, incited by his fear of political and religious turmoil, harshly cracked down upon his perceived opponents. Erasmus believed that the factionalism of the Christian church could be minimised by focusing on a small number of fundamental beliefs upon which all sects could agree; but he found few followers among religious leaders or the general public. Luther's stance was ambiguous and changed over time, but ultimately he came to the view that *public* professions of faith counter to that of the society in which the person lived posed an excessive danger to social and political cohesion.

Thomas More, in *Utopia* (1516), outlined a surprisingly expansive notion of religious toleration in his imaginary realm:

> For king Utopus, even at the first beginning, hearing that the inhabitants of the land were before his coming thither at continual dissension and strife among themselves for their religions; . . . as soon as he had gotten the victory, first of all he made a decree, that it should be lawful for every man to favour and follow what religion he would, and that he might do the best he could to bring others to his opinion; so long as he did it peaceably, gently, quietly, and soberly, without hasty and contentious rebuking and inveighing against others. If he could not by fair and gentle speech induce them to his opinion, yet he should use no kind of violence, and refrain from displeasant and seditious words. To him who would vehemently and fervently in this cause strive and contend, was decreed banishment or bondage.
>
> This law did king Utopus make, not only for the maintenance of peace, which he saw through continual contention and mortal hatred utterly extinguished, but also because he thought this decree should make for the furtherance of religion. (271–72)[17]

This seems a remarkably open-minded conception, but we may be forced to modify our view of More's tolerance when we recognise that, earlier in his treatise, he stated that nearly all human views of deity are roughly similar. Moreover, when he himself attained political power, as Lord Chancellor, he himself had no compunction cracking down on perceived heretics. In Geneva, a year after the execution of Michael Servetus, Sebastian Castellio advocated leniency even against non-Christians. He was promptly exiled by Calvin.

What matters in this debate is not words but actions. Toleration was embraced by few monarchs in Europe, since they adopted the view that religious unity was essential to the preservation of the state. Where toleration—or, more precisely, coexistence—occurred, it was forced upon rulers by the sheer difficulty of forcing large numbers of their citizens to give up their religious preferences and practices. The case of France in the later sixteenth century is of interest. King Charles IX (r. 1560–74) attempted to effect a peace between Catholics and Protestants, but largely failed. This led to decades of religious warfare during his reign and that of his successor, Henry III (r. 1574–89), highlighted by the

17. I have modernised the 1551 English translation by Ralph Robynson of More's Latin text.

murder of 2000 Protestants (Huguenots) on St Bartholomew's Day (August 24) 1572. Further awkwardness resulted from the prospect of a Huguenot ascending to the very throne of France. Furious efforts were made to dethrone him, but he took the crown as Henry IV (r. 1589–1610). Although he converted to Catholicism, chiefly as a gesture of unity, he also issued the Edict of Nantes in 1598, which granted some degree of freedom of conscience throughout France (it applied also to Catholics in Huguenot cities). The edict cannot, strictly speaking, be seen as an instance of religious toleration in principle; it was largely a pragmatic manoeuvre in the face of the brute reality of religious diversity in France. And in one sense it strengthened French Catholicism, since it was widely assumed that Huguenots would eventually convert back to the old faith, and it also strengthened the power and authority of the monarchy.

The Dutch revolt of 1572–1609 was spurred by the atrocities committed by the soldiers of Spain (which still controlled the Low Countries). As a result, Spanish rule was overthrown in Holland and Zeeland, which by then were Calvinist; other provinces remained Catholic. As we have seen, England's alliance with the Dutch led to the defeat of the Spanish Armada in 1588. Ultimately, a Protestant Dutch Republic and a Catholic Netherlands (still controlled by Spain) resulted; the former became a haven of religious toleration in the centuries to come.

Other theologians made explicit pleas for toleration and even of religious freedom. Whereas the former was a negative trait (toleration was seen as a grudging acceptance of dissenting views, even though these were regarded as profoundly erroneous, placing its adherents in jeopardy of eternal punishment in hell), the latter advocated a positive outlook whereby varying religious perspectives were seen as beyond the purview of civil or even ecclesiastical authorities to suppress, since it was impossible to determine where the truth lay.

One of the pioneers of religious toleration in Europe was Sebastian Castellio (1515–1563), a French Catholic who converted to Protestantism around 1540 and worked in Geneva during the period 1541–45, when John Calvin was in charge there. In his prefaces to his Latin (1551) and French (1555) translatons of the Bible, Castellio outlines his views on religious toleration. His opinions were codified in the treatise *De Haereticis* (1554; On Heretics),[18] which largely consisted of passages from a variety of Christian authors from Augustine to Erasmus (including several extracts of his own composition, appearing under pseudonyms) who expressed opposition to religious persecution. The treatise was clearly designed to protest the execution of Michael Servetus the previous year; indeed, Castellio indulges in a bit of mockery by quoting a passage from Calvin's early writing on this point.

In a lengthy preface to the book, Castellio presents his case for toleration: people should follow Jesus Christ in living a life of love and charity; many doctrines in the Bible are obscure and it is not easy to determine who is right; the attribution of heresy against a person only incites blind hatred for that person. Castellio goes on to point out that every sect looks upon adherents of other sects as heretics. In a preface to a French translation of his treatise, Castellio makes the bold claim that the civil magistrate has no jurisdiction over points of religious belief (or unbelief); excommunication is the only appropriate penalty. (This penalty was, indeed, severe enough, as it entailed significant social and economic hardships for those cast out from their church.) But it is worth emphasising that Castellio is no religious sceptic and evinces little doubt of the fundamental doctrines of Christianity.

Calvin replied with a hostile tract against Castellio, and the latter responded with an intemperate and ad hominem attack of his own (this was not published at the time, but it probably circulated widely in manuscript). Here Castellio extends no sympathy to those who deny the Christian religion altogether; as Perez Zagorin notes in summing up Castellio's viewpoint, "Truly impious people such as blasphemers and contemners of the Scriptures are not heretics. If they deny God, blaspheme, and hate holiness and piety, they are punishable by the magistrate, although not for their religion but for irreligion."[19] Castellio is tentatively approaching the notion of the separation of church and state; he is essentially rejecting the notion (propounded most vociferously by Calvin but largely asserted by a majority of Christian magistrates throughout Europe) that religious conformity is necessary for the preservation of the state.

---

18. The full title of Castellio's treatise is *De Haereticis, an sint persequendi?* (Should Heretics Be Persecuted?).

19. Zagorin, *How the Idea of Religious Toleration Came to the West* 118.

A sharply countervailing tendency leading away from toleration was the establishment of inquisitions in various Catholic nations. We have seen that the papacy established an inquisition as early as 1231; but events both preceding and following the onset of the Reformation led to new inquisitions throughout Catholic Europe. Each of these inquisitions (and there were several) developed its own character, so it is worth studying them individually.

Ferdinand of Spain received papal permission to establish the Spanish Inquisition in 1478, chiefly to pursue *conversos*—Jewish citizens who had been pressured to convert to Christianity but whom the authorities suspected (probably with good reason) of continuing to practise Jewish rites in private. The Inquisition got right to business, setting up the *auto-da-fé*—a public ceremony whereby the death (usually by burning at the stake) of heretics was considered an "act of faith" that would encourage others to toe the Catholic party line.

It was in this context that Tomás de Torquemada (1420–1498) emerged to prominence—or notoriety. A Dominican friar, he became Ferdinand's Inquisitor General in 1483. Torquemada vastly expanded the reach of the Inquisition, setting up tribunals throughout Spain. His actions were so severe that the papacy attempted to rein him in, without success. Only his death put an end to his reign of terror, during which an estimated 2000 heretics (most of them Jews) were executed; in addition, 40,000 Jews were expelled from Spain.

It should be noted that the Spanish Inquisition also came down on Catholics, although usually with far less harsh punishments. Its overall agenda, indeed, extended into "the general problem of incorrect religious beliefs among Catholics, the offense of 'scandalous' or 'blasphemous' expression, bigamy, various forms of 'superstition,' sorcery, and witchcraft, and, in the case of Aragón only, the offenses of sodomy and bestiality."[20] Clemency was frequently offered to Catholics in the hope that they would repent and mend their ways. But by the 1520s the Spanish Inquisition quickly shifted its focus toward the nascent Protestant movement.

The Spanish campaign against Jews caused many of them to flee to Portugal, but they were persecuted there as well. King Manoel I (r.

20. Peters, *Inquisition* 86–87.

1495–1521) ordered them expelled in 1496, with the result that no Jews who had not converted to Christianity remained in the country. A Portuguese Inquisition was established in 1536, and over the next two centuries more than 1200 Jews or Judaisers were executed.

In 1542, Pope Paul III (1534–49) established a Roman Inquisition; it gained steam under Pope Paul IV (1555–59). It was only at this time that the papacy formally began to keep a list of "forbidden" books that Catholics were not permitted to read upon pain of excommunication, the *Index Auctorum et Librorum Prohibitorum.* This inquisition's main focus was Protestants. An inquisition was set up in Sicily (then still controlled by Spain) in 1481; it mostly went after Jews and *conversos.* Then in the 1540s it shifted its focus to what it called "Lutheranism," a catch-all term referring to any religious faith other than Catholicism.

A Venetian Inquisition was established in 1547. Unusually, it was operated by a commission that included both lay persons and ecclesiastical authorities. In spite of the city's claims to political and cultural independence from Rome, this inquisition worked closely with Rome's on a variety of logistical and doctrinal matters.

Some of these inquisitions did turn their attention to witchcraft and sorcery, although the Spanish Inquisition's prosecution of such heretics ended in 1614. But Catholic beliefs regarding the existence of suspected witches had been gaining impetus since the early fifteenth century. As early as 1437, Pope Eugenius IV (1431–47) wrote in an official letter that witches entered into a pact with the Devil; this act, in his view, was what made them heretics: it negated a person's covenant with God, as it involved an explicit renunciation of God and scripture.

The issue lay dormant for another half-century. Then, in a treatise written at the request of Pope Innocent III (1484–92), the *Malleus Maleficarum* (1486; The Hammer of Witches), Henrich Kramer[21] outlined the means by which witches were to be tried and on what grounds they were to be convicted. Witchcraft trials did become prevalent in the 1490s onward, in Spain, northern Italy, and elsewhere; but many sceptics of the time questioned some of Kramer's more extreme assertions (the notion that witches could fly or change shapes, among other points)

21. The name of one Jacob Sprenger, a Domenican inquisitor, was added to editions of the work in 1519, long after both Kramer and Sprenger himself had died. It is now widely believed that he had little if anything to do with the preparation of the volume.

without questioning the basic premise of witchcraft. Kramer specifically targeted women as the main perpetrators of witchcraft—a point that had been made in an earlier treatise, Johannes Nider's *Formicarius* (1437–38)—and also asserted that women were more carnally inclined than men, making them susceptible to sexual intercourse by the Devil or by a male demon, the incubus. (Men were susceptible to seduction by a female demon, the succubus.)

What followed upon the publication of the *Malleus* was a roiling debate by those who supported or endorsed the belief in witches with supernatural powers and those who scoffed to a greater or lesser degree at such views. The work of the Dutch physician Johann Weyer is of some interest in this regard. In his treatise *De Prestigiis Daemonorum et Incantationibus ac Veneficiis* (1563; On the Deceits of Demons and on Spells and Poisons), Weyer asserted a psychological analysis of supposed witches, suggesting that they were mentally disturbed. But he nonetheless asserted the reality of the Devil, sorcerers, and other supernatural forces. He did go on to maintain that witchcraft should not be considered a crime; indeed, he went so far as to claim that the very act of burning witches is itself a crime.

The French jurist Jean Bodin wrote a treatise designed to refute Weyer, *De la démonomanie des sorciers* (1580; On Demonomania of Sorcerers), reasserting the idea of the pact with the Devil and maintaining that trials, if conducted properly, would never result in the false conviction of a single witch. Nicolas Rémy (sometimes known by his Latin name Remigius), in *Daemonolatreia* (1595), propounded the view that the Devil could appear in the shape of a black cat or a man, and in the latter role he would lead the Black Mass. He branded those who denied the existence of witches as atheists. Rémy himself claimed to have condemned 800 witches to death. James VI of Scotland (before he became James I of England) wrote *Demonologie* (1598), endorsing witchcraft belief and prosecutions, as did Henri Boguet in *Discours exécrable des sorciers* (1602). On the other side, Reginald Scot (*The Discoverie of Witchcraft*, 1584) spoke out strongly against witch-hunting.

The whole debate culminated with Martin Anton del Rio's *Disquisitiones Magicae* (1599–1600; Disquisitions on Magic), which essentially replaced the *Malleus Maleficarum* as the Catholic handbook for witch-hunting. Witchcraft trials continued throughout the seventeenth century and beyond in both Catholic and Protestant nations, and will be dealt with in subsequent chapters.

F. Secularism in Continental European Literature

The later fifteenth and sixteenth centuries saw the emergence of several titanic figures in the realm of European literature, whether it be Rabelais and Montaigne in France, Tasso and Ariosto in Italy, or Cervantes in Spain. While it cannot be said that any of them exhibit atheistic or even agnostic tendencies in their work, they do exhibit varying degrees of religious scepticism or anticlericalism that set the stage for more radical departures from religious orthodoxy in the coming centuries.

One interesting tendency is the emergence of some notable works of sharp satire, drawing to some degree upon the classical satire of Horace, Persius, and especially Juvenal. Two such works can be noted here. The *Narrenschiff* (1494; Ship of Fools) of Sebastian Brant (1458–1521) is one of the earliest major works of German literature. For all his religious conservatism, he could not escape the humanist tendencies of his time: educated at the University of Basle, he read widely in Latin, Greek, philosophy and law, gaining a licence to practise law. His satirical poem, in 112 chapters, is a long lament on the lapses in faith that led individuals to derelictions of various kinds. This depiction of fools as moral deviants dates back at least to Nigel Wireker's *Speculum Stultorum* (12th century; Mirror of Fools), and, ultimately, back to Socrates and Plato, who deemed all moral failings to be a failure of the intellect. For a conservative like Brant, even seemingly trivial faults (such as "Prattling in Church" [the title of ch. 91]) are all but equivalent to "Contempt of Holy Writ" (ch. 11), "Insolence toward God" (ch. 14), "Speaking against God" (ch. 28), opposition to predestination (ch. 57), "Blaspheming God" (ch. 87), and so on. In one of the lengthiest chapters of the work, on "Decline of the Faith" (ch. 99), Brant laments that Christianity is losing ground to Islam and heresy in general; the Holy Roman Empire is on the wane. The ominous chapter on the Antichrist (103) warns that Holy Writ is being twisted and distorted by nameless individuals to suggest the opposite of what it means; as a result, some books should be burned and their authors banished. Brant concludes: "The Antichrist is very near" (334).

Let us recall that this book was written decades before Luther's emergence. Brant spent his final years wringing his hands about the impending dissolution of European unity triggered by Luther and Zwingli, a unity that was already in trouble because of the depradations of the Turks. In the end, as Edwin H. Zeydel, who translated *Die Narrenschiff,* declares, the work was regarded as "a sort of layman's Bible destined to guide the coming generation of conformists" (32). How successful he was in that effort is an open question.

Brant's work did influence Erasmus's much more famous *Encomium Moriae* (1511; Praise of Folly), although that prose work has a very different agenda. The premise of the book—one that launched Erasmus's career as a humanist celebrity—is that Folly herself speaks on her own behalf, declaring how she is the source of all human life. Would any man or woman, for example, submit to the "halter of matrimony" (19) if they were not endowed with stupidity? Folly is also that which sustains us through all the miseries of life. The fool is never tormented by thoughts of death, hell, and so on.

It is when Erasmus addresses those follies specifically associated with religion that the work gains much interest from our prespective. Much of what Erasmus attacks here would fall under the category of superstition—the veneration of saints' relics, the needless care that people take in planning their own funerals (the implication being that they won't be conscious to perceive these details), and so on. And yet, Folly draws a startling conclusion from these instances of silliness: "So rife, so teeming with such delusions is the entire life of all Christians everywhere" (66). The most fervent atheist could hardly have said it better.

Erasmus was not an atheist, of course, but he does go on to condemn theologians (intolerant, engaging in logic-chopping), monks (wasting their lives in being secluded from the world and secular activity), popes (addicted to wealth, going to war to settle doctrinal disputes), and priests (who also "keep a sharp lookout to harvest their profits" [115]). What is his summation? ". . . it seems to me that the Christian religion taken all together has a certain affinity with some sort of folly and has little or nothing to do with wisdom" (132). One cannot, of course, attribute Folly's statements directly to Erasmus, and by the end of his satirical treatise he may simply be expressing a *reductio ad absurdum* whereby Folly expresses views far more radical than what Erasmus himself espoused.

It is therefore safe to conclude that the *Encomium Moriae* is anticlerical without being anti-religious.

For all that some French writers and scholars continued to use Latin as a mode of expression or drew upon classical literature for inspiration, prose and poetic work in the French language also flourished. The poet Joachim du Bellay's *Deffence et illustration de la langue françoyse* (1549; Defence and Illustration of the French Language) is a landmark in French—and, indeed, European—vernacular literature, defending French as a language as fully capable of rhetorical expression as Latin and Greek. Du Bellay helped to found the Pléiade, a group of French Renaissance poets who, while drawing upon classical sources, advocated originality of thought and conception. Its leading figure was Pierre de Ronsard (1524–1585). Neither du Bellay's nor Ronsard's work is of direct relevance to our enquiry; nor is that of Marguerite de Navarre (1492–1549), author of the *Heptaméron* (published posthumously in 1559), a series of seventy-two short stories modelled upon Boccaccio's *Decameron* but entirely lacking his religious scepticism. Our interest in French literature during this period turns upon two authors, François Rabelais and Michel de Montaigne.

Rabelais (1483?–1553?) was well trained in religion, having served as a monk at a Franciscan priory from 1520 to 1524 and then, after an appeal to the pope, in a Benedictine monastery. In 1528–30 he emigrated to Paris to study medicine, fathering two illegitimate children in the process. By 1532 he was practising medicine, although he did not receive his degree until 1537.

By this time he had already published *Pantagruel* (1532) and *Gargantua* (1535). Later he reversed the order of these books and published them in a revised edition as *Gargantua et Pantagruel* (1542). Book 3 of the ongoing narrative appeared in 1546, Book 4 in 1548. A fifth book appeared posthumously in 1564. This is now regarded as "probably concocted from discarded drafts found in Rabelais's papers."[22]

The exuberance of Rabelais's writing—especially its robust delight in sexuality, scatalogy, and satire and parody of all sorts—is proverbial, but this very characteristic makes interpretation of his work difficult. His religious views have been characterised as anything from atheism to

22. François Cornillat, "Interpretation in Rabelais, Interpretation of Rabelais," in O'Brien, *The Cambridge Companion to Rabelais* 55n18.

covert Catholic orthodoxy, and every gradation in between. It is probably safest at the outset to agree with Edwin Duval that Rabelais was a "Christian humanist in the mold of Erasmus,"[23] attempting to steer a middle ground between the increasingly rigid reformed movement of Luther and his compatriots and the equally rigid Catholic reaction to it.

The premise of Rabelais's sprawling *Gargantua et Pantagruel* is the loose narrative of the trials and tribulations of Gargantua, an immense human-like monster who took eleven months in being born, and his more normal-appearing son, Pantagruel, as they traverse France and other parts of the world in search of adventure. Along the way, they encounter Panurge, a friend who has endured a near-death experience with the Turks, and others who tell their own stories. It is evident that Rabelais is intent on displaying his immense learning in languages (French, Latin, Greek, and Hebrew, among others), philosophy, religious doctrine, and ancient and contemporary history.

In its broadest sense, Rabelais's work can be said to endorse Erasmian humanism against what he deems the "Gothic" scholasticism of the universities of his day and an embracing of the new learning of the Renaissance. Far from anything approaching atheism, he echoes Erasmus in advocating a personal relationship with God nurtured by a study of scripture in the original languages—itself something of a radical stance, since it essentially does away with the entire hierarchical structure of the Catholic church, from the pope on down to monks and secular priests, and disputes the church's role as guardian of Christian doctrine. Book 1 features a sustained polemic against the conversative theological faculty of the Sorbonne (it is not surprising that the university censured his work beginning in 1543) as well as of the monasticism of which Rabelais had had first-hand experience. In later portions of the work he presents another character, Frère Jean, as a sort of ideal monk in contrast to the corrupt, hypocritical monks depicted elsewhere. Analogously, Gargantua founds the Abbaye de Thélème as an idealised monastic institution whose motto is nothing less than "Do what you will" (126). This should not be interpreted as a token of unrestrained hedonism, but rather a sloughing off of the rigid and meaningless restrictions placed on monks' behaviour by Catholic tradition.

23. Edwin Duval, "Putting Religion in Its Place," in O'Brien 93.

Religious satire runs through the work, frequently in a risqué manner that underscores the all-too-human tendencies of the figures who are tasked with carrying out the unrealistic sexual morality advocated by the church. At one point a friar's long penis is compared to a devout Catholic woman's rosary beads (188). Elsewhere, one Grosbeck expounds gleefully on the torturing of heretics:

> Burn them, tear them with pincers, cut with shears, drown, hang, impale, break their shoulders, disembowel, chop to bits, fricassee, grill, slice up, crucify, boil, crush, quarter, smash to bits, unhinge, charcoal-broil these wicked heretics, decretalifuges, decretalicides, worse than homicides, worse than parricides, decretalictones of the devil. (552)

In an exquisite passage, Pantagruel and Panurge venture to the island of the Papimaniacs (i.e., maniacal supporters of the pope), who ask if the visitors have seen "the One and Only" (540). Pantagruel thinks they are referring to God and replies, "Certainly we have never seen Him, and He is not visible to bodily eyes" (540). But it gradually becomes clear that the Papimaniacs are referring to the pope, whereupon the discussion lapses into comic obscenity:

> "We'd kiss his ass with no figleaf, and likewise his balls. For he has balls, the Holy Father, we find that in our beautiful Decretals [papal decrees]; otherwise he wouldn't be pope. So that in subtle Decretaline philosophy this consequence is necessary: he is pope, so he has balls. and if the world ran out of balls, the world would have no more popes." (541)

The satire continues for several more chapters.

An early section, in which Panurge recounts his escape from the Turks, contains several topical references taken from recent history, where the threat of the Ottoman Turks as they increasingly encroached upon European soil was a source of continent-wide panic. Panurge comes close to being roasted alive (a pungent parody of Christian martyrdom) but manages to escape by various ludicrous means, including an episode where he throws lard (with which he had been wrapped when being roasted) at some wild dogs pursuing him. A later episode, where Picrochole engages in a war with Gargantua, has also been seen as a reflection of contemporary history, with Picrochole standing in for the Holy Roman Emperor Charles V; but the religious undercurrent of the satire is evident in a tone of persistent disapproval of these co-religionists battling each other merely for the purpose of territorial gain.

Even more relevant to our purpose is the essayist Michel de Montaigne (1533–1592), although perhaps not in an expected manner. He has often been taken to be a pioneer of Renaissance scepticism, based upon his poignant utterance, "*Que sçay-je?*" ("What do I know?").[24] But the context of this remark has been widely ignored, and Montaigne in fact reveals himself as a thinker desperate to preserve Catholic doctrine and Catholic control of the state against the threatening tides of religious reform, extending all the way to what he blithely labels atheism.

Montaigne, born near Bordeaux and the scion of a noble family, learned Latin at a very early age, even before learning his native French. He gained his title upon the death of his father in 1568. In 1571 he gave up a career in public service to become a fulltime writer. The first two books of his *Essays* appeared in 1580; the second book contained the lengthy "Apology for Raymond Sebond," which shall be our chief focus here. He was elected mayor of Bordeaux (a position his father had held) in 1581, serving for four years. A new edition of his *Essays* appeared in 1588, now containing Book 3.

The "Apology" was ostensibly written to defend the doctrines of Raymond Sebond (1385?–1436), whose treatise—*Theologia Naturalis* (Natural Theology; written 1434–36; published 1484)—Montaigne translated, at the urging of his father, into French (1569). As the title suggests, Sebond maintained that the truths of Christianity can be ascertained by unaided reason as it contemplates the natural world, whose marks of divinity should be available to all.

Montaigne's "Apology" was manifestly written amidst the continuing turmoil of the Reformation, which he flamboyantly states "would easily degenerate into an execrable atheism" (F 320). It is not at all clear how Montaigne justifies such a bizarre view, but that he is manifestly intent on suppressing anything that could by any stretch of the imagination be termed atheism is evident: his mission, he states plainly, is "to establish and prove against the atheists all the articles of the Christian religion"

24. *The Complete Essays of Montaigne* (tr. Donald M. Frame) 393. Subsequent references to this volume will occur in the text, preceded by the initial F.

(F 320).

And yet, Montaigne flatly declares that these articles cannot be defended by human reason; they can only be accepted on faith. It is here that Montaigne's exhaustive knowledge of Greco-Roman philosophy (including the work of such near-atheists as Xenophanes, Democritus, and Epicurus), abundantly revealed throughout his work, weighs upon him:

> And I do not think that purely human means are at all capable of this [proving the Christian religion]; if they were, so many rare and excellent souls, so abundantly furnished with natural powers, in ancient times, would not have failed to arrive at this knowledge through their reason. It is faith alone that embraces vividly and surely the high mysteries of our religion. (F 321)

Indeed, left to itself, reason alone might in the end betray us, since it plainly indicates that our justifications for believing in any religion are weak and adventitious:

> We happen to have been born in a country where it [our religion] was in practice; or we regard its antiquity or the authority of the men who have maintained it; or we fear the threats it fastens upon unbelievers, or pursue its promises. Those considerations should be employed in our belief, but as subsidiaries; they are human ties. Another religion, other witnesses, similar promises and threats, might imprint upon us in the same way a contrary belief.
>
> We are Christians by the same title that we are Perigordians or Germans. (F 324–25)

This is one of the earliest instances of the argument, commonly made over the next several centuries, that one's religious belief is largely dependent upon the accident of our birth.

Montaigne now launches on a monumental and largely tendentious attack upon the efficacy of reason itself. Reason cannot make us happy; even the brightest of us are tormented by "human discomforts" (F 358) that reason has no power to alleviate. Sometimes, indeed, excessive reason can lead to madness (F 363). Knowledge, moreover, does not make us morally good, since history is littered with instances of intelligent people committing dreadful acts. After a wide survey of philosophy from antiquity to his day, Montaigne concludes: "Reason does nothing but go astray in everything, and especially when it meddles with divine things" (F 386). The idea that the disagreements among philosophers is somehow an indictment of the entire displine of philosophy, or of reason itself, is a remarkably anti-intellectualist utterance; and the accusation that reason "meddles with divine things" is manifestly a strategy designed to shield religion from critical scrutiny.

Montaigne's agenda is now clear. He is terrified of the possibility that Sebond's advocacy of reason in ascertaining the "truth" of the Christian religion can, in the hands of atheism (which is "unnatural and monstrous" [F 325]), be turned on its head and used to undermine Christianity, leading to "the frightful and horrible darkness of irreligion" (F 327). It is precisely because, in his view, atheists (whoever they may be) have attempted to overthrow Sebond's arguments that Montaigne must act "to wrest from their hands the puny weapons of reason" (F 327).

Other essays buttress Montaigne's validation of Christianity, and specifically of Catholic Christianity. He regards Catholicism as a rock of stability in civil society; indeed, he conducts a rearguard argument in maintaining the universal scope of the Roman church in defiance of the increasing secular nationalism of the various European states: "We must either submit completely to the authority of our ecclesiastical government, or do without it completely" (F 134–35), he states in an early essay; later he states that Rome "is the metropolitan city of all Christian nations; the Spaniard and the Frenchman, every man is at home there. To be one of the princes of that state one need only be of Christendom, wherever it may be" (F 763). He speaks disapprovingly of the religious flip-flopping in England in the years following Henry VIII's death.

There is some reason to wonder who Montaigne's targets were in his fiery polemics. His repeated attacks on "atheism" in the "Apology" would suggest the widespread diffusion of such radical views, but there is little evidence of that in the historical record. I would argue that it was Montaigne's hostility to the religious ferment engendered by the Reformation that led him to paint his opponents in such lurid colours. Let me provide context for one of my earlier quotations from the "Apology," where he outlines his motivations in translating Sebond's work:

> ... this was when the innovations of Luther were beginning to gain favor and to shake our old belief in many places.
>
> In this he [Montaigne's father] was very well advised, rightly foreseeing by rational inference that this incipient malady would easily degenerate into an execrable atheism. For the common herd, not having the faculty of judging things in themselves, let themselves be carried away by chance and by appearances, when once they have been given the temerity to despise and judge the opinions that they had held in extreme reverence, such as are those in which their salvation is concerned. And when some articles of their religion have been set in doubt and upon the balance, they will soon after cast easily into like uncertainty all the other parts of their belief, which had no more authority or foundation in them than those that have been shaken; and they shake off as a tyrannical yoke all the impressions they had once received from the authority of the laws or the reverence of ancient usage ... (320)

The suggestion here is that the "execrable atheism" Montaigne condemns is more theoretical than real; that Montaigne fears that the tumult Luther has engendered will have its effect, not so much on the learned, but on the uneducated masses who may be infected with irrational scepticism once they begin to note that central pillars of what they took to be the authoritative doctrines of the church are questioned or undermined.

And yet, Montaigne himself unwittingly creates cracks in his fervently constructed edifice in defence of Catholicism. I have already noted the striking assertion that religion may be a product of one's birth. His work in general, apart from the "Apology," is distinguished by its emphasis on the pleasures and traumas of human life in this world; he has singularly little to say about the afterlife or of other central Christian doctrines. As Ann Hartle states, Montaigne largely rejects the "desire for the divine, for eternity and immortality"[25] inherent in both Aristotelianism and the Christianity of Augustine and Thomas Aquinas. And even in the "Apology" he all but admits that the dogma of an immortal soul is essentially unprovable (see F 414f.).

Because of all this—and, perhaps, because later thinkers cherry-picked his utterances, notably *"Que sçay-je?,"* as emblematic of a religious

25. Hartle, *Montaigne and the Origins of Modern Philosophy* 19.

scepticism he clearly did not embrace—Montaigne would become in later centuries a herald of freethought in a manner that would probably have horrified him.

Italian literature in the age of Machiavelli and beyond focuses on two poets, Ludovico Ariosto (1474–1533) and Torquato Tasso (1544–1593), both of whom embody the renewed taste for epic poetry engendered by Renaissance humanism's fascination with the work of such Greco-Roman poets as Homer, Virgil, and Statius. Ariosto's *Orlando Furioso* (1516) deals with Charlemagne and the Franks as they battle the Saracens. The story of Orlando (Roland in French) is of course of mediaeval origin, and Ariosto's utilisation of *ottava rima* is in one sense a homage to Dante; but in other senses the poem could be considered something of a parody of Dante and of the entire chivalric tradition that characterised the Middle Ages, so that the poem's superficial portrayal of Christianity triumphing over militant Islam is repeatedly undercut by tart satire and irony.

Tasso's *Gerusalemme liberata* (1591; Jerusalem Liberated) similarly unearths a mediaeval historical event—the Crusaders' recapture of Jerusalem in 1099—and its depiction of this conflict between Christians and Muslims reflects the author's concerns over the Ottoman Empire's continuing threat to European religious and political sovereignty. The poem is perhaps more religiously orthodox than Ariosto's and may be said to echo not only European worries about Muslim incursions but also some elements of the Counter-Reformation. But Tasso was criticised for his use of supernatural machinery (deriving from his study of Homer and Virgil), although even this element was used to further his emphasis on Christian "truth." But there is a real sense in which Tasso's highly coloured and rhetorical style vaunts spectacle over religious belief in his very long epic.

In Spain, we are met with the formidable figure of Miguel de Cervantes (1547–1616) and his sprawling novel *Don Quixote* (1605–15). But to understand the import of this novel—and its relevance to our enquiry—we must examine the history of Spanish prose fiction extending back a century or more, as Cervantes was manifestly responding to this body of work in his own epochal novel.

It is well known that *Don Quixote* purports to be a text that plays off of the novels of chivalry that had been written in abundance in Spain since the late fifteenth century; the most notable of these was *Amadis de Gaula* (1508), published by Garci Rodriguez de Montalvo, who probably adapted material of much older vintage. This was only one of several genres of romance fiction generated in Spain at this time; others included the sentimental romance, the pastoral romance, the Moorish romance, and the picaresque romance. Even though many of these works were explicitly Christian, conservative clerics condemned them as covert or explicit examples of paganism. One of the most noteworthy of the picaresque romances, the anonymous *Vida de Lazarillo de Tormes y sus fortunas y adversidades* (1554; The Life, Fortunes, and Adversities of Lazarillo de Tormes), is a pungent satire that liberally expatiates on the greed, hypocrisy, and sexual licence of a variety of clerics; not surprisingly, it was placed on the Index in 1559.

Cervantes was educated at a humanist academy in Madrid as a boy, then served in the army in Italy, where he battled the Turks. He wrote a considerable quantity of material, including the pastoral novel *La Galatea* (1585) and as many as twenty plays. The first part of *Don Quixote* was an immediate success, impelling Cervantes to add a second part. Its account of a minor nobleman, Don Quixote, who has been driven "out of his wits" (32) by reading books about knight-errantry (i.e., books of chivalric romance) and undertakes various quests to win the love of a woman he deems Dulcinea, but who in fact is a lowly farm girl, is an imperishable narrative of the tragicomic disjunction of the individual and the society he finds himself in; but its interpretation—especially its relation to the Christianity of Cervantes's time—is a singularly difficult proposition.

What strikes us in reading the novel is the surprising degree to which religion *fails* to dominate the text. In his prologue to Part 1, Cervantes seems to go out of his way to declare that Christian moralising will be absent from his work. He notes that other books are "full of sentences from Aristotle, Plato and the whole herd of philosophers"; on top of which, these books "quote Holy Scripture!" Then, bluntly: "My book will lack all this" (26). Later he quotes an unspecified friend who declares, "nor does it [the novel] set out to preach to anyone, mingling the human with the divine; which is a kind of motley in which no Christian understandiung should be dressed" (29–30). In his opening discussion of the books of chivalry that Don Quixote has devoured, there is no attempt to link them with Christianity. A later passage (Book 1, chs.

5–6) presents a hilarious parody of the Spanish Inquisition, as a priest and a barber conduct what is pointedly called a "public inquisition" (55) over these very books, some of which are to be burned, others consigned to "perpetual banishment" (59) and others to be "delivered . . . over to the secular arm of the housekeeper" (62). (Most of the books are in fact burned.)

The books of chivalry implicitly claimed that the love of a beautiful woman is a metonymy for the love of God—a topos that can be traced back at least to Augustine and to the general Christian embracing of Platonic love as found in the *Symposium*. The notion is, as we have seen, predominant in Dante's *Commedia.* But it is at this point that our interpretative difficulties begin. While it appears that Don Quixote is adhering to this topos, Cervantes has stated plainly at the very outset of his novel that his protagonist is essentially insane and accordingly a buffoon in many of the actions he undertakes; therefore, the true significance of his words and deeds is often the very reverse of their surface meaning. Hence, Cervantes (or the first-person narrator who purports to be the author of the work) lets us know (a) that Don Quixote believed these books to be factually and historically true accounts, (b) that, once he had resolved on his quest to be a knight-errant, he felt obligated to "find a lady to be enamoured of" (34), and (c) that Dulcinea is no princess but merely a "very good-looking farm girl" (35) whose actual name is Aldonza Lorenzo. Indeed, in a later discussion with a traveller, Don Quixote is resolute in declaring that his mission (whatever that exactly may be) signifies that he and other knights-errant "are God's minister's on earth, and the arms by which His justice is executed here" (98); to which the traveller responds:

> "I agree with you . . . but there is one thing in particular about knights errant that seems wrong to me. That is that when they are on the point of embarking on a great and perilous adventure in which there is manifest danger to their lives, never at the moment of attack do they think of entrusting their souls to God, as every Christian in such peril is bound to do. Instead they commend themselves to their mistresses, with as much fervour and devotion as if these were their God, a practice which seems to me to smack somewhat of paganism." (98–99)

Don Quixote violently rejects this accusation, but the overall narrative would seem to endorse the traveller's perspective.

In short, *Don Quixote* is a satire—one more in the long line of "folly" books such as those by Brant and Erasmus we have already studied. This point must be emphasised in opposition to those many critics who have found Don Quixote the character so endearing that they have discounted his "madness" and foolishness and even gone so far as to claim that, even if Cervantes' stated purpose was to ridicule the books of chivalry for their essential falsity (both to historical fact and to moral truth), the novel ends up validating the romantic charm of this kind of narrative. When, in Book 1, chs. 49–50, Don Quixote again defends the chivalry books—especially the supernatural or fantastic elements often found in them—against a canon who attacks them for being both false and implicitly heretical, he cites numerous events in those books that are strikingly, and unnervingly, analogous to various passages in the Bible. As Henry Higuera notes:

> Don Quixote responds . . . with a long, vivid description of a typical chivalric adventure, featuring a lake of boiling pitch, as in Isaiah 34:9 or Revelations 20:9; a marvelous garden, as in Eden; a sun that shines with a new brightness (although not a new sevenfold brightness, as in Isaiah 30:26); and a castle that, along with its walls, battlements, and gates, is built all of gold and precious stones, as in Isaiah 54:11 or Revelations 21:11. These images borrowed from Scripture put the canon in an embarrassing position: are they also impossible to enjoy even as fictions the minute one thinks about them?[26]

There are other pungent episodes of religious satire in the novel. Don Quixote manifestly subscribes to belief in the Devil (and in lesser devils), telling his sidekick, Sancho Panza, in a passage that mocks scholastic petttifoggery: "devils are very crafty. But although they carry smells about them, they do not smell, because they are spirits; and if they do smell, they cannot smell of good things, but only of evil and stinking ones. The reason is that they carry hell with them wherever they are, and can receive no kind of relief from their torments" (419). And

26. Higuera, *Eros and Empire* 147.

in an exquisite passage in Part 2, we are presented with the spectacle of a prophetic ape whose feats are so extraordinary that Don Quixote declares, "this Master Peter, his master, . . . must have made some bargain with the Devil, who has infused this talent into the ape so that he can gain his living by it; and when he is rich, he will give him his soul; for that is what the universal enemy is after" (636).

There is little evidence of what Cervantes' actual religious views were, although it is evident that he had more than a little exposure to Erasmian humanism. Given the dangers of expressing open disbelief in or hostility to Christianity in the Spain of his era, it is understandable that Cervantes would have been circumspect in exhibiting, even in a work of fiction, anything that could be taken as scepticism of scripture or of Catholic dogma. But the mere fact that Don Quixote espouses orthodox beliefs and frequently employs them to justify his own ludicrous ventures into world conquest suggests Cervantes' strong doubts as to the efficacy of Christianity in both the moral and political arenas.

G. Secularism in English Literature

The Renaissance, as a cultural, literary, and intellectual phenomenon, came late to England. The turbulence of the fifteenth century, highlighted by the ongoing Wars of the Roses, produced few writers of any stature aside from Sir Thomas Malory. There was something of a flowering of English poetry in the early sixteenth century, with such figures as Sir John Skelton (1463?–1529), Sir Thomas Wyatt (1503–1542), and Henry Howard, Earl of Surrey (1516?–1547) emerging. Wyatt introduced the sonnet to England. But their work is of little relevance to the development of atheism or secularism in England.

The flowering of literary expression—in poetry, drama, prose fiction, and other forms—during the Elizabethen age is a phenomenon virtually without parallel in English (or, indeed, world) literature, and is accordingly all but impossible to account for. Suffice it to say that the transcendent jewel of this age—the poetic drama of Shakespeare and a constellation of other luminaries—is at least in part a result of the relatively restricted literacy of the citizenry, rendering public spectacles such as plays immensely popular. The talents of these playwrights were expended in ensuring both the pleasing of the audience with vivid action and in attracting a numerically smaller but vital segment of that audience by profundity of thought and a breathtakingly innovative use of simile, symbol, metaphor, and other tropes that the fluidity of the English language at that juncture allowed. As such, Elizabethan drama is a fusion of humanist principles and popular taste. Later in the century, historical chronicles largely replaced mystery plays, enhancing the English people's ongoing pride in their historical and cultural distinctiveness from Europe—a pride that the monarchy's break with the papacy had fostered.

The leading non-dramatic poet of the Elizabethan age was Edmund Spenser (1552?–1599), whose immense and sprawling allegorical poem *The Faerie Queene* (1590–96) is difficult to encompass or even describe in small compass. Without going into details, we can well agree with a leading Spenser scholar, Anthea Hume, in affirming that in this poem, as in his work generally, Spenser reveals "both an enthusiasm for the humanist inheritance and a zealous, even militant Protestantism."[27] Spenser had numerous personal and professional ties to leading Puritans of the 1570s and 1580s, and his earlier poem, *The Shepheardes Calender* (1586)—a long pastoral poem featuring a month-by-month survey of the year from the perspective of a shepherd's life and duties—includes three "ecclesiastical" eclogues (for the months of May, July, and September) that underscore Puritan doctrine regarding the behaviour of the clergy, the superstitiousness of saints' relics, and other matters.

As for the *Faerie Queene,* earlier scholars had proposed a radical disjunction between Book 1 (which purportedly depicts the "order of grace," or the Protestant notion of God's free granting of salvation to human beings regardless of their actions in life) and the "order of nature"—the notion that the "natural man," although he has an innate knowledge of the existence of God, lacks the divine revelation of the "truth" of his redemption by Jesus Christ—that purportedly governs the later books. Hume establishes that there is no such dichotomy: Book 1 portrays the attainment of God's grace; the rest of the poem exhibits the practice of Christian life under that grace.

Nor need we make much of Spenser's extensive use of classical sources in both of his major poems. The pastoral, as we have seen,

---

27. Hume, *Edmund Spenser: Protestant Poet* 1.

emerged in the work of the Greek poet Theocritus and the Roman poet Virgil; but Spenser's immediate influences in *The Shepheardes Calender* appear to have been much more recent writers, including Sir John Skelton and Mantuan (Baptista Mantuanus, 1447–1516). Spenser is one of the signal instances of a Renaissance writer drawing upon classical texts to emphasise Christian teaching, meaning that the mere absorption of such texts is not in itself an indication of religious scepticism or hostility to Christianity. Little of that can be found in Spenser's work, aside from routine condemnations of Catholic dogma and practice, in what would become a commonplace among English writers of all stripes for centuries.

The chief prose writers of the period were Sir Philip Sidney and Sir Walter Ralegh. Sidney (1554–1586)—who in his short life managed to be a poet, courtier, soldier, and even a literary theorist—was, like Spenser, inclined toward Puritanism, which accounts for his objections to Queen Elizabeth's tentative plans to marry the Catholic duc d'Alençon in 1579. Sidney's anti-Catholic bias was markedly enhanced by his witnessing the St Bartholomew's Day massacre of 1572.

Some scholars have claimed that his pioneering critical essay *A Defence of Poesie* (written 1580; published 1595) is a validation of poetry as a kind of replacement of religion by stressing poetry's moral and philosophical value; but it is difficult to see the validity of this argument, since Sidney explicitly declares the Psalms of David and other books of the Bible as among the highest fruits of poetical expression (23, 29). It would be more reasonable to conclude, with Andrew D. Weiner, that the essay is emblematic of "Sidney's Protestant understanding of the reality he perceived."[28]

Sidney's massive prose romance *Arcadia* (existing in two substantially different versions, the *Old Arcadia* [dating to c. 1577–80] and the *New Arcadia* [dating to 1580–86 and published in 1590]) is also an allegory of sorts. This monumental work—written in lavishly evocative prose and popular from the moment it appeared and remaining so for several centuries—deals with Basileus, king of Arcadia, who imprudently asks an oracle for a prediction of his future, in the course of which he hears

28. Andrew D. Weiner, "Sidney, Protestantism, and Literary Critics: Reflections on Some Recent Criticism of *The Defence of Poetry*," in Allen et al., *Sir Philip Sidney's Achievements* 122.

much that appears to bode ill for himself and his family. Accordingly, he flees with his wife, Gynecia, and two daughters, Pamela and Philoclea, to a pastoral realm; but in the end these actions themselves cause the prediction to come true in a different fashion.

The core of the work is both a rumination on the nature of love (romantic, sexual, familial), especially the role of reason and moral restraint in regard to this explosive emotion. The centrepiece of the romance is a debate between Pamela (who, although a pagan, recognises a divine order to existence) and Cecropia, Basileus's sister, who not only openly advocates careless hedonism but also discounts worries about one's future status in the afterlife. In the critical Book 3, chapter 10, Cecropia makes a blasphemous assertion:

> "Be wise, and that wisdom shall be a God unto thee. Be contented, and that is thy heaven: for else to think that those powers (if there be any such) above are moved either by the eloquence of our prayers or in a chafe [i.e., rage] at the folly of our actions carries as much reason, as if flies should think that men take great care which at them hums sweetest, and which of them flies nimblest." (488)

This vaguely Epicurean sentiment—an expression of doubt as to the very existence of a god or, at the very least, a doubt as to whether that god has any concern with the thoughts and actions of the human race—stamps the view as non- or even anti-Christian. In her indignant reply, Pamela rejects the entire notion and condemns Cecropia's "godless mind" (491); later the omniscient narrator chimes in, speaking of Cecropia's "filthiness of impiety" (492).

The kind of discussion Cecropia and Pamela have in this fictional work may or may not echo actual debates among the intellectual and political elite of the period—something that led some contemporary commentators to refer to a "school of atheism" in Elizabethan England. But whether there actually was such a school in any meaningful sense of the term is greatly to be doubted. Critics maintained that it revolved around the charismatic figure of Sir Walter Ralegh. Ralegh (1552?–1618)—nobleman, courtier, poet, historian, and explorer—was for decades involved at the highest levels of the English government before suffering a spectacular fall, undergoing a trial for treason in 1603, shortly after Queen Elizabeth's death, and being imprisoned in the Tower of London. Pardoned in 1617, he undertook his second trip to Guiana, in South America (this followed his failed attempt to establish a colony in Virginia in the 1580s and his first trip to Guiana, in the 1590s); upon his return, as a result of various political machinations, he was imprisoned again and beheaded on October 29, 1618.

The accusation of a "school of atheism" focusing on Ralegh comes from one Robert Parsons in a work published in 1592. A passage of that work reads as follows: "Of Sir Walter Ralegh's school of atheism by the way, and of the conjurer that is M[aster] thereof, and of the diligence used to get young gentlemen to this school, wherein both Moses and our Savior, the Old and New Testament are jested at, and the scholars taught among other things to spell God backward."[29] There is, however, much reason to be sceptical of Parsons's assertion. Elizabeth had, in October 1591, issued a proclamation against Catholics; and Parsons, an English Jesuit, was subsequently one of those accused of being part of a Catholic fifth column if and when the king of Spain were to invade England. By this time Ralegh had already received many favours from the queen, and Parsons's screed may well have been intended to discredit both him and Elizabeth's court as a hotbed of religious deviance; indeed, Parsons went on to accuse her chief adviser, William Cecil (now Lord Burghley), of atheism. Ralegh's hostility to Spain was well known, and this may have added to Parsons's desire to take him down.

The whole issue of "atheism" in Elizabethan England is confused by the multifarious shades of meaning that authors of varying religious and political persuasions gave to it, usually in the course of polemics specifically designed to cast individuals or entire groups of people in a bad light. If any coherent meaning could be attached to the word, it rested not so much on what to us would be the obvious signification (denial of the existence of God) but on denial of the existence of a soul, denial of the immortality of the soul, and a broader moral corollary—that "sin" was meaningless, because there will be no punishment for the individual after death for acts that nature manifestly allows (e.g., incest); as such, they cannot possibly be "forbidden" by a god, since if that were

29. From Parsons's *An Advertisement Written to a Secretary of My L. Treasurers of England, by an English Intelligencer as He Passed through Germany towards Italy* (1592); quoted in Strathman 25.

the case it would be physically impossible to commit them.

It is true that a number of treatises implicitly or explicitly condemning atheism were written by Christian authors during this period. Roger Ascham (1515–1568), whose *The Scholemaster* (written 1563–68; published 1570) is a handbook to the education of (male) English children, goes out of his way to criticise "Italianated" English youths who

> first lustily contemn God, then scornfully mock His Word, and also spitefully hate and hurt all well-willers thereof. Then they have in more reverence the triumphes of Petrarch than the Genesis of Moses. They make more account of Tully's offices than St. Paul's Epistles; of a tale in Boccaccio than a story of the Bible. Then they count as fables the holy mysteries of Christian religion. They make Christ and His Gospel only serve civil policy. Then neither religion cometh amiss to them. (85–86)

This screed was written long before the emergence of Ralegh as a focus of "atheism" in England. If any motive can be attributed to Ascham's screed, it would appear that he is lashing out variously at those who appreciate Greco-Roman culture (and such of its offshoots as Petrarch) and advocate Machiavellianism in politics. It is worth noting that Ascham makes evident that these unnamed individuals "scorn both Protestant and Papist" (86), so that he cannot be alluding merely to doctrinal conflicts within the church.

Philippe de Mornay's *Traité de la vérité de la religion chrétienne contre les athées* (1581; translated into English in 1587 as *A Worke concerning the Trewness of the Christian Religion*) directly attacked atheists among numerous other disreputables.[30] The translation of this work was begun by Sir Philip Sidney and completed by Arthur Golding. John Dove's *Confutation of Atheism* (1605) marked the culmination of this tendency during this period. But the curious thing about all these works as that they name few if any individuals who actually espoused atheism, however that term was defined. This makes one wonder whether there was any body of thinkers who actually espoused such a view.

30. The full title of de Morney's work indicates that his targets are . . . *Atheists, Epicures, Paynims* [a non-Christian, usually applied to Muslims], *Iewes, Mahumetists, and other Infidels.*

A more cogent exposé of Ralegh's alleged atheism is found in the account of a dinner party at the home of Sir George Trenchard in Cerne Abbas, Dorset, in 1593, in which Ralegh, his brother Carew, and others were present. When Ralph Ironside, a clergyman, noted that "death which is properly the wages of sin, is death eternal, both of the body and of the soul also," Carew provocatively responded, "Soul, what is that?" Ralegh then interjected that "I have been a scholar for some time in Oxford, I have answered under a bachelor of art, and had talk with diverse; yet hitherunto in this point (to wit what the reasonable soul of man is) have I not by any been resolved." As the discussion turned to God, Ralegh is alleged to have stated, "Marry, these two be like, for neither could I learn hitherto what God is."[31]

Spectacular as this may sound, it is unlikely that Ralegh is actually asserting doubts as to the existence of the soul or of God. Indeed, it was a commonplace among even the most devout Christian theologians—from as early as Augustine, if not before—to maintain the existence of God and the soul without being able to provide any detailed account of the nature of these two entities.

Indeed, if we examine Ralegh's literary work—some of it published at the time, some centuries after his death—it is difficult to find even the slightest expressions of scepticism of any aspect of Christian doctrine. The central document here is his immense *Historie of the World* (1614). Overall, the work could be read as an emphatic instance of Christian apologetics: here Ralegh asserts God's creation of the world *ex nihilo* and of all the creatures in it; denies the equivalence of God and nature, stating that nature is subordinate to God; acknowledges God's providence and divine justice; and so on. In *A Treatise of the Soul,* unpublished in his lifetime, he explicitly avows the immortality of the soul.

The closest we get to scepticism or freethought in the *Historie* is a vigorous passage in the preface condemning religious disputation and the disinclination of people to lead holy lives:

> And certainly there is nothing more to be admired, and more to be lamented, than the private contention, the passionate dispute, the personal hatred, and the perpetual wars, massacres, and murders, for

31. Quoted in Strathman 47–48.

> religion among Christians; the discourse whereof hath so occupied the world, as it hath well-near driven the practice thereof out of the world. . . . We are all in effect become comedians in religion; and while we act in gesture and voice divine virtues, in all the course of our lives we renounce our persons, and the parts we play. (1.xxix–xxx)

It is true that the *Historie* was written during his confinement in the Tower of London; but it is implausible that Ralegh would have undertaken such an enormous work simply as a means of counteracting his reputation for scepticism.

In some Ralegh's political writings there is some whiff of Machiavellian realism, and this may have laid the seeds for later accusations of his "atheism" by religious partisans. But, even if discussions of the sort that took place at that dinner party in 1593 are to be considered far more radical than they apparently were, the case for a "school of atheism" is exceedingly thin.

The playwright Christopher Marlowe (1564–1593) also came under scrutiny in his day for atheism as well as homosexuality, but both charges seem to be false or, at the very least, much exaggerated. The atheism accusation emerged in a curious manner: in 1593 the playwright Thomas Kyd, under torture, claimed that Marlowe held unorthodox views of both church and state. This incident occurred during the hysteria surrounding an outbreak of the plague. Marlowe was brought before the Star Chamber on May 20, 1593. Richard Baines—who, along with Marlowe, was a member of what was called the "secret service," a group of agents that delivered confidential documents from Elizabeth's court to monarchs or other officials in foreign countries—hurled a wide array of accusations (including the homosexuality claim), among them (a) that religion is used only "to keep men in awe"; (b) that Jesus Christ and his compatriots engaged in free love; (c) that there are contradictions in scripture; and (d) that Marlowe not only holds such views himself, "but almost into every company he cometh he persuades men to Atheism, willing them not to be afeared of bugars and hobgoblins, and utterly scorning both God and his ministers." In conclusion, Baines urges that "all men in Christianity ought to endeavour that the mouth of so dangerous a member may be stopped."[32] But before the Star Chamber or any other judicial body could

32. See Sales, *Christopher Marlowe* 42–43; also J. B. Steane's introduction to his Penguin

take action, Marlowe was killed in a fight in a restaurant.

What are we to make of all this? There is some evidence that Marlowe secretly converted to Catholicism when he attended Cambridge in the 1580s, and it is entirely conceivable that Baines's screed was simply part of a campaign of Protestant propaganda against a Catholic. It is conceivable that Marlowe uttered such sentiments among friends; but since the open expression of atheism was still a capital offence, it seems unlikely that he would be quite so bold about it as Baines indicates.

What is the evidence of his work? In the prologue to *The Jew of Malta* (1589–90), "Machevill" (i.e., the ghost of Machiavelli) states bluntly, "I count religion but a childish toy, / And hold there is no sin but ignorance" (14–15); but it is in the drama above all literary genres that we must practise extreme care in attributing to the author the sentiments of his various characters. The play itself undoubtedly exhibits anti-Jewish prejudice, chiefly by way of condemning Barabas's thirst for money; at one point a character comments that he is "cast off from heaven" (2.3.163), and soon thereafter Barabas condemns himself as a heretic. But in this play where Jews, Christians, and Muslims all battle for military supremacy, "Christians are shown to be every bit as mercenary and opportunistic as Jews."[33]

The two parts of *Tamburlaine the Great* (1587–88) offer some interesting if equivocal evidence. It was this play that led the playwright Robert Greene (*Groatsworth of Wit*, 1592) to accuse Marlowe of making a hero out of an atheist; but Tamburlaine is far from that, unless we adopt the view expressed by some fanatical Christians that all non-Christians are in some sense atheists. Tamburlaine refers to himself grandiosely as the "scourge and wrath of God" (Part 1, 3.3.44), by which he apparently means God's chosen instrument to carry out his decrees and judgments. Beginning as merely a Scythian shepherd, Tamburlaine successively conquers the Persians, the Turks, and the whole of Africa. (The real Tamburlaine, or Timur, had allied himself with Christians to defeat the Turks in Ankara in 1402.) But it is difficult to see how this proto-Nietzschean character can genuinely be considered impious or even anti-Christian: his ruthlessness in war is a trait that any number of Christian military figures exhibited.

Classics edition of Marlowe's *Complete Plays* 13.

33. Sales 110.

In the end, Marlowe's reputation as a religious sceptic must stand or fall on the basis of *The Tragicall History of Doctor Faustus* (probably staged at the very end of Marlowe's life, although the first recorded performance dates to 1597). But this play affords virtually no evidence for any anti-Christian sentiment; indeed, the very opposite is the case. The well-known story—derived by Marlowe from a 1592 English translation of the Faust story originating in Germany in 1587—is about as emphatic an endorsement of the standard Christian view of the dangers of defying God's commandments as could be imagined; moreover, it presents a vivid portrayal of the orthodox conception of witchcraft, sorcery, and devil worship as a literal pact with the Devil.

Doctor Faustus's thirst for power leads him to make such a pact, spelled out in a mystical Latin incantation (1.3.16–22) and signed with his own blood. Although a Good Angel warns Faustus that he is heading toward "blasphemy" (1.1.72), Faustus himself puts on a bold front, claiming that "The word 'damnation' terrifies not me" (1.3.58), and later declares that "hell's a fable" (1.5.130). The figure who enacts the pact is Mephostophilis (so spelled by Marlowe), a "servant to great Lucifer" (1.3.40) who is one of the "unhappy spirits who fell with Lucifer, / Conspired against our God with Lucifer, / And are for ever damned with Lucifer" (1.3.70–72). To demonstrate the reality of hell, Lucifer and his devils come up from that realm and show Faustus the seven deadly sins (1.2.113f.).

Faustus does indeed have an entertaining time of it, appearing as an invisible intruder at the court of the Emperor Charles (i.e., Charles V, Holy Roman Emperor), at which the pope is present. There may well be some anti-Catholic humour at Charles's expense, as Faustus summons up the spirits of Alexander the Great and his paramour. When the Emperor's courtiers attack Faustus, he responds by calling up devils to beat them up.

But Faustus's end is not a happy one. He had sold his soul to Mephostophilis for a period of twenty-four years, and when his death approaches he repents:

> Accursed Faustus, wretch, what hast thou done?
> I do repent, and yet I do despair.
> Hell strives with grace for conquest in my breast.

What shall I do to shun the snares of death? (5.1.68–71)

Not much can be done, it appears. Lucifer and his demons come to him, and Faustus laments that he is endowed with "A surfeit of deadly sin, that hath damned both body and soul" (5.2.40). And more: "For vain pleasure of four and twenty years hath Faustus lost eternal joy and felicity. I writ them a bill with mine own blood, the date is expired: this is the time, and he will fetch me" (5.2.67–71). Just so: "Hell is discovered [i.e., revealed]," as a stage direction indicates (5.2.124–25); his calling upon Jesus Christ (5.2.157f.) is futile, and he is carried down to heaven. The Chorus soberly warns us not "To practise more than heavenly power permits" (5.3.27) lest we meet a similar fate.

To whatever extent we may believe that *Doctor Faustus* reflects Marlowe's own beliefs, it is difficult to maintain that it was written by someone who had extensive doubts about the veracity of the Christian religion. Whether it indicates a Catholic or a Protestant orientation is not entirely clear; even if we assume that there is some harmless if ribald satire directed against the pope, the overall tenor of the play seems Catholic—if only because, at this juncture, it was Catholics who were more vigorously pursuing suspected witches than Protestants, and the play is an accurate reflection of the means by which witches, sorcerers, necromancers, and other miscreants were believed to go about making pacts with the Devil—and what horrible fates they would suffer for doing so.

And now we come to William Shakespeare (1564–1616).[34] As with every other aspect of Shakespeare's life, work, and thought, the subject of his treatment of religion in his plays has been discussed exhaustively and at times with antipodally different results. Matters are not helped by the obvious circumstance that we know little or nothing about Shakespeare's own views on the matter. There is some minimal evidence that his father John and the family of his mother, Mary Arden, were Catholics; but at least some of this evidence is either circumstantial or based on documents that may be forgeries. But his poems and plays make it abundantly clear

34. I will mercifully avoid plunging into the murky waters of the Shakespeare authorship controversy and assume that it was the playwright and actor from Stratford-upon-Avon, and not Sir Francis Bacon, the Earl of Oxford, or any other figure of the time, who actually wrote the plays attributed to him.

that he was intimately familiar with the Bible,[35] the *Book of Common Prayer*, and other documents of the Anglican church. Whether there are more or fewer biblical quotations or allusions in his plays than in those of his contemporaries is an open question.

If Shakespeare's own religious inclinations are now irrecoverable, we are reduced to examining his texts—but the evidence here is singularly ambiguous. This is not only because his transcendent genius (even if expressed in a "popular" medium by an actor/producer who was anything but highbrow) led him to write plays of exceptional subtlety and complexity, but because one of the chief elements of his literary greatness is the manner in which he invests himself fully into the psyches of his characters, whether they be saintly, unmitigatedly evil, or every gradation between; as a result, it is all but impossible to determine which, if any, of the utterances expressed by his characters are echoes of his own views. Nevertheless, some tentative conclusions can be reached.

We are, however, faced with some bold assertions on this issue dating back a century or more. One of the deans of Shakespearean scholarship, A. C. Bradley, threw down a gauntlet in declaring in 1904: "The Elizabethan drama was almost wholly secular; and while Shakespeare was writing he practically confined his view to the world of non-theological observation and thought."[36] Four years earlier, the philosopher George Santayana, in the essay "The Absence of Religion in Shakespeare," wrote: "But for Shakespeare, in the matter of religion, the choice lay between Christianity and nothing. He chose nothing; he chose to leave his heroes and himself in the presence of life and of death with no other philosophy than that which the profane world can suggest and understand."[37] A number of Shakespeare scholars over the past several decades have set out to combat that view, but in the end I believe we are obliged to agree with David Scott Kastan, who wrote in 2014: "Religion in the plays is a psychological and social reality that registers as form, rather than a credal one that registers as belief."[38]

One clue to the role of religion in Shakespeare is offered by the

35. He probably read the Geneva Bible, a translation published in 1560 and produced by English Protestants who had been exiled in the reign of Queen Mary and settled in Geneva.
36. Bradley, *Shakespearean Tragedy* 25.
37. Santayana, *Interpretations of Poetry and Religion* 152.
38. Kastan, *A Will to Believe* 7.

two plays that treat (albeit in an indirect manner) religions other than Christianity: *The Merchant of Venice* (1596–98)[39] and *Othello* (1603?). Both plays are set in Venice, which was widely seen as a booming commercial and cultural centre as well as a sort of nexus between East and West. It featured a religious pluralism that England pointedly lacked (aside from the Catholic/Protestant divide), since Jews had been exiled from the island centuries earlier. Shylock (who is not the titular merchant of Venice; that role belongs to Antonio) embodies the multivalent views of Jews in Elizabethan society: they are condemned for having rejected Christ's teaching (but then, so have Catholics, in the Protestant view), but they deserve a grudging respect for being God's chosen people and the recipients of the Old Testament, forming a necessary chain of continuity from antiquity to the present day. Shylock both emphasises his Jewish identity (religious and ethnic) and famously declares in a poignant speech that he is also emblematic of the human condition:

> I am a Jew. Hath not a Jew eyes? Hath not a Jew hands, organs, dimensions, senses, affections, passions?—fed with the same food, hurt with the same weapons, subject to the same diseases, healed by the same means, warmed and cooled by the same winter and summer as a Christian is? If you prick us, do we not bleed?" (3.1.51–56)

The loftiness of this utterance is, however, confounded by Shylock's comment, immediately following, that both Christians and Jews would exact "revenge" if one were wronged by the other—a point that echoes the OT's "eye for an eye" morality but has been explicitly rejected by Jesus' Sermon on the Mount. In any event, Christianity in *The Merchant of Venice* emerges triumphant; not only is the play littered with antisemitic allusions, but the "mercy" extended to Shylock is predicated upon his forced conversion to the religion that superseded his own.

Othello is one more piece of evidence—if any were needed—of the continuing dread inspired by the Muslim incursions into Europe. Othello himself is a Christian—whether by birth or by conversion is not entirely clear; but he is also a "Moor," a term that customarily denotes a Muslim from Africa. Indeed, his blackness is a central focus in the

39. I cite the probable date of writing or production of Sheskespeare's plays rather than their publication dates, either in quarto editions or in the posthumous First Folio (1623).

play, and not in a positive light; and the fact that he has secretly married the lily-white Desdemona would have been scandalous to Shakespeare's audience. Indeed, almost at the very outset Iago makes a crude reference to the irregularity of the relationship in explicitly racial terms: "Even now, now, very now, an old black ram / Is tupping your white ewe" (1.1.88–89). Nevertheless, Othello is vital to Christian interests because he is leading the Venetian defence of Cyprus against the Ottoman Turks. Remarkably little is said of Othello's religious views, but the audience would not have separated his race from his religion; indeed, it would have linked his blackness with evil, heresy, and damnation. After Othello kills Desdemona, Iago's wife Emilia cries: "O, the more angel she, / And you the blacker devil!" (5.2.131–32). There is no reason to think, however, that Shakespeare shares these prejudices: they are vigorously propounded by Iago, Roderigo, and other characters, but Othello's words and actions largely refute them—until, at least, Iago corrupts Othello's mind and causes him, in the moments before his suicide, to align himself to the "malignant and turbaned Turk" (5.2.349).

It is sometimes stated that the one play of Shakespeare that can be said to embody Christian themes or values is *Measure for Measure* (1603?). The title is generally thought to reflect a passage in Luke: "For with the same measure that ye mete withal it shall be measured to you again" (6:38). But the play does not in fact reflect the "mercy" or tolerance that some have believed it to feature. In this play, Claudio is sentenced to death for "fornication": he had slept with his fiancée Juliet, and gotten her pregnant, prior to completing all the legal paperwork for their marriage. Angelo, the deputy of Duke Vincentio, comes across—and is meant to come across—as a rigid Puritan for his unwavering determination to carry out the sentence; but Isabella, Claudio's Catholic sister, doesn't come across well either, embodying a strident and self-righteous asceticism, valuing her chastity more than her brother's life.

If any play echoes biblical themes, it is *King Lear* (1606), which many scholars have seen as an exemplification of the intolerable suffering of Job. But unlike Job, Lear is in part the author of his own misfortunes, by his selfish demand that his daughters vie in their expression of love for him. As his daughters and their husbands engage in war with one another to gain control of the kingdom (the play is set in a pre-Christian England), Lear's world crumbles all around his ears. There is considerable apocalyptic language in the final acts of the play; indeed, even at the outset Lear calls upon Nature to destroy the world (1.4.230–38). But Lear is in fact impotent to carry out such a goal, and this leads to the Earl of Gloucester's poignantly misanthropic lines: "As flies to wanton boys are we to th' gods; / They kill us for their sport" (4.1.36–37). Lear himself had, curiously, echoed the quasi-Epicurean principle *ex nihilo nihil fit* early in the play: "Nothing will come of nothing" (1.1.90). But the context is obviously not metaphysical. His carrying of the dead Cordelia in his arms is seen as a gender reversal of the *Pietà*—the image of Mary holding the dead Jesus.

There is little doubt that *Hamlet* (1599–1601) presents a substantially greater amount of religious imagery and content than most of Shakespeare's other plays. The presence of the ghost of Hamlet's murdered father is at the core of this scenario. His restless shade appears to be wandering through the Catholic Purgatory:

> I am thy father's spirit,
> Doom'd for a certain term to walk the night,
> And for the day confin'd to fast in fires,
> Till the foul crimes done in my days of nature
> Are burnt and purg'd away. (1.5.9–13)

But there are some curiosities here. In Catholic doctrine, spirits are confined to Purgatory for the crimes *they* committed in life, not those committed upon them. So, in spite of the fact that Protestantism vigorously disputed the very existence of ghosts or restless spirits,[40] we should beware of accepting Stephen Greenblatt's facile formulation that the play is one in which "a young man from Wittenberg, with a distinctly Protestant temperament, is haunted by a distinctly Catholic ghost."[41] It is true that the ghost later laments the failure of his body to be buried in a specifically Catholic manner (including the rare word "Unhouseled" [1.5.77], referring to the eucharist)—a passage that has led enthusiastic scholars to assume that Shakespeare is referring to his own father's adherence to the "old faith"; but Hamlet's own faith is quite a bit more perplexing.

40. See Kastin 126f.
41. Greenblatt, *Hamlet and Purgatory* 240.

His famous soliloquy (3.1.56f.) is an extraordinarily strange utterance. It is almost universally assumed that Hamlet is mulling over the moral, religious, and metaphysical prospects of taking one's own life (a mortal sin in whatever variant of Christianity one espouses) or not doing so; but his rumination is really far broader than that, extending to the basic question of existence versus non-existence. And in this context, the first possibility Hamlet presents is nothing less than the Epicurean "death as oblivion" trope ("To die, to sleep / . . . and by a sleep to say we end / The heartache, and the thousand natural shocks / That flesh is heir to"). Although the "sleep as death" metaphor is a commonplace, even in religious texts, Hamlet here is clearly outlining an utter quiescence of the sort evoked by Book 3 of Lucretius' *De Rerum Natura.* The other possibility Hamlet lays out is a nebulous terror inspired by the thought of some unspecified form of continued awareness beyond death: "To die, to sleep— / To sleep—perchance to dream: ay, there's the rub, / For in that sleep of death what dreams may come / When we have shuffled off this mortal coil, / Must give us pause." Is Hamlet painting a portrait of hell? It does not appear so; all he is suggesting (and it is a suggestion that inspires "dread" that there is "something after death") is merely the extension of consciousness after the death of the body.

If this is not hell, it is not heaven either. The word heaven appears fifty-six times in *Hamlet,* but in Hamlet's own mouth it is largely formulaic, and no idea of his own conception of the beatific afterlife can be derived. Indeed, in one bizarre passage he contemplates killing the praying Claudius and remarks, "And now I'll do it. And so 'a [he] goes to heaven, / And so am I revenged" (3.3.74–75). How the murderer of his father would end up in heaven is not at all clear. In effect, Hamlet's vision of heaven is remarkably free of meaningful content.

In *Macbeth* (1606) we find another celebrated passage that perhaps turns the Bible on its head. His lament after suffering his just desserts is poignant and bitter, and is worth quoting in spite of its familiarity:

> To-morrow, and to-morrow, and to-morrow
> Creeps in this petty pace from day to day
> To the last syllable of recorded time,
> And all our yesterdays have lighted fools
> The way to dusty death. Out, out, brief candle!

> Life 's but a walking shadow, a poor player
> That struts and frets his hour upon the stage
> And then is heard no more. It is a tale
> Told by an idiot, full of sound and fury,
> Signifying nothing. (5.5.19–28)

There may well be numerous echoes of biblical phases here: "thou hast brought me into the dust of death" (Ps. 22:15); "Surely every man walketh in a vain shew" (Ps. 39:6); "we spend our days as a tale that is told" (Ps. 90:9).[42] But all apart from these borrowings (some of which may be questionable), the thrust of the speech is nothing sort of a bleak nihilism that envisions the transience of the entire human race and its utter extinction, both individually and collectively ("And then is heard no more"), in a meaningless and indifferent cosmos. Once again, there is no reason to think that Macbeth's sentiments echo Shakespeare's; but the mere fact that such a speech could be delivered in a public venue in early Jacobean England is remarkable.

We should consider other instances where parody of religion or of the Bible may be present. These appear, understandably, mostly in the comedies. Neither priests nor parsons come off very well in *Love's Labor's Lost, The Merry Wives of Windsor, As You Like It,* and other plays. But perhaps the most pungent satire occurs in *Titus Andronicus* (1588–93), apparently co-written with George Peele. This play deals with a fictional Roman general battling the Goths in the early centuries of the Christian era. The exceptional amount of bloodletting in the play manifestly reflects the influence of Seneca's tragedies, which had been appearing in English translation since 1559. But it is the contention of one scholar[43] that the concluding banquet scene is nothing less than a parody of the Last Supper. Titus has murdered the sons of the Goth queen Tamora and baked them into a pie: this is a clear nod to Seneca's *Thyestes,* but is it also a hideous allusion to the eucharist? As Titus tells his daughter Lavinia:

> And now prepare your throats, Lavinia, come,
> Receive the blood; and when that they are dead,
> Let me go grind their bones to powder small

42. See Milward, *Shakespeare's Religious Background* 102.
43. Mallin, *Godless Shakespeare* 35f.

> And with this hateful liquor temper it;
> And in that paste let their vile heads be baked. (5.2.196–200)

After all, didn't Jesus himself say that the bread and wine are his body and blood? And isn't transubstantiation a kind of cannibalism, as commentators from as early as Tacitus maintained?

There is probably considerably more material on Shakespeare's attitudes toward religion to be mined both from the plays set in ancient Rome (where Shakespeare does a more than credible job in portraying the pagan perspective on the gods) and, especially, the English history plays; but enough has been said to make some broad conclusions on the subject. At a minimum, it is clear that Shakespeare never addressed religion, or the Christian religion, directly in the manner of Marlowe's *Doctor Faustus;* he rarely engaged in anti-Catholic polemic, although that need not imply that he was himself a Catholic; and, in general, his plays do present a largely secular outlook in the sense that the complex social, psychological, political, and cultural issues his characters contend with are resolved in largely human terms without an appeal to God, Jesus, or the doctrines and moral dictates of the Christian religion. This is not to assert anything approaching religious scepticism, much less atheism, on Shakespeare's part; but it does point to the fundamental truth of Harold Bloom's contention that Shakespeare's accomplishment was nothing less than the "invention of the human." There is, however, some reason to doubt whether his influence upon subsequent literature, immense as it is, led his immediate successors to follow him in this specific regard.

The cadre of notable Elizabethan playwrights extends far beyond Marlowe and Shakespeare to include Ben Jonson, Thomas Middleton, Beaumont and Fletcher, Cyril Tourneur, John Webster, Philip Massinger, Thomas Kyd, and several others; but a detailed examination of their work would profit us little. Some of these playwrights continued to work into the Jacobean era, and their work will be examined in the next volume. It is sufficient here to say that several dramatists addressed issues of religion, secularism, and even freethought (as in Tourneur's *Atheist's Tragedy,* 1611) that are worth studying in their place.

H. Renaissance Art and Music

The new spirit awakened by the Renaissance manifested itself not only in literature but in art and music. The rediscovery of ancient texts went hand in hand with the rediscovery or reassessment of the hallmarks of classical art—chiefly sculpture and architecture, since Greco-Roman painting was in relatively short supply. The paint that had worn off ancient statuary created a sense of purity and austerity that augmented the sublime realism of their overall design, especially in the portraiture of the human form. As such, Renaissance art came to be typified by such realism in painting and sculpture, as well as by such key elements from ancient aesthetics as the use of the arch, the various orders of architecture (Doric, Ionic, Corinthian, and so on), and in general a conformation of art and architecture to the human scale as opposed to mediaeval art, whose imposing edifices (especially in church architecture) urged the reader to look toward an omnipotent God whose powers utterly dwarfed the human beings he was thought to have created in his own image. Of course, no new theories of art would have gained traction in the absence of great artists to exemplify it; and the Renaissance engendered an abundance of transcendently brilliant artists who permanently transformed art and established a model for aesthetic excellence that endured for centuries.

One of the earliest and most notable chroniclers of Renaissance art, Giorgio Vasari (1511–1574), in his epochal *Lives of the Most Excellent Painters, Sculptors, and Architects* (first edition 1550; second edition 1568), explicitly criticised the early Christians who, when they took over the reins of the Roman Empire in the fourth century, "not only defaced or threw to the ground all the marvellous statues, sculptures, pictures, mosaics, and ornaments of the false gods of the heathens" (1.xlviii), but went on to characterise Renaissance art as focusing on humanity among other elements. This is not in any way to state that artists suddenly abandoned religious motifs in their work; indeed, painting and sculpture remained predominantly Christian, but sculptures in particular increasingly reflected Greco-Roman models. A much earlier figure, the polymath Leon Battista Alberti (1404–1474), wrote a work, *Della pittura* (1435; On Painting), lavishing praise on recent artists, noting their use of geometry and perspective and recommending the classical traits of restraint, unity, and fidelity to nature. This was as close to a humanist manifesto in art as one is likely to find.

It was in Italian art and architecture that the new values first manifested themselves. Florence was initially the locus for many of the early Italian artists, as its new-found prosperity led to an upsurge of public art and commissions by non-religious sources—especially (after 1434) the Medicis. The architect Filippo Brunellesci (1377–1446), perhaps the first great Renaissance artist, visited Rome in the early fifteenth century to study the ancient sculptures and buildings there. The Pantheon inspired his construction of the dome on Florence Cathedral. Other religious buildings he constructed also embody classical design.

The sculptures of Donatello (Donato di Niccolò di Betto Bardi, 1386?–1466) reveal a strong classical influence, especially in the portrayal of drapery. His celebrated *David* (1440s) mingles Christian imagery (David's defeat of Goliath as a parallel to Christ's defeat of Satan) with imagery taken from Plato, and featuring overall a plainly homoerotic subtext. This fusion of classical and Christian imagery became widespread. The tomb of Leonardo Bruni (1370–1444), is nothing less than a Roman sarcophagus, such as that found abundantly in ancient Rome. Here eagles (representing Jupiter) are found cheek-by-jowl with sculptures of the Virgin and Child. The syncretism extended to architecture, where churches throughout Italy reflected classical elements. It can also be seen in the ducal palace built for Federico da Montelfeltro in Urbino, where two *tempietti* (little temples) were constructed, one devoted to Christianity and the other to the Muses.

In painting, the boldness of the *Expulsion of Adam and Eve* (1420s) by Masaccio (Tomasso di Ser Giovanni di Simone, 1401–1428) in depicting Adam and Eve as full nudes—to say nothing of depicting the wrenching emotions on their faces—stands in striking contrast to the ethos of mediaeval painting. (Fig leaves were painted on the figures at a later date and were subsequently removed.)

The greatest painter of the early Renaissance, Sandro Botticelli (1445–1510), is best known for his *Birth of Venus* (1480?) and *Primavera* (1470s–80s), which evoke in the most exquisite manner the refined eroticism and devotion to nature emblematic of classical myth. There may well be a subtle Neoplatonic contrast between earthly (carnal) love and divine love, and if this interpretation is sound, then it cannot be said that Christian imagery is altogether lacking in these two masterworks; but their portrayal of a Greco-Roman ambiance remains paramount.

With the advent of the High Renaissance toward the end of the fifteenth and into the early sixteenth century, we see the emergence of three transcendently great Italian artists, Leonardo da Vinci, Michelangelo, and Raphael. Leonardo (1452–1519) is the epitome of the Renaissance man, as the diversity of his interests and expertise attest, just as his sketch of *Vitruvian Man* (1485–90) has become an icon of Renaissance humanism. He helped redesign an early mediaeval church (Santa Maria presso San Satiro in Milan) along Renaissance lines, working with Donato Bramante (1444?–1514) on the project. The patent religiosity of *The Last Supper* (1495–98) can be contrasted with the largely secular *Mona Lisa* (1503–15), which features an elaborate geometric design, with a Roman aqueduct in the background.

Michelangelo (1475–1564) was brought to Florence in 1490 under the aegis of Lorenzo de' Medici, and there he studied ancient sculpture and participated in humanist discussions at court. He later went to Rome, where his magnificent sculpture of Bacchus (1497–98) is a pure evocation of classical Roman art. The *Pietà* (1498–1500) in St Peter's, for all its religious content, reflects Renaissance values in the sheer humanity of the figures, notably the detailed musculature of the dead Jesus. His *David* (1501–04) was manifestly inspired by classical sculpture and, in the opinion of one art critic, "exemplifies the humanist dignity of man."[44]

Raphael (Raffaello Sanzio da Urbino, 1483–1520) worked on the Stanza della Segnatura (the papal library in the Vatican), where one of the main frescos was the *School of Athens* (1509–11), a purely classical design with no Christian signification. The architecture in the fresco is Roman, not Greek; the figures are the leading Greek philosophers of the classical period. Pride of place naturally goes to Plato and Aristotle, but Epicurus, Diogenes the Cynic, the Persian Zoroaster, and others are also depicted, reflecting the broadening of interest in Greco-Roman philosophical thought among scholars and literary figures.

In Venice, Giorgione (Giorgio Barbarelli da Castelfranco, 1473?–1510) and Titian (Tiziano Vecelli or Vecellio, 1488?–1576) emerged.

---

44. Adams, *Italian Renaissance Art* 319.

Giorgione's *Sleeping Venus* (1510?) is a classic reclining nude and may symbolise Venice itself. Titian's *Meeting of Bacchus and Ariadne* (1522–23) uses classical myth to underscore the role of the city of Ferrara as the new Athens (the painting was designed for the ducal palace at Ferrara). His *Venus of Urbino* (1538) was clearly inspired by Giorgione.

As a culmination of Renaissance art, the architect Palladio (Andrea di Pietro, 1508–1580) wrote *Quattro libri dell'architectura* (1570; Four Books on Architecture), which provides a theoretical justification for the classicising architecture his work exemplifies. There is, however, in many of his buildings an admixture of Mannerism—a late Renaissance style that featured somewhat recherché elements designed for the appreciation of a specific patron. A certain self-consciousness and artificiality characterise Mannerist paintings and architecture, foreshadowing the Baroque art of the seventeenth century. Michaelangelo's design for the Medici Chapel in the Church of San Lorenzo in Florence (1519–34) is basically classical but with arcane features that only Lorenzo de' Medici might have relished. Michelanglo's monumental *Last Judgment* (1534–412) incongruously features a Charon-like figure carting off damned souls to Hades in his boat. The near-nudity of nearly all the figures in the painting led to charges of impiety from various sources, including Pope Paul IV (1555–59).

Art and architecture elsewhere in Europe was, on the whole, not quite as spectacularly innovative as in Italy, and was in any event significantly influenced by Italian models. In the Netherlands, Jan Van Eyck (1390–1441) and Rogier van der Weyden (1400?–1464) were much appreciated by Italian humanists for their realism and landscape effects. Van Eyck's remarkable *Arnolfini Portrait* (1434) depicts a marriage conducted as a civil ceremony. It is a purely secular portrait: the couple is surrounded by the objects of their domestic life, including a dog and slippers. The only Christian element is a series of tiny medallions surrounding a circular mirror on the back wall, which depict ten episodes from the Passion of Christ. As James Snyder observes, these images "appear as marginal figures of a fading tradition in Christian art, that of the stereotyped religious pictures of the Middle Ages."[45]

Nearly a century later, the Dutch painter Hieronymus Bosch

45. Snyder, *Northern Renaissance Art* 104.

(1450?–1516) attained prominence. As a Catholic, much of his work was inspired by biblical texts, especially Proverbs and the parables in the NT, as exemplified in the sprawling *Table of the Seven Deadly Sins* (1480–85). Bosch has developed a curious reputation over the centuries, and some scholars believe that he was a heretic with deep knowledge of witchcraft; others have seen him as an anti-religious satirist. There is little evidence for either assertion. It is true that Bosch seems fixated on the darker, even the horrific, elements of the human condition even within a religious context, as in the *Triptych of Saint Anthony* (1505–10), with its fantastic hybrid creatures and other bizarre details, all executed with a meticulous realism of a Van Eyck. And his most famous painting, the triptych *Garden of Earthly Delights* (1510–15), remains a subject of controversy as to its overall thrust and meaning. At its most basic level, the painting depicts God's creation of the world, each panel portraying one or more days of the creation. Adam and Eve are in the left panel, as is Jesus Christ. The centre panel depicts descendants of Adam and Eve in the era of Noah. The right panel envisions the horrors of hell. It would appear that the triptych was commissioned by a secular aristocrat, not a religious institution.

Painters in the Netherlands in the early sixteenth century increasingly eschewed religious motifs and focused on scenes from daily life—as in Lucas van Leyden's *Milkmaid* (1510), *Card Players* (1515?), and *Tavern Scene* (1518–20), Quentin Massys's *Money Changer and His Wife* (1514), and so on. Massys's portraits range from the starkly realistic to the grotesque (*The Ugly Old Woman,* 1513). Jan Gossaert alternated paintings on Christian subjects with exuberant renderings of scenes and figures from classical myth, as well as secular portraiture.

In the *Triumph of Death* (1565–66), Peter Bruegel the Elder (1527?–1569) appears to evoke mediaeval notions of the dismal fate awaiting most human beings in the afterlife. But Satan is notably absent from the painting, and it could be taken as an evocation of the horrors of war. Bruegel is known to have taken a great interest in peasant life, and many of his paintings are secular renderings of this motif, notably *Wedding Dance* (1566) and *Wedding Feast* (1568?). Even a nominally religious painting such as *Carnival and Lent* (1559) suggests that the majority of citizens used religious holidays merely as an excuse to have a good time. Bruegel's landscapes are pioneering works evoking nature in conjunction with further studies of peasant life (*Hay Harvest* and *Wheat Harvest* [both 1565]).

In Germany, Albrecht Dürer (1471–1528) fused Italian humanism with a kind of northern Gothic romanticism. His year-long trip to Italy (1494–95) was a transformative experience. The engraving *Adam and Eve* (1504) portrays the central figures with the proportions of the ideal male and female body derived from Greek art. The celebrated *Melencholia I* (1514) is a representation of the torments of creative genius. It reflects the mediaeval idea of the four humours, melancholy being regarded as the most deleterious of them; but the Renaissance interpreted this humour as the sign of artistic genius—a point reflected in the various objects strewn about the main figure, symbolising art and science. Some of Dürer's paintings and engravings from the 1520s reveal analogies with Martin Luther's agenda.

Lucas Cranach the Elder (1472–1553) was a close friend of Luther and sympathetic to his cause. He executed several portraits of Luther. He and his son, Lucas Cranach the Younger (1515–1586), produced a number of frankly propagandist paintings depicting Luther as a heroic figure, with Catholic figures portrayed as evil and corrupt (see *Luther Preaching with the Pope in the Jaws of Hell* [1550?]). But Cranach the Elder also executed a plainly erotic *Venus* (1532) as a full nude, although the portrait has a generally neo-Gothic cast. No doubt he was seeking to satisfy the tastes of the patron who commissioned the painting.

Hans Holbein the Younger (1497–1543) emerged as one of the leading portaitists of his time, noted for his unflinching realism and objectivity. The striking *Christ in the Tomb* (1521) looks like a corpse laid out on a bier. Of this painting a character in Dostoyevsky's *The Idiot* remarks, "Some people may lose their faith by looking at that picture!" (210). He painted numerous portreaits of Erasmus. On a visit to England he painted a famous portrait of Sir Thomas More (1527). He settled in England in 1532. In the turmoil caused by Henry VIII's break from Rome, Holbein sought commissions from wealthy businessmen of the Hanseatic League: these are wholly secular portraits, and much can be said of his famous portraits of Henry VIII himself, which are generally designed to convey his majesty as a ruler, with only glancing allusions to his role as the head of the English church.

Renaissance art in France was heavily dependent on Italian

examples. The Gothic mode in religious art continued throughout the fifteenth and into the sixteenth century, especially so (naturally enough) in ecclesiastical architecture: note the pure Gothicism in the façade of the Church of Notre Dame in Louviers (early sixteenth century) or the Cathedral of Notre Dame de L'Épine (1509–24). But a synthesis of Gothic and Renaissance art (exemplified in the use of such classical elements as the arch) can be seen in the Church of Saint-Étienne-du Mont in Paris (1535–47).

Renaissance principles of lightness, openness, and simplicity are more evident in sixteenth-century chateaux, such as those at Chenonceau (1515–22), Chambord (1519f.), and elsewhere. Then there is the magnificent chateau at Fontainebleau, some thirty miles southeast of Paris. It began as a mediaeval palace in the twelfth century, but Francis I wished it to be renovated in the Renaissance style, even though he did not live long enough to appreciate it in its completed state. The main architect, Gilles Le Breton, effected numerous revisions, especially in the Cour Ovale (oval courtyard). More pertinently, the paintings filling the chateau were executed chiefly by two Italian painters, Rosso Fiorentino (Giovanni Battista di Jacopo, 1495–1540) and Francesco Primaticcio (1504–1570). The majority of Rosso's paintings are on classical subjects. Benvenuto Cellini added some exquisite sculptures, also on classical motifs. Primaticcio contributed both paintings and sculptures. Other classicist painters followed in their wake—Luca Penniu, Antoine Caron, and others—as construction of the chateau continued throughout the sixteenth century.

The Louvre began its existence in the late twelfth century as a military installation, but in 1546 Francis I commissioned its renovation in the French Renaissance style, under the supervision of architect Pierre Lescot and sculptor Jean Goujon. Very few traces of the mediaeval structure now remain.

Renaissance music from the mid-fifteenth to the end of the sixteenth century played its role in the secularisation of European culture. The broad differences between mediaeval and Renaissance music—a substantial development of instrumental music; a greater use of harmony and a "sweetening" of harmonic intervals away from the occasionally harsh dissonances of the mediaeval era; a greater focus on integration of form and content; a greater emphasis on the clarity of verbal utterance in vocal music—constituted, in their way, a parallel to Renaissance art and literature's enhanced devotion to the human over the divine. Sacred music was, of course, written in abundance during this period, but even this music—for all that it often exhibited a conservatism endemic to ecclesiasticism in general—displayed significant traces of modernity.

Music in the earlier decades of this period was of an international cast, but composers gradually evolved means of expression unique to their native lands; as such, they contributed to the development of distinctively national modes of musical expression similar to that found in Renaissance art and architecture and even in political and religious movements. By the end of the era it was possible to speak of English, French, Italian, and other musical traditions that were markedly different from one another. Some of these developments occurred at a surprisingly early stage, especially the progress of the art-song: the French *chanson,* the Italian *frottola,* the German *Lied,* and so on. These songs, overwhelmingly secular in nature, were not merely imitations or adaptations of popular tunes but were highly complex compositions to which the leading composers of the period contributed.

A pair of early composers—Johannes Ockeghem (1410?–1497) and Josquin dez Prez (1440–1521)—symbolise the sharp differences between the old and new schools of composition. Ockeghem's dozen masses hark back to the mediaeval era; Josquin, although he wrote eighteen masses, focused more attention on his hundred smaller-scale motets, which, while still religious in subject-matter, allowed him greater freedom of expression. His close fitting of words to music resulted in a clarity that has been thought to reflect contemporary humanism.

The Italian madrigal of the sixteenth century was a sharp departure from madrigals of earlier eras. Usually they were set to poetic texts—sometimes as solos but more often in four or five voices, with close and complex harmony and polyphony. They were purely secular and therefore afforded a greater range of expression than church music. One of the first great madrigal composers was Cipriano de Rore (1516–1565), a Franco-Flemish musician who worked mostly in Italy and set many of Petrarch's secular poems to music. Late in the sixteenth century, the towering figure of the Italian Claudio Monteverdi (1567–1643) emerges, and his first four books of madrigals (1587–1603) raised this musical form to the highest level of artistry.

In England, the madrigal of the late sixteenth century was only the culmination of a long progression in both sacred and secular music extending back a century. One of the chief figures was Thomas Tallis (1505?–1585), who adapted his music to the fluctuating religious sensibilities of the monarchs of his day—the rebel Henry VIII (who himself was a composer of some ability, mostly of secular songs), the Protestant Edward VI, the Catholic Mary, and the Protestant Elizabeth. His *Lamentations of Jeremiah* exhibits an unprecedented use of poignant emotion in vocal music. William Byrd (1539?–1623), a Catholic, composed secular instrumental music (*My Ladye Nevells Book* [1591], a series of keyboard pieces) and contributed to the celebrated *Fitzwilliam Virginal Book* (1620), a magnificent collection of keyboard pieces by many of the leading English composers of the period. But Byrd also composed several affecting Catholic masses.

But it is in the madrigal that English composers exhibited their greatest virtuosity. Thomas Morley assembled an exemplary anthology, *The Triumphes of Oriana* (1601), as a tribute to Queen Elizabeth. It is a wholly secular paean to a queen that evokes classical myth (each of its twenty-five songs features the concluding couplet, "Then sang the shepherds and nymphs, nymphs of Diana: / 'Long live fair Oriana'"—Oriana being a nickname bestowed upon Elizabeth) and features exquisite word-painting that brings such later composers as Handel and Vivaldi to mind.

The Reformation did not fail to affect the course of musical composition, especially on the Continent. Contrary to popular opinion, Martin Luther was not opposed in principle to music; indeed, he saw in it a means of both education and the fostering of faith. And although he did not object to the continued use of Latin in musical compositions for the church, he himself composed a *Deudsche Messe* (1526; German Mass). The Lutheran church developed the *Choral* or *Kirchenlied* (chorale or church song); a collection of them was published as early as 1524. At this period, Michael Praetorius (1571–1621) was probably only notable composer of Lutheran chorales; he also composed abundant secular and dance music.

The Counter-Reformation spurred a renewed push for Catholic sacred music, and Giovanni Pierluigi di Palestrina (1525?–1594) emerged as the towering figure in church music, and perhaps music as a whole, in the sixteenth century. The immense quantity of sacred music he wrote (more than 100 masses along with 450 motets and other work) generally has a somewhat retrograde or mediaeval quality for all its accomplishment.

Instrumental music began its rise in the mid-fifteenth century with the development of a wide array of instruments, whether they be wind/brass (cornetts, trumpets, krummhorns, etc.), stringed (a whole family of viols), or keyboard (harpsichord, clavichord, etc.). The lute, which had existed for hundreds of years, now became immensely popular among middle-class households, serving both as an accompaniment for vocal pieces or in solo compositions. The English composer John Dowland (1563–1626) became a master of the lute song and solo. Dance music—in the form of the pavane, the canzona, the ballet, and so on—also came into its own, although in many instances the pieces were not literally designed for dancing.

In Venice, instrumental music was centred around the Cathedral of San Marco and represented a glorification of both church and state. The two leading composers, Andrea Gabrieli (1532?–1585) and his nephew, Giovanni Gabrieli (1554?–1612), composed pieces for organ, brass, and other instruments that relied on the resonance of the basilica for its effects; but its ecclesiastical setting did not mean that the compositions were strictly associated with the church (although Giovanni's *Sacrae Symphoniae* [1597] was obviously meant for church services), and they could have been performed in analogous venues of a secular nature. This is music that looks forward to the romantic emotionalism of the Baroque era.

I. Europe's Encounters with New World Cultures

The dynamic spirit of the Renaissance appears to have infected not merely littérateurs and philosophers, but explorers as well. Among the most notable of these were Vasco da Gama, who rounded the Cape of Good Hope and reached India (1497–99); Ferdinand Magellan, who also traversed the Cape of Good Hope in the course of a circumnavigation of the globe (1519–22) around the southern tip of South America (through what are now the Straits of Magellan) and across the Atlantic back to Portugal; and Christopher Columbus, who crossed the Atlantic in the first of four voyages (1492–93) in an attempt to reach Asia, stumbling instead upon islands in the Caribbean and, on later expeditions, portions of central and South America. Hernán Cortés led the first European attempt to settle on the mainland of North America, and his conquest of the Aztec Empire in 1519–21 opened the floodgates to other Spanish conquests: Hernando de Soto and Francisco Pizarro overthrew the Inca Empire in Peru, while Francisco Vázquez de Coronado reached deep into the southwestern United States in an expedition of 1540–42. In the early to mid-sixteenth century, explorers from France, Spain, and England came upon other areas of continental North America—Florida, the Carolinas, Virginia, and elsewhere; but for much of the period from the mid-fifteenth to the end of the sixteenth century, Spain took the lead in colonisation.

To be sure, trade—or, more specifically, the desire to exploit what were believed to be the abundant natural resources of these new lands—was the chief factor motivating the explorers and the European monarchs who sanctioned their voyages; religion may not have been a significant driver of exploration or colonisation, but religious factors inevitably played a role once Europeans encountered indigenous populations. What they found, to their astonishment, was a series of thriving civilisations extending from southern Mexico down through Central America and all along the western coast of South America; and although Columbus himself believed, after a superficial exposure to native cultures, that these peoples had no religion at all, that naïve view was very wide of the mark.

Papal sanction for the enslavement and conquest of "pagan" peoples was manifested at an early stage. In 1455 Pope Nicholas V (1447–55) granted Portugal the authority to seize the territory of "all Saracens and pagans whatsoever, and all other enemies of Christ wheresoever placed." It is no accident that this decree occurred two years after the Muslim incursion into the Balkans. In 1493 Pope Alexander VI (1492–1503), in a breathtakingly broad dictum, granted Spain control of the entire world not already ruled by Christian powers, so that such people would "embrace the Catholic faith and be trained in good morals."[46]

The cultures in Mesoamerica now known as the Incas, Aztecs, and Mayans have their origins in the Neolithic period, but the development

46. See Jennings, *The Invasion of America* 4–5.

of a full-fledged civilisation dates to the centuries covered in this chapter. While there is some evidence of the influence of Asian cultures on the development of Mesoamerican peoples, in large part they were probably of autochthonous growth. The emergence of agriculture (especially the cultivation of corn) dates to as early as 6000 B.C.E. By the first millennium B.C.E., population growth led to the emergence of a stratified society featuring a chieftain, priests, and other offices. Temple-building began around 800–400 B.C.E. A fertility cult seems to have been prevalent, as a means of stimulating the growth of crops. Gods in the form of animals were worshipped.

The Chavin culture in Peru (c. 1000–500 B.C.E.) was a precursor to the Incas; the Olmec culture (c. 1200–400 B.C.E.) was, in the words of one scholar, the "Mesoamerican mother civilization."[47] The Olmecs had a cult based on the snake and the jaguar, both animals symbolising fertility in various guises. Enormous pyramids, with temples at the top, suggest a theocratic society where priest-kings ruled, although there may well have been a parallel war-king as well. The warrior culture that developed, especially in northern Peru, resulted in prisoners of war being ritually sacrificed by being thrown off of mountaintops.

The Incas, during the height of their civilisation (fourteenth to sixteenth centuries) evolved a court religion closely related to the ruling dynasty. Society and government were rigidly hierarchical; the emperor was regarded as divine (the son of the sun) and infallible; but he was expected to act for the benefit and prosperity of the people. The Incas built upon earlier cultures. The city of Tiahuanaco had flourished in the later first millennium C.E., and the Incas probably took over its chief god, Viracocha, a sun god. The Incas also conquered the Chimú culture based around the city of Chanchan; but its influence on Inca religion was negligible.

There were three levels or branches to the Inca religion: 1) the state religion; 2) the gods of conquered tribes, who were subordinated to the Inca gods; and 3) folk religion, focusing on rites of passage (birth, puberty, marriage, and so on) and cycles of vegetation. This last survives to our own day, melded with Roman Catholicism.

The state religion was a complex polytheism. The sun god Inti was

47. Hultcrantz, *The Religions of the American Indians* 169.

not supreme, but was regarded as the ancestor of the ruling dynasty. Other gods pertaining to the moon, thunder, crops, wild animals, and so on were prevalent. An impressive sun temple was built in the capital, Cuzco. The emperor, who personified the sun god, was worshipped as divine; hence he could only marry his sister. The emperor's brother served as high priest. Priests established a detailed calendar of festivals throughout the year, occasionally featuring human sacrifices. Some priests specialised in divination.

There is some mystery regarding the origins of the Mayans, based in present-day Guatemala and southern Mexico. Its civilisation was probably built upon the Olmec culture. The classical period of Mayan civilisation (c. 300–900 C.E.) saw the development of numerous small states ruled by priest-princes. In the absence of major urban centres, there was no concentration of authority, either political or religious. Step-pyramids—notably that at Chichén Itzá in the Yucatán peninsula—are among the most impressive structures in the New World. They were topped by temples where rites and sacrifices were conducted. The interior of the pyramids contained tombs of kings and their court.

Writing was developed to a high degree of sophistication, as were astronomy and mathematics—but these were largely dependent on agrarian or religious needs. Temple-cities surrounding the pyramids were deserted around 900, for reasons that are not entirely clear. The Toltecs, a warrior culture, invaded from the north and took over Chichén Itzá for a time. The Mayans experienced a renaissance around 1200–1450, but had gone into decline when the Spaniards invaded.

Mayan religion dominated every phase of life in the classical period. A multiplicity of gods changed their shape as well as their very nature from one community to the next. An untidy dualism emerged: some gods were deemed good, others evil, but some had both good and evil aspects. The chief god was Itzamma, a sky god who also had some elements of the culture hero. Kinich Ahau was the sun god, as well as a patron of poetry and music. Ixchel was the moon goddess and more generally a goddess of women, hence became a kind of mother goddess. The rain god Chac had a darker side because of the dangers posed by floods and other threats stemming from water. Gods of vegetation (especially corn), the soil, and others existed, while gods of death and war dwelt in the underworld. The death god was Cizin, and he is customarily depicted in a terrifying aspect, with the head of a skull and a thorny spine. The Mayans envisioned thirteen different heavens and nine nether regions, each with its own god.

The Mayan epic *Popol Vuh* recounts a creation myth whereby the gods created earth out of primordial water, and then the human race. The Toltecs imported a snake god, Kukulkan (analogous to the Aztec Quetzalcoatl), who was portrayed as a feathered serpent. His worship came to dominate Chichén Itzá. He was chiefly a war god, reflecting the militaristic tendencies of the Toltecs. Other related gods were also brought in, but they appear to have spurred little interest among the Mayan people. But a radical increase in human sacrifices—previously rare in Mayan culture—occurred during the Toltec domination, followed by ritual cannibalism. Sacrifices (probably of young women) into a huge well (*cenote*) were made when drought or other natural disasters threatened crops.

The Aztecs, who dominated central Mexico, apparently came from the north, probably from the Shoshone and Piute Indians, settling in the Valley of Mexico in the early thirteenth century. They absorbed a number of tribes in the area, including the Zopotec culture, which flourished around 200–800 C.E. This culture practised rituals to ensure fertility of crops, especially corn. Its religion featured numerous specialised gods relating to many aspects of personal and commercial life. The city of Teotihuacan, built by an unknown people before the Aztecs arrived, dates to as early as the third century C.E. In the ninth century it was destroyed and was never fully rebuilt. By the time the Aztecs came, it was abandoned. After the Toltecs withdrew from the region in the mid-twelfth century, the Aztecs moved in. They established the city of Tenotichtitlan (modern-day Mexico City) in the early fourteenth century, as instructed by their patron god, Huitzilopochtli, a sun and war god. An enormous temple to this god was built in a high hill; at its inauguration, an appalling 20,000 prisoners were sacrificed.

The warlike tendencies of the Aztecs were stimulated in part by a need to take over more and more land to feed their growing population. The Aztecs thereby developed sophisticated irrigation systems to promote agriculture. The king had supreme authority in civil, military, and religious affairs. He was thought to be descended from Quetzalcoatl, the god of life. Huitzilopochtli (who may have originated as a sort of hunting god) was not regarded as a Supreme Being; nor was Quetzalcoatl or Tezcatlipoca, a shaman god. This latter was a sky god but had many other functions Ometeotl was a sort of creator god, having both male and female characteristics. Quetzalcoatl was regarded as the creator of humanity and the discoverer of corn, among other attributes. Tlaloc was a god of rain and thunder. Chicomecoatl was the chief goddess of vegetation; Xipe Totec was a more general god of vegetation. Caotlicue gave birth to both gods and humans. She received confessions of sins from human beings. Mictlan, the realm of the dead, situated underground, was ruled by Mictlantecuhtli; he took the form of a skeleton. Gods of mountains, volcanoes, and fire also existed.

Religious rituals were timed to important dates in the agricultural season, especially the planting of corn. Human sacrifices, including children, occurred throughout the year. It was believed that if sacrifices were abandoned, the entire cosmic order would collapse. The Aztec mythology emphasised the value of blood in stimulating the growth of crops, among other benefits.

The European conquest of all these regions was caused by several critical factors, chiefly the colonisers use of firearms, their ruthlessness in killing their enemies, and the spread of diseases to which the native populations had no immunity, resulting in their rapid decimation. European cavalry was also a factor. All these reasons explain why a relatively small number of Europeans were able to overthrow native empires consisting of hundreds of thousands or even millions of people. Only in rare instances—as in Paraguay in the 1530s—was a region jointly settled by Spanish colonists and native tribes without warfare.

Spanish colonists initially focused on regions conquered from the Aztecs and Incas—i.e., central and southern Mexico and Peru. Mexico came to be referred to as New Spain. The Spanish made little effort to destroy the Aztec and Incan culture or even its political system except at the top echelons. But these cultures did become fragmented, and the Spanish made vigorous attempts to suppress native religious practices.

The Christianisation of these regions was facilitated by the native practice of "accepting into their pantheon the primary god of any power that conquered them."[48] Analogously, their military defeat signalled that

48. Kicza, *Resilient Cultures* 84–85.

the god of their people was not as powerful or efficacious as they thought. The Europeans, in their ignorance of the causes of the diseases (notably smallpox) that ravaged the native populations,[49] attributed native deaths to divine punishment and saw in them a further testimonial that the Christian god was validating their conquest.

The paucity of priests or other religious officials who accompanied the European colonists meant that instruction in the tenets of Christianity was at an extremely basic and rudimentary level. As a result, the natives engaged in syncretistic rituals that mingled Christianity with their native faiths. Many of these rituals were public—fiestas, processions, and so on—with the parish church serving as a focal point. Specific saints were revered in different communities, in the belief that these demigods would lend protection to the community or otherwise intervene in their affairs. (It is, however, a myth that the natives believed the Europeans were gods or godlike; Montezuma and other leaders were well aware that they were merely dealing with human beings.)

The Spanish controlled most of South and Central America and the American Southwest, but ultimately ceded control of much of North America to the English and French. Spain did establish a foothold in Florida with the establishment of San Agustin (Saint Augustine) in 1565, ousting a French Huguenot colony in that area. But the Spanish could not be troubled to colonise north of Florida after 1580.

The Portuguese, who had stumbled upon Brazil around 1500, made no effort to colonise the vast area for several decades, using it only as a source of raw materials (chiefly dyewoods). Colonisation only began in earnest in the 1530s. In the course of time a bizarre quasi-Christian cult called *santitade* took root among the natives and led to riots in the 1560s, but the Portuguese ultimately suppressed them. The settlers' towns were controlled by Jesuits, who sought both to convert the natives and to transform their social fabric, introducing Western practices relating to marriage and other domestic customs.

The French explorer Jacques Cartier reached Canada in the 1530s, but colonisation did not proceed until late in the century. Mostly, a series of fur-trading bases were established; Samuel de Champlain established the colony of Quebec in 1608. In contrast to the Spanish, the French

49. The native population of Mexico is estimated to have declined from more than 20 million in 1519 to 1.25 million in 1650.

in general mingled freely with the native population without engaging in bloody battles for supremacy; this was chiefly in order to secure its aid in trading. The Dutch settled the Hudson River area in the early seventeenth century, and the English—aside from Sir Walter Ralegh's failed attempt to establish a colony at Roanoke (1585–86)—also entered New England and the mid-Atlantic region only in the seventeenth century.

J. Renaissance Science and Its Ramifications

In assessing the very existence of something called the Scientific Revolution, emerging in the early to mid-sixteenth century, we are faced with a controversy similar to that associated with the concept of Renaissance humanism; but in this case it is somewhat more clear-cut that the work of Renaissance scientists—Copernicus, Brahe, Kepler, and others—really did constitute a radical break from the past. We have seen that mediaeval science, although it made some notable discoveries, did not radically alter people's conception of the universe or challenge Christianity's stranglehold on how the universe was constituted and to what extent a god had fashioned it. We can state here that few if any Renaissance scientists questioned that last point; but they laid the groundwork for the establishment and vindication of a secular worldview that emerged in the following centuries.

There does not on the surface appear to be much of a relationship between Renaissance humanism and the work of the major scientists of the sixteenth century; but indirect connexions can be detected. Both groups of thinkers subscribed to the notion that knowledge must bear some relevance to human concerns; the "civic humanism" promoted by Erasmus and others was paralleled by the belief among scientists that their discoveries would be of material benefit to the people at large (a point particularly stressed by those who made advances in chemistry, anatomy, physiology, and medicine). Moreover, Renaissance humanism's fascination with Plato, aside from aiding in the ultimate dethronement of Aristotelianism from its position of unquestioned authority, spurred the study of mathematics—a critical component in the pioneering work of astronomers and physicists.

The difficulties that Nicolaus Copernicus (1473–1543), a Polish mathematician and astronomer, faced in the two most radical theories he proposed in his epochal *De Revolutionibus Orbium Coelestium* (1543; On the Revolutions of the Heavenly Spheres)—1) the belief that the Earth revolves around the sun (the heliocentric theory) and 2) the belief that the Earth itself moves (rotates on its axis) rather than remaining stationary—were manifold. He was battling numerous universally held presuppositions whose truth seemed self-evident to anyone who contemplated the matter. The movement of the Earth defied common-sense perceptions: if this were so, why can't we perceive that motion, and why don't objects fly off the Earth? But the heliocentric theory faced the additional barriers of defying Christian doctrine in a multitude of ways—chiefly, the assumption that the Earth is at the centre of the universe, since God had chosen this planet as the object of his special care by fashioning the human race in his own image and blessing it by the creation of the wondrous array of natural objects we see all around us. The notion that stars are not "fixed," also propounded by Copernicus, similarly encountered common-sense objections while also defying a central pillar of Aristotelian physics, which the church had sanctioned as unquestioned and unquestionable. Indeed, it was precisely because the nexus of Aristotelianism, Ptolemaism, and scholastic philosophy resulted in what appeared to be a perfect system impervious to attack at any point that the overthrow of this worldview proved so challenging. And yet, once Copernicus and others did poke holes in that worldview, it collapsed with surprising ease.

It is important to state that Copernicus—who had devised the heliocentric theory as early as the 1510s—did not come up with any new evidence to bolster his contention. Indeed, we have seen that the Ptolemaic theory of cycles and epicycles actually "works" after a fashion in accounting for the seeming anomalies of planetary and stellar motion. The central issue that astronomers had to face was the apparent retrogression of planets from our perspective on Earth; but both the Copernican and the Ptolemaic systems "save the appearances" in this regard. In devising the heliocentric theory, Copernicus first postulated the five known planets (excluding Earth) as revolving around the sun; then, noting a gap between the orbits of Venus and Mars, he placed the Earth there. This scenario simply eliminated the need for Ptolemaic epicycles and therefore resulted in a much cleaner, more economic conception. Indeed, Kepler went on to note that, under the Ptolemaic system, planets would actually have to revolve in bizarre loops and kinks in a manner that defied even common-sense views of planetary motion.

It is impossible to know exactly how Copernicus came up with the heliocentric theory; but Howard Margolis has put forth an intriguing conjecture. Copernicus's discovery was made only about twenty years after Columbus's "discovery" of the land masses constituting the American continents; and even though Columbus himself, to the end of his life, believed that he had reached Asia, other geographers made it plain that the very existence of these new continents necessitated a radical alteration in our conception of the Earth. No longer was Jerusalem the centre of the Earth, with land masses (Europe, Africa, Asia) extending all around it. Is it possible that Copernicus, living through a period when human notions of the Earth's contours had undergone such a radical shift, felt emboldened to envision a new conception of the solar system and the universe at large?[50]

The radical nature of Copernicus's theories was not widely perceived in the immediate aftermath of the publication of his book. There is no clear evidence that Copernicus was afraid to publish his book until he knew he was dying, fearful of the church's reaction; that reaction may have been muted by the fact that Andreas Osiander, a Lutheran priest who shepherded the book into print, wrote an unauthorised preface who essentially stated that Copernicus's central contentions were neither true nor even probable, but were merely being put forth for computational purposes. Copernicus did indeed believe that his views were derived from mathematics, but he went on to state that the movement of the Earth and the heliocentric theory portrayed the physical reality of space and were not merely hypothetical or speculative.

And yet, Copernicus himself was the victim of one key unquestioned assumption—the belief that circular motion was "perfect" and that the planets therefore orbited in a circular fashion—that required subsequent research to correct. In the generation following his death, the Danish astronomer Tycho Brahe (1546–1601) attempted to effect a compromise between the Copernican and Ptolemaic models, whereby the Earth remained at the centre of the universe, with the sun revolving around it;

50. See Margolis, *It Started with Copernicus*, ch. 3.

but the other planets in the solar system revolved around the sun. Brahe did dispense with Ptolemy's notion that the planets were carried around in their orbits on solid spheres, since this might result in the crash of two planets, which was considered an impossibility. But by the time Brahe published his various works (between 1572 and 1588), Ptolemaism had already been discarded by leading astronomers.

Johannes Kepler (1571–1630), an associate of Brahe in Prague, wrote a defence of Copernicanism as early as 1596 (*Mysterium Cosmographicum*), but it was in his *Astronomia Nova* (1609; New Astronomy) that he propounded the theory of elliptical orbits of the planets. This theory effected an even more radical break with Aristotelianism than Copernicanism, since it destroyed for all time the concatenation of assumptions (fundamentally religious in nature, and extending back through Greco-Roman paganism to Christianity) of the "divinity" of circular motion. Kepler was led to this view by two fundamental realisations: 1) the Earth is a planet, and 2) the immensity of the sun compels such an elliptical motion. To some extent he was influenced by English natural philosopher William Gilbert's treatise *De Magnete* (1600; On the Magnet), which asserted that the Earth was an enormous magnet. In the days before Newton's discovery of gravity, magnetism was seized upon by scientists as a means of accounting for the attraction of bodies to one another; and Kepler simply applied this principle as a means of accounting for the sun's harnessing of the planets around itself.

Copernicus's theories were not immediately condemned by the church, possibly as a result of his deliberate cultivation of the favour of several popes during his lifetime; his major book is dedicated to Pope Paul III. But Giordano Bruno had a less happy fate. Bruno (1548–1600), although in his early years a Dominican friar, later became a Calvinist. He espoused numerous daring cosmological theories—notably, that the stars were suns that had planets of their own that might allow for the possibility of life—that would have been outrageously contrary to Christian doctrine, chiefly God's "special" creation of human life on Earth. But it was not for this that he was tried by the Roman Inquisition in 1600: there he was accused of espousing radical views on other central tenets of Christianity, namely the denial of the immortality of the soul, the divinity of Jesus, and transubstantiation. It is unclear whether he actually adhered to these principles, although there seems little doubt that he was something of a pantheist and believed in the transmigration of souls. He was found guilty and burned at the stake in Rome.

The fact that many of the scientists of this period retained vestigial beliefs that we would now call magical or occultist has been used by devotees of religion to minimise their achievements and to suggest that religious or mystical thought was central to their work. There is much exaggeration here, but the facts are undeniable. William Gilbert, in propounding the Earth as a magnet, went on to maintain that as a result our planet is somehow animate and even possesses a soul. Kepler subscribed to numerous theories regarding astrology, the music of the spheres, and so forth. The maintenance of what we would regard as superstitious or irrational elements in the work of these and other scientists—whose radical advances in thought, in fundamental contradiction to church doctrine, cannot be gainsaid—has engendered considerable controversy, but it is fair to say that the prevalence of these apparently outmoded patterns of thought simply attests to the degree to which these thinkers were part and parcel of the intellectual tendencies of their time. It would be unreasonable to expect any of them to shed the presuppositions they found all around them even when they made pioneering discoveries that did indeed challenge contemporary assumptions on the nature of the universe.

Moreover, the early Renaissance witnessed something of a craze not only for the mystical elements inherent in Neoplatonism but also for treatises that were believed to have been written by Hermes Trismegistus (Thrice-Great Hermes) and believed to be of vast antiquity. At a time when the truth of a doctrine was often believed to be related to the early date of its utterance, these hermetic writings (some of which may in fact date to as early as the second century C.E.), with their curious fusion of astrology, magic, and some genuine research in the realms of botany, mineralogy, and other disciplines, exercised a consuming fascination upon some Renaissance thinkers. Jewish cabbalistic writings were also popular.

The effect of all these interests can be seen most visibly in those scientists who laboured in the realms of chemistry, physiology, and medicine, because it was here that the "magical" elements of their thought had the most direct application. I refer to the continued popularity of alchemical thinking among the philosophers of the sixteenth century. Alchemy, in the popular consciousness, conjures up lurid images of robed magicians presiding over bubbling alembics in their attempt to create gold out of "base" metals or to find the Philosopher's Stone that would grant them eternal life; but the more mundane reality was that many chemists or proto-chemists firmly believed in their ability to transform metals, minerals, and other objects by the process of distillation. They drew upon the work of such mediaeval thinkers as Albertus Magnus, Ramon Lull, and Roger Bacon in seeking medical advances that would benefit the entire human race. Gold and silver were seized upon as being incorruptible, and therefore they could be refined to produce an elixir (the Philosopher's Stone) that would prolong human life. (Bacon believed that human blood, when treated in a certain fashion, could produce the same result.)

It is evident that the fatal flaw in the thinking of these mediaeval alchemists, and their sixteenth-century successors, was the continued adherence to the Greek theory of the four elements, a central tenet of Aristotelianism. A wide array of thinkers, from the Presocratics on down, believed that the very fact that some earthly substances were seen to "grow" (such as a piece of coal turning into a diamond) meant that they were alive in some fashion—the ultimate holdover of primitive animism. Nevertheless, alchemy led to much valuable research in chemistry, metallurgy, and other sciences in the fifteenth and sixteenth centuries.

The principal figure in the alchemical movement during this period was Paracelsus (Theophrastus von Hohenheim, 1493?–1541), who pioneered a sort of chemical philosophy that departed radically from some of the central pillars of Aristotelianism. Paracelsus rejected the theory of the four elements, maintaining that there were three first principles—sulphur, salt, and mercury (these terms had a much broader signification for him than they do for us)—whose varied combinations could account for the existence of all the objects of the natural world. Paracelsus also rejected the Galenian theory of the four humours, instead advocating the notion of an *archeus* (life power) inherent in each organ of the body, which causes that organ to behave as it should but can on occasion go awry. To the extent that this theory resulted in a focus on the proper working of individual parts of the body, it represented a notable advance in medical theory.

Andreas Vesalius (1514–1564) wrote a landmark book on anatomy, *De Humani Corporis Fabrica* (1543; On the Construction of the Human Body) that strongly challenged many of Galen's findings. He himself had performed numerous dissections and found many errors in Galen, who up to that point had been regarded with nearly the same reverence as Aristotle, chiefly the result of a dearth of new research in these subjects. Other scholars did important work on the physiology of animals.

The overall effect of these varied scientific discoveries was subtle but pronounced. The "new astronomy" opened up the heavens in such a way as to impress upon intellectuals the notion that our terrestrial globe is only one tiny component of an immense array of stars, comets, and planets—a circumstance that ultimately rendered implausible the notion that God had singled out this one realm for his special care and benevolence. It is still difficult to find any scientist—or other figure in the realm of literature, art, or politics—who could definitely be called an atheist, but the succeeding centuries would see many thinkers espousing atheism, agnosticism, secularism, and freethought more and more openly as evidence of both the natural fabrication of the universe and the deficiencies of religious explanations of it became increasingly patent.

Epilogue

Whether or not there was a "school of atheism" in England—or analogous schools, however informally organised, in Italy, and elsewhere—prior to 1600, it is evident that individuals or groups embracing what was then called atheism were present, in spite of the severe penalties inflicted upon any who openly espoused the idea. Scholars have pointed to numerous tracts by religious figures pointing to the widespread existence of unbelief in their midst; but the issue is rendered perplexing because of the extremely broad scope given to the term atheism in the fifteenth and sixteenth centuries. Far from simply pointing to the denial of the existence of God (a relatively rare phenomenon), the word embraced one or more of the following principles:

1. denial of God's providence (or of any teleological conception of the universe);
2. denial of the immortality of the soul (or of the soul altogether);
3. denial of one of several basic doctrines in the Christian scripture (the divine inspiration of the OT and/or NT; the role of God in human affairs; the divinity of Jesus Christ and the validity of his salvific mission; the "miracles" associated with him; etc., etc.).

Our study has suggested that the number of individuals embracing any of the above was vanishingly small prior to 1600, but that some members of the intellectual elite—philosophers, creative artists, even a few theologians—appear to have done so. The basis of their unbelief might be classified under one or more of the following rubrics:

1. appeal to pagan philosophers (notably Democritus, Epicurus, and Lucretius);
2. used of "unbiased" reason (i.e., reason not based on Christian presuppositions);
3. scientific advance;
4. biblical criticism.

The first two of these were clearly in the forefront; the last two were all but non-existent, since most members of the intelligentsia do not at this time seem to have become aware of the role that, say, the heliocentric theory played in overturning several central pillars of Christian dogma; and the thoroughgoing analysis of the manner in which the OT and NT were set down was still centuries in the future.

The matter is further complicated by the assertion of several Christian conservative thinkers that anyone espousing any other religion but Christianity—whether it be Greco-Roman paganism, Islam, or the other religions that were slowly coming to the attention of Europeans through widening contact with non-Christian cultures around the world—was in effect an atheist. And, as we have seen, Catholics and Protestants occasionally lobbed the "atheist" bombshell at one another—or, at the very least, accused them of adhering to something other than "true" Christianity. But Christian theologians' increasing fears of "atheism," as exemplified in all manner of treatises in the sixteenth century, have led some scholars to believe in the old adage, "Where there's smoke, there must be fire"—in other words, that there were indeed atheists of whatever persuasion scattered throughout European society.

But we must now deal with the gauntlet thrown down more than eight decades ago by Lucien Febvre, who maintained that atheism in the modern sense (the forthright denial of the existence of God) was impossible before the end of the seventeenth century.[1] His argument relies on the assumption that before that time the doctrines of Christianity were so axiomatically accepted that disbelief in them—at least in an intellectually cogent manner—was essentially inconceivable. The evidence I have presented would seem to militate against such

1. See Lucien Febvre, *Le Problème de l'incroyance au XVIe siècle: La Religion de Rabelais* (1942); Eng. tr. by Beatrice Gottlieb as *The Prlblem of Unbelief in the Sixteenth Century: The Religion of Rabelais* (1982).

an extreme view—one that places Febvre in the unenviable position of having to prove a negative. Even if the religious scepticism of such figures as Montaigne and Christopher Marlowe cannot be unequivocally maintained, we have seen others who have come close to denying central tenets of Christian doctrine.

Some scholars have made much of the obscure Frenchman Geoffroy Vallée, who in 1574 was executed for denial of God.[2] Vallée was not an atheist in any meaningful sense of the term; indeed, he was yet another thinker who professed to be returning to what he believed to be the true principles of the New Testament. There is also some reason to doubt Vallée's mental stability. A similar fate met the Italian Giulio Cesare Vanini (1585–1619), who, although educated by the Jesuits and associated with the Carmlites (a Catholic mendicant order dating to the twelfth century), did appear to embrace a number of radical theories:

> He questions whether an immaterial God can create a material world, and whether any spiritual being can communicate with a corporal one; eventually he claims that the only true worship is the worship of nature. He accepts the eternity of matter and mocks the doctrine of creation, presenting instead a case for the origin of mankind, as well as of lesser animals, in putrefaction. He argues against the existence of non-material beings, such as ghosts, demons, spirits, and the immortal human soul. Religions, including Christianity, are fictions, invented by rulers and priests to secure their power; miracles attributed to prayer have natural explanations, reason is instinct, and immorality the product of illness or diet.[3]

This is an impressive list of doctrines that in itself would be sufficient to refute Febvre's thesis, at least in this one instance. Vanini was burned at the stake in Toulouse for blasphemy and atheism.

Trials for atheism in the various European inquisitions do provide evidence of other random individuals accused—and convicted—of what was called atheism; but since we are still centuries away from polling and other means of ascertaining public opinion, it is unclear whether the

---

2. See David Wootton, "New Histories of Atheism," in Hunter and Wootton, *Atheism from the Reformation to the Enlightenment* 13f.
3. Nicholas Davidson, "Atheism in Italy, 1500–1700," in Hunter and Wootton 74.

anecdotal evidence provided by heresy trials points to any widespread dissemination of such views were among the general public. Given that atheism as embodied in a figure like Vanini required substantial educational acquirements that were manifestly lacking in the populace as a whole, it is not at all evident on what basis the average citizen could have embraced a sceptical outlook at this time.

But what we can definitively say is that the multifarious intellectual and cultural tendencies of the age—the rediscovery of a pre-Christian civilisation; the advance of nationalism (which had the effect of minimising adherence to the concept of "Christendom" as a worldwide or even continent-wide phenomenon); the religious turmoil instituted by the Reformation; the increasingly outspoken anticlericalism and scepticism of writers from Chaucer to Boccaccio to Cervantes to Shakespeare; the emergence of secular art, architecture, and music; the advance of scientific enquiry—planted the seeds for full-blown atheism in the coming centuries.

The Reformation may have been critical, although not in the manner in which earlier historians of atheism believed. These scholars had put forth the view that the "freedom of conscience" that Luther and others purportedly vaunted laid the groundwork for the sloughing off of Christian dogma altogether. It should be evident that this notion is not merely naïve but demonstrably false. Luther, Calvin, and their compatriots were hardly interested in freedom of thought—or, rather, they, like so many other religionists over the centuries, advocated it for themselves but denied it to others. But what the Reformation did was to shatter for all time the idea of a unified Christian church. To be sure, the fragmentation of the Catholic church had been in progress for centuries, beginning so early as the schism of the eleventh century; but the Reformation made it abundantly clear that Christianity could now only be a collocation of ever more numerous warring sects whose mutual hostility made it at least possible for some thinkers to imagine a world where the Christian dispensation did not function at all. This is the thrust of one section of Sir Francis Bacon's short essay "Of Atheism" (1597):[4] "The causes of atheism are: divisions in religion, if they be many; for any one main division addeth zeal to both sides, but many

4. The essay was first written in Latin in *Meditationes Sacrae* (1597); Bacon translated it into English for the second English-language edition of his *Essays* (1612).

divisions introduce atheism" (68).

In terms of science, it required the further advances of Galileo, William Harvey, Sir Isaac Newton, and many others in the seventeenth and eighteenth centuries to make anything approaching atheism viable from a purely scientific basis; and, as I have mentioned, the process was not completed until Darwin's theory of evolution at last provided a refutation of the argument from design. The deism that marked the two centuries after 1600 was a significant anticipation of the full-fledged atheism of the French Enlightenment—and that in turn led to English, German, and even American enlightenments that enshrined religious liberty in the founding document of the United States. It was only in the nineteenth century that the "higher criticism" of the Bible and other sacred texts advanced to the point that these writings could be seen as the natural products of their respective eras and cultures. That work continues to the present day.

The ending of this volume at 1600 is largely arbitrary and necessitated chiefly by logistical concerns, as I envision the next volume to be of approximately equal size even though it covers only a period of a little more than four centuries. But the variegated expressions of atheism, agnosticism, rationalism, anticlericalism, secularism, and freethought exhibited during this period—to say nothing of the vastness of the evidence available, in the form of philosophical and religious writing, the work of novelists, poets, and essayists in a multiplicity of languages, the creations of painters, sculptors, musicians, and other artists, and ongoing social, political, economic, and cultural changes that played a role in the development of atheistic thought and practice—will necessitate an even greater level of detail than found in this volume. But at the end of my enquiry I hope to show what a radical change has been effected in Western culture by the shedding of religious belief, whether it be Christianity in all its variants, Judaism, Islam, or other faiths. I will not deny that such a development is, in my judgment, overwhelmingly positive.

Bibliography

Ackroyd, P. E., and C. F. Evans, ed. *The Cambridge History of the Bible, Volume 1: From the Beginnings to Jerome.* Cambridge: Cambridge University Press, 1970.

Adams, Laurie Schneider. *Italian Renaissance Art.* Boulder, CO: Westview Press, 2001.

Albrecht, Michael von. *A History of Roman Literature.* Rev. Gareth Schmeling and the author. Tr. Ruth R. Caston and francis R. Schwartz. Leiden: E. J. Brill, 1997. 2 vols.

Allen, M. J. B.; Baker-Smith, Dominic; Kinney, Arthur F.; and Sullivan, Margaret M., ed. *Sir Philip Sidney's Achievements.* New York: AMS Press, 1990.

Almond, Philip C. *The Devil: A New Biography.* Ithaca, NY: Cornell University Press, 2014.

Asham, Roger. *The Schoolmaster.* London: Cassell, 1902.

Avis, Paul. *Anglicanism and the Christian Church.* Edinburgh: T & T Clark, 1989.

Bacon, Sir Francis. *Essays and New Atlantis.* New York: Walter J. Black, 1942.

Bailey, Cyril. *Epicurus: The Extant Remains.* Oxford: Clarendon Press, 1926.

———. *Religion in Virgil.* Oxford: Clarendon Press, 1935.

Barrow, John. *The Romans.* 1949. Baltimore: Penguin, 1965.

Beagon, Mary. *Roman Nature: The Thought of Pliny the Elder.* Oxford: Clarendon Press, 1992.

Benfell, V. Stanley. *The Biblical Dante.* Toronto: University of Toronto Press, 2011.

Bernstein, Alan E. *The Formation of Hell.* Ithaca, NY: Cornell University Press, 1993.

Bindoff, S. T. *Tudor England.* Harmondsworth, UK: Penguin Books, 1950.

Bloom, Harold. *Shakespeare: The Invention of the Human.* New York: Riverhead, 1998.

Boardman, John. *Greek Art.* 5th ed. London: Thames & Hudson, 2016.

Bowker, John, ed. *The Cambridge Illustrated History of Religions.* Cambridge: Cambridge University Press, 2002.

Bradley, A. C. *Shakespearean Tragedy.* London: Macmillan, 1904.

Brand, Peter, and Lino Pertile, ed. *The Cambridge History of Italian Literature.* Rev. ed. Cambridge: Cambridge University Press, 1999.

Brant, Sebastian. *The Ship of Fools.* Tr. Edwin H. Zeydel. New York: Columbia University Press, 1944.

Brenk, Frederick E. *In Mist Apparrelled: Religious Themes in Plutarch's Moralia and Lives.* Leiden: E. J. Brill, 1977.

Buckley, George T. *Atheism in the English Renaissance.* Chicago: University of Chicago Press, 1932.

Buckley, William F., Jr. *Nearer, My God: An Autobiography of Faith.* New York: Doubleday, 1997.

Bury, J. B. *History of the Late Roman Empire.* 1923. New York: Dover, 1958. 2 vols.

Cary, M., and H. H. Scullard. *A History of Rome Down to the Reign of Constantine.* 3rd ed. New York: St. Martin's Press, 1975.

Castleden, Rodney. *The Stonehenge People.* London: Routledge & Kegan Paul, 1987.

Celsus. *On the True Doctrine: A Discourse against the Chrisstians.* Tr. R. Joseph Hoffmann. New York: Oxford University Press, 1987.

Cervantes, Miguel de. *The Adventures of Don Quixote.* Tr. J. M. Cohen. Baltimore: Penguin, 1950.

Chapman, Stephen B., and Marvin A. Sweeney, ed. *The Cambridge Companion ot the Hebrew Bible/Old Testament.* Cambridge: Cambridge University Press, 2016.

Chaucer, Geoffrey. *The Works of Geoffrey Chaucer.* Ed. F. N. Robinson. 2nd ed. Boston: Houghton Mifflin, 1957.

Clauss, James J., and Martine Cuypers, ed. *A Companion to Hellenistic Literature.* Malden, MA: Wiley-Blackwell, 2010.

Clegg, Brian. *The First Scientist: A Life of Roger Bacon.* New York: Carroll & Graf, 2003.

Cook, J. M. *The Persian Empire.* New York: Schocken Books, 1983.

Cook, John Granger. *The Interpretation of the New Testament in Greco-Roman Paganism.* Peabody, MA: Hendrickson, 2002.

Cornelius, R. M. *Christopher Marlowe's Use of the Bible.* New York: Peter Lang, 1984.

Crossan, John Dominic. *Jesus: A Revolutionary Biography.* San Francisco: HarperSanFrancisco, 1994.

Davies, Brian. *The Thought of Thomas Aquinas.* Oxford: Clarendon Press, 1992.

Davies, Jason P. *Rome's Religious History: Livy, Tacitus and Ammianus on Their Gods.* Cambridge: Cambridge University Press, 2004.

Despland, Michel. *The Education of Desire: Plato and the Philosophy of Religion.* Toronto: University of Toronto Press, 1985.

Digester, Elizabeth DePalma. *The Making of a Christian Empire: Lactantius and Rome.* Ithaca, NY: Cornell University Press, 2000.

Dinter, Martin T., ed. *The Cambridge Companion to Roman Comedy.* Cambridge: Cambridge University Press, 2019.

Doherty, Earl. *The Jesus Puzzle: Did Christianity Begin with a Mythical Christ?* 1999. Ottawa: Canadian Humanist Publications, 2000.

Dostoyevsky, Fyodor. *The Idiot.* Tr. David Magarshack. Harmondsworth, UK: Penguin, 1955.

Dowden, Ken, and Niall Livingstone, ed. *A Companion to Greek Mythology.* Malden, MA: Wiley-Blackwell, 2011.

Dudley, Donald R. *A History of Cynicism.* London: Methuen, 1937.

Erasmus, Desiderius. *The Praise of Folly.* Tr. Clarence H. Miller. New Haven: Yale University Press, 1979.

Esposito, John L., ed. *The Oxford History of Islam.* Oxford: Oxford University Press, 1999.

Fakhry, Majid. *Averroes (Ibn Rushd): His Life, Works and Influence.* Oxford: Oneworld, 2001.

Finley, M. I. *Early Greece: The Bronze and Archaic Ages.* New York: W. W. Norton, 1970.

Frazer, Sir James George. *The Golden Bough.* 3rd ed. London: Macmillan & Co., 1914. 12 vols.

Freely, John. *Before Galileo: The Birth of Modern Science in Medieval Europe.* New York: Overlook Duckworth, 2012.

Freeman, Charles. *A New History of Early Christianity.* New Haven: Yale University Press, 2009.

Friedlander, Paul. *Plato: An Introduction.* Tr. Hans Meyerhoff. Princeton, NJ: Princeton University Press, 1958 (rev. ed. 1969). 3 vols.

Gaunt, Simon, and Sarah Kay, ed. *The Cambridge Companion to Medieval French*

Literature. Cambridge: Cambridge University Press, 2008.

Gautier, Théophile. *The Mummy's Foot and Other Fantastic Tales.* Ed. S. T. Joshi. New York: Hippocampus Press, 2018.

Gies, David T., ed. *The Cambridge History of Spanish Literature.* Cambridge: Cambridge University Press, 2004.

Green, Miranda. *The Gods of the Celts.* Gloucester, UK: Alan Sutton; Totowa, NJ: Barnes & Noble, 1986.

Greenblatt, Stephen. *Hamlet and Purgatory.* Princeton, NJ: Princeton University Press, 2001.

Grout, Donald J. *A History of Western Music.* 2nd ed. New York: W. W. Norton, 1973.

Guthrie, W. K. C. *The Greeks and Their Gods.* Boston: Beacon Press, 1955.

———. *A History of Greek Philosophy.* Cambridge: Cambridge University Press, 1962–81. 6 vols.

Gutzwiller, Kathryn. *A Guide to Hellenistic Literature.* Malden, MA: Blackwell, 2007.

Hadzsits, George Depue. *Lucretius and His Influence.* 1935. New York: Cooper Square Publishers, 1963.

Halbertal, Moshe. *Maimonides: Life and Thought.* 2009. Tr. Joel Linsider. Princeton, NJ: Princeton University Press, 2014.

Hamer, Dean H. *The God Gene: How Faith Is Hardwired into Our Genes.* New York: Doubleday 2004.

Hamlin, Hannibal, ed. *The Cambridge Companion to Shakespeare and Religion.* Cambridge: Cambridge University Press, 2019.

Hampton, Timothy. *Literature and Nation in the Sixteenth Century: Inventing Renaissance France.* Ithaca, NY: Cornell University Press, 2001.

Hanks, D. Thomas, Jr., and Janet Jesmok, ed. *Malory and Christianity: Essays on Sir Thomas Malory's* Morte Darthur. Kalamazoo: Medieval Institute Publications, 2013.

Harden, Donald. *The Phoenicians.* 1962. Rev. ed. Harmondsworth, UK: Penguin, 1980.

Harris, Marvin. *The Rsie of Anthropological Theory.* New York: Thomas Y. Crowell Co., 1968.

Harrison, S. J. *Apuleius: A Latin Sophist.* Oxford: Oxford University Press, 2000.

Hartle, Ann. *Montaigne and the Origins of Modern Philosophy.* Evanston, IL: Northwestern University Press, 2013.

Haugaard, William P. *Elizabeth and the English Reformation.* Cambridge:

Cambridge University Press, 1968.

Hawkins, Peter S. *Dante's Testaments: Essays in Scriptural Imagination.* Stanford, CA: Stanford University Press, 1999.

Henry, John. *The Scientific Revolution and the Origins of Modern Science.* 2nd ed. Houndmills, UK: Palgrave, 2002.

Hess, Richard S. *Israelite Religions: An Archaeological and Biblical Survey.* Grand Rapids, MI: Baker Academic; Nottingham, UK: Apollos, 2007.

Higuera, Henry. *Eros and Empire: Politics and Christianity in* Don Quixote. Lanham, MD: Rowman & Littlefield, 1995.

Hoyland, Robert G., and H. G. M. Williamson, ed. *The Oxford Illustrated History of the Holy Land.* Oxford: Oxford University Press, 2018.

Hsia, R. Po-Chia, ed. *The Cambridge History of Christianity, Volume 6: Reform and Expansion 1500–1660.* Cambridge: Cambridge University Press, 2007.

Hultkrantz, Åke. *The Religions of the American Indians.* 1967. Tr. Monica Setterwall. Berkeley: University of California Press, 1979.

Hume, Anthea. *Edmund Spenser: Protestant Poet.* Cambridge: Cambridge University Press, 1984.

Hunter, Michael, and David Wootton, ed. *Atheism from the Reformation to the Enlightenment.* Oxford: Clarendon Press, 1992.

Insoll, Timothy. *Archaeology, Ritual, Religion.* London: Routledge, 2004,

Inwood, Brad, ed. *The Cambridge Companion to the Stoics.* Cambridge: Cambridge University Press, 2003.

Jennings, Francis. *The Invasion of America: Indians, Colonialism, and the Cant of Conquest.* 1975. New York: W. W. Norton, 1976.

Jones, C. P. *Culture and Society in Lucian.* Cambridge, MA: Harvard University Prss, 1986.

Joshi, S. T. *Classical Papers.* Seattle: Sarnath Press, 2021.

Kastan, David Scott. *A Will to Believe: Shakespeare and Religion.* Oxford: Oxford University Press, 2014.

Kaufmann, Walter. *The Faith of a Heretic.* Garden City, NY: Doubleday, 1961.

Keen, Maurice. *The Pelican History of Medieval Europe.* 1968. Harmondsworth: Penguin, 1969.

Kenney, E. J. *Lucretius.* Oxford: Clarendon Press, 1977.

Kicza, John E. *Resilient Cultures: America's Native Peoples Confront European Colonization 1500–1800.* Upper Saddle River, NJ: Prentice Hall, 2003.

Kiernan, V. G. *Horace: Poetics and Politics.* New York: St. Martin's Press, 1999.

Knox, Peter E., ed. *A Companion to Ovid.* Malden, MA: Wiley-Blackwell, 2009.

Lee, Alexander. *Petrarch and St. Augustine: Classical Scholarship, Christian Theology and the Origins of the Renaissance in Italy.* Leiden: Brill, 2012.

Lloyd, G. E. R. *Early Greek Science: Thales to Aristotle.* New York: W. W. Norton, 1970.

———. *Greek Science After Aristotle.* New York: W. W. Norton, 1973.

McKim, Donald K., ed. *The Cambridge Companion to John Calvin.* Cambridge: Cambridge University Press, 2004.

Macquarrie, John. *Principles of Christian Theology.* 2nd ed. New York: Scribner's, 1977.

Madigan, Kevin. *Medieval Christianity: A New History.* New Haven, CT: Yale University Press, 2015.

Mallin, Eric S. *Godless Shakespeare.* London: Continuum, 2007.

Malory, Sir Thomas. *Le Morte d'Arthur.* Ed. John Matthews. London: Cassell, 2000.

Margolis, Howard. *It Started with Copernicus: How Turning the World Inside Out Led to the Scientific Revolution.* New York: McGraw-Hill, 2002.

Marlowe, Christoipher. *The Complete Plays.* Ed. J. B. Steane. Harmondsworth, UK: Penguin, 1969.

Maurer, Armand A. *Medieval Philosophy.* New York: Random House, 1962.

Milward, Peter. *Shakespeare's Religious Background.* Chicago: Loyola University Press, 1973.

Minns, Denis. *Irenaeus: An Introduction.* London: T&T Clark International, 2010.

Montaigne, Michel de. *The Complete Essays of Montaigne.* Tr. Donald M. Frame. Stanford, CA: Stanford university Press, 1958.

Montemaggi, Vittorio. *Reading Dante's* Commedia *as Theology: Divinity Realized in Human Encounter.* New York: Oxford University Press, 2016.

Moran, Bruce T. *Distilling Knowledge: Alchemy, Chemistry, and the Scientific Revolution.* Cambridge, MA: Harvard University Press, 2005.

More, Sir Thomas. *The Utopia of Sir Thomas More.* Ed. J. H. Lupton. (Includes the 1551 translation of the Latin text by Ralph Robynson.) Oxford: Clarendon Press, 1895.

Morford, Mark. *The Roman Philosophers.* London: Routledge, 2002.

Myers, A. R. *England in the Late Middle Ages.* 1952. 8th ed. Harmondsworth: Penguin, 1971.

Nagel, Tilman. *The History of Islamic Theology.* Tr. Thomas Thornton. Princeton, NJ: Markus Wiener, 2000.

Nauert, Charles G. *Humanism and the Culture of Renaissance Europe*. 2nd ed. Cambridge: Cambridge University Press, 2006.

Nichols, James H., Jr. *Epicurean Political Philosophy: The* De rerum natura *of Lucretius*. Ithaca and London: Cornell University Press, 1976.

O'Brien, John, ed. *The Cambridge Companion to Rabelais*. Cambridge: Cambridge University Press, 2011.

Osborn, Eric Francis. *Clement of Alexandria*. Cambridge: Cambridge University Press, 2005.

———. *Justin Martyr*. Tübingen: J. C. B. Mohr (Paul Siebeck), 1973.

Pallottino, Massimo. *The Etruscans*. Tr. J. Cremona. Ed. David Ridgway. Harmondsworth, UK: Penguin, 1978.

Parker, Robert. *On Greek Religion*. Ithaca, NY: Cornell University Press, 2011.

Parrinder, Geoffrey, ed. *World Religions: From Ancient History to the Present*. New York: Facts on File, 1971.

Parsons, William B. *Machiavelli's Gospel: The Critique of Christianity in* The Prince. Rochester, NY: University of Rochester Press, 2016.

Peters, Edward. *Inquisition*. New York: Free Press, 1988.

Piggott, Stuart. *The Druids*. 1968. Harmondsworth, UK: Penguin, 1974.

Poceski, Mario. *Introducing Chinese Religions*. London: Routledge, 2009.

Price, Robert M. *Deconstructing Jesus*. Amherst, MA: Prometheus Books, 2000.

———, and Jeffrey Jay Lowder, ed. *The Empty Tomb: Jesus Beyond the Grave*. Amherst, MA: Prometheus Books, 2005.

Putnam, Michael C. J. *The Poetry of the* Aeneid. 1965. Ithaca, NY: Cornell University Press, 1988.

Rabelais, François. *The Complete Works of François Rabelais*. Tr. Donald M. Frame. Berkeley: University of California Press, 1991.

Ralegh, Sir Walter. *The History of the World*. Edinburgh: Constable, 1820. 6 vols.

Ranger, T. O., and I. N. Kinambo, ed. *The Historical Study of African Religion*. Berkeley: University of California Press, 1972.

Rankin, David. *Tertullian and the Church*. Cambridge: Cambridge University Press, 1995.

Rist, J. M. *Epicurus: An Introduction*. Cambridge: Cambridge University Press, 1972.

———. *Stoic Philosophy*. Cambridge: Cambridge University Press, 1969.

Rostovtzeff, M. *Greece*. Tr. J. D. Duff. New York: Oxford University Press, 1963.

Russell, Bertrand. *A History of Western Philosophy*. New York: Simon & Schuster, 1945.

———. *Unpopular Essays.* New York: Simon & Schuster, 1950.

Saggs, H. W. F. *The Greatness That Was Babylon.* 1962. Rev. ed. London: Sidgwick & Jackson, 1988.

Sales, Roger. *Christopher Marlowe.* New York: St. Martin's Press, 1991.

Santayana, George. *Interpretations of Poetry and Religion.* New York: Scribner's, 1900.

Scanlon, Larry, ed. *The Cambridge Companion to Medieval English Literature 1100–1500.* Cambridge: Cambridge University Press, 2009.

Schwartz, Seth. *The Ancient Jews from Alexander to Muhammad.* Cambridge: Cambridge University Press, 2014.

Sellar, W. Y. *The Roman Poets of the Republic.* 3rd ed. Oxford: Clarendon Press, 1889.

Sellars, John. *Hellenistic Philosophy.* Oxford: Oxford University Press, 2018.

Serafini-Sauli, Judith Powers. *Giovanni Boccaccio.* Boston: Twayne, 1982.

Shakespeare, William. *The Complete Works.* Ed. Alfred Harbage. New York: Viking Penguin, 1969.

Sidney, Sir Philip. *Arcadia.* Ed. Maurice Evans. Harmondsworth, UK: Penguin, 1977.

———. *A Defence of Poesie and Poems.* London: Cassell, 1891.

Ska, JeanLouis. *Introduction to Reading the Pentateuch.* Winona Lake, IN: Eisenbrauns, 2006.

Steinberg, S. H. *Five Hundred Years of Printing.* 2nd ed. Harmondsworth, UK: Penguin, 1961.

Steinberg, Theodore L. *Reading the Middle Ages.* Jefferson, NC: McFarland, 2003.

Stenton, Doris May. *English Societry in the Early Middle Ages.* 1951. 4th rev. ed. Harmondsworth, UK: Penguin, 1965.

Stokstad, Marilyn. *Medieval Art.* 2nd ed. Boulder, CO: Westview Press, 2004.

Strathman, Ernest A. *Sir Walter Ralegh: A Study in Elizabethan Skepticism.* New York: Columbia University Press, 1951.

TeSelle, Eugene. *Augustine the Theologian.* New York: Herder & Herder, 1970.

Tracy, James D. *Europe's Reformations, 1450–1650.* Lanham, MD: Rowman & Littlefield, 1999.

Trigg, Joseph W. *Origen.* London: Routledge, 1998.

Tylor, Edward Burnett. *Primitive Culture.* 1871. New York: Harper & Row, 1958.

Vasari, Giorgio. *Lives of the Most Eminent Painters, Sculptors & Architects.* Tr.

Gaston Du C. De Vere. London: Macmillan/Medici Society, 1912–14. 10 vols.

Viroli, Maurizio. *Machiavelli's God.* Tr. Anthony Shugaar. Princeton: Princeton University Press, 2010.

Wacher, John. *Roman Britain.* London: J. M. Dent, 1978.

Wade, Nicholas. *The Faith Instinct: How Religion Evolved and Why It Endures.* New York: Penguin, 2009.

Warmington, E. H., ed. *Remains of Old Latin.* Cambridge, MA and London: Harvard University Press/William Heinemann (Loeb Classical Library), 1935–38. 3 vols.

Wheelwright, Philip, ed. *The Presocratics.* New York: Odyssey Press, 1966.

Whitelock, Dorothy. *The Beginnings of English Society.* 1952. Rev. ed. Harmondsworth, UK: Penguin, 1974.

Whitmarsh, Tim. *Battling the Gods: Atheism in the Ancient World.* New York: Alfred A. Knopf, 2015.

Wightman, Gregory J. *The Origins of Religion in the Paleolithic.* Lanham, MD: Rowman & Littlefield, 2015.

Wynne, J. P. F. *Cicero on the Philosophy of Religion.* Cambridge: Cambridge University Press, 2019.

Zagorin, Perez. *How the Idea of Religious Toleration Came to the West.* Princeton, NJ: Princeton University Press, 2003.

Index

Aaron 268
Ab Urbe Condita (Livy) 135, 188–91
Abbas 331
Abbasid dynasty 329, 331
Abelard, Peter 348–49
Abraham 30, 327
Academus 88–89
Accius, L. 152
Achilleid (Statius) 216, 217
Achilles 44, 64, 217
Adam 29, 288–89, 291, 292, 293, 295, 296, 301, 327, 335, 355, 369, 457, 460
Adam and Eve (Dürer) 461
Adonis 131
Adso 358
Adversos Haereses (Irenaeus) 289–90
Aeneas 136, 138, 139n5, 150–51, 164, 180–85, 186–87, 196, 199, 368
Aeneid (Virgil) 150, 180–85, 186–88, 199, 213, 367
Aeschylus 46, 92–93
Aesculapius 147
Aesop 56
Aetia (Callimachus) 127
Aetius 53
afterlife 13–17, 31, 35, 44–45, 84, 120–21, 177, 187, 235, 297–303
Against the Christians (Porphyry) 308
Against the Galileans (Julian) 312
Agamemnon (Aeschylus) 46, 92
agnosticism 79, 311, 322, 351
Agricola, Cn. Julius 224
Ahriman 23
Ahura Mazda 22–23
Aidoneus 65
Akhenaten. *See* Amenhotep IV
Akkadian Empire 19
Akkadian language 18, 21
Alaric 315–16, 318
Alberti, Leon Battista 456–57
Albertus Magnus 343, 344, 349, 477
Albigensians. *See* Cathars
alchemy 477
Alcman 90–91
Alcmene 46
Alcuin 333–34
Alethēs Logos (Celsus) 305
Alexander (Lucian) 239–40, 305
Alexander (bishop of Alexandria) 282
Alexander III (pope) 355
Alexander VI (pope) 400, 466

Alexander of Abonuteichos 239–40
Alexander the Great 17, 19, 24, 28, 100–101, 107, 115, 123, 124
Alexios I Komnenos (Byzantine emperor) 339
Allah 326, 330–31
Almagest (Ptolemy) 249, 342
Amadis de Gaula 435
Ambrose (bishop of Milan) 287, 376
Amenhotep IV (king of Egypt) 17, 30
Ameto (Boccaccio) 370
Ammianus Marcellinus 313
Ammonius 232
Amorites 23
Amorosa Visione (Boccaccio) 370
Amphitryo (Plautus) 155–56
Amun-Ra 17
Anabaptists 407–8, 412
Anacreon 56
Anahita 23
Ananus 257
Anastasius I (emperor of Rome) 317
Anaxagoras 68–69, 71, 76, 79–80, 86
Anaximander 54–55
Anaximenes 55
Andraste 13
Andronicus, Livius 149–50, 152, 157
Andronicus of Rhodes 101
Anglicans 413–17
Anglo-Saxons 381–82
animism 12, 41
Annales (Ennius) 150, 151
Annals (Tacitus) 224–26, 255
Annotations on the New Testament (Valla) 404
Anselm 337, 338–39
Anthony 314
Antichrist 299–300, 335, 358, 417, 425
Antigone (Sophocles) 93–94
Antigonidae 100
Antigonus II Gonatas (king of Macedonia) 129–30
Antiochus III (king of the Seleucids) 28
Antiochus IV Epiphanes (king of the Seleucids) 28
Antiphon 78, 79
antisemitism 285–87, 340–41
Antisthenes 115
Antony, Mark (M. Antonius) 144, 170
Anu 20, 22
Aphrodite 65, 67, 91, 99, 129, 136, 164, 237
Apocolocyntosis Divi Claudii (Seneca) 201–2
Apocolypse of Paul 300
Apocolypse of Peter 300
Apocriticos (Macarius) 309
Apollo 42, 43, 46, 57, 91, 92, 97, 133, 147, 179, 196, 197, 232, 236, 273, 369
Apollonius of Rhodes 127, 128–29, 217
Apologia (Apuleius) 240, 242–43
"Apology for Raymond Sebond" (Montaigne) 430–33
Apology of Socrates (Plato) 81, 84, 86
Apotheosis (Prudentius) 314
"Apotheosis of Arsinoe" (Callimachus) 128
Appendix Vergiliana 185–86
Apsu 20
Apuleius 240–45

Aquinas, Thomas 343, 349–54, 357
Aramaeans 19, 27
Aratus 129–31
Arcadia (Sidney) 440–41
Arcesilaus 122
Archibald, Elizabeth 390
Archilochus 90
Archimedes 125
Ares 65, 140
Argonautica (Apollonius) 128–29
Argonautica (Valerius) 217
argument from design 118, 229–30, 238, 311, 351, 483
Ariosto, Ludovico 434
Aristarchus 125
Aristippus 112
Aristophanes 78, 81, 85, 94, 95–96
Aristotle 49, 50, 51n11, 52, 53, 54, 56–57, 65, 66, 68, 69–70, 73, 82, 83, 100–107, 108, 109, 115, 116, 122, 124, 232, 249, 337, 341, 342, 343, 344, 345, 350, 354, 395, 396, 398, 473, 477, 478
Arius/Arianism 282–83, 291, 316
Arminius 226
Arnolfini Portrait (Van Eyke) 459
Arrian 229
Ars Amatoria (Horace) 197
Ars Poetica (Horace) 192
Artemis 45
Arundel, Thomas 384
Ascham, Roger 443
Asclepius 91, 313
Ashari, Abu l-Hasan al- 336, 337
Asherat-by-the-sea 24
Ashurbanipal 19
Aspasia 80
Assembly of the Gods, The (Lucian) 236
Assyria 19, 20, 21, 21, 23, 27, 29
Astarte 24
astrology 200–201, 247
Astronomia Nova (Kepler) 475
Astronomica (Manilius) 200–201
astronomy 125, 129–30, 200, 249, 342–43, 472–76
Aten 17
Athena 92, 128, 129, 236
Athenodorus 228
Atomists 69–72, 86, 109, 110
Atrahasis 22
Attila (king of the Huns) 316
Attis 169
Atum 14
Augustine 279n27, 281, 287, 288, 289, 291, 292–93, 294, 295–97, 301–3, 314, 315, 318, 322, 339, 349, 357, 358, 367–68, 374, 396, 404, 436, 444
Augustine (archbishop of Canterbury) 382
Augustus (emperor of Rome) 144, 170, 178–79, 180, 183, 185, 195, 196, 199, 202, 204, 224, 251
Aurelian (emperor of Rome) 271
Aurelius, Marcus (emperor of Rome) 135, 230–32, 250, 271, 308, 386
Arthurian legend 363, 388–90
Ausonius (D. Magnus Ausonius) 313–14
Austen, Jane 157
Averroes 337, 339
Avicenna 337Aztecs 469–70

Baal 24, 30
Babylon 18–22, 27, 54
Bacchae (Euripides) 45, 95

Bacchus 147, 458
Bacon, Sir Francis 482–83
Bacon, Roger 343–44, 477
Bailey, Cyril 182
Baines, Richard 445, 446
Bakr, Abu 328
Balder 380
Barrett, C. K. 278
Basic Doctrines (Epicurus) 109, 165n21
Basil 283, 315
Basileus of Tyre. *See* Porphyry
Bastet 15
Batrachomyomachia 132
Becket, Thomas à 383
Bede 343, 381
Belfagor arcidiavolo (Machiavelli) 399
Belisarius 317
Bellerophon (Euripies) 94
Bellum Gallicum (Caesar) 202
Bellum Punicum (Naevius) 160
Beowulf 385
Bernard de Clairvaux 349, 368
Bible 252, 253–69, 278–79, 297–98, 304, 315, 334, 339, 349, 361, 391, 403–4, 406, 413, 415, 421, 440, 449, 454, 480, 483
Bible (Hebrew) 21, 22, 23, 26, 27–32, 261, 264, 278–80, 290–91, 346–47
Big Bang 69, 350–51
Birth of Venus (Botticelli) 457
Biruni, Abu al- 342
Black Death 358, 371
Blish, James 343–44
Bloom, Harold 455
Boccaccio, Giovanni 366n26, 370–73, 427
Bodin, Jean 424
Boethius 321–22, 377
Bogomils 355
Boguet, Henri 424
Boleyn, Anne 412, 413
Boniface VIII (pope) 360
Book of Common Prayer 413, 449
Book of Discipline (Knox) 418
Book of Martyrs (Foxe) 414
Book of the Dead 17
Boorman, John 389
Bosch, Hieronymus 459–60
Botticelli, Sandro 457–58
Boudicca 13, 202
Bradley, A. C. 449
Brahe, Tycho 474–75
Bramante, Donato 458
Brant, Sebastian 425–26
Bruegel the Elder, Peter 460–61
Brunellesci, Filippo 457
Bruni, Leonardo 395
Bruno, Giordano 475–76
Brutus, L. Junius 138
Brutus Albinus, D. Junius 144, 192, 368
Buddhism 56
Bukowski, Charles 95
Bulgarians 317, 318
Burgundians 316
Buridan, Jean 344–45
Burkhardt, Jakob 393
Bury, J. B. 301
Byrd, William 464
Byzantine Empire 325, 326, 332, 339, 375

Caesar, C. Julius 13n9, 143–44, 170, 178, 179, 180, 191, 192, 199,

202, 207, 213–15, 368
Caligula (emperor of Rome) 201, 207
Callimachus 126–28, 169
Calvin, John 43, 408–9, 412, 416, 418, 420, 421, 482
Cambyses 22
Campion, Edmund 417
Canaanites 23, 25, 30
Canterbury Tales (Chaucer) 386–88
Canzoniere (Petrarch) 374
Caotlicue 470
Caracalla (emperor of Rome) 271
Carmen Saeculare (Horace) 192, 196
Carneades 122, 158–59, 161, 170, 173
Carnival and Lent (Bruegel) 460
Carthage/Carthaginians 139, 142–43, 147, 150–51, 160
Cartier, Jacques 471
Cassandra 46
Castellio, Sebastian 419, 420–21
Cathars 355, 356
Catholicism 316, 318–19, 332–35, 405–6, 407, 409–18, 420, 422, 424–25, 432–33, 440, 448, 452, 455, 464
Catiline (L. Sergius Catilina) 170
Cato the Elder (L. Porcius Cato) 138, 146, 160
Cato the Younger (M. Porcius Cato Uticensis) 207
Catullus (C. Valerius Catullus) 168–70
Caxton, William 388, 391
Cecil, Sir William 414–15, 442
Cellini, Benvenuto 462
Celsus 305–8, 312
Celts 11–13, 202–3
Cerberus 43
Cercidas 122–23
Cercylas 91n33
Cernunnos 12
Cervantes, Miguel de 434–38
Champlain, Samuel de 471
Chanson de Roland 362–63
Charlemagne (king of the Franks) 333, 363, 374
Charles V (Holy Roman emperor) 403, 406, 412, 447
Charles VIII (king of France) 402
Charles IX (king of France) 419
Charon (Lucian) 240
Chaucer, Geoffrey 386–88
Chavin culture 467
Chichele, Henry 384
Chicomecoatl 470
Chrétien de Troyes 363
Christ in the Tomb (Holbein) 461
Christian Cosmography (Cosmas) 321
Christianae Religionis Institutio (Calvin) 408
Christine de Pizan 365
Chrysippus 116, 119n58, 120, 121, 161, 193
Church of England. *See* Anglicans
Cicero (M. Tullius Cicero) 54–55, 82, 113, 129, 134, 135–36, 159, 163, 170–78, 189–90, 195, 222, 227, 295
Civilisation of the Renaissance in Italy, The (Burkhardt) 393
Cizin 468–69
Clark, Anna 156–57
Claudian (Claudius Claudianus) 314
Claudius (emperor of Rome) 201–2,

203, 207, 256, 304
Claudius Gothicus (emperor of Rome) 271
Cleanthes 116, 119, 121, 125, 130
Cleisthenes 74–75, 141
Clement III (pope) 335
Clement V (pope) 361
Clement VI (pope) 354
Clement VII (pope) 361, 411–12
Clement of Alexandria 276, 282, 284, 290, 291, 293, 300
Cleombrotus 233–34
Cleopatra 144, 148, 213
Clouds (Aristophanes) 78, 81, 85, 95
Clovis (king of the Franks) 316
Cluny, Abbey of 334, 348, 349, 354, 372
Columba, St. 382n36
Columbus, Christopher 465–66, 474
Commedia (Dante) 366–70, 373, 436
Commentary on the Mishnah (Maimonides) 345, 347
Confessions (Augustine) 295, 302
Confort d'amy (Guillaume de Machaut) 364
Confutation of Atheism (Dove) 443
Conon 128
Consolatio ad Marciam (Seneca) 209
Consolatio ad Polybium (Seneca) 209–10
Constantine (emperor of Rome) 253, 273–75, 282–83, 308, 317, 323, 396
Constantius (emperor of Rome) 275, 276, 283
Constantius II (emperor of Rome) 314
Contra Celsum (Origen) 305
Contra Symmachum (Prudentius) 314
Copernicus, Nicolaus 472–75
Copts 329
Cornutus, L. Annaeus 214, 219, 220
Coronado, Francisco Vazquez de 466
Cortés, Hernán 466
Cosmas 321
Counter-Reformation 410, 434, 464–65
Courtenay, William 384
Cranach the Elder, Lucas 461
Cranach the Younger, Lucas 461
Cranmer, Thomas 412, 413
Crates 115, 121
Cratinus 73
Critias 85
Critolaus 158
Croesus (king of Lydia) 59, 75
Cromwell, Thomas 412–13
Cronos 41, 43
Crossan, John Dominic 264
Crusades 339–40
Cupid 245, 364
Cybele 45, 147, 169, 275
Cyclops (Euripides) 94
Cynics 115–16, 121, 122, 124, 158, 209, 221, 223, 224, 237, 262–63
Cyril 312, 318
Cyrus II (king of Persia) 19, 22, 27

Daemonolatreia (Rémy) 424
Dagon 24
Dallal, Ahmad 341
Danes 383
Dante Alighieri 365–70, 395, 397, 434, 436
Darius I (king of Persia) 27, 75
Darwin, Charles 33n23, 66, 118, 483

David (king of Israel) 26, 258
David (Donatello) 457
David (Michelangelo) 458
Davies, Jason P. 191, 226
De Agri Cultura (Cato) 160
De Anima (Aristotle) 102, 398
De Bello Civilo (Lucan) 213–16
De Civitate Dei (Augustine) 296, 318
De Consolatione Philosophiae (Boethius) 321–22
De Defectu Oraculorum (Plutarch) 233, 234, 242
De Deo Socratis (Apuleius) 241
De Dignitate et Excellentia Hominis (Manetti) 397
De Divinatione (Cicero) 174–75
De E apud Delphos (Plutarch) 233
De Esu Carnium (Plutarch) 234
De Finibus (Cicero) 177
De Haereticis (Castellio) 421
De Humani Corporis Fabrica (Vesalius) 478
De Imitatione Christi (Kempis) 388
De Immortalitate Animae (Pomponazzi) 398
De Institutione Musica (Boethius) 377
De Iside et Osiride (Plutarch) 244
De la démonomanie des sorciers (Bodin) 424
De Legibus (Cicero) 177–78
De Magis (Isidore) 358
De Magnete (Gilbert) 475
De Mirabile Potestate Artis et Naturae (Bacon) 344
De Miseria Humanis Conditionae (Innocent III) 396–97
De Monarchia (Dante) 368
De Natura Deorum (Cicero) 171–75, 177
De Prestigiis Daemonorum et Incantationibus ac Veneficiis (Weyer) 424
De Providentia (Seneca) 211
De Pythiae Oraculis (Plutarch) 233
De Republica (Cicero) 176
De Rerum Natura (Bede) 343
De Rerum Natura (Lucretius) 62, 109, 110–11, 162–68, 186, 187, 200, 453
De Revolutionibus Orbium Coelestium (Copernicus) 473
De Sera Numinis Vindicta (Plutarch) 234
De Superstitione (Plutarch) 233
De Voluptate (Valla) 397
Dead Sea Scrolls 29
Decameron (Boccaccio) 371–73, 427
Decius (emperor of Rome) 271–72
Defence of Poesie, A (Sidney) 440
Deffence et illustration de la langue françoyse (du Bellay) 427
Deism/Deists 68, 89, 344–45
del Rio, Martin Anton 424
Della pittura (Alberti) 456–57
Demeter 43, 46, 96
Democritus 52, 69, 71, 72, 76, 77, 89, 108, 109–10, 354
Demonologie (James VI) 424
Deudsche Messe (Luther) 464
Devil. *See* Satan
Diagoras 80, 310
Dialogues of the Gods (Lucian) 236–37
Diana 169, 196

Diatesseron (Tatian) 278
Didache 262
Diels, Hermann 64, 65
Diocletian (emperor of Rome) 272, 292
Diogenes Laertius 49, 114n51, 116, 117, 121, 122, 161
Diogenes of Babylon 158, 160
Diogenes of Oenoanda 108n46
Diogenes of Sinope 115–16, 123, 172, 263
Dionysius II (tyrant of Syracuse) 87
Dionysius of Halicarnassus 138, 145, 188n42
Dionysus 43, 45–46, 95, 97, 147, 236
Diopeithes 80
Discours exécrable des sorciers (Boguet) 424
Discourses (Epictetus) 229
Discourses (Machiavelli) 399, 400
Discoverie of Witchcraft, The (Scot) 424
Disquisitiones Magicae (del Rio) 424
Djoser 16
Doctor Mirabilis (Blish) 343–44
Doherty, Earl 254n2, 261n11, 265
Domitian (emperor of Rome) 217, 220, 229
Don Quixote (Cervantes) 434–38
Donatello 457
Donation of Constantine 396
Donn 13
Dorians 40
Dostoevsky, Fyodor 461
Dove, John 443
Dowland, John 465
Draco 43
Drake, Sir Francis 417
Druids 12, 202–3
du Bellay, Joachim 427
Dunsany, Lord 196n47
Dürer, Albrecht 461
Duval, Edwin 428
Dyskolos (Menander) 126

Ea 20, 21, 22
Earth Mother 9, 33
Eblis 327, 335
Ecclesiazusae (Aristophanes) 96
Eclogues (Virgil) 180, 367
Edict of Nantes 420
Edward VI (king of England) 413
Egypt 14, 23, 25–26, 27, 97, 148, 223
Egyptian religion 14–18
Einstein, Albert 344
El 24, 30
Elagabalus (emperor of Rome) 271
Elamites 19
Elegia di Madonna Fiammetta (Boccaccio) 371
Elements (Euclid) 124
Elijah 265
Eleusinian mysteries 46, 57, 114
Elizabeth I (queen of England) 412, 414–17, 442, 464
Empedocles 64–68, 71, 164
Enchiridion (Epictetus) 229
Enchiridion Militis Christiani (Erasmus) 403
Encomium Moriae (Erasmus) 426–27
Enki 20, 22
Enlil 20, 21, 22
Ennius, Q. 150, 151–52
Enuma Elish 20
Epic of Gilgamesh 21–22

Epicharmus of Kos 151
Epicharmus (Ennius) 151
Epictetus 229–30, 231
Epicurus/Epicureans 107–15, 116, 117, 121, 122, 123–24, 134, 152, 159, 164–68, 171–73, 176–77, 186, 190, 198, 208, 219, 221, 226, 228, 229, 233, 234, 237, 238, 239, 241, 242, 248, 251, 305, 367, 397, 406, 441, 452, 453
Epistle of Barnabas 286
Epistles (Horace) 192, 193
Épistre de Othéa a Hector, L' (Christine de Pizan) 365
Epistulae (Seneca) 208, 209, 210
Epodes (Horace) 192
Epona 12
Erasmus, Desiderius 392, 397, 402, 403–6, 418, 426–27, 428, 461
Eratosthenes 125
Ereshkigal 20
Erigena, John Scotus 338
Erikson, Leif 378
Eros 64, 129
Errors of the Cathars 359
Essays (Montaigne) 430
Essenes 204
Etruscans 137, 138–41
Euclid 124
Eudoxus 104, 124, 125
Eugenius IV (pope) 359, 423
Euhemerus 123, 151
Euhemerus (Ennius) 151–52
Eumelus 90
Eumenides (Aeschylus) 92
Eunapius 318
Euric (king of the Visigoths) 316
Euripides 45, 94–95, 129
Eusebius 121, 257, 273, 289
Eutyclides 132
Eve 29, 31n20, 288–89, 291, 327, 335, 355, 457, 460
Excalibur (film) 389
Expulsion of Adam and Eve (Masaccio) 457
Ezra 27

Faerie Queene, The (Spenser) 439–40
Farabi, Abu Nasr al- 337
Fasti (Ovid) 197, 199–200
Faunus 140
Febvre, Lucien 480–81
Ferdinand I (Holy Roman emperor) 416, 422
Ferdinand II (king of Aragon) 403
Fibonacci (Leonardo Bonacci) 343
Ficino, Marsilio 396, 397
Fiske, John 4
Fitzwilliam Virginal Book 464
Formicarius (Nider) 424
Fort, Charles 191
Fortuna 152–53, 223
Foxe, John 414
Francis I (king of France) 402, 462
Francis of Assisi 365
Franks 316, 317, 333
Frazer, Sir James George 4, 169, 199–200
Frederick II (Holy Roman emperor) 356–57
Frederick II of Hohenstaufen (Holy Roman emperor) 360
Frederick Barbarossa (Holy Roman emperor) 359–60
free will 110, 293–95
Freyr 381

Frigg 380
Frontinus, Julius 227

Gabriel 326, 327
Gabrieli, Andrea and Giovanni 465
Gaiseric 316
Galatea, La (Cervantes) 435
Galen 161, 249–50, 341, 477–78
Galerius 272–73
Gama, Vasco da 465
Garden of Earthly Delights (Bosch) 460
Gargantua et Pantagruel (Rabelais) 427–30
Gautier, Théophile 16n11
Ge/Gaia 41, 59
Geb 15
Gentillet, Innocent 401
Geoffrey of Monmouth 363
Geographikē Hyphēgēsis (Ptolemy) 249
Georgics (Virgil) 180
Gerard of Cremona 342
Gerusalemme liberata (Tasso) 434
Ghazali, Abu Hamid al- 337
Giacomo da Lentini 365
Gilbert, William 475, 476
Gilgamesh 21–22
Giorgione 458–59
Giotto di Bondone 376
Gnosticism 280–81, 290
Golden Ass, The (Apuleius) 240n82
Golden Bough, The (Frazer) 4
Golding, Arthur 443
Gorgias 76–77, 81
Gossaert, Jan 460
Gothic civilisation 375–76, 461–62
Goujon, Jean 462
Gratian (emperor of Rome) 314
Greek civilisation 11, 37–133, 138, 139–41, 148, 153–54, 155, 158, 160, 250, 276, 313, 341–42, 376, 395–96
Greenblatt, Stephen 452
Greene, Robert 446
Gregory I (pope) 377, 382
Gregory VII (pope) 334–35, 354
Gregory IX (pope) 356
Gregory XI (pope) 361
Gregory of Nazianzus 277
Grosseteste, Robert 343, 344
Guide of the Perplexed (Maimonides) 345, 346–47
Guillaume de Lorris 364
Guillaume de Machaut 364, 378
Guittone d'Arezzo 365
Gutenberg, Johannes 391
Guthrie, W. K. C. 57, 73n19

Hades 42, 43, 46, 65
Hadrian (emperor of Rome) 202, 305
Hadrian (pope) 333
Hamlet (Shakespeare) 452–53
Hammurabi 19, 20, 21
Hanbal, Ahmad ibn 336
Hannibal 143
Hapshepsut 14
Hapy 15
Harris Magical Papyrus 17
Harrison, S. J. 244
Hartle, Ann 433
Hawkins, Peter S. 369n28
Haytham, Ibn al- 342
Hecale (Callimachus) 128
Hecataeus 60, 9

Hecate 129
Hejduk, Julia Dyson 198
Henry II (king of England) 383
Henry II (king of France) 402, 414
Henry III (king of France) 419–20
Henry IV (Holy Roman emperor) 334–35
Henry IV (king of France) 420
Henry VII (king of England) 410–11
Henry VIII (king of England) 411–13, 461, 464
Henry of Lausanne 354
Hephaestus 43, 236
Heptaméron (Marguerite) 427
Hera 42, 65, 129
Heraclitus 59–61, 86
Herakles 46–47, 94–95, 98, 100, 128, 155, 238
Herakles (Euripides) 94–95
Hermes 99, 236
Hermes Trismegistus 476
Herod (king of Judea) 204, 253, 258
Herod Antipas 266, 309
Herodotus 40n4, 47, 96–97
Hertel, Dieter 39
Hesiod 40–41, 43–45, 50, 52, 58, 59, 88, 90, 127, 132, 148, 198
Higuera, Henry 437
Hipparchus (tyrant) 74
Hipparchus of Nicaea 125, 249
Hippias 74
Hippias of Elis 86n28
Hippocrates of Chios 73n20, 124–25
Hippocratus of Cos 73–74, 249, 250
Hippolytus 54, 55
Hippon 72–73
Historia Brittonum (Nennius) 363
Historia Ecclesiastica (Eusebius) 289
Historia Ecclesiastica Gentis Anglorum (Bede) 343
Historia Naturalis (Pliny) 245–46
Historia Regum Britanniae (Geoffrey) 363
Historie of the World (Ralegh) 444–45
Histories (Herodotus) 47, 96–97
Histories (Polybius) 159–60
Histories (Tacitus) 224–26
History of the Wars (Procopius) 321
Hittites 19, 23
Hobbes, Thomas 165
Holbein the Younger, Hans 461
Holy Grail 363, 388, 389
Holy Roman Empire 333, 359, 368, 402, 425
Homer 38, 40, 41–42, 43, 44, 45, 48, 50, 52, 57, 58, 61, 88, 90, 91, 98, 127, 131, 132, 187, 308
Honorius (emperor of Rome) 316
Hooker, Richard 417
Horace (Q. Horatius Flaccus) 108, 158, 191–96, 221
Horus 14, 15, 97
Hubal 326
Huguenots 420
Huitzilopochtli 469–70
Hume, Anthea 439
Hume, David 4, 174, 310
Huns 315, 316, 318
Hus, Jan 362
Hyksos 25, 26
Hymn to Aphrodite (Homer) 136
Hymn to Zeus (Cleanthes) 119, 130
Hymns (Callimachus) 127–28
Hypatia 318

Hyrcanus, John 28

Idiot, The (Dostoevsky) 461
Idylls (Theocritus) 131
Ignatius of Antioch 289
Ignatius of Loyola 410
Iliad (Homer) 38, 39, 40, 41, 46
Incas 467–68
Imami 331
Inanna 20
Inanna-Ishtar 20, 21
Index Auctorum et Librorum Prohibitorum 373n32, 423, 435
Innocent III (pope) 341, 356, 396–97
Inquisition 356, 358–59, 372, 403, 410, 422–23, 436, 475–76
Institutiones Divinae (Lactantius) 284
Irenaeus 281–82, 284, 286–87, 289–90, 291, 293
Ironside, Ralph 444
Isabella (queen of Castile) 403
Isaiah 261
Ishtar 20, 22, 24
Isidore of Seville 358
Isis 15, 24, 148, 244
Islam 326–32, 335–38, 425, 434
Ismailis 331–32
Israelite religion. *See* Judaism
Israelites 23
Itzamma 468
Ixchel 468

James VI (king of Scotland) 424
Jean de Meun 364
Jerome 162–63, 314–15
Jesuits 410, 442
Jesus Christ: death of, 9, 266–67; historicity of, 253–70, 278–79; in Islam, 326, 327; and Jews, 285–87; nature of, 318–19; non-Christian writers on, 255–57, 305–6, 308–9, 311–12; and Peter, 290; relationship to God, 282; Renaissance writers on, 400, 404, 421, 439; resurrection of, 267–68; as saviour, 257–58, 268–69, 291, 292, 298–300, 308, 479
Jew of Malta, The (Marlowe) 446
Jewish Antiquities (Josephus) 256–57
Jewish War (Josephus) 205, 256
Jews 148, 203–6, 222–23, 253–57, 263, 280, 284, 286–87, 308, 310, 319, 327, 328, 340–41, 346, 358, 422–23, 450
Joan of Arc 359n20
John (evangelist) 262, 267, 269, 298
John (king of England) 359
John of Damascus 335
John the Baptist 253, 259, 269, 279, 327
Jones, C. P. 239
Joseph of Arimathea 254, 363, 389
Josephus, Flavius 205, 256–57, 279
Josiah (king of Judah) 27
Josquin dez Prez 463
Judah I 206
Judaism 25–32, 252, 257, 323, 327, 345–47, 397
Judas 253, 260, 265
Judas Maccabaeus 28
Judging of the Goddesses, The (Lucian) 236
Julian (emperor of Rome) 273, 276–

77, 283, 312–13, 314, 324n55
Julian of Norwich 388
Juno 151, 186, 222
Jupiter 137, 151, 155–56, 181, 187, 195, 199, 222, 226
Justin II (emperor of Rome) 320
Justin Martyr 281, 282, 285, 286, 289, 293, 300
Justinian I (emperor of Rome) 317–18, 319–21
Juvenal (D. Junius Juvenalis) 158, 220–24

Kassites 19
Kastan, David Scott 449
Kaufmann, Walter 294–95
Kempe, Margery 388
Kempis, Thomas à 388
Kennedy, E. J. 167
Kepler, Johannes 475, 476
Kharijites 332
Kiernan, V. G. 196
Kindi, Abu al- 336–37
King Lear (Shakespeare) 451–52
Kinich Ahau 468
Kirk, Russell 270
Knox, John 415, 418
Kremer, Henrich 423–24
Kronos 258
Kukulkan 469
Kyd, Thomas 445

Lactantius (L. Caecilius Firmianus Lactantius) 151–52, 284
Laelius, C. 159
Lamentations of Jeremiah (Tallis) 464
Lamprias 234
Landini, Francesco 378
Langland, William 385–86
Last Judgment (Michelangelo) 459
Last Supper, The (Leonardo) 458
Laws (Plato) 88, 89, 177
Le Breton, Gilles 462
Lecky, W. E. H. 4
Leo IX (pope) 334, 356
Leo X (pope) 404, 405, 411
León, Ponce de 34
Leonardo da Vinci 458
Léonin 378
Leontius of Byzantium 319
Lepidus, M. Aemilianus 178
Lescot, Pierre 462
Leucippus 69, 72, 108
Lewis, C. S. 389
Libanius 276
Libation-Bearers (Aeschylus) 92
Lilitu/Lilith 20
Lives of the Most Excellent Painters, Sculptors, and Architects (Vasari) 456
Lives of the Philosophers (Diogenes Laertius) 49
Livy (T. Livius) 135, 136, 138, 147–48, 188–91, 217, 399
Lloyd, G. E. R. 249
"Lock of Berenice" (Callimachus) 127–28
Loki 381
Lollards 384, 388
Lombard, Peter 349, 357
Lombards 318
Longinus 308
Louis VI (king of France) 359
Louis XI (king of France) 402
Lucan (M. Annaeus Lucanus) 213–16

Lucian 235–40, 305, 306
Lucifer 299, 447–48
Lucilius, C. 157–58, 159, 192
Lucius III (pope) 356
Lucius, or the Ass 244
Lucretius (T. Lucretius Carus) 62, 109, 110–11, 113–14, 134, 162–68, 169, 171, 174, 186, 187, 198, 208, 221, 228, 242, 248, 453
Luke (evangelist) 259, 262, 264, 267, 280, 284, 451
Lull, Ramon 477
Luther, Martin 392, 402, 404–7, 408, 411, 425–26, 433, 461, 464, 482
Lutherans 410, 412, 423
Lycurgus 43, 79
Lysias 80

Macarius Magnes 308–9
Macbeth (Shakespeare) 453–54
Machiavelli, Niccolò 399–401, 434, 443, 445, 446
Macrobius 178
Maecenas, C. Clinias 180, 192
Magellan, Ferdinand 465
magic 20, 146, 476–77
Maimonides 345–47
Malleus Maleficarum (Kramer) 423–24
Malory, Sir Thomas 388–90, 438
Manetti, Giannozzo 397
Manichaeism 292, 301, 319, 335
Manilius, M. 200–201
Mannerism 459
Manoel I (king of Portugal) 422–23
Marcion 280–81, 282, 286, 293
Marguerite de Navarre 427
Marduk 20–21
Margolis, Howard 474
Marinus of Tyre 249
Marius, C. 143
Mark (evangelist) 258, 262, 263–64, 267, 284
Marlowe, Christopher 445–48, 455
Mars 13, 136, 140, 179, 203
Marsili, Luigi 395
Martel, Charles 329
Martial (M. Valerius Martialis) 220, 221
Martin of Tours 315
Mary (mother of Jesus) 253, 258, 264, 291, 315, 368
Mary (queen of England) 411, 413–14, 416
Mary Queen of Scots 414, 415, 417, 418
Mary Magdalene 267
Masacchio 457
Massys, Quentin 460
mathematics 124–25, 249, 342
Matthew (evangelist) 262, 264, 267, 284, 286, 298
Maturnus, Firmicus 275
Maximian 272
Maximin 273
Maximus of Ephesus 276
Mayans 468–69
Measure for Measure (Shakespeare) 451
Medea (Euripides) 129
Medes 22
medicine 18, 34–35, 73–74, 239, 249–50, 341–42
Medici family 394, 399, 400, 458, 459
Meditations (Aurelius) 230–32

Meeting of Bacchus and Ariadne (Titian) 459
Megale Syntaxis (Leucippus) 69
Mehmed II (king of the Ottoman Turks) 392
Melancholia I (Dürer) 461
Melanchthon, Philip 406
Meletus 84
Melissus 64
Memmius, C. 168
Mena/Menes 14
Menaechmi (Plautus) 155
Menander 126, 129
Merchant of Venice, The (Shakespeare) 450
Mercury 155–56, 200
Mesoamerican culture 467
Mesopotamia 18
Messe de Notre Dame (Guillaume) 378
Metamorphoses (Apuleius) 240, 242–45
Metamorphoses (Ovid) 197–99
Metaphysics (Aristotle) 101, 103, 104
Methuselah 30
Michael I Cerularius 334
Michelangelo 458, 459
Mictlan 470
Milton, John 370
Mimnermus 52
Minerva 203
Minoans 38–39
Minucius Felix, M. 309–12
Mishnah 206
Mishnah Torah (Maimonides) 345
Mithras 236, 285
Mithridates 143
Mona Lisa (Leonardo) 458
Monophysites 319, 320, 375
Montaigne, Michel de 430–34
Montanism 291–92
Monteverdi, Claudio 463
Montezuma 471
Moralia (Plutarch) 232
More, Sir Thomas 412, 418–19, 461
Morley, Thomas 464
Mornay, Philippe de 443
Morte Darthur, Le (Malory) 388–90
Moses 26, 29, 258, 265, 286, 400, 401
Mostellaria (Plautus) 154–55
Muhammad 326–28, 330–31, 332, 335, 367
Muslims 339–42, 345, 360, 392, 403, 434, 450–51
Mycenaeans 23, 39, 42, 74
Myths and Myth-Makers (Fiske) 4

Nabopolassar 19
Naevius, Cn. 150–51, 153, 213n60
Nafis, Ibn al- 342
Narranschiff (Brant) 425–26
Native American religion 32–35
Natural History of Religion, The (Hume) 4
Naturales Questiones (Seneca) 208, 211
Nebuchadnezzar 19, 24, 27
Neoplatonism 229, 276, 312, 320, 338, 341, 396, 457, 476
Nephthys 15
Nero (emperor of Rome) 201, 207, 214, 229, 255, 304, 305
Nestis 65
Nestorius 318
Newhauser, Richard 384–85

Newton, Sir Isaac 344, 475
Nicene creed 282–83
Nicholas V (pope) 466
Nicholas of Autrecourt 354
Nicomachean Ethics (Aristotle) 102n41
Nider, Johannes 424
Nietzsche, Friedrich 324, 446
Ninety-five Theses (Luther) 402, 405
Ninsun 22
Normans 383
Norse mythology 378–81, 382
Numa Pompilius 137
Nun 14
Nut 15

Ockeghem, Johannes 463
Octavius, C. *See* Augustus
Octavius (Minucius) 309–12
Odes (Horace) 192, 194–96
Odin 379–80
Odoacer 316–17
Odysseus 44, 46
Odyssey (Homer) 38, 40, 44, 46, 149, 182, 187
"Of Atheism" (Bacon) 482–83
Of the Laws of Ecclesiastical Polity (Hooker) 417
Oldcastle, Sir John 384
Olmecs 467
On Mind (Leucippus) 69
On Mourning (Lucian) 240
On Nature (Empedocles) 64, 164
On Nature (Epicurus) 108, 165n21
On Not-Being (Gorgias) 76
On Sacrifices (Lucian) 240
On the Dignity of Man (Pico) 397
On the Error of the Profane Religions (Maternus) 275
On the Gods (Theodorus) 122
On the Holy Spirit (Basil) 283
On the Nature of the Gods (Posidonius) 173
On the Sacred Disease (Hippocrates) 73–74
"One of Cleopatra's Nights" (Gautier) 16n11
Opus Maius (Bacon) 344
Opuscula Sacra (Boethius) 322
Oresme, Nicole 345
Oresteia trilogy (Aeschylus) 92–93
Origen 276, 284, 291, 293, 299, 300–301, 302, 305, 320
Origines (Cato) 138, 160
Orlando Furioso (Ariosto) 434
Orosius 314
Orphism 47, 57, 68
Osiander, Andreas 474
Osiris 15, 17, 97
Ostrogoths 315, 317
Othello (Shakespeare) 450–51
Ottoman Turks 391, 392, 429, 434, 451
Ouranos 41, 59
Ovid (P. Ovidius Naso) 196–200, 370

Pacuvius, M. 152–53
Palestrina, Giovanni Pierluigi de 464–65
Palladio 459
Pan 140
Panaetius 160–61, 162, 176, 209
Pandora 43
pantheism 59, 246, 476
Paracelsus 477

Paradise Lost (Milton) 370
Parallel Lives (Plutarch) 232
Parmenides 61–64, 65, 66, 69, 70, 76–77, 86, 117
Parsons, Robert 442
Patrick, St. 382n36
Paul (apostle) 212, 258, 259–63, 266–68, 269, 279–81, 284, 286, 287–88, 289, 298, 405
Paul II (pope) 396
Paul III (pope) 423, 475
Paul IV (pope) 459
Peele, George 454
Pelagius 297, 398
Peloponnesian War 79–80, 85, 96, 97
Pentateuch 27–28, 29, 346
Pepin the Short (king of the Franks) 333
Peregrinus (Lucian) 306
Pericles 75, 80
Pérotin 378
Persephone 43
Perseus of Macedon 159
Persius (A. Persius Flaccus) 158, 219
Persia 22–23, 24, 27–28, 30, 75, 99–100, 315
Pervigilium Veneris 313
Peter (apostle) 290, 368
Peter of Albano 343
Petrarch (Francesco Petrarca) 373–74, 394, 463
Petronius (C. Petronius Arbiter) 218–19
Phaedo (Plato) 84
Phaenomena (Aratus) 129–31
Pharisees 204, 206
Phidias 98
Philip II (Holy Roman emperor) 403, 414, 416
Philip II (king of France) 356
Philip IV (king of France) 360
Philip of Macedon 99–100
Philistines 25, 26, 27
Philo of Alexandria 256, 279n26, 290
Philo of Larissa 170
Philodemus 114, 172
Philoponus, John 344
Phoenicians 23–24, 27, 40, 50, 139
Phraortes 22
Physica (Anaxagoras) 68
physics 344
Physics (Aristotle) 344
Pico della Mirandola, Giovanni 397–98, 408
Pictor, L. Fabius 138
Piers Plowman (Langland) 385–86
Pietà (Michelangelo) 458
Pilate, Pontius 254, 255–57, 260, 266, 309
Pindar 76, 91–92, 131
Pisistratus 74
Piso, C. Calpurnius 207
Pius II (pope) 361
Pius IV (pope) 414
Pizarro, Francisco 466
Plato 47, 49, 50, 57, 64, 68, 77, 81–84, 85–90, 100, 101, 102–3, 105, 106, 107, 108, 109, 115, 116, 120, 122, 161, 176, 228–29, 232, 240, 241, 242, 244–45, 246, 277, 284, 305, 306, 307, 312, 377, 396, 397, 425, 436, 457
Plautus (T. Maccius Plautus) 153–57, 193

Pliny the Elder (C. Plinius Secundus) 125, 223, 245–48, 251
Pliny the Younger (C. Plinius Caecilius Secundus) 226–28, 248, 255, 303, 304–5
Plotinus 312, 396
Plutarch (L. Mestrius Plutarchus) 54, 119n58, 124, 160, 232–35, 242, 244
Pluto. *See* Hades
Poetic Edda 379
Politics (Aristotle) 105–6
Polybius 159–60, 188n42
Pompey (Cn. Pompeius Magnus) 144, 204
Pomponazzi, Pietro 398–99
Popol Vuh 469
Porphyry 308, 309, 341
Portinari, Bice ("Beatrice") 366
Poseidon 42, 238
Posidonius 160–62, 173, 209
Praetorius, Michael 464
Praxiteles 99
Presbyterians 418
Price, Robert M. 254n2
Primaticcio, Francesco 462
Primavera (Botticelli) 457
Primitive Culture (Tylor) 3
Prince, The (Machiavelli) 399, 400–401
Pro Christiana Religione (Cyril) 312
Procopius 321
Prodicus 79
Prometheus 43, 45, 93, 166, 198
Prometheus Bound (Aeschylus) 93
Propertius, Sextus 222
Prose Edda 379
Protagoras 76, 77–78, 79, 80, 85, 172
Protestantism 405, 416, 448, 450
Prudentius (Aurelius Prudentius Clemens) 314
Psyche 245
Psychomachia (Prudentius) 314
Ptolemies 100, 123, 127–28, 131
Ptolemy (Claudius Ptolemaeus) 125, 249, 342, 473–75
Ptolemy I (king of Egypt) 8
Punic Wars 143, 147, 149–51, 153, 160, 217
Punica (Silius) 217
Purifications (Empedocles) 64, 66
Puritans 416–17, 439, 440, 451
Putnam, Michael C. J. 184n38, 185
Pyrrhus (king of Epirus) 142
Pythagoras 56–57, 59, 60, 61, 63, 67, 87, 102, 118, 176, 306

Q document 262–64, 268
Quattro libri dell'architectura (Palladio) 459
Queste de Saint Greal 389
Quetzalcoatl 469, 470
Quran 326–28, 330–32, 335, 336–38

Ra 14
Rabelais, François 427–30
Rahman III, abd al- 329
Ralegh, Sir Walter 441–45, 472
Rand, Ayn 73
Randall, John Herman, Jr. 102, 103
Raphael 458
Razi, Abu Bakr al- 341–42
Reformation 402, 407–10, 430, 482
Remus 136, 138, 188, 259
Rémy, Nicolas 424

Republic (Diogenes) 123
Republic (Plato) 88
Republic (Zeno) 124
Revelation of John 298–99, 357–58, 369
Rhea 43
Ribadeneira, Pedro de 401
Richards, I. A. 127
Rickles, Don 115
Rist, J. M. 114
Roman civilisation 11, 12–13, 134–251
Roman de la Rose, Le 364
Romulus 136–37, 138, 151, 179, 188–89, 259
Romulus Augustulus (emperor of Rome) 316
Ronsard, Pierre de 427
Rore, Cipriano de 463
Rosso Fiorentino 462
Rudens (Plautus) 156
Rufus, Corellius 227
Rufus, Musonius 229
Rufus, Verginius 227
Russell, Bertrand 51n11, 353
Rutilianus, P. Mummius Sisenna 239

Sabines 136–37
Sacrae Symphoniae (Gabrieli) 465
Sacred Scripture (Euhemerus) 123
Sadducees 204
Safwan, Jahm ibn 336
Saladin 329, 340
Salome 267
Salutati, Coluccio 395
Samson 26
Santayana, George 449
Sappho 91, 194
Saracens 335, 363, 466
Sargon I 19
Sargon II 19
Satan 31, 292, 298–301, 307, 324, 327, 335, 355, 357–59, 367, 423–24, 437–38, 447–48, 460
Satires (Horace) 192, 193
Saturae (Andronicus) 149, 157
Saturn 146, 222
Satyricon (Petronius) 218–19
Saul 26
Savonarola, Girolamo 400
Saxo Grammaticus 379
Sceptics 171
scholasticism 348–49, 394
Scholemaster, The (Ascham) 443
School of Athens (Raphael) 458
Scipio Africanus Aemilianus, P. Cornelius 159, 160
Scipio Cornelius Africanus, P. 143, 159
Scot, Reginald 424
Sebond, Raymond 430–32
Second Sophistic 240–41
Secret History (Procopius) 321
Sedley, David 164
Sejanus, L. Aelius 225
Seleucid Empire 28, 100
Seljuk Turks 329, 339
Sellar, W. Y. 169
Seneca the Younger (L. Annaeus Seneca) 134, 152, 201–2, 206–12, 454
Sennacherib 19, 27
Sentences (Lombard) 349, 357
Servetus, Michael 409, 419, 421
Servius Tullius 137, 141

Seth 15
Severus, Septimius (emperor of Rome) 271
Severus Alexander (emperor of Rome) 271
Sextus Empiricus 72, 76, 79
Seymour, Jane 413
Shakespeare, William 448–55
Shariah 331
Sheol 31, 297, 299
Shepheardes Calender, The (Spenser) 440
Shiites 328, 331
Sibylline Books 147
Sic et Non (Abelard) 349
Sidney, Sir Philip 440–41, 443
Siger of Brabant 353
Silius Italicus 217
Silvae (Statius) 216, 217
Simon Magus 358
Ska, Jean Louis 30
Sleeping Venus (Giorgione) 459
Snyder, James 459
Socrates 48–49, 52, 78, 80, 81–85, 87, 95, 115, 120, 241, 425
Sol Invictus 273, 274, 276
Solomon 26
Solon 74
Somnium Scipionis (Cicero) 176, 177, 178
Sophists 75–81, 82, 85, 86, 95, 97, 159, 241
Sophocles 46, 93–94
Soto, Hernando de 466
soul 16, 57, 60–61, 67, 72, 82–84, 102–3, 111, 120–21, 161–62, 176–77, 209–10, 235
Speculum Stultorum (Wireker) 425
Spenser, Edmund 439–40
Sprenger, Jacob 423n21
Speusippus 100
Statius (P. Papinius Statius) 216
Stilicho 315
Stoics/Stoicism 116–21, 124, 130, 158, 160–62, 171, 173–75, 176, 177, 187, 190, 193, 200, 207–12, 214, 215, 219, 221, 223–24, 228, 230–31, 238, 246, 247, 293, 311
Sturlson, Snorri 379
Suetonius (C. Suetonius Tranquillus) 201, 202–3, 256, 304
Sufism 332
Suleiman the Magnificent (king of the Ottoman Turks) 392
Sulis 12, 203
Sulla, L. Cornelius 143
Sumerian civilisation 18, 20, 21–22
Summa contra Gentiles (Aquinas) 349
Summa Theologiae (Aquinas) 349, 352
Sunnis 328–29, 330
Sura, Licinius 228
Sylvester II (pope) 343
Symmachus, Q. Aurelius 314
Symposium (Plato) 436

Table of the Seven Deadly Sins (Bosch) 460
Tacitus (P. Cornelius Tacitus) 201, 224–26, 248, 255–56, 304
Talib, Ali ibn Abi 328
Tallis, Thomas 464
Talmud 256, 345
Tamburlaine the Great (Marlowe) 446
Tarquinius, Sextus 138

Tarquinius Priscus, L. 137, 141
Tarquinius Superbus, L. 137, 141
Tasso, Torquato 434
Tatian 278
Telamo (Ennius) 152
Terence (P. Terentius Afer) 157
Terpander 90
Tertullian 284–85, 288, 292
Testament, Le (Villon) 365
Testamentum Flavianum 256–57
Tetrabiblos (Ptolemy) 249
Tetzel, Johann 405
Tezcatlipoca 470
Thales 52–54, 55, 62, 66
Thebaid (Statius) 216–17
Theocritus 131–32, 180, 440
Theodora 317, 320, 321
Theodoric I (king of the Visigoths) 316
Theodoric the Great (king of the Ostrogoths) 317
Theodorus (Cynic) 122, 172, 310
Theodosius I (emperor of Rome) 277–78, 283, 314, 315
Theodosius II (emperor of Rome) 318, 320
Theogony (Hesiod) 40–41, 43, 50, 198
Theophrastus 49, 122
Theseus 38, 74, 95, 128, 169
Thesmophoriazusae (Aristophanes) 96
Thomas, Gospel of 266
Thor 380–81
Thoth 15
Thucydides 96–97, 224
Thyestes (Seneca) 454
Tiamat 20, 21
Tiglath-pileser III 19
Timaeus (historian) 150
Timaeus (Plato) 88, 103, 312
Timur (Tamerlane) 392
Tiresias 44, 46
Titian 458–59
Titus Andronicus (Shakespeare-Peele) 454–55
Tlaloc 470
Tolkien, J. R. R. 88
Toltecs 468, 469
Torah 28, 204, 205, 206
Torquemada, Tomás 422
totemism 34
Totila (king of the Ostrogoths) 317
Trachiniae (Sophocles) 46, 94
Tragicall History of Doctor Faustus, The (Marlowe) 447–48, 455
Traité de la vérité de la religion chrétienne contre les athées (Mornay) 443
Trajan (emperor of Rome) 202, 226–27, 255, 304
Tratado de la religion (Ribadeneira) 401
Treatise on the Soul, A (Ralegh) 444
Trenchard, Sir George 444
Trinity 282–84
Triptych of Saint Anthony (Bosch) 460
Triumph of Death (Bruegel) 460
Triumphes of Oriana, The (Morley) 464
Trojan War 38, 39, 84, 127, 128, 133, 136, 152, 181, 193, 196, 217, 365, 368
Tukulti-ninurta I 21
Tusculan Disputations (Cicero) 176
Tutankhamun 17

Twelve Tables 142, 146, 320
Tyche 132, 153
Tylor, Edward Burnett 3
Tyrtaeus 90

Ulfilas 315
Ummayad dynasty 328–29, 332
Uthman ibn Affan 328
Urban II (pope) 335, 339
Urban VI (pope) 361
Utopia (More) 418–19

Valerius Flaccus 217
Valerius Maximus 227
Valhalla 380
Valkyries 380, 381
Valla, Lorenzo 396, 397, 404
Vallée, Geoffroy 481
van der Weyden, Rogier 459
Van Eyck, Jan 459, 460
van Leyden, Lucas 460
Vandals 315, 316, 317
Vanini, Giulio Cesare 481, 482
Varus, P. Quinctilius 226
Vasari, Giorgio 456
Venus 147, 164, 181, 182, 199, 364
Venus (Cranach) 461
Venus of Urbino (Titian) 459
Vesalius, Andreas 478
Vespasian (emperor of Rome) 205, 247
Vesta 145
Vida de Lazarillo de Tormes y sus fortunas y adversidades 435
Vidal, Gore 372
Villon, François 365
Virgil (P. Vergilius Maro) 150–51, 179, 180–88, 199, 213, 366–67, 368, 440
Virococha 467
Visigoths 315, 316, 329
Vita Nuova, La (Dante) 366
Vitruvian Man (Leonardo) 458
Voltaire (François-Marie Arouet) 77, 346
Vulgate 315, 404

Waldensians 355, 356
Waldo, Peter 355
Warrior, Valerie M. 145
Weiner, Andrew D. 440
Weyer, Johann 424
Whetter, K. S. 389
Whitgift, John 417
Wightman, Gregory J. 4n3, 5n6
William I (duke of Aquitaine) 334
William I (king of England) 383
William of Ockham 354
Wireker, Nigel 425
Wisdom of Solomon 31n20
witchcraft 20, 382, 423–25
Witigis (king of the Ostrogoths) 317
Woden 382
Wolsey, Thomas 411
Works and Days (Hesiod) 43
Wyatt, Sir Thomas 414, 438
Wyclif, John 361–62, 384
Wynne, J. P. F. 174–75

Xenophanes 58–59, 60, 61, 63, 95, 246
Xenophon 81, 83
Xerxes (king of Persia) 75
Xipe Totec 470

Yahweh 30, 280, 286

Zacharias 327
Zagorin, Peter 421
Zahrawi, Abu al-Qasim al- 342
Zeller, Eduard 123, 124
Zeno (emperor of Rome) 317
Zeno of Citium 115, 116, 121, 124, 129
Zeno of Elea 64
Zeus 41, 42, 43, 45, 46, 52, 65, 67, 93, 94, 98, 112, 117, 130, 131, 136, 155–56, 236, 237–38, 258–59
Zeus Cross-Examined (Lucian) 237
Zeus the Tragedian (Lucian) 238–39
Zeydel, Edwin H. 426
Zopotec culture 469
Zoroastrianism 22–23, 31, 236, 285, 292
Zosimus 318
Zwingli, Huldrych 406, 426

About the Author

S. T. Joshi (A.B., A.M., Brown University) is the author of *God's Defenders: What They Believe and Why They Are Wrong* (2003) and *The Unbelievers: The Evolution of Modern Atheism* (2011), and the editor of *Atheism: A Reader* (2000), *The Agnostic Reader* (2007), *Icons of Unbelief: Atheists, Agnostics, Secularists* (2008), *The Original Atheists* (2014), and *Advocating Atheism* (2019). He has also edited the atheist writings of H. P. Lovecraft, Mark Twain, H. L. Mencken, and Leslie Stephen, and was the editor of the *American Rationalist* from 2011 to 2017. In addition, Joshi has written numerous critical studies of the literature of supernatural horror and has prepared many editions of works by authors of weird fiction.